D0212188

WEAPONS & WARFARE

WEAPONS & WARFARE

REVISED EDITION

Volume 3

WARFARE: CULTURE AND CONCEPTS

Editor
JOHN POWELL
Oklahoma Baptist University

SALEM PRESS
Pasadena, California   Hackensack, New Jersey

Editorial Director: Christina J. Moose
Acquisitions Manager: Mark Rehn
Acquisitions Editor: Steven L. Danver/Mesa Verde Publishing
Editorial Assistant: Brett S. Weisberg
Research Supervisor: Jeffry Jensen
Photo Editor: Cynthia Breslin Beres
Production Editor: Joyce I. Buchea
Graphics and Design: James Hutson
Layout: Mary Overell

Cover images: The Granger Collection, New York; Library of Congress;
©iStockphoto.com/(Craig DeBourbon, Ian Ilott, Melissa Madia, Adam James Kazmierski)

Copyright © 2002, 2010, by Salem Press

All rights in this book are reserved. No part of this work may be used or reproduced in any manner whatsoever or transmitted in any form or by any means, electronic or mechanical, including photocopy, recording, or any information storage and retrieval system, without written permission from the copyright owner except in the case of brief quotations embodied in critical articles and reviews or in the copying of images deemed to be freely licensed or in the public domain. For information address the publisher, Salem Press, at csr@salempress.com. New material has been added.

∞ The paper used in these volumes conforms to the American National Standard for Permanence of Paper for Printed Library Materials, Z39.48-1992 (R1997).

Library of Congress Cataloging-in-Publication Data

Weapons & warfare / editor, John Powell. — Rev. ed.
   p. cm.
   Includes bibliographical references and index.
   ISBN 978-1-58765-594-4 (set : alk. paper) — ISBN 978-1-58765-595-1 (v. 1 : alk. paper) —
ISBN 978-1-58765-596-8 (v. 2 : alk. paper) — ISBN 978-1-58765-597-5 (v. 3 : alk. paper)
1. Military weapons—History. 2. Military art and science—History. I. Powell, John, 1954-
II. Title: Weapons and warfare.
   UF500.W48 2010
   623.409—dc22

                                                                              2009050491

CONTENTS
WARFARE: CULTURE AND CONCEPTS

ALPHABETIZED INDEX OF ESSAYS

Categorized Index of Essays

CUTTING WEAPONS

ECONOMICS AND TRADE

EIGHTEENTH AND NINETEENTH CENTURIES (1700'S AND 1800'S)

EUROPE AND MEDITERRANEAN

MILITARY THEORY

MIDDLE EAST

MORALITY, ETHICS, AND JUSTICE

WEAPONS & WARFARE

UNCONTROLLABLE FORCES

GEOGRAPHY, WEATHER, AND WARFARE

SOME GEOGRAPHIC CONSIDERATIONS

Warfare takes place within natural contexts that humans can do little to affect. Whether in military action, gathering to fight, campaigning, or fighting in pitched battle, geographical factors such as terrain, food resources, water, weather, and climate have all played major roles in shaping the nature and conduct of organized human conflict. Natural features such as swamps or marshes, ore fields, natural harbors, and mountain passes, or human-made features such as roadways, cultivated fields, and cities have provided both the means for waging war and the targets of territorial aggressors.

Natural resources dictate the availability of military matériel: wood for ships; plentiful grass for herds of horses; and iron, copper, or tin for weapons. Geographic access is necessary for trade that can enhance natural resource deficiencies, and natural trade routes themselves can become military targets, for either control or plunder. In the premodern world, climate tended to dictate where people congregated, and weather tended to restrict military campaigning to the summer months between spring planting and fall harvest.

Human interaction with the landscape shaped the course of warfare in China, the West, and other rather limited regions in the premodern world. Organized cultivation of the land provided rich stocks of food that attracted hungry nomadic peoples who took what they wanted and were able to take. Walled cities, in which people, wealth, and industry concentrated, developed both defensive and offensive capacities that revolutionized military thinking and action. Developed ports became wealthy points of trade and colonial expansion, as well as cradles of naval development and warfare, especially around the Mediterranean basin. Chinese, Persian, Roman, and Incan roads channeled armies quickly within their empires, enabled rapid communication, and consoli-

dated expansion into neighboring areas. Bridges afforded the easy crossing of natural obstacles such as rivers and gorges. Fortification of natural strongpoints along frontiers, coastlines, and travel routes defended political boundaries and economic interests. Finally, great walls such as those of China and Rome's frontier in Britain clearly marked territory and limited depredation by invaders.

Military technology and the changes in thinking and fighting that both drive its development and are in turn affected by it seem to have evolved most rapidly and thoroughly in regions of the world where geographical access encourages contact among varied human groups. Natural obstacles such as heavy forests, jungles, deserts, and mountains tend to insulate peoples from one another and place limitations on effective interactions among even neighboring groups. Where mobility is limited, advances in military technology (and, arguably, in all phases of technology) are likewise limited. Even far-ranging contact by sea, such as that of the Athenians, Vikings, or Polynesians, revolutionized neither the native peoples nor the colonizers. Across the face of the great Eurasian landmass, however, the use of metallurgy, wheeled vehicles, cavalry, and gunpowder technology spread and found ready acceptance along the way. Perhaps because the Western peoples—from Persia to Britain and from Scandinavia to the Sahel—remained in some form of sustained contact from the mid-first millennium B.C.E. through the Persian, Hellenistic, Roman, Celtic, and Islamic empires, major technological innovations developed, took hold, and spread rapidly. Aside from the lack of major geographic obstacles to invasion—the Alps are passable in summer and the Mediterranean is as much a highway as a barrier—early urbanization and intense rivalries both within and among regions account for much of this dynamism.

A range of shifting political and even religious foundations for warring societies may also have played a part in military development. In Mesopotamia, Akkadian king Sargon the Great (c. 2334-2279 B.C.E.) melded the independent, feuding city-states into an empire and created the core of a limited imperial army drawn from throughout the region. In their movement from kingship to functional democracies to imperial subjection, the ancient Greeks shifted from an organization of heroic warriors to a phalanx of citizen shock troops, a force of multiethnic mixed arms with a heavy reliance on cavalry. The Greeks' proximity to and contact with their many neighbors, such as the Persians, Egyptians, Romans, Etruscans, and Carthaginians, resulted in trade, competition, and conflict that necessitated unprecedented innovations. Not least among these areas of development were naval technology and strategy. Rarely outside the West was sustained land and naval competition so fierce and so regular.

Religious considerations drove the Hebrew people to conquer and dominate much of the Levant, and the terrific successes of Islam stemmed far more from aggressive religious fervor than from military innovation or organization. The conflicting desires to create a territorial Hebrew promised land, to spread the Dar al-Islam, and to reconquer the same promised land for Christian purposes from the Dar al-Islam all speak to the geographic expressions and impulses upon which Western religions as well as political entities have relied. The same religious zeal also applied to the Crusaders who were fighting in terrain that was generally unfamiliar, and in far hotter weather than they were used to in Western Europe.

GEOGRAPHIC RESOURCES AND WARFARE

Humans have certain needs for food and shelter that nature must supply. Historically humans largely have occupied a zone of the globe in which climate is conducive to food crops and extremes in temperature and weather are minimal. Some communities shifted from hunting and gathering to herding or domesticating animals and cultivating the soil. After settling in one place, people began to create and store food surpluses and to build permanent shelters. People who remained wanderers (nomadic peoples) or who were

perhaps displaced from their own settlements preyed upon these centers of primitive wealth, necessitating the construction of defensive walls and the earliest cities.

Although cattle raids among the Irish, described in the Irish epic *Táin bó Cúailnge* (late eleventh or early twelfth century; the driving off of the cows of Cooley) exemplify the precivilized expression of tribal rivalry, struggles over cultivated lands and the cities they sustained typified warfare in the ancient world. Surplus in food led to the creation of other forms of valuables through specialization of labor. In some of these settings, warriors stood apart from cultivators, protecting them and living off their labor. In others, the cultivators themselves served as soldiers, denying a basic class distinction. In either case, the initial impulse was defensive, although in the former, the urge to display one's virtues as a warrior or leader may have fueled rivalries or conquests of neighboring lands. In many cultures that practiced primitive warfare, conflicts were strictly limited, highly ritualized, and sometimes relatively bloodless. Resources might have been exchanged but not destroyed or plundered outright. Because of the traditional nature and functions of these battles, little change took place over time. The likeliest events to upset rituals and shape new forms and meanings for organized conflict were major environmental changes (such as disease or sustained weather problems), inmigration, or conquest.

Warrior societies were generally poor materially and relied upon predation for their own wealth. They evolved among cultivators of poor soil, as in the case of the Vikings, or from herdsmen, as did the Central Asian peoples of the steppe. In both of these cases the warriors gained tremendous mobility from clinker-built longships and mounted horses, respectively. In both Viking and steppe nomad societies, trade was as important as plunder, but their native territories provided little of value to others. These warrior groups ranged widely and sought to despoil where defenses were weak; they shared no ritual niceties with their enemies and terrified the people who did. With limited resource bases of their own and without any clear sense of territoriality, these groups could not take and hold power for any sustained period without adapting to the material and social cultures of the conquered, as did the Mongols in China and the Vikings in Normandy. They also chose areas particularly vulnerable to their method of fighting. For the Vikings, the villages near the coast or in river estuaries were regularly attacked, and for the Huns and the Mongols, the open plains of southern Russia had little to inhibit their cavalry.

GEOGRAPHY AND EMPIRE BUILDING

Long-term military success lay, in ancient times, with those who controlled resources and the means of transforming some of them into weapons. Those societies with this power were able to consolidate and control territory that contained raw materials and to defend it from invaders. Indeed, territorial lordship seems to have evolved out of these needs in the Nile Valley, Mesopotamia, China, and parts of the Indus Valley. Land-based empires tended to expand into contiguous areas until forced by geography to halt or to vault barriers. The deliberate expansion of Rome in Italy, of Alexander in the Persian territories, of the Franks in Western Europe, and of Islamic warriors along the Mediterranean littoral and into Persia all followed this pattern.

Lands with valuable resources or connections to other such territories were brought under political and military control. This was one of the reasons for the Carthaginians holding onto Spain and its silver mines, and the Romans keen on attacking England to take control of tin. With trade and ultimately colonization, a society could transcend both its own home territory and its direct neighbors to draw upon far-flung resource centers. Early examples of such societies are the Polynesians, Greeks, Phoenicians, and later the Carthaginians. Seaborne Arabs sailed the Indian Ocean. In more modern times, the Spanish, Dutch, and English all expanded their territory to acquire resources. In each of these cases, expansion into immediately neighboring territories was unfeasible, undesirable, or thwarted, and maritime and naval technology opened distant doors.

The expansion of land-based empires relied upon superior technologies and skillful uses of them, and military organization that could allow operation at a distance from home bases. It also could require adaptation of tactical and sometimes strategic assumptions and factors. Assyrian and Hyksos warriors created and ruled their empires from horse-drawn chariots. Alexander the Great's (356-323 B.C.E.) combination of sarissa-wielding phalanxes and superb cavalry spelled the end for the Persian charioteers and lightly armored infantry. Frankish heavy cavalry bested the lighter Arab horsemen on open fields in central Gaul, and the articulated Roman maniples maneuvered skillfully through rough Italian mountain terrain in ways no massed phalanxes could have. Roman soldiers were also road-builders and connected their conquests directly with urban supply bases and ultimately with Rome itself.

The Assyrians were apparently the first people systematically to utilize protected lines of communication, supply depots, and baggage trains. Alexander's widely ranging army often relied upon supply from both coastal ships and stocked depots, and they suffered tremendously when these failed them. Persian king Xerxes (c. 519-465 B.C.E.) lost his bid for control of southern Greece when his supply ships and their escorts were destroyed at Salamis in 480 B.C.E. In his fourth-century B.C.E. *Bingfa* (c. 510 B.C.E.; *The Art of War*, 1910) the Chinese military theorist Sunzi (Sun Tzu) recommended that the armies of invading commanders carry their own equipment from the homeland but rely on enemy lands for provisions.

Seaborne empires require unobstructed sailing channels that connect the home ports to those of the colonies. Ships had to be adaptable for either trade or battle and ideally could carry on both simultaneously. Ships sought either friendly or directly controlled ports as safe havens along the routes, and those that harbored hostile ships were given a wide berth. Open sea could not be controlled effectively, and individual ships were very vulnerable to predators either alone or in groups. Control of surrounding land could be a factor protecting shipping, but, as Venice discovered in its own Adriatic Sea, it was no guarantee of insulation from bold, swiftly moving enemy fleets.

Ports, as interfaces between land and sea, enjoyed

the strengths and weaknesses of both elements. A stout wall, such as that of Constantinople, could hold enemy armies at bay indefinitely, while supplies could flow in from the sea. A blockading fleet could bottle up the harbor, but unless an army controlled the land approaches to the city, its hinterland could provide for its needs. By its very nature a port city was likely to be well stocked in needed provisions and thus likely to withstand any but the most determined siege. Constantinople fell only when the Turks brought to bear cannons that were capable of breaching its land-side wall in 1453. Ports were, however, vulnerable to raids by fleets that were naturally invisible in the vastness of the open sea or that lay in wait in nearby friendly waters. Before telescopes and artillery, there was little time between spotting raiders and setting out a naval defense, and no way of striking back beyond a bow shot.

Throughout history, invading groups have been drawn to the rich ports of Mediterranean mercantile nations: Iberian pirates in the first century B.C.E., Vandals in the sixth century C.E., Arabs in the ninth, Vikings in the tenth, and feuding Genoese and Venetians in the fourteenth. As trade and conquest extended out of the Mediterranean, ship technology evolved to accommodate oceanic conditions and eventually transoceanic voyages, by which time shipboard cannons and small arms had begun to replace crossbows and javelins. There is an interesting parallel between the development of weapons for use on land and those for sea warfare: Most weapons used at sea were first developed for land fighting. Even the ramming prow began as the battering ram; the Roman *corvus* as a siege tower bridge; Greek fire as a weapon against wooden gates. These modifications make sense if one views a ship as a small, mobile castle at sea.

Although the creation and maintenance of seaborne empires required resources and techniques of attack and defense rather different from those of land-based ones, the fundamental human needs for movement, provisions, and effective weapons remained the same. When peoples such as the Persians, Romans, Arabs, or Byzantines could manage the resources to afford both formidable armies and fleets over the long run, the power of their empires was awesome. For some, such as the fifteenth century Chinese, the matériel was there, but the will to project power and awe was not. For others, such as the Phoenicians and later Carthaginians, vulnerability of the home base spelled doom, while Athens and its empire suffered defeat in the Peloponnesian War (431-404 B.C.E.) when the superb Spartan army allied itself with the Persian fleet.

U.S. Air Force

U.S. and coalition aircraft fly over the southwest Asian desert in 2003.

GEOGRAPHY AND MOBILITY

The ability to build and manage ships enormously enhanced people's ability to treat water as a pathway rather than an obstacle. Wide rivers provided easy downstream movement and ready, if difficult, upstream travel and shipping. When an army in motion needed to cross a river, its width and depth determined the means. When fording proved impossible, bridging on pontoons, usually small boats lashed together, did the trick. The Assyrians were apparently the first to use regular bridge engineers, and the Carthaginians used makeshift bridges during Hannibal's invasion of Italy. However, the Romans developed efficient bridging on the march into an art form. Permanent bridges, though, provided ready access for enemy armies coming from the opposite direction and had to be fortified or guarded with care. Armies could also be ferried across broad expanses of river, but boats brought to or created on the scene were necessarily quite small and light.

Armies that could not use ships to attain their goals were forced to use land routes to maneuver, within both their own and enemy territory. When in motion, the premodern army relied predominantly on human feet and legs, which could traverse a wide variety of terrain and cover great distances when provisions were at hand. Pack animals that could cover the same ground carried supplies but required fodder, which was either carried or found along the way. The Macedonian armies used servants as carriers, but the Roman legions employed about eight hundred pack animals for each legion. Part of the reason for these differing choices may stem from the Macedonians' heavy reliance on cavalry: limited fodder went to Alexander's war horses instead of pack animals. Sledges provided platforms on which provisions and supplies could be carried, dragged by either human or limited animal power.

After armies began using wheeled conveyances, the need arose for fairly smooth and consistent pathways unrestricted by obstacles such as strewn rocks, swamps, or overly steep or narrow passages. Unpaved roads, as found in the Persian Empire, proved perfectly passable in good weather but turned into muddy morasses when heavy rains came. Romans and Chinese created artificial surfaces that retained the road's integrity in all but the worst weather. Carts might be drawn by people or draft animals, such as oxen. The use of horses did not become widespread until after breeders had developed animals of suitable size and strength, and carters had created appropriate harnesses. Progress at human and draft animal speed was steady but slow on easily traversed terrain without steep grades and somewhat faster on paved roadways.

Before horses were ridden, they were harnessed to light chariots. Developed earliest on the Iranian Plateau, horses provided warriors and soldiers much greater speed and range, both prior to and during battle. Organized aggression on a large and mobile scale began with the charioteers. Flat, hard terrain was a necessity, however, and chariots triumphed only where this was in abundance: in Mesopotamia, China, Egypt, and parts of Celtic Western Europe. Before battle, Persian soldiers swept and leveled the field to aid the maneuver of their wheeled warriors. Aryans initially invaded the Indus Valley in chariots, and Mycenean Greeks and Etruscans also used war chariots, but the rocky geography of Italy and Greece limited their usefulness in large formations. Chariots provided platforms from which to shoot arrows or hurl missiles and could easily run down broken formations of lightly armed infantry. Although the fielding and maintenance of a corps of chariots was an expensive proposition, chariot warfare became a standard part of empire building in both China and western Asia. Horses needed large amounts of grass or grain, however, and when dessication set in, as in Mesopotamia, their days were numbered.

Where the availability of grasses allowed, horses were eventually bred, raised, and used for cavalry, first perhaps on the Iranian Plateau around 1400 B.C.E. By around the eighth century B.C.E. horses with backs strong enough to be ridden forward, rather than on the haunches, provided people of the Eurasian steppe between the subarctic northern forest and the great Asian deserts with devastating power and mobility. These horse people had the run of their own vast areas of grass, but were drawn to the civilization and wealth of India, China, and the West. Scythians, Cimmerians, Huns, Mongols, and Turks each in turn terrorized civilized peoples and forced them to adapt to the horseman's threat. However, these were culturally nomadic peoples, and only those Mongols settling in China and those Turks remaining in Asia Minor were transformed into a stable populace. The mobility of the steppe nomads provided their freedom and defined their military tactics: bow-, sword-, and spear-wielding hordes aligned in a great crescent that thundered across the open plain. They were quick to fire their missiles and disperse, reforming and charging again as needed. They could bleed or milk their mounts for food, and as long as the grass was plentiful, they could maintain their control. Beyond the steppe, however, they could not long survive without adapting or retreating.

Arabs and Europeans adopted cavalry as an arm of mixed-force armies, and Western armies gained clear, if limited, mobility from the use of cavalry. Islam was spread as quickly as it was by fervent horsemen who established both the religion and its rulers from southern Gaul to India. These Islamic warriors arrived in desert areas by camel and fought on horseback. Their goal was not territorial conquest per se, but the diffusion of the truth of Islam and worship of Allah. Yet their tremendous mobility spurred the post-Roman West to create its own cavalry, with enormous repercussions for medieval European society and politics. Western cavalry units were quite small relative both to those of the steppe hordes and to the size of their own societies because local Western economies were settled and agricultural rather than nomadic. The warrior class was supported by the agricultural and trading classes, and the European idea of the chivalry of the mounted knight dominated in Europe as part of a larger social, political, and economic reality.

When horsemen introduced themselves into areas previously lacking in horses, such as South Africa, the Americas, and Australia, the enhanced range and speed, as well as accompanying firepower, gave these invaders a huge advantage over local warriors. Nonetheless, areas of extreme heat or cold and mountainous, heavily forested, jungle, and swampy regions have all proven inhospitable as theaters of operation to bodies of cavalry.

In general, the same routes that provided the most direct pathways for merchants, pilgrims, diplomats, and migrating peoples also served the needs of campaigning armies. The paths of least geographical resistance have been trod for centuries, if not millennia. Just as cities are rebuilt time and again upon the ruins of their predecessors for reasons of geography, so battles will repeatedly occur on the same spots as armies vie to enter or defend territory that retains its importance. If the province of Edirne, formerly Adrianople, is the most contested spot on the globe, however, it is not because of its natural resources, but rather because of its position along the southern bridge between Europe and Asia. Similarly, the southern region of Israel has seen conflict from the ancient Egyptians attacking northward, their enemies the Hyksos and later the Hittites moving south to attack Egypt, the Macedonians under Alexander the Great, the Selucids in the Diadochi Wars, the Romans, the Seljuk Turks, the Crusaders, and the Ottoman Turks, as well as, many years later, the French under Napoleon I, the Allies in World War I, and the Arab-Israeli wars of the second half of the twentieth century.

Similarly, in northern France, conflict in that region in the Hundred Years' War (1337-1453) was only a harbinger of future wars: the Wars of Religion (c. 1517-1618), the War of the Spanish Succession (1701-1714), the War of the Austrian Succession (1740-1748), the Seven Years' War (1756-1763), the French Revolution and Napoleonic Wars (1793-1815), and World War I (1914-1918), which have all involved fighting in a relatively small area of land. Nature has provided the obstacles to human movement as well as the highways along which the armies of the world have campaigned.

TERRAIN AND WARFARE

In *The Art of War*, Sunzi stated, "Those who do not know the conditions of mountains and forests, hazardous defiles, marshes and swamps, cannot conduct the march of an army." Of Sunzi's five fundamental factors of war, two are geographical: climate and terrain. The fifth century Roman military historian Vegetius posited that each of Rome's major military arms had its own terrain-specific role: the cavalry had the plains; the navy had seas and rivers; and the infantry had hills, cities, and flat country. The peoples of the great riverine civilizations of China, India, and the West created the great armies of conquest and consolidation. The peoples of the littoral regions of the Aegean, the northern fjords, Oceania, and the Indian coast sent out their seaborne forces for trade, plunder, and colonization. The steppes bred and unleashed on the world the nomadic hordes of charioteers and horsemen. The open terrains of plain, sea, and steppe fostered types of warfare that pitted relatively mobile forces against fixed targets, such as towns, ports, castles, and walls; highly mobile forces, such as fleets and cavalries, against one another; or relatively static armies against each other on the battlefield. Less open terrains, such as mountains, swamps, heavy forests, or jungles, called for conflicts in which neither the massing of troops nor the nimble maneuvering typical of other settings was desired, or even at times possible. Poorer terrain tended to be economically poorer as well, and war tended to flow out of these areas into the wealthier and literally more attractive regions. Territorial defense by the world's early civilizations often meant pacifying the surrounding hills and forests occupied by these outsiders.

Warriors who developed their skills in these less accessible areas had often acquired tactics and weapons that complemented those of the larger armies they joined, as either allies or willing captives. In general, fighting men from these marginal regions were considered "irregular," whether fighting or joining highly organized armies. Mountain and forest terrain lent itself to relatively small, highly mobile, independent parties who would strike and retreat quickly. Such fighters often proved resistant to both authority structures and the discipline necessary to phalanx warfare. Their fluidity and their tendency to raid and ambush, major parts of their strength, have frustrated regular troops from ancient Persia to twentieth century Vietnam. Tu Mu, a ninth century commentator on Sunzi, suggested avoiding or at least scouting areas of danger to chariots and armies: mountain passes, river crossings, and the places where vegetation is luxuriant.

The use of javelins, bows, and slings enabled irregular fighters to engage at a distance, ensuring a buffer that allowed for escape when necessary. The Chinese, Persians, Macedonians, and Romans all incorporated irregulars into their service, adding a needed dimension to their infantry and cavalry arms. The wilderness areas from which irregulars came also provided places of resistance and refuge in times of upheaval or invasion. The difficulty of operating either deterred incursion by regular armies, hampered it effectively, or led to disaster, as in the Teutoburg Forest in 9 C.E., when Germanic warriors annihilated a Roman army that had pursued it too far. In that instance it is thought that the Germans allowed the Romans to enter a narrow defile where the numbers of their attackers would lead to a German victory. Similarly, at Agincourt in 1415, a much smaller English force was able to defeat a larger French one.

By the time of the first Sack of Rome (410 C.E.), the Roman soldier had become increasingly barbarized and was expected to wield the sling, bow, and even darts. Flavius Vegetius Renatus recognized the barbarian origins of the sling in the Balearics and suggested its use derived from the waging of war in stony places. He cited the need for mounted archers to count the same among their enemies and mentioned the origin of the "lead-weighted darts" among the Illyrians. Vegetius also recognized the untrained and undisciplined nature of the *auxilia* soldiers drawn from diverse barbarian peoples. Roman adaptation to the strengths and weaknesses of their enemies had evolved by Vegetius's time, so that the use of concealment and ambush played major roles in his thinking. He believed that good generals would not attack in open battle where the danger is mutual, but rather from a hidden position. Similarly, when the Welsh nationalist leader Owain Glendower faced the English army near Worcester in 1405, neither was prepared to move from a defensive position, and hence no battle was fought. The nature of the battlefield is also of major consideration to the commander and should be studied with regard to its appropriateness to either the cavalry or the infantry.

The difficulties of forcing large groups of foot soldiers to cross desert environments meant that battles in truly desert terrain generally occurred between bodies of men on camels or horses. The heat and lack of water allowed for armies of only limited size, and generally lightly armed and armored characters took part in desert warfare. On the fringes of these areas fought the Byzantine cataphracts and crusading knights, relatively heavy shock troops whose enemies generally wielded the bow and maneuvered agilely into the desert wasteland itself when retreat was warranted. Fluidity and expectations of minimal gains influenced their tactics and strategies, as they did peoples of the mountains and forests. From horseback slings, bolos, and even lassoes could be used by light cavalry to hamper heavy formations in open fields.

CLIMATE, WEATHER, AND WARFARE

In temperate zones early military campaigning was generally a summertime activity, conducted by civilized peoples between the spring planting and the fall harvest. For professional armies, the winter season presented conditions of cold, wind, and precipitation that were best avoided. In spring, flooding rivers often proved impassible, and spring and fall rains turned marching routes into morasses. Chinese, Incan, and Roman roads alleviated some of the last inconvenience, but seasonal campaigning remained the norm. Vegetius recommended conducting naval maneuvers only between late May and mid-September. Foul-weather attacks presented both risks and the opportunity for surprise. Long-term sieges of cities or fortresses had necessarily to last beyond the campaigning season, and while the inhabitants often suffered from lack of food and other supplies, those blockading, relegated to second-class field quarters, often endured worse. Sunzi, who always argued against protracted warfare, advised against sieges of cities under even the best of conditions.

In hotter zones periodic monsoons made military maneuvers all but impossible, and desert conditions affected the size, movement, and armament of military bodies. The Crusaders quickly found that their heavy armor was a deadly encumbrance rather than an aid in the Levant. Lighter clothing and lighter ar-

mor characterize warm-climate warriors and soldiers. As such, lighter weapons could kill them. Native allies often became very important when an empire struck too far north or south from its homeland, and adaptations to local conditions became mandatory. Deaths from dehydration, heat stroke, and unfamiliar diseases had to have been plentiful when men from the temperate zones marched south. One explanation for Attila's (c. 406-453) refusal to march south into Italy is his fear of the area's summertime heat and disease.

Ships at sea are far more vulnerable than land armies to occasional storms, and occurrences of storms breaking up large fleets are not rare in ancient chronicles. Perhaps the most famous is the *kamikaze*, or "divine wind," that destroyed the Mongol invasion fleets that threatened Japan in 1274 and 1281.

It is similar, in some ways, to the divine wind that brought, according to legend, William of Normandy's fleet to England in September, 1066, although modern historians have suggested that his reasons for delaying the attack were not solely dictated by the weather. In spite of these recent reservations about William's actions, conditions on the English Channel were sufficiently variable for the Allied Command for the D-day operation to consult weather forecasters on a daily basis to work out the best time to launch the invasion of France in June, 1944. Prior to the use of professional weather forecasters, soothsayers and fortune-tellers were consulted.

THE HUMAN LANDSCAPE

The development of cities, more than any other human activity, focused military aggression and provided the means for increasing the scope and deadliness of warfare. Cities became targets of predatory nomadic peoples and of each other. Banded together under a single leader, the combined surpluses of a city provided the wherewithal to carry on protracted campaigns of conquest. Between cities stretched roads along which merchants and armies traveled, and urban wealth grew with the trade that followed. The oldest known urban place, Jericho, sported walls

U.S. Coast Guard

More than 100,000 American and British soldiers landed on the Normandy coast of France during the D-day invasion of June, 1944, overcoming the challenges of an amphibious assault.

in its earliest form: walls clearly meant to keep out challengers. The desire to defend and defeat these human landmarks led to an entire branch of military science. Like cities, fortified outposts within which soldiers huddled to defend frontiers and approaches developed defenses appropriate to current siege technologies. At the extreme, these developed into curtain walls.

For Sunzi and his commentators, cities were, like other geographic obstacles, to be avoided by the campaigning army. When cities or large fortifications were not the objective, careful consideration had to be made in deciding whether to attack. Unlike mountains, forests, or marshes, cities and fortifications certainly held people, and probably armed men who could cut supply and retreat lines. The Chinese seem to have assumed rather quick and shallow offensive sallies, on which their supply lines and escape routes would be minimally vulnerable. Alexander

was willing to bypass strongholds, the major exception being Tyre, which he besieged at a great cost in time and energy from January to July 332 B.C.E. Empires and kingdoms tended to fortify along their frontiers, leaving the interior relatively unprotected. The decision of the Roman emperor Aurelian (c. 275-215 B.C.E.) around 270 B.C.E. to build up the city of Rome's walls speaks to the Romans' very real fear of the Germanic tribesmen, as distant as they were. After all, fortified cities were needed along the imperial boundaries, not deep within. Where and when the political geography was fragmented—as in classical Greece, China during the Warring States period, feudal Europe, and Renaissance Italian city-states—every center was vulnerable and had to be defended.

Few premodern city walls were spared the experience of siege, and great innovations accompanied the evolving practice of siegecraft. It has been suggested that the first true professional soldiers evolved from the need for protracted and well-organized sieges. Professional soldiers were neither elite warriors nor citizen soldiers. They brought the patience and skill necessary to invest a fortified area successfully. Weapons and techniques for gaining forced entry developed as simple blockades of city gates proved of little practical use. Egyptians may have used battering rams as early as 1900 B.C.E.; siege towers were depicted from the eighth century B.C.E.; and catapult-like machines for hurling projectiles against the walls or into the protected areas emerged in the fourth century B.C.E. The use of scaling ropes and ladders and the practice of undermining walls are probably of even greater antiquity: The earliest levels of Jericho show signs of a dry moat. Other methods of defense included bastions that jutted out from the walls to provide flanking fire by archers and others; towers that protected vulnerable corners and gates; crenellations; machiocolations; battering (sloping out) of wall bases; and, at least during the high Middle Ages, increasingly ingenious ways of defending gateways. Like other types of military technology, siege engines and defensive forms migrated: The round towers and curtain walls of Edward I's (1239-1307) Welsh castles have their origins in the Islamic Near East.

Geography above all other considerations determined the locations of cities and fortifications. When defense was a major factor, location on hills or along ridges provided the best position from which to resist and repel attackers. After laying siege to Celtic and Etruscan strongpoints, the Romans either destroyed them or forced the inhabitants to move to the valley below, as, for example, at Gubbio in Umbria. Here the medieval citizens relocated to the side of the hill, where the main civic structures remain. Human needs also dictated sufficient living and storage space, a source of fresh water, and easy access in time of peace. When garrisons were consistently small, as in the Roman forts along the Saxon shore or along the frontier of the Sienese Chianti, the needs were small and there was little need for growth. As fortified cities expanded, however, the urban geography changed as the location of the site became less important than the human alterations to it.

Strings of forts marked the Incan and Roman frontiers, but the greatest expressions of the siege mentality were the great walls of the Roman emperors Hadrian (76-138) and Antoninus (188-217) in Britain, and the crowning achievement of Chinese engineering, the Great Wall. The Great Wall stretches for some 4,000 miles and initially linked a series of hilltop fortifications along a border of steppe and mountain, wilderness, and civilized terrain during the Qin (Ch'in) Dynasty (221-206 B.C.E.). Climatic shifts in the region to and from desertification made its reinforcement of a natural physiological boundary irrelevant, and the Great Wall's failure to hold back the Mongol advance is legendary.

BOOKS AND ARTICLES

Contamine, Philippe. *War in the Middle Ages*. New York: Blackwell, 1986.

Durschmied, Erik. *The Weather Factor: How Weather Changed History*. London: Hodder and Stoughton, 2000.

Engels, Donald W. *Alexander the Great and the Logistics of the Macedonian Army*. Berkeley: University of California Press, 1980.

Fields, Nic. *Ancient Greek Fortifications*. New York: Osprey, 2006.

Flint, Colin, ed. *The Geography of War and Peace: From Death Camps to Diplomats*. New York: Oxford University Press, 2005.

Keegan, John. *A History of Warfare*. New York: Vintage, 1994.

Lavelle, Ryan. *Fortifications in Wessex, c. 800-1066*. New York: Osprey, 2003.

Lele, Ajey. *Weather and Warfare*. New Delhi: Lancer, 2006.

McNeill, William H. *The Pursuit of Power: Technology, Armed Force, and Society Since A.D. 1000*. Chicago: University of Chicago Press, 1984.

Nossov, Konstantin. *Hittite Fortifications, c. 1650-700 B.C.* New York: Osprey, 2008.

O'Sullivan, Patrick. *Terrain and Tactics*. New York: Greenwood Press, 1991.

Preston, Richard A., Sydney F. Wise, and Alex Roland. *Men in Arms: A History of Warfare and Its Interrelationships with Western Society*. 5th ed. New York: Holt, Rinehart and Winston, 1991.

Rose, E. P. F., and C. P. Nathanail, eds. *Geology and Warfare: Examples of the Influence of Terrain and Geologists on Military Operations*. Bath, England: Geological Society, 2000.

Stephenson, Michael. *Battlegrounds: Geography and the Art of Warfare*. Washington, D.C.: National Geographic, 2003.

Woodward, Rachel. *Military Geographies*. Malden, Mass.: Blackwell, 2004.

Joseph P. Byrne

CULTURE AND WARFARE

ART AND WARFARE

OVERVIEW

"War art" is a form of artistic expression with warfare as its subject. Historians of art as well as military historians have traditionally interpreted war art in purely mimetic terms, defining it by what they believed it represented: the timeless essence of war. This understanding of war art led to studies that focused on the continuity of the representation of war throughout the ages rather than on culturally specific differences. More recent studies of war art have begun to acknowledge that both war and art are expressions of specific times and places, and scholars are finally acknowledging the role of cultural change in shaping the understanding of both art and war.

SIGNIFICANCE

The cultural turn in the study of war art is important for a number of reasons, not the least of which is that it forces a reconsideration of the complex relationships among art, war, and culture. Furthermore, this change of focus in regard to war art leads to increased reflection on the understanding of change and continuity throughout time. War art has followed a progression over a broad expanse of time, from the ancient world to the present day. The discussion of this progression below is far from comprehensive, but it offers a window into key moments in the evolution of war art.

HISTORY OF ART AND WARFARE

ANCIENT WORLD

Visual representations of war first appeared around 4000 B.C.E. in cave paintings later uncovered in northern Australia; these paintings show what are believed to be groups of warriors hurling spears at each other. War art did not become prolific, however, until the emergence of the Sumerian culture in Mesopotamia (c. 4000-2340 B.C.E.) and the cultures of ancient Egypt (c. 2920-1070 B.C.E.). The artifact known as the Royal Standard of Ur or the Standard of Ur (c. 2600-2400 B.C.E.) shows the chariots of the Sumerian king's army returning to him with the spoils of war, including prisoners, while the king stands motionless at the center of the top panel of this three-paneled work. The king's position in the image highlights his absolute power; all things begin and end with him. The ancient Egyptian artifact known as the Palette of King Narmer (c. 3150-3125 B.C.E.) conveys a similar message of imperial power, but here the king is seen taking direct action: He holds his enemy with one hand while preparing to strike with the other.

Later cultural productions from Greece and Rome did not differ greatly in message from these earlier works, but they moved toward a more sophisticated representation of warfare. The north frieze of the Treasury of the Siphnians, located at Delphi in Greece, is known as the Battle of the Gods and Giants (c. 530 B.C.E.). Despite the mythical subject of this work of art, viewers can envision the battle with much greater facility than they can with such earlier representations of war as the Royal Standard of Ur. Men engage in hand-to-hand fighting in this scene, using swords and spears, and an animal is even depicted biting into the side of one of the soldiers. The realistic portrayal of mythical battles was continued by the Romans, but they began to include elements of more recent history in their war art as well. One example of this Roman method of representation can be found in the *Ara Pacis Augustae* (c. 13-9 B.C.E.), a large sculpted marble altar that was commissioned by the Emperor Augustus (63 B.C.E.-14 C.E.) to celebrate the peace brought about during his reign. The figures on the north and south walls of the altar represent the various segments of Roman society, including the family of the newly crowned emperor, while those on the east and west sides depict episodes from

Roman mythology. Together these scenes are designed to create the impression of peace and stability, but they also suggest imperial power. The *Ara Pacis Augustae* illustrates that war art in the ancient world was primarily a matter of putting state power on display. Consequently, most ancient war art was what today would be considered public art; it took such forms as temples, sculptures, statues, territorial markers, and royal burial chambers, all of which highlighted the role of the ruler as the guarantor of both victory and peace.

MEDIEVAL WORLD

In the medieval period (476-c.1400), war art continued to illustrate the power of the monarch in matters of peace and war, but the added element of Christian belief meant that the secular king would have to share his power with God. Since secular power was subordinate to divine authority, one of the primary sources for war art in this period was the Bible. Medieval Bibles were extensively illustrated with both stand-alone plates and images skillfully blended into the text. Of these "illuminated manuscripts," the Maciejowski Bible (c. 1250), also known as the Morgan Bible, contains some of the most graphic imagery of war found in the art of this period. One set of illustrations depicts the death of King Saul and his sons at Beth Shan. Saul's body hangs headless and partially naked in the top left-hand corner of the page, dominating the viewer's attention. Careful examination of the

North Wind Picture Archives via AP Images

Eugène Delacroix's Liberty Leading the People *commemorates the July Revolution of 1830.*

Time & Life Pictures/Getty Images

Francisco Goya's Third of May 1808: Execution of the Citizens of Madrid *(1814).*

four illustrations reveals the story that explains Saul's gruesome death and the presence of his headless and naked body on the edge of the page. The top two panels show Saul's beheading and the Philistines then raising his headless body above their ramparts as a trophy of war. The two bottom panels show the bodies of Saul's sons being burned and the head of Saul being brought to the Philistine king. The Maciejowski Bible is the product of a world consumed by religious wars, but, like most illuminated manuscripts, it does not make specific reference to contemporary events.

Biblical and Christianized images borrowed from earlier classical texts were the primary subjects of war art in the medieval period. It was not until the emergence of the Renaissance (c. 1400) that historical subjects began to reappear in war art. The painting *The Battle of San Romano* (1454-1457) by Paolo Uccello (1397-1475) is an early example of Renaissance war art. Commissioned by the Florentine leader Cosimo de' Medici (1389-1464) to decorate his home, the work depicts in three separate panels a battle that occurred in 1432 between the armies of Florence and Siena. Despite the painting's lack of depth and the stylized poses of the main characters, Uccello's portrayal of a recent battle marks the beginning of the modern period in war art. From this point on, specific battles or historic events associated with battles became regular subjects of war art.

MODERN WORLD

Two distinct artistic visions of war emerged following the Renaissance. The first continued in the earlier heroic tradition but was updated to meet the needs of that specific time and place. The second was an entirely new view of war that focused on its unheroic aspects, such as the human cost. Although the artists who produced both kinds of works were interested in war art as historic record, they had entirely different focuses and understandings of war.

Jacques-Louis David's (1748-1825) painting *Napoleon Crossing the Alps* (1800) represents the earlier heroic tradition, both in the artist's choice of subject and in the work's execution. The great leader Napoleon I (1769-1821) is at the center of this portrait, preparing to lead his armies across the Alps and on to victory. Also seen, engraved into the rocks on which Napoleon's horse stands, are the names of the two military leaders who had previously crossed the Alps with their armies: Hannibal and Charles the Great. David's painting thus places its subject within an ongoing narrative of military leadership and imperial power. Francisco de Goya's (1746-1848) painting *The Third of May 1808* (1814) is more historically specific than David's, as the title tells the exact date of the events portrayed. The shift of perspective in this painting, from military leaders to civilian victims of war, also radically changes the story about war that it tells. Here war is the bringer of sudden and violent death rather than the preserver of an ancient code of heroism. What little heroism the viewer finds in the painting is in the courage of the main character, who, bathed in an eerie light of unknown origin, kneels upon a pile of the already dead as he awaits his own execution by firing squad.

When compared to the majority of nineteenth century war art, Goya's painting is an anomaly. It was not until World War I (1914-1918) that the pathos-laden and unheroic vision of warfare that his painting represents became the dominant artistic mode in the portrayal of war. This shift in focus coincided with the emergence of photography as a new medium of artistic expression. As photographic technology evolved in the twentieth century, it became possible for nonparticipants to view war in something close to real time. One of the more famous photographs depicting a battle in progress is *Loyalist Militiaman at the Moment of Death, Cerro Muriano, September 5, 1936* (1936), by Robert Capa (1913-1954). The viewer does not see the entire battle but only a moment from it and feels like an intruder as well as a participant in the scene. The photo shows a soldier, presumably attacking the enemy, precisely at the moment when he is shot and about to fall to the ground. Capa does not provide any key to interpreting this photo; rather, he leaves the viewer to ponder the reality of sudden death in war.

Something similar happens to the viewer of photographs taken by Eddie Adams (1933-2004) during the Vietnam War (1961-1975). Adams's most famous photograph is of South Vietnamese brigadier general Nguyen Ngoc Loan shooting an unarmed prisoner during the 1968 Tet Offensive. At first glance, this scene appears to represent a moral outrage as an armed soldier kills a crying and unarmed civilian. The reality, however, is far more complicated, as the man being executed in the photo, Captain Bay Lop, was an officer in a Viet Cong cell responsible for infiltrating Saigon. The inability of the still image to explain fully the events of war was partially responsible for the emergence of moving images and mixed-media works as the dominant forms in war art in the late twentieth century. Films, whether fictional or documentary, are better able than other art forms to show war as a complex experience (involving all five senses) that evades easy interpretation. They are the perfect artistic form for the twenty-first century, which is an age less of certainty than of seeking and doubt.

BOOKS AND ARTICLES

Boneham, John, and Geoff Quilley, eds. *Conflicting Visions: War and Visual Culture in Britain and France, c. 1700-1830*. Burlington, Vt.: Ashgate Press, 2005. Collection of essays addresses the connection between artistic representations of war and nationalism in Britain and France during the period 1700-1830.

Brandon, Laura. *Art and War*. London: I. B. Tauris, 2007. Offers one of the best overviews available on the subject, examining war art from prehistoric times to the early twenty-first century.

Dillon, Sheila, and Katherine E. Welch, eds. *Representations of War in Ancient Rome*. New York: Cambridge University Press, 2006. Collection of authoritative and accessible essays focuses on nationalism in ancient Rome in relation to the war art produced there. Provides some interesting insights into how Roman culture compares with that of ancient Greece in regard to attitudes toward warfare.

Hale, J. R. *Artists and Warfare in the Renaissance*. New Haven, Conn.: Yale University Press. 1990. Contrasts the representations of war produced by artists of northern and southern Europe during the Renaissance.

Malvern, Sue. *Modern Art, Britain, and the Great War*. New Haven, Conn.: Yale University Press, 2004. Focuses on the concepts of witnessing and testimony in showing how the war culture spawned by Britain's experience in World War I not only altered English art but also prepared the way for a post-Holocaust obsession with authenticity and remembrance.

Moeller, Susan D. *Shooting War: Photography and the American Experience of Combat*. New York: Basic Books, 1989. Follows the development of the art of photography alongside the development of warfare. Covers only American photographers, but offers many insights that can be applied to other Western nations.

Paret, Peter. *Imagined Battles: Reflections of War in European Art*. Chapel Hill: University of North Carolina Press, 1997. Presents an informative overview of war art, focusing on a limited number of works that are representative of larger trends in European art with war as its subject.

Sekules, Veronica. *Medieval Art*. New York: Oxford University Press, 2001. Excellent overview of medieval art devotes a chapter to the representation of war in the artworks of the period.

John Casey

COMMEMORATION OF WAR

OVERVIEW

Commemoration relies on objects (such as monuments) and rituals (such as parades) that function as catalysts for remembering specific events. The selection of these catalysts for collective memory depends largely on the values and beliefs of the particular society as well as the nature of the events to be remembered. In the case of war, commemoration has always been challenging, as it is difficult to balance the desire to celebrate victory and martial valor with the equally strong desire to mourn. Modern scholarship on the commemoration of war reflects this age-old challenge, but it also illustrates the radical changes that have taken place in the interpretation of war and shows how those changes have altered the ways in which war is remembered. Personal narratives of remembrance have come to be favored over official state interpretations, as remembering war has come to be understood as the act of memorializing a shared sense of loss.

©Richard Gunion/Dreamstime.com

The Iwo Jima memorial statue in Arlington, Virginia, commemorates the U.S. Marines.

SIGNIFICANCE

An examination of the evolution of war's commemoration is essential to an understanding of the modern perspective regarding war, as the two are inextricably linked. In ancient and medieval times, war was seen as a positive good, and this was reflected in the ways societies chose to remember wars. The Romans named the month of March after their god of war, Mars, and the culture of medieval England incorporated warfare into the fabric of society through the code of chivalry. It was not until the modern period that the view of war as either a necessary evil or the greatest of all disasters came into being, a factor that radically changed how wars would be remembered. The brief and selective history of the commemoration of war that follows shows a few key moments in this process of evolution in both the understanding and the remembrance of war.

HISTORY OF THE COMMEMORATION OF WAR

ANCIENT WORLD

"Sing, O Muse, of the wrath of Achilles"— thus begins one of the earliest works of Western literature, Homer's *Iliad* (c. 750 B.C.E.; English translation, 1611), which also happens to be a commemoration of war. Documenting events that took place during the Trojan War (c. 1200-1100 B.C.E.), the *Iliad* is a written artifact from an earlier oral culture. In oral cultures the poet was both a priest, serving as an intermediary between the gods and humanity, and the keeper of cultural traditions. War was remembered in oral cultures as part of a larger set of norms and mores that were reinforced with each telling of specific tales.

As writing began to replace storytelling, the commemoration of war moved away from ritual retellings of cultural truisms to fixed objects of remembrance. One example of this change can be found in ancient Rome. The *Aeneid* (29-19 B.C.E.; English translation, 1553), created by the poet Vergil (70-19 B.C.E.), pointed back to an earlier oral culture that was connected to the ritual commemoration of war. At the time Vergil wrote his epic, however, Roman culture was experiencing a massive transition, not only from a republican form of government to an empire but also to a form of memory that relied heavily on public monuments. Although monuments had been part of the communal remembrance of war during the Roman Republic (527-509 B.C.E.), it was not until the early years of the empire and the reign of Augustus (27 B.C.E.-14 C.E.) that they were gradually separated from social rituals. Triumph was transformed from an event into an object. Whereas in the Roman Republic the triumph was a procession of

Time & Life Pictures/Getty Images

The Vietnam Veterans Memorial in Washington, D.C., contains the names of American soldiers who died in that conflict, engraved into a wall of polished black marble.

the victorious army through the capital with the spoils of war, in the empire triumph was presented as an accomplished fact. The Column of Trajan (113 C.E.), which was built to commemorate the victory of the emperor Trajan (c. 53-c. 117 C.E.) against the Dacians in what is now Romania, does not require participation to create its meaning. Trajan's victory is already interpreted for the viewer, whose only job is to see and agree with its message. Movement from a republican participatory remembrance of war, however, to the more passive approach of the empire did not lessen the Roman obsession with victory. Like most ancient cultures, Rome saw little use for the recollection of defeat unless it was that of its enemies. Roman commemorations of war were thus designed primarily to put the state's power prominently on display.

MEDIEVAL WORLD

Unless churches are considered to be monuments, the medieval world contained few public memorials of war. Most of the objects of war commemoration created in this period took the form of hand-illustrated books or interior decoration of churches and castles. Also, with the notable exception of the Bayeux tapestry (c. 1077), which depicts the Norman invasion of England in 1066, early medieval remembrances of war focused on ideal warriors and the chivalric code by which they lived rather than on specific real-world wars and battles. Consequently, many commemorations of battles from ancient mythology and history or the Bible were created. For example, a wall painting in the church of San Pietro al Monte, *Civate* (c. 1100) in Como, Italy, shows the archetypal Christian warrior, the angel Saint Michael, slaying the seven-headed dragon from the Bible's book of Revelation. This image would have highlighted for the medieval viewer the necessary connection between Christian belief and martial valor.

An illustration from the Anglo-Norman poet Thomas de Kent's work the *Book of All Chivalry* (1308-1312) seems to represent a complete departure from the Christian iconography mentioned above. This work's illumination shows a well-known historical scene, Alexander the Great fighting the Persian king Darius, but the text helps the viewer interpret the scene properly. Alexander becomes evidence of the classical roots of the Christian warrior's sense of self, which in turn suggests the universal and timeless appeal of the chivalric code.

Because most medieval authors assumed that their audience would be familiar with the chivalric code, few texts from the early medieval period discuss the code with any consistency or at any length. It was not until the late medieval period that explanations of the chivalric code began to appear. One such text is

Christine de Pizan's (c. 1365-c.1430) *Le Livre des fais d'armes et de chevalerie* (1410; *The Book of Fayttes of Arms and of Chivalry*, 1489), which was provided as a guide to the French king Charles VII (1403-1461) and his subordinates. Written at a time when the chivalric code was in a state of decline, this text was intended to ensure not only that wars would continue to be fought in the proper (that is, chivalric) way but also that they would be remembered correctly. Great changes in military science, along with a rising sense of historic consciousness, doomed Christine's project from the start. War was changing dramatically, and so were the ways in which it would be remembered.

MODERN WORLD

Memorials to state power and to ideal warriors did not immediately disappear from modern commemorations of war, but the rising sense of historical consciousness that marked the birth of the modern period led to a greater interest in remembering specific wars and battles rather than timeless ideals. The understanding of history as a force for permanent social change also led to the belief that the names and deeds of ordinary soldiers should be remembered alongside the causes for which they fought. As a result of this specificity, the creators of commemorations of war soon became involved in clashes over the interpretations of particular conflicts.

After the American Civil War (1861-1865), former slave, abolitionist, and orator Frederick Douglass (1817[?]-1895) argued that the Civil War should be remembered as a struggle to free the slaves from bondage. Among the white population of the United States, many Northerners saw the war primarily as an action taken to preserve the nation's political union, while those living in the defeated South thought of the war as the tragic destruction of an entire way of life. A new war over how to remember the Civil War had suddenly replaced the conflict on the battlefields. Over time, however, a compromise was reached. Statues commemorating the common Civil War soldier began to appear in town squares, parks, and cemeteries throughout the United States. These statues largely refrained from interpreting the war; instead they reflected a shared national language of sacrifice.

Such a relatively neutral vision of war also predominated in the monuments created in England to commemorate World War I. "Official" (that is, state) monuments included the *Whitehall Cenotaph* (1920), located near the seat of Parliament in London; the *Cross of Sacrifice* (c. 1918), designed by the Imperial War Graves Commission for cemeteries near the European battlefields of the war; and the *Port Sunlight Memorial* (1921) in Liverpool. These monuments were designed to celebrate English valor and patriotism, but the names of the dead engraved on them remind the viewer that they are also sites of mourning. This juxtaposition of individual suffering and loss with martial valor represents in itself a great change in the nature of modern war commemoration.

Even greater, however, is the growing desire to remember military defeat. The *Vietnam Veterans Memorial* (1982) in Washington, D.C., commemorates a highly unpopular war that ended with what many Americans viewed as a humiliating defeat. A list of names of the fallen greets the viewer at this site; the names, arranged chronologically in the order of death, are carved into a wall of black marble that is set slightly below ground level. This memorial, designed by Maya Lin (born 1959), powerfully displays the human cost of war, but the creation of meaning is ultimately left up to the viewer. The memorial, ironically, represents a move away from monuments and other objects of remembrance and back to a much older participatory form of commemoration.

©June Marie Sobrito/Dreamstime.com

Beams of light shoot up from the sites of the twin World Trade Center towers as a temporary memorial to those who died in the September 11, 2001, terrorist attacks.

BOOKS AND ARTICLES

Ashplant, T. G., Graham Dawson, and Michael Roper, eds. *The Politics of War Memory and Commemoration*. New York: Routledge, 2000. Collection of essays focuses on the commemoration of modern wars and discusses how official narratives often conflict with the memories of minority groups who have experienced the same conflicts.

Blight, David. *Race and Reunion: The Civil War in American Memory*. Cambridge, Mass.: Harvard University Press, 2001. Examines the divergent ways in which the American Civil War was remembered by those who experienced it and, in the process, makes visible the fractures in collective memory at the war's end that made any authoritative national commemoration difficult if not impossible.

Dillon, Sheila, and Katherine E. Welch, eds. *Representations of War in Ancient Rome*. New York: Cambridge University Press, 2006. Collection of authoritative and accessible essays focuses on the Roman state's relationship to war, including how it chose to commemorate past victories.

Faust, Drew Gilpen. *This Republic of Suffering: Death and the American Civil War*. New York: Alfred A. Knopf, 2008. Traces the movement of the Civil War dead from the battlefields to their final resting places, providing some interesting observations on how Americans in the years following the war attempted to mourn the dead and at the same time make sense of the conflict.

King, Alex. *Memorials of the Great War in Britain: The Symbolism and Politics of Remembrance*. New York: Berg, 1998. Examines the various types of war memorials constructed in Great Britain at the end of World War I and shows the difficulty faced by the English people in balancing the desire to present the nation as triumphant while at the same time mourning their war dead.

Strickland, Matthew. *War and Chivalry: The Conduct and Perception of War in England and Normandy, 1066-1217*. New York: Cambridge University Press, 1996. Discusses the relationship between the chivalric code and the waging of war in the early medieval period as well as the impact the code had on how wars were remembered by the Anglo-Norman people.

Winter, Jay. *Remembering War: The Great War Between History and Memory in the Twentieth Century*. New Haven, Conn.: Yale University Press, 2006. Focuses on how World War I has been commemorated by the different European nations that took part in the conflict. Offers an examination of both the official national remembrances of the war and the counternarratives of particular minority groups.

Winter, Jay, and Emmanuel Sivan. *War and Remembrance in the Twentieth Century*. New York: Cambridge University Press, 1999. Collection of essays highlights the various minority-group counternarratives that undermine authoritative national commemorations of war.

John Casey

FILM AND WARFARE

OVERVIEW

Film and warfare have been linked ever since celluloid images were first projected onto a screen. The practice of using cinema as a nationalistic propaganda tool is as old as the medium itself. Beginning in 1896, one-reelers consisting of "actuality" footage were part of traveling exhibits. In 1898, films of fabricated "events" of the Spanish-American War (using toy boats floated in a bathtub) were used to sway public opinion in the United States. In Great Britain, the drama *The Call to Arms* (1902) rallied support for the Boer War (1899-1902) in South Africa. The cinema has provided a mirror for the values of its parent societies. Though documentaries offer direct messages, narrative feature films are often a better barometer of prevalent societal values. A film depicting current events is later valuable as impressionistic historical evidence. Audiences often focus on World War II when thinking of war films, but the entire history of warfare has been represented on the screen.

SIGNIFICANCE

During World War I, Western society experienced one of the first mass propaganda campaigns of the twentieth century. Leaders in Europe and the United States used the burgeoning mass media to rally support for the Allied war effort. The motion-picture industry, just beginning to develop the feature film and its simplistic conventions, became the ideal medium for this campaign. American film producers, who originally depicted warfare to increase ticket sales, were influenced by those presenting positive views of national preparedness.

ANCIENT WORLD

Filmmakers have repeatedly been attracted to "historical" subjects. Audiences have been captivated by images of warfare, and films set in the ancient world have appealed to their spirit of adventure. While some war films set in ancient times are based on "historical fact," motivating their makers to claims of "realism," these productions frequently offer more information about their parent societies than about the civilizations depicted on the screen.

The Battle of Thermopylae (480 B.C.E.) between the Greek city-states and Persia is the centerpiece of *The 300 Spartans* (1962), an epic that inspired Frank Miller to create the graphic novel *300*, a fictionalized version of the battle that was then adapted for a successful computer-enhanced feature film, released in 2007, that favored digital effects over historical accuracy. Alexander III of Macedonia (356-323 B.C.E.) has been the subject of two major films: *Alexander the Great* (1956), a U.S.-British coproduction, and the Oliver Stone epic *Alexander* (2004), which features several battles that flirt with historical facts. The Third Servile War (73-71 B.C.E.), waged by escaped slaves against Rome, is portrayed in Stanley Kubrick's *Spartacus* (1960). Having lost the lead role in *Ben-Hur* (1959) to Charlton Heston, *Spartacus* star Kirk Douglas created his own ancient epic, giving an intense performance amid a flood of historical inaccuracies, including the crucifixion of Spartacus, who supposedly died in battle.

Roman and Egyptian warfare during the reign of Cleopatra VII (69-30 B.C.E.) provides excitement in two films, both titled *Cleopatra*, that contain references to William Shakespeare's *Julius Caesar* (c. 1599-1600): a 1934 Cecil B. DeMille effort and a historically indefensible 1963 disaster featuring Octavian's victory over Marc Antony at Actium (31 B.C.E.). Producer Samuel Bronston and director Anthony Mann made *The Fall of the Roman Empire* (1964), a box-office bomb (set during 180-192 C.E.) rife with historical falsehoods, including the "Battle of the Four Armies" between renegade Roman legions and a force from Armenia and Persia (actually Parthia). Set during the same period, Ridley Scott's

Michael Ochs Archives/Getty Images

Actor Kirk Douglas as Spartacus in the 1960 film of the same name, depicting the gladiator who rebelled against Rome.

Gladiator (2000) opens with a Roman victory over an army of Germanic Barbarians. Responsible for reviving the "historical" epic (including Wolfgang Petersen's *Troy*, 2004, based on the works of the ancient epic poets Homer and Vergil), the film produced the "*Gladiator* effect," increasing public interest in classical subjects.

MEDIEVAL WORLD

Films depicting medieval warfare have frequently been popular with audiences, whose knowledge of "history" often is gained from what they see on the screen. Since the silent era, the legendary King Arthur has been featured in many war-oriented Anglo-American films. Bronston and Mann also made the romanticized *El Cid* (1961), starring Charlton Heston

as the Castilian "master of military arts" who conquered Valencia with a combined Christian and Moorish army (1094-1102). The film vividly depicts an early form of psychological warfare—terrorizing the enemy before attacking suddenly—and the fictionalized ending, with the corpse of the Cid charging into battle, is unforgettable.

The Crusades (1095-1272) have been represented in epics about Robin Hood as well as in Cecil B. DeMille's *The Crusades* (1935) and Ridley Scott's *Kingdom of Heaven* (2005), which prove that "historical accuracy" in films set in the medieval world did not increase much over seven decades. The 1242 Battle of the Ice at Novgorod between Russian peasants and the Teutonic Knights of the Holy Roman Empire is energized by the montage of Sergei Eisenstein and the music of Sergei Prokofiev in the Soviet masterpiece *Alexander Nevsky* (1938).

The story of Joan of Arc has spanned the history of film, from wartime variations during World War I to French epics such as Carl Theodor Dreyer's *The Passion of Joan of Arc* (1928) and Luc Besson's *The Messenger: The Story of Joan of Arc* (1999), which focuses on the teenage Joan's military leadership during scenes featuring anachronistic weaponry. The English perspective during the Hundred Years' War (1337-1453) has been visualized in two adaptations of Shakespeare's *Henry V* (c. 1598-1599): Laurence Olivier's 1944 "wartime version" and a 1989 retooling by Kenneth Branagh featuring a brutal recreation of the Battle of Agincourt (1415).

For *Braveheart* (1995), the epic about William Wallace's role in the Wars of Scottish Independence, director and star Mel Gibson sought optimum historical realism for the battles of Stirling and Falkirk. Members of Clan Wallace appeared as extras, and armorer Simon Atherton provided accurate weaponry. Gibson used rapid editing and thunderous sound to depict the calamity of medieval warfare, creating scenes so shocking in their brutality that they prompted some patrons to flee theaters in 1995. Like most "historical" epics, *Braveheart* was criticized by traditionalist scholars for its revisionism (a tendency less forgivable in the depiction of modern history but unavoidable in a visualization of the thirteenth century).

MODERN WORLD

The English Civil War of the 1640's provided a backdrop for the "historical horror" film *Witchfinder General* (1968) and the epic *Cromwell* (1970), featuring technically impressive though historically inaccurate depictions of the battles of Edgehill and Naseby. In 1939, Hollywood depicted British and Native American attacks in *Allegheny Uprising* (colonial period) and *Drums Along the Mohawk* (revolutionary period). The American Revolution took center stage in *1776* (1972) and *The Patriot* (2000), an ultraviolent and historically inaccurate portrayal in which Mel Gibson plays a variation on *Braveheart*, trading his medieval war hammer for a tomahawk.

In 1927, Abel Gance directed the French silent *Napoleon*, which was groundbreaking in its use of wide-screen battle sequences. France also produced a sound *Napoleon* (1955) that re-created the battles of Austerlitz and Waterloo. A film adaptation of Leo Tolstoy's *Voyna i mir* (1865-1869; *War and Peace*, 1886) was released in 1956 (an Italian-U.S. coproduction), and in 1963-1966 Soviet director Sergei Bondarchuk adapted the work into a four-part series that stands as the most expensive film ever made. In 2003, Russell Crowe starred in *Master and Commander: The Far Side of the World*, a historically detailed adaptation of three Patrick O'Brian novels about Napoleonic maritime warfare.

The Texas War of Independence (1835-1836) has been depicted in many films, including John Wayne's cinematically impressive, historically dubious *The Alamo* (1960) and a 2004 revisionist remake showing the viewpoints of both armies. The Crimean War (1853-1856) inspired Alfred, Lord Tennyson's "The Charge of the Light Brigade" (1854), a poem that has been adapted for two films, a 1936 Warner Bros. adventure starring Errol Flynn and a 1968 British remake. The Indian Rebellion of 1857 provided pro-British colonial warfare for the Hollywood adventure films *The Lives of a Bengal Lancer* (1936) and *Gunga Din* (1939).

The American Civil War was initially represented by Hollywood blockbusters based on pro-Confederate novels. The silent era was revolutionized technically by D. W. Griffith's *The Birth of a Nation* (1915), featuring political and racial stereotypes solidified decades later by David O. Selznick's nostalgic *Gone with the Wind* (1939), which includes some brief scenes of wartime devastation, such as its towering crane shot showing a sea of wounded Confederate soldiers on the streets of Atlanta.

John Huston's 1951 adaptation of Stephen Crane's 1895 novel *The Red Badge of Courage* includes some anachronistic weaponry, but its focus on a young soldier (World War II hero Audie Murphy) horrified by the reality of war was one of the first realistic portrayals of the conflict on film. The Civil War has energized countless Westerns, including Sergio Leone's "spaghetti" epic *The Good, the Bad, and the Ugly* (1966), with Clint Eastwood braving battles while searching for buried Confederate gold. *Glory* (1989), Edward Zwick's powerful, semifactual film about the African American Fifty-fourth Massachusetts Volunteer Infantry, has been praised for providing an antidote to the falsehoods of *Gone with the Wind*.

Western war films often feature (highly stylized) battles between whites and Native Americans. Raoul Walsh's fictionalized film about the life of George A. Custer, *They Died with Their Boots On* (1941), became a heroic vehicle for Errol Flynn, while John Ford depicted several battles in his "cavalry trilogy": *Fort Apache* (1948), *She Wore a Yellow Ribbon* (1949), and *Rio Grande* (1950).

Prior to the U.S. government's establishment of propaganda policy during World War I, feature films created support for the military. *The Brand of Cowardice* (1916) and *The Deserter* (1916) both depicted American men who became like treacherous "foreigners" when they refused to fight. After President Woodrow Wilson declared war in April, 1917, the Committee on Public Information exerted a control over fiction films that was more important than that directed toward the "documentaries" being produced. The most extensive federal involvement in Hollywood films came from the Department of Publicity for the Fourth Liberty Loan Drive. Criticized for his pacifism, actor, writer, and director Charles Chaplin "did his part" by supporting the Third and Fourth Loans, then combined propaganda with comedy in *Shoulder Arms* (1918).

Hollywood's first World War I epic, *The Big Parade* (1925), opens in stereotypical fashion with men anxious for the "fun" of warfare but later features an Allied march through an empty forest that explodes with German machine-gun fire. Another scene captures the appalling stench of no-man's-land when James Apperson (played by John Gilbert) lands in a shell hole with the corpse of an enemy he has just killed. Aerial warfare was staged on a grand scale for William Wellman's *Wings* (1927) and Howard Hughes's *Hell's Angels* (1930), both featuring heroic flyboys in aerial sequences that were remarkably realistic for the period.

Perhaps the most memorable World War I film, Lewis Milestone's *All Quiet on the Western Front* (1930), based on Erich Maria Remarque's antiwar novel *Im Westen nichts Neues* (1929; English translation, 1929), was groundbreaking in its use of the German perspective. The film's horrific images of soldiers being ripped to pieces during combat is surpassed only by the final scene: Amid the mud and blood of the trenches, the protagonist, Paul Bäumer (played by Lew Ayres), is shot to death as he reaches out to grasp a butterfly.

Realizing that Depression filmgoers might be ill served by realistic images of the war's western front, Hollywood filmmakers produced paeans to the heroes of World War I who "made the world safe for democracy," including Warner Bros.' *Sergeant York* (1941). Previously, Warner Bros. had taken risks depicting the challenges faced by veterans, in *The Public Enemy* (1931) and *I Am a Fugitive from a Chain Gang* (1932).

John Ford's *The Lost Patrol* (1934) depicts British cavalrymen battling a deadly, unseen enemy in the sands of Mesopotamia (now Iraq). Aerial warfare energizes Edmund Goulding's *The Dawn Patrol* (1938), which—in the hands of Errol Flynn—reinforces cinematic clichés involving World War I fighter pilots: white scarves flowing in the wind, chivalrous behavior during dogfights, and fatalistic attitudes wrought by impending death. Warner

Bros.' *The Fighting 69th* (1940) chronicles the service of the "Irish" Sixty-ninth Infantry. Amid combat footage involving "Wild Bill" Donovan and poet Joyce Kilmer, James Cagney plays the classic conscript without a cause who is despised by his comrades. After his recklessness leads to several deaths, he redeems himself by waging a mortar assault on the enemy.

Though films set during World War I were prevalent in the years before U.S. entry into World War II, they gave way in 1941 before making a comeback with *The Blue Max* (1966), a British film about German flyers on the western front; the Australian antiwar film *Gallipoli* (1981); and *Flyboys* (2006), a look at American flyers who joined France's Lafayette Escadrille during 1916-1917.

The 1917 Russian Revolution was praised by montage filmmakers Sergei Eisenstein and Vsevolod Pudovkin in *October: Ten Days That Shook the World* (1927) and *The End of St. Petersburg* (1927), respectively. Two years earlier, Eisenstein had directed *Battleship Potemkin* (1925), a depiction of a 1905 mutiny by sailors against their czarist officers. The combination of montage technique and political propaganda made this semifictional military epic one of the most influential films of all time.

During U.S. involvement in World War II, the conventions of the war-film genre were further established, and the influence of these wartime productions can still be seen in films made in the early twenty-first century. The idea for the preparedness comedy *Buck Privates* (1941) began when Lou Costello suggested that moviegoers would be captured by a "soldier picture" capitalizing on the Selective Service and Training Act signed by President Franklin D. Roosevelt in September, 1940. The success of the film led to two more pro-service pictures featuring the comedy team of Bud Abbott and Lou Costello—*In the Navy* and *Keep 'Em Flying*—released prior to the Japanese attack on Pearl Harbor.

Roosevelt's establishment of the Office of War Information in June, 1942, called for Hollywood propaganda, a mandate affecting every film genre. Eventually, even Tarzan, Sherlock Holmes, and the Invisible Man were battling the Axis Powers. By August, 1945, nearly every battleground figured into a script.

Universal Film Co., courtesy National Archives

A scene from the 1918 film The Kaiser, the Beast of Berlin, *which promulgated anti-German sentiment and American support for post-World War I antisedition laws.*

The European theater of operations is portrayed in *Commandos Strike at Dawn* (1942) and *The Story of G.I. Joe* (1945), and the Pacific theater is the focus of *Bataan* (1943) and *Destination Tokyo* (1943). Celluloid war heroes were invented for top stars who stayed home: Errol Flynn (*Desperate Journey*, 1942; *Northern Pursuit*, 1943; *Uncertain Glory*, 1944; *Objective: Burma!*, 1945), Humphrey Bogart (*Sahara*, 1943; *Action in the North Atlantic*, 1943; *Passage to Marseille*, 1944), and John Wayne (*Flying Tigers*, 1942; *The Fighting Seabees*, 1944; *They Were Expendable*, 1945; *Back to Bataan*, 1945).

World War II continued to dominate postwar cinema. *Battleground* (1949), William Wellman's depiction of the Battle of the Bulge, was followed by the fictional *Sands of Iwo Jima* (1950), starring Wayne, and *The Naked and the Dead* (1958), based on Norman Mailer's 1948 novel about his wartime experiences in the Pacific. Submarine warfare was revisited in *Run Silent, Run Deep* (1956), prisoners of war were featured in *Stalag 17* (1950) and *Von Ryan's Express* (1965), and D day was "re-created" on a massive scale in *The Longest Day* (1962), the producer of which, Darryl F. Zanuck, summing up the pseudohistorical content of war films, admitted, "There is nothing duller on the screen than being accurate but not dramatic."

Both theaters of war are represented in the 1970 epics *Tora! Tora! Tora!*, a U.S.-Japanese coproduction about the attack on Pearl Harbor told from both perspectives, and *Patton*, a biography of the general whose military brilliance was undermined by his cavalier treatment of soldiers. D day also is depicted in *The Big Red One* (1980), which is based on director Samuel Fuller's service in the U.S. First Infantry. The German perspective is offered in Wolfgang Petersen's *Das Boot* (1981), an accurate view of U-boat warfare set primarily within the confines of a submarine.

The first twenty-four minutes of Steven Spielberg's *Saving Private Ryan* (1998) have been hailed as the most realistic combat scene in film history. This meticulous re-creation of the landings at Omaha Beach on D day features actual World War II landing craft and weaponry. Spielberg also coproduced the television miniseries *Band of Brothers* (2001), a look at "Easy Company," a parachute regiment attached to the 101st Airborne, based on the 1992 book of the same title by historian Stephen Ambrose and interviews with veterans.

The Korean War and the Cold War are represented in films made over four decades, including films that depict combat (*The Bridges at Toko-Ri*, 1954; *Pork Chop Hill*, 1959), espionage (*The Manchurian Candidate*, 1962), nuclear war (*The Day After*, 1983), and military training (*Top Gun*, 1986). John Wayne attempted to repeat his *Alamo* tribute for soldiers in Vietnam with *The Green Berets* (1968), a counter to the antiwar movement and supported by the presidential administration of Lyndon B. Johnson. Following the withdrawal of U.S. troops from Vietnam, filmmakers created a new, graphically violent subgenre of films depicting the Vietnam War, including *Apocalypse Now* (1979), Francis Ford Coppola's updating of Joseph Conrad's 1902 novel *Heart of Darkness*; *Platoon* (1986), a response to *The Green Berets* based on Oliver Stone's own experiences; and *Full Metal Jacket* (1987), Stanley Kubrick's tale of U.S. Marines at the Tet Offensive.

Hollywood continues to "chronicle" U.S. involvement in foreign conflicts, increasingly focusing on how warfare psychologically affects soldiers. The Persian Gulf War of 1990-1991 is addressed in *Courage Under Fire* (1996), *Three Kings* (1999), and *Jarhead* (2005), while the Iraq War begun in 2003 and the "War on Terror" are explored in *Home of the Brave* (2006), *In the Valley of Elah* (2007), and *Body of Lies* (2008).

In 1965, Frank Sinatra directed the first U.S.-Japanese film coproduction, *None but the Brave*, a war film depicting the viewpoints of combatants on both sides. Four decades later, Clint Eastwood expanded on this idea by directing two innovative companion films, both of which were released in 2006: *Flags of Our Fathers*, the fact-based story of the troops who raised the U.S. flag on Mount Suribachi; and *Letters from Iwo Jima*, based on two nonfiction books, one by General Tadamichi Kuribayashi, who commanded the Japanese garrison during the battle. *Flags of Our Fathers* incorporates vivid battle flashbacks while focusing on the fates of seven U.S. Marines and their Navy corpsman, while *Letters from Iwo Jima* portrays the battle from the perspective of Kuribayashi and his men. Both films were critically acclaimed for their realism and evenhanded historical accounts, with *Letters from Iwo Jima* receiving the lion's share of praise for its empathetic view of the Japanese soldiers.

Books and Articles

Basinger, Jeanine. *The World War II Combat Film: Anatomy of a Genre*. 1986. Reprint. Middletown, Conn.: Wesleyan University Press, 2003. Addresses motion pictures depicting the fighting of World War II as a separate genre of war films. Discusses the evolution of war films in general and provides in-depth discussion of several individual films.

Carnes, Mark C., ed. *Past Imperfect: History According to the Movies*. New York: Henry Holt, 1995. Collection of essays focuses on the historical inaccuracies depicted in motion pictures. Includes several examinations of films in which the action takes place during World War II.

Chadwick, Bruce. *The Reel Civil War: Mythmaking in American Film*. New York: Alfred A. Knopf, 2001. Examines how the revisionist version of Civil War history perpetrated in the late nineteenth century by many writers for magazines and newspapers, as well as novelists and even historians, later came to be depicted in motion pictures as well.

Davenport, Robert. *The Encyclopedia of War Movies: The Authoritative Guide to Movies About Wars of the Twentieth Century*. New York: Facts On File, 2004. Presents brief articles on more than eight hundred films, including cast lists, synopses, and other details.

Eberwein, Robert. *The Hollywood War Film*. Malden, Mass.: Wiley-Blackwell, 2010. Provides an informative, readable introduction to the history of war films as made by American film-makers. Includes an overview of the genre as well as in-depth discussion of individual films depicting wartime action from World War I through the Iraq War of the twenty-first century.

_____, ed. *The War Film*. New Brunswick, N.J.: Rutgers University Press, 2005. Collection of essays by film scholars presents discussion of aesthetic and narrative elements of specific war films. Topics addressed include the conventions of the genre as well as the films' depictions of race and gender issues.

Harty, Kevin J. *The Reel Middle Ages: American, Western and Eastern European, Middle Eastern, and Asian Films About Medieval Europe*. Jefferson, N.C.: McFarland, 1999. Presents synopses and brief analyses of some six hundred films, including silent films and animated works, that depict life in the Middle Ages, including medieval warfare. Supplemented with photographs and bibliographies.

Nollen, Scott Allen. *Abbott and Costello on the Home Front: A Critical Study of the Wartime Films*. Jefferson, N.C.: McFarland, 2009. Focuses on the popular American World War II-era films starring the comedy team of Abbott and Costello. Provides information on each film's story line, production history, and reception.

Scott Allen Nollen

IDEOLOGY AND WAR

OVERVIEW

War has been a universal and almost continuous human phenomenon from the earliest days of human life. The conduct of war until the modern era was mostly a matter for kings, emperors, chiefs, and their warriors. However, in the modern era, the Industrial Revolution, the Enlightenment, and the French Revolution (1789-1793) produced profound changes in the mobilization of populations in a political system for war. Ideas were coalesced into ideologies, which began to be used to motivate people to participate in all manner of causes. Such ideological causes seek to make great changes in the world that would be, according to some intellectual element in the ideology, "just" or "equal" or "national"—or whatever term was needed to mobilize the emotions of the masses.

SIGNIFICANCE

Ideology is a belief structure that forms the minds of "true believers," or ideologues. Ideology so molds their thoughts that it becomes their worldview. It also binds them with similar ideologues and organizes their emotions for action. However, since a questioning attitude about their ideology is often not a part of their thought, their views are often rigid, self-righteous, and closed. The modern world has seen many ideologies that have provided the motives for war or other acts of violence.

HISTORY OF IDEOLOGY AND WARFARE

ANCIENT WORLD

The explicit study of ideologies began with the Enlightenment. However, many scholars across diverse fields believe that ideologies have always existed.

Historically most governments in the world until the American Revolution were kingdoms, empires, or tribal chiefdoms. Kings and emperors usually relied on warrior castes to staff their armies. These arrangements used an ideology based on a social class system to perpetuate people's continual buying into the system. Often, these ideologies build themselves upon religious beliefs or official church teachings in order to justify their existence. One major exception occurred in the ancient Greek democracies. The citizen armies of a Greek *polis* (city-state) involved the whole male population, who accepted the ideology of the supremacy of their city-state, and they were expected to fight in its wars.

Some see religions or the justifications of autocrats, whether kings or some other kind, as ideologies. For example the Ali'i religious system of the Hawaiians functioned as an ideology. It justified the rule of the chiefs, *kahunas* (priests), and the *kapu* (taboo) system. Another example is the Seleucid Empire's use of Hellenism, which functioned as an ideology. It justified using violence against the Jews in support of their political vision (ideology) of a Hellenistic kingdom.

MEDIEVAL WORLD

The fastest-growing religion of the medieval age, Islam, in many ways functioned as an ideology that led followers to engage in warfare to support its expansion throughout the Arab world, and even into parts of Europe. The religion, founded by Muḥammad in the early seventh century, provided a framework for many parts of its followers' lives, from social relationships to the proper conduct and aims of warfare. The Qur'ān gives instruction on, among many other things, the use of jihad (struggle) as a means of expanding the new religion. After Muḥammad's death in 632, warriors inspired by Islamic ideology wrested control of not only Muḥammad's in the Arab Peninsula but also the Levant, Asia Minor, North Africa, and the Iberian Peninsula. In Europe, Charlemagne's capitulary (law or act) of 802 offered an ideological justification of the Holy Roman Empire, including both Popes and temporal rulers. The Crusades also relied on an ideology of warfare in order to justify the conquest of the Holy Land. The ideology put forth by Pope Urban II in 1095 in a sermon that inaugurated the First Crusade emphasized the injustice of Islamic control of Jerusalem and, in a broader sense, provided an ideological rationale for violence through its portrayal of enemies of Christendom and its assertion of divine rewards for those who pursued violence in the name of Christ. This justification of warfare in the name of a religious ideology had a permanent effect on Christianity, and the impact of the Crusades can be seen today in the theological justifications for certain types of warfare.

MODERN WORLD

Although ideologies have been present in human history ever since societies first took shape, their explicit articulation truly began in the revolutions of the late eighteenth century. Both the American and French revolutions produced statements that could be said to have formed an ideology for their movements. Both of these ideologies proved to be persuasive enough to convince people to voluntarily risk, and even lose, their lives in their defense. Specifically, the American and French revolutions share a rejection of monarchy and, by extension, autocracy as a form of government. Taking the place of autocracy was modernism, that is, political ordering that uses human political engineering to create a political system. The effect is to transfer loyalty from the person of the autocrat (usually a king) to the nation and/or a national ideology. The success of these revolutions brought about, for the first time, the study of ideologies.

The first use of the term "ideology" was by Antoine-Louis-Claude Destutt de Tracy (1754-1836) in his *Traité de la volonté* (1815, in *Éléments d'idéologie IV et V*; *A Treatise on Political Economy*, 1817). His ideas were rejected as impractical by Napoleon Bonaparte but were translated into English by Thomas Jefferson. In 1845, Karl Marx (1818-1883) and Friedrich Engels (1820-1895) wrote *Die deutsche Ideologie* (1845-1846; *The German Ideology*,

1938), in which they disagreed with Destutt de Tracy, who had defined "ideology" as the "science of ideas." Instead, Marx and Engels saw ideology as a fabrication by some group (ruling or commercial or other) to justify themselves. Disagreement over the very definition of ideology has grown ever since. For social scientists and especially political scientists, there is no single agreed-upon definition of ideology. There are, however, features of ideologies that are identifiable, and there are also clearly identifiable macro- and micro-ideologies.

Modern, explicitly stated ideologies are often political, materialistic, action-oriented, simple-minded, and mass-oriented. Politically, ideologies use selected sets of political ideas. They use ideas in ways that are simplistic, limited, and closed because they are seeking to move the hearts and minds of the masses to undertake action. In contrast to political philosophies, which teach understanding, ideologies incite to action.

The materialistic aspect of many ideologies arises from their vision of the present and near future. Ideologies often offer followers a hope for material improvements in life that are seen as attainable within a lifetime. Such ideologies promise that political evils will be overcome and replaced with a brave new world of peace and plenty. Ideologies also give solidarity to their followers. Political parties and movements come to a common identity from the ideas they hold, which creates an "ism." Nazism, communism, socialism, fascism, and other political philosophies that define factions or parties are known by their political idea sets. Nationalism seeks to enlist all the people of a political system into its fold.

Ideologies are also action-oriented because they seek to mobilize people into joining the "cause." There is some evil to be ended (global warming, saving the environment, ending poverty, or any number of others), which requires actions that are in line with the specific steps that must be followed to attain the goal. This leads to the creation of organizations that may be political, cultural, civic, economic, social, or even religious in order to put into action steps to reach the common purpose.

The simplistic nature of ideologies is found in the way in which ideas are combined that may or may not be fully coherent. Intellectual rigor is not required for true believers who follow ideologies. As a consequence, symbol manipulation (which is very close to propaganda) enables the leaders of ideology-driven parties to gain support for vague or undetermined goals.

Mass mobilization to achieve the goals of the ideology is the final feature of ideologies. Quite often the mobilization is pitched in terms of war. The ideology uses affective language (language that appeals to emotions) to invite people to join the struggle, the battle, the crusade, the jihad, or even the war. The propagandists of ideologies use simple ideas with significant emotional appeal to mobilize the masses. This joining of people allows opportunities for personal expression to arise.

Revolutionary ideologies in the modern world have created a variety of wars. This is especially the case for the ideologies of liberalism and socialism. The nineteenth century wars of liberation in Mexico and South America were driven by varieties of liberalism that battled against autocratic rule. A number of the revolutions in Europe in the nineteenth century, especially those of 1848, were also revolutionary, their violence aimed at ending ancient forms of rule.

Nationalism—one of the most potent ideologies of the modern world—has been the source of numerous conflicts. In the late eighteenth and nineteenth centuries, as various groups of people in Europe abandoned autocratic forms of government that had ruled for centuries, the mobilization of the masses into nations led—in the case of the French—to a bloody Reign of Terror, then to wars to maintain the Republic, and then to wars to spread the ideology of the revolution, all in the name of the ideology of "liberty, equality, and fraternity." The ideology was a combination of both nationalism and universalism. The revolutionaries and their Napoleonic successor saw themselves as bearers of a universal gift of freedom for all people. The conservative counterrevolution was ultimately successful, instituting a peace designed by the prevailing autocratic powers.

During the Napoleonic Wars (1793-1815), Johann Gottlieb Fichte (1762-1814) delivered his *Reden an die deutsche Nation* (1808; *Addresses to the German Nation*, 1922) becoming the father of German nationalism. He also propounded the idea of the closed economic state in *Der gescholossene Handelsstadt* (1800; the closed commercial state), presenting a theory of economic autarchy, or isolationism. If each nation developed its own economy in isolation, reasoned Fichte, the absence of economic conflicts would bring peace. The vision of isolationism as an application of nationalism was ideological but ultimately ineffective in preventing war.

Nationalism in the nineteenth and especially the twentieth century has been the cause of war. Both the Nazis and the Fascists used it to justify imperialism as territorial expansion. German chancellor Adolf Hitler asserted the Germans' need for *Lebensraum* ("living room," or room to expand the nation), which justified removal of inferior nations (Slavs, Gypsies, Jews, and others). The idea had been proposed in 1897 by Friedrich Ratzel and developed by others before Hitler's rise to power. The racism of the Nazi ideology was used to wage war against "inferior" people.

For Italian dictator Benito Mussolini, expansion was a nationalist goal that would restore Italy to its ancient, glorious past. A new Roman Empire was to be created that would allow for the cultural superiority of Italians, as inheritors of the Romans, to be expressed. The conquest of Ethiopia by the Italian Fascists was an action for spreading Italian nationalism.

The key element that Nazi and Fascist ideologies inherited from their autocratic predecessors was militarism. The glorification of war was hailed as something necessary for the preservation of the state. War was not just a pragmatic instrument of policy but an end in itself. The rise of Nazi and Fascist dictators was due in part to their successful mobilization of the population through militarism. The state would not accept defeat, and scapegoats (Jews, for example) were offered to explain national difficulties. Military aggression appealed to a population suffering from the worldwide depression, offering a promise of victories to come that would change the present and usher in a glorious future.

Democratic governments have also been nationalistic and have engaged in wars of expansion. The

United States' wars with Great Britain (the War of 1812), Mexico (1846-1848), and Spain (1898), as well as its Indian Wars and the Philippine-American War (1899-1902), were conducted as nationalistic campaigns, often with a dose of racism. Other countries have also engaged in nationalistic conflicts; the several wars between India and Pakistan, for example, have had nationalistic ideologies at their base.

While there have been wars justified by religion, the Arab-Israeli wars have been spurred by many factors, including religion (Judaism versus Islam), territorialism (Israel versus Palestine), ethnic rivalries (Jews versus Arabs), and nationalism (Zionism vs. Palestinian Nationalism). The rise of Islamic Jihadists—who are advocates of an ideological version of Islam (Salafism), whether of the Wahhābī type or the Iranian (Hezbollah)—has produced a religious ideology that, in the case of the Wahhābī Ikhwan movement, inspired many to fight battles for King ibn Saud. Modern Salafism, espoused by Osama Bin Laden and others, advocates the use of terrorism in order to achieve its goal of global conquest for Islam as well as a reactionary return to what it holds to be the purity of Islam during the age of Moḥammad and his companions.

In the twentieth century, the post-World War II decades of decolonization have been interpreted as nationalistic wars. The Mau Mau movement in Kenya (1952-1957) and other anticolonial uprisings were nationalistic. During the Cold War, the ideological struggle between Soviet and Chinese communism and the democracies of the West usually played out in areas of the Third World such as Africa, South Asia, and Latin America, where nationalistic groups, whether communist or democratic in their orientation, engaged in proxy wars for their ideological champions.

The communist regimes practiced the revolutionary variety of socialism. The use of violence, both by the ancien régime against revolutionary collaborators and by the revolutionaries to eliminate members of the old order, caused the deaths of millions. The communists waged "class warfare" against their op-

A Nazi poster touts the benefits of euthansia: It says, "This is what this person suffering from hereditary defects costs the Community of Germans during his lifetime. Fellow Citizen, that is your money, too." The banner's largest message touts a future "New People" (neues Volk).

ponents—the wealthy classes, aristocrats, and religious. In the case of the Chinese communists the poor peasants were mobilized to support the liquidation of the Chinese property owners, who were often peasants themselves who happened to own their farms.

Among the collaborators killed by Joseph Stalin (1878-1953), who succeeded Vladimir Ilyich Lenin (1870-1924), were anarchists and other libertarians. While advocates of the use of violence, most were not organized to wage war because they adhered to the theory of Karl Marx that capitalism caused wars and that with the end of capitalism there would be an end to the state and to wars. The state itself was the cause of wars for anarchists.

The list of ideologies ranges widely, from economic ideologies of capitalism and socialism, to political ideologies such as communism, fascism, and liberalism, to other types of ideologies such as racism, environmentalism, pacifism, and many more. While all are ideologies and share ideological characteristics, they also can, under the right conditions, condone violence in some form or other to gain the political changes they seek.

BOOKS AND ARTICLES

Baradat, Leon P. *Political Ideologies: Their Origins and Impact*. Upper Saddle River, N.J.: Prentice-Hall, 2006. Explores the evolution of ideology over three hundred years and looks at how it plays out in politics, society, economy, and military contexts.

Carlton, Eric. *War and Ideology*. Lanham, Md.: Rowman and Littlefield, 1990. A theoretical exploration of why political ideologies so often find expression in warfare.

Cassels, Alan. *Ideology and International Relations in the Modern World*. London: Routledge, 1996. Looks at ideologies in the modern world and how they interact on an international basis.

Kohn, Hans. *Nationalism: Its Meaning and History*. New York: Van Nostrand, 1965. Looks at how nationalism has shaped ideology in the modern world.

Losurdo, Domenico. *Heidegger and the Ideology of War: Community, Death, and the West*. Amherst, N.Y.: Humanity Books, 2001. A focused study of an ideology that was formed to serve a national will.

Vincent, Andrew. *Modern Political Ideologies*. London: Wiley-Blackwell, 2008. Vincent's work is an introductory study of world ideologies over the past two hundred years.

Andrew J. Waskey

LITERATURE AND WARFARE

OVERVIEW

War is life's greatest conflict and the ultimate form of competition. As such, it continues to provide writers with a fertile field for examining the always intriguing complexities of human nature. Warfare is often railed against, and on occasion it has been chic to view it as obsolete. In the overall scheme of things, however, war has generally managed to remain popular. Indeed, the noted philosophers Will and Ariel Durant once calculated that in the past 3,000 years only 268 of those years have been free of war. With this in mind, it is perhaps not surprising that wars have provided grist for some of the world's most enduring literature.

SIGNIFICANCE

Literature that focuses on war recognizes how war affects human behavior through characters created in literature.

HISTORY OF LITERATURE AND WARFARE

ANCIENT WORLD

Organized armies have fought against each other for at least ten thousand years. Either at war or in anticipation of war, military infrastructures have played a key role in the organization of human societies. The earliest civilizations of China, for example, were established by organized armies.

Accounts of the earliest conflicts were preserved in song and story through oral tradition, often setting warfare in a mythological context. Rigvedic hymns of ancient India, for instance, relate tales of the warrior god Indra. A Babylonian epic poem, "War of the Gods," deals with the myth of world creation and the establishment of divine hierarchy, which formed part of a New Year's festival.

The earliest literary work in the Western tradition to deal with war is found in the *Iliad* (c. 750 B.C.E.; English translation, 1611), ostensibly written by Homer (c. 750 B.C.E.), but whether or not it is a work of shared authorship is a moot point. One of the classics of world literature, the *Iliad* deals with the very long and savage war between Athens and Sparta—the Trojan War (c. 1200-1100 B.C.E.)—with the culminating siege of Troy, which dragged on for three decades. The war was originally based on a struggle for control of important trade routes across the Hellespont. However, in the *Iliad*, the story centers on one incident: the Trojans' attempt to recover the abducted Helen of Troy. When Agamemnon—king of the Greeks (who invade Troy), refuses to ransom Chryseis to her father, the god Apollo inflicts a plague of pestilence on them, compelling Agamemnon to return the girl. Not to be entirely thwarted, Agamemnon takes Achilles' prized concubine instead. Dishonored, Achilles withdraws his warriors. War here is depicted as not only mean and bloody but also a process of retaliation and quid pro quo. During this process, when a warrior is slain or an attack is perpetrated, the fury of the combatants escalates. Such endlessly escalating conflict required a resolution, and Homer offered one in the *Odyssey* (c. 725 B.C.E.; English translation, 1614), which tells the story of a survivor of the Trojan War, Odysseus (or Ulysses), who undergoes a series of adventures that function as tests and atonements before he can return home to a joyful reunion with his wife, Penelope. Both the *Iliad* and the *Odyssey* draw heavily on the rich storehouse of Greek mythology, and in so doing provide a "divine" perspective on the issues of loss and redemption surrounding the Greek view of war.

In the *Aeneid* (29-19 B.C.E.; English translation, 1553), war is the context for nation-building: The Roman poet Vergil (Publius Vergilius Maro) uses literature as a sort of genealogical tool to reconstruct the beginnings of the Roman Empire. In this epic poem, the Greek warrior Aeneas has fled his native land following the Trojan War and—after a series of adventures, some harrowing—arrives in Italy, where he proceeds to recount the details of the Trojan War. After defeating the Rutulian leader Turnus in battle and miraculously recovering from a wound received in combat, Aeneas marries Lavinia (daughter of Latinus, king of the Latins) and establishes the new kingdom on the Seven Hills that has been promised to him in a dream.

MEDIEVAL WORLD

The adopted nephew of Charlemagne, the knight Roland, and his bosom friend Oliver, together with their valiant comrades, sacrifice their lives to protect Charlemagne's army by defending the pass at Roncesvalles in the Pyrenees Mountains in 778 C.E. Their epic defense was later immortalized in the anonymous *Chanson de Roland* (c. 1100; *The Song of Roland*).

Among Germanic peoples, one of the most influential works of literature was the *Nibelungenlied* (c. 1200; English verse translation, 1848; prose translation, 1877), set in the fifth century in north-central Europe. Although medieval in origins, the *Nibelungenlied*, like the Homeric writings, draws on numerous myths, including Siegfried's titanic battle with a great dragon, including rituals of ancient worship that are woven throughout the work. War, again, is depicted in the context of national origins and identity, with an emphasis not on realism but on the mythic and glorified aspects of battle, reflecting an ancient Germanic cult of hero worship.

By the late Middle Ages and early Renaissance, the literature of war had begun to depart from the reliance on mythology found in earlier literature and to concern itself more with historical reality. The topic of war continues to provide an opportunity for writers to speak of glory, honor, and courage, but with increasing fidelity to the background against which the story is set. William Shakespeare's *Henry* plays, for example—*Henry IV, Part I* (1592), *Henry IV, Part II* (1597) and *Henry V* (c. 1598-1599)—smoothly blend poetry and history both to glorify England and to explain how the notoriously un-princely Henry V evolved from a rakish and somewhat unprincipled youth into a revered king, the hero of Agincourt. In

the belief that he has as much lawful right to the throne of France as did Charles, the reigning French monarch, Henry V makes his claim for that crown. Insulted by Charles's son, the Dauphin, Henry prepares for war. At the decisive Battle of Agincourt, Henry's leadership carries the day, despite the fact that his army is outnumbered and weakened by illness. Shakespeare glorifies Henry V (r. 1413-1422) and his victory at Agincourt, and his contemporaries may well have regarded the portrayal as an overtly patriotic affirmation of contemporary warfare against Spain. However, many critics have seen in the play's language and portrayals a more ambiguous attitude toward warfare and perhaps a veiled criticism of contemporary events in Elizabethan England (where open criticism of the monarchy and its policies would not have been safe). The play thus illustrates both the growth in literature referencing actual events and the sensitivities, and potential dangers, of doing so.

MODERN WORLD

As world civilizations advanced in age and (especially) technology, these achievements were reflected in world conflicts. Wars increasingly expanded their sphere of impact. Increasingly, battles were no longer confined to unpopulated areas. Accordingly, literature sought to keep pace with the evolution of modern warfare. Although the heroic values present in the literature of ancient and medieval wars was still to be found in literature the realism, the suffering and horror of war became increasingly evident.

As warfare evolved into the so-called modern period, writers sought to present their subjects more realistically. Literary characters provided the opportunity and the voice to reveal a more accurate portrayal of the grim horrors found on the battlefield. In literature as in real life, war as a glorious confrontation of chivalric honor was now depicted as a bloody crucible of suffering and death.

Novels, plays, and poems increasingly began to address not only the external events of war but also the soldier's personal experience of such traumatic events, from courage to cowardice. In Stephen Crane's classic Civil War novel, *The Red Badge of Courage: An Episode of the American Civil War*

(1895), young Henry Fleming finds himself tormented by fear. Having dreamed of glorious battles as a young farm lad, he was at first anxious to taste combat, as are many soldiers who find themselves on the field of war for the first time. Now, as his regiment advances, Henry sees battle as an escape from the boredom of inactivity. Then comes battle, with its cacophony of sounds, followed by an enemy counterattack and panic. Henry flees from the field and now thinks of himself as a coward. In a subsequent battle, he redeems himself, earning the praise of his lieutenant. The novel offers the reader an instructive psychological profile of one young man enduring the chaos, fear, and self-doubt that every soldier must face.

In his 1929 novel of World War I, *Im Westen nichts Neues* (1929; *All Quiet on the Western Front*, 1929), Erich Maria Remarque produced what is generally thought to be the best-known work of antiwar literature published between the two world wars. The novel was subsequently adapted for the screen, starring actor Lew Ayres. So forcefully did the film depict the horror of war that Ayres became a pacifist and later refused to serve in the military during World War II.

Two other haunting and memorable literary statements to emerge from World War I are Lieutenant Colonel John McCrae's poem "In Flanders Fields" (1915) and the poem "Rouge Bouquet" (1918), by Sergeant Joyce Kilmer (perhaps best known for his poem "Trees," 1914). In "Rouge Bouquet," Kilmer memorialized his World War I comrades, who had perished at Rouge Bouquet, near Baccarat in France. Many other poets emerged from this war, including the "war poets" Wilson Owen, who died in battle at the age of twenty-five, and his friend Siegfried Sassoon.

World War I and its fierce trench warfare gave rise to what a group of writers called "the lost generation"; they not only depicted the horror of war but also questioned its value and necessity as a means of resolving disputes between nations. In his novel *A Farewell to Arms* (1929), Ernest Hemingway wrote what many regard as the strongest polemic against war. The story is told through the eyes of a young American officer, Lieutenant Frederic Henry, who is attached to a medical unit on the Italian front. There he meets and falls in love with a nurse, Catherine

Barkley. Wounded, Henry is hospitalized and eventually has surgery on his knee. He and Catherine are together during his rehabilitation. She becomes pregnant. While attempting to avoid capture by the Germans, Henry deserts, and the two manage to reach Switzerland, where Catherine and the baby both subsequently die.

One of the most meaningful works of modern literature to address the subject of war, Norman Mailer's *The Naked and the Dead* (1948), is regarded by some as the best novel of World War II. The author set his story on a South Pacific island, focusing primarily on one platoon of soldiers: their trials and tribulations, their interactions with one another, and

The Granger Collection, New York

The original 1929 front jacket cover for Erich Maria Remarque's All Quiet on the Western Front.

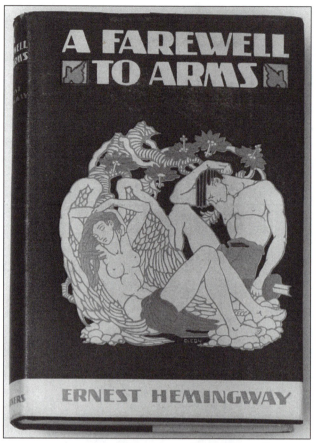

Time & Life Pictures/Getty Images

Ernest Hemingway's A Farewell to Arms.

the same fears and issues with which young Henry Fleming grapples in *The Red Badge of Courage*. In the world of *The Naked and the Dead*, there is little empathy among the members of the platoon, and no sympathy whatever for their Japanese foes. Mailer introduces a second element to his novel, wherein he uses his story as a forum to describe ridiculous army rules and protocols, always the source of irritation for the soldiers. The novel also sets the conflict in perspective by providing background for the campaign and a critique of military judgment.

Satire and comedy have been used in many modern works to depict and condemn war. Critique of war becomes an outright condemnation in Joseph Heller's *Catch-22* (1961), which uses satire to focus on the futility and sheer idiocy of the way in which the military prosecuted war. Heller's main charac-

ter, Yossarian, a bomber pilot based in Italy, has looked at enough sky. He has no interest in heroism, medals, or glory. His one abiding interest is to get rotated home. In what almost appears to be a contrived setup, Yossarian finds that each time he approaches the required number of missions to qualify for rotation home, the higher echelon increases the number. Determined, Yossarian resorts to various deceptions to try to defeat the system. Heller provides a supporting cast of characters every bit as devious as Yossarian. Hilarious in its satiric effect, *Catch-22* speaks against war as loudly as more serious works—but here by casting war as a farce.

The novel *Mister Roberts* (1946), by Thomas Heggen (adapted for the stage in 1948 by Heggen and Joshua Logan, and in 1955 released as a feature film), focuses on life as a soldier, making the audience aware that men in combat must deal not only with fear and suffering but also with the boredom of daily life in the backwater of war. The setting is a supply ship in the South Pacific commanded by a tyrannical captain who cares only about his next promotion. The hero, Lieutenant Douglas Roberts, who longs for a transfer to combat, finally gets his request for transfer approved by the captain—or rather by the members of the crew, who forge the captain's signature in repayment for Roberts's having managed to secure liberty for the crew by agreeing to give up challenging the captain's authority.

The Vietnam War (1961-1975) has occasioned many novels. In these works, realism has continued to be emphasized—including, again, the psychological experiences of the individual soldier. In the case of Tim O'Brien, a Vietnam War veteran, psychological realism renders his novels extremely personal to the point where, at times, the narrative crosses the boundary between actual fact and internal imaginings. *Going After Cacciato* (1978, revised 1989), which won a 1979 National Book Award, examines the conflicting moral imperatives of the Vietnam War when the point-of-view character, Paul Berlin, joins others in his platoon to retrieve the deserter Cacciato (literally "the hunted" in Italian), who has vowed to escape the war by walking to Paris. The actual events in the narrative are seamlessly interrupted by Berlin's fantasies and fears, making the distinction between reality and Berlin's psychological state difficult to discern. The clear sense, however, is that Cacciato, in attempting to carry out his insanely bold plan, is a hero—in some ways a goal to be pursued rather than a criminal to be hunted—as the soldiers grapple with the moral ambiguities of following orders not because they believe in the war but because they need to avoid the fate that Cacciato will inevitably meet when they finally locate him near the Laotian border.

BOOKS AND ARTICLES

Barlow, Adrian. *The Great War in British Literature*. New York: Cambridge University Press, 2000. Elucidates the different ways that World War I has been used in British literature and how that literature has impacted people.

Berkvam, Michael L. *Writing the Story of France in World War II: Literature and Memory, 1942-1958*. New Orleans: University Press of the South, 2000. Looks at the works of literature that portray French life during World War II, after the fall of Paris, showing that not all French resisted the Germans and many later wrote about it.

Chakravarty, Prasanta. *"Like Parchment in the Fire": Literature and Radicalism in the English Civil War*. New York: Routledge, 2006. Uses the literature of English sects during the Civil War to outline the roots of what would later be called liberalism.

Dawes, James. *The Language of War: Literature and Culture in the U.S. from the Civil War Through World War II*. Cambridge, Mass.: Harvard University Press, 2002. Analyzes the ties between language and violence, looking at how words frame the experience and understanding of war.

Griffin, Martin. *Ashes of the Mind: War and Memory in Northern Literature, 1865-1900*. Amherst: University of Massachusetts Press, 2009. Uses the literature of three northern poets and two writers of fiction to investigate the social memory of war and its place in cementing national values.

Jones, Kathryn N. *Journeys of Remembrance: Memories of the Second World War in French and German Literature, 1960-1980*. London: Legenda, 2007. Focuses on the memory of the Holocaust in the literature of France, West Germany, and East Germany during 1960-1980.

Mickenberg, Julia. *Learning from the Left: Children's Literature, the Cold War, and Radical Politics in the United States*. New York: Oxford University Press, 2005. Examines a specific genre of children's books during the 1920's-1960's that went against the Cold War rhetoric to teach so-called radical viewpoints, many of which are now mainstream.

Natter, Wolfgang. *Literature at War, 1914-1940: Representing the "Time of Greatness" in Germany*. New Haven, Conn.: Yale University Press, 1999. Ties German literature about World War I to the rise of a military ethos that persisted through the German defeat and helped prepare the ground for Adolf Hitler's rise and World War II.

Phillips, Kathy J. *Manipulating Masculinity: War and Gender in Modern British and American Literature*. New York: Palgrave Macmillan, 2006. By using examples from the literature from World War I, World War II, Vietnam, and Iraq, this study illuminates how men are goaded into war mentality through the feminization of common traits.

Taylor, Mark J. *The Vietnam War in History, Literature, and Film*. Tuscaloosa: University of Alabama Press, 2003. Uses a case study approach in looking at five episodes during the Vietnam War to examine how returning veterans are regarded in film and literature.

Jerry Keenan

MUSIC AND WARFARE

OVERVIEW

Music, a prime means of expressing the human experience, has been closely connected to warfare from earliest times. Within military establishments, music fosters team spirit, conveys signals, and provides the cadence for coordinated marching. Music also plays a vital liturgical role, invoking God's help in battle and celebrating victory. Less formally, most cultures have created a large genre of "soldiers' music" sung by fighting men and women. A large body of civilian music also reflects on war, ranging from simple tunes about soldiers seen on the street to magnificent orchestral works that conjure up a purified battlefield experience. The nineteenth and especially the twentieth century also saw the rise of antiwar music at both the popular and the concert-hall levels.

SIGNIFICANCE

The scholarly trend of studying "war and society" rather than narrow battlefield history has encouraged investigation of the intersection between music and warfare. Music offers a practically unmined wealth of sources that reveal what society at large has thought of the experience of war—and what the soldiers felt about the matter. Study of music and warfare is, however, still in its infancy. There are major studies of the music of the U.S. Civil War (1861-1865), the two world wars (1914-1918, 1939-1945), and the Vietnam War (1961-1975), but the war music of earlier eras has scarcely been touched.

HISTORY OF MUSIC AND WARFARE

ANCIENT WORLD

The biblical book of Joshua makes it plain that, in the late second millennium B.C.E., the Israelite army was accompanied by trumpeters: "seven priests shall bear before the ark seven trumpets of rams' horns. . . ." (Joshua 6:3). From the context, their purpose seems both religious and military: The trumpets signaled the army, whose great shout brought down the walls of Jericho. Indeed, the first evidence of music in warfare is distinctly religious, as in Numbers 10:9, when the Israelites are instructed to blow trumpets before setting out to war to summon God's help.

It is likely that Egyptian and Mesopotamian armies also used "trumpets" (bored animal horns) for military signals. That other early civilizations also used musical instruments for signals is suggested by the terra-cotta army of China's first emperor, Qin Shihuangdi (died 210 B.C.E.), which includes chariots equipped with large kettledrums.

The ancient Greeks developed a new use for military music: creating a cadence for coordinated action. Hoplite warfare consisted of men marching in very tight ranks carrying spears—they needed to march, not just stroll at their own rates. A fifth century Greek painted vase depicts hoplites marching into battle stepping to the tune of an *aulos* (double flute), which must have been common. The aulos is also attested on warships, setting the beat for rowers. It is very likely that Greek soldiers sang, although the lack of professional standing armies before the fourth century B.C.E. makes it less probable that there was a distinct genre of "soldiers' songs."

Songs about war, most notably Homer's eighth century epic the *Iliad* (c. 750 B.C.E.; English translation, 1611), were, however, enshrined at the heart of Greek culture throughout the classical period and beyond. Schoolboys studied the *Iliad* as poetry, but most people would have experienced it chanted by wandering performers who accompanied themselves on the harp. Oddly, the first extensive song about war is also the first extant condemnation of warfare, as Homer explored the human cost and senseless waste of the Trojan War (c. 1200-1100 B.C.E.).

Evidence becomes better in the Roman period. It

is known that Romans used large metal horns (*tubae*) and kettledrums to convey signals; the contemporary Celts also employed bronze horns. To judge from extant carvings, Roman soldiers at least sometimes also marched to the cadence of horns. Music was employed in the rituals of war, including as accompaniment for the dancing priests of the war god Mars. Rome's chief novelty, though, was clearly attested in soldiers' songs. Rome's professional soldiers sang around the campfire, and traces of their songs have survived. Most notably, the Roman historian Suetonius quotes several songs that soldiers sang during triumphal marches as they processed through Rome. Particularly noteworthy is a ditty produced for Julius Caesar's triumph that might be translated as "See the Bald Adulterer Come," sung by the soldiers in mocking honor of their general.

MEDIEVAL WORLD

The evidence for the intersection of music and warfare gradually improves during the course of the Middle Ages. The idea of armies marching in step was lost to Europe with the fall of the Western Roman Empire, but other forms of war music continued in the Germanic successor states. Especially noteworthy was a substantial body of German-language epic poetry, originally sung, most of which is now lost to us. The oldest literary work in German, the *Lay of Hildebrand* (c. 800 C.E.), which has survived only as a fragment, tells of the beginning of a battle between the hero Hildebrand and his son. Such a tradition is also preserved in the Anglo-Saxon epic *Beowulf* (first transcribed c. 1000), which dates to the same period. Although the hero Beowulf fought monsters, epics also told of battles against human enemies, such as the *Battle of Maldon* (c. tenth century), which commemorates an unsuccessful attempt to repel Viking invaders from England in 991. Far from celebrating war, the tales of Hildebrand, Beowulf, and Byrhtnoth (the English commander at Maldon) all end in tragedy. The songs tell of loyalty in battle but also of the failure of that loyalty and the death of heroes. Later epics, such as the Old French *Chanson de Roland* (c. 1100; *The Song of Roland*), were also performed, as can be seen from notations on the early manuscripts. *The Song of Roland*, commemorating

(and magnifying) a defeat Charlemagne's rear guard suffered in Spain, glorifies warfare rather more than the earlier Germanic epics, but the poem still ends in death and betrayal. Clearly the age of chivalry involved more than just a senseless glorification of war.

The European Middle Ages also shed more light on liturgical music before and after military endeavors. Most notable is the *Te Deum*, a plainchant of thanksgiving to God. While war is not mentioned in the text (which begins: "We praise you, God, we acknowledge you to be the Lord"), it was the custom by the High Middle Ages to hold public religious ceremonies after great military victories, in which the *Te Deum* played a central part. We can also see warriors, most notably Crusaders after 1095, singing hymns while invoking God in processions; unfortunately, few of the lyrics and none of the music in this genre have survived.

A system of music notation was created in the eleventh century, making it possible to imagine what Europe's warlike songs sounded like, although at first few secular tunes were written down. Some of the earliest were propaganda pieces for the Crusades. One of the most haunting was a famous song by the troubadour Marcabru (died 1150) that begins "Pax in nomine Domini" (peace in God's name) and encourages crusading in Spain. The music, with a rising cadence as Marcabru describes how men can have their souls cleansed by fighting for Christ, conveys both excitement and longing.

The short medieval songs that have survived tend to be positive. A notable example is the Agincourt carol, written shortly after England's victory over France on October 25, 1415. It begins:

> Our king went forth to Normandy
> With grace and might of chivalry
> There God for him wrought marvelously
> Wherefore England may call and cry
> Deo gratias [thanks be to God].

The Agincourt carol was widely popular in England and probably facilitated recruitment for King Henry V's ongoing war in France. Not all songs about war and fighting men were positive, however. One of the

A facsimile of the Agincourt carol in the Bodleian Library, Oxford.

most popular songs of the fifteenth century was the French "L'Homme armé" (the armed man). Its text runs:

> The man, the man, the armed man,
> The armed man
> The armed man should be feared, should be feared.

The composer indulged in considerable word painting, raising the pitch as he told of a proclamation that all should be armed and clothing the whole song in an awkward rhythm that hints at how unsettling the presence of soldiers could be.

The greatest innovation in war music of the medi-

eval era, however, came from the Ottoman Turkish Empire, which by the thirteenth century had begun to employ military marching bands. The instruments chosen were loud and abrasive, audible over the noise of men and horses on the move. In its classic configuration, the Turkish band consisted mostly of percussion—bass drum, kettledrum, frame drum, cymbals, and bells—with only harsh trumpets to provide melodies. Such instruments could convey signals, but their most important task was to promote unit cohesion, notably among the elite janissary units, the sultan's famous slave soldiers. Marching in time, at first to foster esprit de corps, became essential as the Turks introduced first the pike and then the musket into their infantry. These long and unwieldy weapons were effective only when the ranks were packed tightly together, so careful drill and coordination were essential to avoid chaos.

MODERN WORLD

Music for drill and marching reentered European armies in the seventeenth century, most closely identified with the military reforms of Gustavus II Adolphus of Sweden (r. 1611-1632). His pike and musket drill gave birth to the drummer boy, a figure familiar on western battlefields for centuries. The military marching band became increasingly complex and formal, until by the eighteenth century most army bands included woodwinds and brass instruments as well as percussion (the first Marquess Cornwallis's band played "The World Turned Upside Down" when he surrendered to the American revolutionaries at Yorktown in 1781). Such bands provided both popular tunes (George A. Custer's band is reported to have played the Irish drinking song "Garryowen" just before the Battle of the Little Bighorn) and specially composed works, such as

"Preussens Gloria" (Prussia's glory), which Johann Gottfried Piefke composed in 1871 for the victory parade at the end of the Franco-Prussian War.

A new development was programmatic concert pieces intended to evoke the experiences of war. Renaissance and baroque composers created bold instrumental works with titles like "The Battle," while classical composers (including Wolfgang Amadeus Mozart and Joseph Haydn) adopted Turkish marches and wrote masses in honor of military heroes (such as Haydn's *Lord Nelson Mass*).

The great flowering of concert war music came in the nineteenth century, though, with great works like Ludwig van Beethoven's *Wellington's Victory* (1813) and Peter Ilich Tchaikovsky's *1812 Overture* (1880), which even incorporates cannon explosions and church bells. The tradition continued into the twentieth century, taking new life in the form of movie sound tracks, such as Sergei Prokofiev's score for the film *Alexander Nevsky* (1938), which celebrates Russia's victory over the Teutonic Knights in the fifteenth century.

The greater availability of sources in the modern era also makes clear what the world's soldiers and sailors were singing. The variety was enormous. Civilian popular songs were always present around the campfires; for example, Teddy Roosevelt's Rough Riders particularly enjoyed "A Hot Time in the Old Town Tonight" during the Spanish-American War (1898). Sometimes popular songs about war were adopted, as when American Revolutionary troops adopted "Yankee Doodle," a ditty originally composed to mock the ragtag colonial levies in the Seven Years' War (1756-1763). Patriotic songs were always popular, such as "Heart of Oak," a Royal Navy march written to commemorate Britain's victories in 1759. The refrain begins: "Heart of oak are our ships, jolly tars are our men," and ends with a resounding "We'll fight and we'll conquer again and again." By the mid-nineteenth century, the first "official" song of a military branch had been created, the "Marine Corps Hymn," in which the singers proclaim, "We will fight our country's battles on the land and on the sea." Such music was used for recruiting as well as among the troops.

Other songs, dear to both civilians and soldiers,

continued to reflect on the high cost of war. Some of the most tuneful came from Ireland, whose sons died for centuries in Britain's foreign wars. The early nineteenth century "Johnny, I Hardly Knew Ye," tells of a young man marching proudly to war, only to return blind and crippled. Based on it, the U.S. Civil War's "When Johnny Comes Marching Home Again" (1863) interjected a somber commentary on the human cost of that war. The text is cheerful:

> When Johnny comes marching home again,
>   Hurrah, hurrah,
> We'll give him a hearty welcome then,
>   Hurrah, hurrah. . . .

The melody, however, tells a different tale, its minor key and dissonance proclaiming that Johnny never in fact came home, and the singers' expectations were doomed to disappointment.

World War I (1914-1918) saw a great outpouring of troop music, both positive and negative, about warfare. Perhaps the catchiest of all the pro-war songs was the American George M. Cohan's 1917 hit "Over There." It proclaims to the world "The Yanks are coming" to join the war, concluding with the bold boast: "We'll be over, we're coming over/ And we won't come back till it's over, over there!" Such a song, penned by an American who had never seen a trench, was simply not enough for the soldiers living through the war, though. The troops wrote their own songs—bitter, often ribald, and harshly critical of their officers. An example is the British "Hanging on the Old Barbed Wire," which tells how sergeants and officers are safe (and often drunk), while the privates are "hanging on barbed wire." It was so inflammatory that the British officers tried to suppress it.

Two novelties stand out in the music of World War II: the conscious manipulation of patriotic ideology by governments and the widespread availability of recorded music. For the first time, troops did not have to make their own music—radios and phonographs provided it for them. The result was certainly a more polished product, like the close harmony of the Andrews Sisters in their 1941 hit "Boogie Woogie Bugle Boy." It could be argued, though, that the authentic voice of the troops was submerged in the process, as, for example, the Nazis blared the music of Beethoven and Richard Wagner from loudspeakers. Similarly, it must be asked how much composed and disseminated works of patriotism, such as the Russian "Svyaschennaya voyna" (sacred war), which proclaimed a longing to drive a bullet into the forehead of the rotten Fascist scum, really reflected the troops' beliefs. Did all Japanese fighters agree with the theme of their music, that no sacrifice was too great for emperor and land, or did the music teach them to hold such beliefs?

In the wars of the late twentieth and early twenty-first centuries, antiwar themes became dominant. Many were produced during the Vietnam War (like Bob Dylan's 1963 classic "Blowin' in the Wind") and have remained popular ever since. The striking Israeli "Ratziti Sheteda" (1979; I wanted you to know), by Uzi Hitman, is also poignant in its longing for peace. Surely the world has rarely heard such a scathing indictment of war as Benjamin Britten's *War Requiem*, composed in 1962 for the consecration of the new Coventry Cathedral, replacing the edifice destroyed by a German bomb.

BOOKS AND ARTICLES

Andresen, Lee. *Battle Notes: Music of the Vietnam War* Superior, Wis.: Savage Press, 2003. Examines how the music of the Vietnam War era reflected the changing public attitudes toward the conflict during the 1960's.

Arnold, Ben. *Music and War: A Research and Information Guide*. New York: Garland, 1993. Looks at the aims composers had in the creation of war-related music.

Bohlman, Philip V. *The Music of European Nationalism*. Santa Barbara, Calif.: ABC-CLIO, 2004. Examines the dialectic between music and European nationalism during the nineteenth and twentieth centuries.

Jones, John B. *The Songs That Fought the War: Popular Music and the Home Front, 1939-1945*. Waltham, Mass.: Brandeis University Press, 2006. One of many books on the music of American conflicts, this one examines how music communicated war aims during World War II.

Pieslak, Jonathan R. *Sound Targets: American Soldiers and Music in the Iraq War*. Bloomington: Indiana University Press, 2009. This work looks at America's most recent conflict, examining changing social attitudes over the course of the war.

Winstock, Lewis S. *Songs and Music of the Redcoats: A History of the War Music of the British Army, 1642-1902*. Harrisburg, Pa.: Stackpole Books, 1970. Using the rise of the British Empire as a case study, this study examines the role that such music played both in the military and in the national consciousness.

Phyllis G. Jestice

RELIGION AND WARFARE

OVERVIEW

Religion, inseparable from warfare throughout human history, has changed in significance over time, between contemporary cultures, or even within a nation or culture. War has at times been a ritual process of religious significance, without any competition between dogmas or beliefs. Religion has been a source of inspiration to soldiers, without war having a particular religious purpose. In certain periods, religious conversion or competition has become the very reason for wars to be fought.

SIGNIFICANCE

As wars are fought by human beings, who are often motivated by religious beliefs, religion can impact warfare as either an arbiter or actual cause for taking up arms. Many wars have been fought, and continue to be fought, in the name of religion, to impose a revealed truth or to resist encroachment.

HISTORY OF RELIGION AND WARFARE

ANCIENT WORLD

Ancient warfare was religious in nature. Peoples, nations, or empires generally had their own tribal or national gods, presumed to fight for their devoted worshippers. It was rare for any conqueror to seek mass conversion from one faith to another. Worship of the suzerain's gods might be demanded as an act of submission or to promote imperial unity, but practice of preconquest cults was generally not questioned. The aid of lesser deities, worshiped by conquered subjects, might even be enlisted at times. Alternatively, a conquered people might transfer loyalty to the victor's gods, which had proved to be the more powerful deities. Ancient cultures did not question the existence of one another's gods but competed for favor and power of any god available.

The major exception was the twelve tribes of Israel and Judah, particularly Judah. The foundation of Judaism was a covenant with a single omnipotent God, gods of other nations being "the work of men's hands." Jewish judges, kings, and priests did not seek to bring other peoples into their covenant, as God's chosen people, but proclaimed that Israel's God was the sole ruler and creator of the universe. Military victory was considered evidence of God's intervening to support his faithful chosen. Defeat, in contrast to many neighboring cultures, was not taken to mean that Israel's god had proved weaker than rival gods. It was God's punishment on Israel's people for failing to live up to their obligations under the covenant. The Zoroastrian faith of successive Persian dynasties, including the Achaemenids, Parthians, and Sāsānians, came closest to playing a similar role, which may have made Persian monarchs amenable to supporting renewal of Judaism and rebuilding of the Temple in Jerusalem, after the Babylonian Exile.

In most of the American continents, ancient warfare, endemic on a low-intensity scale, had less religious character, except for that of the Aztecs and Maya. War in both cultures was a sacred duty to the gods, in itself a ritual of worship. Wars also provided prisoners, who could be sacrificed to the gods. Aztec and Mayan warfare also consolidated smaller states and cities under the rule of ever larger empires.

Aryan invaders of the Indian subcontinent celebrated war in their sacred epics, particularly praising "the all out-stripping chariot wheel," which conquered the previous inhabitants, destroying the Harrapān civilization in the Indus Valley. Division of the population into hereditary *varna* and *jats* was an essential part of the Hindu religion, including a warrior varna, the Kshatriya. The conquered population, variously known as Dravidian, "untouchables," or in recent times Dalit, was deemed ritually unclean in

Hindu cosmology. Although Buddhism was by origin a pacifist faith, arising later in the same region, that did not prevent kingdoms that adopted it as official religion from engaging in war.

Christianity in the Roman Empire, prior to the accession of Constantine, was largely a pacifist faith. Christians often refused military service. Not only were officers and soldiers required to worship Caesar, but also military service was deemed to violate the gospel of reconciliation. Saint Maximilian (274-295 C.E.) wrote, "You can cut off my head, but I will not be a soldier of this world, for I am a soldier of Christ. . . ." Origen (c. 185-c. 254 C.E.) wrote that "we no longer take sword against a nation, nor do we learn any more to make war, having become sons of peace for the sake of Jesus, who is our commander."

There is evidence of Christians serving in the Roman armies after 170 C.E., but many served in police or diplomatic functions rather than in battle. After 416 C.E., only Christians were permitted to serve as soldiers in the Roman army—Christianity having become the empire's official religion. Ambrose (bishop of Milan, 374-397 C.E.) and Augustine (bishop of North Africa, 395-430 C.E.) provided the theology of the "just war." The features of a just war included just cause, proper authority, good intentions, and probability of success.

MEDIEVAL WORLD

Christianity and Islam introduced the first wars motivated by advance of religious doctrine. Sāsānian rulers of Persia at times considered the loyalty of Christians within their empire to be suspect, once the rival Roman and Byzantine empires adopted it as official imperial faith. A distinctly organized Christian hierarchy, particularly adhering to the Nestorian heresy, satisfied the demands of Persian patriotism. Kingdoms and empires professing either Christianity or Islam fought over political, religious, financial, and cultural disputes during several centuries. As each religion fragmented into competing schools or sects, internecine warfare against perceived heresies became a recurrent feature of both Christian and Islamic cultures.

Initially disfavored or persecuted by the Roman emperors, Christianity achieved imperial recognition, and then status as official religion, between the reigns of Constantine the Great (r. 312-337) and Theodosius the Great (r. 379-395). Open state persecution of non-Christians, and of Christians adhering to doctrines considered heresy, became well established in Theodosius's reign. Persecution of Jewish communities made the Jews into enthusiastic allies of Persian armies, then of the new Arabic invaders, bringing Islam to the gates of Jerusalem.

Islam was first introduced to communities outside the Arabian Peninsula by wars of conquest, which established the Umayyad caliphate, and its successor, the ʿAbbāsid caliphate. In the second sura, the Qurʾān enjoins believers to fight against unbelievers "until idolatry is no more and al-Lah's religion reigns supreme," but also that "There shall be no compulsion in religion." Both injunctions were reflected in the subsequent conquest.

A relatively small army, inspired by Islam, based on the temporary political unification of the Arabian Peninsula, fell upon both the Byzantine and Persian empires at an opportune moment. The two long-dominant empires had exhausted themselves with thirty years of warfare. Each had burned the other's temples, including the fire temple near Ganzak and the Church of the Resurrection in Jerusalem. Persecution of Monophysite Christians, as well as Jews, further weakened the loyalty of Byzantine subjects. Fewer than twenty thousand soldiers of the Muslim *umma* conquered all of Persia, as well as Syria and Egypt. At first, the Muslim community was more interested in collecting the *jizya*, a tax on unbelievers, than converting the conquered to Islam. Armies were kept in garrisons, separate from the existing cities. Conquered peoples practicing pagan or polytheistic traditions were likely to be offered a choice of conversion or death, while Christians and Jews were free to practice their faith.

Christianity in Western Europe survived the fall of the Roman Empire by conversion of the invading Germanic peoples, who initially worshiped a Teutonic pantheon analogous to those of the pre-Christian Greeks and Romans. Many tribes, including the Visigoths, adopted the Arian heresy. Conversion of a king, and therefore an entire people, was often inspired by desire for victory in battle. Constantine's set the example; he adopted Christianity before his 312 C.E. victory at Rome's Milvian bridge. Chlodowech (Clovis), king of the Franks, adopted Roman Christianity in 496 during a difficult battle with the Alamanni. His subsequent conquest of the Visigothic kingdom, north of the Pyrenees, marked a triumph of Rome over Arianism.

Religiously motivated wars known as the Crusades began more than four and a half centuries after the establishment of the Islamic caliphate. Before 1000 C.E., the ʿAbbāsid caliphs, leaders of the Sunni branch of Islam, had fallen under the rule of Shīʿite princes, while the Shīʿite Fāṭimids had established a rival caliphate in Egypt. By the later 1050's, Turkish armies were clashing with Byzantine armies, which had taken advantage of the weakened caliphate to regain Tarsus, Antioch, and parts of northern Syria. In the 1060's and 1070's, Turkish armies, nominally acting in the name of the ʿAbbāsid caliphs, established a sultanate ruling Iraq, Iran, and parts of Syria, restoring Sunni ascension. Between 1074 and 1798, Western Europe generated a series of Crusades against the rising Ottoman Turkish Empire.

One feature of the crusades was the formation of professed religious orders dedicated to military purposes. Previously, qualified laymen were considered to have a moral obligation to bear arms in defense of their faith, or specifically at the direction of the Roman church. However, when the Knights Templar (1118-1119) and the Order of the Hospital of Saint John in Jerusalem (1163-1206) became military orders, communities devoted to prayer and service became explicitly institutions of warfare. The notion that the vocation of churchmen denied them the use of force was largely abandoned. The Teutonic Knights, established in 1198, followed a similar pattern.

MODERN WORLD

One demarcation of the medieval from the modern world, at least in western and central Europe, was the

Godfrey of Bouillon, holding a poleax. Leader of the First Crusade in 1095, he became king of Jerusalem.

Protestant Reformation. Following the Council of Trent (1545-1547), Roman popes sought to suppress the Protestant heresy but also fought to reduce the influence of the Habsburg emperors in Italy. While Holy Roman Emperor Charles V fought Protestant German princes from 1531 to 1555, his French (Roman Catholic) rivals often allied with the Protestants and also with (Muslim) corsairs from North Africa. Protestant faith inspired British military rivalry with

Spain, culminating in defeat of the Spanish Armada in 1588 and Dutch independence from Spanish Habsburg rule. In the 1540's, England avoided bankruptcy by funding two-thirds of its military expenses from the sale of confiscated church lands. From 1618 to 1648, a period known as the Thirty Years' War entangled the causes of Protestant religion and German liberty with the national and dynastic aspirations of Sweden, Denmark, France, the Holy Roman Emperor, Habsburg Austria, the Dutch Republic, and Spain.

Library of Congress

An American Bible Society poster designed to solicit public support for a program of providing World War I servicemen with copies of the New Testament.

Since 1700, religion has seldom been the motivator for wars, but it has commonly served as an ideological rationale. The American War of Independence was framed, in part, as an "Appeal to Heaven" from the rule of British monarch George III. Expansion of European colonial empires, in the Americas, Africa, and Asia, was given a veneer of moral purpose by calls to spread the Gospel to the heathen of those continents. Armies, governments, and civilians of almost any belligerent power have invoked prayers for victory and divine protection for those serving in the armed forces. In a world dominated by monotheistic faiths, this means, as Abraham Lincoln said in his second inaugural address, that both sides generally pray to the some God, who cannot answer the prayers of both, and may not answer the prayers of either.

Most modern armies make extensive provision for chaplains to serve the spiritual needs of both enlisted men and women, and officers. Serving as officers in a military chain of command, chaplains are expected to maintain troop morale and serve the assigned military mission, as well as minister to individual soldiers. While some nations have emphasized a single national church in military chaplaincy, a diversity of faiths increasingly requires a variety of chaplains. The United States, with its variety of immigrants, is a model, but Britain has soldiers from dissenting Protestant sects, and a Roman Catholic minority, while many European countries have significant Islamic populations. Germany has established Protestant and Roman Catholic regions, and Latin America has a growing number of evangelical Protestant converts.

A prominent feature of religion in the modern world has been the rise of pacifism in direct opposition to warfare in general. The philosophical basis of pacifism is not modern. Pacifism was never a practical political option, when any valley or city was in constant danger of being invaded by the nearest rival feudal lord, king, or imperial army, for any reason or no reason. The development of large, stable nation-states, with civilian control of the military and periods of substantial peace in parts of the world, gave pacifism a more plausible context. The sheer volume of slaughter in World War I, and the imbalance of colonial wars pitting machine guns against spears, gave pacifism additional moral force. The prospect of worldwide annihilation in an exchange of nuclear weapons gave ominous practical significance to the movement.

Early Christian writers Justin Martyr, Tertullian, Origen, Maximilian, Hippolytus, and Martin of Tours all denounced participation in war as inconsistent with the promise of Christianity, as did Pelagius. The order founded and named after Saint Francis of Assisi was in part pacifist but did not oppose the contemporary Crusades or demand pacifism of the leaders of the Roman church. Humanists such as Thomas More and Desiderius Erasmus also provided some precedent for pacifist thinking, but More, for example, served as chancellor in England, and Erasmus served the Counter-Reformation. Modern religious denominations opposed to war include the Society of Friends (Quakers), Church of the Brethren, and Seventh-day Adventists—but individual members of these churches have served in the military. Among the religiously motivated pacifist organizations of the twentieth century are the Fellowship of Reconciliation, the American Friends Service Committee, the Catholic Worker Movement, and the Catholic Peace Fellowship.

BOOKS AND ARTICLES

Barber, John. *The Road from Eden: Studies in Christianity and Culture*. Bethesda, Md.: Academica Press, 2008. A study of the influence of Reform Theology on Western culture, including warfare.

Fahey, Joseph J. *War and the Christian Conscience*. Maryknoll, N.Y.: Orbis Books, 2005. Presents a scenario in which the U.S. draft is reinstated. Examines the resulting moral and ethical decisions weighed by a female student called for military duty, from four historical perspectives: pacifism/nonviolence, just/limited war, total/holy war, and global citizenship.

Nolan, Cathal J. *The Age of Wars of Religion, 1000-1650: An Encyclopedia of Global Warfare and Civilization*. Westport, Conn.: Greenwood Press, 2006. More than three thousand entries in one thousand pages cover religion and warfare from a global perspective.

Parker, Geoffrey. *The Thirty Years' War*. 2d ed. New York: Barnes and Noble, 1993. An update of a classic work that synthesizes the most important scholarship on the war that has been called Europe's civil war, from politics and major figures to the warfare itself. Maps, chronology, genealogies, and index.

Randsborg, Klavs. *Hjortspring: Warfare and Sacrifice in Early Europe*. Oakville, Conn.: Aarhus University Press, 1995. Examines the ancient Scandinavian ship Hjortspring as an artifact of a defeated raid from the Hamburg region. Looks at this archaological treasure in the context of European pagan religions and warfare, as well as modern nationalism and archaeological theory.

Rao, Aparna, Michael Bollig, and Monika Böck, eds. *The Practice of War: Production, Reproduction, and Communication of Armed Violence*. Oxford, England: Berghahn Books, 2007. Examines warfare from the perspective of ethnographry and anthropology: "The fact is that war comes in many guises and its effects continue to be felt long after peace is proclaimed. . . . It is only over the long view that one can begin to see the commonalities that emerge from the different forms of conflict and can begin to generalize."

Richardson, Glenn. *Renaissance Monarchy: The Reigns of Henry VIII, Francis I, and Charles V*. New York: Oxford University Press, 2002. Compares the most important Western leaders of the Renaissance while asking the question of why warfare was endemic in early sixteenth century Europe.

Riley-Smith, Jonathan. *The Crusades: A Short History*. New Haven, Conn.: Yale University

Press, 1987. A classic, hailed as the most authoritative work on the Crusades, as well as counterpart movements in the modern world. Excellent starting point for students.

Soustelle, Jacques. *Daily Life of the Aztecs, on the Eve of the Spanish Conquest.* Translation by Patrick O'Brian. Stanford, Calif.: Stanford University Press, 1961. Soustelle, an authority on Mexican archaeology and sociology, uses the pictographic system and archaeological artifacts of the Aztecs to present the history of this religious warrior society, from daily life to rituals to conflict and conquest. Illustrated.

Wood, James B. *The King's Army: Warfare, Soldiers, and Society During the Wars of Religion in France, 1562-76.* New York: Cambridge University Press, 1996. Wood brings attention to the military side of the French wars of religion with this analysis of the King's Army.

Charles Rosenberg

TELEVISION AND WARFARE

OVERVIEW

Just as the film *All Quiet on the Western Front* (1930) changed the ways that many people looked at warfare, so the presence of warfare in televised media of various types has once again changed public perceptions. Sometimes television programs can change the ways that the public perceives war, and sometimes they can impact how policy makers conduct war. No matter how one regards the relationship of television and warfare, however, the way that television portrays war—whether in news coverage, documentaries, or dramatic fiction—can have an effect on how war is thought about in the abstract, how it is conducted, and how it is remembered.

SIGNIFICANCE

Although war coverage on television goes back to its roots in the late 1940's, it was in the 1960's when television first began to have a significant impact. In January, 1968, although the war in Vietnam (1961-1975) was controversial, "Middle America" largely supported the war and believed the statements of President Lyndon B. Johnson, Defense Secretary Robert McNamara, and General William Westmoreland: that the end of the war, in victory, was imminent. That all changed when the North Vietnamese Army (NVA) and the Viet Cong (VC) launched what came to be known as the Tet Offensive, attacking more than thirty cities throughout South Vietnam at once during the Vietnamese New Year celebration week, which was traditionally a time of truce. Television crews were there when the VC breached the gates of the U.S. embassy in Saigon.

Although, as a battle, the Tet Offensive had to be considered a loss for the NVA and VC, it proved to be a victory in the long term. The reason for that victory is the key to the significance of television and war:

The American public saw that a victory for their side was not "just around the corner." Public opinion turned quickly against Johnson, McNamara, and Westmoreland. Not long after, Walter Cronkite, news anchor for the Columbia Broadcasting System (CBS), came out against the war, leading Johnson to state, famously, "If I've lost Cronkite, I've lost Middle America."

NEWS COVERAGE

The first American war to be covered on television was not the Vietnam War but the Korean War (1950-1953). However, the television coverage of the Korean War did not have the impact of the coverage of the Vietnam War, for two reasons. First, in the early 1950's, network broadcast signals reached only half of the country, and less than half of the families in the areas to which signals were broadcast actually owned television sets. Second, the footage of the Korean War was provided largely by military cameramen who worked with black-and-white film and within the format established during the 1930's and 1940's for newsreels distributed to movie theaters. Therefore, although much of the footage of the war shot by these cameramen is vivid and often very moving, it reached relatively few viewers and demonstrated very little awareness of the possibilities peculiar to the new medium of television.

By the mid-1960's, when the American involvement in the Vietnam War dramatically escalated, the television networks had expanded and refined their news shows into centerpieces of their programming and had developed large organizations of overseas reporters and cameramen, rivaling the news-gathering capabilities of the major newspapers and newsmagazines. The crews assigned to cover the Vietnam War competed to "scoop" competitors on important or controversial developments. Their reports from the "battle front," which in Vietnam was just about anywhere, often led off the nightly news broadcasts, and because the cameramen used color film, the conflict had an immediacy that was dramatically new. Indeed, because war had never officially been declared against the Viet Cong and the North Vietnamese, reporting was not anywhere nearly as strictly censored as the reporting on World War II (1939-1945) had been. Families often sat eating their TV dinners while they watched some harrowing footage of firefights in which soldiers on both sides were wounded or killed on camera. The blood was red, and the gore was not always edited out. Moreover, because the draft system meant that every neighborhood and most families had someone serving in the war, the television coverage of its brutal realities not only fueled the radical antiwar movement but also, perhaps more significantly, eroded mainstream confidence in the conduct of the war. Indeed, the turning point in public support for the war effort is often identified as Cronkite's declaration that he believed that victory was no longer possible, if indeed it had ever been possible.

Nonetheless, given the protracted nature of the Vietnam conflict, it eventually became a challenge to show or say anything new about it. Because the news reports were still recorded on film that had to be sent to processing centers, it was also difficult to protect a "scoop." In the mid-1970's, the development of videotape and then the rapid expansion and refinement of satellite transmission would have had a dramatic effect on the coverage of the invasions of Grenada and Panama—but those military operations were so focused, suddenly launched, and quickly concluded that the new technologies had relatively little impact on the coverage of the conflicts.

Then, after Saddam Hussein seized Kuwait in 1990, the United States and its coalition of allies took some months to build a sufficient force on the ground and to reduce the Iraqi military capabilities from the air. The military strictly controlled coverage of this prolonged buildup to what was a very swiftly decisive ground war. News organizations subsequently complained that their ability to cover the conflict with any objectivity had been seriously compromised by military controls. The military and political

criticism of reporters such as Peter Arnett, reporting for Cable News Network (CNN)—who remained in Baghdad and provided firsthand reports on the allied air attacks against the military, transportation, and communication facilities in the city (reports that were described as something close to enemy propaganda)—was ultimately mitigated by the American military's own heavy-handed manipulation of the media.

By the time of the war in Afghanistan and the invasion of Iraq, which followed on the terrorist attacks of September 11, 2001, the development of the twenty-four-hour cable news networks created an almost insatiable demand for news and intensified competition among news organizations. In addition, advancements in electronic technologies had turned every cell phone into a camera whose images could very easily be disseminated by e-mail or uploaded to the Internet. The development of blogs and other "new" electronic venues for reportage and news commentary meant that the audience for television news was being further fragmented. Indeed, the Web became a repository for television news clips, whether legitimately or illicitly distributed, and television news programs began to promote "extended" discussions meant exclusively for broadcast on the Web.

Recognizing that all of these developments meant that it could not control coverage of these more geographically dispersed and prolonged conflicts as it had controlled coverage of the first Gulf War, the military developed the strategy of "embedding" reporters with small units. The reporters thus shared the experiences of the troops with whom they traveled and came to see the war largely through their eyes. Coverage of the conflicts was sometimes extremely intense, but each reporter was able to provide a perspective on only a very small part of the conflicts. It is arguable that this strategy diffused and delayed the media attention to the lack of clearly defined strategic goals and plans in both conflicts.

TELEVISION DOCUMENTARIES

Some of the documentaries that have been shown on television were originally developed as newsreel material to be shown in movie theaters. They had a major influence on documentaries subsequently produced for television. For instance, during World War II, the renowned film director Frank Capra produced *Why We Fight* (1942-1945), a seven-part series made for the U.S. government and presenting the case for American involvement in all theaters of the war. Although less overtly propagandistic than Capra's series, the series *Victory at Sea*, a twenty-six-episode series first aired in 1952 and 1953 by the National Broadcasing Company (NBC) and narrated by Walter Huston, and Thames Television's *The World at War*, a twenty-six-episode series first aired in 1973 and narrated by Laurence Olivier, both owed a great deal to the style of Capra's series. That style also carried over to CBS's acclaimed documentary series *The Twentieth Century*, which aired each week from 1957 until 1966. Narrated by Walter Cronkite, each episode covered one of the century's most important political and cultural events or figures. The series was reworked, with Mike Wallace as narrator, for broadcast on A&E in the 1980's. All of these documentaries relied on black-and-white archival footage, inspiring the 1999 documentary series *World War II in Color*.

The two major documentary series about World War I have been *The Great War*, jointly produced by the British, Canadian, and Australian Broadcasting Corporations and chiefly narrated by Michael Redgrave, and *World War I*, produced by CBS and narrated by Robert Ryan. Both series were first aired in 1964, marking the fiftieth anniversary of the start of the war, and both consisted of twenty-six episodes.

The major documentary about the Korean War has been *Korea: The Forgotten War*, aired in 1987. The Vietnam War has been the subject of many compelling documentaries focusing on individual battles and campaigns and particular aspects of the war—from the soldiers who cleared enemy tunnel systems to the use of chemical defoliants to the experiences of prisoners of war. However, the two most significant documentary series that provide a broader perspective on the conflict have been *The World of Charlie Company*, aired on CBS in 1970, and *Vietnam: The Ten-Thousand-Day War*, a twenty-six-

episode series produced by the Canadian Broadcasting Corporation that originally aired between 1980 and 1982. Not surprisingly, the Iraq War of the early 2000's has already resulted in a large number of documentaries. Of those that have aired on television *Baghdad ER*, which aired on HBO in 2006, has perhaps received the most visceral attention and critical acclaim.

War-related documentaries have largely focused on twentieth and twenty-first century conflicts because there is no archival footage from earlier conflicts on which the filmmakers can draw. Most recently lauded for his documentary series on the World War II, titled simply *The War*, Ken Burns had a profound impact on the application of the documentary form to earlier conflicts with his series *The Civil War*. A nine-part series that aired on the Public Broadcasting Service (PBS) in 1990, *The Civil War* remains one of the most popular programs ever aired on that network. *The Civil War* was groundbreaking because Burns recruited well-known actors and actresses to read letters and journals from combatants and their loved ones, which were voiced over actual photographs of the people, battles, and national events associated with the war, skillfully intercut. Moreover, he found commentators on the conflict—notably historian and author Shelby Foote—who made the history truly compelling without indulging in any melodramatic turns. The producers of the documentary series *The American Revolution* were obviously inspired by Burns's success, but they lacked the photographic archives that Burns had available to him. Thus, in this thirteen-part series originally aired on the History Channel in 2006, they employed actors to portray the famous figures and ordinary people from whose perspectives the story of the war is told. Thus, the documentary series moved very close to the television miniseries.

TELEVISION MINISERIES

The two most successful television miniseries have both treated World War II. In the 1970's, Herman Wouk's novels *The Winds of War* (1971) and *War and Remembrance* (1978) were turned into the most costly miniseries in television history. The series featured some major film actors, including Robert Mitchum, who played the scion of a widely dispersed American family that manages to be on the scene in most of the war's major theaters. In contrast, the HBO series *Band of Brothers* (2001) was based on a nonfiction book of the same title by historian Stephen Ambrose and follows an airborne unit from the weeks preceding the D-day landings in Normandy to the mountains of Austria at the war's conclusion.

Other notable miniseries treating wars have included *Julius Caesar* (2002), treating the conflicts that marked Rome's transformation from a Republic to an Empire; *Masada* (1981), depicting the desperate climax of Jewish resistance to Roman rule in 73 C.E.; *John Adams* (2008), dramatizing the second U.S. president's pivotal contributions to the American Revolution; *The Blue and the Gray* (1982), *Gettysburg* (1993), and *Lincoln* (1974), treating the American Civil War; *Holocaust* (1978), personalizing the Nazi genocide against Europe's Jews; *Uprising* (2001), focusing on the Warsaw Ghetto Uprising; *Then There Were Giants* (1994), depicting the Tehran Conference during World War II; *Changi* (2002), documenting the Japanese mistreatment of Australian prisoners of war; *Oppenheimer* (1980), focusing on the physicist who coordinated the effort to develop the atomic bomb; *Nuremberg* (2000), dramatizing the war-crimes trials of surviving Nazi leaders; and *Lord Mountbatten: The Last Viceroy* (1986), capturing the bloodletting that marked the partition of the British raj into the independent nations of India and Pakistan.

BOOKS AND ARTICLES

Anderson, Robin. *A Century of Media, a Century of War*. New York: Peter Lang, 2006. Looks at how modern media have turned war into entertainment, in motion pictures, on television screens, and in video games.

Bullert, B. J. *Public Television: Politics and Battle over Documentary Film*. Trenton, N.J.: Rutgers University Press, 1997. Examines how PBS has carefully shaped the documentaries that it airs, sometimes stifling the freedom of expression and diverse voices that are a part of its mandate.

DeVito, John, and Frank Tropea. *Epic Television Miniseries: A Critical History*. Jefferson, N.C.: McFarland, 2009. Looks the historical development of television miniseries, covering the two-series set that established the standard for war television, Herman Wouk's *The Winds of War* and *War and Remembrance*.

Hoskins, Andrew. *Televising War: From Vietnam to Iraq*. London: Continuum, 2004. From a critical perspective, looks at the ways that the television media have taken advantage of war, sometimes hyping conflict in the name of ratings.

Kilborn, Richard, and John Izod. *Confronting Reality: An Introduction to the Television Documentary*. Manchester, England: Manchester University Press, 1997. Investigates the role of the institutions that produce documentaries in shaping how audiences interpret the images they see, some of the most vivid of which have to do with war.

Mermin, Jonathan. *Debating War and Peace: Media Coverage of U.S. Intervention in the Post-Vietnam Era*. Princeton, N.J.: Princeton University Press, 1999. Uses a case-study format to argue that television coverage of warfare affects not only individual opinions of war but also foreign policy agendas.

Rueven, Frank. "TV in a Time of War." *New Leader*, November/December, 2001, 47-49. This article examines how television, in terms of both news coverage and dramatic series, has shaped views on the War on Terrorism.

Thrall, A. Trevor. *War in the Media Age*. Creskill, N.J.: Hampton, 2000. Investigates the press strategy of the American government from the Vietnam War to the 1991 Persian Gulf War, drawing attention to the increasing importance of the press in the war over political opinion.

Thussu, Daya Kishan, and Des Freedman, eds. *War and the Media: Reporting Conflict 24/7*. Thousand Oaks, Calif.: Sage, 2003. Looks at the historical and contemporary relationships between the media and the military and how the reporter's role has changed along with the changing definitions of war and terrorism.

Martin Kich

SOCIETY AND WARFARE

CIVILIAN LABOR AND WARFARE

OVERVIEW

Military forces often relied on civilians to fulfill labor and support demands, obtaining weapons, food, and other essential items to enable combat troops to focus on warfare. Civilian laborers built and reinforced structures to help troops withstand enemy assaults and prepare offensive maneuvers. Civilian workers represented both voluntary employees and people forced into labor. In the early twenty-first century, many historians analyzed how occupation forces had coerced or overpowered ethnic groups to perform work to achieve military goals. Some scholars evaluated how gender and race affected civilians seeking wartime employment. Economic and political historians considered civilian laborers' impact on industrial production and legislation during wars.

SIGNIFICANCE

Civilian laborers frequently filled manpower shortages at businesses and factories when peacetime workers left for military service. Civilians' work mostly ensured ample production of items, especially weaponry, crucial to military successes. However, fluctuations in civilians' work ethic and inconsistent supplies of laborers impacted the quantity and quality of the military equipment civilian workers manufactured. Some civilian specialists, such as blacksmiths or mechanics (depending on the era in which warfare occurred), applied their professional skills to benefit military troops. Sometimes civilians forced to work for occupying forces sabotaged projects assigned them, hindering enemy troops' effectiveness. Civilian laborers also completed reconstruction work to restore areas damaged by warfare.

HISTORY OF CIVILIAN LABOR AND WARFARE

Many aspects of civilian labor associated with warfare have been universal in different eras. Throughout the history of warfare, civilian laborers supplemented military endeavors in what often became a symbiotic relationship. Military forces relied on civilians to accomplish necessary support services that enabled troops to concentrate on their orders and not be distracted by time-consuming activities such as securing food. Civilians usually wanted military forces to protect them from enemies during wars. Civilian labor varied from formal, organized systems monitored and financed by governments and military leaders to assistance offered spontaneously when citizens encountered military troops in need of supplies and support.

Incentives for voluntary civilian laborers included patriotism and a sense of duty to their leaders or country. Most workers welcomed the opportunity to help relatives, friends, and neighbors fighting in wars by manufacturing war materials useful to military forces. Warfare offered many civilians income sources to support their families. Wartime civilian workers faced risks and suffered injuries and casualties both in home-front industries and during battlefield assignments. Civilian laborers sometimes became prisoners of war or slaves, depending on the era and conqueror when they lived. After warfare concluded, some civilian laborers retained work similar to their wartime employment, while others became unemployed when veterans returned home.

ANCIENT WORLD

Power struggles between leaders of ancient civilizations often provoked military conflicts. Histories of ancient warfare, some of them written by those who were contemporary with the events—including Homer, Thucydides, and Plutarch—and biblical passages described activities of warriors defending their communities or engaging in offensive maneuvers to seize land from rivals. Most accounts omitted details concerning individuals performing labor to assist troops, but generalizations about civilian workers suggested how they participated in warfare. Civilians assisted their communities' military forces by reinforcing shelters, stockpiling supplies, and building roads, trenches, and bridges. Using soil and rocks, civilian laborers constructed defensive structures, including walls around cities and towers for soldiers to post outlooks to detect approaching enemies. Civilian-built barricades protected troops from assaults. Civilian laborers in Assyria and other civilizations aided soldiers by preparing weapons and equipment for sieges. The Bible describes how Solomon forced people he conquered to work to supplement his military resources.

When soldiers traveled to pursue military objectives, their community, including family members and skilled craftspersons and artisans, often followed them. The civilian laborers accompanying Macedonian leader Alexander the Great (356-323 B.C.E.) on his extensive military expeditions were among the best-documented ancient noncombatant workers serving in wartime. A diverse labor group assisted Alexander and his soldiers. Alexander arranged for royal pages to serve him. He ordered servants, known as *ektaktoi*, to monitor his troops' baggage and the livestock transporting it. In addition to overseeing the movement of supplies, the ektaktoi set up tents to shelter troops. Most soldiers provisioned themselves with personal clothing and weapons. Sutlers sold drinks, food, or services to troops not otherwise available. Cooks prepared meals for large groups.

Alexander hired engineers to create weaponry, including catapults, for specific battlefield needs or strategies. Blacksmiths and carpenters contributed their talents to fashion metals and wood into military equipment. Physicians treated battle wounds and sicknesses. Civilians assisted in burying casualties. Some civilian workers met Alexander's intellectual and spiritual demands by serving as historians, scientists, and philosophers to share their observations and insights regarding warfare, foreshadowing the roles of military chaplains, tacticians, and journalists accompanying troops.

Various ancient civilizations' military leaders, particularly those of the Romans and Egyptians, benefited from civilian laborers performing noncombat tasks similar to those provided to Alexander and his soldiers. Many of the roles played by ancient civilian laborers during warfare, including civilians working as spies to obtain military intelligence, continued to be fundamental to military forces in other eras.

MEDIEVAL WORLD

Advances in military organization and weapons technology affected medieval civilian laborers impacted by warfare, who engaged in work resembling that of their ancient counterparts. In Syria, medieval towns were divided into zones to which people were assigned based on their employment status. Zone leaders compensated noncombatant civilians for such services as providing horses for cavalry and transportation, supplying weapons, or performing administrative duties. In 718, when the Umayyad army targeted Constantinople, approximately twelve thousand noncombatant civilian laborers accompanied soldiers into that city. The workers tended mules and camels and distributed food and weapons.

In medieval Europe, monarchs urged civilians to increase livestock breeding for consistent production of swift cavalry mounts and sturdy draft horses for military troops to attain advantages over enemies. Farmers maintained herds to ensure consistent supplies of livestock used for transportation and sustenance. During the late tenth century, weapons manufacturing also experienced changes. Craftspersons, in addition to making more weapons, offered warriors improved designs and varying types to enhance their odds of victory in combat. Regions acquired notoriety for particular weapons, such as Saxony's swords. Medieval ironworkers throughout Europe produced weapons not only for their communities but also to sell to soldiers elsewhere, enhancing local and regional economies.

From the eleventh through thirteenth centuries, civilian laborers accompanied Crusaders traveling to the Holy Land. By the fourteenth century, weapons manufacturing by civilian workers had expanded, and laborers quickly produced quantities of weapons because they used standard designs and materials. During the Hundred Years' War (1337-1453), feudal military forces utilized peasants for such basic labor needs as gathering forage. Sources estimated that peasant laborers formed half of French feudal armies. In the fifteenth century, iron shortages affected civilian weaponry production in Asia, where previously abundant mining resources had ensured plentiful armories. Gunsmiths cast guns from alternate metals, including bronze. Laborers also made bullets and mixed explosives for gunpowder. They assembled wheeled vehicles to transport large weapons to battlefields.

Warfare waged by the Turkic leader Tamerlane, also known as Timur (1336-1405), affected civilian laborers in medieval Iranian communities. *Gullughchi* were civilian servants who performed such tasks as guarding highways, delivering messages, and tending falcons. Camp followers of Tamerlane's armies consisted of such laborers as druggists, saddle makers, and shoemakers. As Tamerlane secured territory with his military forces, he seized the makers of weapons and armor, including Damascus swordsmiths, to work in Samarqand, his empire's capital. These civilian laborers made arms and protective armor to outfit Tamerlane's troops. Tamerlane ordered workers to construct numerous workshops and residences for armorers adjacent to his palace. Timur's siege-warfare tactics destroyed buildings crucial to communities' military strength, such as the citadel in Herāt. Accounts estimated that approximately seven thousand civilian workers reconstructed that structure.

In medieval Italy, craftspersons were renowned for weapons they produced for military troops and horse armor, such as that made in the Milan workshop of Pier Innocenzo da Faerno. In October of 1427, Francesco Bussone, conte di Carmagnola (c. 1385-1432) led Venetian troops at Maclodio. His soldiers subdued the Milanese army, which surrendered. Carmagnola's forces captured ten thousand soldiers and their weapons. Civilian weapons manufacturers in Milan quickly replaced the confiscated arms by producing sufficient weaponry to supply several thousand infantrymen and cavalry soldiers, enabling them to fight victoriously in later battles.

MODERN WORLD

Civilian laborers affiliated with modern warfare experienced more rigid bureaucracy, but women and racial minorities were offered increased opportunities. World War I presented these civilian workers temporary employment as telephone operators, clerks, and medical personnel. After invading France and Belgium in World War I, German troops forced civilians from those countries to work for various labor projects, such as transporting supplies to frontline trenches. In 1915, German military leaders ordered civilian workers to build three defensive trenches in the *Flandern Stellung* and build large concrete structures, which the Germans called *Mannschaften Eisenbetten Understände* (MEBUs). Civilian laborers placed steel in the concrete so the MEBUs could withstand artillery shells.

World War II civilian labor strengthened military forces by providing them sufficient weaponry to fight enemies effectively. In April of 1942, U.S. president Franklin D. Roosevelt selected Paul V. McNutt to direct the War Manpower Commission to oversee procuring civilian labor. Yearly, 53,750,000 U.S. civilian laborers performed work supporting wartime needs. Iconic images of Rosie the Riveter symbolized the influx of North American women into factories to construct aircraft, ships, and munitions crucial for Allied troops to defeat Axis forces. Newsreels depicted the diverse roles the civilian laborers pursued, including agricultural work. Organized labor groups, such as the Transport Workers Union of America, discussed concerns regarding how wartime employment issues affected their members. McNutt dealt with labor strikes, security issues, and absenteeism. Military leaders frequently dismissed McNutt's efforts because he was a civilian, and historians have criticized his administration.

When German troops invaded the Soviet Union in June, 1941, Soviet dictator Joseph Stalin ordered civilians to focus on work that aided troops in what was referred to as the Great Patriotic War. To prevent Germans from disrupting industrial production, Stalin demanded that laborers relocate approximately fifteen hundred factories, steel-rolling mills, and machinery, in addition to 25 million civilian laborers and their families, to eastern areas of the Soviet Union. Nikolai

Alekseevich Voznesensky (1903-1950) outlined plans for evacuating industrial resources, which Council for Evacuation deputy chairman Aleksey Kosygin (1904-1980) oversaw from July through November, 1941. Enemy forces sometimes interrupted transportation by railroad and other vehicles, but eventually most designated Soviet industrial materials were moved. Civilians produced weapons and artillery in Soviet factories. An estimated 11,600 people worked at the Kirov tank factory, which was a significant contributor to Soviet military successes. Soviet workers produced 8,200 airplanes in 1941 and expanded their output to 29,900 airplanes in 1943.

German youths served mandatory two-year German Labor Service terms. In contrast to Allied forces' use of voluntary civilian workers, German military leaders often relied on forced labor. Germans routinely acquired laborers from areas that troops had invaded and occupied. German military personnel also forced many people interned in concentration camps to work; labor of this sort represented one-fourth of civilian laborers working for Germans. German occupation troops also forced civilians to manufacture rope and other utilitarian objects in factories where they had previously worked in peacetime. Japanese military leaders directed forced labor of civilians in Asia to build airfields and military work to sustain troops.

In the twenty-first century, civilian laborers, representing native and international workers—many of them contractors—contributed to work related to the Iraq War. These civilians helped troops by serving in such diverse roles as translators, drivers, and bodyguards. Few civilians expressed interest in performing work associated with warfare in Afghanistan, and as a result, U.S. government officials in the spring of 2009 considered assigning military reservists to those jobs, because they had regularly practiced expertise the military needed, such as engineering, in their civilian employment.

BOOKS AND ARTICLES

Chamberlain, Charles D. *Victory at Home: Manpower and Race in the American South During World War II*. Athens: University of Georgia Press, 2003. Discusses minority civilian laborers' experiences while working in wartime industries, addressing economic, political, cultural, and labor issues.

Kagan, Frederick. "The Evacuation of Soviet Industry in the Wake of 'Barbarossa': A Key to the Soviet Victory." *Journal of Slavic Military Studies* 8 (June, 1995): 387-414. This detailed account notes that historical texts often contain ideologically biased interpretations of the event, stressing that historians should consult primary sources when researching this topic.

Kern, Paul Bentley. *Ancient Siege Warfare*. Bloomington: Indiana University Press, 1999. Comprehensive study of numerous civilizations that incorporates information about civilian laborers based on biblical references and contemporary historians' descriptions.

Kratoska, Paul H., ed. *Asian Labor in the Wartime Japanese Empires: Unknown Histories*. Armonk, N.Y.: M. E. Sharpe, 2005. A collection of essays examining twentieth century uses of civilian labor. States that historians rely on oral and archival records to chronicle these frequently overlooked workers.

Nicolle, David. *The Age of Tamerlane*. Illustrated by Angus McBride. Men-at-Arms Series 222. New York: Osprey, 2003. Refers to civilian laborers who manufactured weaponry and armor. Illustrations depict weapons and protective garments.

Zeiger, Susan. *In Uncle Sam's Service: Women Workers with the American Expeditionary Force, 1917-1919*. Philadelphia: University of Pennsylvania Press, 2004. Analyzes motivations for women to work for military forces and how those jobs presented them with both autonomy and restrictions.

Elizabeth D. Schafer

COUNTERINSURGENCY

OVERVIEW

Counterinsurgency, often referred to as COIN by the U.S. armed forces, refers to the attempt by a government to maintain its legitimacy against an armed uprising of a part of the populace. The insurgents may receive external support as well. The government may utilize military, political, economic, and civic actions in the pursuit of preserving itself in power. The single most significant factor in the effort to maintain political control by government when facing an insurgency is retaining the loyalty of the populace at large. Many of the conflicts fought throughout recorded history possess characteristics that serve to qualify them, partially at least, as counterinsurgencies.

SIGNIFICANCE

An appreciation of counterinsurgency is significant to a broader understanding of warfare in all periods. Many conflicts over the course of history possessed a counterinsurgency component. At the same time, this aspect of warfare is very often overlooked, as much attention is focused on the insurgency dimension and not the manner in which these uprisings are subdued. Likewise, this is the direction toward which many current military theorists see warfare heading in the twenty-first century, with a great emphasis placed on nonstate actors that seek to undermine the legitimacy of established governments.

HISTORY OF COUNTERINSURGENCY

ANCIENT WORLD

Among the earliest counterinsurgencies in the ancient period was that of the Jews against the Seleucid Empire, one of the successor states to the empire of Alexander the Great, in the second century B.C.E. At issue was the ability of the Jews to practice their religion. The revolt finally ended when the Seleucids extended religious tolerance to the Jews. The significance here is that the Seleucids received the loyalty of the Jewish people when they were allowed to practice their religion. The Romans, as well, contended with numerous uprisings of peoples whom they sought to control. These included the revolts of the Celtiberians (195-179 B.C.E. and 153-133 B.C.E.), Quintus Sertorius (c. 123-72 B.C.E.), and the gladiator Spartacus, (109-71 B.C.E.). The Roman solution in these cases was usually quite harsh, including scorched earth, the enslavement of peoples who rose against their control, and the colonization of Romans on their lands in order to disrupt the ability of the restive populace to stand against the empire.

The approaches utilized by the Romans for putting down rebellions failed to be effective in the long run. Many provinces of the empire rose in rebellion on several occasions. One method of counterinsurgency practiced in both the ancient and medieval periods was that of constructing fortifications at strategically significant points. This method met with only limited success.

MEDIEVAL WORLD

During the medieval period in European history, probably the best-documented counterinsurgency is that of Edward I (r. 1272-1307) against the Welsh. Edward sought to confirm his control over their lands. He succeeded in disrupting the control of the Welsh leaders by waging a simultaneous land and sea campaign through which he managed to disrupt their food supply, thus undermining the legitimacy of the local rulers. In addition, he had the leaders of the revolt executed. Edward likewise dealt with the challenges to his authority in the areas of Scotland that were nominally under his control. The Scots were revolting against English rule in some of the border areas, while the English sought to expand their domination of Scotland. In suppressing these challenges to his power, Edward tended to make use of fairly harsh methods.

The Hundred Years' War (1337-1453) as well witnessed a fair amount of counterinsurgency, as there were several major revolts in both England and France. These were very much related to the heavy exactions placed on the peasants of both countries in order to wage the war. In France, the revolt was known as the Jacqueline (1358). This insurgency was put down when the leader, Guillaume Caleb, met with the leaders of the French nobility. He was arrested and decapitated. Much the same fate befell Watt Tyler's rebellion in England (1381). In this case, the rebels were following the lead of the French. When they marched into London, King Richard agreed to meet with them. Watt Tyler was killed in front of his people by the king's men. In both cases, once deprived of their leadership the insurgencies lost their momentum and collapsed.

MODERN WORLD

Among the counterinsurgency campaigns that receive the most attention at the start of the modern period is the fighting in the southern states of the United States during the American War of Independence. In the fighting in this theater, both sides resorted to partisan tactics, and both sought to create some semblance of a legal authority. In the south, especially in South Carolina, political legitimacy devolved into a contested ground after the British capture of Charleston in May, 1781. The Whig government was literally on the run, and the British set up a military government. This was as far as British measures went, however. The British failed to reinstall a civilian authority in any of the former colonies save Georgia, while the American revolutionaries under Nathanael Greene reestablished civilian authority in South Carolina and, through his efforts at restoring order, eventually made the Whig side the one with more legitimacy.

The government of revolutionary France faced a number of internal challenges while simultaneously fighting many of its European neighbors. The most persistent of these came from the northern region known as the Vendée (1793-1800). Here several groups of counterrevolutionaries rose up against the Paris government in defense of the local nobility, and

even more so of their Roman Catholic religion, which the revolutionaries were attempting to suppress. These conditions led to a challenge to the government's authority. Responses to the rebellion at first fell short of the task of breaking its cohesion. At the same time, there were some very harsh methods employed in the region, such as when hundreds of rebels were drowned by Jean-Baptiste Carrier in December, 1793. The task of subduing the revolt fell to General Lazare Hoche. Hoche lived off the land, and in the process he deprived his opponents of resources. He began with fortified bases and then worked to expand his control. Likewise, he took hostages, whom he refused to return unless the rebels returned their arms. These methods proved successful at restoring some level of control to the Vendée. It is worth noting, however, that the revolutionary government did not so much gain legitimacy or even acceptance as simply crush the resistance of the populace. The region would rise again during the latter phases of the Napoleonic Wars (1793-1815).

During the Napoleonic Wars, there were several revolts against the emperor's control. The most famous of these was the revolt in Spain that began May 2, 1808, and eventually played a role in the downfall of Napoleon I. There was a revolt in Prussia as well.

In the early nineteenth century, the Greek Revolt (1821-1828) against Ottoman rule sparked some efforts at counterinsurgency operations on the part of the Turks. To a large extent, these efforts were the same as those used against other insurgents, dividing the population and use of violent repression. What makes the Greek Revolt significantly different is that it was one of the first instances in which a foreign state became involved in supporting the insurgents.

The next counterinsurgency operation worthy of note took place in the late nineteenth century, in 1898; the United States went to war with Spain in what has become know as the Spanish-American War. As a result of the Treaty of Paris (1899), which ended the war, the United States took possession of the Philippines. At first, the transition was peaceful, as the United States had previously backed Philippine rebels against the Spanish. When it became clear that U.S. control over the Philippines would not translate into their independence, the insurgents, under their

F. R. Niglutsch

The comte de La Rochejaquelein leads a group of peasants during the Wars of the Vendée.

leader Emilio Aguinaldo, took to the jungles against American forces. The initial response of the U.S. military was to utilize standard military tactics against the insurgents. Predictably, this approach met with little success. At the same time, there was resort made to the burning of villages and the indiscriminate killing of civilians, all of which served to undermine the legitimacy of the U.S. government. Two factors contributed to obstruct the momentum of the rebellion. First was the capture of Aguinaldo by an American volunteer named Frederick Funston. Second, more humane methods were used to counteract the rebellion, with a greater reliance then placed on civil government.

In Mexico, in 1911, there arose another civil war—actually a combination of two challenges to government power, one in the north, led by Pancho Villa (Doroteo Arango), and one in the South, led by Emiliano Zapata. Zapata's revolt was among the first

insurgencies to place a heavy reliance on certain social classes. The Mexican government responded to the threat with repressive measures that included mass deportations and the confinement of large numbers of the population in concentration camps. In the case of Zapata, while these activities certainly inflicted damage on his movement, they did not destroy it. His resistance collapsed only after Zapata's death in an ambush in 1919.

The aftermath of World War II brought on another series of insurgency and counterinsurgency operations as the Europeans' colonial empires were dismantled through wars of national liberation. The most successful counterinsurgency operation of this period was that of the British in Malaya, referred to as the Malayan Emergency (1948-1960). At first, the British were unsuccessful against the communist-backed insurgents. Then they adopted the plan of

Lieutenant General Sir Harold Briggs. The plan comprised four stages: (1) to create a sense of stability in the populated areas that would lead to solid intelligence on the insurgents; (2) to disrupt the hold of the communist organizations in the populated areas; (3) to isolate the guerrillas from logistical support in the populated areas; and (4) to destroy the insurgents through forcing them into armed confrontations on terms benefiting the government forces. This plan worked very well. Coupled with the military arrangements was support for civilian projects to better the living conditions of the bulk of the Malayan populace.

Finally, in March of 2003, a coalition of nations built around U.S. forces invaded Iraq. The initial military contest was brief and ended resoundingly in favor of the coalition. By the end of the year, however, an insurgency was growing within the country against the occupying troops. Initially, the insurgents inflicted much damage and imposed heavy casualties on the occupying forces. Beginning in 2007, however, there was an increase of troop levels of some 20,000, known informally as the surge. The troops were placed in the most dangerous areas in the country, and by 2009 it appeared that this strategy may have led to a turning point in operations there.

BOOKS AND ARTICLES

Aspery, Robert B. *War in the Shadows: The Guerrilla in History*. New York: William Morrow, 1975. Considered a classic in the field of insurgency and counterinsurgency warfare.

Ellis, John. *A Short History of Guerrilla Warfare*. New York: St. Martin's Press, 1976. A short but useful work that provides much information in a condensed format.

Galula, David. *Counterinsurgency Warfare: Theory and Practice*. London: Praeger, 1964. A classic work that is based on the author's own experiences in several insurgencies in Greece, China, and Algeria.

Linn, Brian M. *The Philippine War, 1899-1902*. Lawrence: University Press of Kansas, 2002. An excellent treatment of the Philippine insurgency that examines it in great detail.

Lynn, John A. "Patterns of Insurgency and Counterinsurgency." *Military Review* 85, no. 4 (July/August, 2005): 22-27. An excellent brief introduction to the subject.

McCuen, John J. *The Art of Counter-revolutionary War*. St. Petersburg, Fla.: Hailer, 2005. This study encompasses a solid discussion of the theory and practice of counterinsurgency warfare.

Metz, Steven, and Raymond Millen. *Insurgency and Counterinsurgency in the Twenty-first Century: Reconceptualizing Threat and Response*. Carlisle Barracks, Pa.: U.S. Army War College, 2004. Places the war on terror in historical context.

Sepp, Kavlev I. "Best Practices in Counterinsurgency." *Military Review* 85, no. 3 (May/June, 2005): 8-12. As the title states, the work provides a clear discussion of the most effective techniques for dealing with insurgencies.

Taber, Robert. *War of the Flea: The Classic Study of Guerrilla Warfare*. Dulles, Va.: Potomac Books, 2002. Looks at counterinsurgency from the insurgents' perspective, describing their strengths and how these can be overcome.

Trinquier, Roger. *Modern Warfare: A French View of Counter-Insurgency*. New York: Praeger, 1964. Based on French experiences, this work advocates unrestrained methods for disrupting insurgencies.

James R. McIntyre

EDUCATION, TEXTBOOKS, AND WAR

OVERVIEW

Military veterans and officers instruct soldiers how to fight effectively in combat. Lessons often include lectures or textbook assignments describing military history and exercises to enhance physical strength and agility and acquire skills with weapons. Military education emphasizes discipline and organization to achieve warfare goals. Nonmilitary schools incorporate warfare discussion in curricula for varying objectives. While some educators tell pupils facts, other teachers present versions to satisfy government requirements. In the early twenty-first century, some military historians shifted from institutional studies of how specific military academies, service branches, and governments educated troops to examining warfare's role in diverse cultures, people's perceptions of war, and educational depictions influencing them.

SIGNIFICANCE

Education provides credentials for soldiers to advance professionally within the military. Academic accomplishments reinforce peers' and subordinates' respect for officers' authority. Military histories educate commanders to make decisions such as when to go to war, continue fighting, or withdraw forces. Textbooks, intended for either military personnel or school-age students, deliver narratives designed to achieve specific goals. While military textbooks train soldiers, many school history textbooks emphasize positive aspects and ignore controversial topics. Some educational resources misrepresent military history intentionally with rhetoric and propaganda to promote nationalism. Ideas presented by textbooks shape how students view warfare and influence their attitudes toward their country's military forces—motivating them, for example, to consider serving as adults.

HISTORY OF TEXTS, EDUCATION, AND WAR

Throughout history, boys participated in games and activities such as hunting as a form of early military training. Formal educational experiences prepared soldiers and officers for warfare. Handbooks and instructional guides provided information soldiers needed to perform their duties and respond to wartime demands. Some military schools incorporated military history and theory into lectures and assigned books, often written by instructors and veterans, for cadets to study. Troops bonded by sharing training, rituals, and sacrifices. Warfare impacted people according to the historic period and geographical region in which they lived and how essential military power was for their leaders to secure control. Civilians' comprehension of history and awareness of military books and tacticians' concepts often shaped cultural responses to warfare.

As social ideas regarding childhood changed, educational opportunities for children expanded in the nineteenth and twentieth centuries. Many schools used textbooks that featured notable military figures, battles, and wars. Lessons often emphasized military role models and successes from ancient times through contemporary events to encourage children to be patriotic citizens and feel pride for their country. Discussion of atrocities and defeats was often omitted or dismissed as irrelevant. Publishers, authors, and educators exhibited varying degrees of accountability regarding textbooks' role in educating children about warfare.

ANCIENT WORLD

Historians consider Sunzi's *Sunzi Bingfa* (c. fifth-third century B.C.E.; *The Art of War*, 1910) to be the first known military text. Initially available in ancient Chinese territories, this work influenced contemporary military and political leaders and extended its impact through time, continuing to shape

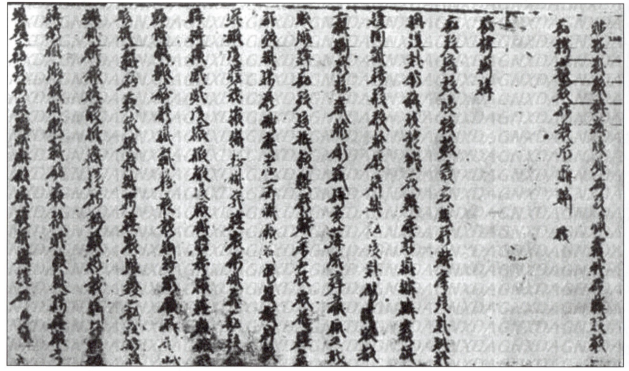

A Tangut script of Sunzi's Art of War *(c. 510 B.C.E.), one of the oldest texts on military theory.*

warfare in the twenty-first century. Sunzi (Sun Tzu; c. 544-c. 496 B.C.E.), whose identity many historians question, emphasized the role of warfare in maintaining effective governments to prevent their failure and submission to other powers. The text, no matter who wrote it, contains universal principles that have been appropriated in warfare for centuries since it was written. In ancient China, Qin emperor Shi Huang credited *The Art of War* for tactics to conclude military strife during the Warring States period. Translations expanded the influence of *The Art of War* to diverse cultures and commanders in other eras. Many modern U.S. military school curricula adopted *The Art of War* as a strategy textbook.

Ancient military narratives influenced Alexander the Great (356-323 B.C.E.) of Macedonia and empowered him as a general. His father, King Philip II, arranged Alexander's military training, ordering teachers to instruct his son in horsemanship and weaponry. Philip secured philosopher Aristotle's services as Alexander's academic tutor. Aristotle's lessons encouraged discussion of historic events, including battles.

Aristotle gave Alexander a copy of the *Iliad* (c. 750 B.C.E.; English translation, 1611), by Greek poet Homer, with annotations he had added. The *Iliad* shaped Alexander's view of warfare. Fascinated by Homer's depiction of the Trojan War (c. 1200-1100 B.C.E.), Alexander admired the protagonist, Achilles, from whom Alexander believed he was descended, and aspired to achieve similar triumphs. Alexander possibly also read military accounts by historians Herodotus, Thucydides, and others describing actions during the fifth century B.C.E. Peloponnesian War and Persian Wars.

Those texts influenced how Alexander responded to his early military actions and envisioned his responsibilities as a leader, planning logistics and organizing personnel at the Battle of Chaeronea (338 B.C.E.). Alexander trained his soldiers much the way his father had, instructing troops regarding battle formations and how to use pikes, swords, and other weapons. He emphasized drills to prepare his warriors, many of whom engaged in training to fulfill requirements demanded of citizens, for potential battlefield situations and reinforce discipline. When Alexander's army reached such Trojan War battle sites as Troy in 334 B.C.E., Alexander, whose copy of the *Iliad* accompanied him on military campaigns, paid tribute to the warriors who had fought at those sites and visited Achilles' tomb.

Other ancient military handbooks influenced contemporaries' perception of war. Many ancient people were constantly confronted with warfare and its obligations and incentives, such as assuring citizenship through service. Britannia governor Sextus Julius Frontinus (35-c. 103 C.E.) wrote *Strategematicon libri iii* (late 80's C.E.; *Strategematicon: Or, Greek and Roman Anecdotes, Concerning Military Policy, and the Science of War*, 1811), which shaped commanders' ideas on the deployment of military troops. Arrian (c. 89-155 C.E.), noted in *Tactica* (c. 136/137; on tactics) that the Romans had adapted some military moves from the Celts. In the late fourth century, Flavius Vegetius Renatus (fl. fourth century), a Roman finance minister, compiled the most enduring ancient military handbook, *Epitoma rei militaris* (c. 384-389 C.E.; *The Military Institutions of the Romans*, 1767), usually referred to as *De re militari*, which he created to instruct military and government leaders. Historians lack proof that Vegetius's handbook affected how ancient commanders conducted warfare, but it became part of the medieval military canon.

MEDIEVAL WORLD

Army and naval commanders during the Middle Ages were aware of books written by ancient military historians and tacticians. Vegetius's *De re militari* was a frequently mentioned ancient text in medieval military histories and often was copied for military and political figures. Literate medieval people read *De re militari* because it provided access to Roman thought and concepts. Roman military information intrigued medieval readers curious about ancient warfare and its possible applications to their military needs. Contemporary sagas, such as the *Slovo o polku Igoreve* (c. 1187; *The Lay of Igor's Host*, 1902), revealed that medieval people had contrasting cultures regarding warfare; during the Middle Ages, people were motivated to fight by different factors, including honor, glory, dutifulness to rulers, chivalric expectations, and religious beliefs.

Some copyists revised ancient handbooks to meet conditions in their location and time. Freculph, bishop of Lisieux (fl. ninth century), gave his edited copy of Vegetius's handbook to Charles the Bald, stating that it could help military leaders form effective fighting techniques to resist Viking attacks in the mid-ninth century. By the thirteenth century, a French translation of Vegetius's handbook was distributed. In the fifteenth century, craftspersons used the printing press to produce copies of *De re militari*. Various histories stated that notable medieval commanders took copies of Vegetius's handbook into battle, but no evidence verifies that they applied this guide in combat.

About 856, King Lothair II commissioned Rabanus Maurus (c. 780-856), a scholar and church leader, to appropriate Vegetius's work to write a revised handbook entitled *Recapitulatio* (recapitulation). Rabanus selected text that was relevant to medieval warfare, including such topics as weaponry, strategies, and tactics. Other medieval military handbooks included one credited to Emperor Maurice (Flavius Tiberius Mauricius, c. 539-602) entitled *Strategikon* (*Maurice's Strategikon: Handbook of Byzantine Military Strategy*, 1984), which was distributed around the year 600. The Frankish count Nithard (790?-844), whose grandfather was Charlemagne, wrote *Historiae*, or *De dissensionibus filiorum Ludovici pii* (c. 843; on the dissensions of the sons of Louis the Pious), in which he described military training and drills for Carolingian horse soldiers. Students might have had access to these handbooks at military schools, especially at the Carolingian monastery, Saint-Riquier, where *milites* (soldiers) associated with the royal family lived and trained. Despite references to Vegetius, Rhabanus, and other military theorists in histories, sources are unclear on whether medieval military officers actually read those books and utilized their concepts in warfare.

Contemporary reception of *Dell'arte della guerra* (1521; *The Art of War*, 1560) by Niccolò Machiavelli (1469-1527), is better known. Machiavelli, who served the Florence government as a secretary, modeled his book on *De re militari*, copied some of Vegetius's concepts, and discussed such medieval figures as Francesco Sforza and Cesare Borgia. Many of Machiavelli's contemporaries were more familiar with those of his works that focused on politics, but *The Art of War* generated greater immediate impact than its medieval predecessors by shaping Florence's military organization and warfare objectives. Machiavelli's treatist suggested that using citizens instead of mercenaries as soldiers could educate the populace about warfare's realities, develop civic values, and reinforce people's commitment to serve. Machiavelli stated that personal involvement with warfare would unify populations and prepare citizens to defend their government loyally and unconditionally, unlike foreigners hired to fight. Many scholars emphasize that Machiavelli's *The Art of War* introduced modern concepts relevant to military theory and practice.

MODERN WORLD

By the nineteenth century, warfare had begun a transition which Carl von Clausewitz (1780-1831) ad-

dressed in his book *Vom Kriege* (1832; *On War*, 1873). Clausewitz stressed the role of government policies in shaping warfare. Notable officers who stated that they had applied Clausewitz's concepts to their military strategies include Helmuth von Moltke (1800-1891). Although many British and American military leaders criticized Clausewitz, the Vietnam War (1961-1975) altered resistance to Clausewitz's theories as commanders realized how governments' decisions affected military performance. At the U.S. Army War College, Colonel Harry Summers conducted a Clausewitz study and published *On Strategy: A Critical Analysis of the Vietnam War* (1982). Many military colleges incorporated *On War* into their curricula.

Critics and supporters wrote articles and books examining, and often misinterpreting, Clausewitz's works. Sir Basil Henry Liddell Hart (1895-1970) was one of Clausewitz's most vocal critics. He denounced Clausewitz for promoting total war, which Liddell Hart thought had shaped World War I commanders' actions and caused high casualties. Liddell Hart urged armies to become mechanized with tanks. Some historians credited Liddell Hart's writings with inspiring German officers, including Erwin Rommel, to create Blitzkreig tactics. Liddell Hart emphasized the need for more historical warfare studies in educational curricula in his *Why Don't We Learn from History?* (1944).

Before World War I, some U.S. educators wanted high school boys to receive military instruction that would condition them physically and mentally for war and to provide their communities security. Teachers belonging to the American School Peace League spoke against that training. Those pacifists were mostly successful in preventing mandatory military education in U.S. schools, but many countries prepared their students educationally for potential warfare roles.

Courtesy, USMA Public Affairs Office

The United States Military Academy, looking north along the Hudson River.

Courtesy, U.S. Air Force Public Affairs

Basic cadets salute during their first reveille formation at the United States Air Force Academy in Colorado Springs, Colorado.

After World War II, the Japanese Ministry of Education told educators to ink out military sections in textbooks to appease U.S. occupation forces. The Supreme Command for the Allied Powers (SCAP) required new Japanese textbooks written by professional historians to replace educational resources deemed to be unsuitable. In 1946, historian Saburō Ienaga (1913-2002) wrote *Shin Nihonshi* (1947; new Japanese history), which emphasized themes of democracy, pacifism, and truth. His book *Taiheiyō sensō* (1968; *The Pacific War: World War II and the Japanese, 1931-1945*, 1978) acknowledged Japan's war crimes in Nanjing, China.

During the 1950's, Japan's education ministry rejected books it considered contrary to values they wanted Japanese children to acquire, including Ienaga's books (unless he would agree to revise them).

By the mid-1960's, Ienaga initiated litigation against the ministry, stating its textbook selection was unlawful. He complained that the ministry had insisted he revise discussion of Japan's military aggression against China, Korea, and the Philippines. In the 1990's, Tokyo University education professor Nobukatsu Fujioka publicly endorsed textbooks that glorified and often embellished Japanese history and excluded historical figures and events he considered negative.

Japan's supreme court affirmed the ministry's textbook selection as constitutional in 1997 but stated that all revision demands should be compatible with historical scholarship. Fujioka established the Atarashii Rekishi Kyōkasho o Tsukurukai (Japanese Institute for Orthodox History Education), which produced a textbook incompatible with historical facts. The ministry's approval of that textbook provoked criticism throughout Asia. Numerous Japanese historians and educators stated that it inaccurately perpetuated myths and included flawed interpretations. Most Japanese school districts refused to use it. Historians worldwide voiced concerns about textbooks presenting military history responsibly to students.

BOOKS AND ARTICLES

Bassford, Christopher. *Clausewitz in English: The Reception of Clausewitz in Britain and America, 1815-1945*. New York: Oxford University Press, 1994. Interprets responses to Clausewitz's ideas and how changing public attitudes toward warfare influenced reactions to his writing.

Hein, Laura, and Mark Selden, eds. *Censoring History: Citizenship and Memory in Japan, Germany, and the United States*. Armonk, N.Y.: M. E. Sharpe, 2000. Essays analyze textbook depictions of wars, events, and national histories, including provocative images often omitted.

Lindaman, Dana, and Kyle Ward. *History Lessons: How Textbooks From Around the World Portray U.S. History*. New York: The New Press, 2004. Excerpts present varied perspectives and distortions about warfare from educational material used in diverse countries' schools.

McNeilly, Mark. *Sun Tzu and the Art of Modern Warfare*. New York: Oxford University Press, 2001. Applies Sunzi's tactical principles to discussion of significant historic battles and commanders, comparing those ideas with other military strategists' concepts.

Nicolle, David. *Armies of Medieval Russia, 750-1250*. Illustrated by Angus McBride. Men-at-Arms Series 333. New York: Osprey, 1999. Explores reasons soldiers fought, with cultural references to warfare. Illustrations feature contemporary images.

Zeiger, Susan. "The Schoolhouse vs. the Armory: U.S. Teachers and the Campaign Against Militarism in the Schools, 1914-1918." *Journal of Women's History* 15, no. 2 (Summer, 2003): 150-179. Examines attempts to incorporate military education into mainstream curricula in context with issues associated with warfare.

Elizabeth D. Schafer

PARAMILITARY ORGANIZATIONS

OVERVIEW

Prior to the establishment of standing armies, groups of people armed themselves for their own protection, and essentially this is the origin of the many paramilitary organizations that have existed since ancient times. These groups had commanders and "officers" who held military ranks, and they were armed, but the difference between them and armies was that central authorities did not control the paramilitary organizations and they operated on a basis similar to that of some militias today. During the late twentieth century, the term "paramilitary group" tended to be used for armed groupings, which come together for a political purpose, often armed illegally. However, there are many instances in which the division between paramilitary groups, militias, and other armed groups are blurred.

SIGNIFICANCE

Throughout history, paramilitary groups have played a major role in determining political control of particular parts of countries, and they have been prominent in local affairs. They have been especially important in civil wars, the control of civilians, and keeping some governments in power, as well as unseating (or attempting to unseat) others. In full-scale warfare, they are usually "outgunned" if they are fighting regular armies, although the nature of paramilitaries has often meant that they can blend into the general civilian population, which, in turn, has meant that they have had success in guerrilla warfare, insurgencies, and periods of civil strife.

HISTORY OF PARAMILITARY ORGANIZATIONS

ANCIENT WORLD

In the ancient world, militias and local armies effectively controlled towns. However, with the emergence of large empires, localities continued to have means to protect themselves from local banditry or sudden incursions from their neighbors by raising small forces. Owing to the scanty nature of information from much of the ancient world, there is academic debate over the exact nature of some of the military forces that operated and whether or not they had a degree of central control. An example is the army of Hannibal (247-182 B.C.E.), which, although it was referred to as the Carthaginian army, may in fact have its origins in a paramilitary force raised by his father, Hamilcar Barca, in Spain. By contrast, the soldiers raised by Marcus Licinius Crassus in Rome in 71 B.C.E., against Spartacus, although paid for by Crassus himself, were put at the disposal of the Roman government (admittedly led by Crassus) and were therefore not paramilitaries. There is also clear evidence that some of the armies during the "barbarian" invasions of the Roman Empire operated with sufficient autonomy to imply that they might also have been paramilitary forces. Indeed the fall of the Roman Empire—essentially with the collapse of central authority—led to the formation of regionally based military groups to protect cities, towns, and villages.

MEDIEVAL WORLD

The lack of central authority in the medieval world resulted in the formation of local militia groups and essentially in the paramilitary groups as they exist in the modern world. This occurred in parts of Germany, along the eastern borders of Europe, and for periods in France. In England, the Wars of the Roses (1455-1485) were essentially a battle between paramilitary forces raised by respective landowners. As the feuding families of medieval and Renaissance Italy needed their own soldiers, their paramilitaries, often augmented by the hiring of mercenaries and alliances with regional powers, came to dominate Italian politics for centuries. Mercenary bands such as the White Company of Sir John Hawkwood in the fourteenth century were also paramilitary groups, as were the followers of Cesare Borgia in Italy after the death of his father, Pope Alexander VI. Also in Spain during the Reconquista, paramilitary forces operated from regional powers that were involved in alliances with and against the Moors from the twelfth to the fifteenth century.

MODERN WORLD

The European voyages of discovery led to the establishment of large colonial empires and powerful chartered companies such as the British East India Company and the Dutch Vereenigde Oost-indische Compagnie (VOC, or Dutch East India Company). Most of these companies maintained their own armed forces (and navies), which had military ranks and raised soldiers both from the homeland and in their new possessions. These sometimes fought alongside colonial armies. This was particularly the case with the armies and navies of the British East India Company, which did not integrate its armed forces with those of the British Army and British India until 1858. Prior to this, and certainly before the 1830's, the British East India Company was involved in waging wars of aggression without needing to get prior agreement from the British government.

In the cases of civil wars such as aspects of the Thirty Years' War (1618-1648) and the English Civil Wars (1642-1651), councils and wealthy individuals raised their own forces, which were sometimes put at the disposal of the main commanders but often were involved in local skirmishes or the defense of their own property or town, making them effectively paramilitaries.

The best-known paramilitary forces have operated in the twentieth and twenty-first centuries. In Germany after World War I, there were problems

with law and order. The result was that certain groups were formed, the most famous being the Freikorps, which first appeared in December, 1918, mainly composed of former soldiers and taking the name from a similar force that had appeared in the eighteenth century. Essentially the storm troopers and the Sturm Abteilung (SA) of Ernst Röhm, during the period of the rise to power of the Nazi Party up until 1931 and during the German occupation of much of Europe, operated as paramilitary groups. Certainly the Blackshirts in Italy, who helped Benito Mussolini come to power in 1922, had a similar role. There were also pro-Fascist groups in other countries who marched in uniform and sometimes, when possible, carried weapons. These included the Falange in Spain, the Blue Shirts in Ireland, the Blackshirts of Sir Oswald Mosley in Britain, and possibly even the New Guard in Australia. Certainly not all the paramilitary groups were of the political right; socialist, communist, and anarchist militia groups operating in Spain during the Spanish Civil War (1936-1939) usually supported, and often fought alongside, the Spanish Republican forces but occasionally fought against each other. It could even be argued that the International Brigade during that war was essentially a paramilitary group, especially given that it drew people of many nationalities and followed various commanders.

During World War II, the Germans sponsored many paramilitary groups who fought alongside them in parts of Russia, the Balkans, and other parts of Europe. Some of these groups, especially in the Baltic, in Poland, and in the Ukraine, became heavily associated with the atrocities against Jews and other people there. While many of the groups fought alongside the German forces, and quite clearly had the support of them, sometimes their exact nature is still debated by historians. Mention should also be made of the Fascist Militia in France, which operated on a paramilitary basis, again with the support of members of the Vichy government (but often not at its behest). On the opposite side during the war, the partisans in Yugoslavia, Albania, and Italy, as well as other countries, essentially operated as paramilitary groups, as did some Free French forces in 1944 and 1945.

Following the Chinese Revolution of 1911 and the fragmentation of the country, many warlords established their own "armies," again as paramilitary groups, sometimes allied with the government but often able to control civilians in areas that had achieved a degree of local autonomy. One example is the group led by Zhang Zulin (Chang Tso-lin, also known as the Old Marshal or Mukden Tiger) in Manchuria. His forces were armed and trained, controlled a significant part of the country, but only loosely took orders from the central government. As a result, technically until the Northern Expedition, the armies loyal to the Guomindang (Kuomintang) from southern China were also essentially paramilitaries.

In Ireland, there were also paramilitary groups formed along religious and political lines. The Irish Republican Army, which was led by people holding military rank, and for official occasions dressed in uniforms, was also a paramilitary group—although labeled by its opponents as a terrorist organization. While it served to oppose the British army first in Ireland and later in Northern Ireland, the Ulster Defence Association was established in 1971 to support British rule in Northern Ireland, and uniquely it was a legal organization with its commanders able to use military ranks, although they were not allowed to use weapons.

During the civil war in Lebanon from 1975, many militia groups emerged, including Amal for the Shīʿites, the Druze militia of Walid Jumblatt, the Falangist militia of Pierre Gemayel and then Bashir Gemayel, and later Hezbollah. All these groups were effectively paramilitary groups, as were the Palestinians based in Lebanon during much of this time. Discussion of paramilitary groups in Lebanon is also problematic because of the success of some paramilitary leaders who have attained political power. This could be seen with the election of Bashir Gemayel, leader of the Falangist militia, as president of Lebanon and then, after his assassination, the election of his brother Amin Gemayel and the subsequent assumption of power by Michel Aoun. As commanders of one of the most powerful paramilitary groups in the country, they were also heads of the government.

In many cases there are also instances when secretive paramilitary forces have been used to work alongside the official military but in roles from which the military have shrunk. These include militia groups in Indonesia involved in "the Killings" in 1965 and the destruction of East Timor in 1999, and the "death squads" in many Central American countries during the 1980's.

Many paramilitary groups have emerged in Africa. Some have been made up of colonists opposed to independence, such as the Algerian supporters of the 1960 Barricades Revolt in Algiers. In the 1990's, paramilitary militia-style groups in regions of Africa gained considerable notoriety, among them the Interahamwe in Rwanda and the Janjaweed in the Darfur region of Sudan. Although both these groups operated with significant support from their local governments, they operated with considerable local autonomy. To complicate matters, attempts for independence by people in Biafra and Katanga led to wars that the central governments in Nigeria and the Congo, respectively, saw as resistance to "illegal" paramilitary groups rather than the suppression of independence movements. Similar arguments can be made over whether the African National Congress (ANC), National Union for the Total Independence of Angola (União Nacional para a Independência Total de Angola, or UNITA) in Angola, the Mozambican National Resistance (Resistência Nacional Moçambicana, or RENAMO), and the Polisario Front are, or were, paramilitary groups. In South Africa as it moved toward majority rule in the early 1990's, the Afrikaner Weerstandsbeweging (AWB), led by Eugène Terre'Blanche, which was opposed to the end of apartheid, effectively turned itself into a militia, with its supporters wearing military-style clothing, carrying weapons, and becoming involved in events such as driving into Bophuthatswana in 1994 as part of the paramilitary Afrikaner Volksfront. Similarly, it could be argued that the Zulu groups, armed with "traditional weapons," were effectively a paramilitary group, as possibly were the "war veterans" involved in land seizures in Zimbabwe in the 2000's.

BOOKS AND ARTICLES

Caballero Jurado, Carlos. *The German Freikorps, 1918-23*. New York: Osprey, 2001. This work covers the organizations formed by returning World War I veterans, who feared a communist revolution in postwar Germany.

Flackes, W. D. *Northern Ireland: A Political Directory*. London: Ariel Books, 1983. Contains a listing of the makeshift organizations that have come and gone throughout the Troubles.

Katz, Samuel M., and Lee E. Russell. *Armies in Lebanon, 1982-84*. New York: Osprey, 1985. Details the history and organization of the various terrorist groups in Lebanon during their time of highest activity.

Norton, Augustus Richard. *Hezbollah: A Short History*. Princeton, N.J.: Princeton University Press, 2007. In addition to providing information on how the organization developed, the book looks at the various military, nonmilitary, and charitable parts of the larger group.

Thomas, Nigel. *Partisan Warfare, 1941-45*. New York: Osprey, 1983. Profiles the various paramilitary groups, such as the French Resistance, that played such an important role during the invasion of Europe during World War II.

Windrow, Martin. *The Algerian War, 1954-62*. New York: Osprey, 1997. Looks at the various groups that fought against French colonialism, eventually succeeding in driving the Europeans out.

Justin Corfield

THE PRESS AND WAR

OVERVIEW

The notion of the fourth estate—the "press" (or the "media")—has evolved over human history from oral recitation through the advent of print to the current digital age. The ability of the press to cover conflicts has also evolved, as have the objectives of those who announce and write history, including modern journalists and others who purport to report the "news." Issues specifically attached to the media during wartime have included how to obtain and disseminate information to the public, the inevitable conflict between the media and the state, and their competing interests during wartime. The role of technology has had a particular impact—from the invention of the printing press (fifteenth century) to the modern era of the Internet—on how information is gathered and distributed by the media from the battlefield to people's living rooms and how the public is influenced by the media's coverage of war.

SIGNIFICANCE

The relationship between the media and the state during wartime has often blurred the distinction between information and propaganda and created the conflict between censorship and the "right to know." Both institutions have competing agendas: the state's desire to control the distribution of information, especially information that might be embarrassing or harmful to wartime objectives; and the media's mission to obtain the truth and to inform the public. It is especially during the last 150 years, with the rise of democracies and the accelerating pace of technology, that the conflict between the media and the state during wartime has intensified.

HISTORY OF THE PRESS AND WAR

ANCIENT WORLD

In the ancient world, all news was spread by word of mouth. Even with the advent of writing, the great majority of ancient peoples were illiterate, and thus all information was restricted to an elite of scribes and rulers. The stories behind the great epics of the Greeks, such as Homer's *Iliad* (c. 750 B.C.E.; English translation, 1611), were originally told orally and retold through the generations. It was through trade that people were exposed to information and ideas. In ancient Greece, the *agora* of Athens and other cities served as a forum where all kinds of news was exchanged.

Getty Images

CNN's Peter Arnett reports from Iraq during the Gulf War in 1991.

Ancient Romans received their daily news at the Forum through reading placards. The placards fed the Romans' desire for news about life abroad. Most of all, the baths were a favorite gathering place for Romans of all classes, where they could exchange news and the daily gossip. The *Acta Senatus* and the *Acta Diurna* served as the means by which Romans could learn about their government and their empire. Julius Caesar (100-44 B.C.E.) had written treatises on the Germanic tribes he encountered in his campaigns in Gaul, but they did not have the current feel of a modern newspaper. Unlike the modern newspaper, however, placards reported facts only randomly, without any kind of editorial oversight. There was no criticism of government policies during peace or war.

MEDIEVAL WORLD

The collapse of the Roman Empire meant a total breakdown of society. Because of the collapse of the political order, the infrastructure and security that made an urban and cosmopolitan way of life possible simply disappeared. In Western Europe, people were reduced to a far simpler way of living. Between 500 and 1000 C.E., invasions by "barbarian" tribes made the world of the "Dark Ages" unpredictable. Life was more isolated, and information much harder to come by. Knowledge of the first few centuries of the Middle Ages survived only through the work of a handful of monks and chroniclers.

By the High Middle Ages, between about 1000 and 1300, Western Europe had recovered a degree of civilization with the rise of towns, but nowhere near the same level of sophistication that had thrived under the Romans. Tales of war, courtly love, and chivalry became popular as minstrels and troubadours spread news about far-off lands through verse and song.

MODERN WORLD

The emergence of the modern newspaper can be traced to the seventeenth century. Prior to this, town criers and heralds announced royal proclamations. Eventually, they would be replaced by circulars and printed journals. The precursors of the newspaper were the *nouvellistes*, who scoured the country for the most recent news, which included news about politics, literature, the arts, and the mundane. The nouvellistes also recorded the wars of Louis XIV.

In 1631, a physician named Théophraste Renaudot (1586-1653) founded the *Gazette de France*, the first modern newspaper. His goal was "to get at the truth." The earliest examples of wartime correspondence were letters, called *corantos*, that dated from the Thirty Years' War (1618-1648), mixed with personal stories and travelogues. These letters were duplicated through the printing press and were distributed to a larger public. The prototype of the wartime correspondent was an anonymous writer for the *Swedish Intelligencer* who reported the accounts of King Gustavus Adolphus. Like modern newspapers, the *Swedish Intelligencer* had a bureau in London, but unlike modern journalists, the writers of the *Swedish Intelligencer* did not go out to the field to get first-hand information; instead, they depended on the word of gentlemen of high rank and on other secondary sources.

After the Thirty Years' War, newspapers began acquiring their present characteristics. Newspapers began establishing foreign bureaus where people would pass on firsthand accounts. By the eighteenth century, newspapers were becoming the dominant source of information. English newspapers could freely publish without censorship, while French and other European newspapers were kept under political scrutiny. When it came to wartime, however, all newspapers were under tight government restrictions and were almost entirely dependent on the government for information.

The wars of the French Revolution (1789-1793) and the Napoleonic Wars (1793-1815) opened an opportunity for the development of war correspondence. The events of the French Revolution attracted British journalists, who reported as "our Correspondent in Paris." One prominent example is that of Robert Cutler Fergusson, who was in Paris between 1792 and 1793 to report, firsthand, history-making events such as the massacre of the Swiss Guards by the women of Paris, the attempted flight of the royal family, and the meetings of the Legislative Assembly, which ultimately convicted Louis XVI and Marie-Antoinette. French newspapers recorded the activi-

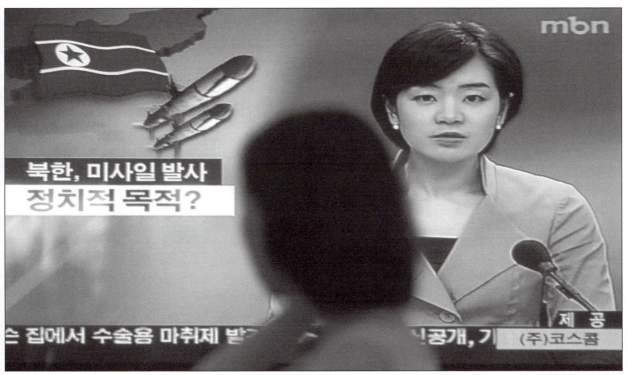

AFP/Getty Images

A pedestrian passes by a television screen in Seoul during a report about a North Korean missile launch on July 4, 2009.

ties of Napoleon's armies, based on the information provided them by the official bulletins posted by Napoleon Bonaparte (1769-1821). These dispatches were also printed in English newspapers, with the caveat that they might be unreliable, since they came from French sources. English journalists countered French bulletins by pointing out their inconsistencies; however, any other sources beyond those of Napoleon's armies proved very difficult to obtain.

Official information from generals and admirals did not make for exciting reading to the larger public. For example, during the Peninsular War (1808-1815), Arthur Wellesley, the the duke of Wellington (1769-1852), provided such dull and uninspiring dispatches that they gave the impression of defeat, when in fact the British were successful in hampering Napoleon's objectives in Spain. Another challenge to war correspondents was the slow pace of mail couriers. Newspapers had to be mindful of placating postal officials, both foreign and domestic, or risk missing a

"scoop." The Continental System established by Napoleon had the unintended effect of making British newspapers prized on the Continent. By the end of the Napoleonic Wars, British newspapers such as *The Times* had refined their information-gathering methods and themselves became the source of information for the British government when it sought updated information on Napoleon's forces.

By the middle of the nineteenth century, the modern newspaper was undergoing an evolution: The formerly haphazard means of gathering information were becoming more structured and standardized, leading to the sophisticated media organizations recognized today. American journalists such as George William Curtis for *The New York Times*, Margaret Fuller for *The New-York Tribune*, Charles A. Dana, William Cullen Bryant, and Theodore Sedgwick competed with their European counterparts for breaking news on the battlefield. Correspondence on the Mexican War (1846-1848) showed that American journalism had come of age. First, the new technology of photography allowed this conflict to be the first to be photographed. American war correspondents—unlike their dignified and restrained European counterparts—reported directly from the battlefield and even fought on the battlefield. George Wilkins Kendall of the New Orleans *Daily Picayune* captured a Mexican flag and acquired the title of major. American newspapers jostled with each other to get the first scoop on the latest fighting. The telegraph, which had just been invented at the outset of the war, had not yet realized its potential. Thus, newspaper agencies still depended on courier services. Coverage of the Mexican War suited every appetite for news, describing everything from the tactical and strategic aspects of the conflict to human-interest stories and letters to home.

The Crimean War (1853-1856) marked a turning point in wartime correspondence. Newspaper organizations began the organized practice of using a civilian reporter to inform the general public. The age of the newspaper correspondent dawned with William Howard Russell (1820-1907). His journalistic career began when he was hired by *The Times* in 1841 to cover elections in Ireland. He first covered the Crimean War in 1854, when editor John Thaddeus Delane (1817-1879) of *The Times* assigned him to cover a British force in Malta. When Russell arrived at Gallipoli, he saw firsthand the conditions of the British army, which was supposed to be fighting the Russians. He was dumbfounded at the unsanitary conditions the injured soldiers had to endure and the incompetence of the officers, who came from the aristocracy. Upon observing these conditions, he faced the dilemma of whether to publish his findings to *The Times*. Delane encouraged Russell to continue reporting. As the editor, Delane selected which of Russell's reports were fit for public consumption and which he would distribute privately to the government, which led to the collapse of an entire cabinet.

Another effect of Russell's reports on the lot of the ordinary British soldier was that they inspired Florence Nightingale to lend her services, which in turn led to the modern nursing profession. While Russell was reporting on the conditions of the British army, the British government, perhaps instigated by Prince Albert, sent royal photographer Roger Fenton (1819-1869) to counter Russell's reports on incompetence and suffering. Fenton portrayed British soldiers as happy and well dressed in order to maintain public support for the Crimean War. The Crimean War established the practice of the special correspondent, the role Russell most exemplified. His example would be emulated by future war correspondents throughout the rest of the nineteenth century, from the American Civil War to the Boer War.

World War I (1914-1918) witnessed the maturation of the wartime correspondence, as well as the increasingly intertwined relationship between the state and the press. Initially, the Allied and Central Powers attempted to accommodate war correspondents by accrediting journalists and providing tours of the battlefields and military positions. However, as the war progressed, the governments of the Allies and the Central Powers reined in journalists by providing only the sort of information that was deemed suitable by the military censors. Propaganda was crucial in maintaining public support of the war. Casualties were downplayed, even fudged. Both the Allies and the Central Powers painted their respective causes in the most favorable light possible, while portraying the enemy as less than human. God was on everyone's side, and the war was described as a war for civilization. The British were especially adept in demonizing the Germans. The *Financial Times* reported on June 10, 1915, that the German army had put a bounty on the children of the Belgian king, Albert. The Bryce Commission reported alleged German atrocities committed in Belgium. Among them included accounts of rape, butchery, and murder. Because the report bore the name of Lord Bryce, a scholar and former ambassador to the United States, the atrocities gained credibility among the British and American public, arousing anti-German sentiment. A decade later, many of the allegations were proved to be exaggerated or false.

World War II (1939-1945) proved to be far more destructive than the first, and the ability of the government to control information was even greater because of advances in technology in the twenty years since the guns had fallen silent at the western front. In response to the development of shortwave radio, the

British Ministry of Information established protocols for the control of information in 1936; its objective was to make the next war a "newsless" war. Correspondents' movements would be restricted by the military. Censors would keep unflattering information away from the public view. The Germans took their cue from the example set by during British World War I, creating an elaborate propaganda machine directed by Joseph Goebbels (1897-1945). The military establishment carefully screened all material written by correspondents and intimidated anyone who wrote unfavorable news about the German war effort.

The United States also established measures to prevent the leaking of sensitive information. Despite its democratic institutions, the U.S. government resorted to propaganda as a means to bolster public morale. Such practices dated to the Creel Commission during World War I. During the World War II Pacific campaign, for example, General Douglas MacArthur's return to the Philippines was publicized with photographers and newsreel cameras. At the same time, however, the news of the Holocaust found a skeptical audience. Having been raised on the German atrocity stories of World War I—subsequently discredited—the Allied public assumed that stories of the concentration camps were mere propaganda. As in World War I, journalists during World War II were their own censors, glorifying their own countries at the expense of the truth.

After World War II, the Grand Alliance broke down into superpower tensions between the United States and the Soviet Union. The witch hunts of McCarthyism led Americans to fear the spread of communism throughout Eastern Europe and the Third World. Unlike World War II, in which the enemy was clearly established, wartime coverage of conflicts in Africa, Asia, and Latin America was ambiguous for journalists because of the nature of the client-state relationship of the Cold War.

The Korean War (1950-1953) was such a war. Journalists found it difficult to understand the objectives of this conflict, which killed 2 million Koreans and 300,000 troops under the United Nations. Military censorship hampered journalists' ability to obtain facts, as in previous wars.

In the 1960's, technology revolutionized the dissemination of information as television and satellite communication brought the war to people's living rooms. The Vietnam War (1961-1975) was broadcast into the homes of Americans every evening. As the public watched, the reality of war—battles, casualties, maimed and dying children, and soldiers returned in body bags—mounted in the evening news.

Hulton ArchiveGetty Images

War correspondent Walter Cronkite reporting from Vietnam during the Tet Offensive in 1968.

American public opinion turned against the war, and for the next decade and a half the experience of the Vietnam War, for both soldiers and civilians, made the United States reluctant to engage in any major conflict.

With the end of the Cold War came new conflicts. The Persian Gulf War (1990-1991) marked a return of the United States to the field of war. Journalists once again were restricted by the military establishment and were fed information without the opportunity to investigate its veracity, though they were allowed to be present to report the impact of Saddam Hussein's bombs falling as the U.S. troops entered Kuwait. This was the first major conflict the United States had been involved with since the advent of twenty-four-hour cable news organizations, such as

Cable News Network (CNN). Americans no longer had to wait for the evening news to know what was happening; now the newest developments were in front of the American public as they happened.

By the mid-1990's, the Internet was making the reporting of events even faster. This was clearly evident during the American invasion of Iraq in 2003, as journalists "embedded" in military units reported their stories instantaneously. With the advent of embedded journalism, the objectivity of the reporting came into question, as the idea of an embedded journalist reporting negatively on the actions of the unit with which he was traveling was unthinkable. Regardless of the changes on the battlefield, the conflict between the military and the public's right to know continues.

BOOKS AND ARTICLES

Aronson, James. *The Press and the Cold War*. Indianapolis, Ind.: Bobbs-Merrill, 1970. Concentrates on the role played by radical journalists in raising public awareness during the Cold War, especially during the Vietnam War.

Badsey, Stephen, ed. *The Media and International Security*. Portland, Oreg.: Frank Cass, 2000. Presents the proceedings of a 1995 conference, including presentations by academic scholars, members of the media, and representatives of the armed forces.

Kennedy, William V. *The Military and the Media: Why the Press Cannot Be Trusted to Cover a War*. Westport, Conn.: Praeger, 1993. Argues that American journalists have largely failed to acquire proper training to cover military matters, and that this failure was dramatically evident in their coverage of the 1991 Persian Gulf War.

Knightly, Phillip. *The First Casualty: The War Correspondent as Hero, Propagandist, and Myth-Maker from the Crimea to Iraq*. Baltimore: Johns Hopkins University Press, 2004. Probably the standard-bearer for historical examination of the media's coverage of wars, this volume has been updated with nearly every significant conflict that has appeared since its first edition in 1975.

Matthews, Joseph. *Reporting the Wars*. Minneapolis: University of Minnesota Press, 1957. The first book-length treatment of the history of the coverage of wars.

Salmon, Lucy Maynard. *The Newspaper and the Historian*. New York: Oxford University Press, 1923. Reprint. New York: Octagon Books, 1976. This groundbreaking study examines the interaction between the philosophy of a particular newspaper and its coverage of various conflicts.

Sweeney, Michael. *Secrets of Victory: The Office of Censorship and the American Press and Radio in World War II*. Chapel Hill: University of North Carolina Press, 2001. A case study looking at the U.S. Office of Censorship's role in how information was presented during World War II, in both formal and informal settings.

Dino E. Buenviaje

PROPAGANDA

OVERVIEW

Propaganda, simply put, is the manipulation of opinion. This, however, is the only thing simple about it. In its nuances and implications, propaganda's basic appearance belies its utter complexity. To begin with, the propagandist aims to communicate messages at the level of the emotions rather than thought. The more emotional the message is, the more successful the propaganda will be in persuading its audience. It is important to avoid logical thought; members of the target audience must become so enchanted with the message that they are seduced into a state of willing disbelief. Confusion and deception, rather than discussion and debate, rule the day for this subterfuge. Through the telling of partial truths and the omission of others, the propagandist attempts to shape perceptions, manipulate cognitions, and directly control the behavior of the intended audience.

While propaganda can be utilized by governments or groups to push forward social agendas or movements, it holds its most powerful potential in warfare. In warfare, propaganda often conveys a message concerning a real or imagined threat. Here propaganda is aimed at two targets: the nation's own citizens and the enemy.

SIGNIFICANCE

Propaganda has taken as many different forms as there are societies in which it has been used. In its broadest sense, propaganda is information intended to persuade or orient its audience toward a certain way of thinking. Some examples are personal, such as the tattoo-covered Caddo warrior, whose body attests to every victory, accomplishment, or god worshiped. Some are thunderous, such as Hannibal's titanic war elephants advancing across the Italian plain. Some are deafening, such as the "rebel yells" of Confeder-

National Archives

A World War II poster reminds Americans never to reveal sensitive information to anyone, because "loose lips sink ships."

ate soldiers proclaiming that a charge was about to ensue. Some are subtle, such as the poster of a coquettish woman announcing that if she were a man she would join the U.S. Navy. Some are persistent, such as North Korean radio, announcing good morning from the Great Leader as the Sun peeks over the horizon. Some are selective, such as the media's decision to show jetliners colliding into the World Trade Center but not to show civilians leaping from windows and plummeting to their deaths. All of these examples of propaganda, while seemingly disparate, have a common purpose: They serve to rally a group of people around an image or to manipulate the morale of an common enemy. All are forms of propaganda.

Both the people of Imperial China and their enemies saw the power of the emperor in the Great Wall. Later, the great cathedrals that filled Europe were symbolic not only of the Christian godhead but also of the worldly power of the Roman Catholic Church and the Papacy. In the 1930's, during the worldwide Great Depression, different ideologies were displayed through building projects to demonstrate the supremacy of their causes. The Soviet Union built the world's largest fixed-wing aircraft, the Tupolev ANT-20; Nazi Germany built the world's largest airships, the Zeppelins; and at the same time, the German Volkswagen, or "people's car," crossed the Third Reich on the Autobahn. To buoy up the the capitalist democracy of America during the economic crisis, President Franklin D. Roosevelt spent on great public works projects, and the federal government subsidized artists who painted murals and actors who presented plays in the Art for the Millions program. Such projects not only put people to work; they reinforced the greatness of America in the minds of the nation's downtrodden citizens. For the Soviet Union, the hammer and sickle provided a strong image of plebeian empowerment. Nazi Germany took a Sanskrit symbol, the swastika, turned it at an angle, and made it the symbol of the National Socialist (Nazi) Party and "Aryan" purity. The United States adopted the bald eagle as the country's symbol: an image of fierce beauty and proud independence, flying above others and symbolizing what many consider great about America. Propagandists, in sum-

mary, work to remove all doubt about the superiority of a society by focusing that greatness into symbolic images.

HISTORY OF PROPAGANDA

ANCIENT WORLD

In the ancient world, the success of a society depended on many things, but predominantly on the size of the population. One of the ways this was promoted was to persuade the people that they were somehow set apart. Historically, building the notion of the "greatness" or "moral superiority" of the group has been accomplished in many ways—from early tribal organizations that taught that the gods held their people in special favor to later civilizations in which the leaders themselves claimed some form of divine right. To doubt the group's moral superiority, therefore, was to doubt the gods, tantamount to a form a sacrilege. As civilizations advanced, architecture was used as a physical symbol to illustrate the greatness of the state.

Methods of communication enhanced the ability of civilizations to broadcast their superiority, especially the development of written forms. At first these symbols were limited to pictographs that recounted the greatness of the society. Early examples can be found in the prehistoric cave paintings at Lascaux, France, where a landscape filled with bounty was depicted. As language continued to develop into the written word, the fact that literacy was limited to the elites forced the propagandists to continue to rely heavily on representative (rather than abstract) symbols for expression. Although Ramses the Great was possibly the most famous of the Pharaohs for his building projects, by no means was he the only one to undertake projects to assure his greatness through the ages. Almost every Egyptian ruler had murals painted and reliefs sculpted depicting the favor of the gods upon their society. Edifices ranging from the brightly painted temple walls to the tall obelisks recounted the favor the gods showed the Pharaoh and, by extension, the people of Egypt. This form of propaganda was not limited to the civilizations of the

Mediterranean basin; symbols propounding greatness can also be found among other ancient peoples, from the triumphal arches of the Romans to the image-laden walls of Temple of Warriors at Chichén Itzá.

MEDIEVAL WORLD

The collapse of the Western Roman Empire marked the entry of Europe into the medieval age. With the breakdown of large-scale infrastructure in the West, a void was created that was filled by the increasing power of the Roman Catholic Church, the development of the feudal system, and the growth of aristocracy and monarchy. Each of these elements of society used some form of propaganda to justify its position of authority.

The Church built symbol-laden cathedrals, which—beyond their gargoyles, statuary, and ornate stained-glass windows—spoke to parishioners of God's grace and favor for his people. Feudal lords built impregnable fortifications both for the protection of their people and as tangible expressions of their greatness. These fortifications, with their tall, thick walls of stone surrounded by defensive moats, were designed to deter enemies who might attack not only physically but also psychologically, with their stark, daunting appearance. Armor slowly developed until it reached the pinnacle of defensive propaganda: the metal plate of the knight. Weapons, such as the crossbow, were developed that were so dangerous—and whose possession was so effective as a propaganda tool—that the Church attempted to outlaw them. Because building and supporting armies with the latest technologies took resources, the escalating need to "out-might" the enemy eventually led to the formation of centralized nation-states under the governance of monarchs. As strong governments reappeared, the focus could be expanded beyond merely survival and the modern age arrived.

During the late tenth through twelfth centuries the Crusades against the Islamic "infidels" of the Middle East and North Africa were promoted by the Roman Catholic popes as a struggle behooving all good Christians. Beginning with his speech at Clermont in 1095, for example, Pope Urban II used his power of the pulpit and graphic language (re-rendered here from the account of Robert the Monk, about twenty-five years later) to call on Christian soldiers to fight Muslims in the Levant who were killing Christians and destroying churches:

> When they [the infidels] wish to torture people by base death, they perforate their navels, and dragging forth the extremity of the intestines, bind it to the stake. . . . On whom therefore is the labor of avenging these wrongs and of recovering this territory incumbent, if not upon you? You, upon whom above other nations God has conferred remarkable glory in arms, great courage, bodily activity, and strength to humble the hairy scalp of those who resist you. . . .

What prompted this appeal was not only a call from Byzantine emperor Alexius I for defenses against Turkish incursions but also the (quite political) hope on the part of the Papacy to reunite Christendom after its schism in 1054, thus solidifying the power of the Church to achieve a theocracy over Western Europe, Eastern Europe, and the kingdom of Jerusalem. Not insignificant in this effort was the popes' fear of the increasing secular powers of feudal kings and their vassals. For all these reasons, Urban II preached a sermon that rivaled the intensity of the speeches of Adolf Hitler eight and a half centuries later. The frenzied audience responded, "Deus volt!" ("God wills it!").

Perhaps the most important tool of propaganda developed near the end of the Middle Ages, with the arrival of Johann Gutenberg's printing press in 1453. The ability to mass-produce printed documents quickly made possible the dissemination of the written word to a populace that formerly was not (and could not afford to be) literate. Like today's Internet, the printing press revolutionized—created, really—mass communications. Within a few decades, the number of books in Europe increased from thousands to millions and literacy was on the rise, increasing dramatically by the sixteenth century. In the meantime, one of the first uses of the printing press was during the religious upheavals known as the Protestant Reformation and the ensuing Counter-Reformation. The printing press made possible the dissemination of propaganda images to an illiterate population, often casting the pope, as the representative of the Roman Church, in a negative light. Lucas Cranach's *Whore of Babylon* and Albrecht Dürer's series of what would now be called political cartoons, *Passion of the Christ and Anti-Christ* (the anti-Christ being the pope), are examples. As literacy increased, bills, pamphlets, and other writings disseminated Protestant and Catholic propaganda messages to the mass populace. Perhaps the most important of these was the Ninety-five Theses of Martin Luther himself—widely considered to be the spur to the the Reformation.

MODERN WORLD

During the modern age, propaganda has become more vivid and widely used, as an ongoing revolution in communications media has allowed for the easier distribution of inflammatory imagery and messages. Should the government need its population to take action against a real or perceived threat, the focus of propaganda becomes the unquestioned supremacy of the group. Propaganda has continued to be used to dehumanize and incite hatred toward the enemy—an enemy that can be either external or internal (that is, anyone who stands against the ideal the propagandist supports). To this end, the propagandist manipulates the use of symbols. The enemy is reduced to a malicious, dehumanized caricature.

Some groups used these tactics simply to put forth their agendas. The Grangers (later the Farmer's Alliance), for example, promulgated images of the fat eastern capitalist draining the wealth of the hardworking western farmers. Immigrants were often caricatured by xenophobic nativist (anti-immigrant) Americans as evil-looking beasts; the Irish in the mid-nineteenth century, the Chinese during the late nineteenth century, and Mexican Americans in the early to mid-twentieth century are among these groups. Both Native Americans and African Americans have been the victims of such propaganda from the arrival of Europeans in North America, suffering the double atrocities of oppression and slavery as well as hatred incited by propaganda. Today, some might even consider the portrayal of a greedy, uncaring tobacco industry as nothing more than a type of propaganda that paints the "enemy" with a broad brush as merchants of death.

Combining language with imagery and symbols has allowed propagandists to increase their effectiveness. As a greater percentage of the population became literate, the power of words was used to advance propagandists' positions. For propagandists, the message was best kept simple and short. Like visual forms of propaganda, the words had to be clear, concise, and repeated—hammering home the same emotional message. With the advance of technology, the modern propagandist had a wide assortment of rhetorical tools on which to draw to persuade the people, from transparent appeals to fear, prejudice, or groundless personal attacks to subtler messages that associate positive imagery with behaviors the propagandist wishes to promote or negative imagery with groups the propagandist wishes to demonize.

An excellent example of how a small minority used the power of language, stereotype, frustration, and fear to further its message can be seen in the reporting of the 1770 Boston Massacre. After the conclusion of the French and Indian War (1763), the American colonists were frustrated by Britain's imposition of new taxes, increased regulation, and insufficient government services, which were seen as threats to the prosperity the colonials had enjoyed. However, with no unity among the colonies, this displeasure was too diffuse to find effective expression. On March 4, 1770, British soldiers, in self-defense, fired on an agitated mob of more than four hundred American colonists in Boston, Massachusetts. When the smoke cleared, five bodies lay dead. Samuel Adams, leader of Boston's Sons of Liberty, knew that this incident was "propaganda gold." Adams pursued many avenues to turn an action of civil disobedience into martyrdom. First, he gave this incident a name: the Boston Massacre. Turning to fellow Son of Liberty and well-known silversmith Paul Revere, he commissioned Revere to create a lithograph, an image that depicted an image the propagandists wanted to reinforce in the minds of the colonists. The British soldiers were reduced to mere caricatures: faces frozen in devilish grins, firing on command into innocent townspeople. One of the civilian targets was depicted as innocently walking his dog. (It is noteworthy that, although Crispus Attucks, a mixed African and Native American, was one of the first to die, all victims portrayed were white.) Despite the fact that the event took place at night, the picture painted it as occurring during the day. Despite, or perhaps because of, such inaccuracies, this piece of propaganda was very effective. The colonies unified, and the tax was repealed. Through "committees of correspondence," news and suspicions surrounding the British continued to flow through the colonies. In 1773, when the British passed the Tea Act to save their struggling East India Company, the colonial reaction was immediate and intense. Although the new law actually would have made tea cheaper, the propagandists were able to paint it as a devious trick by the British to force the colonists to pay one more duty. The

R. S. Peale and J. A. Hill

Paul Revere's engraving of the Boston Massacre of 1770.

conversion of the colonials to the revolutionaries' cause was so effective that anger and riots in some areas took place against attempted landings of the new and cheaper tea, culminating in the famous Boston Tea Party of December, 1773.

Through the utilization of words and imagery, newspaper magnate William Randolph Hearst helped foment the 1898 Spanish-American War by carrying sensational stories of Spanish atrocities against the Cuban people. Such stories, combined with imagery and music, prepared the American people for the reality of war. Hearst's papers, it has been argued, issued so many fabricated or at least exaggerated stories of atrocities in Cuba that his "yellow journalism" can be seen as manufacturing the rationale for a war of imperialism on the part of the United States. When Hearst sent illustrator Frederic Remington to Cuba to record mutilations and other horrors perpetrated by the Spanish, Remington sent Hearst a telegram: "Everything is quiet. There is no trouble here. There will be no war." Hearst's now famous reply was immedi-

ate and unequivocal: "Please remain. You furnish the pictures and I'll furnish the war." When Hearst's newspapers carried the story of the explosion on the USS *Maine* in Havana harbor on February 15, 1898, an enhanced color lithograph accompanied the text, along with a jingoistic headline, "Remember the *Maine*!" So powerful was this report that, despite the fact that the President William McKinley was hesitant, a declaration of war sailed through Congress.

World Wars I and II offer some of the most famous instances of propaganda, on both sides. During World War I, the Creel Commission in the United States, for example, propagated the characterization of Germans as "vile Huns." In the years leading up to World War II, Jews and other ethnic groups were made scapegoats for every imaginable wrong suffered by the German people. The Nazi regime, headed by Adolf Hitler, found a populace willing to be persuaded, under the direction of propaganda minister Joseph Goebbels, that whole ethnic populations were unfit to live and that Germans who could consider

Library of Congress

The New York World *two days after the USS* Maine *exploded in Havana harbor.*

lets as the Voice of America, Radio Free Europe, and Radio Liberty, the U.S. government broadcast messages crafted to entertain, inform, and, of course, warn against the dangerously aggressive Soviet Union, portraying it as a system that sought to brainwash citizens in any territory it acquired. The Soviet Union, for its part, happily used the image of the fearless juggernaut the West provided, employing Radio Moscow to broadcast its own messages that the West was a place of moral decadence whose governments were dominated by greedy capitalists who exploited the citizenry, leaving them to live in conflict and poverty.

In the so-called War on Terror (following the attacks on the Pentagon and World Trade Center on September 11, 2001), propaganda continued to be employed. This global conflict, however, has produced an interesting form of propaganda, almost a sterile "anti-propaganda." If propaganda is the manipulation of facts, it is interesting to note what facts are presented to the American people. With an almost sanitized coverage of the war over much of the media, many Americans have

themselves part of the pure "Aryan" race were destined to rule the world. As a result, the deaths of six million Jews and approximately one million others were blinked at by a brainwashed citizenry.

Propaganda became global during the Cold War (1945-1991). The propaganda produced during the second half of the twentieth century, a period of brinkmanship and détente, was nationalistic and ideological. The governments of both the United States and the Soviet Union employed any and every media outlet they could to reinforce, remind, and ultimately convert other nations to their point of view. The United States Information Agency was created to spread its message of freedom. Utilizing such out-

enjoyed a comfortable mental separation from the conflict (unlike what they experienced during the Vietnam War [1961-1975], when images of battle and carnage could be seen daily on their television sets and the draft threatened sons, brothers, and boyfriends). Moreover, Americans were asked to sacrifice nothing as the War on Terror began in 2003: Soldiers were not drafted; food and personal items were not rationed. Likewise, caricatures of zealous terrorists have not been presented. At times it seems as though the only propaganda use of the conflict occurs when a political party sees an opportunity to further its agenda. Once pulled out of the box, however, the War on Terror and its attendant conflicts have just as quickly been stuffed back inside: to be forgotten or dropped. The media, perceiving the citizenry's lack of appetite for coverage of seemingly endless and goal-less conflict, after the initial years have tended to report on the war with the same emphasis they give to the death of a pop musician, using the events to fill gaps in the twenty-four-hour news cycle. With no casualties seen or advancements toward a clear victory heralded, it seems as if this lack of coverage may be a new, postmodern form of propaganda by omission.

In the twenty-first century, the proliferation of information transmitted by handheld communication devices—such as "smart" cell phones equipped with still and video cameras whose images are easily uploaded to Web sites on the Internet such as YouTube—vies with editorially vetted sources of information such as established news agencies. The speed with which information, confirmed or unconfirmed, is globally transmitted both facilitates and complicates the propagandist's purpose. What is clear is that information must be consumed responsibly, and dispassionately, if the peoples of the world are to perceive, and protect themselves from, the intention behind the message.

BOOKS AND ARTICLES

Aldrich, Richard J. *The Hidden Hand: Britain, America, and Cold War Secret Intelligence.* New York: Overlook Press, 2002. Details the covert activities by British and American intelligence units beginning in World War II and continuing as the enemy changed from Germany to the Soviet Union during the Cold War.

Edwards, Mark U. *Printing, Propaganda, and Martin Luther.* Berkeley: University of California Press, 1994. Addresses the question of to what extent the Reformation was a "print event" by examining Protestant and Catholic pamphlets c. 1518-1530, made possible by the proliferation of Gutenberg's movable-type printing press.

Eisenstein, Elizabeth L. *The Printing Press as an Agent of Change: Communications and Cultural Transformations in Early Modern Europe.* 2 vols. New York: Cambridge University Press, 1979. Examines the advent of printing and its impact as a force for social change, especially during the Renaissance, the Reformation, and the rise of modern science.

Fleming, Thomas. *Liberty! The American Revolution.* New York: Penguin Putnam, 1997. Presents the story of the coming of the American Revolution from the personal perspectives of both loyalists and patriots, including propagandists such as Samuel Adams and Paul Revere.

Konstam, Angus. *San Juan 1898.* New York: Osprey, 1998. Examines the Spanish-American War, including the use of propaganda in promoting both the explosion of the U.S.S. Maine and the Rough Riders' charge up San Juan Hill.

Krivitsky, Walter G. *In Stalin's Secret Service: Memoirs of the First Soviet Master Spy to Defect.* New York: Enigma Books, 2000. The autobiography of the first top Soviet intelligence officer to defect to the West, whose life came to an end at the hands of a Soviet assassination squad.

Leighton, Marian. *Soviet Propaganda as a Foreign Policy Tool.* London: Freedom House, 1991. An analysis of the development of Soviet propaganda and its expression on the world stage.

Maier, Pauline. *From Resistance to Revolution: Colonial Radicals and the Development of American Opposition to Britain, 1765-1776.* New York: W. W. Norton, 1991. A detailed account of the rise of the ideology that led to the American Revolution, including the activities of the Sons of Liberty and Committees of Correspondence, which used propaganda as tools to increase the feeling for revolution.

O'Neill, William L. *A Democracy at War: America's Fight At Home and Abroad in World*

War II. New York: Free Press, 1993. Analyzes American involvement in World War II through the lens of the war fought to transform the American people from isolationism to a war mentality.

Snyder, Alvin A. *Warriors of Disinformation: American Propaganda, Soviet Lies, and the Winning of the Cold War—An Insider's Account*. New York: Arcade, 1995. Written by the former director of the United States Information Agency's Television and Film Service, this account details the American propaganda campaigns against Soviet Communism during the 1980's.

Zacour, N. P., and H. W. Hazard, eds. *The Impact of the Crusades on Europe*. Madison: University of Wisconsin Press, 1989. Includes a chapter, "Crusade Propaganda," that examines the use of propaganda and its reception during the Crusades.

Andrew Reynolds Galloway and Steven L. Danver

REVOLT, REBELLION, AND INSURGENCY

OVERVIEW

The legal framework of war may be the only place where a serious and spirited debate over the differences between revolt, rebellion, and insurgency can occur. However, for those who happen to be leading a revolt, planning a rebellion, or participating in an insurgency, the subtle distinctions between the three can be important. A revolt is defined as an attempt to break away from or rise against established authority. Rebellion goes further, suggesting the manner and extent to which that person will resist those government demands. Insurgency is that state of resistance which, while clearly a challenge to established order, lacks the organizational aspects of a revolution. History is full of examples of all three.

SIGNIFICANCE

While it would be easy to dismiss revolt, rebellion, and insurgency as events cut from the same cloth, there is a slight, but nonetheless important, distinction. Only insurgency would seem to offer any outside credibility, which might entitle it not only legal recognition from other nations but also material support, and quite possibly legal protection in the event of failure. If one is facing a well-entrenched opposition and the odds of success appear slim, being able to win acceptance as an insurgent movement could offer some very important perquisties, including the chance of avoiding execution in the event of failure.

HISTORY OF REVOLT, REBELLION, AND INSURGENCY

ANCIENT WORLD

No doubt Roman leaders in charge of the security of their empire spent more than one sleepless night worried about the Middle East, and with good reason. The Great Revolt, also known as the First Jewish-Roman War, lasted seven years and, while a failure, revealed the obstacles an occupying force faced in trying to pacify an area. Starting in the year 66 C.E., over alleged religious tensions between Jews and Greeks, it quickly grew to include an antitax protest and even featured random attacks on Roman citizens in Caesarea. Roman troops were rushed in to restore order but were attacked and turned back by local forces. Fearing the defeat might embolden others to join the revolt, Emperor Nero ordered a full-scale invasion to crush it. In 67 C.E., 60,000 Roman troops attacked Galilee, and its destruction convinced many that resistance was futile. Year by year, town by town, the Roman legions restored order, until the only remaining holdout was Masada, to which the Romans laid siege (70-73 C.E.). When the legions finally broke through the fortresses' defenses, they found that the defenders had taken their own lives rather than surrender. Masada's fall signaled that the revolt was over, crushed by overwhelming force and quite possibly hampered by its inability to win new supporters or outside help.

MEDIEVAL WORLD

Runnymede may seem like a strange name to some people, but to others it is the home of one of the most significant rebellions of the medieval world. It was at Runnymede in England that the people of Britain successfully forced their king to acknowledge that the rule of law surpassed his power as monarch.

In 1066, the Normans had conquered England and in the process established a highly centralized form of government that put tremendous power in the hands of the king. The system seemed to work until the early thirteenth century, when John of England became king. He suffered a series of military setbacks, which cost him valuable lands in France and required him to raise taxes to mount a counterattack. He also ran afoul of the Catholic Church over the selection of the Archbishop of Canterbury. It had always been the king's choice, but bishops decided they wanted more of a say. The controversy resulted in King John's excommunication by Pope Innocent III and the threat of an invasion by Spain. The bishops got their choice, and John returned to the good graces of Rome by declaring England and Ireland papal territories and then renting them back for an annual tribute. Noblemen, worried about how the higher taxes might affect their holdings and enraged by the king's unilateral surrender of sovereignty to a foreign power, may have been pushed over the edge and into rebellion. In 1215 they gathered their forces and marched on London, finding the gates open to them and a receptive population waiting for them. Many of the city's residents, though not in outright rebellion, shared the nobles' outrage concerning the king's behavior. Together this coalition executed by all accounts a relatively peaceful rebellion, forcing King John to meet them, acknowledge certain limits to his power (in the Magna Carta), and grant the nobles certain control over his actions.

MODERN WORLD

The Arab Revolt of 1936-1939 is a good example of a revolt that failed to achieve its goals. It was a revolt by committee, trying to forge a coalition among groups without giving much thought or shedding much light on what it would do if successful.

Britain had controlled the area in the Middle East known as Palestine since the end of World War I, alternately administering and disciplining Palestinian Arabs and Jews. The Balfour Declaration (1917) had determined that at some point the region was to be designated a homeland for Jews, with some consideration given to the national aspirations of Arabs. Both sides wanted a homeland that excluded the other. The Arab Revolt of 1936-1939 was the first sustained violent uprising of Palestinian Arabs in more than a century. Thousands of Arabs from all classes were mobilized. The revolt began with spontaneous acts of violence committed by followers of an Arab religious leader who had been killed by the British in 1935. In April, 1936, the murder of two Jews led to escalating violence. At that point, Arab political parties formed a committee. It called for a general strike, nonpayment of taxes, and national independence. Coinciding with the strike, Arab rebels, joined by volunteers from neighboring Arab countries, took to the hills, attacking Jewish settlements and British installations in the northern part of the country. By the end of the year, the movement had assumed the dimensions of a national revolt. The British shipped more than twenty thousand troops into Palestine, and by 1939 the Zionists had armed more than fifteen thousand of its people in their own nationalist movement. Even though the arrival of British troops restored some semblance of order, the armed revolt continued. A British government task force was sent to Palestine to investigate the situation and reported in July, 1937, that the revolt was caused by an Arab desire for independence. The task force recommended that the region be partitioned, separating Jews from Arabs, and further recommended the forcible transfer of the Arab population from the pro-

F. R. Niglutsch

Revolutionaries defending barricades in Paris during the July, 1830, revolution.

posed Jewish state. The Arabs were horrified by the idea of dismembering the region and particularly by the suggestion that they be forcibly transferred. As a result, the momentum of the revolt increased. In September, 1937, the British were forced to declare martial law, and many Arab officials were arrested. Although the Arab Revolt continued well into 1939, high casualty rates and firm British measures gradually eroded its strength. According to some estimates, more than five thousand Arabs were killed, fifteen thousand wounded, and fifty-six hundred imprisoned.

Although it signified the birth of a national identity, the revolt was unsuccessful in many ways. The general strike, which was called off in October, 1939, had encouraged Palestinian Jews to become more self-reliant, and the Arabs of Palestine were unable to recover from their sustained effort of defying the British administration. Their leaders were killed, arrested, or deported, leaving the dispirited and disarmed population divided. Palestinian Jews, on the other hand, were united and cooperated with British forces in fighting the Arabs. In the end the revolt failed because of a leadership vacuum and inability to articulate a vision for a political structure to supplant the British authority.

If revolts are the poor relations of forceful change, rebellion may be their more successful cousins, but just barely. Like revolts, rebellions involve open defiance of the established order. Rebellion, however, also involves a clear use of armed force and attempts to publicize its objectives so people know what the ruckus is all about.

The Chechen Rebellion in Russia is a good example. Chechnya declared its independence in 1991 as the Soviet Union was collapsing. However, it was unable to free itself from the Russian Federation, led by Boris Yeltsin. The First Chechen War lasted from 1994 to 1996, when Russian forces attempted to stop Chechnya from seceding. The Russians outmanned and outgunned the Chechen rebels but could not outmaneuver them, and they were therefore unable to smash the resistance. In 1996 the Russian government signed a peace treaty with Chechnya's military leaders, who proclaimed the rebellion a success. The Chechen people elected a president and a coalition government and went about the business of running their own country. The independence was short-lived, however, apparently faltering when Chechens decided to export their rebellious notions to neighboring Dagestan. This time the Russians responded in a more organized fashion, coordinating air and ground operations first to eject the Chechens from Dagestan and then to invade Chechnya itself. The Russian incursion disrupted Chechnya's rebel movement and claimed the life of its president. By 2000, Russia had installed a pro-Moscow government in Chechnya, ending the rebel movement indefinitely.

In the eyes of the world—or at least in the eyes of those who recognize international law—insurgency may be the most legitimate form of resistance to an existing order. To engage in insurgency is to participate in a revolt against a government in a manner less organized than a revolution. Revolutions are more cerebral; they leave paper trails of those who have spoken of them, written about them, and even planned them. Insurgencies are more action-oriented, headed by leaders sometimes characterized by dedication, swagger, and daring and pitted against seemingly overwhelming odds. Fidel Castro and his insurgent forces in Cuba or Ho Chi Minh and his insurgent forces in Vietnam might come to mind. In the beginning, neither Castro nor Ho and his forces were able to control large areas of territory, but they certainly were capable of offering stiff resistance to the Cuban and French governments, respectively.

The question of how insurgents should be dealt with in the event of their success (or failure) is at issue: Recognition by third parties? Summary execution? At the very least, international law has instructed its adherents that insurgencies can be recognized as wars against the established order. At the same time, recognition of an insurgency expresses the belief by third parties that the insurgents should not be executed if captured and that they should be entitled to prevent the opposition from gaining access to supplies from neutral nations. In their insurgency against the French, Ho Chi Minh and his followers enjoyed the support of the Soviet Union and the People's Republic of China, and they diligently attempted to deny France the supplies it received from a seemingly neutral party, the United States. In the end the insurgency prevailed, and Ho went on to bigger things.

In the tangled maze of revolts, rebellions, and insurgencies, with their confusing mix of terms, one thing seems clear: It is how others see them that really counts.

BOOKS AND ARTICLES

Brinton, Crane. *Anatomy of a Revolution*. New York: Vintage, 1965. Takes the theories developed in international law and applies them to specific cases that have become the benchmarks of twentieth century political upheaval.

Defronzo, James. *Revolutions and Revolutionary Movements*. Boulder, Colo.: Westview Press, 2007. Offers a modern look at the subject Brinton discussed four decades before, suggesting that the changing global political environment offers some subtle yet important changes to the picture Brinton originally limned.

Fenwick, Charles. *International Law*. New York: Appleton-Century-Crofts, 1948. Good for a legal understanding of the terms. Fenwick gives helpful insights into how the international community defines and responds to revolt, rebellion, and insurgency.

Karnow, Stanley. *Vietnam: A History*. New York: Penguin, 1997. Takes a comprehensive look at how the Vietnamese insurgent movement developed, back to the time when China was the country's chief nemesis.

Morris, Benny. *Righteous Victims: A History of the Zionist-Arab Conflict, 1881-2001*. New York: Vintage Books, 2001. Provides further proof of the difficulties inherent in executing a victorious revolt or rebellion by examining the various Jewish-Arab conflicts over control of Palestine prior to World War II.

Moss, George Donelson. *Vietnam: An American Ordeal*. New York: Prentice Hall, 2008. Insurgency is explored both directly and indirectly. Touches briefly on the insurgent struggle in Vietnam, first against the French and then against the United States.

Rocca, Samuel. *The Forts of Judea, 168 B.C.-A.D. 73*. New York: Osprey, 2008. Reconstructs the particulars surrounding the first Jewish-Roman War, sometimes referred to as the Great Revolt. Astute readers will note that between the lines Rocca provides a cautionary tale on the difficulties of staging a successful revolt in the absence of a broad base of support and effective communications.

Schultz, Richard. *Insurgents, Terrorists, and Militias: The Warriors of Contemporary Combat*. New York: Columbia University Press, 2006. Offers contemporary commentary about conflict.

Smith, Sebastian. *Allah's Mountains: The Battle for Chechnya*. London: Tauris Parke, 2001. Examines Chechnya's insurgent movement and the Russian response.

John Morello

WAR'S IMPACT ON ECONOMIES

OVERVIEW

Although most histories focus on the battles that ac-company wars, few address the economic impact those conflicts have on the societies involved or the neutral parties connected to them. Land produced most human "wealth" before the twentieth century, but cities and towns have been the centers of com-merce, grain stores, and treasury as well as political power. Destroying or consuming crops imposed hardship on a population, but sacking cities reduced a civilization's financial reserves, all but eliminating its ability to recover. Disease, starvation, and the mass removal of population as slaves followed, in-tensifying the damage. Civil wars have proven par-ticularly devastating for the loser.

SIGNIFICANCE

A conflict's impact on the participants' economies often has lasting effects beyond the conflict itself. Wars that endured with no particular victor ex-hausted the participants, leaving them too weak to withstand an outside power—or the economic price and deprivation imposed on the population led to the destruction of the established political order, even in cases where no conquering army occupied the land. China's and Europe's dynastic collapses illustrate the political upheaval created by war's economic and corresponding political impact, as does the post-World War II breakup of Europe's colonial empires.

HISTORY OF WAR'S IMPACT ON ECONOMIES

ANCIENT WORLD

In ancient times, war's primary economic impact fell on the invaded territory. The Egyptian, Sumerian city-state, Hittite, Assyrian, and Persian armies plun-dered the areas they invaded, making exceptions when cities opened their gates without resistance. However, while marching through their own territo-ries, these armies drew from imperial grain stores or, in the case of Egyptian troops, were supported by grain ships. Nonetheless, the armies' supplies came at the expense of the civilian population.

In their wars against each other, Greek city-state armies lived off the land when they marched into hos-tile territory but rarely sacked cities except as punish-ment. Chinese armies also lived off the land, but the sacking of cities was rare after the Warring States period of the third to fourth centuries B.C.E. Most Chi-nese conquerors were as concerned with governing the territory they seized as they were with taking it in the first place. They deployed with a supply train that provided at least some of their food supplies, reduc-ing their reliance on local resources. South Asian, Southeast Asian, and Japanese armies relied almost entirely on local food supplies as they marched. Al-though the extent of the economic damage varied ac-cording to army size and the duration of a campaign, few regions recovered quickly from the passage of any army, friendly or hostile, but the latter left a path of ruin from which it took years to recover.

The Imperial Roman Army was the first European army to rely heavily on a military supply system, but early Roman armies followed the practices of other European militaries, living off the land most of the time. However, the development of a disciplined army quartermaster system limited the army's reli-ance on local supplies, reducing frictions with poten-tially allied city-states. Before that, Rome's wars on Carthage first destroyed that commercial empire's navy and merchant marine, severely disrupting its trade and financial power. The Second Punic War (218-201 B.C.E.) devastated both Rome's and Car-thage's economies, but Rome's naval supremacy en-abled it to continue its foreign commerce, denying Carthage the resources and ability to support Hanni-bal's campaign on the Italian peninsula. Moreover,

Rome's superior diplomacy prevented Hannibal from drawing more than a handful of Italian city-states to his side. He eventually was forced to return home, but the devastation he inflicted on Rome's economy drove the Senate to seek Carthage's permanent removal as a threat. The resulting Third Punic War (149-146 B.C.E.) ended with Rome salting the fields around Carthage, sacking the city, and thereby permanently destroying its capacity for trade and war.

Rome's expansion after that came at the expense of conquered lands, as plunder and populations sold into slavery fed Rome's coffers. Captured wealth peaked in the first century after Julius Caesar's death, but as Rome's borders stabilized and conquest gave way to consolidation, the absence of seized riches began to tell on the Roman treasury, a factor exacerbated by the empire's numerous civil wars, which disrupted internal trade and destroyed farmland. The barbarian invasions further decimated Rome's agricultural and mineral production. The exact cost may never be calculated with certainty, but descriptions of the looting, destruction, and casualties suggest the barbarian incursions cost Rome more than 25 percent, and possibly as much as 40 percent, of its productive capacity between the third and fifth century C.E. The same can be said for the Eastern Empire, which survived Rome's fall, leaving Byzantium in a constant state of constrained finances despite its later monopoly on the European silk trade.

MEDIEVAL WORLD

While the "Dark Ages" followed Rome's demise at the end of the fifth century, Asia saw extensive trade and wealth, with India and China each producing roughly 23-25 percent of global economic activity into the twelfth century. The Islamic armies' sweep across North Africa and the Holy Land destroyed the traditional Afro-European trading patterns in the seventh and eighth centuries and that between Europe and the Middle East during the late eleventh century. The Mongol and Muslim invasions also disrupted trade between Europe and Asia during that century, and the Mongols all but destroyed the trading empires of central Asia. They wiped out entire city populations and laid waste to the countryside around enemy cities as a terror tactic. Although the

Crusades initially were called to help the Eastern Roman Empire retake the Holy Land from Islam, the First Crusade's looting and other excesses perpetrated on the march through Byzantine territory severely damaged Byzantium's wealth and agricultural production, significantly reducing the empire's economic base. The Eastern Empire never fully recovered from the seizure of the capital and looting of the treasury during the Fourth Crusade (1202-1204). Forced to grant tax concessions to Genoa and Venice and sell the rights to its silk monopoly, Byzantium, or Constantinople as it was known after the fifth century, was but an empty shell when the Ottoman Turks conquered the empire's remnants in 1453. However, the Crusades also opened European eyes to the culture, trade, and knowledge of the East, and that renewed knowledge led to the Renaissance that ultimately drove Europe's technological and industrial development in later centuries and, eventually, leadership over global affairs.

MODERN WORLD

The modern era began with the Thirty Years' War, which killed more than one-third of Germany's population, all but eliminated central Europe's commerce, and by some estimates consumed nearly half of northern Europe's production between 1618 and 1648. The human and economic costs influenced European, especially German and Austrian, thinking well into the nineteenth century. The period was marked by limited wars in which armies depended on stored supplies, paid for the materials they acquired from local communities, and relied on maneuver, rather than highly destructive and expensive combat, for victory.

That period of European warfare lasted until Napoleon reintroduced the concept of total war to Europe in the late eighteenth century. Napoleon's use of mass conscript armies living off the land and employment of concentrated artillery devastated the countryside of his opponents. His methods proved his undoing in Russia, where the czarist armies employed scorched-earth tactics to deny Napoleon food supplies and shelter for his troops, but the Russian victory came at the expense of starving its own population. More than one million Russians may have died from hunger and disease following the French invasion, and Russian agricultural production did not return to prewar levels until five years later.

In Asia, European incursions and China's civil wars destroyed what once was the world's richest economy and empire. Most economists believe that China produced more than 25 percent of the world's gross domestic product (GDP) in 1700. The depredations of the Opium Wars (1839-1842, 1856-1860), nine rebellions, and the First Sino-Japanese War (1894-1895) had reduced China's economy and power to a fraction of its former self by the nineteenth century's end. Those conflicts, along with Europe and America's Industrial Revolution and domination of global trade, had reduced China's proportion of global economic output to less than 10 percent of the total. China's post-World War I civil war, World War II, and Maoist economic policies further decimated the country's economy. Meanwhile, the West's pursuit of weapons technology and national mobilization would set the stage for the most expensive conflicts in history.

America's Civil War (1861-1865) served as a harbinger: Both sides mobilized and committed their manpower as best their economies and political structures could support. The Northern armies destroyed millions of acres of cropland, the South's limited industrial capacity, and its transportation system, while the Union blockade all but terminated Southern trade with the outside world. The South's agriculture-based economy collapsed months before its armies, and it took more than eighty years for the region to regain its prewar standards of living and economic production.

World Wars I and II were industrial wars in which entire populations sacrificed to maintain their countries' or empires' war efforts. Those wars consumed more than 40 percent of the participating countries' economies and destroyed most of Central Europe's productive cropland. Food shortages swept across Europe throughout World War I and after the war, because farmhands were conscripted into service in the belief that larger armies would ensure a short war. Additionally, the destruction of Eastern Europe's farmland and diversion of fertilizer nitrates to production of explosives cut agricultural production by

40 percent. The war's cost drove all the participants into near bankruptcy. All of Europe's major empires fell as their entire societies collapsed from the weight of supporting those war efforts, giving rise to several revolutionary movements across the globe. Japan and neutral America gained from the participants' need for their loans, industrial production, and raw materials. Shielded by distance from joining the costly fighting in Europe, Japan acquired territories in China and the Western Pacific, gained further access to new military technologies, expanded its merchant marine to handle the escalating trade in war materials, and expanded its shipyards to meet French and British shipbuilding requirements. Although the United States did not gain any territory, its neutrality in the war's early years enabled it to transition from a debtor to a creditor nation. By the time America entered the war in 1917, France, Britain, and Russia owed the United States more than $16 billion, equal to about 15 percent of America's gross domestic product.

World War II proved even more expensive and destructive. The massive bombing of that war, Russia's scorched-earth policies, and German looting of its occupied territories destroyed more than 70 percent of Europe's total industrial capacity. Spared invasion and bombing, the United States was the only country to end the war with a larger industrial capacity than it had at war's start. Germany and Japan lost more than 90 percent of their industrial capacity and Russia more than 50 percent. Britain's economy shrank nearly 16 percent during the war, and its war debt approached 50 percent of GDP. By war's end, France's transportation networks were all but destroyed, particularly in the north, and would take a decade to rebuild. The same could be said for Germany's, Japan's, and Russia's. Italy's limited prewar industrial base suffered some damage but largely was spared by the country's September, 1943, surrender, which came before the Allied bombing campaign reached fruition. In fact, more than half of the world's total economic output was either destroyed or expended in World War II.

Except for civil wars, the conflicts that followed World War II have been more limited, but the growing cost of armaments has ensured that war's cost remains high. More important, today the world's poorest nations (such as the Democratic Republic of the Congo, Eritrea, Somalia, and North Korea) are those that have been afflicted by conflict or have allocated excessive resources to readiness for war. The Arab-Israeli wars have suppressed economic growth among all the participants, and only extensive foreign aid and other forms of outside funding have kept them from bankruptcy. High oil prices have enabled the Arab nations to draw almost unlimited credit and provide funding to the so-called frontline states facing Israel. Coming at a time when the United States was addressing its social inequities, the Vietnam War (1961-1975) imposed an expanding deficit on the United States and destroyed South Vietnam's economy. North Vietnam reportedly expended nearly 40 percent of its GDP on the war and sustained that effort only with support from the Soviet Union, Warsaw Pact nations, and China.

However, the costliest wars of the twentieth century's second half were the incessant civil wars that plagued Africa. The nearly twenty years of fighting that afflicted Angola, the Democratic Republic of the Congo (DRC), the Côte d'Ivoire (Ivory Coast), Liberia, Rwanda, and Somalia have cost more than 5 million lives and may have deprived those countries of the equivalent of fifty years of GDP. Somalia remains a failed state. Angola's oil revenues have funded the de-mining and reconstruction efforts that may enable it to recover by 2015, but of the others, only Rwanda and Liberia remain completely at peace and are making progress toward recovery.

Elsewhere, Afghanistan's and Iraq's economies have been all but crippled by constant conflict since 1979, and only the latter's potential for expanded oil production offers the promise of fully funded recovery before 2020.

All indications suggest that the incessant local conflicts across the globe will continue to drain global resources well into the 2010's. The probability of massive nuclear war may have receded since the Cold War ended in 1991, but national and domestic rivalries and irredentist movements promise to sustain the world's level of conflict into the foreseeable future. For example, Pakistan's economy remains severely depressed by its enduring conflicts with domestic extremist elements and the government's concurrent and enduring focus on potential conflict with India. Pakistan will remain dependent on foreign aid and credit until both those issues are resolved. Afghanistan's internal conflicts cost about $35 billion a year, and the country requires more than $70 billion in assistance to repair the damage inflicted by thirty years (and counting) of nearly constant warfare within its borders. India, the Philippines, and Thailand face continuing separatist movements, some religious-based and other ideological, costing them up to 25 percent of their defensive budgets or about 3 percent of their GDPs. Terrorism in all of its forms reportedly has forced governments and organizations around the world to spend more than $200 billion on security alone and up to another $100 billion in military and security operations against terrorist groups and movements. Barring a sudden and rapid end to those movements, the price and economic impact probably will continue to rise.

BOOKS AND ARTICLES

Barber, John, and Mark Harrison. *The Soviet Home Front, 1941-45: A Social and Economic History of the USSR in World War II*. New York: Longman, 1991. Investigates how the Soviet leadership during World War II withstood the stresses to its political and economic system while being invaded by Nazi Germany, to rally its people to defeat Adolf Hitler's armies.

Broadberry, Stephen, and Mark Harrison. *The Economics of World War I*. New York: Cambridge University Press, 2005. A contextualized study that examines how European nations mobilized for war, how their economic strength impacted the war's course, and how their wartime economies impacted postwar economic growth.

Campagna, Anthony. *The Economic Consequences of the Vietnam War*. New York: Praeger,

1991. Looks at events leading to the war from an economic standpoint, from the Eisenhower administration's views on the French conflict in Indochina to the Nixon presidency.

Cohen, Jerome B. *Japan's Economy in War and Reconstruction*. New York: Institute of Pacific Relations, 1949. Presents a history of Japan's economic development from the last few years before World War II, through the war, and then into the "miracle" resurgence of the postwar years.

Finley, M. I. *The Ancient Economy*. Berkeley: University of California Press, 1973. Argues that the ancient Mediterranean powers lacked the economic structure to conduct warfare in the same way as modern nations.

Harrison, Mark, ed. *The Economics of World War II: Six Great Powers in International Comparison*. New York: Cambridge University Press, 1998. Presents chapters written by different economists on the impact of World War II on the economies of the United Kingdom, the United States, Germany, Italy, Japan, and the Soviet Union.

Singer, Clifford. *Energy and International War: From Babylon to Baghdad and Beyond*. Hackensack, N.J.: World Scientific, 2008. Examines the history of warfare involving energy resources, from ancient times to the present and into the future. Resources at the core of these conflicts have included slaves, gold, silver, iron, coal, oil, and other mineral resources. Challenges the notion that resource wars are endemic to industrial society.

Taylor, Alan M., and Reuven Glick. *Collateral Damage: Trade Disruption and the Economic Impact of War*. Working Paper W11565. Cambridge, Mass.: National Bureau of Economic Research, 2006. Looks at the effects of war on trade with other nations, beginning in 1870.

Weinstein, Jeremy, and Kosuke Imai. *Measuring the Economic Impact of Civil War*. CID Working Paper 51. Cambridge, Mass.: Harvard University Center for International Development, 2000. Seeks to examine civil wars empirically, particularly how they impact economic growth through negatively impacting investment.

Carl Otis Schuster

WOMEN, CHILDREN, AND WAR

OVERVIEW

Since ancient times, although men have predominated in leading and fighting in wars, women and children have been involved as well. Women have participated in war as leaders and combatants. They have formulated strategies and have supported militaries by providing services as scavengers, cooks, seamstresses, laundresses, informants, vendors, prostitutes, clerks, nurses and doctors, technicians, pilots, and morale boosters, among other roles. They have been casualties of war, suffering abduction, sexual assault, injury, and death. Children, even the very young, have accompanied armies, have served in support roles and as soldiers, and have been bounty and victims of war.

In studying wars and children, it is necessary to keep in mind that the definition of what constituted a "child" as distinct from an "adult" has differed across cultures and over time. The 1989 United Nations Convention on the Rights of the Child defined a "child" as "below the age of eighteen years unless under the law applicable to the child, majority is attained earlier."

SIGNIFICANCE

Portrayals of men in historical and recent accounts as the principal actors in war have tended to minimize women's and children's participation. With few exceptions, women and children have appeared in depictions of war primarily as relatives who remained at home when male soldiers departed for combat, and as victims of war atrocities, subjected to capture, rape, and murder. Influenced by women's movements in the latter half of the twentieth century and efforts by scholars to uncover the histories of and give voice to groups that previously received little attention, scholarship published in the late twentieth and early twenty-first centuries has broadened the scope of women's and children's involvement in wars beyond the roles of exceptional women and child leaders and warriors, families left behind when armies go on campaign, and victims of war. While such accounts recognize war in most societies over the ages as a predominantly masculine activity, largely entailing combat between adult males, they demonstrate that wars have relied heavily on women and children for justification, services, and morale. Such studies increase the understanding of why and how wars are waged, and of the effects of war beyond official combatants.

National Archives

A young boy learns about how to use a ration book during World War II.

HISTORY OF WOMEN, CHILDREN, AND WAR

ANCIENT WORLD

Ancient writings and artifacts provide evidence of women and children accompanying militaries and being involved in wars. However, the scarcity of written records, embellishments and other alterations in later accounts, and the challenges of analyzing archaeological objects can make it difficult to determine women's and children's activities with certainty. For example, the Egyptian queen Hatshepsut (c. 1503-1458 B.C.E.), who also ruled as a king and coregent with her stepson, might have led a military campaign to Nubia (now Sudan), but this remains speculation, even in the light of recently discovered evidence. Chinese writings and artifacts tell of women soldiers and military leaders, among them the general Fu Hao (c. 1200 B.C.E.) and Wei Hua Hu (also known as Hua Mulan, c. third century C.E.). Greek and Roman historians wrote of legendary events, passed down from oral accounts, said to have occurred centuries before they were transcribed. The Greek historian Herodotus (fifth century B.C.E.) wrote of Sammu-ramat, queen mother of Neo-Assyria in the ninth century B.C.E., conducting military campaigns against Babylonia and India. Modern scholarship, however, asserts that it is not possible to verify reports of Sammu-ramat's military exploits and notes that she and other Neo-Assyrian queens wielded power only through male relatives.

The Old Testament contains numerous stories of women and children's involvement in wars, as collaborators with male enemies, plunder, defenders, and fighters. One story is that after attacking the Midianites, the Israelite leader and prophet Moses (c. 1250 B.C.E.) allowed soldiers to keep thousands of virgin girls as spoils of war but ordered all boys and women to be killed. A famous biblical story is that of Deborah (twelfth century B.C.E.), an Israelite judge, prophet, and military leader who helped to plan and conduct an attack against the Canaanites. One must bear in mind that the historical authenticity of biblical figures and events often has been difficult to ascertain. That said, biblical accounts can offer insight into how earlier peoples conceived of roles of, as well as restrictions on, women and children in warfare.

Near-contemporaneous Greek and Roman writers left accounts of women's and children's involvement in wars and relationships with soldiers. Scholars in later ages have used these writings as well as other evidence in their studies of this topic. Ancient Greeks told of women warriors and of women defending their towns when attacked by outside armies. Roman officers could marry and were allowed to bring families to forts, archaeological evidence for which exists, for example, from the Vetera I fort in the Lower Rhine region (c. first century C.E.). It was not until c. 197 C.E. that ordinary Roman soldiers could enter into legal marriage, although before then many maintained households with women and children. The evidence from Vetera I also raises the possibility of women and children at commercial sites at the fort, perhaps as vendors catering to the Roman army. Greek and Roman leaders complained of large numbers of women (including prostitutes) and children encumbering the travel of armies, but some also expressed the view that family members motivated male soldiers to fight.

Roman authors also described women who fought on the side of the Romans' opponents. Plutarch (46-c. 119 C.E.) described a battle between the Romans and the invading Cimbri (believed to be a Germanic or Celtic people) in France in 102 B.C.E. in which Cimbri women fiercely defended themselves against Roman attackers. Another historian, Tacitus (c. 56-120 C.E.), wrote of Germanic women exhorting their men to fight the Romans.

MEDIEVAL WORLD

As in previous ages, women and children in medieval times assisted soldiers, accompanied militaries in their travels, and played various roles in supporting wars. Combat remained chiefly a male domain, although exceptional girls and women engaged in warfare. The best known of these is Joan of Arc (c. 1412-1431), a French farmer's daughter who during the Hundred Years' War (1337-1453) claimed that Christian saints had come to her in visions instructing her to aid in ousting the English from France. At approximately age seventeen, dressed in armor, she led

F. R. Niglutsch

Red Cross nurses arrive in Athens during the Greco-Turkish War (1897).

French soldiers in the Battle of Orléans (1429), driving the English from the city. However, in 1430 the Burgundians captured Joan and sold her to the English, who accused her of witchcraft and heresy and also condemned her for wearing men's clothes. In 1431, the English burned her at the stake in Rouen. In 1920, the Catholic Church made Joan of Arc a saint.

In Europe and other regions, women and chil-dren less renowned than Joan of Arc played roles in preparing for, participating in, and supporting wars. Women and children accompanied men in the Crusades, between the late eleventh and thirteenth centuries, to remove Muslims from power and establish Christianity in Jerusalem and other sites in Palestine considered holy to Christians, as well as to convert non-Christians to Christianity. In the Crusades and other wars, women and children performed arduous labor for armies, carrying heavy supplies, digging ditches, collecting wood for fires, and washing garments and linens.

In *Le Livre des fais d'armes et de chevalerie* (1410; *The Book of Fayttes of Arms and of Chivalry*, 1489), the Venice-born writer Christine de Pizan (c. 1364-c. 1430), who spent most of her life in France, examined tactics and rules of warfare. Among the topics she discussed was training the children of knights and common people in the use of arms and in other skills so that they would be able to fight effectively and defend against invaders. Indeed, adults considered children's playing at war and with fencing swords, and hunting, as training for combat.

Christine de Pizan articulated the assumptions of many of her predecessors and contemporaries, that women were weak and, along with children and aged men, of little use in warfare, even in defense during the siege of a fortress (although she did suggest that women might aid in boiling water to pour on would-be invaders). In an imagined discussion with an expert on matters of warfare, Christine de Pizan's interlocutor observed that "those who follow the military custom" should be "ashamed to imprison women, children, helpless and old people." As to the question of whether it would be just for an enemy to hold a child for ransom, the response was that "reason does not agree that innocence should be trifled with; for it is evident that the child is innocent and not guilty in anything connected with war." Thus, like other scholars before, during, and after the Middle Ages, Christine de Pizan's depiction of warfare as essentially constituting conflict between men obscured the roles played by women and children and positioned them mainly as encumbrances and victims.

MODERN WORLD

Although in modern times males continued to dominate in waging war, occasionally women led armies or, as heads of state, saw their countries through war. Queen Njinga Mbande of Angola (1582-1663) led her military against Portuguese slave traders. The rani of the Indian district of Jhansi, Lakshmi Bai (born c. 1830), who previously had cooperated with British officials, in 1858 led battles in a rebellion against them, losing her life. Despite the complexity of her relationship with the British, she became an enduring symbol of Indian resistance to colonial rule. Golda Meir (1898-1978) served as prime minister of Israel during the 1973 Arab-Israeli War, which began when Egyptian and Syrian forces launched a surprise attack on Israel on Yom Kippur, a Jewish holy day. In 1982, when Argentina attempted to reclaim the Falkland Islands, a British territory located in the Southern Hemisphere, British prime minister Margaret Thatcher (born 1925) oversaw the dispatch of United Kingdom forces to the archipelago and succeeded in retaining it.

According to the eminent military scholar Barton Hacker, "During the decades that spanned the end of the nineteenth century and the start of the twentieth, Western armies became almost exclusively male, perhaps for the first time in history." Women still provided crucial support for professional Western militaries, but they were physically more separated from male soldiers than in previous eras, when they had lived and worked with them in close proximity. In independence and revolutionary movements in various parts of the world, however, women participated as combatants as well as in support roles, as in uprisings against colonial governments in Latin America in the early 1800's and China's Taiping Rebellion (1850-1864).

National Archives

A woman works as a riveter at Lockheed Aircraft Corporation in Burbank, California.

In the latter part of the twentieth century, women in numerous countries attained official status as soldiers in their nations' armed forces, among them the United States (1948), the United Kingdom (1949), Canada (1951), Germany (1975), Norway (1977), the Netherlands (1979), and Spain (1988). Most countries did not draft women or allow them into direct combat. As of 2006, the countries that did draft women were China, Eritrea, Israel, Libya, Malaysia, North Korea, Peru, and Taiwan. In some societies, the inclusion of women as official members of the armed forces resulted from recognition of their effectiveness in World War II and from evolving views of gender equality. Besides serving as official members of armed forces, women in the twentieth century participated in wars as resistance fighters and guerrillas—for instance, against the Germans in World War II and in anticolonial and civil wars in Africa and Asia.

Although sexual assaults against women and children, and sometimes against men, had occurred in wars since ancient times, the 1998 Rome Statute of the International Criminal Court declared that rape, forced pregnancy, and other forms of sexual violence constituted crimes against humanity and war crimes. These weapons of war had been recently used against girls and women, many of them Muslim, in conflicts in the former Yugoslavia during the 1990's, and against Tutsi girls and women in the 1994 Rwandan genocide.

In modern times, changing attitudes about childhood and about protecting children from warfare gained traction in many countries. Children's advocates sought the protection of children in international and civil wars from conscription, dislocation, hunger, disease, poverty, torture, sexual assault, psychological trauma, land mines, and other risks to their well-being. The 1989 United Nations Convention on the Rights of the Child declared that states could not recruit children under the age of fifteen years into their armed forces. However, boys and girls served as soldiers into the early twenty-first century in Burma, Colombia, Nepal, Sri Lanka, Somalia, Sudan, and more than a dozen other countries. Australia, Canada, the United States, and several European countries allowed seventeen-year-olds to serve in their militaries in noncombat roles.

NARA

In a now-famous World War II poster, Rosie the Riveter enjoins women to support the war effort.

BOOKS AND ARTICLES

Allison, Penelope M. "Engendering Roman Spaces." In *Space and Spatial Analysis in Archeology*, edited by Elizabeth C. Robertson et al. Calgary, Alta., Canada: University of Calgary Press, 2006. This article illustrates the challenge of using archaeological evidence to ascertain and evaluate the presence of women and children at Roman sites.

De Pauw, Linda Grant. *Battle Cries and Lullabies: Women in War from Prehistory to the Present*. Norman: University of Oklahoma Press, 1998. A detailed, wide-ranging, and highly informative examination of women's (and, to a lesser extent, children's) support of militaries and involvement in wars around the globe and across millennia.

Filipovi , Zlata, and Melanie Challenger, eds. *Stolen Voices: Young People's War Diaries from World War I to Iraq*. Foreword by Olara A. Otunnu. New York: Penguin Books, 2006. First-hand accounts from adolescents and young adults who experienced the effects of war in Europe, Asia, the Middle East, and the United States.

Fraser, Antonia. *The Warrior Queens*. New York: Alfred A. Knopf, 1989. A history of exceptional women rulers in wars from antiquity through the late twentieth century.

Hacker, Barton C., and Margaret Vining, eds. *A Companion to Women's Military History*. Leiden, the Netherlands: E. J. Brill, 2010. Edited by historians at the Smithsonian Institution in Washington, D.C., this collection of essays examines women's support of militaries and engagement in warfare, from the European medieval era through the early twenty-first century.

Li, Xiaolin. "Chinese Women Soldiers: A History of Five Thousand Years." *Social Education* 58, no. 2 (1994): 67-71. A summary of Chinese women's military roles from ancient to modern times. Li shows that although Chinese women led militaries as long ago as c. 1200 B.C.E., fought in defense of homes and in uprisings, and performed vital work for armies, the modern Chinese military remains male-dominated, and women do not serve in combat positions.

Marten, James, ed. *Children and War: A Historical Anthology*. New York: New York University Press, 2002. This collection consists of twenty-one topical essays by scholars of history, psychology, and other academic disciplines on children's experiences of war, cultural beliefs regarding children and war, and teaching children about wars.

Rosen, David M. *Armies of the Young: Child Soldiers in War and Terrorism*. New Brunswick, N.J.: Rutgers University Press, 2005. Rosen, an anthropologist and legal scholar, scrutinizes the complex subject of child soldiering by considering perplexing questions such as whether a universal age of adulthood can be established and the extent to which children exercise self-determination in serving as soldiers. Chapters on Jewish child partisans in World War II, child soldiers in Sierra Leone's civil war (1991-2001), and Palestinian children's militant opposition to Israel illuminate the experiences, perspectives, and problems of child soldiers.

Donna Alvah

SCIENCE AND WARFARE

BIOLOGY, CHEMISTRY, AND WAR

OVERVIEW

Science and war have always developed side by side. New inventions were often made during war or to further bellicose goals. Scientists were tasked with inventing weapons that could kill the enemy more efficiently or ways to protect their governments' own forces. Biology is the science of all living organisms. Biological warfare, also known as germ warfare, is the use of viruses, bacteria, or other disease-causing living organisms as biological weapons (bioweapons). Chemistry deals with the structure, composition, and properties of all kinds of matter and the reactions they may cause in interaction. The use of nonliving toxic products as weapons is considered chemical warfare. Both biological and chemical weapons can occur in nature and be employed as weapons, which tended to happen in ancient and medieval times. In modern times, science and technology have been applied to develop such weapons and the means of delivering them.

SIGNIFICANCE

Both biological and chemical weapons are considered to be weapons of mass destruction (WMDs), since they are designed to kill millions of people, and thus they pose a grave threat to humanity as a whole. Sometimes called "the poor man's atom bomb," the sheer existence of these weapons inflicts fear, and because the threat of their use is a potent means of intimidation, their effect can be more psychological than real. Whoever is in possession of such weapons will have the upper hand in any conflict, at least once conventional means fail, and this makes the party possessing chemical or biological weapons a potential aggressor, feared by neighbors. These WMDs not only threaten annihilation and defeat; their inhumane nature has also led to their banishment in the modern world.

HISTORY OF BIOLOGY, CHEMISTRY, AND WAR

ANCIENT WORLD

Early recorded uses of bioweapons include the poisoning of wells by toxic plants during the First Sacred War in Greece (595-586 B.C.E.) and by the Roman commander Manius Aquilius in 130 B.C.E. Wells were often poisoned by placing poisonous plants, dead horses, or even killed persons in them. In sea battles, catapults, or ballistae, were sometimes loaded with snakes, which were lobbed onto the decks of enemy ships and caused panic aboard that confined space.

According to archaeological evidence, bitumen and sulfur crystals were ignited by the armies of ancient Persia to give off a dense, poisonous smoke that killed Roman soldiers. Sunzi's *Sunzi Bingfa* (c. fifth-third century B.C.E.; *The Art of War*, 1910) and Hindu books describe ways to poison wells, create toxic smoke, and poison weapons. The effect of such weapons seems to have been limited, however.

MEDIEVAL WORLD

In medieval times, the poisoning of wells continued. Even though the exact mechanisms of infection remained unknown, it was clear that disease could spread from animals to people or from person to person. Aggressors, when laying siege to a town, would catapult sick or dead animals into the town, hoping that the carcasses would infect the inhabitants. Victims of the bubonic plague (Black Death) or decomposing corpses were also shot into besieged towns, as were feces. During the Siege of Caffa in 1346, the besieging Mongol forces catapulted cadavers of plague-infested animals into the city. However, the plague most likely first affected the attackers. Thousands were killed, according to eyewitnesses. The Black Death spread from there toward Constantinople, Italy, and France. It is unclear whether and to what extent the use of bioweapons contributed to this pandemic.

Gunpowder, a chemical invention and hence a form of chemical weapon, revolutionized warfare. Military units were now able to fight numerically superior forces, fortifications could be breached more easily, and small groups of skilled knights gave way to mass formations of riflemen.

MODERN WORLD

In the fifteenth through eighteenth centuries, Europeans colonizing the Americas, perhaps unbeknownst to them at first, brought many diseases with them to the New World, and these essentially functioned as biological weapons, even when they were not initially intended as such. Smallpox epidemics raged among indigenous Americans, and there have been allegations that British commanders spread the disease deliberately to quell Native American uprisings. While it is a fact that smallpox had a very high morbidity rate among Native Americans, because of their complete lack of immunity to the virus, and thus affected them more than the European settlers, those allegations cannot be proved in most cases. However, some evidence exists to support the intentional use of the smallpox virus against Native Americans. In 1763, during Pontiac's Rebellion, one "Mr. McKee" and Captain Simeon Ecuyer, the commanding officer at Fort Pitt, gave "two blankets and a handkerchief out of the Small Pox Hospital" to Delaware chiefs with the "hope it will have the desired effect."

Smallpox caused many casualties during the American Revolution (1775-1783), and there are allegations that it was spread deliberately by both sides. Again, there is no way to prove this today, and analysts still argue whether this kind of biological warfare took place or events occurred naturally. Native Americans, for their part, poisoned wells by throwing killed animals in them, a method repeated during the American Civil War (1861-1865). Additional proposals were brought forward to produce various types of chemical weapons during the Civil War, but it was thought that battlefield doctors and nurses would have a difficult time dealing with the effects of these weapons, and the proposals were shelved. Other nations drew back from chemical weapons as well. Some in the British military, during

the Crimean War (1853-1856), proposed to use cyanide, but it too was rejected.

During the Second Sino-Japanese War (1937-1945), the infamous Japanese Army Unit 731 conducted experiments on thousands of people in occupied China. The unit was formed and headed by General Shirō Ishii (1892-1959). Ishii started with experiments in 1932 and was given control of his own research facility in 1936. He was appointed chief of the Biological Warfare Section in 1940 and headed Japan's bioweapons program, the largest of any nation during the war, until the end of the war. He received immunity from prosecution in 1946. During World War II, Japanese Army Unit 731 (with up to three thousand men) and other special units tested various agents on Chinese prisoners of war as well as civilians, usually disguising the tests as vaccinations or claiming that they were for medical research. Around 400,000 people are thought to have perished in these "experiments" and deliberate attacks. In October, 1940, bubonic plague was spread in the Chinese cities of Qu Xian (Chü-hsien) and Ningbo, killing twenty-one and ninety-nine people, respectively. Another attempt in November in Kinhwa did not lead to a breakout of plague. By the end of 1941, prisoners of war were infected with typhoid. Anthrax was used in May, 1942, in retaliation for the Doolittle raid, but when the disease also spread to retreating Japanese troops, Ishii was relieved of command of Unit 731. As efforts to develop an aerosol failed, rats and insects were infested with bubonic plague and set free in cities or dropped in ceramic bombs.

Programs to weaponize diseases, including various forms of plague and anthrax, were carried out by other states as well. Such efforts continued after World War II. The U.S. program was headed by George W. Merck (1894-1957) and Ira Baldwin (1895-1999), who became the first director of the U.S. Biological Warfare Laboratories in Maryland in 1943. There are allegations of bioweapons, developed under Baldwin, being used during the Korean War by the United States.

Chemical weapons are most widely associated with World War I. German scientists developed various types of WMDs for this conflict, although the term "gas war," often applied to this war, is somewhat misleading. The chemical agents used were mostly liquids or aerosols; some of these agents would develop into a gas only over time or were delivered as a fine spray that looked like a gas. Methods of deployment varied. First, canisters with the liquids were brought up to the front and opened, facing the enemy, where it was hoped that the wind would blow the gas or aerosols toward enemy lines. In many cases, shifting winds inflicted more casualties on the side that had deployed the chemical weapons. Later, grenades were filled with the chemical agents and fired against the enemy. Upon impact, they burst apart and spread the liquids. Airplanes were also used to spray the chemical weapons over large areas.

Chlorine gas was first used on April 22, 1915, by the German army at the Second Battle of Ypres (1915) on the western front. The German army deployed some 5,700 cylinders north of Ypres, containing nearly 170 tons of chlorine. The gas was released, forming a gray-green cloud that drifted toward French colonial troops, who broke ranks. The Germans used gas on three more occasions during that battle. Some ninety men died immediately from gas poisoning in the trenches, more than two hundred were wounded, and sixty of them later died. As the Germans were also afraid of the effects of the gas and lacked reinforcements, the break in the front lines could not be exploited. These scenes would be replayed often during the remainder of the war. "Gas attacks" in the end had more of a psychological than a truly military effect.

Lethal in high doses, its smell and color made chlorine a relatively ineffective weapon, as it could

AP/Wide World Photos

Israeli students wear gas masks in 2003 during a drill to prepare them for the possibility of a chemical attack.

easily be spotted. Phosgene, more lethal and harder to detect, was later used. Both agents caused harm to the eyes and lungs of victims, leading to asphyxiation. Perhaps the most notorious chemical weapon deployed in World War I was the so-called mustard gas (dichloroethyl sulfide), which stuck to surfaces for hours. This weapon, a vesicant (blistering agent), attacked the eyes and lungs and functioned as a systemic poison. The use of gas masks during the war resulted in its being responsible for relatively few fatalities, but its use was feared and lethal to those unprotected, and it would later be used against poorly equipped armies in Ethiopia (1935-1936) and the Iran-Iraq War (1980-1988).

A leading scientist on the German side was Fritz Haber (1868-1934). After research in the field of fertilizers and explosives, Haber developed chlorine gas for chemical warfare. His wife, Clara, committed suicide after she learned of the effects the weapon had in Ypres. Together with Carl Bosch (1874-1940), Haber developed the Haber process, which can be used to extract nitrogen from the air to use in fertilizers under conditions of low temperature and high pressure. For this achievement he was awarded the Nobel Prize in Chemistry in 1918, despite also being the "father of the Gas War." A Jew, Haber fled Nazi Germany in the 1930's.

Most states worked on chemical weapons in the interwar period and had huge stockpiles of them ready for use by World War II (1939-1945). These ultimately were not used, as both sides feared the effects of these horrendous weapons. After the war, more powerful toxins were developed, mostly "nerve agents." These compounds would cause muscle spasms, ultimately leading to failure of the respiratory or circulatory system. The compound known as VX, tasteless and odorless, with the texture of motor oil, was one such nerve agent. When entering the body, it blocks an enzyme that triggers nerve pulses; the victim then suffers severe muscle contractions, which ultimately lead to death.

During the Vietnam War (1961-1975), the United States used various types of chemical agents, such as Agent Orange—not against persons but as defoliants, to deforest the jungle areas in Southeast Asia. The detrimental effect upon animals and also people, due to its high content of dioxin, was unintended and discovered only later.

In 1988, Iraqi dictator Saddam Hussein (1937-2006) used poison gas against Kurdish civilians in Halabja during the Anfal campaign. Kurdish villages were bombed by the Iraqi Air Force with multiple agents,

AP/Wide World Photos

Pictures of a mangrove forest in Vietnam both before (top, in 1965) and after (in 1970) treatment with the herbicide Agent Orange.

most likely including mustard gas, and the powerful nerve toxins sarin, tabun, and possibly VX. Some five thousand civilians were killed in this incident alone. Iraq also used poison gas during the Iran-Iraq War. Western sources did not at first believe this and even claimed that Iran, not Iraq, had used the weapons. The United States later referenced this use and ability to manufacture such chemical weapons to make the case that Iraq still possessed WMDs.

On March 20, 1995, the Japanese Aum Shinrikyo sect used sarin gas for a terror attack on the Tokyo subway system, the first modern use of a WMD by terrorists. This incident shocked the world and highlighted how vulnerable civilian populations were to chemical and biological attacks.

Today, both biological and chemical warfare are covered by conventions under the auspices of the United Nations. The 1992 Convention on the Prohibition of the Development, Production, Stockpiling, and Use of Chemical Weapons and on Their Destruction, administered by the Organization for the Prohibition of Chemical Weapons, and the 1972 Biological Weapons Convention, signed by more than one hundred countries, outlaw the storage, stockpiling, and use of these weapons.

BOOKS AND ARTICLES

Barenblatt, Daniel A. *Plague upon Humanity: The Secret Genocide of Axis Japan's Germ Warfare Operation*. New York: HarperCollins, 2004. Summary of the known facts about Japan's biological warfare capability, carefully developed with the direct support of the emperor and tested in China.

Endicott, Stephen, and Edward Hagerman. *The United States and Biological Warfare: Secrets from the Early Cold War and Korea*. Bloomington: Indiana University Press, 1998. The authors present an impressive array of evidence that the military and executive branch lied to Congress and the public about the development of biological weapons and even used them in Korea.

Harris, Sheldon H. *Factories of Death: Japanese Biological Warfare 1932-45 and the American Cover-Up*. New York: Routledge, 1994. Meticulous research on Japan's secretive experiments on live human beings and U.S. complicity in covering up the truth after World War I.

Jones, Simon. *World War I Gas Warfare Tactics and Equipment*. New York: Osprey, 2007. Explains practical details, such as the means and tactics of delivery, the effects and influence on the battles, and the race to produce better protection for the troops on both sides, of this type of warfare, which became one of the dominant aspects of World War I.

Mangold, Tom, and Jeff Goldberg. *Plague Wars: A True Story of Biological Warfare*. London: Macmillan, 1999. Covers research facilities and scientists in the former Soviet Union, the United States, and other countries.

Mayor, Adrienne. *Greek Fire, Poison Arrows, and Scorpion Bombs: Biological and Chemical Warfare in the Ancient World*. Woodstock, N.Y.: Overlook Duckworth, 2003. Shows that biological and chemical weapons saw action in battles long before the modern era.

Robinson, P. J., and M. Leitenberg. *The Rise of CB Weapons*. Vol. 1 in *The Problem of Biological and Chemical Warfare*. Stockholm: SIPRI, 1971. Detailed account of research and development in biological and chemical warfare worldwide and the often little-known use of biological and chemical weapons.

Williams, Peter, and D. Wallace. *Unit 731: Japan's Secret Biological Warfare in World War II*. New York: Free Press, 1989. Explains this infamous unit and its projects in China.

Thomas Weiler

MEDICINE ON THE BATTLEFIELD

OVERVIEW

Military medicine aims to keep soldiers and sailors fit enough to fight. While it is likely that battlefield medicine has existed as long as humans have fought over territory, the subject has received comparatively little attention in the historical record. Much of this gap is attributable to poor record keeping as well as a general lack of interest; few people besides military physicians have demonstrated any interest in military medicine. Most accounts of military medicine over the centuries are found in nonmedical writings, such as memoirs, histories of battles, and diaries as well as works of art.

SIGNIFICANCE

Military medicine on the battlefield cannot be viewed in the narrow confines of a field of combat. It encompasses the treatment of injuries sustained on the battlefield, from spear wounds to gunshot wounds, as well as the side effects of such injuries, such as shock and infection. Medicine on the battlefield begins with the recruitment of troops who are healthy enough to fight on the battlefield. It continues with the maintenance of the health of fighters through adequate sanitation, the provision of safe foods, and the availability of clean water. It proceeds with the treatment of the wounded on the field and in hospitals. Battlefield surgeons have also shaped public policy to ensure better treatment of the wounded.

HISTORY OF MEDICINE ON THE BATTLEFIELD

ANCIENT WORLD

In the ancient world, killing technology and defensive technology were fairly well balanced. As a re-
sult, ancient battlefields were not more dangerous than modern battlefields. Soldiers had an excellent chance of surviving attacks by axes, swords, javelins, and spears. Nevertheless, war wounds appear to have been a constant threat for ancient men. Classical literature gives the impression of nearly continuous warfare in the ancient world. The treatment of war wounds is the only kind of medical activity mentioned in the *Iliad* (c. 750 B.C.E.; English translation, 1611), the earliest Greek source available. Hippocrates (460-377 B.C.E.), the Greek father of medicine, advised that "He who would become a surgeon should join the army and follow it."

Broken bones were the most common battlefield injuries. Ancient Egyptian and Sumerian medical texts discuss broken bones extensively, indicating that military physicians were quite familiar with them. The injured soldier had the greatest risk of dying from the side effects of battlefield injury: tetanus, gas gangrene, and septicemia. The tetanus bacterium is commonly present in soil and is found in greater numbers in richly manured soil, which was typical of agricultural societies of the ancient world. The ancient medical practice of leaving the wound unsutured for several days before closing was likely to produce far fewer tetanus infections than the process of rapid closure used from the medieval period to World War I. Gangrenous wounds likely produced 100 percent mortality. Ancient military physicians repeatedly cleansed wounds for several days before closure, thereby removing necrotic (dead) tissue and greatly reducing the risk of gangrene. Again, this habit disappeared after the fall of Rome with the result of a high death rate until World War I. Septicemia or blood poisoning is caused when bacteria enter the bloodstream. Wounds to arteries and major veins caused the greatest risk of septicemia. Until the invention of antibiotics in the twentieth century, septicemia almost always killed.

Available data on wound mortality and infection produce a rough statistical profile of the causes of battlefield death. Of 100 soldiers wounded in action, 13.8 would die of shock and bleeding within two to six hours. The numbers were lower for Roman soldiers. Like other ancients, the Romans knew to use a tourniquet to stop bleeding and prevent shock. Unlike their peers, the Romans had the organizational skills to move the wounded quickly from the battlefield to a hospital where physicians could tie off the severed arteries. Another 6 percent of the wounded would likely contract tetanus, and 80 percent of those would die within three to six days. About 5 percent would contract gangrene, of whom at least 80 percent would die within a week. Septicemia struck less than 2 percent of soldiers but generally killed them all within ten days. Most soldiers died of disease rather than the result of combat, which would remain the case until the twentieth century: Ignorance about such dangers as typhus and dysentery, as well as improper nutrition, ensured this greater risk.

MEDIEVAL WORLD

The same four major factors—shock and bleeding, tetanus, gangrene, and septicemia—would serve as the leading causes of death among military wounded until the twentieth century. The near-total disintegration of Western culture following the fall of Rome in 476 C.E. resulted in the loss of most medical knowledge until the Renaissance. The only significant development is found in the Byzantine military, which provided each battalion with its own detachment of two physicians, a general practitioner and a surgeon. The medical staff was augmented by eight to eighteen medical orderlies, who served as combat medics and stretcher bearers. The Byzantines copied the Roman practice of immediate medical treatment. Unlike the Romans, they gave medical personnel a gold bonus for every wounded soldier rescued from the battlefield and brought to the medical tent.

The Islamic world practiced medicine based upon the Qurʾān. Since the Qurʾān prohibited dissection, medical personnel lacked a thorough knowledge of the body, as did physicians in the West. Fevers and infection were treated by bleeding and purging, again similar to Western practice. Surgery was akin to butchery, with amputation being accomplished by

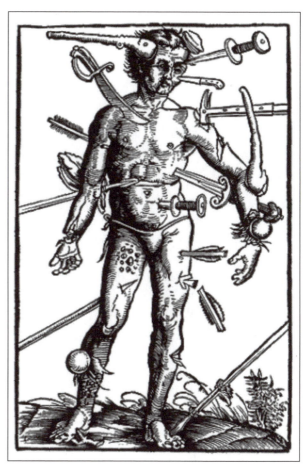

An illustration from an early sixteenth century German field manual for wound treatment, by Hans von Gersdorff, shows typical wounds. The image is by Hans Wechtlin.

repeated blows with a short sword or mallet, after which the limb was submersed in boiling pitch or oil to cauterize the limb. Bone setting was crude, with the result that the limb was often left distorted. However, since Islamic medicine relied more upon drugs than surgery, the Arabs developed superb pharmaceutical knowledge. They used hemp fumes as anesthetics and preoperative compounds to induce sleep before surgery.

In the Renaissance, the military barber-surgeon emerged as a familiar figure in Western armies. Prior to about 1453, Western armies often relied upon "cutters," men who followed the troops and tended the wounded for a fee extracted from the soldier him-

AP/Wide World Photos

U.S. Marines get plasma transfusions during the 1945 invasion of Okinawa.

self. These cutters were typically the only source of medical care for the common soldier. The barber-surgeons, many of whom had probably begun as cutters, acquired a high level of medical craftsmanship, especially in surgery. They needed this skill to deal with the shattered bones produced by the new invention of gunpowder. Amputation proved the most common treatment for gunshot-induced compound fractures, in which there is an open wound of the soft parts leading down to the break in the bone. Such fractures became the most common battlefield injury. A French barber-surgeon, Ambroise Paré (1510-1590), developed the best technique for performing battlefield amputations. He used ligature prior to amputation, as the Romans had done. Instead of plunging the limb into boiling oil, Paré treated the amputation with a mixture of egg yolk, oil of roses, and turpentine. Paré's patients had lower infection rates, but few other physicians adopted his humane techniques until the nineteenth century.

Infection remained a major killer of soldiers. Often,

Renaissance surgeons would remove a bullet by enlarging the wound and then probing for the missile with fingers or unsterile probes, increasing infection rates. Physicians would also stuff gunshot wounds with all sorts of foul materials to create pus that would presumably heal the injury. Infection often resulted. Gunpowder also created burns, and the most popular treatments were vegetable and animal ointments that usually induced blistering and scarring.

MODERN WORLD

Until the late eighteenth century, surgeons did some field surgery, but the wounded were typically gathered after the battle and brought to the surgeon. Military leaders feared that any attempt to remove the wounded would disrupt the fighting integrity of the unit. The wounded often lingered for hours and sometimes days before being evacuated. This situation did not improve until the Napoleonic Wars (1793-1815), when Baron Dominique-Jean Larrey (1766-1842) invented "flying ambulances" that located, treated, and evacuated the wounded under fire.

The state of medical knowledge was also advancing in the eighteenth century. Surgery stopped being a technical craft practiced by physicians of a lower order while medical publishing expanded. In this century, governments accepted the obligation to provide and pay for the military medical care of the common soldier. In 1776, military surgeon John Jones (1729-1791) published the first American textbook on surgery as well as the first American medical book. Jones, who had served colonial troops during the French and Indian War (1754-1763), treated Revolutionary War soldiers as a surgeon with the Continental Army. His book *Plain Concise Practical Remarks on the Treatment of Wounds and Fractures* (1776) provided a guide to surgery and advice on hygiene. As Jones realized, in times of revolution, recruits were eager to join the fighting, with the result that large numbers of marginally healthy adults with poor sanitary habits entered military service.

Eighteenth century military medicine benefited from a number of new techniques. Styptics were commonly used to stop minor bleeding. Pressure sponges, alcohol, and turpentine were used to treat minor wounds. Cauterization of arteries was still practiced but with less frequency, since the invention of locked forceps. The screw tourniquet made thigh amputations possible and greatly reduced the risk associated with amputations below the knee. Military surgeons place greater emphasis on preparing limbs for prosthesis as flap and lateral incision amputations became common procedure.

In the early nineteenth century, military doctors began to record what they observed with the aim of changing public policy and improving the health of the army. As an additional concern, the deaths of soldiers overseas proved to be a burden to the taxpayer. In 1863, the Royal Commission on India estimated that Great Britain lost £588,000 annually from sickness among the troops in India alone. The financial impact of disease prompted more governments to focus their resources on the improvement of military medical care.

The most common battlefield injury continued to be compound fractures from bullets and cannonballs propelled by gunpowder. Many such fractures were infected, since there was a likelihood that pieces of clothing, contaminated soil, and other substances would enter the wound. Treatment proved very difficult. During the American Indian Wars of the late nineteenth century, Louis Anatole LaGarde (1849-1920) realized that the act of firing a bullet does not, as had previously been thought, sterilize a projectile and that bullets can therefore induce sepsis from a wound. He published his discovery in 1893. In World War I (1914-1918), the British Army began using the Thomas splint and the U.S. Army employed the army leg splint. The patient was saved from shock, pain, and other symptoms that had made bone fractures frequently fatal. In 1918, the death rate from such injuries in evacuation hospitals dropped to 17.5 percent, an improvement of 40 to 50 percent over the rate in the first months of the war. In 1923, Hiram Orr, a Nebraskan who had served with both the British and the American forces in France during World War I, proposed a "closed treatment" for broken bones by encasing the leg splint in plaster of Paris casts. Orr's treatment received its first military test during the Spanish Civil War (1936-1939). José Trueta (1897-1977), a Spanish surgeon, reported that of 1,073 gunshot fractures treated with casts, only six patients died. He also noted the almost complete absence of gas gangrene, a notorious killer among the wounded in previous wars.

Largely because of advances in military medicine during World War II (1939-1945), the death rate for combatants dropped dramatically. In the 1945 Battle of Iwo Jima, 32.6 percent of the U.S. Marines became casualties, making the campaign the bloodiest in the history of the Marine Corps. If the same casualties had been suffered by Union forces in the Civil War (1861-1865), the death rate would have been 14.6 percent. The overall death rate among wounded U.S. sailors and Marines for all Pacific campaigns stood at 2.3 percent. The improved figures resulted from administering first aid on the scene of battle, speedily evacuating the wounded, providing whole-blood transfusions, and using penicillin. In 1943, wounded U.S. soldiers returning from the Pacific became the first group of soldiers to receive the newly invented antibiotic. Tests on American soldiers in 1943 and 1944 revealed that penicillin reduced the death rate from staphylococcal infections from 75 percent to 10 percent while limiting infection from wounds and burns.

In the subsequent decades, military physicians improved their treatment of shock with readily available blood and transfusions. Vascular surgeons were used on the front lines for the first time during the Korean War (1950-1953). During the Vietnam War (1961-1975), helicopters with trained corpsmen aboard quickly evacuated the wounded to hospitals. Of the wounded who were still alive upon reaching a hospital, 97.5 percent survived. The Iraq War (beg. 2003) led to improvements in the treatment of combat trauma, particularly vascular injuries.

BOOKS AND ARTICLES

Anderson, Robert S., and W. Paul Havens, Jr., eds. *Internal Medicine in World War II: Infectious Diseases and General Medicine*. Washington, D.C.: Department of the Army, 1968. This textbook covers the treatment of World War II combat injuries.

Freemon, Frank R. *Gangrene and Glory: Medical Care During the American Civil War*. Urbana: University of Illinois Press, 2001. This is a heavily illustrated and highly readable account of the challenges facing Union and Confederate medical forces.

Gabriel, Richard A., and Karen S. Metz. *A History of Military Medicine*. 2 vols. Westport, Conn.: Greenwood Press, 1992. A superb survey of military medicine from the dawn of recorded time to the end of the twentieth century.

Griffin, Alexander R. *Out of Carnage*. New York: Howell, Soskin, 1945. An engaging contemporary account of World War II battlefield medicine.

Jadick, Richard, and Thomas Hayden. *On Call in Hell: A Doctor's Iraq War Story*. New York: New American Library, 2007. Jadick is a career U.S. Marine who volunteered in 2004 to serve as a battalion surgeon in the Iraq War. Jadick and his men followed military units through the streets of Iraq in order to reach and stabilize wounded soldiers quickly.

Kaplan, Jonathan. *The Dressing Station: A Surgeon's Chronicle of War and Medicine*. New York: Grove Press, 2001. Kaplan, trained as a surgeon in South Africa, recalls his frontline medical experiences in apartheid South Africa, Kurdistan, and other places where undeclared wars raged.

Littleton, Mark R. *Doc: Heroic Stories of Medics, Corpsmen, and Surgeons in Combat*. New Plymouth, New Zealand: Zenith Press, 2005. Littleton recounts stories of medical professionals, including nurses, from World War I to the Iraq War.

McCallum, Jack E. *Military Medicine: From Ancient Times to the Twenty-first Century*. Santa Barbara, Calif.: ABC-CLIO, 2008. This is an encyclopedia that opens with a general history of medicine before proceeding to nearly two hundred entries on various aspects of military medicine.

Nessen, Shawn Christian, Dave Edmond Lounsbury, and Stephen P. Hetz, eds. *War Surgery in Afghanistan and Iraq: A Series of Cases, 2003-2007*. Washington, D.C.: Department of the Army, 2008. The first scholarly work to cover military medicine in the Afghanistan and Iraq wars, this book covers one hundred cases of combat trauma.

Salazar, Christine F. *The Treatment of War Wounds in Graeco-Roman Antiquity*. Leiden, the Netherlands: E. J. Brill, 2000. The first book to address military medicine in the ancient world.

Caryn E. Neumann

PSYCHOLOGICAL EFFECTS OF WAR

OVERVIEW

In the anticipation of conflict, as well as during the fighting itself and afterward, there have long been known to be psychological effects on the people—both combatants and noncombatants—affected by conflict. In the ancient and medieval world, this was little understood, because there was not much understanding of the workings of the mind or of mental illnesses, although the effect of the nature of the cruelty in war would have led to trauma that would have been noticed by all. Much of the work on the psychological effects of warfare started with World War I (1914-1918), when, for the first time outside a siege situation, people were involved in fighting over many weeks or months.

SIGNIFICANCE

The topic of war's psychological impact took on significance gradually over the course of the twentieth century. During World Wars I and II, many instances of "shell shock" (combat fatigue) were reported, but not seriously addressed, by the psychological establishment. However, with the return to the United States of large numbers of American veterans after the Vietnam War (1961-1975), the massive number reporting psychological problems caused the issue to receive more of a focus. Diagnoses of post-traumatic stress disorder (PTSD) skyrocketed, and both practicing and academic psychologists began to address the needs of returning soldiers (though the effects of warfare on civilian groups, who are often just as seriously damaged as soldiers, received far less attention).

HISTORY OF THE PSYCHOLOGICAL EFFECTS OF WAR

ANCIENT WORLD

In the ancient world—although little was known about the workings of the mind—enthusiasms, shock, and trauma would have been noticeable. Many of the writings of the Greeks and the Romans pay great respect and honor to those who fought for their city or country. Nevertheless, many people clearly did whatever they could to avoid conflict, and most, such as the ancient historian writer Flavius Josephus, rejected the idea of "honorable" wartime service or suicide in favor of living, albeit in a Roman-dominated world.

Even though there are many examples of wanton cruelty, such as the brutal "games" in the Colosseum in Rome and other arenas where people fought each other or wild animals, there were still many Romans who shunned these events. Most Romans, moreover, if we are to believe the writings that survive, were far from the fighting, while some who wrote of war, like Julius Caesar, could reflect on the events from the relative safety of battlefield command. Being so far from the scenes of cruelty and killing, and aware that these battles served to build the empire, the citizens of Rome certainly entertained great war fever and rejoiced in their triumphs; those involved in the fighting themselves, however, often felt very differently. One early recorded example of obvious trauma was during Caesar's siege of Alesia in 52 B.C.E. The Gauls, holding out but running short of food and desperate, forced their women and children out into the no-man's-land between the Gallic fortifications and those of the Romans, leaving them to die.

Certainly Caesar and the Romans also understood the need to terrify people who opposed the Romans, and they did this by their triumphal marches through Rome, after which large numbers of captives were murdered in public, while some of their number were allowed to return home to tell people of the horrors they had seen and the mighty power of the Romans. Similar tactics would be followed by countless armies throughout history.

MEDIEVAL WORLD

In Europe during the "Dark Ages" and the later medieval period, there are many examples of wanton cruelty to terrorize people. During the Viking raids on England in the eighth, ninth, and tenth centuries, the tactic of desecrating the bodies of the dead served to frighten their opponents; likewise, the Mongols, Saracens, and Crusaders sacked whole cities in the expectation that other cities would quickly surrender.

Since ancient times, people had lived in fortified settlements throughout the world, and this continued into the Middle Ages as a defensive measure against both invasions and civil wars. Castles were built to provide protection, and hence were regarded as comforting symbols of safety, but also to intimidate, and thus could also be seen as signs of oppression. The motte-and-bailey castles in Norman England and the great castles built by Edward I in Wales were intended to overawe the population and show them who ruled the regions where they were built.

Hatred of people from rival kingdoms was combined with the concept of treason: the support of war against one's own rulers. In many cases, wars clearly wreaked havoc on the ordinary people, especially those in unprotected villages. Attacks by English raiders traumatized Joan of Arc during her childhood, and the earlier persecution of the Cathars in southern France was conducted with such ferocity that its aim was clearly to create trauma in those who harbored "heretical" or unpopular beliefs, or who supported those who did.

MODERN WORLD

During the Renaissance, there were efforts on the part of theorists and philosophers to rationalize and advocate this use of terror in war. Niccolò Machiavelli wrote about this, and Cesare Borgia practiced it. There were also clear campaigns of hatred against individual groups of people, especially Jews, who were blamed for many conflicts and other troubles during early modern Europe. In other cases the scapegoats

were Protestants (as in the St. Bartholomew's Day Massacre in 1572) or Catholics (as in the English Civil War of the 1640's). Oliver Cromwell's destruction of Drogheda and Wexford also served to traumatize the people in Ireland into submission. Moreover, one should not exclude the actions of the Spanish in the Americas or the many European countries involved in the slave trade.

Throughout western Russia, in Flanders, and in many other parts of the world, fortified homesteads and farms were the norm until the early twentieth century. This sense of being potentially under attack at any time did much to affect the lives and lifestyles of these populations, who spent much of their lives worrying about when the next war might erupt. The French writer Guy de Maupassant's short story about the elderly lady trapping a Prussian soldier in her cellar reflects the effects such wars had on ordinary people.

If the trauma from war became well known in modern times, so also were modern governments able to harness the will of their own people in wartime by demonizing their opponents. William Randolph Hearst was able to use his newspapers to whip up a frenzy over war between the United States and Spain, and Joseph Goebbels in Nazi Germany ran the propaganda ministry, dedicated to getting people to follow the dictates of a government leading its people into war. Hatred of the enemy—whether blamed on the alleged behavior of the German soldiers in Belgium in 1914 or the anti-Semitism that was to lead to the Holocaust—must be counted among the psychological effects of war.

As for the soldiers themselves, until World War I little was known about what became called "shell shock," now known as combat fatigue. Much of this ignorance was because knowledge of the workings of the human mind was in its infancy, not really identified as an area of study until the early twentieth century. Also, until World War I, many modern military campaigns (excluding sieges) sustained only short periods of fighting. A study was made of two British soldiers who served in Spain in the Peninsular War (1808-1815) against Napoleon. Both qualified for fifteen clasps—the maximum awarded to any individual—since both had served in fifteen battles. In the case of one of them, James Talbot, although he had survived fifteen battles, researchers found that he probably had been under fire for as much as twenty-four hours in his eight years of service. His regiment also suffered 123 killed in action. By contrast, the trench warfare of World War I saw men under fire for more than a week at a time, and as many men were killed each week in a regiment as were killed in the entire the Peninsular War some one hundred years earlier.

The idea of stress on soldiers in war—not just trauma in seeing their friends and other people being killed—was first recognized during the American Civil War (1861-1865); certainly civil wars have tended to be particularly traumatic, since they divide families and test friendships. In the Second Boer War (1899-1902), the judicial case of the Australian soldier Breaker Morant made mention of the psychological stress he and his co-accused suffered after they found the butchered body of a colleague. During the Russo-Japanese War (1904-1905), the Russians started to view war stress as a mental disease.

In 1915 in France, it was quite clear that many British (as well as French and German) soldiers were suffering from shell shock and other disorders related to combat stress. Although the British first used the term "not yet diagnosed (nervous)" (NYDN), and they set up centers several miles behind the battle lines to treat the mounting number of soldiers suffering from trauma and mental disorders, at the same time the British army was involved in executing some three hundred of their own soldiers for cowardice, many of them clearly victims of shell shock. There were also mutinies in the British and French armies, as well as the French navy—many of these becoming the subject of antiwar films.

After World War I, many of the soldiers returned to their homes shattered by what they had seen. With shell shock and trauma, many returned to families who had been largely untouched by the fighting, and few talked about their role in the war except to other soldiers. Many became mentally ill, and there were asylums throughout the world to treat people for shell shock and other psychological problems in the war.

National Archives

Lebanese-born James Thaber listens to President Dwight D. Eisenhower announce that he is sending U.S. troops to Lebanon in July, 1958; atop Thaber's radio is a picture of his son, a recent recruit into the U.S. Army.

Some soldiers also turned to alcohol. There were large numbers of suicides of former soldiers during the 1920's and 1930's, as well as violence against family members, especially wives and children. Some murders were clearly also related to the traumatic scenes many soldiers had encountered during the war.

World War II (1939-1945) was generally supported by the American and Allied populations, but, like the soldiers of World War I, many veterans of the later war returned to a world in which the social codes of the time discouraged sharing and verbal processing of their experiences, and like their earlier counterparts, many men elected to bury the horrors they had witnessed and move on with their lives—often finding, however, that the experiences of an entire, formative chapter of their youth were impossible to suppress and inevitably emerged through coping behaviors that led to alcoholism and emotional problems. In one sense, however, these veterans held an advantage: The nation was grateful, as evidenced by passage of the G.I. Bill and clear public support not only of the war effort but also of returning veterans.

After World War II, there were wars throughout the world that proved unpopular in their home countries. Some veterans from the Vietnam War found themselves ostracized when they returned home to the United States or to Australia. After Vietnam, soldiers often turned not only to alcohol but also to drugs (to which in many cases they had been introduced during the war). Likewise, veterans of the Iraq War—another war far less popular at home than World War II—became morose over their rejection by the same society that had sent them to war. In the case of Vietnam, and perhaps also in the case of Iraq, the society's lack of support for war veterans relative to their counterparts in World War II may also have occurred because these wars generally were considered lost, inadvisable, or at least not won in a clear victory.

However, what distinguishes more recent conflicts is that there have been many attempts to deal with the traumas experienced by their veterans. Not only has individual treatment become available to many soldiers, but there are also attempts to establish a "fair" end to any conflict. From ancient times, the end of a conflict meant that the victors were allowed to exert vengeance on the losers, in any way they wanted. In 1975, for example, when the Khmer Rouge communists captured the Cambodian capital of Phnom Penh, they evacuated the city of its two million inhabitants and turned the country into, essentially, a labor camp for their class enemies. By contrast, the Nuremberg and Tokyo trials at the end of World War II were designed to demonstrate a victory of justice over vengeance, when those deemed to be war criminals were arraigned in open court and, if found guilty, were jailed and in some cases executed. For many people these trials provided some form of closure based in law, in the same way that the Truth and Reconciliation Commission did in South Africa at the end of the war and civil insurrection there.

For the veterans themselves, recognition of posttraumatic stress and other mental and emotional disorders, not only after the conflict but also during combat, has increasingly led enlightened militaries to acknowledge and treat such cases while they are occurring. Identifying and counseling cases of PTSD is seen as not only important for the individual soldier but also essential for the military effort as a whole. The home society and family are also becoming increasingly aware of such psychological issues as veterans return to civilian life. Although no amount of counseling and treatment can address some of the psychological effects that will stay with veterans for their lifetimes, the recognition that such issues exist has served to bring them into the open and encourage both the society to offer help and veterans to seek it out.

BOOKS AND ARTICLES

Allison, William, and John Fairley. *The Monocled Mutineer*. London: Quartet Books, 1978. Explores the life of Percy Toplis, a World War I deserter from the British army.

Cosmopoulos, Michael B., ed. *Experiencing War: Trauma and Society from Ancient Greece to the Iraq War*. Chicago: Ares, 2007. Presents ten academic papers from a 2004 conference, with the goal of raising awareness of the catastrophic impact of war and violence on individuals and society as a whole.

Egendorf, Arthur. *Healing from the War: Trauma and Transformation After Vietnam*. Boston: Houghton Mifflin, 1985. Written by a psychologist and Vietnam veteran. Egendorf explores what is necessary for healing to take place for Vietnam vets to overcome their memories of the war.

Haythornthwaite, Philip J. *The World War I Source Book*. London: Arms and Armour, 1992. A good general coverage of World War I, looking at the impact that weapons and conditions on the front had on soldiers.

Krippner, Stanley, and Teresa M. McIntyre. *The Psychological Impact of War Trauma on Civilians: An International Perspective*. Westport, Conn.: Praeger, 2003. As the evolution of warfare in the twentieth century increasingly impacted civilian populations, questions began to arise as to how best to treat their illnesses, which can be very different from those experienced by soldiers.

Justin Corfield

WARFARE, MORALITY, AND JUSTICE

COLLABORATION IN WAR

OVERVIEW

Collaboration in war refers to the willful cooperation of local populations or elites with a foreign invader in a time of war. This can involve "fifth columns"—underground groups coordinated in advance of an invasion—or the impromptu recruitment of puppet regimes and auxiliary military forces in occupied territory. Collaboration is endemic to warfare, but its conflation with treason is a relatively recent Western development. Most scholarly work on the subject focuses on the motivations behind collaboration in the modern era, citing factors such as ideology, internal religious or ethnic divisions, material motives, and basic survival instinct. Both the invader and the collaborator are agents in the process.

SIGNIFICANCE

Invading armies often seek the collaboration of enemy populations in order to limit casualties and expenditure of resources. Subversive activity by collaborators behind enemy lines can hasten the collapse of a defending force. Likewise, by co-opting local administrative personnel, an invader can improve security, exploitation, and communications in its occupied territories at relatively little cost. Regardless of motive, wartime collaboration can result in significant and lasting changes for a population. Whether successful or not, the presence of collaboration may ultimately force a society to redefine itself, both politically and culturally.

HISTORY OF COLLABORATION IN WAR

ANCIENT WORLD

Collaboration has existed in some form as long as groups of people with divided loyalties and survival instincts have been in conflict with one another. Before the rise of the modern nation-state, such behavior did not necessarily have the ugly connotations it has today.

The Greek historian Herodotus (c. 484-c. 425 B.C.E.) demonstrates some concept of collaboration in his account of the Persian Wars, but its significance should not be exaggerated. Numerous Greek towns submitted to the Persians during Xerxes' invasion in 480 B.C.E. Free Greek city-states labeled them "Medizers" (the Greeks referred to Persia as Medea). The Persians gained troops and logistical support from most of the towns they occupied, not out of ideological consensus but for survival. Early resistance was crushed—towns were razed and populations enslaved—prompting widespread compliance. Based on the calculations of Herodotus, 15 percent of Xerxes' force at the Battle of Thermopylae (480 B.C.E.) was Greek. Persian victory at the battle was achieved when Ephialtes, a Greek seeking a reward, showed Xerxes a route through the mountains to outflank the Spartan defenders. Medizing continued even after the defeat of the Persian fleet at Salamis. Greeks provided the shock troops for the Persian forces at the Battle of Plataea in 479 B.C.E. The victorious free Greeks did not seek vengeance upon the Medizers, which suggests that Panhellenism was not yet so advanced for this type of collaboration to be deemed treasonous. If one's primary loyalty lay with one's city-state, Medism was more reflective of opportunistic alliance making than it was of collaboration.

Greek loyalty to the city-state was made evident in the Peloponnesian War (431-404 B.C.E.), fought between Athens and Sparta and their allies. According to Thucydides (c. 459-402 B.C.E.), the war began with an example of collaboration. A small Theban force was able to seize the town of Plataea when a local faction opened the gates at night, hoping to use the Thebans to kill off a rival faction and obtain power for themselves. In this case, collaboration came as the result of internal local politics, but it did not end well for the plotters. When the Plataeans realized how few Thebans there were, they revolted and massacred the foreigners.

The Romans had stronger notions of collaboration. They used the legend of Tarpeia as a warning for potential traitors or collaborators. During the war with the Sabines, Tarpeia, the daughter of the commander defending Rome, let the Sabines into the citadel. According to one of the versions told by Livy (c. 59 B.C.E.-17 C.E.), Tarpeia demanded the heavy gold bands that the Sabines wore on their left arms as payment. Not willing to reward a traitor, the Sabines piled their shields—also worn on their left arms—upon the girl, crushing her to death.

In their later campaigns of expansion, the Romans actively sought the collaboration of local auxiliaries, especially in the form of cavalry, which they lacked. From the point of view of the collaborators, however, such acts did not constitute treason. Troops in auxiliary units were primarily loyal to their leader, who might well choose to ally with the Romans against other tribes for personal gain. Thus, Julius Caesar conquered Gaul with the help of other Gauls, but their tribal nature meant that, like the Greek Medizers, they were more allies than collaborators.

MEDIEVAL WORLD

The medieval period saw few developments in Western concepts of collaboration. Despite the bonds of chivalry, the feudal system ensured that loyalties remained at the level of the individual, between lord and vassal. Small armies serving for short periods of time on expeditions with limited aims provided little opportunity for large-scale collaboration. Hugh of Maine provides a typical example of medieval collaboration. In 1091, Hugh, a vassal of Matilda of Tuscany, informed the Holy Roman Emperor Henry IV of an impending attack, enabling the latter to defeat Matilda's forces at Tricontai.

Religious wars, such as the Crusades, provided the conditions for a broader range of collaboration, but religious motives often coalesced with personal and political ones. Armenian Christians supplied the Crusader armies besieging the Turkish-held city of Antioch in 1097. Their main intention, however, was to gain the Crusaders as allies in their attempt to

break free from the Christian Byzantine Empire and form an independent kingdom in Cilicia. When Antioch fell to the Crusaders in 1098, it was with the help of an Armenian named Firouz, who served in the Turkish garrison but was disgruntled that the local emir had confiscated his wealth. Firouz opened the gates to the city, and other Armenian residents took part in the massacre that ensued against the Turkish population.

MODERN WORLD

The centralization of military and political authority in Europe that followed the 1648 Peace of Westphalia brought new perspectives on collaboration. These developments broadened the scope and ramifications of treason, especially for the nation-states that had risen by the nineteenth century. If primary loyalties were to be directed toward higher legal authorities and broader communities, collaboration with a clearly defined foreign power had greater significance than before. In addition, technological and organizational developments increased the geographic range of wars and public participation within them, creating new opportunities and the likelihood for more types of collaboration.

The age of revolution brought new, ideological motives for collaboration. Napoleon may never have taken his republican rhetoric seriously, but he actively used it to gain the collaboration of different national groups in his campaigns. His invasion of Italy in 1796 saw local radicals rise up against the ancien régime. Similarly, Napoleon's "liberation" of Poland won the support of some nationalistic Polish nobles, including Prince Józef Antoni Poniatowski (1763-1813), who would reach the rank of marshal in Napoleon's Grand Armée. Despite this, the French never attained the level of collaboration they desired within their occupied territories. Because of Napoleon's focus on the exploitation of these countries for the war effort, the reforms and independence desired by collaborators never materialized.

Napoleon's conquests were not equaled until World War II, which solidified modern notions of collaboration. Because so much of Europe and Asia was occupied, collaboration was widespread. Furthermore, because of the brutality represented by

Nazi expansion, this collaboration was imbued with moral connotations that have permanently attached themselves to the concept. For these reasons, World War II provides the best case study to categorize the various types of collaboration in the modern world and to explain the different motives behind them.

World War II introduced a new term for collaborators. During and since the conflict, collaborators came to be referred to as "quislings." The name of the Norwegian collaborator Vidkun Quisling (1887-1945) became synonymous with treasonous collaboration. Interestingly, though, one of the most famous collaborators in history was also one of the most inept. Quisling's Fascist-style National Union Party was politically irrelevant in 1939. Realizing that his only chance of success was through foreign help, Quisling lobbied the Germans to invade Norway. The Germans had their own reasons for an incursion into Scandinavia and initially wanted nothing to do with Quisling, whose value was limited by his lack of popularity. Nonetheless, with the fall of Oslo in April, 1940, Quisling committed the treasonous act of proclaiming himself head of a new Norwegian government. He was a complete failure. His efforts to Nazify the country only fueled resistance, and he never gained independence of command from the German occupation authorities. After the war, the Norwegian court convicted Quisling of treason, and he was executed by firing squad.

Other groups collaborated with the Nazis on ideological grounds, but without subordinating their ideas so completely to German chancellor Adolf Hitler's worldview. French marshal Henri-Philippe Pétain (1856-1951) signed an armistice with the Germans in 1940 and headed the collaborationist French government in Vichy partly out of defeatism and the conviction that he was saving France from an even worse fate. However, Pétain and other Vichy leaders also hoped to institute a patriotic national revolution in France to replace republicanism. Disaffection with the Third Republic had been fairly widespread before the war, which gave the Vichy regime some degree of popular backing until Hitler ordered the complete occupation of France at the end of 1942. Pétain's death penalty after the war was commuted to life imprisonment.

German and Italian occupation forces were able to use religious and ethnic divisions in the Balkans to their advantage, gaining collaborators to help administer and police the conquered territories. A fascist regime was established in Croatia, headed by Ante Pavelić (1889-1959), to free the Axis from the direct occupation of that country. When Pavelić's regime proved incapable of maintaining security against the communist-led partisan movement, the Italians had few qualms against using Orthodox Serbian Četniks as auxiliaries. The Četniks themselves were royalist or nationalist guerrilla fighters opposed to Axis occupation, but they saw communism as the greater evil. These examples demonstrate the frequently ambivalent nature of collaboration.

As the war progressed and partisan resistance became greater, local auxiliaries became increasingly important to Axis policies in occupied Europe. Large numbers were recruited in the occupied Soviet Union—far more, in fact, than the Soviet partisans themselves could muster—more out of the need to feed themselves and their families than out of support for the Nazis, who envisioned their eventual reduction to slavery. It was nonetheless this widespread form of collaboration that Europeans found most difficult to come to grips with after the war. Particularly disconcerting was the predominant role of local auxiliaries in the Holocaust. These forces, rather than German units, were frequently used in the rounding up and execution of Jews in Eastern Europe. As in previous eras, the most important motive behind collaboration during World War II was survival. Although collaboration was widespread, Hitler's ideological aims and overbearing nature ensured that it could never be total.

Collaboration remains an important goal of occupation forces in present operations, though for very different aims and in new ways. In Afghanistan, North Atlantic Treaty Organization (NATO) forces seek the cooperation of village elders in formulating reconstruction plans, thereby promoting the creation of democratic traditions at the local level. This type of collaboration faces the same challenge it did in previous times: the need to balance the aims of the occupier with that of the occupied. Collaboration has always been a two-sided affair.

BOOKS AND ARTICLES

Dean, Martin. *Collaboration in the Holocaust: Crimes of the Local Police in Belorussia and Ukraine, 1941-44*. New York: St. Martin's Press, 2000. Dean catalogs the actions of Belorussian and Ukrainian auxiliaries in the antipartisan campaign and genocide in the east. These forces outnumbered their Nazi colleagues.

Ghazarian, Jacob G. *The Armenian Kingdom in Cilicia During the Crusades: The Integration of Cilician Armenians with the Latins, 1080-1393*. Richmond, Surrey, England: Curzon, 2000. Ghazarian traces Armenian efforts to form an independent kingdom in Cilicia between the eleventh and fourteenth centuries. Part of their strategy was to ally with the Crusaders against their former masters.

Gillis, Daniel. *Collaboration with the Persians*. Wiesbaden, Germany: Franz Steiner, 1979. In one of the few works to deal explicitly with concepts of collaboration in the ancient world, Gillis analyzes the actions of Greek Medizers in the Persian War.

Hoidal, Oddvar K. *Quisling: A Study in Treason*. Oslo: Norwegian University Press, 1989. Hoidal's is the most thorough account of the archetypal collaborator: Vidkun Quisling. Alongside biography, Hoidal ably places Quisling in his Norwegian and European context.

Jackson, Julian. *France: The Dark Years, 1940-1944*. New York: Oxford University Press, 2001. Dividing his focus between collaboration and resistance in occupied France, Jackson argues that the Vichy regime enjoyed some popular backing.

Tomasevich, Jozo. *War and Revolution in Yugoslavia, 1941-1945: Occupation and Collaboration*. Stanford, Calif.: Stanford University Press, 2001. Tomasevich focuses on Pavelić's regime in Croatia, arguing that his collaboration was misguided: The Axis would never have allowed the complete independence Pavelić desired.

Nicolas G. Virtue

GENOCIDE

OVERVIEW

Combining the Greek word *genos* ("race" or "tribe") with the Latin *cide* ("killing"), Raphael Lemkin (1900-1959), an obscure Jewish lawyer and refugee from Nazi-occupied Europe, coined the word "genocide" in 1944. Born near Wołkowysk (now Volkovysk) in the Białystok (Belostok) region of what was then Russian Poland, Lemkin—who developed an early fascination with state-sponsored mass atrocities and subsequently became a crusader for an international law to criminalize and punish what he initially characterized as "barbarity" and "vandalism"—defined genocide in his 1944 book *Axis Rule in Occupied Europe* as "the destruction of a nation or an ethnic group" via "a coordinated plan of different actions aiming at the destruction of essential foundations of the life of national groups, with the aim of annihilating the groups themselves." Though controversial from its birth, Lemkin's term was incorporated into the indictments prepared for the 1945-1946 Nuremberg trials of major Nazi war criminals. Moreover, in 1948, thanks in part to Lemkin's continuing efforts to make genocide a legal crime, the newly established United Nations adopted the Convention on the Prevention and Punishment of Genocide, which declared genocide a crime under international law; enumerated the acts (including murder, causing serious physical or mental harm to group members, intentionally inflicting conditions on groups designed to produce complete or partial destruction, imposing measures aimed at preventing births within groups, and transferring by coercion children from one group to another) that constituted genocide; and declared such acts to be punishable.

SIGNIFICANCE

Building on more than a decade of research and writing on the Holocaust, serious scholarly study of geno-
cide began in the early 1980's. Since that time, historians, political scientists, sociologists, and others have created a distinct field, commonly labeled "genocide studies," which has done much to broaden the world's knowledge and understanding of specific genocides throughout history, as well as to identify the contexts, including war, in which genocide has occurred. In fact, much scholarship argues that genocide and war are "Siamese twins" and therefore should not be treated as separate phenomena, as has frequently been the case. Ample evidence for this assertion can be found throughout history, as war, both international and civil, has time and again created circumstances and conditions that allow perpetrators opportunities to annihilate, either in whole or in substantial part, specific victim groups while facilitating their efforts to do so.

HISTORY OF GENOCIDE

The twentieth century has been characterized as "the century of genocide," with good reason. Several indisputable cases of genocide, as defined by Lemkin, the 1948 U.N. convention, and other sources—notably Nazi Germany's persecution and systematic mass murder of an estimated six million European Jews—date to the twentieth century. However, recent scholarship, specifically that which accepts a broader definition of the term and thus takes a more inclusive approach in identifying instances of genocide, argues that genocide was not exclusive to the twentieth century; that, in fact, it has occurred throughout history; and that examples, frequently intertwined with warfare, are to be found in the ancient world, the medieval world, and the pre-twentieth century modern world.

ANCIENT WORLD

According to an increasing number of scholars, the Assyrians, a highly militaristic people native to northern Mesopotamia, perpetrated genocidal acts during the first millennium B.C.E. Between 1000 and 665, while conquering a vast empire in western Asia, which included their Mesopotamian homeland, much of southern Asia Minor, Syria, Palestine, and Egypt, the Assyrians deliberately massacred entire populations, irrespective of age, gender, and physical condition, and conducted mass deportations, forcibly resettling conquered populations, either in whole or in part. Designed to warn those who might dare resist in the future and/or to eliminate those who had already resisted, the practices of mass murder and deportation—"ethnic cleansing," to use twentieth century terminology—were fundamental to the Assyrian way of war.

Other examples of genocide in the ancient world commonly cited by genocide scholars include atrocities committed by the Athenians against the population of Melos in the fifth century B.C.E. and by the Romans against the Carthaginians in the second century B.C.E. In the former case, Athenian forces captured Melos, an island located in the Sea of Crete, in 416 B.C.E., after which they killed all men deemed capable of bearing arms, enslaved the women and children, and introduced Athenian colonists. In the latter case, Roman military forces destroyed the North African city of Carthage in 216 B.C.E., killed an estimated 150,000 Carthaginians—of a total population of somewhere between 200,000 and 400,000—and poured salt into the land surrounding the city to destroy its arability. What is significant about these cases is that war served as the context for both. The Athenian actions, maybe best characterized as "gendercide," were triggered by Melos's refusal to ally itself with Athens, at that time involved in the Peloponnesian War (431-404 B.C.E.) against Sparta, while those of Rome came at the end of the Third Punic War against Carthage (149-146 B.C.E.) and should be seen as the Roman decision that there would be no fourth contest with their chief rival for dominance in the western Mediterranean.

MEDIEVAL WORLD

During the medieval era, Christian Crusaders perpetrated mass slaughters that some scholars interpret as genocidal. Major targets and victims included Muslims, who were deemed infidels; Jews, who were held responsible for the crucifixion of Jesus; and those Christians who had accepted doctrines and taken positions labeled heretical by the Roman papacy. The First Crusade (1095-1099), launched by Pope Urban II (r. 1088-1099) for the ostensible purpose of reclaiming the Holy Land from the Seljuk Turks, witnessed some 100,000 Crusaders from across western Europe descend upon the Byzantine Empire, rout the Seljuks, and liberate the city of Jerusalem. During their trek to the east, the Crusaders massacred entire Jewish communities, especially those located in the German Rhineland, while in the aftermath of their victory at Jerusalem they put to the sword thousands of Muslims, Jews, and Christian heretics. More than a century later, Pope Innocent III (r. 1198-1216) initiated a crusade against the Albigensians (1209-1229), Christian sectarians in southern France who criticized the Catholic Church's material wealth, advocated clerical poverty, and called for the translation of the Scriptures into vernacular languages. Innocent III's forces destroyed the Albigensian heresy via the mass killing of the sect's adherents and the appropriation of their property for the Catholic Church.

Scholars also attribute genocide to the Mongols, who, after their unification by Genghis Khan (c. 1155 or 1162-1227) at the beginning of the thirteenth century, proceeded to conquer a vast Eurasian empire that stretched from the shores of the Pacific Ocean in the east to the banks of the Danube River in the west and included China, central Asia, portions of the present-day Middle East, the territories of Russia, and parts of eastern Europe. Like the Assyrians of the first millennium B.C.E., the Mongols made mass murder of entire populations—designed to terrorize future targets of attack and conquest into submission—an integral component of their way of war. Contemporary accounts, especially those pertaining to the Mongol conquest of the Russian principalities (1237-1241), paint a gruesome picture of the mass death and absolute devastation that accompanied the "Devil's horsemen."

MODERN WORLD

While evidence for genocide in both the ancient and the medieval worlds is circumstantial, highly problematic, and subject to differing interpretations, evidence for genocide in the modern world is far more conclusive, and thus scholars who investigate modern genocides stand on much firmer ground when they interpret specific cases of mass atrocity as genocide. However, the modern era has its share of so-called disputed, as opposed to denied, genocides, including the annihilation of indigenous peoples during the European conquest of the Americas (fifteenth and sixteenth centuries), the Atlantic slave trade (sixteenth to nineteenth centuries), the Committee of Public Safety's crushing of the Vendée uprising (1793) during the French Revolution, the "rubber terror" (1880's-1890's) of Belgian king Leopold II (r. 1865-1909) in the Congo Free State, the German suppression of the Herero revolt (1904) in southwest Africa, the Ukrainian famine (1932-1933), the Allied strategic bombing campaigns (including the atomic bombings of Hiroshima and Nagasaki) in Europe and Asia during World War II (1939-1945), and the ethnic cleansings conducted by the Serbs in Croatia, Bosnia-Herzegovina, and Kosovo (1991-1999) during the so-called Wars of Yugoslav Succession. What cannot be contested is that the twentieth century witnessed the leaders of the Ottoman Empire commit genocide against the Armenian population of the empire; the leadership of Nazi Germany perpetrate genocide against Europe's Jews and several other victim groups; Pol Pot (1928-1998) and the Khmer Rouge leadership of Cambodia carry out a genocide that targeted the country's ethnic minorities, Buddhist monks, and suspected political opponents; and the Hutu leadership and population of Rwanda engage in genocide against the Tutsi population of the country.

Getty Images

In 1492, countless Jews either were burned alive or expelled from Spain after refusing to convert to Christianity.

What is especially relevant is that in three of these cases—the Armenian genocide, the Nazi genocides, and the Rwandan genocide—war allowed the perpetrators to commit their premeditated crimes.

World War I (1914-1918), generally considered the first "total war," provided the background for the Armenian genocide of 1915, which produced the deaths of somewhere between 1 and 1.5 million people and which wiped out the Armenian communities of Anatolia and historic western Armenia within the Ottoman Empire. Perpetrated by the "Young Turks"—who had seized power in Istanbul in 1908 with the aim of saving the empire, the so-called sick man of Europe, which appeared on the verge of extinction—the assault against the Armenians involved the mass murder of the adult male population and the deportation, primarily by forced marches, of the women and children to the Syrian desert. Those among the Young Turks' leadership most culpable—minister of the interior Mehmed Talât Paşa (1874-1921), minister of war Enver Paşa (1881-1922), and minister of the navy Ahmed Cemal Paşa (1872-1922)—justified these harsh measures by accusing the Armenians of disloyalty and treason, claiming that they had collaborated with the Russian Empire, against whom the Ottomans were at war. In reality, however, the attempted destruction of the Armenian population of the Ottoman Empire must be understood both as the culmination of the escalating persecution of the Armenians that had begun during the reign of Abdülhamid II (r. 1876-1909) and as a component of the Young Turks' program to transform the empire into an homogenous Turkic state based on one people and one faith. War provided Talât and his associates the opportunity to resolve what he and others described as "the Armenian question."

Initiated by Nazi Germany and its fanatical leader Adolf Hitler (1889-1945)—who aspired to effect a global demographic revolution that would allow allegedly racially superior pure-blooded Germans, the so-called Aryans, to dominate the world—World War II (1939-1945) offered the führer and his associates the opportunity to eliminate those peoples deemed racially inferior, biologically defective, and politically and ideologically oppositional. Consequently, the Nazi regime murdered more than 200,000 mentally and physically disabled people (described as "life unworthy of life" and "unproductive eaters"), somewhere between 250,000 and 500,000 Sinti and Roma (labeled "asocial" and "racially inferior"), and several million Poles and Russians (characterized as "subhuman"). The chief targets and chief victims of German genocidal actions, however, were Europe's Jews, whom Hitler held responsible for Germany's defeat of 1918 and for the country's subsequent political and economic problems, and whom he saw as simultaneously the most inferior of races and the single greatest threat to the continued existence of the Aryans. Committing themselves to the "Final Solution of the Jewish Question" in 1941, and thus the physical elimination of the entire Jewish race, the Nazis, with help from collabora-

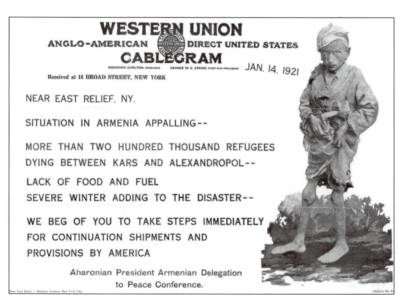

Library of Congress

Threats to Armenian survival in Turkey continued long after the genocide of 1915; residents of the neighboring Armenian homeland faced new challenges when the Soviet Union was formed in the early 1920's, as shown by this 1921 appeal for American help.

National Archives

These starved prisoners died en route to the Dachau concentration camp, while they were packed like sardines in freight cars.

tors from across Europe, proceeded to murder, primarily by mass shootings and mass gassings conducted in specially established death camps, approximately two-thirds of Europe's Jewish population before the Third Reich's military defeat finally brought this genocide—characterized as "unique" by some, "unprecedented" by others—to a conclusion.

At the end of the century, civil war in the central African country of Rwanda served as the context for a genocide characterized by one expert as "in some ways without precedent." Beginning in 1990, the civil war pitted Paul Kagame's (born 1957) Rwandan Patriotic Front, a guerrilla organization formed by Tutsi refugees in Uganda that aimed at restoring Tutsi control in Rwanda, against the Hutu government of Juvénal Habyarimana (1937-1994). In April, 1994, less than one year after an uneasy peace, the Arusha Accords, had been negotiated, Habyarimana was killed when his plane was shot down as it approached Kigali airport. Although responsibility for Habyarimana's assassination remains unresolved, Hutu extremists in the late president's inner circle, the government, and the army—Colonel Théoneste Bagosora (born 1941) in particular—used the event

AP/Wide World Photos

In Rwanda, human skulls on display, many of which show evidence of deep gashes. The killings were the result of the 1994 Rwandan genocide, the mass murders of several hundred thousand Tutsis and Hutu political moderates by Hutus subscribing to the Hutu Power ideology.

to justify a final reckoning with the Tutsi and those Hutu who sympathized with them. Blaming the murder of Habyrimana on Tutsi rebels, the Hutu extremists unleashed the Presidential Guard, the army, and the notorious Interahamwe (Hutu militia) against the "cockroaches" and their supporters. What followed was a "hurricane of death" during which innocent men, women, and children were killed in the most brutal and barbaric of fashions. Though the Hutu per-

petrators ultimately lost power when Kagame's forces seized Kigali in July and failed in their effort to exterminate the Tutsi population, they managed to murder somewhere between 800,000 and 1 million people, roughly 10 percent of Rwanda's population and 75 percent of the Tutsi population, in only one hundred days. As one scholar notes, "the daily killing rate was at least five times that of the Nazi death camps."

BOOKS AND ARTICLES

Bergen, Doris L. *War and Genocide: A Concise History of the Holocaust.* 2d ed. Lanham, Md.: Rowman and Littlefield, 2009. Explains the motives that drove Nazi policy from 1933 to 1945 and demonstrates the link between war and the Third Reich's persecution and murder of Jews and other target groups.

Jones, Adam. *Genocide: A Comprehensive Introduction*. New York: Routledge, 2006. A good beginning point for those interested in the history of genocide and major components of genocide studies.

Lemkin, Raphael. *Axis Rule in Occupied Europe: Laws of Occupation, Analysis of Government, Proposals for Redress*. Washington, D.C.: Carnegie Endowment for International Peace, 1944. The work that introduced genocide to the world.

Markusen, Eric, and David Kopf. *The Holocaust and Strategic Bombing: Genocide and Total War in the Twentieth Century*. Boulder, Colo.: Westview Press, 1995. Focusing on the Nazi murder of Europe's Jews and the Allied bombing of Germany and Japan during World War II, the authors argue against treating genocide and war as separate phenomena.

Shaw, Martin. *War and Genocide: Organized Killing in Modern Society*. Cambridge, England: Polity Press, 2003. Demonstrates the close connection between war and genocide and argues that there exists a fine line between "degenerate war" and genocide in modern history.

Totten, Samuel, William S. Parsons, and Israel W. Charny, eds. *Century of Genocide: Critical Essays and Eyewitness Accounts*. 2d ed. New York: Routledge, 2004. Written by leading experts and accompanied by primary documents and first-person accounts, this compilation of essays examines major twentieth century genocides.

Bruce J. DeHart

MERCENARIES

OVERVIEW

Mercenaries are soldiers who serve not their own country, city-state, tribe, or clan but rather another group, purely for financial gain or other benefits. Most often (but not always), mercenaries are recruited and employed during wars and other conflicts. They can be found among the armies of organizations that lack the military manpower, popular support, or military technology to maintain a sufficiently powerful force drawn from the nation's own citizenry or the group's own members. The use of mercenaries is well documented in many wars throughout history.

Today, mercenaries face legal restrictions under international law: U.N. Resolution 44/34 prohibits the recruitment, training, and employment of mercenaries for purposes of overthrowing a government. Unlike the soldiers of the nation's own army, mercenaries are not guaranteed protection under the Geneva Conventions. Despite this, mercenaries can still be found on the battlefields of Africa and other areas where national political authority is in question and international scrutiny is limited or nonexistent.

SIGNIFICANCE

Typically, the use of mercenaries rises during a period of constant warfare or during the declining years of a kingdom, empire, or country, when they are seen as a ready source of trained military manpower, but falls out of favor during periods of strong governments. Their employment carries political and operational risks, since their only loyalty is to money or plunder and thus that loyalty cannot be ensured when their compensation becomes unreliable during periods of hardship or in the face of heavy losses. Thus, mercenaries have thrived during periods of limited warfare and political instability but have suffered when those conflicts are settled or the political situation has stabilized to a point where concerns about the presence of these armed foreigners with uncertain loyalty outweighs that of potential defeat.

HISTORY OF MERCENARIES

ANCIENT WORLD

The Egyptian Pharaoh Ramses II is the first ruler known to have hired mercenaries. He used some eleven thousand paid "auxiliaries" during his military campaigns in the fourteenth century B.C.E. Indeed, Egypt first started employing mercenaries as scouts and light infantry during the Old Kingdom and continued the practice through the New Kingdom period. Nubian, Syrian, and Canaanite light troops supported most of the Egyptian campaigns in the Levant, even serving as the Pharaoh's personal security detachment.

However, the best-known mercenaries of the pre-Roman era were those of Greece. Greek hoplites and Cretan archers served in the armies of Persia, Egypt, and even Carthage throughout the classical period. Alexander the Great included mercenary archers and Thracian infantry in his army. He also employed Greek mercenaries hired to remain with him for his Bactria and India campaigns after he sent the city-state contingents home. The Balearic Islands provided another source of mercenaries, primarily slingers, and the Nubian kingdom provided mercenary light cavalry units to the Egyptian and Carthaginian empires. Gallic tribesmen also hired out as mercenaries, constituting the bulk of Hannibal's army when he invaded the Italian peninsula.

The Roman Republic and early Roman Empire employed few mercenaries; even their auxiliary troops were considered part of the Roman Army and were recruited from among the empire's population, if not its citizens, although auxiliaries could earn citizenship through their service. However, manpower shortages and political considerations drove the later Roman Empire and its Byzantine successor to recruit entire foreign mercenary contingents into their forces, the best known of which is Byzantium's Varangian Guard of Norsemen. Rome's employment of German tribes to man its army contributed to the empire's fall when the tribal contingents' leaders turned on Rome. Mercenary contingents followed leaders who could deliver pay or plunder.

MEDIEVAL WORLD

The so-called Dark Ages probably saw mercenaries serving under the more aggressive local leaders, who paid with plunder. William the Conqueror included Flemish mercenary archers among his troops when he invaded England in 1066. Crusading armies included mercenaries among their infantry and auxiliary forces. Virtually every kingdom in Europe and North Africa employed mercenaries from the eleventh to the nineteenth century.

Elsewhere, pre-shogunate Japan's fighting clans and the kingdoms of Southeast Asia employed mercenaries to reinforce their armies. The Nungs, an ethnic Chinese group spread across Indochina, served Annamese, Laotian, and Khmai kingdoms of Indochina. India's kingdoms also used mercenaries, and China's Ming Dynasty hired contingents of Manchu and central Asian horsemen to support its armies.

Lacking the resources to train and maintain standing armies, kings and emperors hired mercenaries as required. In Europe, this gave rise to "free companies," or military companies led by "captains of fortune," who hired out their troops for specific contractual periods and often to the highest bidder. Typically, the fighting was ritualized and tightly controlled, with troops fleeing when the battle's momentum turned against them. Trained soldiers were difficult and expensive to replace. Their captains often withdrew their units from the battle lines if

they thought the risks were too great or their casualty rates became excessive. Despite this, mercenary companies prospered across Europe.

By the fifteenth century, some ethnic groups, cantons, and regions became known for their specialized mercenary forces. For example, the Flemish and Genoese were noted as crossbowmen, while England and Wales provided archers. Switzerland's pikemen were perhaps the most famous and popular mercenaries, dominating Europe's battlefields from the fifteenth to the seventeenth century. German principalities recruited and trained competing pikemen

Leonardo da Vinci's 1480 drawing of a condottiero *(literally, "contractor"), a mercenary soldier contracted by Italian city-states and the Papacy between the late Middle Ages and the mid-sixteenth century.*

U.S. Air Force

The World War II group known as the Flying Tigers were sometimes called mercenaries because they were private contractors fighting for a combination of monthly pay and a bounty for every Japanese plane they shot down. The fronts of their airplanes were painted to resemble sharks, as seen in the middleground.

companies called *Landsknechts*. Specially trained musketeers supported the pikemen as armies tried to balance the ratio of "firepower" and "shock" components of their forces. It was the combination of mercenary musketeers and pikemen that ended the mounted knights' reign over Europe's battlefields. However, musket and pike drill required great skill and intense discipline, something feudal levies and few royalist officers had the time, patience, or motivation to achieve.

MODERN WORLD

By 1750, up to two-thirds of Imperial France's army consisted of foreign mercenary contingents and as much as 20 percent of Britain's army was such. The German musketeers and riflemen were the most feared of those contingents, but their use in suppressing civil disorder generally proved counterproductive. In fact, British use of German mercenaries in the American Revolution turned many colonists against the Crown. Revolutionary France's use of mass levies of troops and Napoleon's adroit use of those forces all but ended Europe's large-scale employment of mercenaries. By 1830, France and Spain were the only countries utilizing foreign mercenaries in their armies, although Britain's East India Company employed mercenaries across what became colonial India. That practice, too, ended when India became a crown colony and the East India Company's military components were disbanded.

The rise of nationalism accelerated the decline of mercenaries in Europe, but civil wars in China, Central America, and South America inspired hundreds to hire out to political factions and in some cases try to become local warlords and rulers in their own right. Typically, mercenaries were hired for their technical expertise with specific weapons, such as machine guns and artillery. Mercenary pilots hired themselves out to China's warlords during the post-Republic civil war era, and both Ethiopia and China hired mercenary pilots to fight the Italians and Japanese, respectively, in the 1930's. In fact, General Claire Lee Chennault's famous Flying Tigers were mercenaries fighting for a combination of monthly pay and a bounty for every Japanese plane they shot down.

The post-World War II breakup of Europe's colonial empires provided many opportunities for mercenary employment as newly formed nations sought immediate military expertise either to suppress competing political movements or to secure disputed border areas. "White" mercenaries, so called because they were primarily Caucasian, fought in civil wars across Africa throughout the 1950's and into the 1980's. In some cases, they were successful in ending conflicts without excessive bloodshed, such as in the Congo in 1964, where South African mercenary Michael Hoare led a mercenary unit that worked in concert with Belgian paratroopers to rescue more than one thousand Europeans threatened by a rebel group called the Simba that had become notorious for murdering civilians. Separatist Biafra hired mercenary soldiers and pilots during the Nigerian Civil War (1967-1970), as did Southern Sudan when it tried to break away from the Arab-led regime in Khartoum during the first Sudanese Civil War (1955-1972). Postcolonial Angola saw one of its factions employ mercenaries during the struggle for power after the Portuguese withdrawal in 1974. Funded by the United States through its Central Intelligence Agency (CIA), the operation was a dismal failure, and six of the captured mercenaries were executed in 1976. This was followed later by the aborted mercenary coup in the Seychelles and two mercenary coups in the Comoros Islands, which were overthrown by the French military. The 1980's saw little mercenary activity in Africa, although several Middle Eastern countries hired foreigners for oil-field security and to maintain their high-technology military equipment.

The 1990's saw a resurgence in mercenary activity. Sierra Leone employed a private security firm, Executive Outcomes, to train its troops and suppress several insurgent groups. Although this effort was successful, political pressure from its African neighbors and concerns about the return of mercenary armies to the continent led Sierra Leone to cancel the contract in 1997. More recently and more controversially, in 2004 Zimbabwe arrested a group of sixty-seven mercenaries en route to Equatorial Guinea, where they reputedly were destined to support a coup attempt. Funded by unknown benefactors who allegedly included former British prime minister Margaret Thatcher's son Sir Mark Thatcher, the former South African soldiers were supposed to link up with local regime opponents and place opposition leader Severo Moto in power. Most were sent to prison, where they would await trial on various charges.

The day of mercenaries does not appear to be over, although the bulk of their service today is related more to training and maintenance than to direct combat roles. Private security, or military, companies (PMCs), such as Blackwater, DynCorp International, Executive Outcomes, and Sandline International, have deployed military specialists and security personnel to Afghanistan, Angola, Bosnia, Croatia, Haiti, Indonesia, Iraq, Kuwait, Sierra Leone, and Somalia. Although their industry is considered unsavory, as long as there is a need for specialized military expertise, mercenaries will find employment in areas were political sovereignty is unsettled and the outcome of a conflict is considered critical to someone willing to pay.

BOOKS AND ARTICLES

Griffith, G. T. *Mercenaries of the Hellenistic World*. New York: Arno Press, 1984. Discusses the presence of mercenaries in Greek armies going back to Mycenaean times, who contributed to the development of Greek warfare by bringing with them different styles of fighting.

Lee, Michael Lanning. *Soldiers of Fortune from Ancient Greece to Today*. New York: Presidio Press, 2005. Looks at the history of mercenaries from ancient Egypt to the American use of private military companies in the modern Iraq War.

Percy, Sarah. *Mercenaries: The History of a Norm in International Relations*. Oxford, England: Oxford University Press, 2007. Argues that the use of mercenary armies by nations, although with a long and illustrious history, has been gradually frowned upon in modern international relations.

Scahill, Jeremy. *Blackwater: The Rise of the World's Most Powerful Mercenary Army*. New York: Nation Books, 2007. Traces the history of one particular private military company, its use both in the aftermath of Hurricane Katrina and in the Iraq War, and the controversies that have surrounded the organization.

Thompson, Janice R. *Mercenaries, Pirates and Sovereigns*. Princeton, N.J.: Princeton University Press, 1994. Takes on the idea that modern states are the source of violence by tracing the histories of irregular armies throughout modern conflicts.

Ventner, Al. *War Dog: Fighting Other People's Wars*. Havertown, Pa.: Casemate Publishers, 2006. Looks at the use of mercenary forces in the modern world through an examination of a South African private military company, Executive Outcomes.

Carl Otis Schuster

Peace Movements and Conscientious Objection to War

Overview

Peace movements are a loose assemblage of groups and individuals, often with dissimilar programs but in accord on seeking to reduce conflict or end war by achieving some change in foreign policy. Conscientious objection, termed pacifism in 1901 by the French war opponent Émile Arnaud, can be either the absolute renunciation of war or the opposition in principle to a specific war or governmental program on religious, philosophical, humanitarian, or social-justice grounds. Current historiographical trends include conflict management, which involves writings focused on achieving peace through negotiation, mediation, arbitration, international law, and arms control and disarmament; social reform, which involves writings seeking to change political and economic structures and ways of thinking; and world order transformation, which involves writings on world federation, better economic and environmental relationships, and a common feeling of security.

Significance

Peace movements and conscientious objection are significant concepts in relation to the overall understanding of military conflict and the nature of warfare because of the fear of global annihilation. Estimates put the total number of people killed by organized violence in the twentieth century, both military and civilian, between 167 million and 188 million. This would calculate to be roughly five thousand lives lost every single day for one hundred years. The goal of those engaged in peace efforts is to eliminate or at least restrict armaments, conscription (draft), nuclear proliferation, imperialism, racism, and war itself. Peace movements and pacifists are also part of a social-reform movement, presenting alternatives to the policies they oppose, which call for the elimination all forms of structural violence resulting in death and oppression.

History of Peace Movements and Conscientious Objection

Ancient World

In the ancient world, international relations did not exist. Greek city-states coexisted in a casual manner, moving between hostilities and calm without much distinction. Every four years, ongoing hostilities were interrupted by a truce prohibiting Greeks from making war. The establishment of the Olympic Games was a by-product of this truce. Perhaps the first to secure lasting peace was the Amphictyonic League. City-states that joined agreed not to wage war with one another or cut off another's water supply. The Peloponnesian Wars (431-404 B.C.E.), moreover, generated strong sentiments for peace among the citizens of Athens and Sparta.

In ancient Rome, however, conquest and domination was a way of life. During the first few centuries C.E., Christians were persecuted for refusing to serve in the Roman legions. The early Christian church considered military service as "idolatry" and taught that the renunciation of arms was part of the teachings of Jesus. In the ancient world, though, the idea of peace rarely passed beyond the stage of individual thought and was never an organized endeavor.

Medieval World

During the Middle Ages, the Roman Catholic Church attempted to limit war among Christians on the European continent. Two religious doctrines prevailed in the name of peace: the "Truce of God," which forbade warfare on Sundays and "holy days" (from which derived the modern term "holidays"), and the "Peace of God," which prohibited combat in certain holy places. However, one must not overlook the Church's promotion of the Crusades and the prosecution of "just wars" as conveyed in the fifth century by Saint Augustine in his *De civitate Dei* (413-427; *The City of God*, 1610) and later adapted and explicated upon by Saint Thomas Aquinas in his thirteenth century treatise *Summa theologiae* (c. 1265-1273; *Summa Theologica*, 1911-1921).

The appearance of traditions of absolute pacifism took place during the latter Middle Ages and the Reformation. These traditions were marked by a very strong antistate attitude. The Waldensians in the twelfth century and the sixteenth century Anabaptists were opponents of organized rule and vigorously persecuted by the Catholic Church and the state. The Anabaptists—Mennonites, Moravians, Dunkers, and later the Church of the Brethren—were entirely German-speaking from Central Europe and based their doctrine of nonresistance on what they called *Wehrlosigkeit*, which meant renunciation of war and refusal to participate in politics.

MODERN WORLD

The historical origins of peace movements as they are known today began during the Thirty Years' War (1618-1648) in Europe. The gradual formation of nation-states, along with the development of professional armies in support of European monarchs, led some thinkers to question the desirability of society's militarization. One of the first European thinkers to question the need for large standing armies was the Dutch jurist Hugo Grotius (1583-1645). Witnessing the expansion of large armies on the continent that far outnumbered his native population, Grotius wrote *De jure belli ac pacis* (1625; *On the Law of War and Peace*, 1654). Although he recognized the prospects for international war, his work was the first to draw a sharp distinction between what was war and what was peace.

Later in the seventeenth century, pacifist sects relying on religious grounds of conscientious objection transplanted their beliefs in the New World. The best-known American sectarian peace group was the Society of Friends (originally founded in England by George Fox around 1650). Led by William Penn, who won a large tract of land from the king of England and called his settlement Pennsylvania in the 1680's, the Friends (Quakers) believed that civil authority should flow directly from the power of the people's experience of "inner light" (direct personal knowledge of the good). What drew them together were their common hatred of war and violence, belief in nonresistance as a way of life, and love for Christ. One of the most famous proponents of Quaker pacifism was the eighteenth century Friend from Mount Holly, New Jersey, John Woolman, who preached against slavery and criticized raising taxes for war purposes. During the American Revolution (1775-1783), Quakers made conscientious objection (later known as passive nonresistance) an effective philosophical instrument.

Meanwhile, in Europe, at the end of the eighteenth century, one of the most important philosophical contributions to the principles of peace appeared. In *Zum ewigen Frieden: Ein philosophischer Entwurf* (1795; *Perpetual Peace: A Philosophic Essay*, 1897), German philosopher Immanuel Kant (1724-1804) laid the empirical groundwork for examining the necessary conditions for peace. Kant focused specifically on the dangers of armaments. He also argued that as society advances, reason and logic will further moral perfection. A product of the eighteenth century Enlightenment, Kant insisted that universal truths are independent of time and place, and because of humanity's ability to utilize rational principles, certain fixed principles, such as peace, will eventually prevail.

At the conclusion of the War of 1812 and the end of the Napoleonic conquests on the European continent in 1815, the first organized peace movements were formed in the United States and Great Britain. In the United States, an organized endeavor that was both religious and humanitarian, but not specifically tied to any one sectarian group, emerged under the leadership of New England sea captain and Harvard graduate William Ladd (1778-1841). Perhaps the world's first national peace organization, the American Peace Society coordinated activities among the fifty or so peace groups. In England, the London Peace Society led the way, composed mainly of Quakers. On the European continent, moreover, the ideas for the establishment of permanent arbitration tribunals and a federation of nations advocated by thinkers such as Pierre Dubois (c. 1255-c. 1312) and the Abbé de Saint-Pierre (1658-1743) were widely popularized. The Holy Alliance of Czar Alexander I also seemed to be an indication that such ideas might be workable. In large measure, nineteenth century organized peace movements were products of the United States and Great Britain and would remain so for much of the twentieth century as well.

One of the most important advocates of peace during this period was the "Learned Blacksmith" from Connecticut, Elihu Burritt (1810-1879). During the Oregon Crisis between Britain and the United States in the mid-1840's, Burritt cooperated with Friends and other peace activists in England in an exchange of "friendly addresses." This exchange was carried out between British and American cities and involved merchants, ministers, laborers, and women. Burritt himself carried two "friendly addresses"—with impressive lists of signatures—one from Edinburgh, Scotland, and another from women of Exeter, England, to Washington, D.C., where Senator John C. Calhoun and other senators applauded this "popular handshaking" across the Atlantic. In addition, Burritt founded the largest and most uncompromising nonsectarian pacifist organization yet known among Western peace seekers: the League of Universal Brotherhood. By 1850, this "world peace society" had collected seventy thousand British and American signatures for its pledge of complete disavowal of war.

In the aftermath of the American Civil War (1861-1865), European peacemaking efforts had a profound impact on the American quest to eliminate war. Attempts to promote the importance of international law in Europe occurred roughly at the same time that the American Peace Society began widespread propaganda for arbitration. Sir Randal Cre-

mer (1828-1908), a tireless British peace advocate and labor organizer who was instrumental in furthering Anglo-American arbitration negotiations, organized a vast peace congress in Paris in 1878. With spokespersons from thirteen countries, this congress called for a court of arbitration and for an international commission to estimate the armaments of each nation. The congress placed emphasis on the cost of wars to workers and the need for strike action to prevent war, proposing that the peace societies in various countries be federated. Subsequently, Cremer and Frédéric Passy (1822-1912) of France established the Inter-Parliamentary Union in 1889, and their efforts led to the Lake Mohonk Conferences on International Arbitration in the United States (founded 1895). The work of European and American arbitrationists and internationalists led to the creation of 130 new international nongovernmental organizations in the last quarter of the nineteenth century—and, as peace historians have pointed out, to the very term "international organization."

Antidraft riots in New York City in 1863.

During these same years, inspired by the movement for international arbitration, European peace activists also created their own international network. Though not organized as peace movements the way they were in Great Britain and the United States, peace societies sprang up in France, Italy, Germany, Belgium, Denmark, Sweden, Norway, and even czarist Russia, thanks in large part to Count Leo Tolstoy (who would become most famous for his novel *Voyna i mir* [1865-1869; *War and Peace*, 1886]). In 1892, peace societies created the International Peace Bureau in Bern, Switzerland, as a clearinghouse for publicizing their differing philosophies. Until 1914, peace workers lectured throughout the Continent, wrote books and pamphlets criticizing military expenditures, developed peace curricula for schools, and held meetings nearly every year, at which peace resolutions were submitted to foreign ministries.

The movement for international arbitration also became widely popular in the United States at the start of the twentieth century. Among the most influential organizations were the American Society of International Law, the Carnegie Endowment for International Peace (CEIP), and the World Peace Foundation (WPF). These organizations were specialized agencies for transmitting the experts' knowledge of peace to the masses and encouraging conciliatory gestures among governments. At the same time, the Hague Peace Conferences of 1899 and 1907 created the hope that disarmament and arbitration would end wars forever.

The outbreak of World War I in 1914, however, presented serious challenges to the rights of conscientious objectors as well as the two major organized peace movements. In Great Britain, Edward Grubb (1854-1939), a theologian, Friend, and social reformer, played a prominent role in establishing the No-Conscription Fellowship (NCF). The NCF waged a vigorous battle in its efforts to protect the right of conscience and in breaking down barriers separating religious and nonreligious war resisters. Largely through Grubb's efforts, the British government reexamined its views on the treatment of war resisters and absolute pacifists, adopting an entirely new policy that recognized their legal rights to exemption from state service.

During the war, the National Peace Council (NPC) served as the arm of the peace movement in England and the most recognizable peace organization in Europe. Founded in 1908, the NPC was a coalition of voluntary organizations that acted as a check on the government's attempt to militarize the populace and stifle dissent. The NPC encouraged an end to the conflict and looked forward to the establishment of some type of international peacekeeping organization. After the war, moreover, the establishment of the Peace Pledge Union in the 1930's secured numerous adherents to its pledge: "I renounce war and will never support or sanction another."

In the United States, the administration of President Woodrow Wilson respected the rights of the historic peace churches. However, nonreligious war resisters received harsh treatment and imprisonment. Many were beaten and placed in strip cells at federal prisons such as Alcatraz and Fort Leavenworth. Those found guilty of violating the Selective Service Act went to prison. When findings with respect to the treatment of imprisoned war objectors became public, President Wilson issued an executive order requiring the elimination of such harsh penalties.

The organized peace movement in the United States became divided between liberal internationalists who supported the war and pacifists who opposed it. Ultimately, this division resulted in a reorganized peace movement that would be led by groups such as the religious Fellowship of Reconciliation (originally founded in England in 1915 but establishing headquarters in the United States after World War I), the Women's International League for Peace and Freedom (the first American female to receive the Nobel Peace Prize, Jane Addams, was a member), the War Resisters League, and the American Friends Service Committee. These new organizations were born during and immediately after the war and considered peace as something more than the absence of armed conflict. Their creation defined the "modern" peace movement in America.

The leading peace advocate of the "modern" movement during this period was Abraham J. Muste (1885-1967). Labeled "America's No. 1 Pacifist" by *Time* magazine in 1939, Muste elevated peace action and connected it to labor and economic issues. His form of nonresistance would later inspire a peace strategy known as direct action. Muste played a prominent role in the Christian nonviolence movement in twentieth century America and, with the Fellowship of Reconciliation, established effective relationships with peace societies in Europe, East Asia, and South Africa.

By the late 1930's, as fascism and militarism took hold in Europe, organized peace movements—still located in Britain and the United States—once again split apart. Devoted pacifists opposed the use of arms, while internationalists considered the defeat of German chancellor Adolf Hitler and Japanese aggression a necessity for establishing world order. Unlike Great Britain, which had come to grips with the issue of conscientious objection, the United States required some form of alternative service to bearing arms. A Civilian Public Service camps program was established and paid for by the Historic Peace Churches. Still, this approach did not satisfy absolute pacifists, and the controversy continued for the duration of the war.

After World War II (1939-1945), the reality of atomic and then nuclear warfare, highlighted by the Cold War, led to the establishment of new peace groups in the United States, such as the Committee for a SANE Nuclear Policy, as well as disarmament groups on the European continent such as Great Britain's Direct Action Committee, which sponsored the annual Aldermaston marches. These peace organizations were committed to halting aboveground nuclear testing and encouraged disarmament talks between the principal nuclear powers. In addition, both the success of the nonviolence movement of Mohandas K. (Mahatma) Gandhi in India and antinuclear awareness promoted by the *hibakusha*, Japanese survivors of Hiroshima and Nagasaki, influenced the peace movement's role in Third World countries.

The most dramatic peace protests of the twentieth century took place in the United States during the

NARA

A young woman offers a flower to a military policeman at the Pentagon during an anti-Vietnam War demonstration in 1967.

Vietnam War (1961-1975). Massive antiwar demonstrations frequently took place in major cities, and direct action strategies were carried out to disrupt the machinery of government. Opposition to the war was widespread on college campuses. To a considerable extent, the antiwar movement was fueled by resentment over the draft as many young men questioned the legitimacy of the war. As a result, U.S. Supreme Court decisions gave wider latitude to the meaning of conscientious objection and no longer adopted a rigorous policy of alternative service.

The 1980's witnessed the peace movement in the United States and on the European continent calling for a freeze on the deployment of missiles and halting development of more nuclear warheads. What provoked such a sharp response was the growth of antinuclear movements in Western Europe. In 1981, massive protests were carried out in various Western European cities aimed at stopping a plan by the North Atlantic Treaty Organization (NATO) to deploy intermediate-range nuclear missiles in five European nations. Major demonstrations were conducted in Paris, Rome, London, Amsterdam, Brussels, and Bonn. British historian and left-wing social critic E. P. Thompson (1924-1993) became the leading intellectual light of the movement against nuclear weapons. He rallied the British peace movement and took the lead in numerous Aldermaston marches. His writings also inspired American pacifists, who initiated a series of direct action campaigns aimed at defense plants, submarine bases, missile sites, and the Pentagon. In America, moreover, scientist Randall Caroline Forsberg (1943-2007) led the way in calling for a nuclear freeze.

In June, 1982, the movement for a nuclear freeze was dramatically illustrated at a disarmament rally in New York City. More than 700,000 people participated, making it the largest political demonstration in U.S. history. The campaign's grassroots impact was enormous as the freeze referendum appeared on state ballots across the nation. "It represented," in the words of one reporter, "the largest referendum on any issue in American history; sixty per cent of the voters supported the resolution." Although the freeze

movement did not achieve its ultimate goal, the antinuclear arms movement did result in a change in attitude, both at home and abroad. It provided a badly needed political platform in support of arms control and disarmament.

The wars in Iraq and Afghanistan that began after the terrorist attacks of September 11, 2001, have also witnessed massive antiwar demonstrations. Among the salient aspects of this peace movement have been the sheer size of protests and its global scale. Prior to the commencement of military action in Iraq in 2003, peace demonstrations were larger than those that opposed the Vietnam War at its height. One of the unique aspects of this peace movement, particularly in the United States, has been its online organizing, which has helped many antiwar groups succeed in their efforts to mobilize at the grass roots. This peace movement has emerged as a force for organizing,

Getty Images

In San Francisco, people of all ages demonstrate against the imminent U.S. invasion of Iraq in 2003.

raising money, and influencing politicians and the media through blogs and e-mail messages. Using conference calls and e-mail messages to the U.S. Congress are new weapons for these protest movements, as peace workers aim to influence votes rather than gather in mass demonstrations.

Thus, the peace movement that emerged after 9/11 has embraced the notion of advancing international collective political struggles in novel as well as traditional ways. The interconnectedness associated with globalization and new communication technologies has elicited new opportunities to forge a global collective identity. No longer are organized peace movements primarily the domain of the United States and Great Britain alone. While military theorists believe that the future of warfare will revolve around social and communication networks worldwide, antiwar groups are demonstrating that theory as they get out the message of peace and justice.

One of the most important developments involving the issue of conscientious objection is that governments have moved away from a strict interpretation of "conscience" based on religion to a more secular understanding of people's views regarding a particular war. With respect to peace movements, it is safe to say that their importance has grown globally in size and stature, given the realities of modern warfare and the possibilities for nuclear annihilation. No longer are peace movements confined to nations composed of traditional peace societies and organizations. While peace movements, historically, may not have been effective in preventing all wars, it is clear that they have been responsible for informing publics as to the destructiveness of modern warfare.

BOOKS AND ARTICLES

Beales, A. F. C. *The History of Peace: A Short Account of the Organized Movements for International Peace.* New York: Dial Press, 1931. A survey of the peace movements in the United States and Great Britain to World War I, with primary emphasis on the London Peace Society.

Brock, Peter, and Nigel Young. *Pacifism in the Twentieth Century.* Syracuse, N.Y.: Syracuse University Press, 1999. A revised and expanded version of one of Brock's earlier works, *Twentieth Century Pacifism* (1970), analyzing pacifist ideals and peace movements throughout the twentieth century in Europe and the United States.

Carroll, Bernice, Clinton F. Fink, and Jane E. Mohraz, eds. *Peace and War: A Guide to Bibliographies.* Santa Barbara, Calif.: ABC-CLIO, 1983. A massive annotated bibliography covering topics on peace and war from 1785 to 1980 from a transnational perspective.

Chatfield, Charles. *The American Peace Movement: Ideals and Activism.* New York: Twayne, 1992. A historical survey of the organized sectarian movement to the 1980's campaign against nuclear weapons through the lens of social movement theory.

Cooper, Sandi. *Patriotic Pacifism: Waging War on War in Europe, 1815-1914.* New York: Oxford University Press, 1991. Examines the role of citizen peace activism by focusing on national and international societies, schools and curricula, and the effects of peace movements on the political process in Europe during this period.

Cortright, David. *Peace: A History of Movements and Ideas.* New York: Cambridge University Press, 2008. A valuable work discussing the meaning of peace, origins of peace societies, and internationalism, with an emphasis on religion, democracy, social justice, morality, and disarmament.

DeBenedetti, Charles. *The Peace Reform in American History.* Bloomington: Indiana University Press, 1980. Expanding and updating the classic work by Merle Curti, *Peace or War: The American Struggle, 1636-1936* (1936), this survey emphasizes peace work as part of the larger reform movement in American society.

Ferrell, Robert H. "Peace Movements." In *Encyclopedia of American Foreign Policy*, edited by Alexander DeConde et al. New York: Charles Scribner's Sons, 2002. Offers a brief overview of the origins of peace movements and American foreign policy efforts in the realm of international relations.

Howlett, Charles F., and Robbie Lieberman. *A History of the American Peace Movement from Colonial Times to the Present*. Lewiston, N.Y.: Edwin Mellen Press, 2008. The most comprehensive survey of the struggle for peace and justice in America to date, with an emphasis on achieving social and economic justice; contains a thirty-two-page bibliographic essay on peace scholarship.

Wittner, Lawrence S. *Confronting the Bomb: A Short History of the World Nuclear Disarmament Movement*. Stanford, Calif.: Stanford University Press, 2009. An abridged version of Wittner's award-winning trilogy *The Struggle Against the Bomb*, which stresses the effectiveness of grassroots movements worldwide in challenging and thwarting the nuclear desires and ambitions of the great powers.

Charles F. Howlett

PRISONERS AND WAR

OVERVIEW

The four Geneva Conventions of 1949 and their Protocol I of 1977 constitute the legislation covering the protection of war victims. "Lawful combatants" who fall into the hands of the enemy either because they surrender or because they are wounded, sick, or shipwrecked have entitlement to the status of prisoners of war. The capturers must intern them in prisoner-of-war camps, which must be located far from the combat zone. The capturers must hold prisoners in good health and treat them humanely. Prisoners also have a set of rights, which the Third Geneva Convention spells out in detail—for example, against violence, intimidation, or insult.

SIGNIFICANCE

The recognition of individuals having rights as prisoners of war has evolved along with the changing nature of warfare and more broadly with the recognition and development of universal individual human rights.

Library of Congress

Indian prisoners are marched away from their homeland by U.S. troops under the command of General George Custer. The U.S. warfare against and removal of Native Americans throughout the nation constituted one of the most shameful legacies of American history.

HISTORY OF PRISONERS OF WAR

ANCIENT WORLD

Economies of the classical world had slave labor as their basis. A person's wealth and status typically corresponded to the number of slaves he or she owned. Prisoners constituted booty from war and had value as such; they were considered loot and became chattel. Prisoners were therefore kept alive because they were valuable, but they had no rights. They were tools with voices.

MEDIEVAL WORLD

The chivalric code in feudalism was a system of rules regulating behavior between the nobility, including their treatment as prisoners of war. Nobles captured in battle were valuable hostages who could be ransomed by their fiefdoms. The members of lower social orders captured in war who had no access to economic resources for their own ransom therefore had no rights, were a burden, and were treated as such.

MODERN WORLD

Until the modern era, the devices available for mutual enforcement of the traditional laws of warfare included "belligerent reprisals" (a reprisal is a breach of international law by one state in return for another breach). This barbaric instrument included maltreatment of prisoners of war. Belligerent reprisals against prisoners of war and innocent civilians are now universally illegal but still frequently occur.

Article 4 of the Third Geneva Convention relative to the treatment of prisoners was ratified in Geneva, Switzerland, on August 12, 1949, and entered into force generally on October 21, 1950. It defines "prisoners of war" as persons belonging to one of the following categories, who have fallen into "the power of the enemy":

(1) Members of the armed forces of a Party to the conflict as well as members of militias or volunteer corps forming part of such armed forces.

(2) Members of other militias and members of other volunteer corps, including those of organized resistance movements, belonging to a Party to the conflict and operating in or outside their own territory, even if this territory is occupied, provided that such militias or volunteer corps, including such organized resistance movements, fulfill the following conditions: (a) That of being commanded by a person responsible for his subordinates; (b) That of having a fixed distinctive sign recognizable at a distance; (c) That of carrying arms openly; (d) That of conducting their operations in accordance with the laws and customs of war.

(3) Members of regular armed forces who profess allegiance to a government or an authority not recognized by the Detaining Power.

(4) Persons who accompany the armed forces without actually being members thereof, such as civilian members of military aircraft crews, war correspondents, supply contractors, members of labour units or of services responsible for the welfare of the armed forces, provided that they have received authorization from the armed forces which they accompany, who shall provide them for that purpose with an identity card similar to the annexed model [sic].

(5) Members of crews, including masters, pilots and apprentices, of the merchant marine and the crews of civil aircraft of the Parties to the conflict, who do not benefit by more favorable treatment under any other provisions of international law.

(6) Inhabitants of a nonoccupied territory, who on the approach of the enemy spontaneously take up arms to resist the invading forces, without having had time to form themselves into regular armed units, provided they carry arms openly and respect the laws and customs of war.

According to legal scholar Antonio Cassese, in its decision in the case of *Kupreskic et al.* the International Criminal Tribunal for the former Yugoslavia (ICTY, 2000) restated, and the international community widely accepts, that the 1949 Geneva Conventions lay down universal, international community obligations. Article 1, which is common to all four Conventions, obliges any state "contracting Party" to the Geneva Conventions "to respect and ensure respect" for the Conventions "in all circumstances." All states are under obligation to demand cessation of serious violation of the Conventions, as well as to demand punishment of the culprits, even if not directly engaged as belligerents in the conflict.

Other forms of "grave breaches" of the laws of warfare in the Geneva Conventions include refusing quarter to peoples wanting to surrender, the use of weapons that international law prohibits, and the torture of captured enemies in order to obtain information. Typically only international tribunals or the national jurisdiction of the adversary prosecutes systematic, grave breaches, also called "system criminality."

The Conventions institute the requirement that the countries that have signed on to the Conventions, known as states parties, act to repress systematic criminality occurring anywhere. This instrument involves the condemnation of an entire system of government for misbehavior involving the highest authorities in place in a country. No state legal system used this legal instrument until forty years after it came into force. States parties began resorting to it subsequent to the work of the ICTY and the International Criminal Tribunal for Rwanda in the 1990's. Still, national courts have refrained from claiming universal jurisdiction over systematic violations of the Conventions regarding treatment of prisoners of war, wherever they occur. They have confined themselves to the more traditional, territorial forms of their jurisdiction in practice for prosecuting grave breaches of the Geneva Conventions, using universal jurisdiction only if the state of a court had enacted national legislation that allows it.

The development of traditional international law historically shows that the interest of the Great Powers has been to exclude from the category of "lawful combatants" any person who is not a member of a regular army. Since the second half of the twentieth century began, the Great Powers have fought numerous "brushfire" wars, where their large, professional, standing armies invade a smaller country, usually defended by "irregular" or "insurgent" forces. During the nineteenth century, small and medium-sized powers demanded international legal concessions to recognize the role of militias and volunteer corps, as well as for the entire civilian populations, as lawful combatants. They thereby succeeded in preventing the Great Powers from obtaining sovereign rights over the territory the Great Power had invaded, since control of the territory was often still contested by an irregular, but legally recognized, fighting force.

This compromise granted the status of lawful combatant not only to regular armies but also to militias and volunteer corps. For combatants from a *levée en masse*—those who spontaneously take up arms to resist an invading army without the time to organize themselves—only two conditions are necessary to be a lawful combatant and therefore to hold rights as a prisoner of war: (1) to carry arms openly, and (2) to respect the laws and customs of war, including clear visible differentiation of military personnel from the civilian population.

Until World War II, mainly regular armies fought wars. In 1949, the Third Geneva Convention added in Article 4.A.2 a new category of irregular, lawful combatant holding the right to prisoner-of-war status: partisans, that is, "organized resistance movements, belonging to a party to the conflict and operating in or outside their own territory, even if this

U.S. Department of Defense

A U.S. POW is interrogated by a North Vietnamese officer in 1973, during the Vietnam War.

AP/Wide World Photos

An Iraqi POW at Abu Ghraib prison in Baghdad was forced to stand on a box, arms outstretched, in one of several cases of abusive treatment later litigated under the Uniform Code of Military Justice.

instead allowing the mere wearing of an insignia or any outward token, along with the open carrying of weapons, to signify combatant status. These requirements can be met either during or immediately prior to an attack. If combatants fail to fulfill the insignia or weapons-bearing requirement, they are still entitled to prisoner-of-war treatment, but they become vulnerable to punishment for violating Article 44.3.

The 1977 protocol relaxed these requirements further with regard to such situations as "wars of national liberation" and "military occupation." In these situations, the second sentence of Article 44.3 requests only that a combatant carry arms openly "(a) during each military engagement, and (b) during such time as he is visible to the adversary while he is engaged in a military deployment preceding the launching of an attack in which he is able to participate." If combatants are not satisfying the second sentence of Article 44.3, and the opposing forces capture them in the course of a war of national liberation or in territory under occupation, they then forfeit their status of lawful combatants and therefore cannot enjoy prisoner-of-war treatment. Therefore, someone who hides a gun and draws it to fire on occupying soldiers loses prisoner-of-war status if he or she was, in fact, part of a military operation. If the combatant is a disguised, failed suicide bomber as part of a planned military operation, then he or she also logically loses prisoner-of-war status. By contrast, if the combatant acted spontaneously and on his or her own, then he or she still receives prisoner-of-war status.

The adoption of Article 47 at the Geneva Conference (leading to the 1977 Protocol) constituted official recognition in paragraph 1 that "a mercenary shall not have the right to be a combatant or a prisoner of war." The definition of prisoners of war came under challenge with the development of the concept of "unlawful combatant" to refer to irregulars who refuse to wear identification markers or who openly carry weapons in order to identify and differentiate themselves from the civilian population. As a result,

territory is occupied"; partisans must have a direct link to a party in the conflict.

The legal debate over irregular, guerrilla fighters became particularly important after 1949, with the rise of guerrilla warfare within the framework of interstate wars or wars of national liberation. The debate led the 1974-1977 Geneva Convention negotiations to adopt a compromise formula: The combatants also "are obliged to distinguish themselves from the civilian population while they are engaged in an attack or in a military operation preparatory to an attack" (Article 44.3, first sentence). This formula relaxes the "distinction from civilians" requirement, the claim of the U.S. government during the administration of President George W. Bush was that such prisoners did not have prisoner-of-war status under the Geneva Conventions. Granting this status would also imply granting political recognition to the political authorities on behalf of whom they were agents. To ensure that they were not subject to U.S. legal state responsibility to adhere to the Geneva Conventions in their treatment, many were interned at Guantánamo Bay, Cuba, to keep them outside U.S. territorial legal jurisdiction.

For the purpose of safeguarding their interests and impelling adversaries to abide by international law, including treatment of their prisoners of war, the 1949 Geneva Conventions codified and improved on international practice with regard to the designation of "Protecting Powers" by belligerents for ensuring humanitarian treatment of their prisoners. Traditionally, each of the belligerents could appoint a third state as a Protecting Power, but the consent of both belligerents was necessary. An advance of the 1949 Convention was in the provision for "Substitutes for the Protecting Powers," declaring that the Detaining Power (the state detaining the enemy wounded, shipwrecked, prisoners of war, or civilians) is under the obligation to accept "the offer of the services of a humanitarian organization, such as the International Committee of the Red Cross, to assume the humanitarian functions performed by Protecting Powers under the present Convention."

BOOKS AND ARTICLES

Burrows, Edwin G. *Forgotten Patriots: The Untold Story of American Prisoners During the Revolutionary War*. New York: Basic Books, 2008. Tells the story of the approximately twenty-five thousand members of the Continental Army who were held as prisoners of war in New York City. Estimates are that some 70 percent of those prisoners died, totaling more than the number of soldiers who died in battle.

Gillispie, James M. *Andersonvilles of the North: The Myths and Realities of Northern Treatment of Civil War Confederate Prisoners*. Denton: University of North Texas Press, 2008. Both Southern and Northern captors held large numbers of prisoners of war during the Civil War and were vilified by those they held. This study does for Northern captors what other studies have done for places like the Southern prison at Andersonville: It shows that they were far less cruel and oppressive than their image.

Krammer, Arnold. *Prisoners of War: A Reference Handbook*. Westport, Conn.: Praeger, 2008. A good, general history of prisoners of war from ancient times to the modern era.

LaGrandeur, Philip. *We Flew, We Fell, We Lived: The Remarkable Reminiscences of Second World War Evaders and Prisoners of War*. London: Grub Street, 2007. Presents the stories of forty soldiers' experiences in Nazi prisoner-of-war camps.

Lloyd, Clive L. *A History of Napoleonic and American Prisoners of War, 1756-1816: Hulk, Depot, and Parole*. Woodbridge, Suffolk, England: Antique Collectors' Club, 2007. One of the only sources on the experiences of prisoners of war during the European and American conflicts of the late eighteenth and early nineteenth centuries.

MacDougall, Ian. *All Men Are Brethren*. Edinburgh: Tuckwell Press, 2009. Discusses various parts of the experiences of French prisoners of war held in Scotland during the Napoleonic Wars.

Spiller, Harry. *American POWs in World War II: Twelve Personal Accounts of Captivity by Germany and Japan*. Jefferson, N.C.: McFarland, 2009. Twelve prisoners of war during World War II describe their experiences, recounting harrowing tales of forced labor, disease, and brutality.

Benedict E. DeDominicis

WAR CRIMES AND MILITARY JUSTICE

OVERVIEW

Humans have committed war crimes against one another since wars were fought with clubs and stones, and for centuries war crimes were accepted as part of the horrendous price of waging war. As war evolved, so did a body of treaties and laws that sought to regulate the treatment of soldiers and civilians involved in war. The Hague Conventions were international treaties negotiated at the First and Second Peace Conferences at The Hague, Netherlands, in 1899 and 1907, and were, along with the Geneva Conventions, among the first formal statements of the laws of war and war crimes in international law. Article 147 of the Fourth Geneva Convention defines war crimes as:

> Willful killing, torture or inhuman treatment including . . . willfully causing great suffering or serious injury to body or health, unlawful deportation or transfer or unlawful confinement of a protected person of the rights of fair and regular trial, . . . taking of hostages and extensive destruction and appropriation of property, not justified by military necessity and carried out unlawfully and wantonly.

International lawyers stipulate that this is the basic definition of war crimes.

Since war crimes are associated with war, military tribunals or military commissions are used to try people in military custody or those accused of violating a law of war. Courts-martial generally have jurisdiction over members of their own military. Military tribunals usually provide quick trials under the conditions of war, but critics say these trials occur at the expense of justice. Military tribunals do not satisfy most protections and guarantees of the U.S. Bill of Rights, but many presidents of the United States have used them and Congress has authorized them.

SIGNIFICANCE

World War II brought sweeping changes to populations and places and new definitions and understandings of war crimes. This global conflict transformed the concept of war crimes, necessitating a practical means of defining them and determining the punishments for them. Chief among the reasons for this transformation were the Nazi murders of seven million people, mainly Jews, and the Japanese murders and mistreatment of both civilians and prisons of war. The Allied powers prosecuted the Nazis for their war crimes at the Nuremberg Trials in 1945 and 1946, and twelve Nazi leaders were executed as a result. Japanese perpetrators were also tried, in Tokyo in 1948, and seven Japanese commanders were hanged, although Japanese emperor Hirohito was excluded from the prosecutions.

The idea that an individual can be held responsible for the actions of a country or that nation's soldiers is the core concept of war crimes. Genocide, crimes against humanity, and mistreatment of civilians or combatants during war all fall under the category of war crimes, with genocide being the most severe of these crimes. The trials at Nuremberg and Tokyo set the precedents for the cases that the modern-day tribunal in The Hague hears.

Since World War II, the issue of war crimes has become even more pressing with the outbreak of smaller wars all over the globe. The United Nations established tribunals to try crimes against humanity in the former Yugoslavia and in Rwanda. The U.S. Senate, on March 13, 1998, unanimously passed a resolution urging the United Nations to create a tribunal to indict and try Saddam Hussein as an international war criminal for "his crimes against humanity." Congress also passed the War Crimes Act of 1996, which defines and punishes offenses against the law of nations and violations of both the Geneva and Hague conventions. This U.S. law granted jurisdiction over these war crimes to federal district courts but did not intend for the act to override the long-standing jurisdiction of American military commissions and general courts-martial over war crimes.

HISTORY OF WAR CRIMES AND MILITARY JUSTICE

ANCIENT WORLD

The ancient world did not have a codified definition of war crimes. The nature of warfare guaranteed that war crimes were committed in almost every war fought, and both religious and civil leaders were often guilty of war crimes, at least by their modern definition.

The Massacre of Thessalonica provides one example. In 390 C.E., the citizens of the Greek city Thessalonica rose in revolt against the ruling Romans, and Emperor Theodosius I took immediate action. The flash point of the uprising occurred when Botheric, a Gothic general in the emperor's army, ordered a popular charioteer arrested for trying to seduce a servant of the emperor or the general himself. The charioteer went to prison, but the citizens of Thessalonica demanded his release. In the following chaos, Botheric was killed, and then the emperor intervened and ordered executions. The emperor's intervention came too late, and angry Gothic troops massacred seven thousand people in Thessalonica's hippodrome.

This event exemplifies issues that modern theorists of war crimes and debaters over the power of military tribunals are still addressing: How should retaliatory actions during war be defined, and who should determine the punishment of the perpetrators? Theodosius I ruled Rome, but according to the Catholic Church, he had to answer to the Supreme Being. In fact, the Church excommunicated Theodosius I and readmitted him to the Eucharist only after he had spent several months in public penance.

MEDIEVAL WORLD

During medieval times, either kings or military commanders in charge of campaigns issued ordinances of war, which laid down the ground rules governing conflicts. Many of these ordinances dealt with matters that might in later centuries be considered to be war crimes. For example, in 1385, Richard II of England set out in his Durham Ordinances rules that prohibited robbery, pillage, and the killing or capture of unarmed persons belonging to the Church and of unarmed women. In 1419, Henry V put out his Mantes Ordinances, which barred soldiers from entering a place where a woman was lying and prohibiting them from robbing women. Lower-class tenant farmers were protected, and the capture of children below the age of fourteen, unless they were the children of persons of rank (because they would bring a high ransom), was also prohibited. Not all monarchs or lords were so inclined to limit the activities of their soldiers, and such ordinances were issued only on a case-by-case basis.

MODERN WORLD

In the twentieth century, "war crimes" have come to be defined by international conventions, the Geneva Conventions and the Hague Conventions, which had evolved over the course of the late nineteenth and early twentieth centuries. Following World War II, the atrocities perpetrated by aggressor states reached not only international proportions but also levels of inhumanity that offended most modern human sensibilities. Hence, in the 1950's and later, the Geneva Conventions were refined to define war crimes and their prosecution, and the International Criminal Court at The Hague was set up to hear tribunals involving those who have perpetrated "ethnic cleansing" and other atrocities.

Even democratic governments can be guilty of genocide and war crimes. The Trail of Tears—the forced relocation of Native Americans from their homelands in the southern United States to Indian Territory (present-day Oklahoma) in the western United States—is a significant example. In 1831, the Cherokee, Chickasaw, Choctaw, Creek, and Seminole tribes, together known as the Five Civilized Tribes, were living as autonomous nations in the American South. By 1839, with the Cherokee removal, all of them had been forced to walk hundreds of miles west to live on reservations in Indian Territory.

President Andrew Jackson pressured the Cherokees to sign a removal treaty. Jackson's successor, Martin Van Buren, imposed the terms of the treaty by allowing Georgia, Tennessee, North Carolina, and Alabama to raise an armed force of seven thousand troops, composed of militia, regular army, and volunteers. General Winfield Scott (later famous for his role in the Civil War) led the army, which rounded up thirteen thousand Cherokees and forced them to march more than one thousand miles—mostly on foot and without shoes, moccasins, or adequate clothing—to face the harsh winter weather of the Indian Territory. Approximately fifty-five hundred Cherokees died during this trek, now called the Long March (1834-1835).

During these tumultuous times, the Cherokee John Ross (1790-1866) proved to be the dominant spokesperson for his people. Of about seven-eighths Scottish ancestry, Ross had grown up in Cherokee and frontier American environments and had earned great wealth and an elite place in the Cherokee Nation. He represented the Cherokee Nation to the U.S. government, especially in the Cherokees' cases before the Supreme Court. Ross's life and career shone a glaring spotlight on many nineteenth century European American assumptions about Native Americans and race, revealing the willingness of white American citizens, as well as the U.S. government, to engage in war crimes and de facto genocide before modern definitions of war crimes identified their acts as such.

Another war, the American Civil War (1861-1865), highlighted the uneven relationships between war crimes, military tribunals, and practical applications of justice. Samuel Alexander Mudd (1833-1883), a physician, practiced medicine in Maryland and in 1865 was implicated and imprisoned for aiding and conspiring with actor John Wilkes Booth and others in the assassination of President Abraham Lincoln. Lincoln had used the exigencies of war to justify suspending the writ of habeas corpus and allowing controversial, and some claimed illegal, military tribunals to try both civilians and soldiers. In an ironic twist of history on May 1, 1865 (about two weeks after Lincoln was assassinated), President Andrew Johnson authorized one of the controversial tribunals to try the assassins. Historians agree that Dr. Mudd knew Booth well, and some believe that Mudd knew about and actively participated in the conspiracy. The authorities arrested Mudd, and the military tribunal, mostly based on circumstantial evidence, found him, along with seven others, guilty of conspiracy to murder Lincoln. Mudd was sentenced to life imprisonment at Fort Jefferson, 70 miles west of Key West, Florida, in the Gulf of Mexico. President Johnson pardoned Mudd on February 8, 1869, partially because of his heroic efforts to fight a yellow fever epidemic in the prison.

The story of Lieutenant William Calley, a U.S. Army officer who was found guilty of ordering the My Lai Massacre on March 16, 1968, during the Vietnam War (1961-1975), illustrates the potent and potentially disastrous mixture of political expediency and justice. Born in 1943 in Miami, Florida, William Laws Calley, Jr., enlisted in the U.S. Army in July, 1966. He arrived in Vietnam in 1967 as a second lieutenant of infantry and was the leader of First Platoon Company C, First Battalion, Twentieth Infantry of the Twenty-third Infantry Division of the United States. On March 16, 1968, Calley ordered his men to kill everyone in the village of My Lai, a small Vietnamese village. In the ensuing bloodbath, the soldiers killed at least five hundred villagers, mostly women and children. Calley was court-martialed in November 1970, and as his defense claimed that he was following the orders of his immediate superior, Captain Ernest Medina. In March, 1971, the jury convicted Calley of the premeditated murder of twenty-two Vietnamese civilians and sentenced him to life imprisonment at hard labor. Medina was acquitted.

Twenty-six officers and soldiers were initially charged for their part in the My Lai Massacre, but Calley was the only one convicted. Many Americans were outraged at his conviction and believed that the court-martial had not been just. On April 1, 1971—the day after Calley's sentencing—President Richard Nixon ordered Calley transferred from prison to house arrest at Fort Benning, pending appeal of his sentence. Secretary of Defense Melvin Laird protested this leniency, and the prosecutor, Aubrey Daniel, wrote, "The greatest tragedy of all will be if political expedience dictates the compromise of such a fundamental moral principle as the inherent unlawfulness of the murder of innocent persons."

After more military interventions and another review by President Nixon, Calley served only three years of his sentence. Judge J. Robert Elliott of the federal district court granted him habeas corpus on September 25, 1974, along with immediate release, and further reviews and appeals upheld the habeas corpus writ. Some legal arguments contend that the outcome of the My Lai courts-martial reversed the Nuremberg and Tokyo war crimes tribunals, which

set a historic precedent by establishing the principle that no one can use "following orders" as a defense for committing war crimes. *The New York Times* quoted Secretary of the Army Howard Callaway as stating that Calley's sentence was reduced because he (Calley) honestly believed that he was following orders. This reasoning directly contradicts the standards of the Nuremberg and Tokyo war crimes tribunals, which executed German and Japanese soldiers for murdering civilians.

The United States' invasion of Iraq in 2003 applied another wartime litmus test of the Geneva Con-

NARA

Defendants at the Nuremberg Trials circa 1946 are (left to right, front row) Hermann Göring, Rudolf Hess, Joachim von Ribbentrop, Wilhelm Keitel, and (left to right, second row) Karl Dönitz, Erich Räder, Baldur von Schirach, and Fritz Sauckel.

ventions. In 2004, stories of physical, psychological, and sexual abuse of prisoners began to surface from the Abu Ghraib prison in Iraq, including a *60 Minutes II* news report and a *New Yorker* article by Seymour Hersh. The personnel of the 372nd Military Police Company of the United States Army and other government agencies were identified as the perpetrators.

Donald Henry Rumsfeld (born 1932), an American businessman, served as the thirteenth secretary of defense under President Gerald Ford and the twenty-first secretary of defense under President George W. Bush (2001-2006). When the stories about Abu Ghraib broke, he addressed the Senate Armed Services Committee on May 7, 2004:

> These events occurred on my watch. As secretary of defense, I am accountable for them. I take full responsibility. It is my obligation to evaluate what happened, to make sure those who have committed wrongdoing are brought to justice, and to make changes as needed to see that it doesn't happen again. . . . To those Iraqis who were mistreated by members of U.S. armed forces, I offer my deepest apology. It was un-American. And it was inconsistent with the values of our nation.

BOOKS AND ARTICLES

Belknap, Michael R. *The Vietnam War on Trial: The My Lai Massacre and the Court Martial of Lieutenant Calley*. Lawrence: University Press of Kansas, 2002. Excellent retelling of the My Lai story through the prism of law that provides new perspectives on the Vietnam War.

Best, Geoffrey. *War and Law Since 1945*. Oxford, England: Clarendon Press, 1997. Discusses the relationship between war and international law.

Edwards, William C., and Edward Steers, eds. *The Lincoln Assassination: The Evidence*. Champaign: University of Illinois Press, 2009. One of the premier publications in the field of Lincoln assassination studies. A gold mine of original records and primary sources.

Jinks, Derek. *The Rule of War: The Geneva Conventions in the Age of Terror*. New York: Oxford University Press, 2008. A guide to the Geneva Conventions for the general reader.

Jones, Adam. *Genocide, War Crimes, and the West*. London: Zed Books, 2004. Explores the involvement of the United States and other liberal democracies in actions that are conventionally depicted as the exclusive province of totalitarian and authoritarian regimes.

Madariaga, Isabel de. *Ivan the Terrible*. New Haven, Conn.: Yale University Press, 2005. A definitive, thorough biography that explores the complex character of Ivan IV.

Maga, Tim. *Judgment at Tokyo: The Japanese War Crimes Trials*. Lexington: University Press of Kentucky, 2001. Discusses the important precedents set by the Tokyo trials and establishes what constitutes war crimes and how they can be prosecuted.

Meron, Theodor. *War Crimes Law Comes of Age*. New York: Oxford University Press, 1998. A collection of essays in which the world's authority on issues of international humanitarian law contemplates topics ranging from Renaissance war ordinances to the Nuremberg trials to war crimes in the Balkans, Nicaragua, and the current world.

Purdue, Theda, and Michael D. Green, eds. *The Cherokee Removal: A Brief History with Documents*. 2d ed. New York: Bedford/St. Martin's, 2004. A multifaceted, succinct account of this complicated story in American history.

Strasser, Steven, ed. *The Abu Ghraib Investigations: The Official Independent Panel and Pentagon Reports on the Shocking Prisoner Abuse in Iraq*. New York: Public Affairs, 2004. A judicious account of Abu Ghraib and the Geneva Conventions.

Kathy Warnes

BEHIND THE BATTLEFIELD

CRYPTOGRAPHY

OVERVIEW

Cryptography encompasses use of letters, numbers, symbols, and words to form coded messages. Military personnel utilize cryptography to transmit orders to officers and troops on land, sea, or in air as well as to mislead enemies who intercept messages. Historians have analyzed the role of cryptography in warfare, often soon after major conflicts occurred, with scholars revising interpretations as information regarding secret code-breaking work became declassified and participants divulged their contributions. World War II and espionage were the focus of much historical scholarship examining cryptography in the late twentieth century. Early twenty-first century histories discussed digital aspects of encrypting military information and assessed cyber vulnerabilities affecting military forces.

SIGNIFICANCE

Since ancient times, military forces have benefited from various forms of cryptography, which allows sensitive information to be transmitted without informing the enemy and which can also deliberately misinform the enemy, in the effort to win battles and wars. Codes disguising military information have enabled victories over enemies who were unaware when and where troops would attack, their strength, and other crucial facts. Moreover, the ability to intercept and decipher enemies' encrypted messages has alerted commanders to invasions so they can plan defenses and revise strategies. Military cryptanalysts have deciphered enemy messages regarding destruction of supply lines necessary for transportation of both military and civilian resources so officers could order strikes to stop enemies before they could act. Military leaders unaware of their opponents' plans have often experienced defeat.

HISTORY OF CRYPTOGRAPHY

Warfare has been influenced by cryptography for centuries. Although applications have varied, military forces in different eras have appropriated universal aspects of cryptography to transmit secret information. Basic ciphers often involved substitution of letters in a word or the rearrangement of their order. The frequency of specific letters and patterns has alerted cryptanalysts to the enemy's encoding key, so they could convert the remaining letters. Some cryptographers assigned words unique codes, which they

Greg Goebel

A four-rotor Enigma machine.

recorded in code books accessible to people composing messages and translating them; code books were vulnerable to being misplaced or theft by enemies. Knowledge of keys became essential for effective cryptography.

Ciphers and techniques associated with cryptography advanced as people recognized more complex ways to conceal messages with elaborate combinations of codes and sophisticated technology, such as machines and computers, devised to generate or decipher coded messages. Military cryptographers have constantly sought more secure encryption methods to outwit code breakers. Cryptanalysts honed their skills to comprehend meanings in otherwise nonsensical text. Military code specialists developed strategies to prevent enemy cryptographers from realizing their codes had been broken unless such awareness could be manipulated to confuse enemy officers. Codes associated with warfare throughout history have rarely proved impossible for enemies to decipher.

ANCIENT WORLD

Humans in ancient civilizations first utilized cryptography to protect secrets in communications from economic and political rivals, particularly during combat. Early methods often relied on people's insights regarding how to confuse enemies. Julius Caesar (100-44 B.C.E.) explained in *Comentarii de bello Gallico* (52-51 B.C.E.; *The Gallic Wars*, in his *Commentaries*, 1609), that he had disguised a communication to his Roman military officers fighting in Europe to prevent enemies from comprehending the message if they secured access to it. Aware that Cicero, overwhelmed by opposing forces, was thinking of surrendering, Caesar prepared a message to reassure his officer that he was sending reinforcements. Concerned about the enemy learning that more Romans were en route, Caesar wrote his message with Latin vocabulary formed with Greek letters. Cicero, fluent in both languages, announced Caesar's news to his soldiers, who rebounded to resist enemy attacks. Caesar also used substitution ciphers, in which pairs of letters corresponding with each other could be used to encode words. The "Caesar shift" that ancient historian Suetonius describes involved corre-

lating letters with those three positions away, such as writing the cipher letter D for the text letter A.

Polybius created a grid with the alphabet placed in five columns and numbers from one through five written along the top and also descending on the left side to designate the rows and columns in which letters were located. The two numbers associated with each letter formed the cipher. Polybius stated that signalers could consecutively hold specific amounts of torches representing letters to send messages coded with his system to troops on the battlefield.

Other Romans used transposition ciphers, which rearranged letters to create nonsensical words or entire sentences that confused enemy readers. Most ancient cryptographic systems were vulnerable to being unraveled by the enemy, who occasionally would decode messages when recognizing the correct order of letters in a jumbled word or analyzing messages for patterns of the most common vowels and consonants, which could help determine the cipher technique that had been applied to a message.

Ancient historians such as Plutarch and Herodotus recorded incidents involving secret messages and cryptographic devices associated with warfare. For example, the Spartans in the fifth century B.C.E. provided military leaders with a wooden device called the *scytale*, which they wrapped with a parchment or leather strip circling it along the length of the scytale. A message was then written on the parchment or leather, with letters spanning the different wrapped strips. The strip was removed from the scytale and delivered by a courier to the military official for whom it was intended, who would then wrap the strip around his own scytale, which had to be of the exact same diameter. Without a corresponding scytale, the writing on the strip was indecipherable. Military victories attributed to scytale communications included that of Spartan military general Pausanias over Persian forces after he received troops requested through this form of encryption.

Demaratus, the ruler of Sparta exiled in Persia, alerted Greeks that the Persian ruler Xerxes' forces were planning an invasion. Demaratus etched his message on pieces of wood, which were coated in wax to hide his words. Persian guards did not suspect anything strange about those boards en route to the recipients. Demaratus's clever approach succeeded in preparing Greeks to repel Persian efforts to conquer their territory.

In *Aineiou poliorketika* (after 357 B.C.E.; *Aeneas on Siegecraft*, 1927), Aeneas the Tactician described placing holes in disks in patterns to conceal messages that could be deciphered by threading a cord in the holes.

MEDIEVAL WORLD

During the Middle Ages, mathematicians and scientists created methods of encryption that were more complex than their ancient predecessors. Many of these encoded messages were used in military communications to outwit increasingly adept code breakers. By the late fourteenth century, governments were using ciphers for diplomatic correspondence in an effort to thwart spies.

In Italy, architect and engineer Leon Battista Alberti (1404-1472) devised a disk consisting of two rings with the alphabet printed on both. A person encoding a message set the rings and coded a few words with the corresponding letters, then moved the rings to code more text. Recipients deciphered messages by using a similar cipher disk and awareness of how they needed to adjust their device as they translated. Alberti innovated polyalphabetic cipher methods and discussed cryptography in his text *De componendis cifris* (c. 1466; *A Treatise on Ciphers*, 1997).

The Italian city-states sought cipher experts to create keys for codes and read rivals' messages, appointing people to positions of cipher secretary and cryptanalyst. In Venice, the Council of Ten and its secret police force maintained power and selected cryptanalyst Giovanni Soro (died 1544) in 1506 as Venice's cipher secretary. He skillfully cracked codes, including one used in a request that Holy Roman Empire army commander Mark Anthony Colonna had sent to Emperor Maximilian I, telling him he needed more funds, thus revealing that force's weakness.

In *Polygraphia* (1518), Johannes Trithemius (1462-1516) described a method of altering cipher keys as each letter was enciphered to produce more secure messages. Blaise de Vigenère (1523-1596), in *Traicté des chiffres* (tract on ciphers), examined contemporary cryptography and described coding messages with his tableau technique, which used twenty-six rows and columns in which letters shifted to the next position in each succeeding column and row. About 1550, Italian mathematician Gerolamo Cardano (1501-1575) publicized a concept in which the key for enciphering words in a message changed for every word following the first. Also trained as a physician, Cardano created masks with slots for writing portions of a secret communication on paper. The message, concealed when other text was written around it, was revealed only if a mask with the proper slots was available to the recipient. The Knights Templar used ciphers to write letters representing credit because they did not carry currency when they traveled on military crusades to the Holy Land.

MODERN WORLD

In the seventeenth century, French cryptologist Antoine Rossignol (1600-1682) contributed his skills to create and crack codes for King Louis XIII. In 1626, Rossignol examined an intercepted encoded letter that Huguenot leaders in Réalmont had written during their siege of that city. Rossignol decoded the letter, which revealed that the Huguenots were considering surrendering. Rossignol gave French representatives the deciphered message to show the Huguenots their dire situation was known, thus securing Réalmont for the French army. Rossignol continued his cryptographic services for the king and military. His son, Bonaventure Rossignol, also pursued cryptography. The pair devised a cipher using syllables instead of letters to encode royal messages. They emphasized capturing enemies' coded messages for military purposes, resulting in the creation of the Cabinet Noir, a group of cryptanalysts devoted to decoding intercepted diplomatic communications. Other European nations established similar cryptography services, which provided useful military intelligence during warfare.

By the nineteenth century, technological advances were having a great impact on military cryptography. The telegraph resulted in officers ordering cryptographers to encrypt messages prior to their subsequent transcription into Morse code. Auguste Kerckhoffs (1835-1903) contributed articles about cryptography to the *Journal of Military Science*,

(591)
1535
15/11-jwa

HEADQUARTERS,
AMPHIBIOUS FORCE, PACIFIC FLEET,
CAMP ELLIOTT, SAN DIEGO, CALIFORNIA

March 6, 1942

From: The Commanding General.
To: The Commandant, U. S. Marine Corps.

Subject: Enlistment of Navaho Indians.

Enclosures: (A) Brochure by Mr. Philip Johnston, with maps.
            (B) Messages used in demonstration.

1.   Mr. Philip Johnston of Los Angeles recently offered his services to this force to demonstrate the use of Indians for the transmission of messages by telephone and voice-radio. His offer was accepted and the demonstration was held for the Commanding General and his staff.

2.   The demonstration was interesting and successful. Messages were transmitted and received almost verbatim. In conducting the demonstration messages were written by a member of the staff and handed to the Indian; he would transmit the messages in his tribal dialect and the Indian on the other end would write them down in English. The text of messages as written and received are enclosed. The Indians do not have many military terms in their dialect so it was necessary to give them a few minutes, before the demonstration, to improvise words for dive-bombing, anti-tank gun, etc.

3.   Mr. Johnston stated that the Navaho is the only tribe in the United States that has not been infested with German students during the past twenty years. These Germans, studying the various tribal dialects under the guise of art students, anthropologists, etc., have undoubtedly attained a good working knowledge of all tribal dialects except Navaho. For this reason the Navaho is the only tribe available offering complete security for the type of work under consideration. It is noted in Mr. Johnston's article (enclosed) that the Navaho is the largest tribe but the lowest in literacy. He stated, however, that 1,000 — if that many were needed — could be found with the necessary qualifications. It should also be noted that the Navaho tribal dialect is completely unintelligible to all other tribes and all other people, with the possible exception of as many as 28 Americans who have made a study of the dialect. This dialect is thus equivalent to a secret code to the enemy, and admirably suited for rapid, secure communication.

NARA

A letter of recommendation for a Navajo enlistee emphasizes his ability to speak the Navajo dialect, which is "completely unintelligible to all other tribes and all other people."

U.S. Army

Comanche code talkers for the Fourth Signal Company, U.S. Army Signal Center, Ft. Gordon.

which were compiled into the text *La Cryptographie militaire* (1883; military cryptography). Kerckhoffs sought more secure ways to telegraph messages during wars, emphasizing that military ciphers should use keys that could be easily memorized, could be adapted for changing situations, and could remain secret.

Modern warfare involved numerous cryptography experts and events. During World War I, French code breaker Georges-Jean Painvin (1886-1980) worked in the Bureau du Chiffre (cipher bureau) to decipher German codes during crucial military operations in spring, 1918. Painvin evaluated German messages transmitted during combat in northern France and detected patterns of letters and digits that helped him discover the cipher used. Herbert O. Yardley (1889-1958) developed the World War I Cipher Bureau to support the U.S. military. He interacted with European cryptanalysts, including Painvin, to enhance American cryptography methods. Yardley wrote *The American Black Chamber* (1931), which revealed how code breaking enhanced U.S. military intelligence during warfare.

The British Government Code and Cypher School (GCCS) established its headquarters at Bletchley Park. Most Axis countries (Germany, Italy, and Japan) encoded their military communications with the so-called Enigma machine, which could created millions of ciphers. In the late 1930's, Polish mathematician Marian Rejewski (1905-1980) and associates told British and French officials how their technology helped decipher Enigma messages during the interwar period. World War II Bletchley Park cryptanalysts, mostly linguists and mathematicians such as Alan Turing, focused on the more complex Enigma ciphers German military branches used for orders, particularly those directing U-boat missions, which were disrupting North Atlantic Allied shipping. Engineer Thomas H. Flowers (1905-1998) built a digital computer, Colossus, to process encrypted German messages. Using Colossus computers, Bletchley Park cryptanalysts decoded more than 2.5 million communications during the war, which helped the Allied military prepare maneuvers in Europe, including the June, 1944, Normandy invasion.

In the Pacific, Leo Rosen created a facsimile of Japan's cipher machine. William F. Friedman (1891-1969), the U.S. Army Signals Intelligence Service chief, and Frank Rowlett (1908-1998) cracked Purple, the Japanese cipher used for diplomatic communications. Access to decoded Japanese military orders enabled U.S. naval pilots to hit the plane trans-porting Admiral Yamamoto Isoroku, the Imperial Japanese Navy's Combined Fleet commander. Cryptanalysts' work contributed to the American victory in the Battle of Midway in 1942. Approximately 420 Navajos served as code talkers, using their complex language to encipher communications in battles the U.S. Marines fought on Pacific islands. Officers credited the Navajos for American troops successfully securing Iwo Jima, among other strategic victories, which helped the Allies defeat Japan. The Japanese were unable to break the Navajo code.

Military cryptography embraced emerging technological advances, such as those of the digital revolution. Code experts applied mathematical functions, such as algorithms, to encode and decipher information digitally. The U.S. Military Academy's mathematical science department began publishing the journal *Cryptologia* in 1977. Codes were used to protect nuclear materials, electronic data associated with military procedures and records, and the Milstar satellites deployed for military communications.

Cryptography was utilized in the Vietnam War (1961-1975) and played an important role in the 1964

Bletchley Park, north of London, where the Enigma codes were cracked.

Gulf of Tonkin incident, where it was used to obtain congressional approval for nearly unlimited U.S. action in Vietnam. A part of the verification process that supported the idea that North Vietnamese torpedo boats attacked two American destroyers was the use of deciphered North Vietnamese communication. A National Security Agency report, declassified in 2006, revealed that it was likely that the communications were incorrectly deciphered.

Modern communication monitoring really hit its stride with the Persian Gulf War (1990-1991), as "traffic analysis" allowed Americans listening to massive amounts of communication to decipher Iraqi war plans. However, American cryptographic experts may have eventually become victims of their own success, as nations wishing to avoid American eavesdropping operations have returned to lower-tech ways of personally delivering messages.

BOOKS AND ARTICLES

Churchhouse, Robert F. *Codes and Ciphers: Julius Caesar, the Enigma, and the Internet*. New York: Cambridge University Press, 2002. A chronological discussion of cryptography from its ancient origins through the early twenty-first century, noting military and espionage applications.

Copeland, B. Jack, ed. *Colossus: The Secrets of Bletchley Park's Codebreaking Computers*. New York: Oxford University Press, 2006. Articles written by cryptography experts include perspectives from such prominent figures as Thomas H. Flowers, describing technological developments to decipher Enigma messages.

Kahn, David. *The Reader of Gentlemen's Mail: Herbert O. Yardley and the Birth of American Codebreaking*. New Haven, Conn.: Yale University Press, 2004. In this pioneering military cryptanalyst's biography, a renowned cryptography historian offers insights and corrects errors in the cryptography literature that are often reiterated.

Kozaczuk, Władysław, and Jerzy Straszak. *Enigma: How the Poles Broke the Nazi Code*. New York: Hippocrene Books, 2004. Examines Polish mathematicians' cryptography training and accomplishments, the Polish Cipher Bureau, and their impact on British cryptanalysts.

Meadows, William C. *The Comanche Code Talkers of World War II*. Austin: University of Texas Press, 2002. Comprehensive study of Native Americans who served Allied military forces by using their languages to encipher and translate messages.

Showell, Jak P. Mallmann. *German Naval Code Breakers*. Annapolis, Md.: Naval Institute Press, 2003. This illustrated history presents details unavailable in most secondary sources regarding the German Naval Radio Monitoring Service intercepting Allied communications in warfare.

Elizabeth D. Schafer

DIPLOMACY

OVERVIEW

Diplomacy can be defined as the conduct of relations between sovereign entities such as nation-states, empires, and kingdoms. Diplomacy takes the form of negotiations between duly appointed agents, known as diplomats. Diplomacy is relevant to an understanding of all aspects of war, since diplomats are closely involved with war origins, the conduct of war, and the conclusion of hostilities. Historical studies of diplomacy have traditionally focused on the study of state papers and documents. In recent years, historians have widened the scope of the study of diplomacy to include all aspects of exchanges between states, including cultural and social contacts.

SIGNIFICANCE

Diplomats are heavily involved in negotiations that precede the outbreak of wars. No student of World War I, for example, could come to a proper understanding of that war without developing a familiarity with the war's origins. During wartime, diplomats are actively engaged in attempting to win the active, or passive, support of neutral states. In coalition wars, or wars between alliance systems, diplomats are responsible for maintaining the strength of the coalition through the ups and downs of war. Diplomats discuss peace proposals with the enemy and take the leading role in talks that conclude the war. Postwar peace conferences, such as the Paris Peace Conference of 1919, are likewise the responsibility of diplomats.

HISTORY OF DIPLOMACY

ANCIENT WORLD
Diplomacy in the ancient world consisted of emissaries who were sent by the ruler of one state to the ruler of another state on a specific mission. Emissaries might be used to negotiate trade agreements, arrange dynastic marriages, or conduct discussions aimed at resolving a conflict. In order to lend credibility to the mission, emissaries were always members of the ruling elite or members of the ruler's family. Empires, such as those of the Assyrians (which reached its peak around 650 B.C.E.) and Persians (which dominated the Middle East by 513 B.C.E.), needed to manage relations with tributary states or with rival states on their borders. Diplomacy was particularly intense when a network of states of roughly equal power emerged, such as the Greek city-states of the Peloponnesian War (431-404 B.C.E.). Diplomats were usually ranked according to the importance of their mission and their social standing. When the mission was completed, emissaries would return home.

MEDIEVAL WORLD
Diplomacy in the medieval world followed patterns established in the ancient world. One of the most frequently cited examples of medieval diplomacy is the relationship between Charlemagne (742-814), king of the Frankish Empire, which governed most of western and central Europe, and Hārūn al-Rashīd (763/766-809), ruler of the ʿAbbāsid caliphate, which included modern Iran, most of the Middle East, and North Africa. In China, the diplomacy of the Ming Dynasty, which emerged in 1368, involved the management of relations with subordinate, tributary states that existed on the periphery of the empire. The same could be said for the diplomacy of the Ottoman, Mughal, and Persian empires. The Papacy was particularly active diplomatically, at one point maintaining a permanent mission at the Byzantine court. Permanent diplomatic missions would become a hallmark of the modern conception of diplomacy.

MODERN WORLD
Most scholars would trace the origins of the modern system of diplomacy to Renaissance Italy. By the time of the Renaissance, the Italian peninsula was di-

F. R. Niglutsch

The court of the influential French minister Cardinal de Richelieu, who was a dominant diplomatic figure during the reign of Louis XIII.

vided into a number of city-states, which engaged in frequent bouts of warfare. Venice emerged as a major commercial power in the Mediterranean by the fourteenth century. All the Italian city-states needed accurate information from their rivals in order to keep ahead of the intrigues that dominated the Italian peninsula at the time.

Venice, in particular, required information on foreign markets and the activities of its competitors. Such needs led to the stationing of agents, or ambassadors, in foreign capitals on a permanent, not temporary basis. The concept was soon adopted across Europe. Written reports by ambassadors and their subordinates had to be analyzed and filed on receipt in the home country. Governments established foreign ministries, staffed by bureaucrats, to process incoming reports and send out instructions. The heads of these ministries, known as foreign ministers or foreign secretaries, emerged as some of the most

powerful members of the cabinets of European states. Diplomacy continued to be dominated by the aristocracy. Commentators wrote books giving advice to rulers on the practice of diplomacy and statecraft. Perhaps the most famous of these works is *Il principe* (1513, pb. 1532; *The Prince*, 1640), by Niccolò Machiavelli (1469-1527).

Prominent practitioners of diplomacy included France's Cardinal de Richelieu (1585-1642). Richelieu served as chief minister to King Louis XIII from 1624 to 1642. Richelieu put forward the concept of *raison d'état*, by which he meant that the good of the state is supreme. Diplomacy, according to Richelieu, must be conducted free of sentiment or ideology. Alliances, he held, should be made and broken according to the interests of the state. Critics denounced Richelieu for his alleged lack of morality, but Richelieu merely replied that the good of the state was the ultimate in morality.

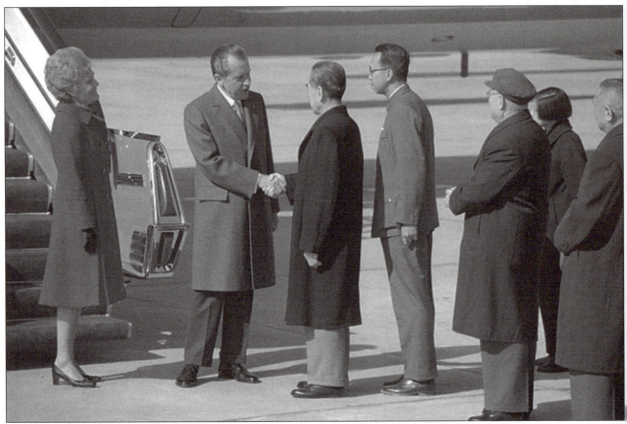

White House photo by Byron Schumaker

U.S. president Richard M. Nixon is widely credited with having helped open China to the West during the height of the Cold War.

The Peace of Westphalia of 1648, which ended the Thirty Years' War (1618-1648), is often cited as the first diplomatic conference. The treaty explicitly recognized and formalized the principle of state sovereignty. States now had the right to govern their affairs, free of interference from outside powers. By the eighteenth century, observers of international affairs, such as the Scottish philosopher David Hume (1711-1776), began articulating a concept known as "balance of power." The new doctrine held that international relations should be dominated by a number of states of equal power that could restrain the ambitions of any one power that tried to dominate the others.

Restoring the balance of power in Europe was the main aim of the Congress of Vienna (1815), the most important diplomatic conference of the nineteenth century. The Congress of Vienna, held at the end of the wars of the French Revolution (1789-1793) and the Napoleonic Wars (1793-1815), tried to restore peace to Europe after many years of turmoil. Dominated by the Austrian foreign minister Prince Klemens von Metternich (1773-1859), the Congress redrew the borders of Europe. Metternich hoped that the five great powers of Europe (France, Britain, Austria, Prussia, and Russia), acting in concert, could maintain stability in Europe. Metternich's "Concert of Europe," however, sought to maintain the rule of authoritarian, antidemocratic empires increasingly at odds with awakening nationalist and liberal sentiments in Europe.

By the 1860's, the concept of Realpolitik came to dominate diplomacy. Major practitioners of Realpolitik included Count Camillo Cavour (1810-1861) prime minister of the Italian state of Piedmont; Louis Napoleon (Napoleon III, 1808-1873), emperor of France; and Otto von Bismarck (1815-1898), chancellor of Prussia and then Germany. Realpolitik returned to the style of diplomacy advocated by Richelieu. Once again, national interest assumed supreme importance in the conduct of diplomacy. Treaties and moral obligations could be thrown overboard if the situation demanded. Cavour succeeded in uniting the scattered Italian states using the methods of Realpolitik. Louis Napoleon was less successful in his diplomatic career, and France was defeated in the Franco-Prussian War of 1870-1871. Louis Napoleon's enemy, Bismarck, chancellor of the German state of Prussia and an unapologetic practitioner of Realpolitik, masterminded the unification of the German states and the defeat of France. The new German state became the center of diplomacy in Europe.

Bismarck put Germany at the center of a web of alliances designed to maintain Germany's predominant position in Europe. In 1884 he presided over the Berlin Conference, which established the ground rules for European expansion into Africa and Asia at the end of the nineteenth century. Diplomacy in Europe now had dramatic, worldwide consequences.

The era of classical diplomacy, when diplomats came from similar aristocratic backgrounds and shared common assumptions about the conduct of diplomacy, came to an end with the outbreak of World War I in 1914. The war left nine million dead and large areas of Europe devastated. Public opinion increasingly condemned "old diplomacy," with its secret alliances and treaties, and held diplomats responsible for the outbreak of war. President Woodrow Wilson (1856-1924) of the United States advocated a new style of "open diplomacy." The Paris Peace Conference of 1919, called to redraw the map of Europe following the war, established the League of Nations, one of Wilson's most important ideas. The League would substitute the rule of law for anarchy and brute force in international relations. Member nations were required to submit disputes to the League for peaceful resolution. Aggressors faced sanctions and possible military action. Hopes soared that a new era in international affairs had arrived. In 1928 practically all the independent states of the world signed the Kellogg-Briand Pact. Signatories to the pact promised to renounce the use of war as a means for settling disputes. Arms control conferences, such as the Washington Naval Conference of 1921-1922, promised to end expensive arms races.

Unfortunately, the League of Nations was hobbled from the start by the absence of the United States, which withdrew into isolation after 1919. The League proved unable to withstand the challenges of aggressive and expansionist states, such as Japan, Italy, and Germany in the 1930's. In 1931, Japan conquered the Chinese region of Manchuria with impunity. Fascist Italy, led by Benito Mussolini (1883-1945), invaded Ethiopia in 1935, a final discrediting of the League.

The worsening international situation in the late

NARA

The Camp David Accords (1978), signed by Egyptian president Anwar el-Sadat (right) and Israeli prime minister Menachem Begin (left), were witnessed by U.S. president Jimmy Carter and paved the way for the 1979 Israel-Egypt Peace Treaty.

1930's, with Nazi Germany under Adolf Hitler (1889-1945) challenging Britain and France, saw the rise of summit diplomacy. Air travel, along with modern communication, meant that leaders could conduct their own face-to-face meetings with foreign leaders to resolve crises. Accordingly, British prime minister Neville Chamberlain (1869-1940) flew to Germany three times in 1938 to negotiate a solution to the crisis over Czechoslovakia. War broke out a year later, but summit diplomacy remained as a key characteristic of modern diplomacy. During World War II (1939-1945), Allied leaders met repeatedly to plan the course of the war.

The numerous crises of the ensuing Cold War ensured that the practice continued. The meetings of Soviet and American leaders always received massive publicity and press coverage. The Cuban Missile Crisis of 1962, which brought the world to the brink of a nuclear war, reinforced the need for instant communication between leaders. President John F. Kennedy (1917-1963) and Soviet premier Nikita Khrushchev (1894-1971) set up a telephone "hot line" to ensure clear communication in a crisis.

Face-to-face meetings between world leaders remain the preferred means of diplomacy in the twenty-first century. International institutions such as the United Nations, the European Union, and the North Atlantic Treaty Organization (NATO) also serve as important venues for diplomacy. Ambassadors and foreign ministries continue to play important roles, if slightly diminished compared to the age of classical diplomacy. The vast increase in the number of independent states since 1945 has ensured that the practitioners of diplomacy today are far more diverse and varied in their backgrounds and worldviews than in the past.

BOOKS AND ARTICLES

Afflerbach, H., and D. Stevenson, eds. *An Improbable War? The Outbreak of World War One and European Political Culture Before 1914*. New York: Berghahn Books, 2007. Recent collection of essays examining the defining diplomatic crisis of the twentieth century.

Kissinger, Henry. *Diplomacy*. New York: Simon and Schuster, 1994. A survey of diplomacy by the former U.S. secretary of state, one of the most foremost practitioners of twentieth century diplomacy.

Lawford, Valentine. *Bound for Diplomacy*. Boston: Little, Brown, 1963. Memoir of a British diplomat of the 1930's, witness to the rise of Hitler.

Mosslang, Markus, and Torsten Riotte, eds. *The Diplomat's World: A Cultural History of Diplomacy, 1815-1914*. New York: Oxford University Press, 2008. A collection of essays showcasing the new "cultural" approach to diplomacy.

Nicolson, H. *Diplomacy*. London: Thornton Butterworth, 1939. A study of diplomacy by a British politician and member of the British delegation to the pivotal 1919 Paris Peace Conference.

Rich, N. *Great Power Diplomacy, 1814-1914*. New York: McGraw-Hill, 1992. A classic diplomatic history of a period when European powers dominated the world.

Paul W. Doerr

Financing War

OVERVIEW

Finance can be defined as the way goods or services are funded. Historically, financing of war, which is an expensive activity, has been achieved in a number of ways in order to pay for the logistics and the personnel of military forces. Three major ways of financing war are taxation, borrowing, and money management. Today the study of war finance is usually included under the heading "defense economics."

SIGNIFICANCE

Since war is as old as humanity, the financing of war has varied through the ages. It is also an expensive activity: As Sunzi (Sun Tzu) noted in his book, *Sunzi Bingfa* (c. fifth-third century B.C.E.; *The Art of War*, 1910), written during China's Warring States period, an army is kept for a thousand days to be used on one day—that is, the army (or navy) must be paid for more than a thousand days, but then all is spent in one day, when it is probably destroyed.

The method for financing war can contribute to the ultimate success of the combatants. The French Army under Napoleon I traveled on its stomach by foraging, which was simply taking from the local agrarian populations whatever food it could find. During the Iberian campaign, the British practice of paying in gold sovereigns for its supplies bought goodwill among civilian populations.

Many revolutions, civil conflicts, and wars have been won because the victors had superior resources for sustaining war over a long period of time, enabling them to exhaust the vanquished. Ultimately this is how the West defeated the Soviet Union in the fifty-year Cold War (1945-1991) between the communist bloc and the West. In the end, President Ronald Reagan moved the United States into an arms race that bankrupted the Soviet Union but caused no special financial damage to the West.

HISTORY OF FINANCING WAR

ANCIENT WORLD

Probably the most basic way in which war has been financed has been through plundering. Tribal chiefs, bandit chiefs, or other leaders—who if successful enough came to be called kings—would gather an armed body of men who would raid their neighbors, their enemies, or even distant victims. The goal was to take what could be found and then return.

Raids are temporary. The Bedouins of the Arabian, Syrian, and North African deserts, as well as other nomadic groups, would usually steal livestock, women, children, and portable goods in order to trade them at home. However, when raids turned into permanent invasions, then the method of finance changed into demands for tribute. The conquered would be forced to finance their own subjugation, with tribute payments in kind, in precious metals or gems, or even in people.

Armies in ancient times supported themselves by capturing the supplies of other armies. The Greeks, after the Battle of Marathon (490 B.C.E.), were astounded at the riches they had captured from the Persians. Many armies, especially guerrilla groups, have financed themselves with captured weapons and matériel.

Capturing slaves was another method for financing war, used in both ancient and medieval times. Captured sites would yield not only valuable objects as booty but also soldiers and civilians who could be sold into slavery. The slaves would be exploited as servants, laborers, sacrificial victims, and even sexual objects.

MEDIEVAL WORLD

The feudal system required that kings and their vassals provide protection for the people of their estates. Despite that obligation, kings and vassals turned to those people for military service rather than hiring trained soldiers—hence, service to the lord of the

BANQUE DE L'UNION PARISIENNE
7, RUE CHAUCHAT _ PARIS

Valmy

Pour que la France soit victorieuse comme à Valmy!
Pour la libération du territoire!
SOUSCRIVEZ TOUS
AU 4ᵉ EMPRUNT NATIONAL

VISA Nᵒ 13636.   DEVAMBEZ.IMP.PARIS

Library of Congress

The Battle of Valmy was touted as the first step in the French Revolution and was used in this poster to encourage French citizens to buy war bonds "so that France will be victorious as at Valmy."

need of the kings to secure authority for taxes levied on the "commons" (common people) in order to finance wars. War financing through gifts has been far less common than financing through some form of coerced "taking," ranging from plundering to taxation.

MODERN WORLD

Whenever governments have grown large enough to impose taxes, these taxes have on occasion been used to finance wars. High taxes that have been paid unwillingly in wars that have continued for a long period of time have often caused enough political instability to destroy governments.

Wars have also been financed by loans. The American Revolution was financed in part by loans obtained from bankers in Europe. The use of loans to finance the revolution also occurred at the local level. Many Revolutionary War soldiers, for example, borrowed against their farms. This activity was to contribute to an uprising of Revolutionary War veterans in Shays's Rebellion in 1786. Some classical economists, such as Adam Smith, author of *The Wealth of Nations* (1776), opposed financing wars through loans because they believed it masked the costs of wars. Their opposition was not motivated by pacifism but by a practical belief that paying directly for wars would reduce both their occurrence and their duration. Also during the American Revolution, the British used an old method for recruiting armies, the hiring of mercenary troops (in this case, from Germany).

Money management during the revolution also involved inflationary printing of money. American colonists were accustomed to manufacturing their

manor in the form of military service was a method for financing war in economies that were essentially agrarian. At times wars were also financed by kings from out of their own personal incomes. The development of the English parliament arose from the own money as a way to have enough specie and other forms of cash available for business in economies that suffered from the mercantilist policies of the British Empire. Continental currency was printed and used among the revolting colonists. Eventually the Continentals generated inflation sufficient to earn the expression "not worth a Continental damn." Inflation, nevertheless, would continue to be used to finance wars.

On the high seas, another form of indirect funding was used until the Paris Declaration Respecting Maritime Law was signed on April 16, 1856. The declaration outlawed letters of marque and reprisal. Letters of marque had frequently been issued by governments to privateers, allowing them to wage war at sea against the merchant and naval vessels of the enemy country or countries. The letters of marque gave the privateers legal authorization for activities that otherwise would have been treated as piracy. The ships that were seized and their cargos could be sold in home ports or neutral ports as prizes of war. The privateers' ship owner, captain, and crew would share in the profits as well as in the dangers of naval warfare. Hence, letters of marque generated inexpensive ways for governments to finance naval warfare.

During the American Civil War (1861-1865), both the North and the South issued currency to finance the war. In the North the currency was popularly known as "greenbacks." In the South it came to be called Confederate money. Both also instituted taxes, although the South taxed lightly compared to the North. Both also seized the "contraband" of the other's supporters as well as the public material or money of their respective governments. Bank robberies in raids were used to acquire funds. A raid on St. Albans, Vermont, by Confederate cavalrymen targeted three banks and netted more than $200,000.

With the entry of the United States into World War I, the U.S. government again resorted to borrowing in order to finance the war effort. Financing wars grew enormously at this time, when the French and British used the financial services of J. P. Morgan (through the House of Morgan) to provide loans for the purchase of war supplies. In the process, the Morgan bank became a virtual sutler to the Allied effort, letting contract for herds of livestock, food, ammuni-

tion, and other war supplies. The Morgan bank also was seen by isolationists, pacifists, and others as an arms merchant that profited from the blood of others.

Borrowing to finance war is limited only by the amount of credit that a government can get, and defaulting on war debts is a funding tactic that has been used historically many times. The Fifth Amendment to the Constitution of the United States repudiated Confederate War debts, a default upheld by the Supreme Court in *Principality of Monaco v. Mississippi* (1934) to the loss of British bond holders and others.

Library of Congress

A poster by Winsor McCay exhorts Americans to support World War I; the American soldier is defended against the threats of "devastation," "starvation," "war," "pestilence," and "death" by the shield of liberty loans.

Bank loans were not enough, however, so campaigns to fund the war with "liberty bonds" (debt securities) and (in Canada) "victory bonds" were marketed to citizens. Even before the United States entered World War II, it began selling war bonds identified as Series E, F, and G bonds. Canada financed half of its war costs though war bonds. Bonds had three advantages: they financed the war, reduced inflationary pressures, and enlisted patriotic fervor. Germany also used drives to sell the public war bonds, called *Kriegsanleihe*. The Nazis financed much of their war effort with bonds, and the Austro-Hungarian Empire conducted nine drives.

The method used by the United States to raise the more than $300 billion it spent fighting the Axis powers in World War II combined borrowing and taxation with Federal Reserve management of the money supply to increase war finance while keeping inflation low. The taxation transferred spending from individuals to the government. However, its spending put money into the bank accounts of millions of military personnel, war production personnel, and others, thereby raising the bank reserves of the nation's banks. By managing the reserve requirements, the Federal Reserve was able to provide banks with liquidity for war loans to industry, to the government, and to individuals. In all, about a third of the funding came from borrowing, a third from taxation, and a third from expansion of the money supply, which allowed for more borrowing and taxation. Such methods would be used later to finance the Cold War as well as the wars in Korea (1950-1953) and Vietnam (1961-1975).

Clandestine warfare has at times been funded from both legal and illegal sources. The Central Intelligence Agency (CIA) laundered money through the Pakistani Inter-Service Intelligence (ISI) to fund a ghost war against the Soviets in Afghanistan (1979-1989). Purely illegal funds have been generated by "blood diamonds," drugs, smuggling, and other black-market commodities. The ill-gotten gains have been used to fund terrorist groups.

In modern times, defeated nations occasionally have been compelled to pay reparations, such as those imposed on Germany after World War I, thereby paying the victors' war costs. This is another form of tribute—which can prove counterproductive in the long run, as demonstrated by German resentment after World War I, when the 1919 Treaty of Paris, which proved punitive to Germany, actually helped sow the seeds of World War II. A representative to the Paris Peace Conference of 1919, economist John Maynard Keynes, resigned in protest over the imposition of reparations upon Germany. It was a failure, he believed, to finance the peace with reparations. Financing of war recovery is a war cost, one that is necessary to establish a prosperous peace.

During the Cold War, the use of mercenaries was transformed into proxy wars between communists (mainly the Soviet Union) and the West (primarily the United States and Western Europe). In a number of places, the manpower for the war was local, but the combatants' equipment and wages were supplied by the Soviet Union or the United States in the form of military aid funded by tax monies from the two superpowers. The U.S. policy of "containment" mandated support for local wars against communist-backed aggressors, theoretically to stave off the worldwide spread of communism. Such an approach was cheaper than a larger power struggle between the main Cold War opponents and, given the advent of nuclear weapons, perceived to be safer as well.

BOOKS AND ARTICLES

Gilbert, Charles. *American Financing of World War I*. Westport, Conn.: Greenwood, 1970. Looks at World War I finance as an example of government pursuing policies that are expedient in the short run rather than beneficial in the long run.

Keynes, John Maynard. *The Economic Consequences of the Peace*. New York: Skyhorse, 2007. The foremost economist of the early twentieth century, Keynes takes the Western allies to task for their imposition of heavy reparations on Germany at the end of World War I, as counterproductive to the recovery and long-term peace of Europe.

Murphy, Henry Clifford. *The National Debt in War and Transition*. New York: McGraw-Hill, 1950. Gives an analysis of the use of savings bonds to finance the war effort in the United States shortly before, during, and after World War II.

Samuel, Lawrence R. *Pledging Allegiance: American Identity and the Bond Drive of World War II*. Washington, D.C.: Smithsonian Institution Press, 1997. Examines how different groups of Americans, defined by race and class, participated in the war effort through the purchasing of war bonds, and how that played into their racial, class, and national identities.

Steil, Benn, and Robert E. Litan. *Financial Statecraft: The Role of Financial Markets in American Foreign Policy*. New Haven, Conn.: Yale University Press, 2006. Outlines, in a thorough and systematic way, how international capital has been and still is used by Western nations as a tool to implement foreign policy.

Taylor, Leonard B. *Financial Management of the Vietnam Conflict, 1962-1972*. Washington, D.C.: Department of the Army, 1974. Lays out the various aspects of the financial management of Army operations during the Vietnam War.

Andrew J. Waskey

INTELLIGENCE AND COUNTERINTELLIGENCE

OVERVIEW

Simply put, intelligence (or "intel") is information that has been processed, evaluated, and analyzed. Intelligence exists to support policy makers and military leaders in a variety of ways. Basically, intelligence is concerned with issues related to national security and is normally collected and processed in secret. Counterintelligence (CI) is the effort made by intelligence organizations to prevent foreign intelligence services from gaining information about them or disrupting their activities. CI efforts are also directed at preventing other intelligence services from conducting espionage within a nation's borders. The military also conducts CI in order to carry out protective measures at home and among units deployed abroad.

SIGNIFICANCE

The role of intelligence and the agencies that conduct intelligence activities can be broken down into four primary components. The first is to prevent a potential enemy from achieving strategic surprise. Second is to provide policy makers with knowledge that has been collected and assessed by experts, usually over a long period of time. This is especially important in governments where the leadership is transitory. The third role is to support the policy-making process. Decision makers require current intelligence in order to determine what policies they may wish to carry out. Timely intelligence can offer critical background information, help determine risk, and enable leaders to consider the potential risks and rewards of the decisions they are considering. Finally, there is the need to keep secret the methods of collecting intelligence as well as the information needs of decision makers. Governments and the military need to keep some information secret from others and, at the same time, have ways of getting information from those who wish to keep their knowledge confidential. This makes having intelligence services vital, for both civilian and military organizations.

HISTORY OF INTELLIGENCE AND COUNTERINTELLIGENCE

ANCIENT WORLD

The importance of good intelligence has been understood throughout history. The ancients of the Middle East, the Egyptians in particular, had sophisticated intelligence organizations. The Egyptians were among the earliest to employ codes, specialized inks, and other methods for communicating secretly in writing, for example. Other ancients in the Middle East also carried out intelligence activities. According to the Bible, the Hebrews relied on the use of spies as they entered the Promised Land.

The Greeks and Romans relied heavily on intelligence to govern and defend their respective civilizations. The story of the Trojan horse is a classic example of the use of deception to defeat an enemy. The Greek city-states routinely spied on one another, seeking intelligence about military strength and defensive capabilities. The Romans were very dependent on intelligence, especially after the creation of the empire. Rome routinely conducted espionage activities against its neighbors in order to gauge their respective strengths and weaknesses. Agents also were used to try to induce potential enemies to ally themselves with Rome. Counterintelligence activities had more of a political connotation as rival factions within the government often plotted against one another.

The legendary ancient Chinese general Sunzi

(Sun Tzu) commented on the importance of learning about one's enemies and the use of spies to gather intelligence. Writing in *Sunzi Bingfa* (c. fifth-third century B.C.E.; *The Art of War*, 1910), Sunzi outlined methods for establishing espionage networks and for the recruitment of defectors. Kauṭilya (also known as Cāṇakya or Chanakya, fl. 300 B.C.E.), in ancient India, also noted the value of intelligence gathering. During the feudal period in Japan, ninjas often served as spies for samurai warlords. In general, however, intelligence processes were at the mercy of the skills and the interests of individual rulers.

MEDIEVAL WORLD

The fall of the Roman Empire and the onset of the Middle Ages meant that intelligence was focused primarily on military operations or on keeping an eye on one's vassals. To what degree feudal lords engaged in intelligence activities is difficult to say, as there are no surviving records of such endeavors. The only real full-time intelligence community to come into being in the Middle Ages was created by the Roman Catholic Church. The onset of the Crusades led the Church to engage in a variety of intelligence operations including spying, sabotage, and even rescue missions to free prisoners of war. At the same time, the increase of religious fervor sparked by the Crusades led to the Inquisition, which could be thought of as a counterintelligence effort directed against heretics and dissenters. Domestic spying was a vital part of the Inquisition; secret police forces were used by the Church and the Spanish monarchy to root out heresy and political dissent.

As nation-states began to emerge, intelligence began to take on a greater level of organization. Niccolò Machiavelli wrote of the importance of intelligence to rulers who wished to protect their power. Ivan the Terrible (Ivan IV) created Russia's first secret police system in the sixteenth century. In England, Queen Elizabeth I relied on the skills of Sir Francis Walsingham to provide her with intelligence. Referred to as the Queen's "spymaster," Walsingham was one of the first to utilize intelligence methods in a modern sense. He developed an organization that collected intelligence throughout Europe, penetrated the Spanish military, and used counterintelligence methods to defend Elizabeth from domestic plots. The intelligence community created by Walsingham is noteworthy for its reliance on academics, linguists, scientists, engineers, and other experts for both the gathering and the analysis of intelligence. During the Thirty Years' War (1618-1648), the Cardinal de Richelieu in France played an important role in the establishment of French intelligence. He used domestic spies judiciously in order to defend the monarchy from potential enemies, and his spies abroad not only provided intelligence culled from other European monarchs but also worked to deceive them with false information.

MODERN WORLD

Intelligence began to take on forms that are more recognizable in today's world. A series of revolutions and wars from the seventeenth through the nineteenth century led to an increasing appreciation of intelligence and counterintelligence and the use of clandestine and covert operations. George Washington was especially aware of the importance of good intelligence, and he worked diligently to learn about the intentions of the British during the American Revolution (1775-1783). Washington proved to be a most capable spymaster: He successfully organized and supervised spy rings, recruited agents, organized deceit and deception operations, helped develop the codes and disappearing inks his spies used, and even served as his own intelligence analyst. Washington fully understood the importance of secrecy in intelligence operations in order for them to be successful. Later, as president, he oversaw the intelligence activities of the United States—the first American president to do so—and thereby established the precedent of executive control of the intelligence function.

A diplomat named William Wickham (1761-1840) oversaw British intelligence efforts against France during the French Revolution (1789-1793) and Napoleonic Wars (1793-1815). Operating from his diplomatic post in Switzerland, Wickham organized spy rings and supported operations designed to restore the French monarchy. Although these attempts failed, Wickham continued to operate spy rings that provided the British with key information about French military activities until the French learned of his spying and got the Swiss to have him removed from his post. British agents also carried out several unsuccessful attempts to assassinate Napoleon Bonaparte during his reign as emperor. Intelligence was equally important to the French. Counterintelligence was carried out by Joseph Fouché, who had enemy agents discredited or killed. Napoleon also oversaw intelligence operations, supervising spies and organizing operations designed to deceive enemy commanders. Likewise, under the direction of Prince Klemens von Metternich, Austria devel-

oped an effective intelligence organization to keep tabs on domestic and foreign threats. By the 1850's, Prussia was relying on its secret police to guard that nation's national security, and later it used espionage to help prepare for German unification. The use of an extensive network of spies was a major factor in the German defeat of France in the Franco-Prussian War (1870-1871).

Intelligence played a vital role in the American Civil War (1861-1865). Both the North and the South utilized spies, but new technologies also began to revolutionize intelligence activities. Both sides made use of balloons in order to conduct aerial reconnaissance. The telegraph not only allowed for speedier communications but also led to more sophisticated encryption and code-breaking efforts. False messages were often transmitted from captured telegraph stations. Both sides even tapped each other's telegraph lines. Information was acquired not only from spies but also from prisoners of war, documents taken from the battlefield dead, and newspapers.

Prior to the outbreak of hostilities in 1914, Germany had undertaken massive spying efforts in France and Great Britain. German spies sought to obtain military secrets as well as confidential political and industrial information. In addition to its espionage activities during World War I, Germany also conducted sabotage operations not only against its opponents but also against neutral nations, such as the United States.

The British responded to reports and rumors of German espionage by creating the Secret Service Bureau to counter the German intelligence-gathering efforts. By the eve of World War I, the British Secret Service had largely broken up Germany's spy rings, and it continued to identify

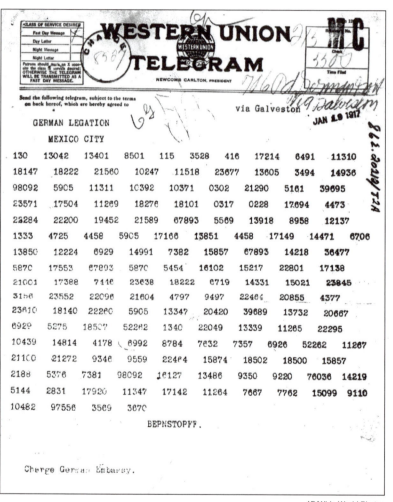

AP/Wide World Photos

The decoding of the so-called Zimmermann note, an intercepted German telegram that proposed an alliance of Germany, Mexico, and Japan against the United States, led the Americans to declare war on Germany on April 6, 1917.

and apprehend enemy agents during the war. Counterintelligence efforts also were directed at protecting vital ports, factories, and warehouses from enemy saboteurs. In the United States, the responsibilities of the Federal Bureau of Investigation (FBI) were expanded to include counterintelligence activities. Both sides relied heavily on encryption and codebreaking techniques for intelligence and counterintelligence purposes. The interception and decoding of the "Zimmermann note" by the British was a significant counterintelligence victory that contributed to the entrance of the United States into the war.

Technological advances, particularly in communications, made the need for accurate intelligence, delivered quickly, a necessity for all of the belligerents. Equally important was counterintelligence. The outcome of battles was often the result of good intelligence or counterintelligence. In the secret war of intelligence, the Allies won a decisive victory over the Axis powers. The Ultra project, for example, enabled the British to decipher German codes and contributed to the successful defense of Great Britain against the German air offensive of 1940, and to the defeat of Erwin Rommel and his German forces in Africa. The ability of the U.S. Navy to break Japan's naval codes led to an American victory at the Battle of Midway (1942). The Allies were able to perform successful deceit and deception operations against the Germans, and a variety of covert operations were carried out by the British Special Operations Executive (SOE) and the American Office of Strategic Services (OSS). Aerial reconnaissance came into increasing use as well. Although the Axis powers conducted numerous intelligence activities as well, their efforts were not as successful as those of the Allies.

There were failures, however. The successful Japanese attack at Pearl Harbor was the result of a massive intelligence failure on the part of the United States. Information was not shared between intelligence offices, and American analysts assumed that the disparity in strength between the two nations would keep the Japanese from risking war with the United States. In addition, the war-making capabilities of the Japanese were seriously underestimated.

Finally, despite their alliance with both countries, Soviet spies penetrated the British and American atomic bomb projects.

Prior to World War II, the United States had no real intelligence organization to speak of. The Japanese bombing of Pearl Harbor on December 7, 1941, had demonstrated the need for a structured intelligence function within the government, and this led to the establishment of the Central Intelligence Agency (CIA) in 1947. The United States was the last of the world's major powers to create a national intelligence agency, and the CIA quickly took up its role in gathering foreign intelligence and conducting covert and clandestine activities abroad. Other major intelligence agencies included the Soviet Komitet Gosudarstvennoi Bezopasnosti (Committee of State Security, or KGB), Britain's MI6, China's Central Department of Social Affairs (now the Ministry of State Security), and Israel's Mossad.

Decades of distrust between the United States and the Soviet Union and the destruction of the balance-of-power system in World War II helped bring about conflict between the United States and the Soviet Union. The Cold War would result in a great deal of intelligence activity between the United States and the Soviet Union, along with their respective allies. The competition for intelligence between the two sides was intense. Massive espionage networks sought to gather intelligence and engaged in counterintelligence operations against each other. The Soviets tended to rely more on human intelligence (HUMINT), or spies, for acquiring intelligence, while the United States emphasized technology to a greater degree. The establishment of the National Security Agency in 1952 and its mission of collecting foreign signals intelligence (SIGINT) and cryptanalysis reflected the American focus on technology as a primary collection resource.

Aerial reconnaissance, such as U-2 and SR-71 overflights of the Soviet Union and other nations, provided the United States with critical information about their missile and nuclear capabilities, and both sides eventually used orbiting satellites to monitor compliance with nuclear and arms reductions treaties, movements of military units, and the general state of affairs within other nations, as well as for intercepting communications. Spies such as Julius and Ethel Rosenberg, Aldrich Ames, and Robert Hanssen in the United States, and Kim Philby and Klaus Fuchs in Great Britain, turned over atomic and other secrets to the Soviet Union, while Soviet military officers such as Oleg Penkovsky and Pyotr Popov provided British and American intelligence with vital information about Soviet military and intelligence capabilities and operations.

The end of the Cold War brought new challenges for intelligence agencies, particularly the rise of international terrorism. The penetration of terrorist cells is difficult for a variety of reasons, not least of which is that members of terrorist organizations are known to one another or have contacts who can vouch for them. Therefore intelligence agencies often rely heavily on a variety of other techniques, including SIGINT, imagery intelligence (IMINT), and financial research and analysis, to monitor terrorist organizations and apprehend their members.

Besides terrorism, nations face other threats to their security, and they will continue to seek out intelligence about the intentions and capabilities of enemies, potential enemies, and even friendly nations. In addition, border security issues, internal dissent, competition for natural resources, the proliferation of weapons of mass destruction, the resurgence of piracy, and numerous other regional and global issues will make intelligence a vital function of governments for a long time to come.

BOOKS AND ARTICLES

Andrew, Christopher, and Vasili Mitrokhin. *The Sword and the Shield: The Mitrokhin Archive and the Secret History of the KGB*. New York: Basic Books, 2000. Presents the story of what *The Washington Post* called "one of the most extraordinary events in the intelligence game since the Soviet Union collapsed," KGB espionage activities, based on the archives of KGB researcher and defector Vasili Mitrokhin.

_____. *The World Was Going Our Way: The KGB and the Battle for the Third World*. New York: Basic Books, 2000. This volume is the second installment of the history of postwar espionage based on the Mitrokhin archive, secret KGB documents through which the late coauthor revealed the Soviet Union's activities in Africa, Asia, and Latin America. Photographs.

Black, Ian, and Benny Morris. *Israel's Secret Wars: A History of Israel's Intelligence Services*. New York: Grove Press, 1992. Designed for specialists and spy buffs, a history of five decades of Israeli intelligence, from internal conflicts to victories in spying on Arab neighbors.

Dorril, Stephen. *MI6: Inside the Covert World of Her Majesty's Secret Service*. New York: Free Press, 2002. A history of Her Majesty's secret service that debunks myths and reveals a more fumbling organization than legend would suggest. Documents activities conducted for the United States as well as various assassination plans and spy operations.

Knightley, Philip. *The Second Oldest Profession: Spies and Spying in the Twentieth Century*. New York: W. W. Norton, 1980. A history of spies and spying, from the first modern intelligence agency, established in 1909, to the present day, with emphasis on Britain, France, Germany, Russia, and the United States. Knightley is unsympathetic to elaborate espionage operations, considering them expensive and corrupting.

Lowenthal, Mark W. *Intelligence: From Secrets to Policy*. 4th ed. Washington, D.C.: CQ Press, 2009. A primer on intelligence (including boldfaced key terms, reference lists, and useful appendixes) that considers both the history of intelligence gathering and the impact of intelligence institutions on public policy decisions.

Richelson, Jeffrey T. *A Century of Spies: Intelligence in the Twentieth Century*. New York: Oxford University Press, 1997. Written by a senior fellow at the National Security Archive, this volume examines both technological and human intelligence and their impact on history, decade by decade: from Adolf Hitler through the Cold War to economic espionage.

Volkman, Ernest. *The History of Espionage*. London: Carlton Books, 2007. An investigative reporter and former executive editor of *Espionage* magazine provides an overview of spying from ancient times to the world after the terrorist attacks of September 11, 2001.

Weiner, Tim. *Legacy of Ashes: The History of the CIA*. New York: Doubleday, 2007. A Pulitzer Prize-winning *New York Times* correspondent uses archives and interviews with CIA insiders (such as former chiefs Richard Helms and Stansfield Turner) for this history of the agency. Weiner argues that the CIA has, in the main, done more damage than good when it became distracted by gadgetry and covert actions under presidential influence while neglecting its mission to provide accurate intelligence.

Wise, David. *Nightmover: How Aldrich Ames Sold the CIA to the KGB for $4.6 Million*. New York: HarperCollins, 1995. Wise, an acclaimed espionage expert, rehearses the Ames case and the mole-hunt team that brought him to justice. The damage inflicted achieves a human dimension as Wise tells the tragic stories of the CIA operatives whom Ames identified.

Gregory Moore

INTERNATIONAL ARMS TRADE

OVERVIEW

The international arms trade exists for weapons to be made in one country and sold for use in another country or occasionally to be transshipped to a third party. The reason for this has often been that the source country has an extensive manufacturing capacity, usually for high-grade weapons, or that it is not possible to manufacture weapons in the country where they will be used. A third sector of the international arms trade follows a conflict when unused weapons may be sold to another party.

SIGNIFICANCE

Since ancient times, the international arms trade has been very important, because if one side in a conflict has access to better weaponry, that gives them the military edge in conflicts. Also in terms of the money spent on weapons, it has been estimated that some 2 percent of the world's gross domestic product is spent on weaponry, leading to the emergence of a military industrial complex. In 2007, it was estimated that nearly $33 billion (in U.S. dollars) was spent on weapons in that year. In 2008, that amount declined significantly, to about $14.3 billion, and by 2009 it was expected that the financial constraints on many countries would continue to cause a diminution of the international arms trade. However, the arms trade will remain important for military as well as economic reasons well into the foreseeable future.

HISTORY OF THE INTERNATIONAL ARMS TRADE

ANCIENT WORLD

There is much evidence that there was an extensive international arms industry during ancient times. Much of this concerned the development of particular armaments, notably the use of bronze and then iron. When the metal was developed in one area, entrepreneurs were involved in selling some of the weapons in rival countries. This was certainly the case with the introduction of iron (used by the Hittites) into ancient Egypt. It has also been suggested that the spread of the technology associated with iron helped transform the African continent, leading to small groups of people able to dominate particular societies in central, east, and southern Africa.

The largest military powers in the ancient world—the Assyrians, Achaemenid Persians, Macedonians, Carthaginians, and Romans, as well as the armies of ancient China—had to ensure that they held the military edge over their opponents, and this often involved the purchase of weapons or the materials to make weapons (such as tin from Cornwall or from Southeast Asia) to help furnish the large war machines. For example, items that could be easily transported, such as battleships, had to be made near the source of the materials (here, wood) required for their construction.

Animals were used in war in the ancient world, and the procurement and then the training of animals often involved significant cross-border trade. Such animals included war elephants, horses, and camels. As part of the international arms trade in the ancient world (a situation that has continued through to the present day), trained personnel were hired by a second country to accompany particular armaments to ensure that they were used correctly. This was often the case with siege machines, but also with simple weapons that required a particular skill, such as the Balearic slingers and crossbowmen in China.

MEDIEVAL WORLD

Greater trade in medieval times allowed for the increasing manufacture of weapons, and the decline in the large empires and creation of city-states led to changes in the international arms trade. Some parts of Europe—especially northern Italy and central Germany—became favored locations for the manufacture of armor, both for its durability and for its style. It became customary for members of royal families and the nobility to import armor from these places, as is evident in armories around Europe and the Mediterranean.

The Crusades led to increased manufacture of weapons for export, with the Knights Templar and the Knights Hospitaller both stockpiling within their castles in the Holy Land large numbers of weapons manufactured in Europe. It has been suggested that the wealth of these two Crusader orders led to the largest-scale mass manufacture of weapons since the end of the Roman Empire. Their enemies, the Seljuk Turks, developed the use of Damascus steel, a technology that was heavily guarded, but this secret did not prevent many rulers in the Middle East, the Mediterranean, and northern India from wanting to equip their armies with weapons made from Damascus steel.

Gradually within Europe, in the German and Italian states, the emergence of an arms industry led to the manufacture for sale of crossbows and later artillery—and in the early modern period, harquebuses. The need to have trained soldiers using them led not only to the purchase of the weapons but also often to the hiring of mercenary bands. It was essentially the development of firearms from the harquebus that led to the international arms trade as it is today.

MODERN WORLD

In the early modern period, the heavy use of firearms by one side over the other gave the side that possessed them such a major military advantage that it rapidly became necessary for all armies to be re-equipped with such weaponry. Because of the complicated nature of firearms manufacture, some craftsmen specialized in making firearms, which were then sold to armies and paramilitary groups. As a result, the international sale of such weapons spread throughout the world, equipping armies, often with weapons sourced from a range of countries. During periods of particularly fierce hostility—such as the Wars of Religion in France from 1562 to 1598, the Thirty Years' War (1618-1648), and the English Civil Wars (1642-1651)—the need for firearms and also gunpowder led to a lucrative trade in which neutral countries or states recognized that they could make fortunes in the provision of firearms and cannons.

The provision of large standing armies in Europe during the late seventeenth and early eighteenth centuries led to the uniform equipping of entire armies. As a result, many major countries began to establish their own arms industries, which quickly developed the ability to sell surplus weapons to other nations. After the major wars of the period—the War of the Spanish Succession (1701-1714), the War of the Polish Succession (1733-1735), the War of the Austrian

U.S. Marine Corps

An AK-47 rifle, one of the most popular weapons of the international small-arms trade.

Succession (1740-1748), and the Seven Years' War (1756-1763)—there was often an abundance of weapons at the end of fighting, and this generated an arms industry of its own.

Many of the weapons were sold to places that lacked the industrial capacity or manufacturing ability to make their own weapons—parts of North America, the Caribbean, South America, and Africa—and some groups able to buy weapons from Europe were able to create secondary empires of their own. The export of weapons to Asia led to a transformation in that continent, with some groups able to reequip their armies quickly and others unable to do so.

The French Revolution (1789-1793) and Napoleonic Wars (1793-1815) coincided with a period of industrialization in Europe, starting in Britain, which led to that nation's becoming one of the leading arms exporters. At the end of the Napoleonic Wars, it was the ability of people in South America to buy many of the surplus weapons that led to the successful wars of independence that saw the countries of South and Central America gain their independence—and for some of them, their own arms industries. By the mid-nineteenth century, British arms sales contributed significantly to the international arms trade. Although many of the weapons made were used throughout the British Empire, a large number were sold overseas.

Although companies had operated since medieval times making arms, the nineteenth century saw companies such as Blyth Brothers in Limehouse, London, start to focus heavily on manufacture of weapons for sale overseas. The arms industry soon came to be linked heavily with the foreign policy of the country in which companies were located. There was a worry that the weapons could be used against the armed forces of the manufacturing country. Thus the introduction of export permits generally resulted in bans placed on the sale of weapons to countries that were likely to go to war with that of the manufacturer.

AP/Wide World Photos

Lieutenant Colonel Oliver North, a central figure in the Iran-Contra affair, testifies before a joint House-Senate panel in 1987. North, a Marine officer working for the National Security Council, was accused of directing a secret U.S. operation to sell arms to Iran and secretly diverting the profits to the Contras, a group trying to overthrow the government of Nicaragua. He was found guilty of crimes arising from the affair, but his conviction was overturned.

By the late nineteenth century and early twentieth century, a number of major arms manufacturers had emerged. In Britain, Vickers and Armstrong (which subsequently merged) made goods ranging from small weapons to battleships. In Germany, Krupp and other major industrial firms, such as Blohm and Voss, dominated the German production. The manufacture of various machine guns, such as the Maxim gun and the Nordenfelt gun, also led to increased sales as countries again sought to rearm. In addition to the manufacturers themselves, there were dealers who traveled the world offering weaponry for sale. Such marketing efforts led men such as Sir Basil Zaharoff to be accused of causing wars.

After World War I, the press focused particularly on Zaharoff and the role he had played in that war. The international arms trade was denounced by speakers such as the Reverend Charles Coughlin in the United States, who linked war profits with the U.S. involvement in World War I. Profits from arms sales to other countries were denounced, as they helped encourage conflict, and the constant need to rearm as weapons became obsolete led to many countries being unable to afford to spend money for the welfare of their own people—a criticism that has continued to the present day.

The emergence of new nation-states after World War I helped increase the international arms trade. Some of the smaller countries were not large enough to manufacture their own weapons and were forced to acquire arms from overseas. This situation continued after World War II, with many countries gaining their independence. The constant reequipping of armies in Latin America and Africa by foreign arms dealers led to an emerging body of literature outlining the role played by the international arms trade. As well as the main manufacturers—the United States, the United Kingdom, France, the Soviet Union/Russia, and then China—there were a number of other countries that became heavily involved in the international arms trade, such as Czechoslovakia, Chile, Argentina, and also, because of their peculiar circumstances, South Africa and Israel. The latter two both manufactured their own weapons to prevent reliance on foreign imports, but to finance their arms industries, they began a trade in exporting their weaponry—with the added benefit to purchasers that the weapons had generally been tested in combat.

In the period from the 1960's to the present day, the international arms trade has continued to be an important part in the extension of the political and foreign policy goals of many countries. The sale of arms from one country to another tended to signify political support rather than a mere financial transaction, and similarly there were organized boycotts of sales of weaponry, such as the United Nations' sanctions on the apartheid government in South Africa. Countries and companies involved in breaching such sanctions were often blacklisted, as in the case of those who supplied the Iraqi government of Saddam Hussein in the run-up to Operation Desert Storm in 1991. As a result, many companies have become involved in the international arms trade, seeking to sell their weapons to countries that have difficult reputations and often selling those arms through middlemen in a country that can provide the requisite "end-user certificates" to prove that the weaponry is to be used by that country and not sold to another. This illegal sale of weaponry has led to the arming of militia and paramilitary groups around the world.

BOOKS AND ARTICLES

Laurance, Edward J. *The International Arms Trade*. New York: Lexington Books, 1992. Written at the time of the first Gulf War, this volume examines arms trading in the light of international realtions theory to analyze the impact of the international arms trade on policy makers.

Levine, Paul, and Ron Smith, eds. *The Arms Trade, Security, and Conflict*. New York: Routledge, 2003. A collection of papers by world experts considering the economics as well as security impact of the arms trade.

Navias, Martin, and Susan Willet. *The European Arms Trade*. New York: Nova Science, 1996.

Examines the arms export and trade policies of the United Kingdom, Germany, France, and the European Union from several perspectives. Index.

Sampson, Anthony. *The Arms Bazaar: From Lebanon to Lockheed*. Rev. ed. London: Hodder and Stoughton, 1991. From Vickers and Krupp to Lockhead and Northrop, Sampson looks at arms scandals in the Middle East, the role of arms trader Adnan Khashoggi, the buildup of arms sold to Iran, and the impact of the first Gulf War.

Yihdego, Zeray. *The Arms Trade and International Law*. Portland, Oreg.: Hart, 2007. A research fellow in law at Oxford Brookes University presents an authoritative and thorough overview of the impact of small arms and light weapons (SALW) on the post-Cold War modern world, which takes a hard look at the numbers (700 million SALW worldwide, traded by 99 nations and involving 1,000 companies). Argues that these unregulated weapons constitute a looming crisis and that there is an imminent need to address them legally at both the national and international levels.

Justin Corfield

MILITARY ORGANIZATION

OVERVIEW

Military organization refers to the way a nation-state structures its armed forces. Organization reflects the way a military perceives and develops its strategic mission and provides systematic command and control at the tactical level. An efficient organizational structure also includes administrative and logistical components, making the creation, maintenance, and application of effective military power possible. In order to understand organization, three major parts must be examined: the bureaucratic, usually centered in a nation's department of defense or ministry of war; the armed forces, usually breaking down into branches of service (cavalry, artillery, infantry) as well as unit relationships such as the battalion and division; and the command hierarchy/rank structure.

SIGNIFICANCE

Understanding a nation's military organizational structure reveals a great deal about how a military perceives and seeks to accomplish its mission. The United States, for example, with a large industrial base, has a table of organization and equipment that seeks to maximize technology and avoid casualties. This is a logical outgrowth of the principles of the Enlightenment on which the United States was founded. The Vietnamese, on the other hand, have an organizational structure that reflects *dau tranh*, which emphasizes the need to carry the struggle to the enemy at all costs.

Additionally, in many societies, the rank system mirrors the social structure; for example, in the Prussian army the landed gentry, the Junkers, generally held officerships, while the enlisted ranks were the peasantry, who in civilian life worked under them.

HISTORY OF MILITARY ORGANIZATION

ANCIENT WORLD
The most famous of the Greek military formations was the phalanx—a mass of troops equipped with long spears or pikes. Each line, or *stoechis*, consisted of sixteen to twenty-five troops, and each phalanx was eight to thirty-two lines deep. The largest formation, the *taxis*, consisted of between five hundred and fifteen hundred troops and was commanded by a general. A general's council or a single commander in chief led the entire army, usually consisting of more than one taxis.

Military reforms by Gaius Marius in 106-107 B.C.E. standardized Roman military organization, training, and equipment and introduced a self-contained, combined arms unit, the legion, that could operate independently or as part of a larger army. Not simply reliant on mass, the legion could use a variety of tactics that enabled it to outmaneuver the unwieldy phalanx. While the composition of the legion varied widely, in general the basic unit was the *centuriate*, consisting of sixty to one hundred troops and commanded by a *centurion*. Two centuriates were a *maniple*, commanded by the senior centurion; six to eight centuriates formed a *cohort*, commanded by the senior centurions of the legion. There were ten cohorts per legion. The overall commander was the *legatus legionis*.

The centuriate consisted of heavy infantry, whose main weapons were the pilum, or javelin; a short sword, or gladius; and a heavy shield, which could be used to form a tight defensive line. Light infantry, the *velites*, were used to confuse and harass the enemy. In addition, cavalry, the *equites*, and auxiliary troops filled out the legion, giving it a strength of approximately 5,126 troops.

MEDIEVAL WORLD
Medieval European armies reflected the social organization of their day. The elites in the armies, the

knights and heavy cavalry, generally came from the nobility or royal classes, and the common soldiery, the infantry, typically came from the peasantry. Most nobles and royalty did keep a retinue of professional men at arms, commanded by a sergeant at arms. Men at arms were generally expensive to maintain, and a king's ability to wage war depended greatly on the nobles who had sworn loyalty to him and the manpower they themselves could generate. With the exception of mercenary armies, which had a definitive command-and-control structure, most medieval wars were fought by armies that had strong social and political loyalties but little in the way of professional training or effective organization. The result was often disastrous. At the Battle of Agincourt in 1415, for example, the French outnumbered the English by three to one. Charles I d'Albret was unable to coordinate his reserves or his men at arms with the heavy cavalry effectively, and the result was a French defeat.

The French defeat underscored another important development in the medieval period: the rise of specialized, professional troops. English longbowmen, largely credited with the English victory at Agincourt, were highly trained. The inclusion of such troops could often turn the tide in battle, and in the Middle Ages the development of artillery—at first catapults, ballistae, and trebuchets but also battering rams and siege towers—gave an increasing edge to those armies that could afford them. By the eighteenth century, the development of cannons had created a specialized niche in European armies.

In the 1620's, the Manchus developed the four-banner system, which became the main organization for China (expanded to eight banners in 1642) until the end of the Qing Dynasty in 1911. Originally a means of controlling the Manchus, each banner became a means of civil administration after the establishment of the Qing Dynasty in 1644. In military terms, each banner army was independent and answered directly to the emperor. The smallest unit was *niru* (three hundred men). The next was *jalan* (consisting of five nirus), and five jalans constituted a *gusa* (banner). There were banners for the Manchus, the Han Chinese, and the Mongols. In 1631 a separate Chinese artillery corps was formed.

MODERN WORLD

The modern system of military organization can be traced to the French defeats in the middle of the eighteenth century. Maurice, comte de Saxe, the French general in Flanders during the War of the Austrian Succession (1740-1748), reorganized the French army into columns to be used to outflank and outmaneuver rather than annihilate an enemy. He also experimented with mixed arms units, combining cavalry, artillery, and infantry in a single operation. During the Seven Years' War (1756-1763), Victor-Maurice de Broglie (the duc de Broglie) published *Instruction pour l'armée du roi commandée par le maréchal duc de Broglie* (1761; instruction for the army of the king, commanded by the marshal the duke of Broglie), which separated the army into four divisions. Each division would have a quarter of the brigades under overall command, and a lieutenant general would command each. Each division would also be self-sufficient and have cavalry, artillery, and infantry resources at its disposal. This organization proved effective; however, de Broglie's system was dropped after his death, mostly because of pressure by noble officers who wished to preserve the French army as a bastion of privilege.

In 1772, the organizational ideas of Saxe and de Broglie were revived and developed by Count Jacques de Guibert, whose *Essai général de tactique* (*General Essay on Tactics*, 1781) called for a mixed formation of line and column depending on the tactical situation, a reform of the supply system, and an emphasis on speed. Artillery should be massed to concentrate on an enemy's weakest spot, and a reserve should be maintained. In 1779, the *Défense du système de guerre moderne* (defense of the system of modern war) developed these ideas further and called for a "nation in arms" that is, a nation willing and able to commit all of its resources to winning a war. Guibert's tactical ideas, and the organizational reforms they required, became the basis of a reformed French army, with one exception. The corps, consisting of two to four divisions and completely self-sufficient, was introduced by Napoleon in 1806. During the French Revolution (1789-1793) and the Napoleonic era, this army would conquer Europe and force all other European militaries to adopt similar organizational structures.

Modern military organization varies from army to army, but all have a similar outline. The basic unit of maneuver in the U.S. Army is the squad, consisting of five to seven troops. In communist armies, the three-man fire team is the smallest unit, but the squad remains the basis of operations. Each squad is led by a noncommissioned officer, usually a corporal or sergeant. Four squads make up a platoon, led by a sergeant first class and officered by a second lieutenant. Five platoons comprise a company, usually with one platoon devoted to heavy weapons, such as a mortar or heavy machine gun. Captains command companies.

Two to five companies are a battalion; three battalions are a brigade. In some armies, battalions are organized into regiments. In the U.S. Army, while each battalion retains its regimental identity, its organizational identity remains with the brigade to which it is attached. For example, the second brigade of an infantry division might contain First Battalion, Second Infantry Regiment; the First Battalion, Third Infantry Regiment; and First Battalion, Sixth Infantry Regiment.

Each brigade consists of infantry and armor elements. An infantry brigade consists of two infantry battalions and one armor battalion; an armor brigade consists of one infantry battalion and two armor battalions. There are usually two to three brigades in a division. The number of infantry to armor brigades determines if the division is infantry or armored. A colonel or brigadier general usually commands a brigade. A lieutenant general or major general commands a division.

In addition to the brigade structure, each division usually has an armored cavalry squadron, an aviation unit, and a divisional artillery battalion attached, in addition to transportation, logistical, and health/hospital services.

The company/battalion structure is for the infantry. Artillery units are organized into batteries rather than companies, and cavalry and armored cavalry units use troops rather than companies and squadrons rather than battalions.

Modern armies are still organized into corps, but usually by geographic locale. For example, most U.S. Army elements in Germany during the Cold War were part of VII Corps. An organization of corps is an army.

BOOKS AND ARTICLES

Biddle, Stephen. *Military Power: Explaining Victory and Defeat in Modern Battle*. Princeton, N.J.: Princeton University Press, 2004. On the more theoretical side, Biddle examines the history of the modern system, the impact of technology in force employment, and the resulting changes in training and organization.

Brown, Howard G. *War, Revolution and the Bureaucratic State: Politics and Army Administration in France, 1791-1799*. Oxford, England: Clarendon Press, 1995. Examines the political and bureaucratic genesis of French Revolutionary and Napoleonic military organization.

Center of Military History. *FM 100-2-3: The Soviet Army—Troops, Organization, and Equipment*. Washington, D.C.: Department of the Army, 1991. The Center of Military History and the U.S. Department of the Army publish excellent studies and field manuals, which furnish detailed organizational structures on individual militaries. This volume remains a thorough reference to the organizational structure of the Red Army.

Chaliand, Gérard. *The Art of War in World History: From Antiquity to the Nuclear Age*. Berkeley: University of California Press, 1994. Because of the unique nature of national militaries, it is beyond the scope of this essay to survey all relevant works on the history, theory, and evolution of individual military organizations. As a beginning point for the student of military organization, however, Chaliand's study addresses this problem using primary documentation and is especially valuable for its inclusion of both non-European and Enlightenment military thinkers.

Dague, Everett. *Napoleon and the First Empire's Ministries of War and Military Administration*. Lewiston, N.Y.: Edwin Mellen Press, 2006. Examines the political and bureaucratic genesis of French Revolutionary and Napoleonic military organization.

Doughty, Robert, and Ira Gruber, eds. *Warfare in the Western World*. 2 vols. Lexington, Mass.: D. C. Heath, 1996. While primarily an operational survey, this work demonstrates the evolution of and relationship between modern organization and tactical employment.

Elting, John. *Swords Around a Throne*. New York: Free Press, 1988. Another excellent resource on the armies of the French Revolution and Napoleon.

Forrest, Alan. *Soldiers of the French Revolution*. Durham, N.C.: Duke University Press, 1990. Provides superb descriptions of the organization, composition, and employment of the armies of the French Revolution and Napoleon.

Griffith, Paddy. *The Art of War of Revolutionary France*. London: Greenhill Books, 1998. Solid coverage of the French Revolution and Napoleon.

Howard, Michael. *War in European Society*. New York: Oxford University Press, 1976. The study of organization is bound up in a fuller study of military history. Howard's book provides an excellent overview of how military force developed from the Middle Ages to the present.

Ralston, David B. *Importing the European Army: The Introduction of European Military Techniques and Institutions into the Extra-European World, 1600-1914*. Chicago: University of Chicago Press, 1990. Examines the social and economic impact of European military organization on Russia, the Ottoman Empire, Egypt, China, and Japan.

Stofft, William, ed. *American Military History*. Washington, D.C.: Center of Military History, 1989. For the student of modern military organization, this volume provides an excellent overview the Army as well as the Reserve and National Guard organizations.

Everett Dague

STRATEGY

OVERVIEW

Simply stated, military strategy is the planning, coordination, and implementation of a set of actions, or tactics, that are aimed at defeating the enemy in an individual engagement or in a war as a whole. Although many have written on the topic since then, it might have best been broken down in 1838 by the French general Antoine-Henri de Jomini:

> Strategy is the art of making war upon the map, and comprehends the whole theater of operations. . . . Strategy decides where to act; logistics brings the troops to this point; grand tactics decides the manner of execution and the employment of the troops.

Of course, within that definition, endless permutations are possible and, indeed, probable.

SIGNIFICANCE

An understanding of tactics is essential for anyone seeking to develop a comprehensive evaluation of why wars have been won and lost. For example, if one seeks to understand why the Nazis lost World War II when they seemed to have achieved such a stunning victory so early in the war, a look at Adolf Hitler's war strategy, and specifically his fascination with waging war against the Soviet Union, is absolutely crucial. In the modern world, military strategy may not be the only factor in determining the outcome of a conflict, but it remains a vital field of inquiry by generals and historians alike.

HISTORY OF TACTICS

ANCIENT WORLD
Although wars have been fought dating to ancient times, one of the most influential early codifications of the principles of military strategy was written around 500 B.C.E. by the Chinese philosopher Sunzi (Sun Tzu) in his *Sunzi Bingfa* (c. fifth-third century B.C.E.; *The Art of War*, 1910). In this masterwork, Sunzi developed thirteen principles of military strategy, devoting a chapter to each. These included calculations, doing battle, planning attacks, formation, force, army maneuvers, ground formation, fire attacks, and using spies. His ideas have influenced many throughout the world and still are read today.

In the West, military strategies developed along with the rise and fall of civilizations over the millennia. Though the ancient Sumerians and Greeks developed strategies to defeat their enemies, the development of strategies reached a high point with the Macedonian leaders Philip II (382-336 B.C.E.) and his son Alexander the Great (356-323 B.C.E.). Philip II tactically utilized infantry and cavalry together to weaken his foes and, in concert with large-scale planning and long-distance communication, expanded his empire. Using a large-scale strategy that employed both warfare and diplomacy, Philip was able to unite most of the city-states of Greece in his League of Corinth. Picking up where his father left off, Alexander took his father's tactical and strategic innovations and employed them on an even larger scale, dominating much of the known world during his brief lifetime, expanding the Macedonian Empire by driving northward into Europe, southward into Egypt, and eastward, conquering the entire Persian Empire. Alexander employed surprise, meticulous planning, and effective communication as a means of implementing his strategies.

The Carthaginian commander Hannibal (247-182 B.C.E.) is generally considered to have been both a brilliant tactician and a supreme strategist. Facing the Romans in the Second Punic War (218-201 B.C.E.), Hannibal developed a victorious strategy that can be seen not only in such battles as the one at Cunnae (216 B.C.E.), but also, in a larger sense, in his complete reorganization of the Roman Army to deal with the forces and strategies that he innovated. Luring the Romans into engagements in terrains where he knew his forces had an advantage, Hannibal came closer than anyone else in the ancient world to conquering Rome. Eventually, however, the Roman general Quintus Fabius Maximus employed his own strategy, specifically designed to wear Hannibal down gradually by cutting off his supply lines, engaging him only in small skirmishes that diverted his attention, and avoiding a direct conflict with his powerful army.

The Roman emperor Julius Caesar (100-44 B.C.E.) was the first Roman to combine civil and military power, so that he could implement his strategic vision with both the political and military arms of the Roman government. Following a war of conquest through Italy that consolidated his power, turning the Roman Republic into the Roman Empire, Caesar executed his brilliant conquest of Gaul, not only cutting off his opponents' military supply lines but also patiently waiting until they had exhausted their water supply. Fear of Roman power was implemented ruthlessly as a strategy, as he often cut off the heads of surviving opposing soldiers as a warning to others not to rebel against Rome.

MEDIEVAL WORLD

During the seventh century C.E., it was the Islamic world that was expanding, and that expansion was largely directed by the Prophet Muḥammad's greatest general, Khālid ibn al-Walīd (died 642 C.E.). After honing his strategies in helping Muḥammad expand his new religion throughout the Arabian Peninsula, Walīd oversaw the invasion and conquest of both the Persian Empire and the Roman province of Syria within three years. Seeking to fight against many smaller foes before they could unite into a large army, Walīd defeated tribes seeking to escape the Muslim hegemony. Planning attacks from multiple sides while making sure that there were no enemies on his own flanks and marching his own forces through inhospitable deserts that his foes thought he could not, he completed the conquest of Persia in 633 C.E. and of Roman Syria the following year.

The early medieval period was a low point in the application of strategy in Europe, as the feudal system gradually dominated, with its emphasis on defense, castles, and sieges. However, to the east, the Mongol leader Genghis Khan (c. 1155 or 1162-1227) employed psychological strategies of terrorizing his opponents into submission. By implementing a scorched-earth policy along with mounted archers and cavalry, Genghis conquered Arab, Persian, European, and Asian armies with his highly mobile forces and revolutionized warfare with the rapidity of his movement. Using terror and biological means to subdue fortified cities, successor khans kept order through terror as well.

New technologies such as the longbow and gunpowder inevitably changed the character of European warfare during the late medieval period, but if there was one person who truly bridged the medieval and modern periods, it was Gustavus II Adolphus (1594-1632) of Sweden. In the Thirty Years' War (1618-1648), Gustavus pioneered strategies that led to victories over the forces of the Holy Roman Empire. Maintaining infantry and cavalry with mobile artillery and logistics in coordinated attacks, Gustavus used nationalism and a standing army to create and expand the Swedish Empire into the third largest nation in Europe, behind only Spain and Russia. Like Genghis Khan, he used maneuverability to create a very aggressive military strategy that downplayed defense and overcame the stagnant and static medieval fortifications and other defense strategies, utilizing the new firepower of carbines and artillery to great effect.

MODERN WORLD

During one of the first wars of the modern era, the Seven Years' War (1756-1763), Frederick II of Prussia (Frederick "the Great," 1712-1786) began the transformation of war based on small-scale engagements to one based on large, expansive strategies that required massive logistical support and a highly disciplined, maneuverable army. Employing the basic tenets of modern warfare, the concentration of forces at a weak point along the lines of his opponent, Frederick used artillery to soften the lines in advance of his assault. Pressing his attack in order to exhaust his opponents and fighting off multiple opponents by keeping his forces extremely mobile within his own interior areas, Frederick employed strategies that took advantage of his knowledge of the terrain and the best ways to exploit it to create weak points in his opponents' forces.

However "great" Frederick was, his legacy, and most others', pales in comparison to the giant of military strategy in the early modern world, Napoleon Bonaparte (1769-1821). Despite the growth in the size of armies because of the implementation of conscription, Napoleon was able to implement high maneuverability to achieve a strategy of scorched earth and terrorized civilian populations. The mobility of Napoleon's forces allowed him to dictate the order of battle, where his opponent would be enticed to strike, and how to find his opponents' weakest points to win the battle. Cutting his opponents' supply and communication lines sped their defeat. Warfare based on lines of soldiers was shown to be ineffective in the face of Napoleon's cavalry surrounding the lines, cutting them off from their reserves. With the judicious use of mobile forces in strategic locations, Napoleon was routinely able to defeat much larger, linear forces. Perhaps no greater compliment can be paid to Napoleon's strategies than to note that they inspired the rise of the study of military strategies, which saw the first two modern masterworks of military strategy, Carl von Clausewitz's *Vom Krieg* (1832; *On War*, 1873) and Jomini's *Traité des grandes opérations militaires* (1805, 5 volumes; *Treatise on Grand Military Operations*, 1865).

Napoleon also influenced later military strategists during the American Civil War (1861-1865), such as Union generals Ulysses S. Grant and William Tecumseh Sherman and Confederate generals Robert E. Lee and Thomas "Stonewall" Jackson. However, advances in technology meant that the weapons of war were much more efficient and could fire much more rapidly, necessitating larger-scale strategies that could be implemented only by the political leaders of the belligerent nations. The impact of communications technologies, such as the telegraph, allowed political leaders to work more directly with military commanders. Working with the Union's political leaders, Grant and Sherman used scorched-earth strategies and highly mobile forces, along with naval blockades and the destruction of supply and communication lines, to surround Lee's forces and bring about the end of the war.

If the technological changes of the nineteenth century revolutionized military strategy, by the early twentieth century consistent change in military technology would continue to transform strategies with each and every large conflict. At the beginning of World War I (1914-1918), the forces implemented strategies learned from the conflicts of the late nineteenth century, only to be overwhelmed by the large artillery pieces developed. This necessitated the retreat of forces on both sides into trenches, which would characterize the rest of the conflict. World War II would see the addition of the elements of powerful tanks and airpower, resulting in massive tactical and strategic, and eventually atomic, bombing, again necessitating massive changes to war strategies. However, a return to an emphasis on mobility and concentration of forces accompanied the new technologies. The unified German forces (Wehrmacht), acting under Hitler's directives, implemented Blitzkrieg (literally, "lightning war"), a sudden, surprise attack of overwhelming force, often employing coordinated air and ground forces—which proved to be an extremely effective offensive strategy. Fortunately, Hitler's fixation on the conquest of the Soviet Union proved to be his undoing.

With the hesitancy of the United States and the Soviet Union to engage directly during the Cold War (1945-1991), for the latter half of the twentieth century warfare took a less technological turn, as exemplified by the conflict in Vietnam from the 1950's to the mid-1970's. Despite massive technological superiority, guerrilla warfare caused the United States to employ a series of unsuccessful strategies, causing frustration not only among soldiers but among the American public as well. Guerrilla warfare dominated many of the small-scale conflicts of the last half of the century, especially in locations where the landscape lent itself to easy concealment.

Technology came to the fore once again with the two Gulf Wars of the 1990's and 2000's. The use of so-called smart bombs and the massive implementation of the "surge" in Iraq—a significant influx of "boots on the ground"—led to military superiority in Iraq, although the lessons of Vietnam continue to be taught, in that indirect, small-scale engagements by a force committed to a conflict by ideology or religion can keep a large, technologically advanced force off its stride, extending a conflict until the superior force, or the nation behind it, tires of the conflict and withdraws.

The counterstrategies employed by insurgents and ideologically driven guerrillas have fallen under the rubric of "terrorism," which expands the war from the arena of the battlefield to all areas of daily life, in a strategy that employs any tactic necessary—from the hijacking of civilian airlines to their use as projectile bombs to car-bombings of hotels and cafés to suicide bombings—to wage psychological as well as ideological war. The strategies of terrorism encroach on the entire fabric of a society by diverting that society's resources to long-term (not just temporary) counterstrategies involving heightened security in order to ensure safety in transportation, trade, and other economic and civic infrastructures. Time will tell if a military strategy is ever developed to overcome a small-scale, guerrilla army that wages a war on ideological grounds.

BOOKS AND ARTICLES

Bose, Partha. *Alexander the Great's Art of Strategy Lessons from the Great Empire Builder.* New York: Gotham, 2003. Uses historical episodes from the life and conquests of Alexander the Great to illustrate his mastery of strategy on a large scale.

Chaliand, Gérard, ed. *The Art of War in World History: From Antiquity to the Nuclear Age.* Berkeley: University of California Press, 1994. Assembles a collection of writings on the strategic aspects of warfare from across the ages, including writings from modern times as well as from ancient Europe, the Middle East, and Asia.

Collins, John M. *Military Strategy: Principles, Practices, and Historical Perspectives.* Washington, D.C.: Potomac Books, 2001. Uses historical examples to demonstrate how different war strategies have worked in the past in order to predict how they may work in the future.

Gartner, Scott Sigmund. *Strategic Assessment in War.* New Haven, Conn.: Yale University Press, 1999. Looking at the wars of the twentieth century, analyzes how armies implement their strategies and adjust them in response to their opponents' strategies.

Gray, Colin S. *Modern Strategy.* New York: Oxford University Press, 1999. Examines the evolution of military strategies over the course of the twentieth century to illustrate that strategy is ever changing.

Liddell Hart, B. H. *Strategy.* 2d rev. ed. New York: Plume, 1991. One of the classic works on strategy, written by one of the foremost military strategists of the twentieth century, Liddell Hart's famous "indirect strategy" emphasized mobility and lightning warfare, with the implementation of a massive, decisive force in order to win the war quickly.

Luttwak, Edward N. *Strategy: The Logic of War and Peace.* Rev. ed. Cambridge, Mass.: Belknap Press, 2002. Also centering on the "indirect strategy," Luttwak looks at the strategic relationship between war and peace, noting how war strategy depends not only on what the opponent does but also on what is politically feasible with the general public.

Marston, Daniel, and Carter Malkasian, eds. *Counterinsurgency in Modern Warfare.* New York: Osprey, 2008. Presents a history of major conflicts, from British action in Ireland during the 1910's to the Iraq War of the 2000's, where strategy proved key in determining the victor.

Paret, Peter, ed. *Makers of Modern Strategy from Machiavelli to the Nuclear Age.* Rev. ed. Princeton, N.J.: Princeton University Press, 1986. Revised from its original 1943 publication, this collection presents twenty-eight essays, from some of the foremost military historians, on the topic of strategy.

Steven L. Danver

TACTICS

OVERVIEW

Military units preparing for and in battle are governed by the overall *strategy* of the campaign. All component elements of a military force in a campaign maneuver fight within an operational plan. At the sharp end (in contact with the enemy), all personnel use *tactics* to achieve their aim—in movement around the battlefield, in defense, and in attack.

SIGNIFICANCE

To a great extent, tactics have always been influenced by the technology available at the time. From rock to rifle to rocket, tactics have evolved to use what is available to inflict the most damage on the enemy while preserving lives on the user's side. The evolution of battlefield weapons and their increasing range and power have affected tactics directly. Another significant factor in tactics is mobility: Both defenders and attackers need to be able to move freely about the battlefield; failure to maintain freedom of movement can easily lead to defeat.

HISTORY OF TACTICS

ANCIENT WORLD

Tactics are governed by weapons to a large extent, and the range and firepower of those weapons. In the period of early warfare, available weapons were limited in range to below the total range of vision. This meant that anyone out of range of bow or catapult was safe to move. Tactics developed to bring the enemy within range by maneuver and speed of deployment.

Weapons available in the pre-firearm period included the sword, bow and arrow, spear, javelin, lance, and siege engines. Men en masse on foot moved slowly and were difficult to maneuver once a battle had begun. The answer was to mount some men on horses, giving them a greater speed on the battlefield and a greater range on reconnaissance.

Cavalry became, as training and tactics improved, the masters of the shock effect. Horses could be trained and could attack en masse, and a cavalry charge was very effective in breaking the ranks of defending infantry. Initially the defenses against cavalry were limited to spear, pike, and bow; it was the bow that finally began the decline of cavalry, for well-trained archers were capable of breaking up a cavalry charge long before it reached the defender's front line.

For the defender, one of the best protections was walling and towers, the castle, keep, fortified town, or house. Tactically the defender has the advantage in that he has internal lines of communication (and therefore freedom of movement), and the static defenses of thick walls and towers often defeated the attacker. Here, however, technical developments led to the invention and development of siege engines of considerable power, capable of slowly but finally demolishing even the thickest walls. Other tactical methods of defeating the wall including mining underneath it.

The art of static defenses reached its peak with the detailed designs of Sébastien Le Prestre de Vauban (1633-1707), although the very last such constructions were seen as late as the twentieth century in the Maginot line (named after André Maginot, 1877-1932) in eastern France and similar defensive works.

MEDIEVAL WORLD

The arrival of firearms on the battlefield further limited the effect of cavalry, although initially the range and firepower of these early weapons were limited, and musketeers were normally protected from cavalry by pikemen, who stood to their front.

The first military firearms were designed perhaps more to frighten the horses than to have killing effect. Both handheld and heavier weapons were developed, and cannons served well to reduce static defenses. The rate of fire, accuracy, and general effect of the weapons was limited, but technology made great strides in improving the characteristics of these equipments.

Tactics throughout the ages have always been crucial in determining how much damage each side can do to the other in battle. The side with the most soldiers and the best weapons could normally be expected to prevail, but there are occasions when small groups that were better armed and equipped were able to inflict disproportionate damage on much larger forces. The use by the British army of machine guns in nineteenth century colonial warfare and the Spencer rifle (invented by Christian Spencer in 1860) in the American Civil War are examples of this.

MODERN WORLD

In the nineteenth century, changes to firearms began to create a need for changes in tactics. Firearms became more effective. The rate of fire was increased, accuracy improved, and the arrival of the breech-loading rifle, the machine gun, and quick-fire cannon would affect tactics more rapidly than had been seen before.

Breech-loading rifles meant that no longer did infantry have to stand to fire; earlier muzzle-loaded weapons had to be reloaded with the soldier standing up. The ability to reload lying down meant that infantry were less obvious on the battlefield and hence better protected against enemy cannon fire. Defenders began to dig into the ground to lower their silhouettes and to protect themselves even more, and attacking infantry had to move toward the enemy across ground that was covered by the defenders' fire.

The cannon on the battlefield had, for a long time, been limited in effect by its lack of maneuverability, but manufacturing techniques slowly overcame this problem and guns were soon able to keep up with the cavalry by being horse-drawn on highly mobile and stable carriages. Breech-loading methods improved the rate of fire, higher standards of manufacture increased accuracy, and the cannon became the field gun with considerable effect upon bodies of troops present on the battlefield.

The invention of the machine gun spelled the end of massed troop formations, although this was not fully understood in the nineteenth or early twentieth century. Units with machine guns issued to them often failed to use them, despite the obvious advantage of a high rate of sustainable fire, still preferring to fight battles with verve and élan rather than brains.

World War I (1914-1918) saw the technology of war show how utterly ruthless it could be against masses of men. No matter how great the attacker's superiority in numbers, machine guns, artillery, and barbed wire spelled the end of millions of lives. The problem for the tacticians of this war was that technology had supplied weapons of defense that were far superior to the weapons of attack. In most cases, the attackers were armed simply with rifle and bayonet and were faced by increasing numbers of defending machine guns, deep belts of barbed wire, and artillery defense plans that left the attackers dead and dying in front of the defending trenches.

Trenches in World War I were redolent of the earlier wall defenses of the Middle Ages and earlier. Siege warfare existed between the two sides on the western front, and although major attacks were made, they failed in the main in the first three years of the war because the defender had the advantage, although it must also be recognized that the more senior officers on both sides (particularly the British commander, Field Marshal Douglas Haig, Viscount Dawick) were still convinced of the value of cavalry (against machine guns, barbed wire, and guns) to make the breakthrough and develop the attack into a rout. This was simply impossible. What was needed was a breakthrough weapon.

That weapon was the tank. Invented by the British, and much promoted by Winston Spencer Churchill, the tank was seen to be capable of breaking through the enemy defenses unscathed, and accompanied by infantry, to lead the breakthrough into the enemy gun lines and rear, whereby victory would be won. However, technology here lacked the ability to provide sufficiently reliable tanks, and the defenders soon realized that they could fight against tanks. Nonetheless, the idea bore eventual fruit and led to the infantry-tank warfare of World War II.

Once more, tactics were to undergo changes to incorporate the new tanks and the very new concept of air power. The Germans demonstrated their new tactics in Poland, Denmark, Holland, and France in 1939 and 1940, and it seemed that there was no real answer to Blitzkrieg. The combination of infantry, tanks, artillery, and aircraft caused a remarkable effect on the battlefield. The "empty battlefield" of World War I became even more essential in this war for the reason that movement, concentrations of troops, and defensive positions were all vulnerable to air attack, shelling, or an infantry tank attack combined with supporting weapons.

The pace of tactics had changed dramatically; no longer did battles proceed at the pace of the infantry but rather at the speed of the motor vehicle (and later, with the arrival of paratroops and "vertical envelopment," at the speed of the aircraft). The need for rapidity of movement now became paramount, and infantry, to keep up with the tanks, had to be carried in trucks—or, better still, in armored personnel carriers, a concept of Sir Basil Henry Liddell Hart (1895-1970) and Major General John F. C. Fuller (1878-1966), completely adopted by the Germans, especially Colonel General Heinz Guderian (1888-1954). Artillery also needed to move faster, and so was towed or even self-propelled in semiarmored vehicles.

Tank battles were fought tank against tank, but by the side of this was a developing ability for the infantry to destroy tanks themselves with easily movable antitank guns and, later in the war, man-portable "fire and throw-away" antitank weapons, as well as the "bazooka" and similar weapons. Tanks were becoming hunted as well as hunters.

In the air, enormous strides were made in developing weapons to make air-ground cooperation a reality. Initially air support was provided by, for example, the Junkers Ju87 Stuka dive-bomber. In the course of the war, rocket-firing aircraft could knock tanks out, and even strategic bombers were used (sometimes not very effectively) to aid ground troops.

Modern tactics are a combination of the well-tried and -tested fire and movement technique (some men fire at the enemy, while the others move forward tactically) and a mobility that is fundamental to gaining surprise on the battlefield. The delivery of troops unexpectedly on the battlefield was always a great contributor to success; paratroops were used for this purpose, but nowadays air-landed troops (from aircraft or helicopter) can often tip the scales in favor of the side using them (whether as attacker or defender).

Infantry are now almost invisible on the battlefield, whether moving or in defensive positions; night as cover has disappeared with the appearance of light-intensification and infrared equipment, and tanks can engage the enemy by heat signature alone. Artillery can deliver devastating, concentrated fire, which will totally demoralize any defender.

In the air, target identification sometimes remains a problem, but the delivery capability and capacity are tremendous, and one aircraft can drop a payload of immense value to the troops on the ground. Air-lifting troops both to make an assault and to put "boots on the ground" can proceed so quickly that rapid buildups of troops are possible in a very short time.

Tactics seem to have developed out of all recognition, but in fact they remain the same: to engage the enemy on the battlefield and to defeat him. If anything, tactics are very personal to soldiers, because if the tactics are effective they will kill the enemy; if not, then they will be killed. Only the technology has changed, meaning that speed is now of the ultimate essence: speed of movement, rate of firepower, speed in gaining and using intelligence, speed in reacting to enemy threat. On the ground, however, it all comes down to getting into such a position that defeat of the enemy can be achieved. When it comes down to the basic level, it is the soldier on the ground who counts, and if the tactics are faulty or the training deficient, then soldiers will die.

BOOKS AND ARTICLES

Clausewitz, Carl von. *On War*. Edited and translated by Michael Howard and Peter Paret. Princeton, N.J.: Princeton University Press, 1976. Considered perhaps the greatest work on the theory of warfare, Clausewitz's treatise not only is classic but also remains current. The paperback edition of this translation offers a useful index.

Drury, Ian. *The Civil War Military Machine: Weapons and Tactics of the Union and Confederate Armed Forces*. New York: Smithmark, 1993. The first Civil War book to focus on small arms (handguns and rifles), field and siege artillery, naval ordinance, and ships. More than four hundred color illustrations show Union and Confederate weapons, battles, landscapes, forts, and naval vessels, many in cross section.

Eady, H. G. *Historical Illustrations to Field Service Regulations*. Vol. 2. London: Sifton Praed, 1927. Although difficult to locate, an invaluable resource.

Gaulle, Charles de. *The Army of the Future*. Foreword by Walter Millis. London: Hutchinson, 1940. A translation of de Gaulle's *Vers l'armée de métier* (1934), in which the French general advocated the creation of a mechanized, professional army.

Haughton, Andrew. *Training, Tactics, and Leadership in the Confederate Army of Tennessee: Seeds of Failure*. Cass Series—Military History and Policy 5. Portland, Oreg.: Frank Cass, 2000. Focuses on the South's army structure, from officers to privates, and their daily military lives during the Civil War.

O'Sullivan, Patrick. *Terrain and Tactics*. Contributions in Military Studies 115. New York: Greenwood Press, 1991. Discusses military tactics in the light of geographical concepts, a field known as military geography. O'Sullivan considers many different geographic settings and how they pose advantages and disadvantages, including a survey of the geography of war from 1945 through guerrilla and insugency tactics of the late twentieth century.

Samuels, Martin. *Doctrine and Dogma: German and British Infantry Tactics in the First World War*. Contributions in Military Studies 121. New York: Greenwood Press, 1992. Describes German and British infantry tactics, training, and leadership during World War I. Especially interesting for its comparison of the two nations' value systems and their reflection in military practice and achievement. Of particular interest to military historians and professional officers.

Steiger, Rudolf. *Armour Tactics in the Second World War: Panzer Army Campaigns of 1939-41 in German War Diaries*. New York: Berg, 1991. Primary documents form the basis for this description of World War II tank tactics, with particular emphasis on Operation Barbarossa, based on the files of the Germans' second Panzer Army.

Sun-tzu. *The Illustrated Art of War*. Translated by Samuel B. Griffith. New York: Oxford University Press, 2005. This ancient work is still read and consulted for its timeless insights, and it formed the basis of several of Mao Zedong's twentieth century military theories.

David Westwood

RESEARCH TOOLS

WAR FILMS

The following films are important in the study of military history. They are selected for their value in representing the conflict and/or the period in question, and they are arranged in roughly chronological subsections, within which they are arranged alphabetically by title. An * (asterisk) denotes a foreign production; a ^ (caret) denotes a television production.

ANCIENT GREECE

Alexander
Released: 2004

Alexander the Great began his conquest of the known world in 334 B.C.E. His Asian campaign, which pitted his Macedonian army against Persians, Bactrians, Scythians, and East Indians, lasted until 326 B.C.E. Unfortunately, of the myriad battles and sieges he fought, *Alexander* depicts only two: Gaugamela (331 B.C.E.) and Hydaspes River (326 B.C.E.). The decision to emphasize Alexander's personal life robs the film of much of its value as a war film; however, there are few other films about the campaigns of Alexander. The film is successful in accurately portraying the scale of the massive Battle of Gaugamela, arguably Alexander's most important victory, while close-up shots are excellent in portraying the Macedonian phalanx in battle, as well as the extent to which Alexander relied on his cavalry.

The 300 Spartans
Released: 1962

In 480 B.C.E., during the Second Greco-Persian War, three hundred Spartan warriors under King Leonidas held off the advancing Persian army of Xerxes at the Battle of Thermopylae (480 B.C.E.). While much older than the more recent release of *300* (2006), *The 300 Spartans* is much more objective in its portrayal of both the battle and the two armies involved (although neither film makes mention of the Spartan enslavement of the Helots, while at the same time depicting the battle as one of freedom versus slavery). The more recent film has a better depiction of phalanx warfare, as well as an explanation of the Spartan *agoge* and warrior culture, but its depiction of the Persians as beasts and demons makes *The 300 Spartans* a better choice.

ANCIENT ROME

Spartacus *and* **Gladiator**
Released: 1960 and 2000 respectively

Taken together, these films provide an accurate depiction of the Roman legion and Roman warfare. Though the former is primarily fiction and the latter is based on the Third Servile War (73-71 B.C.E.), each nicely complements the other. *Gladiator*'s opening battle scene shows the Roman legion in action up close, while the battle scene at the end of *Spartacus* shows an absolutely astounding portrayal of legion tactics and maneuvers from a distance. In addition to their depictions of warfare, both go into some detail in portraying the politics of Rome and, of course, the role of Roman blood sports. Which film is superior is a matter of preference.

MIDDLE AGES AND CRUSADES

Alexander Nevsky*
Released: 1938

The Battle of the Ice (also known as the Battle of Lake Peipus) took place in 1242. It was fought between the Teutonic Knights and the Republic of Novgorod as part of the northern Crusades. Alexander Nevsky led the Novgorod army to victory against the invading Teutons on the frozen lake. The climactic scene comes when the weight of armored knights becomes too much for the ice to bear and the Teutons break through, drowning under the ice. This film, a Soviet production, is not only a masterful piece of propaganda but also one of the first epic war movies. It is a useful film both because of the period it depicts and because of the period that created it.

Braveheart
Released: 1995

Mel Gibson's film about the life of William Wallace is both a blessing and a curse. Historically speaking, *Braveheart* is plagued with many significant inaccuracies, something Gibson acknowledged as necessary in order to enhance cinematic value; however, *Braveheart*'s numerous battle scenes (Stirling Bridge, 1297; Falkirk, 1298; and Bannockburn, 1314) are massive, intense, and thoroughly engaging. They also provide a depiction of a major turning point in military history: the use of pikes by infantry to defeat charging cavalry. *Braveheart* is a good visual supplement for study of the Scottish Wars of Independence.

Henry V
Released: 1989

On Saint Crispin's Day, 1415, Henry V of England took the field against a French army twice as large and made up of mounted knights, yet at the end of the day the English had won a decisive victory. The Battle of Agincourt, as it is known, is one of the most important battles in history because it demonstrated that, armed with longbows, peasant infantry could defeat cavalry, thus threatening the social hierarchy of Europe. The entire film traces the events leading up to the battle, the battle itself, and the battle's significance. Though the battle scene is only a fraction of the film, it aptly depicts the impact of both the longbow and the thick mud that covered the field and hindered the French against their lighter-armored opponents. Because the film is based on Shakespeare's play and follows it closely, the language will be difficult to follow for some. Kenneth Branaugh (Henry V) and his fellow actors, however, bring both language and action to life.

Kingdom of Heaven
Released: 2005

Beginning in 1095, the Crusades served as a centuries-spanning source of conflict between Christian and Muslim. In 1187, Saladin the Saracen laid siege to the city of Jerusalem, which was defended by an army under the command of Balian of Ibelin. *Kingdom of Heaven* tells of Balian's rise to the status of noble and Crusader, his journey to the Holy Land, and his unsuccessful defense of Jerusalem. The film provides a nice visual portrayal of medieval warfare, especially siegecraft, and reveals some of the complex politics involved in the governance of the Crusader states.

The Messenger
Released: 1999

Joan of Arc is one of the most famous individuals in French history. Her victory at Orléans in 1429 marked a turning point in the Hundred Years' War (1337-1453) between England and France. *The Messenger* not only provides a brief but adequate background to the Hundred Years' War, along with good visuals for medieval warfare and siegecraft (particularly the use of the culverin), but also explores Joan's mentality, visions, and belief that she was chosen by God to push the English out of France.

FEUDAL JAPAN

The Last Samurai
Released: 2003

This film is a double-edged sword. On one side, it is an excellent portrayal of the Japanese transition from feudal warfare and weapons to those of the modern age, intermixing the social, military, and political consequences of the transition. The film's portrayal of the Japanese warrior code of bushidō and its many battle scenes are tremendous; however, the portrayal of the opposing sides is too skewed (as in *The Patriot*). The Japanese samurai and peasants are shown to have had a perfect life until those awful, modernizing Western nations came along. However, if one can look past the revisionist history, the film has a lot to offer.

Ran*

Released: 1985

Ran is an excellent film for bringing feudal Japanese warfare to life. The film offers excellent visuals, both in its epic battle scenes and in its beautiful costumes. The battle scenes, though sometimes gory to the point of being comedic, accurately depict the formations, tactics, and weapons of the Japanese warlords, in particular their use of the harquebus. The introduction of firearms is a pivotal point in military history, and the film shows why. *Ran* is also useful in depicting the samurai warrior code of bushidō. The film's only real drawback is that it is based on William Shakespeare's *King Lear* (c. 1605-1606) and therefore is not historically based.

THIRTY YEARS' WAR

Alatriste

Released: 2006

In the most expensive Spanish-language production to date, based on the series of novels by Arturo Pérez-Reverte *Las aventuras del Capitán Alatriste* (1997-2006; the adventures of Captain Alatriste), a quarter century of the seventeenth century Spanish Empire and religious wars are depicted, including the Battle of Rocroi (1643).

The Last Valley

Released: 1970

Despite its enormous importance to history, the Thirty Years' War remains a scantly used setting for war films. *The Last Valley* is one of the few existing films to be set during the war, and although there are no epic battle scenes, the film provides a good visual context for the viewer and does contain one battle scene, which provides a basic depiction of seventeenth century warfare. Additionally, the complexity of the political and religious aspects of the war, especially religious zeal, are nicely conveyed through the interaction and dialogue of the characters.

ENGLISH CIVIL WARS

Cromwell

Released: 1970

England is locked in civil war. Forces loyal to King Charles I fight against the armies of Parliament, led by Oliver Cromwell. This film covers the entirety of the war, from its earliest causes clear through to the execution of Charles and beginning of the Interregnum. Its numerous battle scenes are impressive both in scale and in detail, showing the pike-and-shot tactics of the time period. The largest battle scene depicts the Battle of Naseby (1645) and the Loyalist defeat at the hands of the New Model Army (another important aspect of the war that is treated in adequate detail in the film).

FRENCH AND INDIAN WAR (SEVEN YEARS' WAR)

The Last of the Mohicans

Released: 1992

Based on James Fenimore Cooper's novel, *The Last of the Mohicans* is set during the Seven Years' War (known in North America as the French and Indian War). The plot is set in the American colonies and revolves around the successful French siege of Fort William Henry (1757) and the subsequent massacre of the retreating British troops by some of France's Indian allies. Containing battle and siege scenes, *The Last of the Mohicans* vividly portrays colonial-era warfare. The ambush scene near the end of the film is especially useful in illustrating the differences between the unconventional tactics employed by the Indians and their effectiveness against traditional European-style fighting. The only drawback is that it covers only the war in the colonies when the war was truly global.

AMERICAN REVOLUTION

April Morning
Released: 1988

The film adaptation of Howard Fast's novel, this better-than-average portrayal of the beginning of the war depicts a boy's coming-of-age as the colonists stand up to the British on Lexington Green.

Drums Along the Mohawk
Released: 1939

Newlyweds settle in the Mohawk Valley just as the revolution is erupting, and the young husband goes off to war; the film ends on a bright note with the birth of a new nation. Though a fictionalized and sentimental chronicle, this classic, directed by John Ford, offers a rich depiction of frontier life during the war. Props had to be made from scratch, and many are true to historic detail. Flintlock muskets, however, were those actually used during the era—the prop department tracked them down in Ethiopia, where they had been used to fight the Italians during World War II.

John Adams^
Released: 2008

Based on the book by David McCullough, this acclaimed biographical television miniseries (HBO) chronicles Adams's role as Founding Father, including the Revolutionary War period, beginning with the Boston Massacre.

Johnny Tremain
Released: 1957

The first adaptation of Esther Forbes's novel portrays the beginning of the American Revolution from the perspective of a young man whose views on the war change as he evolves into a revolutionary. Emphasizes the human perspectives on the war, from both sides.

The Patriot
Released: 2000

As a film about the course and causes of the American Revolution (1775-1783), *The Patriot* falls flat. It is too critical of the British, too praising of the colonists, too focused on the southern theater of war, and too idealistic in its depiction of race relations and slavery. However, the film is accurate in its portrayal of the military aspects of the war, particularly the difficulties of the Continental Army in maintaining adequate numbers and discipline. While the character of Benjamin Martin is so perfect that he is unbelievable, he is loosely modeled after the real soldier Francis Marion. Additionally, the scenes of the Battles of Camden (1780) and Guilford Courthouse (1781) are excellent portrayals of the traditional close-order formations and tactics used by European armies in the colonial era. The Camden scene also shows how cavalry are effectively used to break a wavering line and run down the fleeing troops.

1776
Released: 1972

The film version of the stage musical, depicting the Founding Fathers and America's first congress.

NAPOLEONIC WARS

Master and Commander
Released: 2003

Set during the Napoleonic Wars, *Master and Commander* explores the war at sea with a twist; it is the British vessel that is at a disadvantage in size and armament and must rely on the skill and wit of its crew to defeat the French. Although the story is fictional, it is excellent in its portrayal of naval warfare in the Napoleonic era, as well as depicting and explaining every aspect of life at sea, from ship conditions and nautical terminology (for example, why speed at sea is measured in knots) to maritime medicine and class distinction.

Voyna i mir (war and peace)
Released: 1967

In 1812, Napoleon led his Grande Armée into Russia; it returned later that year in pieces. Both the United States and the Soviet Union produced epic films based on Leo Tolstoy's novel *Voyna i mir* (1865-

1869; *War and Peace*, 1886), but the 1956 American version, in limiting the film's duration (though it is still more than three hours long), also limits its depiction of key battles such as those at Austerlitz and Borodino. The 1967 Soviet version requires a full day to watch, but it is more comprehensive and detailed in explaining the history behind Napoleon's fatal invasion of Russia and allows the story of the breaking of Napoleon to be told by the country that broke him.

Waterloo
Released: 1970

The last battle of the Napoleonic Wars, Waterloo (1815) pitted the French under Napoleon against the British and Prussians under the duke of Wellington (Arthur Wellesley) and Gebhard Leberecht von Blücher. The film begins with Napoleon's return from exile and ends almost immediately after the battle. The first hour sets the stage for the battle. The remaining half of the film is devoted entirely to the battle itself and presents it on a scale that is worthy of its subject. *Waterloo* is fantastic for showing the battle on a remarkable scale (using twenty thousand extras to flesh out the armies); one particular scene beautifully shows the use of the infantry square as a defense against cavalry.

TEXAS WAR OF INDEPENDENCE

The Alamo
Released: 2004

In 1836, Antonio López de Santa Anna's Mexican army besieged the tiny garrison of Texans and Tejanos at the Alamo. Although the battle ended in defeat for the defenders, it has become a famous battle in Texas and American history as a symbol of defiance in the face of overwhelming odds. A 1960 version starring John Wayne remained the only film dedicated to the Alamo for more than forty years; however, the film's length, gross inaccuracies and exaggerations, and the fact that the climactic battle scene occupied only a small portion of the film's three-hour duration makes Ron Howard's 2004 release a better choice, though not perfect. Addition-

ally, Howard's version carries the story through to the pivotal Battle of San Jacinto (1836).

AMERICAN INDIAN WARS

Geronimo^
Released: 1993

With the Louisiana Purchase in 1803 and victory in the Mexican War in 1848, the United States achieved its dream of stretching from the Atlantic to the Pacific; however, as settlers moved west, the conflict with the Indian tribes—a conflict that began with initial colonization—flared up again. During the Indian Wars, no Indian warrior became more notorious than the Apache warrior Geronimo. Many films and documentaries have been made about Geronimo; famously, the 1962 version starring Chuck Connors as Geronimo had no Native Americans in the cast. This 1993 television release did feature Native Americans and offers the best explanation for Geronimo's motivations and actions.

THE OPIUM WARS

Lin Tze-hsu (the opium war)
Released: 1959

This film depicts the events leading up to, and the initial stages of, the conflict between Great Britain and imperial China known as the First Opium War (1839-1842) and is a valuable tool for three reasons: First, it was the only feature film about the Opium War for nearly fifty years (until the release of *Yapian zhanzheng* in 1997); second, it is a Chinese film and thus tells the story from a non-Western perspective; third and most important, the film was made shortly after the communist takeover of China and is a blatantly anti-West, anticapitalist, and anti-imperialist propaganda film, ending on a victorious note for the Chinese and not mentioning the eventual British victory. The film is useful in teaching about the time it was made, the time it portrays, and the concept that history, particularly military history, can be written differently depending on one's perspective.

CRIMEAN WAR

The Charge of the Light Brigade
Released: 1968

Far superior to the 1936 Hollywood production of the same name (in terms of both historical accuracy and overall presentation), this film portrays the disastrous British cavalry attack known as the Charge of the Light Brigade, which took place at the Battle of Balaclava (1854) during the Crimean War, in which the British charged a fortified Russian artillery position, suffering casualties of nearly 50 percent. The battle, and the characters best associated with it (Lord Cardigan and Lord Raglan in particular), are wonderfully brought to life. The only drawbacks to the film are its abrupt ending, which comes just moments after the attack, and the numerous Monty Python-esque animation scenes that harm the film's authority by making it appear comic.

AMERICAN CIVIL WAR

The Birth of a Nation
Released: 1915

D. W. Griffith's epic film about the reconstructed South and the origins of the Ku Klux Klan is as impressive as it is controversial. The impressiveness of the opening battle scene is rivaled only by the film's gross misrepresentations of the Klan's heroism and the beastliness of the freed slaves. This film is included on the list because of its impact at the time of its release more than its representation of war. *The Birth of a Nation* was a film that affected society at the time of its release by rewriting history. It stands today as an example of the power that film has to influence the course of history as well as our remembrance of it.

The Civil War^
Released: 1990

Perhaps the definitive Civil War documentary, Ken Burns's meticulous compilation of documents, photographs, traditional music, letters, and history brings the full extent of the war—from battles to personal stories to impact on Native Americans—alive using primary sources. Nine parts comprise hours of historical detail on the seemingly endless course of the war, humanized and brought to life.

Gettysburg
Released: 1993

The Battle of Gettysburg (1863) was the largest battle of the Civil War. *Gettysburg* devotes four hours entirely to the battle, from the initial skirmish just west of Gettysburg to Robert E. Lee's exclamation, "It's all my fault." The attention to detail and historical accuracy makes this an excellent film for anyone interested in the subject, though it is rather lengthy; however, several key events in the battle (the defense of Little Round Top and Pickett's charge, for example) receive special attention and round out the film nicely.

Glory
Released: 1989

After Lincoln issued the Emancipation Proclamation in 1863, the Union Army allowed African Americans to join the Union fight in the American Civil War (1861-1865). The first all-black unit in the army was the Fifty-fourth Massachusetts Regiment under the command of Colonel Robert Gould Shaw. Beginning with a scene of the Battle of Antietam (1862), *Glory* tells the story of the Fifty-fourth from its creation to its brave but disastrous attack on Fort Wagner. Not only is the film's subject significant, but its battle scenes illustrate the ferocity of Civil War combat, especially hand-to-hand fighting. The film also clearly explains that although the North allowed blacks in the military, there was still much racial tension between blacks and Northern whites.

Gone with the Wind
Released: 1939

In terms of its contribution to film history, *Gone with the Wind*, America's first epic in color and the most popular film in American history, is a masterpiece. In regard to historical representation, the film is both a blessing and a curse. Based on Margaret Mitchell's 1936 novel of the same name, *Gone with the Wind* is the perfect film for depicting white society in the antebellum South; however, its portrayal of slavery and the causes and conduct of the Civil War is highly skewed. Like *The Birth of a Nation*, *Gone with the Wind* is an excellent example of how film can re-write the past, and its popularity reveals the extent to which the rewriting of history can be accepted.

ZULU WAR

Zulu
Released: 1964

After the disastrous defeat at Isandhlwana (1879), the British troops in southern Africa braced for a final knockout blow at the small outpost of Rorke's Drift. Over the course of two days (January 22-23, 1879), the small garrison of around 150 British successfully held off an army of more than four thousand Zulu. In making his argument for a "western way of war," Victor Davis Hansen pointed to the Battle of Rorke's Drift as an example of superior discipline in battle. The entire film, but in particular the last battle scene, does an excellent job of showing how discipline, es-pecially the efforts of sergeants and other noncom-missioned officers to keep the soldiers from breaking and fleeing, contributed to the British victory.

BOER WAR

"Breaker" Morant*
Released: 1980

At the beginning of the twentieth century, the British Empire went to war against Dutch farmers (Boers) in the southern tip of Africa. Because the Boers could not fight toe-to-toe with the British Army, the (second) Boer War (1899-1902) was an unconventional war and required the British to adopt unorthodox tactics in order to defeat the Dutch Kom-mandos. *"Breaker" Morant* is based on a true story and, though focusing on a court-martial (meaning the majority of the film is courtroom drama), the events leading up to the courtroom are told in flashbacks that display very well the aspects of the war that made it so unconventional.

RUSSIAN REVOLUTION AND CIVIL WAR

Battleship Potemkin
Released: 1925, as *Bronenosets Potyomkin**

In the wake of their disastrous defeat at the hands of the Japanese in the Russo-Japanese War (1904-1905), there was a great deal of social unrest through the Russian Empire. In 1905, sailors aboard the bat-tleship *Potemkin* rebelled at the horrible conditions they were forced to endure. Director Sergei Eisenstein was commissioned by the Soviet government in 1925 to make the film (known in the United States as *Bat-tleship Potemkin*) as a propaganda film. Not only is the film an excellent piece of Soviet propaganda; it also is considered a masterpiece. The scene on the Odessa Steps is considered a landmark scene in the history of film.

Dr. Zhivago
Released: 1965

In the last years of World War I, the Russian peo-ple revolted against the czar. Following the collapse of the monarchy and withdrawal from World War I, Russia sank into a brutal civil war pitting the Reds (Bolsheviks) against the Whites (Mensheviks), with the majority of the population caught in the middle. *Doctor Zhivago*, though focusing primarily on a love story rather than political and social events, provides an excellent representation of life in Russia during the Russian Revolution and Civil War. Viewers will draw the most from the film if they brush up on early twentieth century Russian history, but even without that effort, the film has much to offer.

WORLD WAR I

All Quiet on the Western Front
Released: 1930, 1979 (television)

Based on Erich Maria Remarque's famous war novel *Im Westen nichts Neues* (1929), *All Quiet on the Western Front* is the classic World War I film. Depicting the fighting between the French and the Germans from the German viewpoint, the film not only shows the brutality of trench warfare but also illustrates the patriotic fervor that led millions of young men on both sides to enlist, as well as the disparity between what the German home front was being told and the actual situation. Of the two versions, each has its advantages. The original version follows the novel more precisely and is a film classic, but color film and improved special effects make the 1979 version better for providing a visual of trench warfare on the western front.

Gallipoli
Released: 1981

In 1915, the British attempted to break the deadlock of trench warfare in Europe and knock the newly entered Turkey out of the war in a single stroke. Soldiers of the Australian and New Zealand Army Corps (ANZAC) assaulted the Turkish positions at Gallipoli in an attempt to wrest control of the Dardanelles away from Turkey. The film is a bit slow at the beginning but does an excellent job of showing the impossibility of trench warfare and the catastrophic Battle of Gallipoli (1915-1916).

Hell's Angels
Released: 1930

Considering the film's age, *Hell's Angels* is a remarkable film. Though incredibly exepensive, director Howard Hughes captured some amazing aerial footage in his filming of Great War dogfights. Most of the scenes involving aircraft are shot with real planes, not models, giving the film enhanced authority and authenticity. The film also illustrates the Zeppelin raids over London, a topic often left out of World War I lectures. The accompanying love story does little to enhance the film, but viewers who stick it out to the end will get to witness a wide-shot aerial battle between the British Royal Flying Corps and the infamous Red Baron's Flying Circus.

Joyeux Noël* (merry Christmas)
Released: 2005

One of the most remarkable events of World War I took place on Christmas Eve, 1914. The British, French, and German troops in one section of the front put down their weapons and fraternized with the enemy. The Christmas Truce, as it was called, witnessed soldiers who only a day before were shooting at each other now sharing family pictures, exchanging gifts, and even kicking around a soccer ball. When news of the unofficial truce reached respective headquarters, it was quickly ended and fighting resumed. The Christmas Truce was never repeated. *Joyeux Noël* was a collaborative effort of German, French, and British filmmakers to bring to the screen an excellent portrayal of one of the most curious and positive events of the war.

La Grande Illusion*
Released: 1937

Jean Renoir's classic antiwar film is set in World War I. Though there are no battle scenes, the film still portrays the brutal reality of war through the terrible toll it extracts from those who fight it, showing that the "grand illusion" is that war is noble and glorious. Like many other films in this list, *La Grande Illusion* has been included because of what it says about the time in which it was produced more than about the time depicted in the film. In 1937, Fascist aggression was pushing Europe toward war. Renoir's film was a reminder of what happened the last time Europe went to war.

Lawrence of Arabia
Released: 1962

Taking place in the Middle East during World War I, this film, though long (four hours), brings to life one of the most dynamic and controversial figures of the time period. *Lawrence of Arabia* is a biography of the wartime career of British officer Thomas E. Lawrence. Not only does it depict the guerrilla-style desert warfare between the British, with their Arab allies, and the Turks, but it also explores Lawrence's attempts at fostering Arab nationalism. The Turkish front was not the decisive theater in the war, but the impact of Lawrence's actions remains today.

Sergeant York
Released: 1941

Alvin York fought with the U.S. Army in the trenches of World War I and distinguished himself by becoming a highly decorated war hero despite being a pacifist and conscientious objector. His most notable achievement (and the climactic scene of the film) was his single-handed capture of 132 German soldiers. *Sergeant York* is an excellent film, not only because of its subject matter but also because it is a good example of film as propaganda. The film was produced in 1941, just when the United States was faced with the possibility of fighting another war in Europe but before Pearl Harbor tipped the scales in favor of intervention. The film portrays a quiet, simple man, wanting only to live in peace but forced to take up arms in defense of freedom.

SPANISH CIVIL WAR

Land and Freedom
Released: 1995

This film is a collaborative effort between the United Kingdom and Spain and depicts the civil war that erupted in Spain between 1936 and 1939. The war was one of political ideology (primarily fascist vs. communist) and as such was incredibly brutal. Not only does the film excellently portray the hatred between the two groups; it also brilliantly illustrates the divisions and dissension within the loyalist force (those opposing Generalissimo Francisco Franco), which contributed a great deal to Franco's eventual victory. It also includes the International Brigades, another crucial aspect of the Spanish Civil War, by centering the story on the life of a British communist who goes to Spain to fight.

WORLD WAR II

Action in the North Atlantic
Released: 1943

Despite its enormous importance to the war effort, the task of the U.S. Merchant Marine in keeping Britain and the Soviet Union supplied with arms and equipment seldom receives much attention in war films. This film, however, is wholly devoted to the perilous journey across the submarine-infested Atlantic Ocean. By 1943, the Battle of the Atlantic was just beginning to turn in favor of the Allies. *Action in*

the North Atlantic, though propagandistic, does a good job of showing the various aspects of the war at sea: secrecy, submarines, the convoy system, depth charges, and liberty ships. It is excellent for showing antisubmarine warfare.

Band of Brothers^
Released: 2001

Based on the book by Stephen Ambrose, *Band of Brothers* was an HBO miniseries about the exploits of the 101st Airborne Division in World War II from basic training to shortly after the war ended. The 101st took part in almost every major battle in the European theater, including Normandy, Market Garden, and the Battle of the Bulge. The series was enormously successful and is an excellent source because of its comprehensiveness, historical accuracy, and riveting presentation of the use of paratroopers in modern warfare.

Bataan
Released: 1943

The Japanese attack on Pearl Harbor in 1941 was just a part of a massive offensive in the South Pacific that included an attack on the American-controlled Philippine islands in 1942. The outnumbered and outgunned garrison retreated to the Bataan Peninsula, where they fought a desperate and ultimately unsuccessful struggle. This was one of the first wartime films made by the United States, and although telling a story with an unhappy ending, *Bataan* was made to encourage Americans to continue the fight, even when things looked bleak.

Battle of Britain
Released: 1969

The Battle of Britain (1940) was one of the pivotal battles of World War II. The Royal Air Force and the German Luftwaffe battled for aerial supremacy over the English Channel. *Battle of Britain* is a stunning film that not only provides excellent visuals of World War II-era aerial combat but also explains other important aspects of the battle, such as the role of radar and the international squadrons that supplemented the Royal Air Force. (For an excellent film retelling the Battle of Britain from the viewpoint of one of these international squadrons, see the Czech production, 2001's *Dark Blue World*). In addition, the film also portrays the devastation of the Blitz, Germany's switch from military to civilian targets.

Battle of the Bulge
Released: 1965

In the winter of 1944, Germany launched a massive attack (Operation Wacht am Rhein) against the Allies in Western Europe, hoping to turn the tide. The attack faltered and instead of moving the entire front it only pushed through in the center, creating a large bulge, hence the name. The end of the film contains a large tank-battle scene that does a good job of showing tank combat. Another important part of the battle, and the film, is the German use of spies to disrupt Allied transportation and communication during the offensive.

The Best Years of Our Lives
Released: 1946

This film begins after the war has already ended, so there are no battle scenes, and almost no "action," yet it is a valuable "war film" because it addresses one of the most important aspects of any war: when Johnny comes marching home. This film tells the story of three different returning soldiers (one Army, one Navy, one Air Force) and shows the trials and difficulties that each has, both physically and mentally, when they try to integrate back into society. Demobilization is an important part of any war, and this is one of the few films devoted entirely to it.

Bridge on the River Kwai
Released: 1957

Prisoner-of-war (POW) films are an essential part of World War II. For the Pacific theater, *Bridge on the River Kwai* and *The Great Raid* (2005) focus on POW camps, while Steven Spielberg's *Empire of the Sun* (1987) looks at civilian internment camps. Of these, *Bridge on the River Kwai* is the best choice, not only because of its good depiction of the brutality of Japanese POW camps but also because of its excellent portrayal of how concepts of right and wrong can be severely skewed in wartime (as exemplified by

Alec Guiness's character, who initially resists the Japanese attempts to put POWs to work and unwittingly ends up fully cooperating in the end).

A Bridge Too Far
Released: 1977

After the successful D-day landings, Field Marshall Bernard Law Montgomery concocted Operation Market Garden, a plan that, if successful, would end the war by Christmas of 1944. The plan was for American and British paratroopers to capture strategic bridges across the major rivers in the Netherlands, paving the way for an invasion of Germany. *A Bridge Too Far*, based on the book by journalist Cornelius Ryan, is an excellent retelling of the event and includes both the Allied and German perspective. It is one of the standards of World War II films.

*The Burmese Harp**
Released: 1956, as *Biruma no tategoto*

Based on Michio Takeyama's novel, *The Burmese Harp* begins in the last days of fighting between the British and Japanese in World War II. The film is important, not because of the time period it depicts but because of the time period in which it was produced. The film was made shortly after the American occupation ended and portrays the war in Asia from the Japanese perspective. It makes a very clear distinction between the "warmongers" in the army and the majority of Japanese soldiers, who did not want to fight. It is a film that works hard to reverse the warrior image that the Japanese constructed during the war.

Catch-22
Released: 1970

Taking place on the Italian Peninsula in the later years of World War II, *Catch-22* is an adaptation of Joseph Heller's novel about the American bombing efforts from Italy after the fall of Benito Mussolini. As a sharp criticism of war (Vietnam in particular, with which the film was contemporaneous) and the people who run it, *Catch-22* is unconventional and comedic in its portrayal of war and the American military. The absurdity of the characters and events in the film are meant to express the absurdity of war.

The very term "catch-22" entered the English vocabulary as a result of Heller's unorthodox and comedic approach to war criticism.

Das Boot* (the boat)
Released: 1981

Whereas *Action in the North Atlantic* tells the story of the war in the Atlantic from the perspective of the U.S. Merchant Marine, *Das Boot* shows the war from the view of the German U-boats that hunted Allied ships from beneath the waves. Wolfgang Peterson's intention was to make an antiwar film that not only showed the terror of war at sea but also drew clear distinctions between Nazis and Germans. It is an excellent film for showing life and combat onboard a submarine. The more recent *U-571* (2000) is another good film for depicting World War II submarine warfare, but its historical inaccuracies make *Das Boot* a better choice.

Defiance
Released: 2008

An important, though often forgotten, aspect of World War II on the eastern front is the role of the partisans. Many bands of these guerrilla fighters, composed of Jews, communists, Eastern Europeans, and other groups deemed "undesirable" or "subhuman" by the Nazis, fought against the Germans for the majority of the war. This is an excellent film for depicting the lives and various difficulties of the partisans in World War II.

The Desert Fox
Released: 1951

See "Cold War" section below.

The Great Dictator
Released: 1940

Charles Chaplin's personally funded critique of Nazi Germany appeared on the silver screen only one year after the war in Europe officially began but before the United States' entry. In typical Chaplin style, the film uses slapstick comedy to attack Adolf Hitler, Benito Mussolini, and fascism in general. Although there are no battle scenes, the film is an excellent resource for an illustration of Nazi Germany's foreign and domestic policies through Chaplin's unique comedic style.

The Great Escape
Released: 1963

Films about German prisoner-of-war (POW) camps present an interesting problem. Unlike those depicting Japanese camps, the spectrum for films about German camps (outside Holocaust films) ranges from the adventurous, such as *Von Ryan's Express* (1965), to the wildly comedic 1960's television program *Hogan's Heroes*. However, the best choice is *The Great Escape*. Based on real events, the film depicts the attempt of British and American POWs to stage a massive escape. Though the story does not exactly have a happy ending (few of the men actually succeed), *The Great Escape* is an excellent film for showing life and conditions in a German POW camp.

The Grey Zone
Released: 2001

Though not a war film per se, *The Grey Zone* depicts the Holocaust as the consequence of combining nationalism, modernity, industrialism, and warfare. No list of war films would be complete without at least one film that addresses the Holocaust, and this one—not Steven Spielberg's *Schindler's List* (1993)—is the best choice. It is based on the Jewish inmates at Auschwitz who helped run the gas chambers and crematoria in exchange for a few months' stay of execution. It is the best choice because it is as dramatic and graphic as *Schindler's List*, but it explores more of the complex issues related to the Holocaust, such as the fine line between collaboration and survival and other moral questions posed by the Holocaust.

Hadashi no Gen* (barefoot Gen)
Released: 1983

On August 6, 1945, an American B-29, *Enola Gay*, dropped the world's first atomic bomb. The Hollywood production *Fat Man and Little Boy* (1989) retells the story of the bomb's construction, and many other American films allude to the bomb, but to see a film about the impact of the bomb we must turn to Japanese anime. As the only cartoon on the list, *Hadashi no Gen* lets viewers experience the bomb, and all the devastation that went along with it, from the eyes of those who experienced it. Written by a survivor of the bombing of Hiroshima, the film not only depicts the explosion itself (in graphic detail), but also the unforeseen consequences, such as radiation poisoning, nuclear fallout, and the social chaos that resulted from the weapon that ushered in the nuclear age.

Kanal*
Released: 1957

In 1944, the German army was in retreat. As the advancing Red Army entered Poland, partisans in the city staged a massive uprising, hoping for help from the approaching Soviets. Unfortunately, the Soviets halted outside Warsaw, allowing the Germans time to crush the uprising. *Kanal*, a Polish production, is the first film about the uprising (not to be confused with the Warsaw Ghetto uprising in 1943). The film depicts the hopelessness of the struggle as well as the determination of the Poles to fight on, even when defeat is inevitable.

Letters from Iwo Jima *and* Flags of Our Fathers
Released: Both 2006

Iwo Jima was the bloodiest battle in United States Marine Corps' history, waged on one of the last islands to be taken before the Japanese mainland could be invaded. Both the attacking Marines and the Japanese defenders fought tenaciously for control of it. In representing this battle on film, director Clint Eastwood made not one but two films, each telling the story of the fight for Iwo Jima, one film for each side. The two versions ought to be viewed as two halves of the same film. The battle scenes are epic and detailed, showing the brutality that characterized the war in the Pacific, but the films' greatest contribution is that they show both sides of the same story and demonstrate that history depends on viewpoint.

The Longest Day
Released: 1962

As the film adaptation of Cornelius Ryan's book, *The Longest Day* rests alongside 1969's *Battle of Britain* and 1977's *A Bridge Too Far* as the classics of epic World War II films. The film tells the story of Operation Overlord (the Normandy invasions, or D day), the largest amphibious assault in history, from both the Axis and the Allied sides, leaving out very little detail. The film provides an excellent background to the planning and execution of all facets of the operation, including paratroopers, deception tactics, the role of the weather, and the confusion and weakness of the Axis response.

Memphis Belle
Released: 1990

Beginning in 1942, the United States Army Air Force took part in the air war against Germany by conducting daylight bombing raids using the B-17 "Flying Fortress." *Memphis Belle*, like many war films, is double-edged. Nearly the entire film is devoted to the actual mission, giving viewers a chance to experience every aspect of a daylight mission from takeoff to touchdown. The disadvantage of the film is that while it claims to be based on a true story, the story has been so altered as to leave only the name of the plane as historically accurate. This is an excellent film for showing an example of the air war, but not for telling the story of the *Memphis Belle*.

Midway
Released: 1976

In June of 1942, the American and Japanese navies fought a battle in which neither fleet actually saw the other. The entire engagement was a dual between aircraft launched from carriers just off the coast of the island of Midway. The battle resulted in a resounding victory for the United States and critically crippled the Japanese ability to pursue the war in the South Pacific. *Midway* is entirely devoted to this pivotal battle and reaffirmed what Pearl Harbor demonstrated: that the aircraft carrier was now the king of the seas. Additionally, the film successfully weaves stock footage into the battle scenes, making them more authoritative.

Patton
Released: 1970

General George S. Patton was one of the most colorful and controversial figures of World War II. Having fought the Axis powers from Africa all the way to Germany, Patton earned a reputation as one of the best generals of the war. Although the film takes a few liberties here and there, *Patton* brings to life one of the United States' most famous military figures through the brilliant performance of George C. Scott. The film portrays Patton's brilliance in combat, his eccentricities off the battlefield, and his personality and ego clashes with Field Marshall Bernard Law Montgomery.

Roma, città aperta (Rome, open city) *and* L'Armée des ombres (army of shadows)
Released: 1945 and 1969 respectively

After the fall of France in 1940, those men and women who continued to resist both the Germans and the Vichy government formed the Maquis, the French Resistance. As an important part of World War II, no film list would be complete without a film about the Resistance. This film, which covers the middle war years when the Resistance was small and particularly vulnerable, provides an excellent illustration of the cloak-and-dagger world in which the Maquis had to operate. Like *L'Armée des ombres* (1969), *Open City* is a film about the clandestine resistance efforts in occupied Italy. Though not as famous as the Maquis, the Italian Resistance faced many of the same trials and suffered many of the same pains as the French Resistance.

Saving Private Ryan
Released: 1998

Operation Overlord was the largest amphibious assault in history and involved American, Canadian, and British troops storming the beaches of northern France, guarded by Germans and Ostbattalionen (conscripts from Eastern Europe). To gain a better understanding of the history surrounding the Allied invasion of Normandy, *The Longest Day* is the best choice, but *Saving Private Ryan*, through improved special effects, attention to detail, and stripping away of the "sanitized" depictions of war, portrays the battle so vividly and with such intensity that it not only revolutionized battle scenes but also traumatized many war veterans who saw the film.

Since You Went Away
Released: 1944

Along with *The Best Years of Our Lives*, *Since You Went Away* is a film that reminds its audience that war is not just about "over there." In many ways this film is simply producer David O. Selznik's *Gone with the Wind* retold in a World War II setting. The entire film takes place on the home front and shows what civilians, particularly the families of soldiers, must go through in wartime. Although romanticized, the film does address issues such as rationing, women in the war industry, recruitment, scrap metal drives, and the pain of receiving a telegram from the War Department.

Sink the Bismark!
Released: 1960

World War II marked the end of the battleship's dominance of the seas with the emergence of the aircraft carrier; however, the naval war in the Atlantic had few carriers. The German battleship *Bismark* threatened to devastate the Allied shipping that was keeping Britain in the war; thus, it became important for the British navy to "sink the Bismark." *Sink the Bismark!* is an excellent film for showing pre-carrier warfare and illustrating how navies fought before the advent of the aircraft.

So Proudly We Hail! *and* Cry Havoc
Released: 1943 and 1947 respectively

The war brought numerous opportunities for women to challenge traditional stereotypes given them by society, both by working in the war industry at home and by serving in the armed forces abroad as nurses. Both films tell the story of army nurses in the Philippines. As the release dates reveal, not only did these films recognize women in the war effort; they also served to encourage more women to do the same. There are not many other films wholly devoted to women's wartime service; *Cry Havoc* and *So Proudly We Hail!* are as essential to any collection of war movies as women's efforts were to the war itself.

Stalingrad*

Released: 1993

The Battle of Stalingrad is arguably the decisive battlefield of World War II. It lasted through the winter of 1942-1943 and saw some of the most intense urban combat of the war as the Germans fought the Soviets for control of the gateway to the Caucasus and the city named for Stalin. By February, 1943, the German army at Stalingrad and thus the war in the east were broken. The German production *Stalingrad* portrays the battle from the perspective of the Germans who fought it and depicts the bloody fighting and horrible conditions under which they fought.

Talvisota* (the winter war)

Released: 1989

Shortly after the Germans invaded Poland in 1939, the Soviet Union used the nonaggression pact with Germany to launch an invasion of Finland. For the next two years the Finns fought a desperate and little-known war against the Red Army. The Soviets had such superiority in men and matériel that their victory seemed a foregone conclusion, but to the shock and dismay of the Soviets, the Finnish soldiers succeeded in defending their homeland and won the Winter War. *Talvisota*, a Finnish production, is the first and only major film to depict the war and does so splendidly.

The Thin Red Line

Released: 1998

After the Battles of Midway and Coral Sea destroyed Japan's ability to expand its empire, the United States had the task of rolling back Japanese gains in the Pacific. The "Island-Hopping" campaign began with the attack on Guadalcanal in the Solomon Islands. Based on James Joyce's novel, *The Thin Red Line* depicts the fight for Guadalcanal and not only is an excellent film for portraying the brutality of the war in the Pacific (as well as atrocities committed by both sides) but also addresses the mentality of the men fighting, showing that soldiers are not simply mindless machines.

Thirty Seconds over Tokyo

Released: 1944

Following the attack on Pearl Harbor, the United States wanted to take some sort of immediate, punitive action against the Japanese. The result was the Doolittle Raid, a bombing raid over Tokyo comprising 16 B-25 "Mitchell" bombers, which would attack the city and then fly to safety in unoccupied China. Although ineffective strategically, the Doolittle Raid was a big morale boost for the United States following the shock of December 7. This film adequately depicts the raid's planning, training, and execution.

To Hell and Back

Released: 1955

Audie Murphey was America's most decorated soldier in World War II and in many respects is to World War II what Alvin York was to World War I. Murphy rose from private to lieutenant and earned almost every medal the United States had to offer. The film, based on his war autobiography of the same name, follows Murphy's life from his adolescence through the end of the war. The battle scenes are good, but not spectacular. This movie is included, like *Patton* and *Sergeant York*, because of the importance of the individual to American military history.

Tora! Tora! Tora!

Released: 1970

On December 7, 1941, carrier-based planes of the Japanese Navy laid waste to the American fleet at Pearl Harbor. Although the more recent film *Pearl Harbor* (2001) makes use of computer graphics and better special effects to make a much more action-packed battle scene, *Tora! Tora! Tora!* is by far the better film for explaining the reasoning, planning, and execution of the attack (and the battle scene is well done). As a collaborative effort between the United States and Japan, the film tells the story from both sides objectively and remains the best film made about the "day of infamy."

The Tuskegee Airmen^

Released: 1995

Along with women, World War II provided the black community with opportunities to challenge social stereotypes. The Tuskegee Airmen were the first black fighter pilots in the U.S. Army Air Force; they saw combat in both North Africa and Italy. Although the only nondocumentary film on the subject, *The Tuskegee Airmen* is an excellent film for showing the trials and difficulties associated with race relations during the war in general, as well as telling the story of America's first black fighter squadron.

Der Untergang* (the downfall)
Released: 2004

In the last days of World War II, Adolf Hitler retreated into his Berlin bunker to lead the futile last-ditch defense of the city. This film, a German production based on accounts by those who lived in the bunker with Hitler during those last days, is an excellent representation of the final days of the Third Reich as well as an illustration of the devastation of urban combat. Because most of the army had been killed or captured, Berlin's defenses had to be heavily supplemented by the Volkssturm, the militias made up of teenage boys and old men, and the film nicely illustrates the use of those forces.

Valkyrie
Released: 2008

In July of 1944, a small group of Adolf Hitler's top officers plotted to kill him. Though this event forms a large part of the film *The Desert Fox*, *Valkyrie* is devoted entirely to the planning and failed execution of the attempt. The film does a good job of establishing that the officers involved were motivated, not for any moral concerns, but because they thought Hitler was leading the country to ruin militarily. The film also offers a nice contrast to *The Desert Fox*, because the two illustrate a long-standing debate over the role of Erwin Rommel in the assassination attempt. *Desert Fox* places him at the center, while *Valkyrie* makes no mention of him at all.

A Walk in the Sun
Released: 1945

After defeating the Germans in Africa, the Allies moved on to Sicily and then the Italian Peninsula, where the fighting bogged down in conditions similar to the trenches of World War I (though in Italy the majority of the Axis forces were German). War has been described as "long periods of boredom punctuated by moments of sheer terror," and *A Walk in the Sun* portrays that beautifully. Opening with a brief battle scene when American forces land on the beaches in Italy, the rest of the film is simply "a walk in the sun" until the final battle scene: an assault on a farmhouse occupied by the Germans.

Windtalkers
Released: 2002

As the United States continued to fight the Japanese in the Pacific, the American military had problems with maintaining security. Japanese intelligence continually broke American radio codes, severely hampering the American effort. To solve the problem, the United States began using Navajo Indians as radio operators to prevent the Japanese from cracking the code. The code talkers played an important part, not only in winning the war, but also in the advancement of race relations back on the home front, and although *Windtalkers* is not the best film about the war in the Pacific theater, the subject of its plot makes it an important film.

COLD WAR

The Day After^
Released: 1983

One of the most controversial films of its day, aired on television, *The Day After* depicts the grim aftereffects of a nuclear bombing in Lawrence, Kansas, at the height of the antinuclear movement that characterized the Cold War period.

The Desert Fox
Released: 1951

Erwin Rommel led the Afrika Korps against the British and Americans in North Africa. Although ultimately failing in Africa, Rommel has became a legend both in German and in British and American history, partly because of his skill as a general, partly because of his supposed involvement in the July plot to assassinate Adolf Hitler. *The Desert Fox* is included because of the time period it represents, rather than the time it depicts. Produced in 1951, *The Desert Fox* was an early Cold War film. The Soviet Union replaced Nazi Germany as the arch-enemy of the United States, and divided Germany emerged as the likely battleground for a struggle between the United States and the Soviet Union. This film is an excellent example of the backpedaling that had to be done to turn former World War II enemies into Cold War allies.

Dr. Strangelove
Released: 1964

Although completely fictitious, the context and themes of *Dr. Strangelove* are completely accurate. Just two years before the film's release, the United States and the Soviet Union came within inches of nuclear war during the Cuban Missile Crisis. This film explores the tension and fears of nuclear holocaust while poking fun at the generals and politicians who ultimately made the decisions that would lead to or avert a nuclear war. In playing on the fear of nuclear attack and the impotency of all but a few to do anything about it, director Stanley Kubrick appropriately subtitled his film *Or, How I Learned to Stop Worrying and Love the Bomb.*

Fail Safe
Released: 1964

Released almost simultaneously with the classic film *Dr. Strangelove* (whose director, Stanley Kubrick, is said to have complained to studio executives that the nearly identical story line plagiarized his film—and won first release), *Fail Safe* is the dead-serious counterpart to Kubrick's eerie send-up, showing U.S. bombers headed toward Russia after a faulty order to drop the nuclear bomb cannot be reversed. The two can be regarded as complementary treatments of a similar scenario, both released only two years after the Cuban Missile Crisis—but the tone of *Fail Safe* is unrelentingly grim and chilling.

The Hunt for Red October
Released: 1990

The story line of *The Hunt for Red October* follows a high-ranking Soviet officer's attempts to de-

fect to the United States and the United States' attempt to prevent the defection from leading to open war. Like the later production *Crimson Tide* (1995), *The Hunt for Red October* has a wholly fictitious story line, but both films are excellent for showing life on a submarine and portraying modern naval warfare. The much later *K-19: The Widowmaker* (2002) is also a good submarine film and gives the Soviet perspective in a more historically based setting.

The Missiles of October
Released: 1974

This 150-minute docudrama details the events leading up to and during the Cuban Missile Crisis of October, 1962. It is based on Robert F. Kennedy's book *Thirteen Days* (1969).

Thirteen Days
Released: 2000

For two weeks in October of 1962, the United States and the Soviet Union came as close as they ever would come to starting World War III over the Soviet positioning of missiles in Cuba. *Thirteen Days* tells the story of the Cuban Missile Crisis from the initial discovery of the missile sites to the peaceful resolution and does an excellent job of conveying the tension of the crisis and creating an engaging film without making too many sacrifices to historical accuracy. Although bearing the same title as Robert F. Kennedy's book, this film is based on the book *The Kennedy Tapes* (1997), by Ernest May and Philip Zelikow.

KOREAN WAR

The Bridges at Toko-Ri
Released: 1954

Although Germany began experimenting with jet aircraft during World War II, jets did not come into their own until the Korean War five years later. *The Bridges at Toko-Ri* was the first film in which American moviegoers would have been able to see jets on the silver screen, introducing them to modern aerial combat as well as a detailed depiction of launching and landing jets from aircraft carriers. However, being first does not also mean being the best: *Top Gun* (1986) is much better at depicting aerial combat using modern jet aircraft.

M*A*S*H
Released: 1970

Set during the Korean War, *M*A*S*H* is a unique war film. First, it takes place in a field hospital and portrays the battles waged in the operating room after the battles on the frontline end. Battlefield medicine is an essential part of any war, but *M*A*S*H* is one of the only films dedicated to it. Second, as a comedy, *M*A*S*H* belongs to that very small group of films that critique war through humor and satire; third, the film introduces the helicopter, a new technology at the time; finally, it is a product and reflection of its time. Written, filmed, and released while the United States was embroiled in the Vietnam War, the movie, later to become a long-running television series, can be seen as much as a commentary on Vietnam as a show set in the Korean conflict.

Retreat, Hell! *and* Pork Chop Hill
Released: 1952 and 1959 respectively

The Korean War matched U.N. forces (predominantly South Korean and American) against communist North Korea and its Chinese allies. In choosing a film about the experience of American soldiers in combat, the choice is a toss-up between *Pork Chop Hill* and *Retreat, Hell!* Historically speaking, *Retreat, Hell!* is a better film for showing the course of the war from General Douglas MacArthur's landing at Inchon to the Battle at the Chosen Reservoir, but in regard to battle scenes, *Pork Chop Hill* is the better choice. The best option would be to watch these two together, thus combining the strategic overview with combat close-up.

Taegukgi hwinallimyeo*
Released: 2004

The Korean War pitted the North Koreans and their Chinese allies against United Nations forces consisting of South Koreans, Americans, British, Canadians, and a half dozen other countries. What makes this film so essential is that it portrays the war as a *Korean* war. Most other major films about the Korean War portray the American effort against the Chinese. This film however, portrays the film as a civil war and does an excellent job, not only in utilizing the filming techniques that made the battle scenes of *Saving Private Ryan* so surreal but also in making an antiwar statement by emphasizing the brutality of war and showing both North and South Koreans committing atrocities.

VIETNAM WAR

Apocalypse Now
Released: 1979

Francis Ford Coppola's rendition of Joseph Conrad's 1902 novel *Heart of Darkness* is a scathing criticism of the Vietnam War. As the story develops, the film blurs the line between friend and foe and leaves the viewer questioning the war's purpose, conduct, and goals. Not only is the film's message blatant, but the images and script have had a tremendous impact on American popular culture. Even today, people who have never seen the film quote lines from it.

Born on the Fourth of July
Released: 1989

This film is Oliver Stone's second Vietnam-based project and, like its predecessor *Platoon* (1986), is highly critical of the Vietnam War, showing the terrible price that the war extracted from those who fought it. Based on the life of Vietnam veteran Ron Kovic, *Born on the Fourth of July* shows not only the chaos of Vietnam (such as friendly fire and the killing of civilians) but also the chaos the war unleashed at home as the American people turned against the conflict.

The Deer Hunter
Released: 1978

As one of the first films to challenge the Vietnam War portrayed in *The Green Berets* (1968), *The Deer Hunter* excellently examines the physical and mental impact that the war had on those who fought it. There is only one short combat scene, yet the movie is intensely gory in its depiction of the actions of both American and Vietnamese soldiers, suggesting that in Vietnam there were no "good guys" and no "bad guys," just a mass of senseless violence characterized by numerous scenes in which people play Russian roulette for money.

Dien Bien Phu*
Released: 1992

The siege of the French fortress at Dien Bien Phu began in March, 1954, and ended two months later. The Viet Minh, with help from communist China, besieged the fortress and slowly strangled it into submission. The battle was significant because it signaled the end of French control in Vietnam, and the beginning of the path toward eventual American involvement. *Dien Bien Phu*, a French production, is one of the only films available about the battle.

Flight of the Intruder
Released: 1991

Nearly every set in movies about the Vietnam War represents the ground and recounts the war from the standpoint of the men who waded through the jungles and rice paddies. However, airpower was a big part of the American effort in Vietnam, and thus *Flight of the Intruder* makes the list to provide a film about the war from the viewpoint of the pilots who flew the air raids always seen in the ground films.

Full Metal Jacket
Released: 1987

Like *Platoon* (1986), *Apocalypse Now* (1979), and *The Deer Hunter* (1978), Stanley Kubrik's *Full Metal Jacket* is a classic antiwar, anti-Vietnam film. The film is best known for its first thirty minutes, which are dedicated to depicting life in a marine boot camp, and the breaking down of the individual in order to rebuild him as a killer. The film also contains a scene depicting the Tet Offensive, the massive Viet Cong attack of South Vietnam in January of 1968.

The Green Berets
Released: 1968

The Green Berets is John Wayne's pro-Vietnam, pro-American propaganda film, released (coincidentally, on July 4) shortly after the Tet Offensive in an attempt to gain support for the war. The film depicts the war as a good war, the Americans as fighting a just cause, and the war itself as harsh but not overly brutal or bloody; there are also clear distinctions between "good guy" and "bad guy." The war portrayed in *The Green Berets* is very different from, and is seriously challenged by, almost every Vietnam film that follows.

Platoon
Released: 1986

Oliver Stone's first anti-Vietnam film has become, arguably, *the* anti-Vietnam film. The film depicts the actions of one platoon in Vietnam and illustrates the myriad conflicts and problems within the army itself, to say nothing of difficulties fighting the enemy—problems such as insubordination, drug addiction, fragging, and atrocities against the Vietnamese, to name a few. Although no specific historical battle is portrayed, the film gives an excellent depiction of the guerrilla tactics that characterized the war, as well as a few scenes showing the elaborate tunnel system that the Viet Cong used with great success.

We Were Soldiers
Released: 2002

Near the close of 1965, the United States had its first, and one of the only, pitched battles against North Vietnamese regulars in the Ia Drang Valley. *We Were Soldiers* is the story of the Ia Drang battle and not only provides an excellent portrayal of the conflict but also highlights the introduction and role of the helicopter, a technology that has come to characterize the Vietnam War. This film is also important because it is a reaction against anti-Vietnam films and an attempt to return to the war as portrayed in *The Green Berets*.

CAMBODIAN CIVIL WAR

The Killing Fields
Released: 1984

As the war in Vietnam intensified, it spilled over into neighboring Cambodia. The communist Khmer Rouge took over the Cambodian government and began a systematic cleansing of political enemies, intellectuals, and anyone who posed a threat to the regime. A full one-third of the population of Cambodia was killed in the Khmer Rouge's "killing fields." *The Killing Fields* is the only feature film to explore Pol Pot's murderous regime; thus it is an essential component of any list of films dealing with war.

WAR OF ALGERIAN INDEPENDENCE

The Battle of Algiers* (La battaglia di Algeri)
Released: 1966

The end of colonialism was characterized by war. This film depicts the Battle of Algiers, France's victory in defeating the National Liberation Front and maintaining control of Algeria in the short-term, but ends noting that Algeria eventually gained its independence. The film is an excellent depiction of the terror tactics and atrocities committed on both sides, and it shows just how violent anticolonial struggles could be. The film takes a few historical liberties but overall is historically accurate.

ARAB-ISRAELI CONFLICT

Kippur*
Released: 2000

In October of 1973, Egypt and Syria jointly attacked Israel on Yom Kippur. *Kippur*, an Israeli-French production, is based on the actual experiences of a helicopter rescue team as they evacuate the wounded from the battlefield. There are very few films about the Arab-Israeli conflict readily available, and what makes *Kippur* stand out is its ability to turn the viewer into a participant. The film also contains many long, unbroken scenes that help make the experience real, chaotic, and sometimes necessarily boring, rather than jumping from action to action as many war films do.

FALKLANDS WAR

An Ungentlemanly Act^ *and* Iluminados por el fuego* (blessed by fire)
Released: 1992 and 2005 respectively

The fight for the Falkland Islands (or the Malvinas, to the Argentineans) began in April of 1982. The war lasted only a few months and ended in a British victory. Each of these films is biased in favor of the country that produced it, but together they paint a good picture of the entire conflict as well as demonstrate that history changes depending on who is telling it. *An Ungentlemanly Act* focuses primarily on the initial Argentinean invasion. Only the last five minutes of the film address Britain's counterattack and eventual reconquest of the island. *Iluminados por el fuego* begins in the midst of the war, after the British returned in force, and carries through to the postwar era.

FIRST GULF WAR

Jarhead
Released: 2005

Of the handful of films set in the First Gulf War—including *Courage Under Fire* (1996) and *Three Kings* (1999)—*Jarhead* is the best choice. It follows a unit of Marine snipers from boot camp to the end of the war. There is not much combat, and no epic battle scene caps the film, but that is what makes *Jarhead* valuable. Battles in the First Gulf War were few and far between, which was good for civilians at home but was torture for Marines trained to fight and kill; simply waiting for the unknown was worse than confrontation with a physical enemy. The film also explores the soldier's anguish over life back home. *Jarhead* is a new type of war film that focuses primarily on the war within the soldier rather than the soldier within the war.

YUGOSLAVIAN CIVIL WAR

No Man's Land*
Released: 2001

With the death of Tito in 1980, Yugoslavia descended into chaos as nationalist sentiment, historical precedent, and religious differences led to brutal conflict between Croats, Serbs, Bosnian Muslims, and other ethnic groups. *No Man's Land* not only presents an excellent depiction of the violence of the war and the intense hatred between the various sides but also exposes the impotence of the United Nations to maintain peace and reach a peaceful compromise. The film, telling the story of only a handful of characters fighting over a single trench, provides an allegory for the war.

SOMALI CIVIL WAR

Black Hawk Down
Released: 2001

In 1993, the United States military staged a small raid in the city of Mogadishu, hoping to capture important figures in the government of Warlord Mo-hamed Farrah Aidid. The raid went smoothly until the local militia shot down a Black Hawk helicopter that was providing support for the raid. The rescue mission turned into a two-day battle between a small group of Army Rangers and Delta Force soldiers against the entire city militia in what is now known as the Battle of Mogadishu. The film is a graphic and detailed example of late twentieth century warfare.

RWANDAN CIVIL WAR

Hotel Rwanda
Released: 2004

During the decolonization of Africa, many parts of the continent erupted in violence. One of the most shocking examples occurred in Rwanda, where in 1994 Rwandan Hutus killed one million of their Tutsi compatriots in one hundred days. As demonstrated by *The Grey Zone* (2001) and *The Killing Fields* (1984), modern war has made genocide possible. What makes the genocide in Rwanda different (and prompts its inclusion on this list) is that the United Nations, though pledged to prevent genocide, failed to take adequate measures to stop it.

Chris Thomas

WAR LITERATURE

The following works are important in the study of military history. They are selected for their value in representing the conflict and/or the period in question, and they are arranged in roughly chronological subsections, within which they are arranged alphabetically by title.

ANCIENT WORLD

Anabasis
Author: Xenophon
First published: 386-377 B.C.E., as *Kyrou anabasis*

Anabasis chronicles the determined survival of an army of ten thousand Greek mercenaries stranded in northern Mesopotamia by the death of the claimant to the Persian throne who hired them. Although the author's account of the mercenaries' endurance against enormous military odds and great geographical obstacles is clearly colored by self-interest, the narrative is so stirring that it is said to have provided the literary inspiration for Philip of Macedon and Alexander the Great's shared conviction that they could conquer the Persian Empire with a relatively small but highly disciplined Greek army.

The Art of War
Author: Sunzi (Sun Tzu)
First published: c. 510 B.C.E., as *Bingfa*

This treatise on waging war consists of thirty-six stratagems covering everything from geopolitical strategy to battlefield tactics to the practice of espionage. In all of these areas, Sunzi advises caution over bellicosity. He argues for short wars with broad support among the population and warns against the corrosive effects of protracted conflicts. He argues for the clever manipulation of all possible advantages in everything from topography to weaponry, for the mitigation of the limitations of one's own forces, and for the concentration of force where the enemy is most vulnerable. That many of these ideas have become truisms is a testament to Sunzi's lasting influence.

The Gallic Wars
Author: Julius Caesar
First published: 52-51 B.C.E., as *Comentarii de bello Gallico* in *Commentaries*

This classic work of military commentary and Latin prose consists of seven books, with each book covering one year of Caesar's seven-year campaign to subdue Gaul. Written in the third person, the narrative focuses not only on the major battles but also on the logistical preparation, intelligence gathering, political maneuvering, and tactical ingenuity that enabled Caesar's always greatly outnumbered forces to defeat the Celtic tribes. For all of their ferocity, however, the Gallic tribes had been decimated by long, ongoing conflicts with Germanic tribes, and they remained unable to overcome their tribal divisions for any extended period.

The History
Author: Herodotus
First published: c. 424 B.C.E., as *Historiai Herodotou*

Known as the "Father of History," Herodotus originally published his *History* in nine volumes. His primary subject was the Greco-Persian Wars of the fifth century B.C.E., which ensured the continuing independence of the Greek states and their formative role in the development of Western culture. He also, however, traveled widely throughout the Mediterranean world, and his histories include not only what he learned, first- and secondhand, about the lands that he visited but also what he learned about lands that lay beyond those he visited. Thus, he provides many of the earliest European references to regions such as sub-Saharan Africa and India.

History of the Peloponnesian War

Author: Thucydides
First published: 431-404 B.C.E., as *Historia tou Peloponnesiacou polemou*

Establishing many of the fundamental elements of modern historiography, Thucydides attempted to provide an objective history of the Peloponnesian War, despite the fact that he had been a combatant and could be expected to be biased toward the side on which he fought. The war was fought between the Delian League, led by Athens, and the Peloponnesian League, led by Sparta. The war ended Athens's preeminence and opened the way for the Macedonian conquest of Greece less than a half century later. Covering the first twenty-one years of the twenty-seven-year conflict, *History of the Peloponnesian War* has been divided into eight books. It is assumed that Thucydides was still working on the project when he died.

Iliad

Author: Homer
First published: c. 750 B.C.E.

The oldest surviving work in the Western literary canon, this epic poem describes the extended Greek siege of Troy, a major port in Asia Minor. Focusing on the martial achievements of the heroes on both sides and the dramatic deaths of many of the noteworthy combatants, the poem presents the great warrior as a sort of demigod. The greatest of all these warriors is the Greek Achilles, against whom no Trojan hero, not even Hector, can stand. The war and the poem conclude with the Greeks' apparent withdrawal and their "gift" to the besieged city of the so-called Trojan horse. Actually filled with Greek warriors who, under cover of darkness, open the city's gates to the returning mass of the Greek army, the Trojan horse has become a symbol for any audacious deception.

The Mahabharata

Author: Vyasa
First published: c. 400 B.C.E.-200 C.E., *Mahābhārata*

One of the two great epics in Sanskrit that define much of the cultural and religious traditions of Hin-

duism, the *Mahabharata* includes more than 100,000 verse lines and 1.8 million words. On a basic narrative level, this epic poem is a chronicle of the struggle for royal succession in the Kuru kingdom of Hastinapura, a struggle that reached its great climax in the Kurukshetra War. The contending claimants to the throne are the Kaurava and the Pandava branches of the royal bloodline. Despite incredible demonstrations of valor by the great warriors on both sides during the war, the Pandava are ultimately victorious. Commentators have often drawn parallels between this Sanskrit epic and the *Iliad*.

Masters of Rome

Author: Colleen McCullough
First published: 1990-2007

Best known for *The Thorn Birds* (1977), the melodramatic family saga about the development of Australia, McCullough followed its tremendous commercial success, including its adaptation as an extremely popular television miniseries, with a complete change of direction. In the seven novels of her painstakingly researched series Masters of Rome, McCullough chronicles the fall of the Roman Republic and its transformation into an imperial state. The seven novels include *The First Man in Rome* (1990), *The Grass Crown* (1991), *Fortune's Favorites* (1993), *Caesar's Women* (1996), *Caesar: Let the Dice Fly* (1997), *The October Horse* (2002), and *Antony and Cleopatra* (2007).

Memoirs of Hadrian

Author: Marguerite Yourcenar
First published: 1951, as *Mémoires d'Hadrien*

Working from the fact that the Roman emperor Hadrian wrote an autobiography that was lost to history, Yourcenar provides a fictional version of that autobiography in this, her most acclaimed novel. Epistolary in form, the novel is framed as a letter from Hadrian to his presumptive successor, Marcus Aurelius. After years of immersing herself in Roman history and culture, Yourcenar was able to create and sustain a voice for Hadrian that won over classicists as well as more general readers, re-creating the milieu that he shaped at a level far beyond the usual "costume novel."

Spartacus
Author: Howard Fast
First published: 1951

Fast transformed the leader of the largest slave revolt in Roman history into a champion of egalitarian, progressive ideals. The novel is divided into two types of sections. Those told in the past tense present the recollections of Roman leaders of the failed attempts to quell the uprising and the terror it created throughout Italy. These accounts exhibit the political machinations and the class consciousness that eventually subverted the core values of the Roman Republic and led to the rise of the imperial state. The other sections are told in the present tense from the rebels' very different perspective. In contrast to the Roman vilification of Spartacus as a barbarous agent of civil disorder, to his followers he is an iconic figure, the embodiment of valor and honorableness.

MEDIEVAL WORLD

Genghis
Author: Conn Iggulden
First published: 2007-2008

Called the Conqueror series in the United Kingdom, this series includes *Birth of an Empire* (2007), *Lords of the Bow* (2008), and *Bones of the Hills* (2008). It reconstructs the rise of Genghis Khan from the leadership of a small nomadic tribe to the master of the largest empire in human history. The series is notable both for the extensiveness of Iggulden's research and for his unobtrusive integration of that research into the narratives. Projecting this as a seven-volume series, Iggulden has indicated that he will focus on Kublai Khan in the fourth through sixth novels.

Ivanhoe
Author: Sir Walter Scott
First published: 1819

The most enduring work by the prolific and popular Scottish novelist, *Ivanhoe* is a Romantic historical novel set in twelfth century England. The title character is a Saxon knight who not only supports Richard, the Norman king of England, but also accompanies him on his crusades to the Holy Land. Ivanhoe and the Lady Rowena, a direct descendant of the last Saxon king, are very much in love, but Ivanhoe's father, who is also Lady Rowena's guardian, has disinherited him for his support of a Norman king and is scheming to marry her off to Lord Æthelstane, the most powerful Saxon lord in England.

Poem of the Cid
Author: Unknown
First published: c. 1140, as *Cantar del mío Cid*

The hero of this great epic poem is based on Rodrigo Díaz de Vivar. He emerged at the head of a private army of knights in the midst of the political chaos that marked the eleventh century efforts of the Spanish states to reconquer the Iberian Peninsula from the Moorish states. Rodrigo had to anticipate the shifting alliances and conflicts among the Spanish states, the Moorish states, and the outside forces that attempted to take advantage of the chaos. In the poem, this Machiavellian figure becomes a great patriot whose fidelity to his king and the nascent notion of a Spanish state is rewarded with ingratitude and even perfidy.

Romance of the Three Kingdoms
Author: Luo Guanzhong
First published: mid-fourteenth century, as *Sanguo zhi yanyi*

This epic novel treats the political turmoil and the military campaigns that followed the Yellow Turban Rebellion against the Eastern Han Empire. The three kingdoms of the title—Wei, Wu, and Shu—enter into a precarious and frequently broken truce. The fortunes of each of the kingdoms are shown to rise and fall not simply on the skills of their kings but even more on the skills of the military advisers serving those kings. The novel chronicles the many schemes and battles that lead eventually to the defeat of both the Shu and Wu kingdoms by the Wei and the ascension to power of Ssu-Ma Yen as the first Emperor of China.

The Saracen Blade

Author: Frank Yerby

First published: 1952

Although he has been much criticized for refusing to address issues of race in his fiction and although his early efforts and even some of his later novels can rightly be dismissed as historical romances or costume novels, Yerby was actually a fairly accomplished writer of historical novels. *The Saracen Blade* is a competent and even insightful treatment of the Crusades. Beyond some melodramatic inventions, Yerby demonstrates an awareness of the broad cultural conflicts that formed the backdrop to the specific battles and other historical events. Moreover, he takes pains to present a culturally balanced view of those events, representing with some nuances both the Christian and the Muslim perspectives on them.

The Tale of the Heiki

Author: Kakuichi

First published: 1371, as *Heike monogatari*

This classic epic of Japanese literature first appeared in oral versions, with the bulk of the composition being attributed, in the folk tradition, to a monk named Yukinaga. The most widely read and first authoritative written version, however, was completed by Kakuichi two centuries after the events described in the work. The main theme of *The Tale of the Heiki* is the Buddhist concept of impermanence, especially as it is reflected in the shifting centers of military and political power and in the stature of individual warriors. The work is a stylized account of the Gempei Wars (1180-1185), in which the Taira clan first defeated the Minamoto clan and then was defeated by it.

SPANISH CONQUEST

Aztec

Author: Gary Jennings

First published: 1980

Jennings's novel is the first in a five-novel series, which also includes *Aztec Autumn* (1998), *Aztec Blood* (2002), *Aztec Rage* (2006), and *Aztec Fire*

(2008). The series chronicles the history of Mexico from the height of the Aztec Empire just before the Spanish conquest to the Mexican war for independence from Spain. The first novel is an account of the conquest from the point of view of an elderly Aztec survivor, filtered through the point of view of a Spanish bishop who is writing a report to the Spanish king. Since Hernán Cortés's conquest of Mexico is often regarded as one of the most improbable military adventures in history, *Aztec* fills a fictional void in attempting to reconstruct events from the perspective of the conquered.

FRENCH AND INDIAN WAR (SEVEN YEARS' WAR)

The Last of the Mohicans

Author: James Fenimore Cooper

First published: 1826

The Last of the Mohicans is one of Cooper's most enduring novels and one of the best-known novels about the French and Indian War. The novel emphasizes that most of the war was fought on the frontier, by colonial and Native American surrogates rather than by the French and British forces per se. In the wilderness setting, treachery and savagery reduced adherence to the "rules" of European warfare to a tragic sort of foolhardiness. In the novel's focal event, the British garrison at Fort William Henry surrenders, and the French allow the British safe passage out of the wilderness. The Huron allies of the French nonetheless ambush the British column and massacre almost everyone in it.

AMERICAN REVOLUTION

Drums Along the Mohawk

Author: Walter D. Edmonds

First published: 1936

One of the best-known novels about the American Revolution (1775-1783), *Drums Along the Mohawk* is set in the Mohawk River Valley of upstate New York, at that time the frontier between colonial settlements and the territory of the Iroquois. Allied with the British and the Tory colonists who remained loyal to the British crown, the Iroquois terrorized the colonial settlers. Moreover, when the settlers banded together to present an effective fighting force, they had to leave their homes, their crops and animals, and sometimes their wives and children defenseless.

NAPOLEONIC WARS

Horatio Hornblower series
Author: C. S. Forester
First published: 1937-1967

Chronologically, this is the second novel in the eleven-novel series following Horatio Hornblower's experiences as a British naval officer during the Napoleonic Wars. Published in 1952, *Lieutenant Hornblower* was the seventh novel of the series in order of publication but seems to have been the pivotal novel in terms of securing the popularity of the series on both sides of the Atlantic. Chronologically, the other novels in the series include *Mr. Midshipman Hornblower* (1950), *Hornblower and the Hotspur* (1962), *Hornblower and the Crisis* (1967), *Hornblower and the Atropos* (1953), *Beat to Quarters* (1937; also known as *The Happy Return*), *Ship of the Line* (1938), *Flying Colours* (1938), *Commodore Hornblower* (1945), *Lord Hornblower* (1946), and *Admiral Hornblower in the West Indies* (1958).

Master and Commander
Author: Patrick O'Brian
First published: 1969

This is the first in a series of twenty novels featuring Captain Jack Aubrey and surgeon Stephen Maturin, serving together with the British navy during the Napoleonic Wars. Considerably different from the film adaptation in 2003, the novel follows the career of the warship *Sophie* from helping to protect a convoy of British supply ships to preying on French merchant ships to a vicious battle with a Spanish warship to its dramatic capture by a squadron of French warships. The novel establishes three hallmarks of the series: O'Brian's great interest in the intricacies of naval politics, in the physical workings of ships of the period and the ways in which their crews functioned, and in the individual personalities of his characters.

Richard Sharpe series
Author: Bernard Cornwell
First published: 1981-2006

Set during the Napoleonic period, Cornwell's series follows the title character across several continents and a broad range of adventures and misadventures. Sharpe is introduced as a private serving with the British East India Company in India, serves in the extended campaigns against the French in Portugal and Spain, participates as a field-promoted officer in the Battle of Waterloo, and visits St. Helena and meets Napoleon on his way to Chile on a privately commissioned mission. The series was not initially published in chronological order. It eventually included twenty-one numbered novels and three numbered short stories, from *Sharpe's Tiger* to *Sharpe's Devil*.

War and Peace
Author: Leo Tolstoy
First published: 1865-1869, as *Voyna i mir*

The greatest war novel ever written, *War and Peace* treats Napoleon's invasion of Russia, which to that point was the greatest military undertaking and the greatest military debacle in human history. Told from the Russian point of view, with much attention to the class structure of Russian society, this twelve-hundred-page novel is equal to Napoleon's grand ambition and the size of his Grande Armée to the vastness of the Russian landscape and of the desolation left by the retreating Russian's "burned earth" policy and the great scope of the Russian effort, materially and morally, to drive the Antichrist from the motherland. Every ambitious war novel written since *War and Peace* has inevitably been compared to it and has been found wanting.

AMERICAN INDIAN WARS

The Court-Martial of George Armstrong Custer

Author: Douglas C. Jones
First published: 1976

The first novel by Jones, and the first novel in the trilogy that includes *Arrest Sitting Bull* (1977) and *A Creek Called Wounded Knee* (1978), *The Court-Martial of George Armstrong Custer* received the Golden Spur Award from the Western Writers of America. A speculative work of historical fiction, the novel proceeds from the premise that Custer managed to survive the massacre of most of his troopers at the Little Bighorn and was subsequently placed on trial for the recklessness with which he had placed his command in jeopardy.

The Panther in the Sky

Author: James Alexander Thom
First published: 1989

Thom has made a career out of writing historical novels about the opening of the American frontier in the first half of the nineteenth century. His most commercially and critically successful novel, *The Panther in the Sky* is a fictionalized biography of Tecumseh. Within the framework of chronicling the Shawnee chief's formative experiences, his decision to ally his tribe with the British during the revolutionary War and the War of 1812, and his partially successful attempt to unite the tribes of the Old Northwest against American expansion, Thom provides a poignant view of a still vibrant culture on the verge of near extinction.

COSSACK-POLISH CONFLICT

Taras Bulba

Author: Nikolai Gogol
First published: 1835, revised 1842

In this short novel, Gogol chronicles the military campaigns waged by the title character against the Poles, who are determined to dominate the Ukraine.

A moving tale of determined armed resistance, a deeply ingrained spirit of independence, and a nascent sense of national spirit, the novel presents the Cossacks as archetypal Russians, with Taras and his sons playing out the sort of conflicts that often occur between great men and the sons who tragically attempt to emulate them or bitterly reject them. Thus, for all of its considerable historically accurate detail, the novel provides an idealized, if not distorted, view of the Cossacks before they became an instrument of Russian imperialism and oppression.

The Trilogy

Author: Henryk Sienkiewicz
First published: 1884-1888

Although Sienkiewicz received the Nobel Prize in Literature in 1905, he is remembered today primarily as the author of the international best seller *Quo Vadis* (1896). In his trilogy, Sienkiewicz synthesized the conventions of the historical epic with aspects of naturalism, then a relatively new literary movement derived from the controversial theories of scientific determinism. *Ogniem i mieczem* (1884; *With Fire and Sword*, 1890) focuses on a Cossack revolt against Polish rule. *Potop* (1886; *The Deluge*, 1891) treats a catastrophic Swedish invasion of Poland. *Pan Wołodyjowski* (1888; *Pan Michael*, 1893, also known as *Fire in the Steppe*, 1992) depicts the seventeenth century conflicts between Poland and the Ottoman Empire, which halted the Ottoman advance into eastern and central Europe.

INDIAN COLONIAL WARS

"Gunga Din"

Author: Rudyard Kipling
First published: 1892

The best known of Kipling's *Barrack-Room Ballads*, "Gunga Din" focuses on the hard existence and unexpected nobility of an Indian water carrier for the British forces on the Afghan frontier. The poem exploits the fact that the title character is regarded as an inferior by most soldiers in the army that he serves and that, when he is noticed, it is generally as the target of indignities. The narrator of the poem, however, recounts how this unlikely figure heroically gave his life to save the lives of the narrator and many of his fellow soldiers.

The Siege of Krishnapur
Author: J. G. Farrell
First published: 1973

Set during the Indian Mutiny or Sepoy Rebellion of 1857, Farrell's novel focuses on the siege of a small fictional town. Told from the points of view of the British residents of the besieged town, the novel shows how those residents struggle to continue their daily lives without the Indian laborers on whom so much of their social rituals and basic comfort depend. Despite the inevitable leveling effects of the siege, the residents are also unable to let go of their class consciousness. Even cholera, scurvy, and general starvation are not enough to subvert completely their ingrained notions of who they are—which is, ironically, what dooms both the town and the rebellion to which it falls victim.

Crimean War

"The Charge of the Light Brigade"
Author: Alfred, Lord Tennyson
First published: 1855

As part of his duties as the British poet laureate, Tennyson produced poems on events of national interest. This poem celebrates the heroism of British cavalry that charged down a valley into Russian artillery fire during the Battle of Balaclava. The battle occurred during the Crimean War, which is now largely remembered as the only conflict involving most of the major European powers between the Napoleonic Wars and World War I. Tennyson's poem turned a military debacle into an iconic, if tragic, demonstration of national character.

American Civil War

Amalgamation Polka
Author: Stephen Wright
First published: 2006

In what may be the first truly postmodern novel to treat the American Civil War, Wright focuses on the misadventures of Liberty Fish, an abolitionist who, as soon as he is old enough, predictably enlists in the Union army. What makes Liberty's situation rich with ironic possibilities is the fact that, although his parents are staunch abolitionists, his maternal grandparents are unapologetic slave owners, and his paternal grandparents are textile manufacturers who owe their fortune to slave-produced cotton from the Southern plantations. Wright stresses that despite the unprecedented scale and complexity of this terrible conflict, it both created and was created out of complicated, multilayered antagonisms that divided individual families and the tangled internal conflicts with which its combatants struggled even as they raised arms against each other.

Andersonville
Author: MacKinlay Kantor
First published: 1955

For this historical novel about the horrors endured by Union prisoners of war in the prison camp near Andersonville, Georgia, Kantor received the Pulitzer Prize. Although Kantor drew on historical sources (such as 1879's *Andersonville: A Story of Rebel Military Prisons*, by John McElroy) that were largely biased in favor of Northern antipathy toward the Confederates, his novel is notable for his attempt to present balanced portraits of the key historical figures, especially the vilified camp commandant, Henry Wirz. Likewise, the novel provides a broad spectrum of fictional figures representative of the factions among the prisoners and even among the residents of the surrounding countryside.

Cold Mountain

Author: Charles Frazier
First published: 1997

Set in the closing months of the American Civil War, this debut novel by Charles Frazier juxtaposes the stories of W. P. Inman, a wounded Confederate veteran who decides to desert, and his love interest, Ada Monroe, who has moved from Charleston to the supposed safety of the mountains of North Carolina. As Inman travels the 250 miles to Cold Mountain and Ada, he confronts all sorts of scurrilous characters and is hounded by the Home Guard. Meanwhile, Ada has to cope with her father's death and survives largely because of her growing friendship with a mountain woman named Ruby Thewes. The lovers reunite but only long enough for her to become pregnant with his child.

The Killer Angels

Author: Michael Shaara
First published: 1974

In this sprawling novel, Shaara attempted to describe the Battle of Gettysburg from the perspectives of as many of the combatants as possible. The result is an intimate sense of the intensity with which the battle was fought, the confusion that very often caused opportunities to be lost or advantages to be gained by both sides, and the terrible carnage that the soldiers on both sides somehow managed to endure even when it became clear that the battle was moving toward some climactic slaughter—which turned out to be Pickett's Charge. The novel received the Pulitzer Prize and was adapted for a landmark television miniseries.

The March

Author: E. L. Doctorow
First published: 2005

In his previous novels, Doctorow has experimented with the conventions of the historical novel and has brought a postmodern sensibility to his treatment of historical subjects and to his fictional reconstruction of historical eras. In this novel, which depicts General William Tecumseh Sherman's devastating march across Georgia in the fall of 1864, Doctorow explores the paradoxes in Sherman's public persona, the ambiguities in his personal character, and the complexities in his temperament. Sherman is more a focal than a truly central character, however, for the novel presents characters representative of the many types of people affected by the devastation of a sixty-mile-wide and three-hundred-mile-long section of Georgia by sixty thousand loosely controlled troops.

The Red Badge of Courage

Author: Stephen Crane
First published: 1895

The best-known and most critically acclaimed novel about the American Civil War, *The Red Badge of Courage* was a largely imaginative work, inspired by Crane's fascination with photographs of the battlefields and his dissatisfaction with the generally dry reminiscences of veterans. The short novel focuses on a young soldier named Henry Fleming. In his second battle, he breaks from the Union lines as the Confederates attack. Finding himself among either other deserters or the wounded, he is embarrassed by his lack of a wound. However, an argument with an artilleryman leaves him with a gash in the head, and when he returns to his unit, his injury is accepted as a battle wound. In the next day's battle, Fleming becomes almost recklessly courageous, inspiring his fellow soldiers and impressing their officers.

SPANISH-AMERICAN WAR

Cuba Libre

Author: Elmore Leonard
First published: 1998

Leonard's novel was published on the hundredth anniversary of the event that made the Spanish-American War inevitable, the explosion on the battleship *Maine* in Havana harbor. Although Leonard had begun his career as a novelist writing Westerns, this foray into the genre of the historical novel at the height of his fame as a crime novelist surprised reviewers and readers. However, the novel explores familiar Leonard themes—in particular, the way that most moneymaking schemes inevitably become more complicated and corrupting. In this instance, two cowboys set out from Arizona to deliver thirty-one horses to a Cuban plantation. When the purchaser reneges on the deal, they keep trying to recoup their losses and end up in the middle of the wars between the Spanish and the Cuban insurgents and then between the Spanish and the invading Americans.

BOER WARS

Ladysmith
Author: Giles Foden
First published: 1999

In this, one of the most significant novels about the Boer War, Foden focuses on the lengthy Boer siege of the British town of Ladysmith. The siege followed some early Boer victories over the British, which surprised not just the British military and government but also observers from all over the world. The outcome of the siege became a critical issue for the British and the Boers, not only because the town was located near the Boer republics and strategically important but also because of the psychological effect of a clear victory for the Boers or even a stalemate for the British.

RUSSIAN REVOLUTION AND CIVIL WAR

Doctor Zhivago
Author: Boris Pasternak
First published: 1957

Pasternak's epic novel treats the Russian Revolution and the Civil War between the Red and White forces that followed it. In the half decade between 1917 and 1922, imperial Russia was wrecked and the Bolsheviks created the Soviet Union at the cost of several million of lives. Most of the dead not were combatants but civilians unable to escape the carnage or unable to survive on the devastated landscape that was its aftermath. Pasternak's protagonist, a physician and a poet, represents those who somehow managed to survive but at a considerable physical and psychological cost.

MEXICAN REVOLUTION

The Underdogs
Author: Mariano Azuela
First published: 1916, as *Los de abajo*

Written while Azuela served as a surgeon with Pancho Villa's forces in northern Mexico in the mid-1910's, this novel is not only the most significant work about the decade-long Mexican Revolution but also one of the most influential works of social protest in Mexican and Latin American literature. Azuela conveys the massive dislocations of the population caused by the almost continuously shifting alliances that made each successive leader's hold on power very tenuous. Likewise, he captures the extraordinary brutality of the conflict, which was fueled as much by feverishly confused ideologies as by ideological fervor.

WORLD WAR I

All Quiet on the Western Front
Author: Erich Maria Remarque
First published: 1929

One of the most highly regarded novels to come out of World War I, *All Quiet on the Western Front* is also one of the few German novels about that war to have been made widely available in translation. It focuses on a group of school friends who are encouraged to enlist for idealistic reasons that quickly seem bitterly delusory amid the carnage of trench warfare. When the soldiers return to their homes on leave, they realize that in going off to save their homeland, they have lost all connection to home.

Birdsong
Author: Sebastian Faulks
First published: 1993

This novel is the middle volume of Faulks's French Trilogy, which also includes *The Girl at the Lion d'Or* (1989) and *Charlotte Gray* (1998). The most commercially successful and critically acclaimed novel of the trilogy, *Birdsong* has, moreover, been one of the most popular and most highly regarded British novels of the last quarter century. The main character is Stephen Wraysford, and the primary focus is on his experiences during World War I, especially during the great British offensive along the Somme. A parallel narrative concerns the efforts of his granddaughter, Elizabeth, to learn about his wartime experiences more than a half century later.

The Blue Max

Author: Jack D. Hunter
First published: 1964

Hunter's first novel charts the rise and fall of Bruno Stachel, a German fighter pilot during World War I. Unlike most of the original fighter pilots, who were aristocrats, Stachel comes from a working-class background and begins his wartime service as an infantryman. When the air losses create a demand for pilots, he not only seizes the opportunity to escape the carnage of the trenches but also becomes determined to compile the twenty "kills" required to win the Blue Max, an award reserved for Germany's most highly honored air aces. Stachel's ruthless pursuit of his goal involves him in all sorts of machinations—military, political, socioeconomic, and sexual.

The Case of Sergeant Grischa

Author: Arold Zweig
First published: 1927, as *Der Streit um den Sergeanten Grischa*

Part of the six-volume series *The Great War of White Men*, this satiric novel follows the title character, a Russian soldier being held in a German prisoner-of-war (POW) camp, as he makes his escape and attempts to make his way back to his homeland. When he is eventually captured, he identifies himself as a deserter to avoid being sent back to the POW camp. Because he is illiterate, however, he has been unable to read the posted notices that deserters who have failed to report to German authorities are to be shot as spies. What follows is a trial and then a series of reversed decisions as the military bureaucracy tries to decide whether he ought to be executed.

Clerambault: The Story of an Independent Spirit During the War

Author: Romain Rolland
First published: 1920, as *Clérambault: Histoire d'une conscience libre pendant la guerre*

Most remembered for his ten-novel cycle *Jean Christophe* (1904-1912), Rolland received the Nobel Prize in Literature in 1915. Five years later, this novel presented a powerful indictment of all wars. The major character struggles to come to terms with his son's death in combat during World War I. Throughout the novel, father and son are out of step. Initially, the father is skeptical about the causes and ramifications of the war, while his son is stirred deeply by a sense of the momentousness of the war. Then as the son experiences the horror of the trenches and becomes profoundly disenchanted, the father finds himself searching for ways to express his heightened patriotism. In the end, the main character embraces pacifism and is accused of being traitorous.

Collected Poems

Author: Rupert Brooke
First published: 1915

One of the best-known British poets of World War I, Brooke was twenty-seven when he died of blood poisoning on his way to the battlefield at Gallipoli. He had experienced relatively little of the horrors of the trench warfare that would transform much of northern France into a muddy, carnage-strewn wasteland. Shortly before he died, Brooke wrote a series of patriotic sonnets that captured the intense patriotism and naïveté of prewar Britain. The most remembered of these sonnets are "Peace," "Safety," "The Dead," and "The Soldier," considered by most to be Brooke's signature poem.

The Complete Poems of Wilfred Owen

Author: Wilfred Owen
First published: 1963, edited by C. Day Lewis

Owen served on the western front in 1916 and 1917, participating in the Battle of the Somme. While recuperating from shell shock, Owen met Siegfried Sassoon, who influenced Owen's composition of a series of poems in which he sought to describe his own wartime experience and to emphasize the "pity" underlying all battlefield experience. Only a few of these poems were published before Owen returned to the front, where he perished one week before the Armistice. His best-known poems include "Anthem for Doomed Youth," "Dulce et Decorum Est," and the never completed "Strange Meeting."

The Enormous Room
Author: E. E. Cummings
First published: 1922

In this autobiographical novel, Cummings re-creates his four-month imprisonment in France during World War I. A volunteer ambulance driver, Cummings was the recipient of a series of letters from another driver who in very strong terms denounced the war. Although Cummings himself was simply the recipient of these letters, he along with the writer was imprisoned on suspicion of disloyalty to the Allied cause. Following American diplomatic intervention, Cummings was released and returned to the United States just as the entry of American troops into the Allied effort on the western front was escalating.

A Farewell to Arms
Author: Ernest Hemingway
First published: 1929

Hemingway's novel is set in northeastern Italy, in the region surrounding the Isonzo River, where a series of great battles were fought between the Italian and Austro-Hungarian forces during World War I. The main character is Frederic Henry, an American serving as a volunteer with the Italian ambulance corps. While he is recuperating from wounds, he falls in love with an English nurse, Catherine Barkley. Eventually he returns to the front lines, but the anarchic brutality that follows an Italian retreat from the Isonzo convinces him to flee to neutral Switzerland with Catherine, who is pregnant with their child. The child is stillborn, and Catherine dies in childbirth.

The Good Soldier: Švejk
Author: Jaroslav Hašek
First published: 1921-1923, as *Osudy dobrého vojáka Švejka za světove války*

When the Czech writer Jaroslav Hašek died of tuberculosis in 1923, he had completed only four of the projected six books about Švejk (often rendered as Schweik). The four completed books have subsequently been published for the most part as a single book. The tone of the work is clearly satiric, with Schweik repeatedly demonstrating the ridiculousness of the Austro-Hungarian military, its other institutions, and the continued viability of the empire itself. Hašek is able to sustain the satire because Schweik remains an ambiguous figure; that is, one is never sure whether he is a clever malcontent or is simply an imbecile who accidentally or coincidentally makes those around him seem ridiculous.

"In Flanders Fields"
Author: John McCrae
First published: 1915

The best-known poem about World War I, "In Flanders Fields" was written by a Canadian physician, John McCrae, who was serving as a battlefield surgeon with the British forces in Belgium. Following the very costly Second Battle of Ypres, during which one of McCrae's closest friends was killed, McCrae wrote "In Flanders Fields" as a memorial to his dead friends and, by extension, to all of the war dead. A practiced poet and a military veteran who had served during the Boer War, McCrae captured the terrible pathos of war while avoiding the usual bromides about the glorious sacrifices made by the war dead. In the last year of the war, McCrae himself died from pneumonia.

Parade's End
Author: Ford Madox Ford
First published: 1924-1928

Ford may be most remembered for *The Good Soldier* (1915), which remains one of the most cited illustrations of the use of an unreliable narrator, but this tetralogy of novels about a British officer's experiences in the trenches during World War I is arguably his masterwork. The main character is Christopher Tietjens, the scion of prominent family of Tory gentry, and the novels trace his deepening preoccupation with sustaining both his commitment to the war and his determination to conduct himself honorably. The four novels of the tetralogy include *Some Do Not* (1924), *No More Parades* (1925), *A Man Could Stand Up* (1926), and *The Last Post* (1928).

Paths of Glory

Author: Humphrey Cobb
First published: 1935

Published in the mid-1930's when another world war seemed to be increasingly inevitable, *Paths of Glory* offered a scathing indictment of military culture and command structure. Set in World War I, the story hinges on a French general's first ordering an impossible attack against a German position and then ordering the execution of forty arbitrarily selected French soldiers as a punishment for the "cowardice" evident in the failure to achieve the attack's objective. In Stanley Kubrick's film adaptation, Colonel Dax, the commander of the units that spearheaded the attack, provides an uncompromisingly moral perspective, but in Cobb's novel, he is more ineffectual, mitigating only by degrees what is unambiguously morally outrageous.

Regeneration Trilogy

Author: Pat Barker
First published: 1991-1995

Barker's highly regarded trilogy includes *Regeneration* (1991), *The Eye in the Door* (1993), and *The Ghost Road* (1995). The first novel was a finalist for the Booker Prize, and the third novel received that prize. The trilogy about World War I is set primarily in a British army hospital, where a psychiatrist named W. H. R. Rivers attempts to treat soldiers suffering from shell shock. One of his patients is the aristocratic poet Siegfried Sassoon, whose commitment to the facility has kept him from being tried for treason for publicly expressing his increasingly virulent antiwar sentiments. At the opposite end of the spectrum is the working-class character Billy Prior, whose premonitions about his terrible death in the trenches manifest themselves first in indiscriminate sexual affairs and then in bisexuality.

A Soldier of the Great War

Author: Mark Helprin
First published: 1991

The title character, now an elderly man on his way to visit his daughter, impulsively joins a much younger man on a seventy-kilometer walk to their destinations. Along the way, the title character reminisces about his life and, in particular, recounts his experiences during World War I. Having enlisted in the navy to avoid the carnage of the ground war, he was assigned to a riverboat patrolling first near the Austrian front to monitor enemy movements and then in Sicily to apprehend deserters. He himself eventually becomes a deserter, barely escapes execution, serves with the infantry, is wounded, falls in love with a nurse who is killed in an air attack on her hospital, and ends up after the war in Vienna, tracking down the pilot responsible for her death.

Three Soldiers

Author: John Dos Passos
First published: 1921

One of the most significant American novels about World War I, *Three Soldiers* is, in contrast to the modernist experimentation with form and language in *Manhattan Transfer* (1925) and *The U.S.A. Trilogy* (1937), a work set squarely in the realist tradition. The three soldiers of the title are Andrews from Virginia, Chrisfield from Indiana, and Fuselli from California. The novel describes the ways in which the soldiers' training and the authoritarian regimen of military life combine to reduce their sense of individuality and of the significance of their individual fates. Despite their very different temperaments and ambitions, all three soldiers are left irreparably brutalized by their experiences in uniform.

Under Fire

Author: Henri Barbusse
First published: 1916, as *Le Feu*

Written while Barbusse was still serving in the trenches with the French army during World War I, *Under Fire* imitates the form and style of a journal, and its narrator moves anecdotally from one day's experiences to the next. The narrator is a member of a squad of French "volunteers" who responded patriotically to the German invasion and try to maintain their sense of purpose in the midst of a conflict that has acquired a scope terribly beyond any cause. The novel is notable for its unsparingly realistic descriptions of the hardships of life in the trenches and the carnage of trench warfare.

The Wars

Author: Timothy Findley
First published: 1977

The recipient of the Governor-General's Award for fiction, Findley's novel stands as one of the major Canadian works about World War I, even though it was published just short of six decades after the Armistice. Like Wallace Stegner's *Angle of Repose* (1971), *The Wars* is framed as a historian's reconstruction of past events—in this case, the mysteries surrounding the last days in the life of a young officer named Robert Ross. Stationed on the western front, Ross is increasingly traumatized by the cumulative effect of his wartime experiences. Following his gang rape by a group of soldiers, he "madly" sets free a corral of horses and shoots dead the officer who tries to stop him. He and the horses are eventually caught in a barn, and when it is set on fire, Ross suffers terrible burns, from which he ultimately dies.

CHINESE CIVIL WAR

The Sand Pebbles

Author: Richard McKenna
First published: 1962

After serving in the U.S. Navy for more than twenty years, McKenna began to write fiction, producing primarily novels and short stories in the science-fiction genre. This novel is one of the few works in which he drew directly on his own military experience, and he died before the novel was adapted for a very successful film starring Steve McQueen. The title of the novel is a colloquial rendering of the name of the river gunboat on which the main character is serving, the USS *San Pablo*. While patrolling the Yangtze River in the late 1920's, the gunboat becomes enmeshed in the rising tensions and increasingly open conflict between the Chinese nationalists and communists.

SPANISH CIVIL WAR

For Whom the Bell Tolls

Author: Ernest Hemingway
First published: 1940

The best-known novel about the Spanish Civil War of the 1930's, *For Whom the Bell Tolls* is set among the partisans fighting behind the Fascist lines on behalf of the Republican cause. The main character is Robert Jordan, a munitions expert with the International Brigade, who is sent to join a group of partisans who are to provide support in his demolition of a bridge. The Republican forces are set to launch an offensive, and destroying the bridge will prevent the Fascists from rushing reinforcements to the sector against which the offensive is being launched. The novel emphasizes the psychological strain that this merciless conflict exerted on combatants and civilians alike.

Homage to Catalonia

Author: George Orwell
First published: 1938

In this memoir of his experiences during the Spanish Civil War, Orwell focuses as much on the divisions on the Republican side as on the battles fought between the Republican and Fascist forces. A communist who was opposed to Stalinism, Orwell joined the POUM militia on the Republican side, but in less than a year after his arrival in Spain, the Republican leadership had outlawed POUM because the Republican cause had become increasingly dependent on Soviet aid and dominated by Soviet "political advisers." After barely escaping a Stalinist "purge" of anti-Stalinist elements on the Republican side, Orwell became a lifelong critic of totalitarian communism.

SINO-JAPANESE WAR

Empire of the Sun
Author: J. G. Ballard
First published: 1984

The protagonist of this autobiographical novel is Jim Graham, a British boy who is living with his parents in Shanghai when the Japanese overwhelm the city. Separated from his parents, Jim is eventually picked up by the Japanese and sent to a civilian detention center. The novel chronicles the ways in which he learns to survive by his wits and sometimes manages to survive by sheer luck. Despite his awareness of the brutality of his Japanese captors, the boy inevitably admires their proud bearing and martial discipline. The novel vividly depicts the deprivation of the war's final months and the uncertainty of its closing weeks.

Music on the Bamboo Radio
Author: Martin Booth
First published: 1997

Like J. G. Ballard's *Empire of the Sun*, Booth's novel treats the Sino-Japanese War that merged into the broader war in Asia and the Pacific between the Allies and the Japanese. Also, like Ballard, Booth has chosen to depict these events through the perspective of an English boy separated from his parents by the Japanese attack against the city in which they are living, in this case Hong Kong. Unlike Ballard's protagonist, however, Nicholas Holford ends not in a detention camp but adopted by a Chinese family, and he becomes increasingly involved in sabotage and other clandestine activities of Chinese Communist partisans.

Red Sorghum
Author: Yan Mo
First published: 1992

Set in rural China during the period of the Japanese invasion and occupation, *Red Sorghum* was originally published as a series of four short novels. The sorghum crop is at the center of the novel, literally as well as symbolically, for the survival of the Chinese village depends on it, but the fields in which it is planted are the scene of both a Japanese massacre and a nearly suicidal but successful retributive attack by the peasants and partisans. Yan's narrative style is modernist in its experimentation with chronology and point of view, but his style owes much to Magical Realism. The color red is omnipresent, from the sorghum itself to the flamboyantly vivid descriptions of the mutilating effects of violence.

WORLD WAR II

Armageddon
Author: Leon Uris
First published: 1964

In this, his fifth, novel, Uris provides a contemporary history of the city that a quarter century earlier had become the monument-dominated capital of Adolf Hitler's Third Reich. The grandiose plans of Hitler and his architects had just begun to be realized, however, when the city became a favorite target of the Allied air war against Germany. Then, although largely reduced to ruins, it became the setting for the war's climactic and bloodiest battle. Following that apocalyptic framing of Hitler's suicide, it then was rebuilt, but as an occupied and militarily divided city that became a symbolic as well as actual focal point of Cold War tensions.

Battle Cry
Author: Leon Uris
First published: 1953

Based on Uris's own combat experience as a Marine, this novel focuses on a communications company of the Sixth Marine Regiment, following its members from boot camp through some of the bloodiest battles of the Pacific campaigns in World War II—Guadalcanal, Tarawa, and Saipan. The novel is narrated by the company's battle-hardened sergeant, and it follows the pattern of many GI novels in emphasizing the ethnic diversity among the men in the company, which includes a farm boy from Indiana, a Native American, and a Chicano.

Beasts of No Nation
Author: Uzodinma Iweala
First published: 2005

Relatively young boys have sometimes been enlisted into armies desperate for manpower (such as the German Home Guard in the closing months of World War II), but the forced recruitment of very young boys, even preadolescents, as a deliberate strategy for creating an easily indoctrinated fighting force is a relatively recent phenomenon seen primarily among insurgents in a number of African and several Asian nations. Iweala's novel is set in a West African nation. It is narrated by a boy soldier who loses his childhood and almost loses all sense of himself amid the commonplace horrors of a war as ill-defined as his terror-sustained allegiance to his commander.

A Bell for Adano
Author: John Hersey
First published: 1944

That Hersey's novel, published in wartime, was awarded the Pulitzer Prize in 1945, as World War II was drawing to a close, suggests the sort of appeal that it initially had. The novel is set in Italy after the Americans and British have driven the German forces back to the Italian mainland. The main character, an Italian American officer, becomes committed to replacing the bell in a village church that had been confiscated by the Fascists to be melted down and recycled into munitions. Although still admired for its craftsmanship, the novel has been increasingly regarded as the sort of approbative tale that is, in effect, a type of relatively benign propaganda.

Black Rain
Author: Masuji Ibuse
First published: 1966, as *Kuroi ame*

In Japan, Ibuse remains an important literary figure of his generation, though he has not achieved the stature, through translation into English and other Western languages, of some of his contemporaries. Drawing on the diaries of survivors of the atomic bombing of Hiroshima, Ibuse created a masterpiece of documentary realism in *Black Rain*. The central characters are an elderly man and his niece, whose determined attempts to reconstruct their lives from the absolute devastation of the bombing are shadowed by the specter of the long-term effects of the "black rain," or radioactive fallout from the atomic blast.

Bomber
Author: Len Deighton
First published: 1970

Although Deighton may be best known for his series of Cold War espionage novels featuring Bernard Samson, he is also the author of several novels and nonfiction books about World War II. Indeed, according to several critics, *Bomber* may be his most accomplished novel. It focuses on a single Royal Air Force bombing raid against the German industrial plants in the Ruhr Valley. The chapters follow the progress of the raid from hour to hour, and the suspense is heightened by the crews' increasing awareness that the raid is not going as planned.

The Bridge over the River Kwai
Author: Pierre Boulle
First published: 1952, as *Pont de la rivière Kwai*

Although Boulle's novel won the Prix Sainte Beuve and was adapted for an acclaimed film, it has continued to generate controversy. The novel deals with the hurried construction of a railroad between Bangkok, Thailand, and Rangoon, Burma, to support the Japanese conquest of Burma during World War II. The massive project was completed with almost no heavy machinery. Instead, the Japanese relied on native conscripts and Allied prisoners of war to complete the work with rudimentary tools. The controversy surrounds Boulle's suggestion that Allied officers in effect collaborated with the Japanese in an ill-conceived effort to protect their men.

The Brotherhood of War
Author: W. E. B. Griffin
First published: 1983-2001

Griffin is the pseudonym of William Edmund Butterworth III, who has written more than a half dozen popular series of novels, most of which focus on the military. This series of nine novels follows a group of American Army officers who initially served as lieutenants during World War II and remained in the military through the immediate post-Vietnam era. The series is notable because its primary emphasis is not on the combat experiences of these officers, though that certainly is described, but, instead, on the tactics and strategies required to work changes through the military and political bureaucracies.

The Caine Mutiny
Author: Herman Wouk
First published: 1951

This Pulitzer Prize-winning novel has also been commercially successful and critically acclaimed in its adaptations to stage and screen. The *Caine* is an outdated destroyer refitted to serve as a minesweeper. The story centers on a mutiny that occurs while the ship is under the command of Captain Queeg, a petty tyrant, who uses the service manual to intimidate and humiliate his subordinates. Much worse, he seemingly exhibits cowardice under fire and, at the time of the mutiny, during severe weather. The genius of Wouk's story is that he shows that the mutineers have their own character flaws and self-serving motives.

Castle Keep
Author: William Eastlake
First published: 1965

Just before the Battle of the Bulge, a loosely organized group of American soldiers are taken out of the front lines and billeted at a Belgian estate for much-needed rest and recuperation. Initially the owners of the estate welcome the soldiers as protectors, but when the German offensive in the Ardennes begins and the American commanding officer decides to turn the estate into a fortified position, the owners recognize that he is putting at great risk not just the lives of his soldiers and their own lives but also the estate and all of the irreplaceable artwork and family heirlooms that their mansion contains. The novel also explores the tension in each soldier between conditioned discipline and unit cohesion, and self-assertion and self-preservation.

Catch-22
Author: Joseph Heller
First published: 1961

This antiwar novel was published just before the escalation of the Vietnam War and is associated with the antiwar movement. However, it is actually a novel about World War II. Specifically, it satirically treats the experiences of American bomber crews in the Mediterranean theater. The title, which has passed into the general lexicon, refers to the circular logic of bureaucratic policies. Specifically, if an airman contends that he is too crazy to fly any more missions, he has, in effect, proved his sanity because no sane person would want to continue flying missions, given the losses that the bomber force is suffering. The main character, a bombardier named Yossarian, struggles against the insanity of his wartime experience until he finally decides that his only viable option is to "disappear."

Cryptonomicon
Author: Neal Stephenson
First published: 1999

This massive novel (918 pages in hardcover) presents two parallel stories. The first follows the efforts of the British cryptographers based at Bletchley Park who eventually cracked the complex codes produced by the Nazi Enigma machine. That extremely complex device was used to communicate with the U-boat fleet that was devastating the British merchant fleet, the United Kingdom's main source of military supplies and foodstuffs. The second story is set in the near future and concerns an effort to use computer-driven cryptography to create an impenetrable data center in a nation called Kinakuta, which resembles the East Indian Kingdom of Brunei.

"The Death of the Ball Turret Gunner"
Author: Randall Jarrell
First published: 1945

Given the great scope and length of many of the most acclaimed American novels about World War II, it is ironic that this, one of the best-known American poems about the war, is only five lines long. The ball-turret gunner operated a machine gun that swiveled 360 degrees within a plexiglass hemisphere attached to the bottom of the B-27 bombers that were the mainstay of the American forces in the costly air war against Germany. The gunner was an easy target, and the ball turret was often very difficult to escape when a bomber was badly damaged.

The End of My Life
Author: Vance Bourjaily
First published: 1947

Bourjaily's first novel caused reviewers to make complimentary comparisons to Ernest Hemingway's *A Farewell to Arms* (1929), and for several decades it was regarded as one of the best American novels about World War II. The novel's standing has, however, declined in proportion to the decline in Bourjaily's broader reputation as a novelist. An autobiographical novel, *The End of My Life* presents the experiences of Skinner Galt, an ambulance driver in North Africa, who eventually recognizes that whatever meaning war may have on a political level, it is always an exercise in horrible absurdity for the individual soldiers.

Execution
Author: Colin MacDougall
First published: 1958

One of the most acclaimed Canadian novels about World War II, *Execution* was MacDougall's only novel. It follows a Canadian infantry unit through the course of the Italian campaign, and, dramatically and thematically, it revolves around two executions. The first is the execution of two Italian deserters that the Canadians have adopted into their unit as cooks and genuinely like. The second is the execution of one of their own, a goodhearted but mentally limited soldier who has become involved with a group of soldiers engaged in the black market who murder an American.

Fires on the Plain
Author: Shōhei Ōoka
First published: 1951, as *Nobi*

Set in the Philippines following the American invasion to retake the islands from the Japanese, this novel vividly details the experiences of a single Japanese soldier, Private Tamura. Ostracized by the soldiers in his unit, Tamura decides to desert and finds himself caught between the ambiguous battle lines, between soldiers on two sides who equally despise him and among a civilian population conditioned to hate him. His only recourse is to flee ever more deeply into the jungle, where survival is a more primal exercise and spectral experience than it is even on the battlefield.

From Here to Eternity
Author: James Jones
First published: 1951

Jones's first novel remains his best known. The first in a somewhat loosely connected trilogy, *From Here to Eternity* focuses on a group of American soldiers stationed in Hawaii in the months leading up to the Japanese attack on Pearl Harbor. The main characters are Sergeant Milt Warden, who becomes involved in an affair with the wife of his commanding officer, and Private Robert E. Lee Prewitt, who resists all sorts of pressure to fight on the company's elite boxing team. Though it focuses of these and other individual soldiers, the novel is ultimately concerned with the prewar army as a self-defined institution.

The Gallery
Author: John Horne Burns
First published: 1947

Set in Naples after the American occupation of the city, the novel treats the relationships among American soldiers and between those soldiers and the civilian population in and around the Galleria Umberto Primo, an arcade of shops and bars at the center of the city. The novel's opening and closing sections are called the "Entrance" and "Exit," and the intervening chapters shift between nine chapters called "Portraits" and eight transitional sections called "Promenades." Each "Portrait" focuses on the tensions that define an individual character, and each "Promenade" recounts, in the first person, a soldier's experiences from the North African theater to Sicily to the invasion of Italy.

Guard of Honor

Author: James Gould Cozzens
First published: 1948

This Pulitzer Prize-winning novel by Cozzens has long been regarded as one of the more significant American novels about World War II. Drawn broadly from Cozzens's own experience as an information officer for General Henry H. "Hap" Arnold, the commander of the U.S. Air Forces during the war, the novel remains one of the few to focus on the stateside military during the war. It centers on three days' events on a Florida air base, emphasizing the ways in which the military bureaucracy and the personalities of individual officers intersect to define each other.

Gunner Asch Tetralogy

Author: Hans Hellmut Kirst
First published: 1954-1955, 1964

A committed Nazi who gradually became increasingly disaffected by the regime's excesses and its corruption of German institutions, Kirst is now best known for his suspense novels, such as *Night of the Generals* (1963), but all of his novels have satiric elements, and the satire is very close to the surface in the Gunner Asch novels, for which he first received international acclaim. The first three novels were published as a trilogy called *Zero Eight Fifteen* (1955-1957). They include *The Revolt of Gunner Asch* (1955), *Forward, Gunner Asch!* (1956), and *The Return of Gunner Asch* (1957). These novels concern the increasingly absurd experiences of the title character, an enlisted man serving on the eastern front. A fourth volume, *What Became of Gunner Asch* (1964), follows the protagonist into the postwar years.

Hiroshima

Author: John Hersey
First published: 1946

Now considered a forerunner of such movements or genres as the New Journalism, the nonfiction novel, and creative nonfiction, this slender volume sparely but movingly documents the aftermath of the dropping of the first atomic bomb on the Japanese city of Hiroshima. Originally written as a four-part article for *The New Yorker*, Hersey's book was not the first account of the atomic bombing, but it was the first account to focus on the recollections of Japanese survivors. Ironically, this aspect of the narrative, which has ensured its continuing appeal, was originally a point of concern for critics who thought that Hersey was characterizing the "enemy" too sympathetically.

The Hope *and* The Glory

Author: Herman Wouk
First published: 1993 and 1994 respectively

This pair of novels has not achieved anywhere near the commercial success or even the critical recognition of Wouk's earlier pair of novels about World War II, *Winds of War* (1971) and *War and Remembrance* (1988). Nonetheless, these novels are marked by a thorough, albeit pro-Israeli, understanding of the historical events and figures that shaped the first four decades of the existence of the modern state of Israel. *The Hope* covers the events from the 1948 War of Independence up to the Six-Day War of 1967, while *The Glory* covers events from the Yom Kippur War (1973) through the peace agreement between Israel and Egypt. The complicated love lives of the two main fictional characters provide contrived melodrama that is the novels' main weakness.

Johnny Got His Gun

Author: Dalton Trumbo
First published: 1939

This antiwar novel was published in 1939 as World War II became inevitable, but the novel actually concerns an American soldier, Joe Bonham, terribly—almost inconceivably—injured by a shell blast in the trenches of World War I. Bonham has lost all of his limbs and, because of massive injuries to his face, all of his senses except for the ability to feel someone touching him. Nonetheless, his mind remains intact, and the novel presents his thoughts as he comes to terms with the horror that he is completely isolated in what remains of his own body. The novel was withdrawn from publication after Nazi Germany invaded the Soviet Union, and because Trumbo was blacklisted during the 1950's it was not released again until the Vietnam era.

The Jukebox Queen of Malta

Author: Nicholas Rinaldi
First published: 1999

The tiny, British-controlled island of Malta became strategically important during World War II because it lay across the supply routes from Fascist Italy to Libya, where the German Afrika Korps had reversed early British victories and was threatening Egypt and the Suez Canal. The island was subjected to one of the longest sieges of the war, with German bombers reducing many of the mostly stone buildings to rubble. The main character is an American radio operator who begins a passionate relationship with the title character, a woman who travels around the island repairing jukeboxes.

King Rat

Author: James Clavell
First published: 1962

Clavell's first novel is drawn from his own experiences as a prisoner of war held for three years by the Japanese at the notorious Changi Prison in Singapore. The title character is an American corporal, generally referred to as "the King," who has transformed his detention into a business opportunity and has created a thriving business in black-market goods. The ranking British officer in the camp rightly views this black market as an exploitation of other prisoners' miseries, and he becomes determined to prove that the King is guilty of collusion with the enemy. The pivotal character is the narrator, a young British officer named Peter Marlowe, who cannot help but admire the King's ingenuity and audacity but ultimately recognizes their moral cost.

Mister Roberts

Author: Thomas Heggen
First published: 1946

Like Herman Wouk's *The Caine Mutiny* (1951), Heggen's novel has been adapted very successfully for stage and for film. Also like *The Caine Mutiny*, it focuses on the tensions between the captain and the crew, not on a big warship such as a carrier, battleship, or cruiser, but on a support ship. Unlike the destroyer converted to a minesweeper in *The Caine Mutiny*, however, the ship in *Mister Roberts* is a cargo ship operating far from the widely scattered battlefronts of the Pacific theater. The story presents a battle of wits between the well-meaning title character, respected by the crew but yearning for a combat assignment, and the ship's captain, protecting his ship's "clean" record by perversely exerting his authority.

The Naked and the Dead

Author: Norman Mailer
First published: 1948

Mailer's first novel remains the most highly regarded American novel about World War II. Set on a Japanese-held island on which American forces have landed, the novel features a broad range of characters, but the three focal characters are the aristocratic and fascist-leaning General Cummings; his well-born but more egalitarian aide, Lieutenant Hearn; and the battle-hardened but hardly heroic Sergeant Croft. The novel provides ample illustrations of the brutality of combat in the Pacific, as well as manifold evidence of the disjunction between the abstraction of painstakingly developed campaign strategies and the fluid realities of the battlefield. It vividly explores the connections and disjunctions between the characters' civilian lives and their military experiences.

The Painted Bird

Author: Jerzy Kosinski
First published: 1965

In his first and most enduring novel, Kosinski chronicles the experiences of a Jewish-looking young boy who is sent by his parents from a Polish city into the ostensible safety of the countryside. The peasants with whom the boy seeks refuge are typically as anti-Semitic as the Nazis, and his survival is something of a miracle resulting from completely accidental turns in circumstance, the intercession of a few beneficent individuals, and the boy's own increasing store of survival skills. In the end, he is adopted into a Russian military unit and finds a father figure in an accomplished sniper. The novel's closing provides a hopeful note about the boy's capacity to transcend at least some of the trauma of his formative experiences.

Partisans

Author: Alistair MacLean
First published: 1982

Not as well known as *The Guns of Navarone* (1957), *Partisans* also treats the Yugoslavian theater during World War II, but it provides a more nuanced sense of the very complicated range of contending forces in that conflict. Although all Yugoslavian partisan groups are ostensibly resisting the German and Italian occupation of their country, their military strategies and actions are directed as much against each other as against the occupiers. The three main partisan groups are the Communists; the Serbian Chetniks, who support the reinstatement of the Yugoslav monarchy; and the Croatian Ustashe, who have a fascist ideology. MacLean's protagonist is clearly a Nazi hater, but beyond that his allegiances and aims are very ambiguous.

The Polish Officer

Author: Alan Furst
First published: 1995

The third novel in Furst's Night Soldiers series, *The Polish Officer* is set primarily in Poland after the German and Soviet conquest and partition of that nation. The main character, Captain Alexander de Milja, is an expert mapmaker who becomes a pivotal figure in the Polish underground and its attempts to support the Polish government in exile. He takes the lead in concealing Poland's gold reserves from the Nazis and Soviets and in smuggling those reserves through Romania to Great Britain. While emphasizing de Milja's courage and ingenuity, Furst also conveys the physical and psychological strain caused by his clandestine activities and his recurring impulse simply to save himself regardless of the cost.

Run Silent, Run Deep

Author: Edward L. Beach, Jr.
First published: 1955

Drawing on his own extensive service as a submariner during World War II, Beach wrote this novel in the middle of a lengthy and distinguished military career. It presents a vivid depiction of the experiences of American submariners in the Pacific theater during World War II. The central characters are Commander P. J. Richardson and his executive officer, Jim Bledsoe. Richardson is obsessed with sinking the Japanese destroyer that destroyed the submarine he had previously commanded as well as several others, and the crew begins to question his decisions. Bledsoe shifts from second-guessing Richardson to pursuing his objectives after Richardson is accidentally disabled after suffering a fractured skull.

Slaughterhouse-Five

Author: Kurt Vonnegut, Jr.
First published: 1969

With this novel and *Cat's Cradle* (1963), Vonnegut made the dramatic transition from a little-known writer of speculative fiction to one of the leading literary voices of the counterculture period. In *Slaughterhouse-Five*, he startled readers by synthesizing aspects of historical and speculative fiction. The novel includes a lengthy and harrowing account of the American bombing of Dresden, seen through the perspective of American prisoners of war, who were afterward employed in the collection and disposal of the corpses of some of the tens of thousands caught in the firestorm. Like *Catch-22* (1961), this novel about World War II became a major antiwar work of the Vietnam era.

The Soldier

Author: Richard Powell
First published: 1960

Set in the Pacific in the months following the American entry into World War II, this novel focuses on the effects of the war on the career of Lieutenant Colonel William A. Farralon. His assignment to a remote Pacific post serves as an unmistakable indication that his career is on a downturn. However, after the Japanese attack on Pearl Harbor and most of the other American and European bases in the Pacific and Southeast Asia, Farralon takes advantage of a series of opportunities to distinguish himself. By the end of the war, he has risen to the rank of general, and his earlier fall from favor has been permanently eclipsed by his wartime service.

The Thin Red Line
Author: James Jones
First published: 1962

In this loose sequel to *From Here to Eternity* (1951), Jones re-presents the major characters from that novel under similar names. This novel provides a fictional account of the Guadacanal campaign—in particular, the Battle for Hill 53. Jones emphasizes that the sense of unit cohesion provided the individual infantryman's only psychological defense against the isolating terror of hand-to-hand combat in the hellishly tropical environment. In his later nonfiction study of the war and the art that it inspired, Jones contrasts the battle for Guadacanal, the outcome of which depended very much on the efforts of very small groups of Marines, with the corporatization of the war effort at Saipan, Iwo Jima, and Okinawa, the outcomes of which were never in doubt—however much their ultimate cost in blood and matériel may have been miscalculated.

The Tin Drum
Author: Günter Grass
First published: 1959, as *Die Blechtrommel*

The Tin Drum is the first novel in Grass's acclaimed *Danziger Trilogie* (1980; *Danzig Trilogy*, 1987), which also includes *Katz und Maus* (1961; *Cat and Mouse*, 1963) and *Hundejahre* (1963; *Dog Years*, 1965). Although the late revelation of Grass's service with the Waffen-SS has somewhat compromised his standing as a critic of the Nazi regime, *The Tin Drum* remains the most inventive and trenchant critique of that regime yet written. A work of Magical Realism predating the definitive Latin American experiments with that style, *The Tin Drum* is the autobiography of its main character, Oskar Matzerath, who decides not to enter the adult world and remains physically a child even as he ages. His most prized possession is a tin drum, which he protects at all costs and through which he communicates with an increasingly deranged world.

A Town Like Alice
Author: Nevil Shute
First published: 1950

The protagonist of this novel is Jean Paget, an Australian woman who is in Malaya at the time of the Japanese invasion and is detained for the duration of the war with a group of European women and children. During the course of their detainment, they are helped by an Australian prisoner of war who steals food and other supplies that keep them alive and then accepts the punishment for those actions without implicating them. That punishment is so severe that Jean mistakenly assumes that he has not survived the war. The rest of the novel describes the convoluted process by which they are eventually reunited and the terms on which they decide to build a life for themselves in a rural Queensland community.

V-Letter and Other Poems
Author: Karl Shapiro
First published: 1944

Although Shapiro had a long and distinguished career, his literary reputation has faded to the point that it would come as a surprise to most students of modern American poetry that at the end of World War II he was widely regarded as one of the most accomplished and promising poets of his generation. Awarded a Pulitzer Prize, this collection was written while Shapiro was serving with the U.S. Army in the New Guinea campaign. Imitating the style and form of the letters that military personnel sent to their loved ones back home, the poems convey both the immediacy and the terrible strangeness of the war's horrors. Likewise, they suggest the soldiers' growing sense of disconnection from home and their increasingly desperate need to maintain some sense of connection to life beyond the war.

The War Lover
Author: John Hersey
First published: 1959

Hersey's novel chronicles twenty-three bombing raids by a B-27 crew over German targets during World War II. It focuses on one bomber pilot who is either admired or reviled by his fellow pilots, their crews, and his superior officers. Although he repeatedly exhibits great skill and daring, his need continually to push the limits becomes increasingly regarded as recklessness and dangerous self-indulgence, especially since others seem to pay for the chances he takes while he survives unscathed. Critics of the novel have praised Hersey's attention to technical and sociological detail, but they have also suggested that the density of detail is detrimental to the literary value of the novel.

War of the Rats

Author: David L. Robbins
First published: 1999

One of the few noteworthy American novels about the eastern front of World War II, *War of the Rats* depicts the titanic battle for Stalingrad in all of its terrible scope and ghastly particulars. The city had quickly been reduced to rubble, and soldiers on both sides were fed into prolonged battles for individual city blocks and even individual buildings. Despite the firepower of the masses of mechanized weapons employed in the battle, the fighting was largely hand-to-hand and medieval in its ferocity. The novel provides a microcosm of the battle through the contest of skill and wits played out between the most celebrated German and Soviet snipers.

Williwaw

Author: Gore Vidal
First published: 1946

This novel is notable because it is the debut effort of a long, prolific, and distinguished literary career, because it was regarded as the first "literary" novel about World War II to be published, and because it is the only significant novel to treat the Aleutian theater of the war. Vidal wrote the novel while serving with the Navy on a supply ship. The title refers to a strong wind that blows down from the snow-covered coastal mountain peaks and collides with the warm air rising up from the sea, creating violent storms and currents. Given that the war in the Aleutians claimed far fewer lives than the weather, among all branches of the military, it is important that Vidal's novel is meteorologically as well as psychologically accurate.

The Winds of War

Author: Herman Wouk
First published: 1971

This immensely popular novel and its sequel, *War and Remembrance* (1988), are each nearly a thousand pages long, reflecting Wouk's ambition to capture the whole scope of World War II as powerfully as he had captured it in microcosm in *The Caine Mutiny* (1951) two decades earlier. The novel is unified by being presented through the eyes of the widely scattered members of a single family, that of Victor "Pug" Henry, a naval officer who becomes a sort of personal emissary of and troubleshooter for President Franklin D. Roosevelt. This strategy no doubt increased the popularity of the novels, but for critics, it stretched credibility and made many aspects of the novel seem contrived, despite Wouk's obvious efforts to ensure historical accuracy.

The Young Lions

Author: Irwin Shaw
First published: 1948

Of all of the acclaimed American novels about World War II, Shaw's *The Young Lions* has perhaps suffered the most precipitous decline in critical appreciation. Shaw was a real pro as a novelist, and his manipulation of the conventions of the realistic novel make some of his late novels a delight to read. This novel is perhaps a little too obviously "well made" in its presentation of the intersecting stories of three soldiers: a self-indulgent but charming product of privilege named Michael Whiteacre, a working-class Jew named Noah Ackerman, and a German officer named Christian Diestl.

COLD WAR

The Manchurian Candidate

Author: Richard Condon
First published: 1959

Condon has been described as one of the most paranoid novelists ever. Certainly this landmark novel of the Cold War captured the profound distrust on both sides of the conflict. The novel begins with the capture of a platoon of American soldiers by the Chinese during the Korean War. The soldiers are brainwashed into believing that Sergeant Raymond Shaw, an unlikely hero, has saved them from being massacred. Shaw receives the Medal of Honor, but after they all return to the United States, his captain, Bennett Marco, gradually uncovers the truth that Shaw has been programmed to perform a political assassination.

Once an Eagle

Author: Anton Myrer
First published: 1968

Although not highly regarded by literary critics, Meyer's best-known novel is one of only two works of fiction on the recommended reading list for the U.S. Army's Officer Professional Development program. The novel follows the careers of two officers over three decades, from World War I to the beginnings of the Cold War in the years immediately following World War II. The two officers are very different in temperament and mores. Sam Damon is an upright person in both his personal and his professional relationships; in contrast, Courtney Massengale is a much more Machiavellian character who has very little sense of personal loyalty. The novel provides an intimately knowledgeable account of how the military bureaucracy operates.

The Red Wheel

Author: Alexsander Solzhenitsyn
First published: 1983-1991, as *Krasnoe koleso:*
   includes *Avgust chetyrnadtsatogo*, 1971,
   expanded 1983 (*August 1914*, 1972, expanded
   1989); *Oktiabr' shestnadtsatogo*, 1984
   (*November 1916*, 1999); *Mart semnadtsatogo*,
   1986-1988 (partial translation as *March 1917*,
   2006); *Aprel' semnadtsatogo*, 1991 (partial
   translation as *April 1917*, 2006)

Solzhenitsyn will be most remembered for his two works about the Stalinist penal camps, *Odin den' Ivana Denisovicha* (1962; *One Day in the Life of Ivan Denisovich*, 1963) and *Arkhipelag GULag, 1918-1956: Opyt khudozhestvennogo issledovaniya* (1973-1975; *The Gulag Archipelago*, 1974-1978). However, *The Red Wheel*, his cycle of novels covering the

years from the Russian entry into World War I to the collapse of the Russian monarchy in 1917, is a massive work of literary as well as historical merit. *The Red Wheel* includes *August 1914*, *November 1916*, *March 1917*, and *April 1917*, with the middle novels consisting of two volumes each. Solzhenitsyn had originally planned to carry the series through 1922, or the Bolsheviks' consolidation of power at the end of the civil war and Lenin's personal decline due to a series of strokes.

Smiley's People

Author: John le Carré
First published: 1980

This is the third novel in le Carré's Karla Trilogy, which also includes *Tinker, Tailor, Soldier, Spy* (1974) and *The Honourable Schoolboy* (1977). All three focus on British intelligence agent George Smiley and provide a perspective on Cold War espionage dramatically different from the glamorous, high-adventure doings in Ian Fleming's James Bond series. If le Carré is the master of the Cold War novel of intrigue, then this portrait of a career spy who is not permitted to settle quietly into retirement is his masterwork. Although Smiley maneuvers in a world in which violence is a very real and ugly hazard, the emphasis is on his experienced understanding of the subtle surface indications that some clandestine scheme is being orchestrated.

ARAB-ISRAELI CONFLICTS

Exodus

Author: Leon Uris
First published: 1958

A novel with epic sweep, *Exodus* depicts the violence that preceded and followed the declaration of a Jewish state in Palestine. It begins with the efforts of Jewish underground groups to smuggle refugees and weapons into Palestine in anticipation of independence, and their violence against the British forces that had been garrisoned in Palestine to prevent the Jews and Arabs from prematurely intensifying their inevitable conflict. Criticized for its consistent characterization of the Jews as courageous and its general demonization of the Arabs, the novel presents its Jewish protagonist, Ari Ben Canaan, as a very human but undeniably representative figure.

KOREAN WAR

The Bridges at Toko-Ri
Author: James Michener
First published: 1953

The Bridges at Toko-Ri focuses on the experiences of carrier pilot Harry Brubaker. Having survived much air combat during World War II, Brubaker had just begun to settle comfortably back into civilian life when he was recalled to service in the Korean War. By the time that the mission to destroy the heavily defended bridges at Toko-Ri is announced, Brubaker is suffering from combat fatigue and has become haunted by the foreboding that he will not survive many more missions. Although he manages to destroy the last of the bridges, his plane goes down and he is killed by the Chinese infantry who have shot down the helicopter sent to rescue him.

The Hunters
Author: James Salter
First published: 1957

Like James Michener's *The Bridges at Toko-Ri*, Salter's first novel focuses on the air war over Korea, but Salter is much more interested than Michener in the way a fighter wing functions—in how the fighter pilots compete for recognition and their alliances and conflicts shape how they are led and how long they manage to survive. Despite the complex tactics on which each wing is trained and despite each pilot's dependence in combat on the wingman with whom he is paired, flying fighters is ultimately a solitary test of the pilot's skill, courage, endurance, and temperament. Salter's protagonist, Cleve Connell, eventually downs a notorious MiG pilot known as "Casey Jones" but cannot provide confirmation of the "kill" and so attributes it to his own downed wingman.

M*A*S*H
Author: Richard Hooker
First published: 1968

Published at the height of the Vietnam War, adapted for an experimental film directed by Robert Altman, and providing the basis for one of the longest-running and most acclaimed television series of all time, this novel was based on Hornberger's experiences as a battlefield surgeon during the Korean War and was actually more an irreverent take on military life than a pointedly antiwar work. Following on the success of the film and television series, however, Hornberger—using the pseudonym Richard Hooker—wrote two sequels in 1972 and 1977, and collaborated with William E. Butterworth on a series of twelve novels, published between 1974 and 1977, that followed the mobile army surgical hospital (MASH) surgeons to the far corners of the world.

War Trash
Author: Ha Jin
First published: 2004

Ha Jin's highly regarded novel treats the Korean War from the Chinese perspective. The novel is framed as the memoir of its protagonist, Yu Yuan. Drafted into the Chinese army after the Communist takeover of China, he finds himself among the hundreds of thousands of troops sent across the Yalu River to drive back the United Nations forces that had routed the North Koreans. In addition to relating Yu's experiences on the march and in battle during a bitterly cold winter, the novel treats his eventual capture by U.N. forces and his extended detention as a prisoner of war.

COLONIAL WARS

The Dogs of War
Author: Frederick Forsyth
First published: 1974

The discovery of significant plutonium deposits in a small African nation governed by a dictatorial regime leads a British industrialist to underwrite a mercenary force to remove the existing government and to replace it with one more disposed to sell the mineral rights under favorable terms. The novel details the ways in which the mercenary force is recruited, given some cohesion as a unit, equipped and supplied, and clandestinely transported to the target nation. The novel is purportedly based on Forsyth's own failed attempt to use a mercenary force to seize the small nation of Equatorial Guinea and to offer it as a haven for the Nigerian insurgents defeated in the Biafran War.

The Four Feathers
Author: A. E. W. Mason
First published: 1902

Following the Mahdi's conquest of Khartoum and the death of "Chinese Gordon," the British forces massed in Egypt under Lord Kitchener to defeat the Mahdi's forces, who were driven equally by religious fervor and anticolonial resentments. The protagonist of this novel resigns from his unit as it is about to be shipped overseas and is justifiably reviled for his cowardice. Seeking to redeem himself, he travels on his own to the Sudan, where, in order to pass himself off as a native, he disfigures himself, infiltrates the Mahdi's forces, and provides critical assistance to his former comrades in arms.

Guerrillas
Author: V. S. Naipaul
First published: 1975

One of Naipaul's most unsparing, harrowing novels, *Guerrillas* concerns an uprising against the continuing colonial influence on a Caribbean island. The three main characters are Roche, a South African exile with progressive political views; his disaffected lover, an Englishwoman named Jane, who mistakes her own world-weariness for depth of understanding and reliable judgment; and Jimmy, a political radical who disdains Roche and Jane but is willing to use them, and anyone and anything available to him, to promote his cause and his own movement toward the centers of power. The novel explores the ease with which the comfortable certainties of daily life can be undermined.

CUBAN REVOLUTION

The Death of Che Guevara
Author: Jay Cantor
First published: 1983

In this very ambitious first novel, Cantor has sought to re-create fictionally the life of the Cuban revolutionary, Che Guevara, who has become an increasingly iconic figure since his pointless death while attempting to breathe life into a listless Bolivian insurgency in 1967. Cantor constructs the story around a broad range of historical documents, from personal diaries and correspondence to news accounts and government reports. Almost all of these documents, however, are Cantor's fictional creations, and taken together, they add layers of complexity and possibility to the portrait that the novel provides of this personally and culturally enigmatic figure.

VIETNAM WAR

Dispatches
Author: Michael Herr
First published: 1977

This book, a seminal work of the New Journalism, was published a decade after Herr traveled to South Vietnam to report on the Vietnam War for *Esquire*. The essays that he produced for that magazine as well as for *Rolling Stone*, *New American Review*, *New York*, and *Crawdaddy* were revised extensively and synthesized into the continuing narrative of the book. Nonetheless, that narrative consists largely of vignettes that convey, often with ironic or horrific immediacy, the "grunt's" view of the war. The power of the narrative derives from Herr's identification with the average soldier and his recognition that however close he comes to the fighting, he is more a witness than a combatant.

Going After Cacciato

Author: Tim O'Brien
First published: 1978, revised 1989

The most acclaimed American novel about the Vietnam War, *Going After Cacciato* combines the documentary realism of O'Brien's other books about the war with an extended episode of Magical Realism. The novel is divided into three types of chapters. The narrative is organized around ten "Observation Post" sections, set in November, 1968. In these sections, the main character, Paul Berlin, reflects on the ironies, paradoxes, improbabilities, and hard realities of the war. These sections also provide a narrative frame for the other two types of sections: his memories of his unit's harrowing experiences in combat between June and October and an extended fantasy about his unit's pursuit across two continents of the AWOL soldier Cacciato.

Meditations in Green

Author: Stephen Wright
First published: 1983

In this, his first novel, Wright presents the recollections of a veteran of the Vietnam War who is attempting, through meditation exercises in which he focuses on plants, to recover some sense of emotional and moral equilibrium. His recollections of the war include characterizations of officers too self-centered to inspire confidence in their leadership and of soldiers too young to cope with the alternating boredom and terror of war without using mind-altering drugs or retreating into varying degrees of psychotic detachment. The focal event involves an effort to locate and recover the remains of an intelligence patrol crew presumed lost when their helicopter went down. The bodies are found gruesomely mutilated and displayed.

No Man's Land

Author: Duong Thu Huong
First published: 2005

Perhaps the most internationally known Vietnamese dissident writer, Duong Thu Huong supported the North Vietnamese and Viet Cong cause during the Vietnam War. Following the reunification of the country, however, she became a critic of the abuses of power and the corruption that she felt had become endemic within the communist regime. Though not pointedly political, her once popular novels were banned, and she was imprisoned several times. In *No Man's Land*, a missing-in-action North Vietnamese soldier returns home fourteen years after the end of the war. Although he has been physically and psychologically damaged by his wartime experiences, which are presented in flashback, his wife is pressured into leaving her current husband and their son, both of whom she loves dearly, and to endure the privations and humiliations of life with him.

Paco's Story

Author: Larry Heinemann
First published: 1986

When this, Heinemann's second novel, won the National Book Award, it was generally regarded as a very surprising choice. Like Heinemann's first novel, which had been published nine years earlier, *Paco's Story* concerns the experience of a Vietnam veteran. The title character is seeking a respite in which he can recuperate physically and psychologically from his wartime experiences. Although he finds a job washing dishes in a small-town restaurant operated by a sympathetic veteran of World War II, he cannot escape the stigma of having served in an unpopular war or the memories of the atrocities that he and his fellow soldiers committed in Vietnam. Much of the novel is narrated by the ghosts of the men in Paco's unit who died in Vietnam.

The Quiet American

Author: Graham Greene
First published: 1955

A truism about the Vietnam War has been that American involvement dated from the defeat of the French at Dien Bien Phu. In actuality, the United States supplied almost all of the military matériel used by the French against the Viet Minh, and American concern with checking Soviet influence, more than any American interest in preserving pre-World

War II European empires, drove U.S. involvement in Vietnam from its clandestine beginnings. Narrated by Thomas Fowler, a world-weary British journalist, Greene's novel explores the enigmatic character of Alden Pyle. Nominally an American aid worker, Pyle is clearly working for the Central Intelligence Agency to ensure that a South Vietnamese alternative to the Viet Minh will be available if the French do not prevail in the largely guerrilla war against them. Pyle is murdered, but not before he gets Fowler's beautiful Vietnamese mistress.

The Sorrow of War
Author: Bao Ninh
First published: 1993

Framed as a novel within a novel, *The Sorrow of War* presents a "fictional" account of the wartime experiences of Kien, a North Vietnamese veteran of the Vietnam War. The survival of any long-serving veteran of that prolonged conflict would be something of a miracle, but in several instances, Kien has been the only survivor of firefights, shellings, and bombings that have killed every other member of his unit. His extraordinary luck is, however, juxtaposed to the loss of his lover, whom he has known since their idyllic childhood, and the unreliability of others whom he has trusted.

Tree of Smoke
Author: Denis Johnson
First published: 2007

A recipient of the National Book Award, Johnson's novel seems a high mark in a steadily distinguished, if idiosyncratic, literary career. Certainly, *Tree of Smoke* stands out in a body of work consisting of very spare novels on eccentric subjects. It is a long and lushly descriptive fictional treatment of the Vietnam War. The main character is Skip Sands, an agent with the Central Intelligence Agency who serves in Vietnam from 1965 to 1970, or from the dramatic escalation of American involvement to the post-Tet Offensive recognition that deescalation, if not defeat, was inevitable.

FIRST GULF WAR

We Pierce
Author: Andrew Huebner
First published: 2003

The most significant literary work written about the Gulf War of the early 1990's, *We Pierce* is a fictionalized memoir or autobiographical novel drawn from Huebner's own family history. The narrative focuses on two brothers, Sam and Smith Huebner. Sam is politically progressive, a teacher and writer whose emotional demons are exhibited in his deepening alcohol and drug abuse. Forgiving to a fault in terms of family issues, Sam paradoxically is very dogmatic in his political views, including his opposition to the Gulf War. In contrast, Smith serves with distinction as part of a tank crew during the conflict. Although he refuses to address the issues in their parents' marriage and their upbringing, he has a contented marriage and does everything that he can to ensure that his own children's home life is stable.

AFRICAN CIVIL WARS

Johnny Mad Dog
Author: Emmanuel Boundzéki Dongala
First published: 2005

Dongala explores the world of the "boy soldiers" who have become commonplace among the combatants in Africa's civil wars because they are one of the largest segments of most African populations, because they are more easily indoctrinated than adult "recruits," and because they can be more easily conditioned to witnessing and committing atrocities. The novel is drawn from Dongala's experiences during the Republic of the Congo's civil war in the late 1990's. The title character has became a despicable, sociopathic character, and Dongala emphasizes how little he and his kind feel any connection to their country, its people, or its future.

The Rebels' Hour

Author: Lieve Joris

First published: 2008

Published variously as a nonfiction novel and as a work of creative nonfiction, Dutch journalist Joris's book resulted from extensive reporting on and a complex understanding of the conflicts of central Africa and, in particular, the Democratic Republic of the Congo—previously referred to as Zaire, the Belgian Congo, and the Congo Free State. The focal character is a Tutsi named Assani. Originally from Rwanda, his family fled from the Hutu genocide into the eastern Congo, where the ethnic conflicts in Rwanda and Burundi became intertwined with an equally vicious cycle of civil war. Assani was recruited by Lawrence Kabila, whose largely Tutu force overthrew the infamously corrupt and pro-Hutu Mobuta regime, shortly before Kabila himself was assassinated.

AFGHAN WARS

The Kite Runner

Author: Khaled Hosseini

First published: 2003

The story of the unlikely friendship of two boys in Afghanistan—one rich and one poor—is set against the backdrop of Afghanistan from the end of the monarchy through the wars of the present.

Martin Kich

LEXICON

Abteilung. German term for a detachment or battalion in either the German (later West German or East German) or Swiss armed forces. During World War II (1939-1945), an Abteilung was generally for a unit of about 1,000 soldiers and was used in the Waffen-SS and other groups.

Aircraft carrier. A large, motorized warship with a flat topdeck to serve as a runway for fixed-wing aircraft. Invented by the British in 1918, developed by most major navies in the 1920's and 1930's, and first used in World War II (1939-1945), its effectiveness was dramatically proved at Pearl Harbor in December of 1941, and then the Battle of Midway, in June of 1942, when planes from three American carriers, *Enterprise*, *Hornet*, and *Yorktown*, commanded by Admiral Raymond A. Spruance, destroyed four Japanese carriers, *Akagi*, *Hiryu*, *Kaga*, and *Soryu*, commanded by Admiral Isoruku Yamamoto. The carrier immediately superseded the battleship as the primary instrument of naval firepower.

Amabutho. This term is often used interchangeably with "regiment" for Zulu armies. The number of warriors in this unit ranged from 900 to 4,000.

Antiaircraft gun. A machine gun, often with two or more barrels for wide-pattern fire; pedestal-mounted with rapid 360-degree traverse in fixed batteries, land vehicles, or ships; designed for accurate, long-range, high-angle fire to shoot down enemy aircraft. Developed late in World War I (1914-1918) and popularly known as "ack-ack" (both from its sound and from British signalmen's variant pronunciation of its acronym, AA), it was a standard weapon in World War II (1939-1945) but was superseded by guided antiaircraft missiles in the late twentieth century.

Antiballistic missile (ABM). Developed by the United States in the late 1950's and widely deployed by both the United States and the Soviet Union by the 1970's, any guided missile, either ground-launched, sea-launched, or air-launched, with a nuclear warhead designed to explode in the vicinity of incoming enemy missiles, rendering them harmless. ABM systems were supposed to be severely limited as a provision of the 1972 Strategic Arms Limitation Talks (SALT I), but verification proved difficult.

Antimissile missile. Any missile intended to destroy an incoming enemy missile before it can do any damage. Satellite-guided antimissile missile systems were a fundamental component of President Ronald Reagan's Strategic Defense Initiative (SDI), known as "Star Wars," in 1983, but their technology was still not practical decades later. Antiballistic missiles are a special type of antimissile missile.

Antitank gun. A rifled firearm specifically designed to destroy tanks. The earliest, in 1918, was the German 13.3-millimeter Mauser Tankgewehr bolt-action rifle, firing armor-piercing bullets. By World War II (1939-1945), antitank weaponry was recognized as very important. Most were field pieces, such as the German 37-millimeter Panzerabwehrkanone (PAK36) and the Soviet 100-millimeter M-1944, all firing armor-piercing shells. After World War II, recoilless guns, mortars, and rocket launchers firing guided armor-piercing missiles replaced antitank guns.

Arbalest. Originally, after about the eleventh century, the French word for crossbow, derived from two Latin words, *arcus*, or bow, and *ballista*, or big, rock-shooting crossbow. Around 1400, the term also began to mean a particular type of large, very powerful, heavy-draw Northern European crossbow, whose bow was shorter than average and either reinforced with steel or made entirely of steel.

Arban. The smallest unit in the Mongol army, consisting of 10 soldiers.

Armor-piercing shell. Special antitank or antiship artillery ammunition, in two varieties: kinetic and chemical. The former is a hard, high-velocity, usually pointed shell that punctures the armor and then explodes inside the target; the latter is designed to explode either near or on the armor, shattering it from the outside. Development of armor-piercing ammunition was necessitated by the introduction of ironclad warships in the American Civil War (1861-1865) and tanks in World War I (1914-1918).

Army. A general term to describe the land force of the defense forces of any country. In the Byzantine Empire, an army consisted of 9,000 soldiers (or three *meroi*). In the British army, specifically, "army" refers to a land formation that consists of more than one corps. In the latter case, the armies are given numerical prefixes, such as First Army and Second Army.

Army group. A land-force formation that includes two or more numbered armies. An example of an army group occurred during the German invasion of the Soviet Union in 1941; army groups were given geographical descriptors: Army Group South, Army Group North, and so on. Army Group Africa consisted of Italian and German soldiers. In all these cases, army groups were commanded by a field marshal. The Japanese army in World War II (1939-1945) was divided into six army groups; and during the Sino-Japanese War (1937-1945) and the Chinese Civil War (1946-1949), there were also army groups, which might have anywhere between 500,000 and 1.5 million soldiers. After World War II, armies of the North Atlantic Treaty Organization (NATO) were formed into army groups combining soldiers from a variety of allied countries.

Artillery. Sometimes called ordnance, the term comprises all firearms, or weapons powered by explosions, that must be operated by more than one soldier for maximum effectiveness, such as cannons, most rockets, and most missiles, as well as some pre-gunpowder heavy siege weapons such as catapults, onagers, trebuchets, and large varieties of the crossbow. Artillery is traditionally classified as either heavy or light.

Assagai. A short-handled, long-bladed, double-edged traditional spear of the Zulu nation of South Africa. Used mainly as a multiple thrusting weapon,

it could also be hurled as a javelin or wielded for slashing. It fit well into the standard "chest-and-horns" assault and surround tactics of the Zulu, in which a large body of troops in close ranks would run suddenly at the enemy to gain advantage in hand-to-hand combat, as they did when they destroyed the British at Isandhlwana in 1879.

Assault helicopter. A versatile fighting aircraft developed by the United States in the 1950's, first used extensively in the Vietnam War (1961-1975) and refined by the Soviet Union in the 1970's. The mainstay of modern air cavalry, its tactical equipment includes computerized search-and-destroy weapons, antitank guns, machine guns, rockets, air-launched minelaying systems, and sophisticated navigation devices for rapid, ground-hugging flight. Among the most prominent types are the Soviet Mi-24 and Mi-28 and the American Apache and Black Hawk.

Assault rifle. Fully automatic rifle that can fire either single-shot or rapid fire, developed by many nations during World War II (1939-1945) but primarily by Mikhail Kalashnikov (b. 1919) for the Soviet Union between 1941 and 1944. His AK-47, named for the year of its invention, is the most famous weapon of this type. Others include the Israeli Uzi and the American M-16. Most models have a straight stock to prevent the recoil from pushing successive shots gradually too high during rapid fire.

Atomic bomb (A-bomb). An extremely powerful explosive device involving the fission of radioactive elements, invented during World War II (1939-1945) by an American team of scientists in fulfillment of the secret, federally funded Manhattan Project. It was first tested on July 16, 1945, at Alamogordo, New Mexico; first used on August 6, 1945, when the United States dropped Little Boy, a uranium bomb, on Hiroshima, Japan; and used for the second and last time in the twentieth century on August 9, 1945, when the United States dropped Fat Man, a plutonium bomb, on Nagasaki, Japan.

Automatic firearm. Any firearm that loads automatically, usually from either a bandolier belt or a magazine, and fires more than one shot for each squeeze of the trigger. The reloading process is typically powered by the energy from each previous shot, as hot gas, recoil, or blowback. The first sustained use of automatics in warfare was as the various Browning, Maxim, Spandau, and Vickers heavy machine guns that caused millions of casualties in World War I (1914-1918).

Ballista. A gigantic crossbow used in both ancient and medieval warfare, developed by the Romans but patterned after the mounted crossbows invented by Archimedes. Tactically employed as a catapult, it was cocked with a winch and ratchet, usually wheeled, and capable of hurling bolts or stones of up to about 10 pounds (4.5 kilograms) accurately for relatively long distances (about 400 yards or meters) at tolerably low trajectory.

Ballistic missile. A large, long-range guided missile, usually with a nuclear warhead, developed by the United States in the late 1950's, self-propelled by a rocket engine on a high-trajectory, often stratospheric, course, and guided in its upward arc but usually free-falling in its descent. Its earliest prototype was the Nazi VZ (Vergeltungswaffe Zwei) rocket, used with a high explosive warhead against London from September, 1944, to March, 1945.

Ballistite. Smokeless powder introduced in 1887 by Alfred B. Nobel (1833-1896) and consisting of 40 percent low-nitrogen nitrocellulose and 60 percent nitroglycerin. The product could be manufactured as small flakes and was a common propellant for firearms until after World War II (1939-1945). In the English-speaking world, cordite, a similar mixture invented shortly after ballistite, was more common.

Band. This term, often referring to warrior bands, was used to describe the many Native American military units during the nineteenth century.

Bangalore torpedo. An indefinitely long metal tube, consisting of a series of short lengths screwed together, with an explosive charge at one end and a fuse inside the tube. By pushing it slowly toward or under its target, demolition teams could remain in positions of cover and cut paths through barbed wire, neutralize minefields, or blast fortifications.

The Allies, notably the amphibious forces on D day, used it extensively during World War II (1939-1945).

Banner. A unit within the Manchu army, the vast majority originally mounted, who would follow a particular banner in battle; altogether there were eight banners. During the Qing (Ch'ing) Dynasty in China (1644-1912), it came to represent a military unit within the Chinese army consisting of thousands of soldiers, almost exclusively of Manchu descent. Manchu soldiers came to be known as bannermen.

Barbed wire. Thick wire with sharp metal points built in at regular intervals, first patented in the United States in 1867, first used for civilian purposes to mark boundaries, and extensively deployed as a defensive obstacle in both world wars. Since the late twentieth century, varieties have been manufactured with embedded fiber-optic cable so that computerized sentry systems can determine precisely where the enemy breaches it and immediately direct defensive fire to that spot.

Barrage balloons. Defensive antiaircraft apparatus used in both world wars, especially by the British. Small balloons trailing long cables or nets were tethered at high altitude in the hope that enemy aircraft attacking below the balloons would catch their wings on the dangling obstacles.

Baselard (*or* basilard). A double-edged European dagger common from the fourteenth to the sixteenth centuries, typified by two prominent crosspieces, one at the pommel, or the end of the hilt, the other at the guard, or the joint between the hilt and the blade.

Battalion. An infantry unit that is commanded, in the case of the U.S. and British armies, by a lieutenant colonel. Within the British army, over time, its size has changed considerably. Traditionally at full strength it was similar to that of a Roman legion, around 1,000 soldiers. In the Australian army in World War I (1914-1918), it had, at full strength, about 1,000 soldiers. For the German army in World War I, battalions were subdivisions of regiments, usually with three battalions in a regiment, numbered I, II, and III. Overall, a German battalion had, at full strength, 23 officers,

3 regimental medical officers and paymasters, and 1,050 other ranks. By 1917, because of the shortage of soldiers, most battalions had about 750 soldiers in them. In the U.S. Army, battalions can have as little as three companies (300 soldiers) or as many as 1,200 soldiers.

Battering ram. An ancient and medieval siege engine for breaching enemy walls, consisting of a large pole, usually a tree trunk, with a metal head, sometimes pointed, slung horizontally from ropes under a sturdy frame so that it could be swung back and forth with great force. The frame, covered with water-soaked hides to prevent defenders from burning it, could be wheeled up to the target wall by soldiers underneath it, chocked, and put to work.

Battery. A unit of artillery, commanded by a major. To some degree the equivalent of a company of infantry or a squadron of cavalry.

Battle-ax. A slicing and chopping weapon invented in the Stone Age when someone lashed a sharp stone to the end of a stick, developed throughout the Bronze Age, and nearly perfected during the Iron Age, when more sophisticated versions evolved from both the mace and the hand ax. Although warriors needed great strength to wield it well, it proved popular in all pre-firearm cultures, especially in the eighth to eleventh centuries among the Vikings, who revered their axes and often gave them proper names, such as Skarphedin's gigantic Rímmugýgr, or "Ogress of War," in *Njal's Saga*.

Battleship. A gigantic, armored, motorized ship bristling with long-range, large-caliber, breech-loading cannon, mounted mostly in turrets, intended primarily for ship-to-ship combat. It dominated naval warfare from the late nineteenth century until the aircraft carrier was proved superior at Midway in 1942. Before 1906 it was relatively slow, with the intermediate battery larger than the main battery, but thereafter the standard was the dreadnought, faster, larger, more heavily armed and armored, and with its strength disproportionately concentrated in the main battery.

Bayonet. An edged weapon attached to the muzzle of a firearm, usually a musket or rifle, first used in Europe in the seventeenth century to substitute for a pike. The earliest, the plug bayonet, was inserted into the muzzle itself. The socket bayonet includes a sleeve to fit over the muzzle; the sword bayonet has a regular sword hilt with an adapter slot that slides under the barrel; and the integral bayonet is permanently affixed to the firearm. Bayonet tactics evolved into complex and deadly offensive maneuvers in the eighteenth and nineteenth centuries. Since the twentieth century, bayonets have mostly been multipurpose survival knives conveniently detachable from a soldier's personal weapon.

Bazooka. An American recoilless antitank weapon, the M9A1, common in World War II (1939-1945). A short-range, handheld, direct-fire, line-of-sight weapon firing unguided projectiles, it was superseded after the war by more sophisticated recoilless guns and especially by mortars firing guided antitank missiles.

Big Bertha. Any of several large German howitzers mounted on railway cars and used extensively in World War I (1914-1918) on the western front until 1916, when the newer Allied heavy artillery outranged them. The designation especially refers to the Krupp 42-centimeter L-14, because Gustav Krupp's wife's name was Bertha.

Bilbo. A high-quality, wide-bladed, double-edged, fancy Spanish rapier of the Renaissance, so called from the place of its manufacture, Bilbao, Spain.

Bill. Type of pole arm whose head includes a regular spear point, a hook for unhorsing mounted knights or cavalrymen, and numerous perpendicular spikes. One of the first pole arms, it evolved from the pruning hook, or billhook, and was in use from the early Middle Ages until the end of the eighteenth century. Many variants exist, some resembling the voulge, with a small ax-blade instead of the spikes, but the required feature is the hook.

Biological weapons. Organic substances introduced into enemy areas by bombing, artillery, or infiltration, designed to cause debilitating disease outbreaks. Sometimes, but not quite accurately, known as germ warfare, the employment of such weapons includes loading medieval trebuchets with dead horses, tampering with water supplies, and releasing noxious aerosol particles in enemy airspace. Among the diseases that could be caused by these tactics are cholera, influenza, anthrax, typhoid, dysentery, encephalitis, malaria, typhus, yellow fever, bubonic plague, and smallpox.

Bireme. A galley with two banks of oars. Shortly after the naval ram was invented, around 800 B.C.E., the Greeks and Phoenicians developed fast galleys to exploit this weapon. More oarsmen meant more speed and power, but, since single-banked ships long enough to hold crews of more than 50 were impractical, the bireme was developed around 700 B.C.E., with an upper bank of oars on outrigger fulcrums so as not to interfere with the lower bank. It was between 25 and 35 meters long, carried a crew of about 100, and reached top oared speeds between 7 and 9 knots per hour.

Blockbuster. A popular name for the high-capacity bomb, the giant aerial bomb dropped by both the Allies and the Germans in World War II (1939-1945), so called because each one was capable of demolishing an entire city block. Developed first and best by the British, the largest could hold 22,000 pounds (10,000 kilograms) of TNT (trinitrotoluene), RDX (cyclo-1,3,5-trimethylene-2,4,6-trinitramine), PETN (pentaerythitol tetranitrate), or some combination of these explosives.

Blowgun. A long, straight, thin, smallbore, hollow tube through which light projectiles, usually darts, are driven with amazing accuracy to surprising distances, solely by the force of rapidly but smoothly exhaled breath. Independently developed by many preliterate tropical cultures, such as those of Malaysia, Indonesia, and Brazil, its darts are sometimes poisoned, and a flared mouthpiece is often added to concentrate the breath for more power.

Blunderbuss. A short-range, short-barreled, muzzle-loading, smoothbore, personal firearm developed in either Holland or England early in the seventeenth century and common through the eighteenth, characterized by a flaring muzzle to facilitate loading and to scatter the shot, which could be either a single bullet or a pellet load. Extremely inaccurate, with the effect of a sawed-off shotgun or scattergun, it was typically used as a defensive or deterrent weapon for property owners, ships' officers, and stagecoach drivers.

Bofors gun. A type of light, mobile, antiaircraft gun, usually 40 millimeters, intended for use especially against low-flying planes, and named after the Swedish company that introduced it in the 1930's. Naval varieties are typically mounted with double, quadruple, sextuple, or octuple barrels.

Bolt-action rifle. Any breech-loading rifle that uses the manual action of a sliding bolt to open the breech block and eject the spent cartridge. The bolt handle is pushed up out of a slot to unlock the breech and down into the slot to lock it. The weapon can be either repeating, if it can take a magazine, or single-shot, if it cannot. Typically, the repeaters have military application, while single-shot bolt-actions are for sport. Developed in the 1860's and 1870's, bolt-action weapons were the norm in the Second Boer War (1899-1902) and World War I (1914-1918).

Bomb. Any offensive explosive device designed to detonate only under certain conditions, but especially, since World War I (1914-1918), one dropped from an airplane, thrown, or otherwise delivered aerially, but not by artillery.

Bombard. A primitive smoothbore mortar, probably dating from the early fifteenth century, characterized by a narrow powder chamber; an extremely short, sometimes flaring, barrel; and a huge-caliber bore, sometimes as wide or wider than its length.

Bomber. An aircraft designed to drop explosive devices accurately on target. The first bombers were observation planes dropping handheld bombs early in World War I (1914-1918). By the end of that war, both sides had specialized planes for bombing missions, particularly the British DeHavilland and the German Gotha. The Spanish Civil War (1936-1939) and World War II (1939-1945) were the first wars in which airpower played a dominant role, and during their courses, aerial bombing became a carefully studied science.

Booby trap. An offensive obstacle designed to kill, maim, or terrorize unsuspecting soldiers or passersby. Extensively used by the Viet Cong against the Americans in Vietnam, by native populations against invading forces, by fortress defenders, and by terrorists, the wide variety of booby traps includes car bombs, mines, mail bombs, pitfalls, nets, tripwires, spikes, spring traps, snares, positioned firearms, and time bombs.

Boomerang. An aboriginal Australian, aerodynamically enhanced throwing stick, designed in two basic forms: one flying a curved path and returning to the thrower, and the other flying a straight, far, end-over-end path but not returning. The former is used mainly for hunting and exhibitions, the latter for war. War boomerangs exist in many styles but are generally heavier and may have cutting edges or protuberances. Some throwing sticks, similar to boomerangs, were found in the tomb of the Egyptian Pharaoh Tutankhamen.

Bouncing bomb. This device, created by the British inventor Barnes Wallis, was designed to penetrate the defenses of the German dams in World War II (1939-1945). The idea came to Wallis when he watched a boy skimming a stone at a village pond; he used it effectively in the dam-buster raids Operation Chastise in May, 1943.

Bow. Invented in the Stone Age, a simple combination of string and spring to hurl projectiles, usually arrows, much farther, more powerfully, and more accurately than they could be thrown by hand. The shape, tension, material, length, weight, and curve of a bow all affect its spring energy. Bows are of four basic kinds: simple, made of a single piece; backed, two pieces of different materials glued together; laminated, three or more pieces of the same material glued together; and composite, three or more pieces of different materials glued together.

Bowie knife. An American single-edged fighting knife about 20 inches long overall, named for American frontiersman James Bowie (1796-836), but actually designed by his brother, Rezin. Evolved from the frontiersman's hunting knife and the straight-bladed "Arkansas toothpick," it featured a simple hilt; a flat, wide crossguard with a prong at each end angled about 45 degrees toward the point; a tempered steel blade, mostly straight, but, from the point toward the hilt about 3 inches, convex in front and concave in back; and a strip of soft metal, such as brass, inlayed along the back of the blade to catch enemy blades. It was edged blade-length in front and along the concave portion in back.

Breechloader. Any firearm that loads its ammunition through the rear of the barrel. Attempted for centuries, but barely practical in time for the Crimean War (1853-1856) and the American Civil War (1861-1865), it soon thereafter superseded muzzle-loaders and made repeating arms and automatic weapons possible.

Bren gun. A British light machine gun, the Bren Mk1, first produced in 1937 and used extensively in World War II (1939-1945). Because the British based its design on the Czech ZB/vz26, invented eleven years earlier, they coined its name from the "Br" in Brno, where the Czech gun was made, and the "En" in Enfield, where the British gun was manufactured. The Royal Small Arms Factory, Enfield, North London, was founded in 1804 and has been responsible for a great number of historically important weapons.

Brig. A sailing, two-masted, square-rigged, wooden warship, related to the nonnaval brigantine, smaller than a frigate but bigger than a sloop of war or corvette, carrying between 12 and 32 guns on one or one and a half decks. Brigs were common from the eighteenth century until the end of the age of sail.

Brigade. An army unit that, in the British army, is an operational formation led by a brigadier (or brigadier-general). The number of soldiers serving in a brigade varies tremendously. Essentially a brigade has to consist of two or more fighting units, along with an operational formation structure. In the Australian army in World War I (1914-1918), a brigade consisted of four battalions (4,000 soldiers at full strength), and three brigades formed one division. After World War II (1939-1945), in the North Atlantic Treaty Organization (NATO), a brigade would consist of 4,000-5,000 soldiers, but in the Swiss and Austrian armies, there could be as many as 10,000 soldiers in a brigade. Words similar to "brigade" are used in other countries; in the Estonian army, for example, a *brigaad* includes 8,750 infantry soldiers.

Broadsword. A large, straight European sword dating from the early Middle Ages, usually double-edged, often two-handed, intended for slashing, chopping, and cutting, rather than thrusting.

Browning automatic rifle (BAR). An American light machine gun, the .30-06-caliber M-1918A2, invented by John M. Browning (1855-1926). Weighing only 20 pounds, air-cooled, with gas-powered reload and a bipod at the muzzle, it was well known as the squad automatic of World War II (1939-1945).

Bunker-busting bomb. A bomb developed to penetrate targets buried deep underground. Although prototypes of this bomb were used in the Gulf War in 1991, their first major use was by the U.S. military in Afghanistan in 2002.

Caltrop. A small, throwable, defensive obstacle consisting of four metal spikes protruding from a central vertex, each at an angle of 120 degrees to the other three, so that whichever three form a tripod on the defended ground, the fourth will be sticking straight up. At Bannockburn in 1314, Robert the Bruce devastated the English cavalry with caltrops.

Canister shot. A type of case shot, preloaded into a brittle tin shell designed to disintegrate immediately upon firing and thus add its own fragments to the antipersonnel pattern of projectiles. It differs from grapeshot by being sealed in a container and from case shot by specifically incorporating a tin shell. Its advantage over both was ease of loading.

Cannon. A firearm too big to be carried by an individual soldier, an artillery piece, invented early in the fourteenth century, that exists in three basic forms: gun, howitzer, and mortar, which are distinguished by caliber, trajectory, projectile velocity, range, and barrel length.

Carbine. A rifle with a short barrel designed to be convenient for cavalrymen. Developed by the French during the wheel-lock era, it achieved its greatest renown in the nineteenth century, when early breech-loading carbines such as the Sharps, Enfield, Springfield, and Winchester became standard British and American cavalry issue.

Carronade. A short-barreled, large-caliber, relatively lightweight, smoothbore naval cannon, inaccurate but highly effective at short range, introduced by the Carron Company of Scotland in 1779 and common until the mid-nineteenth century.

Case shot. Short-range, wide-dispersion, antipersonnel muzzle-loading artillery ammunition. Consisting of small metal balls or shards and common during the last hundred years of the muzzle-loading era, it differs from grapeshot by being sealed in a container, which would either break, burn, or disintegrate as soon as the charge was fired, thus allowing the load to spread. A variety of case shot sealed specifically in a tin shell is canister shot.

Catapult. An ancient and medieval artillery engine using a lever to hurl large projectiles. Its power came from a leaf spring; the torsion of a twisted skein, as in the onager; or a huge counterweight, as in the trebuchet. Made obsolete by the development of the cannon, catapults nevertheless remained fairly common in warfare until the sixteenth century and were used as recently as World War I (1914-1918) to hurl grenades into enemy trenches. The term also refers to devices used to launch planes from aircraft carriers.

Cell. Although usually used to describe political groupings in which secrecy ensured that members of the cell did not know the identities of other members in order to avoid infiltrators and people who had been captured, this term was also applied to the soldiers in the National Liberation Front for South Vietnam (Viet Cong) during the Vietnam War (1960-1975).

Chain shot. A type of ammunition for smoothbore, muzzle-loading cannons. Compact when loaded but expanding when fired, it was designed for naval use in the sixteenth century to cut the rigging of enemy ships. Later it was also used by ground troops as an antipersonnel charge.

Chariot. An ancient attack vehicle, a two-wheeled backless cart with high front and sides, pulled by usually one or two but sometimes as many as four horses. It could contain either a single occupant, who both drove and fought, or two, one to drive and the other to shoot arrows, thrust spears, or slash with his sword. At Gaugamela in 331 B.C.E., the Persians used chariots with protruding scythes affixed to rotate with the axles, but the maneuvers of Alexander's phalanxes snagged the scythes with one another and rendered the chariots ineffective.

Chassepot. A bolt-action 11-millimeter rifle invented in 1866 by Antoine Alphonse Chassepot (1833-1905) and carried by French soldiers in the Franco-Prussian War (1870-1871). Based on the Dreyse needle gun, which was standard in the Prussian army after 1848, it used a combustible paper cartridge. When the trigger was pulled, a needle pierced the cartridge from behind before hitting the primer and firing the charge.

Chemical weapons. Organic or inorganic agents, usually delivered by shell, intended to poison the enemy. Safety for the attacker is often achieved through the binary system, whereby two ingredients are kept isolated from each other within the shell until impact, when they combine to create the poison. Since World War I (1914-1918), various provisions of the Geneva Conventions and other international treaties have limited chemical warfare, especially the use of poison gas.

Cheval de frise (*pl.* chevaux de frise). Literally, a Frisian horse, a late medieval and early modern defensive obstacle consisting of many long spikes protruding radially from a central log, barrel, or other convenient cylindrical object serving as an axis. A good anticavalry defense for musketeers, it could safely be moved into position by four soldiers, two at each end. Not much used after the eighteenth century, it was finally superseded by barbed wire in the late nineteenth century.

Claymore. A gigantic two-handed Scottish broadsword with a blade up to 6 feet long. The traditional blade of Scotland, known in Gaelic as claidheamh mòr, it was developed in the late Middle Ages and used extensively throughout the Renaissance and early modern era.

Club. A short, stout, heavy, sticklike object, usually wooden, with a large knob on one end to crush skulls or break bones. Of prehistoric origins, it could have either a plain, blunt warhead or a spike driven through the warhead for added deadliness. Almost exclusively a weapon of traditional, preliterate, or aboriginal cultures, it nevertheless

appeared also in more advanced cultures as armor-breaking weapons: the mace and the war hammer. Perhaps the most famous club is the Irish shillelagh, cut from the blackthorn tree.

Cluster bomb. Developed by the Soviet Union in the 1930's and common since the 1960's, an aerial bomb that jettisons its casing at a predetermined altitude to release dozens or even hundreds of small bombs, or bomblets, typically used as an antitank, antivehicle, or antipersonnel weapon.

Cohort. Consisting of approximately 480 soldiers (except for the first cohort of every legion, which had 800 soldiers), this term for a unit in the Roman army was subsequently used to describe a body of soldiers, of varying sizes, who were designated a particular task, like a column.

Column. A division of an army, often with no specific number of soldiers, that had the job of moving to a particular place, especially for sieges or for a specific task.

Company. In late medieval and early Renaissance times, this term often referred to the subunit of an army with a separate commander, such as Sir John Hawkwood's White Company, and there was no specific number of soldiers. Gradually the term "company" come to signify a subunit of a battalion or regiment, and in the case of the British army, it has, at full strength, 120 soldiers, commanded by a major. A company is further divided into two or more platoons. In the German army, the company is the subunit of a battalion, usually with twelve companies in an infantry battalion, making a total, at full strength, of about 80 soldiers.

Composition B. Also called cyclotol, a castable mixture of 40 percent TNT (trinitrotoluene) and 60 percent RDX (cyclo-1,3,5-trimethylene-2,4,6-trinitramine), insensitive to temperature and shock, commonly used as a military explosive because of its tremendous power to crush and shatter. It was the usual load of Allied bangalore torpedoes in World War II (1939-1945).

Composition C. Plastic explosive consisting of 80 percent RDX (cyclo-1,3,5-trimethylene-2,4,6-trinitramine) and 20 percent plasticizing agent, designated C-1 through C-4 according to which plasticizer is used. Like all practical military explosives, it is insensitive to environmental conditions, safe to handle, and long-lived. It is frequently used in land mines.

Cordite. An efficient form of smokeless powder invented in Britain in 1889 by Sir Frederick Augustus Abel (1827-1902) and Sir James Dewar (1842-1923), consisting of nitroglycerin, guncotton, petroleum jelly, and acetone pressed into thin brown cords. Similar to ballistite, it was used extensively in small arms ammunition throughout the twentieth century.

Corps. In the ancient Egyptian army, a corps consisted of some 4,000 soldiers. During the eighteenth and nineteenth centuries, within the British army, the term was often used interchangeably with "regiment," when reference was being made to an infantry regiment. From the late nineteenth century, the "corps" referred to an army formation that consisted of two or more divisions but was itself smaller than an army. Traditionally in military books and maps, a Roman numeral was ascribed to the Corps: VI Corps, VII Corps, and so on. In the German army in World War I (1914-1918), at the start of the war, a German corps consisted of two divisions, each of 17,500 soldiers. There were also instances when specific units in the British, Australian, or Canadian armies had special corps that kept the former use, making them similar in size to regiments, that is, 1,000 or more soldiers. Examples of these include the Camel Corps, Medical Corps, Veterinary Corps, and, in the case of the German army in World War II (1939-1945), the Afrika Korps.

Crossbow. A shooting weapon invented in China about 500 B.C.E. and known in Europe by the end of the first millenium, consisting of a short, thick bow transversely attached to a wooden stock that featured a trigger, a groove to guide the projectile, and usually a detachable cranking mechanism to draw the string. Its ammunition was either stones, pellets, or short arrows called bolts or quarrels. With a range of about 400 yards (370 meters), it was so accurate and powerful that in 1139 the Lateran Council banned its use against Christians. After the Battle of Crécy in 1346, the British preferred the longbow, which could shoot six times as fast, but the crossbow, with its longer range, remained dominant on the Continent through the fifteenth century. By the mid-sixteenth century, it was obsolete in warfare, superseded by firearms, although it is still occasionally used by commandos because it is silent and also for its range and accuracy.

Cruise missile. A tactical, self-propelled, ground-hugging, guided missile developed by the United States and the Soviet Union in the 1960's and 1970's. A "smart bomb," capable of pinpoint accuracy, it can carry either nuclear or nonnuclear warheads and can be launched from land, sea, or air. The American sea-launched Tomahawk and the air-launched ALCM turbofan-powered cruise missiles proved devastating against Iraq in the 1991 Persian Gulf War.

Culverin. A long, smoothbore, muzzle-loading, medium- to large-caliber European field cannon of the fifteenth to seventeenth centuries. Since cast iron technology was not yet dependable for large objects, its barrel was not cast but constructed of overlapping and superimposed hoops of wrought iron. A typical culverin had a 6-inch bore and fired an 18-pound ball.

Cutlass. A short, curved, wide-bladed saber with a thrusting point and a stout hand guard, developed in Europe in the seventeenth century, remotely related to the English falchion of the thirteenth century, and used mostly in naval warfare and by pirates.

Dagger. Next to stones, probably the most ancient of all weapons, originally made of chipped flint. A sharp-pointed, straight-bladed knife intended primarily for stabbing, it can be held with the little finger toward the blade for powerful downward stabbing or with the thumb toward the blade for more versatile thrusting and slashing.

Davach. A subunit within the Irish army in early medieval times, which included enough soldiers to man one fighting ship.

Defoliant. Any chemical weapon intended to destroy plant life and thus prevent the enemy from taking cover in the forest or living off the land. The most notorious was Agent Orange, used extensively by the United States in Vietnam and subsequently discovered to have debilitating long-term side effects on exposed personnel.

Depth charge. An antisubmarine high explosive device, first used in 1916 by the British against the German U-boats in World War I (1914-1918). Since World War II (1939-1945), depth charges have been standard armaments on destroyers, destroyer escorts, and PT boats. Typically, several are catapulted overboard simultaneously in different directions, set to explode at different depths to maximize the chance of hitting the target either directly or with shock waves.

Derringer. A small, easily concealable, short-barreled, medium- to large-caliber, usually single-shot rifled pistol, first manufactured about 1850 by Henry Deringer (1786-1868) of Philadelphia. With the *D* lowercased and another *r* added, the name became generic. John Wilkes Booth (1838-1865) used a derringer to assassinate Abraham Lincoln (1809-1865).

Destroyer. A fast, relatively small, motorized warship of the twentieth century, intended to defend fleets and convoys from all sorts of attack: surface, undersea, and air. It is armed with a great variety of weapons, including torpedoes, depth charges, antiaircraft guns, medium-caliber cannons, and sometimes missiles.

Destroyer escort. A motorized warship, smaller and usually slower than a destroyer, developed by the United States early in World War II (1939-1945) to support destroyers in their mission to defend fleets and convoys. Since 1975, it has been also known in the U.S. Navy as a frigate.

Detachment. A loose term to define a military unit assigned to another command on the battlefield; there is no set size.

Detail. A military unit within the British army, run from headquarters, for transport, intelligence, catering, or another purpose.

Dirk. A dagger used by the British navy in the eighteenth and nineteenth centuries and by Scots generally since the Middle Ages. This traditional Scottish weapon, regularly issued to regimental pipers, is characterized by a wide, straight, symmetrical, double-edged, tapering blade about one foot long. The genuine Scottish dirk has no guard, but the naval dirk does.

Dirty bomb. A device that uses conventional explosives to disperse radioactive material. Although tests have taken place in the United States, it is believed that the weapon is still speculative.

Dive-bomber. A small, maneuverable, propeller-driven airplane capable of steep, steady dives and abrupt, rapid climbs, intended to drop bombs accurately at low altitude and escape before antiaircraft fire or enemy fighter aircraft could bring it down. Armed with either bombs or torpedoes, it is especially effective for attacking ships broadside. Dive-bombing originated as a tactic in World War I (1914-1918) but achieved prominence in World War II (1939-1945) through such planes as the German Junkers Ju-87 Stuka, the Japanese Aichi D3A and Yokosuka D4Y, and the American Douglas SBD Dauntless and Curtiss SB2C Helldiver.

Division. In early modern times, a division was an administrative grouping made up of a number of infantry regiments, with no set size. During the eighteenth century, within the British army, a division was a subset of a battalion similar to what became known as a platoon. Since the late nineteenth century, a division in the British army, along with those of many other countries, has come to be a field formation comprising two or more brigades. In addition to these brigades, there is a divisional command structure that often has extra units assigned to it. In the Australian army during World War I (1914-1918), a division consisted of three brigades, and each brigade consisted of four battalions, making the number of soldiers in a division, when at full strength, around 12,000. In the German army in World War I, a division, at full strength, consisted of 8,407 infantry, 170 cavalry, 1,363 artillery, 838 pioneers, 757 divisional troops, and 108 in the divisional headquarters.

Drone. An unmanned aerial vehicle used in reconnaissance missions and also for remote-controlled bombing. Its task is to fly into areas where it would be risky to send crewed aircraft. Much use of drones has been made by the United States in Iraq and in Afghanistan, and by Israel.

Dumdum bullet. A hollow-point or soft-nosed bullet designed to expand quickly upon impact, causing tremendous internal damage and leaving a horrible exit wound. Developed around 1891 by the British at their colonial arsenal in Dum Dum, India, near Calcutta, they used it in India and the Sudan in the 1890's until it was banned by the Hague Convention of 1899.

Dynamite. Powerful high explosive invented in 1867 by Alfred B. Nobel (1833-1896), consisting of an inert, porous substance saturated with nitroglycerin. Its greatest advantage is rendering nitroglycerin safe to handle, but because it cannot be stored for long periods without becoming unstable, it has limited military application.

Elephants. A type of pachyderm that not only provided transportation for soldiers and equipment but also functioned as the first "tanks." Used in warfare in India from prehistoric times and by the Persians against the Greeks in the fourth century B.C.E., elephants gained military importance, most famously in their role in Hannibal's crossing the Alps to attack Italy in 218 B.C.E. Elephants, aside from being monstrously strong, are fearless, difficult to kill, and a terror to enemy horses.

Equite. An elite Roman cavalry unit designed to protect the emperor and other high-ranking individuals.

Explosive projectile. Any hurled device designed to explode either on impact or at a predetermined point in its flight. Not limited to artillery shells, they may include hand grenades, long-range guided missiles, and even medieval firepots.

Falchion. A short, single-edged sword popular from the thirteenth to the sixteenth centuries in Europe, featuring a wide, heavy, straight-backed blade, a convex cutting edge near the point, and usually an S-shaped crossguard. It evolved into the cutlass.

Falconet. A very light, smoothbore, muzzle-loading, small-caliber European field piece of the sixteenth and seventeenth centuries, characterized by a long, narrow, cast-metal barrel, usually

bronze. The largest known was a 3-pounder (that is, it fired a 3-pound ball). The name means "little falcon."

Fanika (or Fahnlein). A Finnish term used to describe a military unit in the Swedish army that follows a single banner into battle. Traditionally it consisted of about 1,000 soldiers, similar to a battalion, but during the Thirty Years' War (1618-1648) there were only some 500 soldiers in each fanika.

Farm tools. Throughout history, when large numbers of peasants either revolted or were impressed into service, their weaponry included their familiar tools from home. Scythes, sickles, threshing flails, pitchforks, and pruning hooks were extensively used in such conflicts as the Crusades (1095-1270), the Thirty Years' War (1618-1648), and the French Revolution (1789-1799). Minor modifications turn a sickle into a curved dagger or a pruning hook into a pole arm.

Fasces. A bundle of rods holding an ax. Used in war, it became the symbol of the authority of the Roman Republic and came to have significance similar to that of the later parliamentary mace in Britain and former British colonies. During much of the first half of the twentieth century, it was adopted as the symbol of the Italian Fascist Party.

Felucca. Slender, swift, lateen-rigged, wooden sailing ship of the Mediterranean, developed in the sixteenth or early seventeenth century. Favored by the Barbary corsairs until their demise at the beginning of the nineteenth century, it typically carried ten to fourteen guns (seldom, as many as twenty).

Field piece. Any light or medium-weight cannon designed to be highly mobile and versatile in the thick of battle. The term especially refers to the horse-drawn cannons of the muzzle-loading era. Most of the victories of Napoleon I involved his expert use of such artillery.

Fighter aircraft. Early in World War I (1914-1918), personnel in observation planes would fire pistols at enemy observation planes. Soon, two-seater planes were equipped with a swivel machine gun for the copilot. In 1915 Anthony Fokker (1890-1939) invented for the Germans a gear system to allow mounted machine guns to fire forward without hitting the propeller, thus creating the first practical fighter planes. Ideal fighters are small, fast, and maneuverable. Propeller fighters such as the Japanese Mitsubishi Zero, the German Messerschmitt, the British Spitfire, and the American Flying Tiger reached their zenith in World War II (1939-1945) and were superseded by jets in the late 1940's.

Fighter jet. Although developed first by the Germans and later by the Allies during World War II (1939-1945), jet fighter aircraft did not see much action until the Korean War (1950-1953). Outstanding jet fighters include the Russian MiG (Mikoyan-Gurevich) series and the American F-11 Tiger, F-86 Sabre, and F-104 Starfighter.

Firepot. An ancient and medieval incendiary weapon, consisting of a ceramic container filled with an inflammable substance. Flung from a catapult, onager, or trebuchet, it was designed to ignite easily upon impact.

Fireship. A derelict wooden sailing ship or barge, set afire and sent among the enemy's wooden ships. It represented an effective and common naval tactic from ancient to early modern times.

Flail. A type of mace with one, two, or three warheads, usually solid iron spheres studded with spikes, attached to a thick, reinforced wooden handle by short lengths of chain. It was used for the same purpose as the mace, to crush armor, but the chains provided a whiplike effect that added velocity and force to the warhead.

Flak. Invented by the Germans in 1936, the 88-millimeter Flugabwehrkanone (FLAK36) automatic cannon, with an effective range of about 26,000 feet (8,000 meters), was the standard Nazi antiaircraft gun of World War II (1939-1945) and the basis of several later antiaircraft and antitank weapons. Allied airmen soon applied the term to antiaircraft fire in general, especially the hazardous flying debris from exploding antiaircraft shells.

Flamethrower. An offensive incendiary device whereby a single infantryman can safely and effectively shoot a stream of burning liquid from a high-pressure nozzle to distances of about 200 feet (60 meters). Developed during World War I (1914-1918) and used extensively in World War II (1939-1945) and Vietnam (1961-1975), it was a significant advance in military technology because fire is often dangerous for the attacking and attacked armies alike. Soldiers using flamethrowers typically wear flameproof armor, head to toe.

Fleet. Either the entire navy of any country or a substantial group of ships involved in a military action, under the command of an admiral.

Flintlock. A muzzle-loading firearm ignition mechanism, invented around 1610 and common from 1650 until the end of the muzzle-loading era in the mid-nineteenth century, a simple improvement of the snaphance, from which it differs by being single-action rather than double-action. When its trigger is pulled, the hammer pushes the pan cover away from the pan, thus creating sparks, igniting the primer, and firing the weapon.

Fragmentation bomb. Invented during World War I (1914-1918), an artillery shell or aerial bomb whose thick but brittle metal casing is scientifically designed to shatter upon impact, sending jagged debris in all directions as antipersonnel projectiles.

Francisca. A throwing ax used by the Franks in the early Middle Ages and by some Germanic peoples and the Anglo-Saxons in England. French in origin, a double-headed version of the francisca was used during World War II (1939-1945) by the pro-German Vichy government.

Frigate. A sailing, square-rigged, three-masted wooden warship larger than a brig but smaller than a ship of the line. It usually carried between twenty and forty-eight guns on two decks. The USS *Constitution*, "Old Ironsides," launched in Boston in 1797, was a forty-four-gun frigate. From 1950 to 1975, the U.S. Navy designated some large destroyers as frigates, and after 1975 the Navy used the term to refer to destroyer escorts.

Fusil. A light, small-caliber, French flintlock musket of the seventeenth century. British soldiers armed with these weapons were called fusiliers. Subsequently, *fusil* became the ordinary French word for rifle.

Galleon. A warship developed in Spain and England in the fifteenth century, trimmer and more streamlined than the floating fortresses of the fourteenth century. Without their high, overhanging forecastles and poops, but with three or four full-rigged masts, it was the first ship able to hold position against the wind while delivering broadsides to the enemy. The British were victorious over the galleons of the Spanish Armada in 1588 not only because of the weather but also because Sir Francis Drake's galleons were smaller, shallower, faster, and more maneuverable. The galleon was superseded in the seventeenth century by the British man-of-war.

Galley. A long, low, slender, shallow-draft warship of the eastern Mediterranean, usually rowed but equipped with a single square sail. Developed in Greece, Crete, or Phoenicia around the ninth century B.C.E. and later adopted by the Romans, it was the primary warship until the fall of the Roman Empire. With the foremost part of the prow at or just below the waterline reinforced and sharpened, its basic tactics involved ramming the enemy ship broadside; then it could be boarded, sunk, or set afire. Galleys were used in war as recently as the Battle of Lepanto (1571).

Garand rifle. A semiautomatic .30-06 caliber rifle invented in the 1930's by John C. Garand (1888-1974), engineer at the U.S. Armory, Springfield, Massachusetts. Also called the M-1, it had an eight-round magazine. When the U.S. Army made it the standard infantry weapon in 1936, it was the world's first semiautomatic rifle to be so honored. American ground troops carried it in World War II (1939-1945) and the Korean War (1950-1953).

Gas shell. A basic element of chemical and biological warfare, an artillery projectile filled with poison gas released at or just before impact. Used extensively in World War I (1914-1918), armed chiefly with mustard gas, phosgene, or lewisite, it differs from a gas grenade in that it is fired rather than thrown. Even though military poison gas was outlawed by the 1925 Geneva Protocol, most countries have continued to develop such weapons.

Gatling gun. A primitive machine gun invented in 1862 for the Union army in the American Civil War (1861-1865) by Richard Jordan Gatling (1818-1903), characterized by several, usually six to ten, revolving barrels that were cranked around to produce rapid fire. The Gatling gun was superseded by the machine guns of Hiram Stevens Maxim (1840-1916) in the 1890's, but the Gatling principle was employed for airborne and antiaircraft weapons in the late twentieth century, when very high rates of fire, in excess of six thousand rounds per minute, were desired.

Gladius. A short, straight thrusting sword carried by the Roman infantry legions. From its name derives the word "gladiator." It was superseded in battle by the spatha in the Christian Roman Empire.

Glaive. A type of pole arm whose head consists of a single blade resembling that of a sword. Common variants include a curved, single-edged, saberlike blade and a broadsword blade. It was developed by the French during the High Middle Ages and used primarily for slashing.

Grapeshot. A type of spreading antipersonnel and anticavalry muzzle-loading artillery ammunition, consisting of ten or twenty loose, grape-sized, solid metal balls packed as a group into a cannon. Very common in warfare from the eighteenth century until the end of the muzzle-loading era, it differs from case shot and canister shot by not being sealed in a container. The effect was like that of a giant shotgun. The Russians fired grapeshot into the Light Brigade at Balaklava in 1854.

Greek fire. An early medieval, and perhaps ancient, incendiary mixture of unknown ingredients, usually delivered by catapult in breakable containers and extensively used in naval warfare because it was unaffected by water. Some say it ignited on contact with saltwater and was first used in 673 by the Byzantines defending Constantinople against the Arabs. Others, who discount the story that Archimedes set Roman ships afire with mirrors during the Second Punic War (218-201 B.C.E.), suggest that he may have been the inventor and first user of Greek fire.

Grenade. A small bomb, either thrown by hand or launched from a hand-carried device. Developed in Europe in the sixteenth century, it originally contained either gunpowder or an incendiary mixture, but later versions contain smoke screens, poison gas, or other chemical agents. Grenades are detonated by percussion, impact, or a short fuse activated just before throwing or launching.

Grenade launcher. Dating from the fifteenth century and in constant military use ever since, any short-barreled, wide-bore, muzzle-loading, personal firearm designed to throw grenades farther and more accurately than they can be thrown by hand. Some muskets and rifles can be temporarily converted into grenade launchers with specialized muzzle attachments. The 40-millimeter American M203 grenade launcher, standard infantry equipment in the 1990's, is easily combined with the M-16 rifle to create a double-barreled weapon.

Guided missile. Developed by the United States, the Soviet Union, and many other industrialized nations after World War II (1939-1945), a self-propelled, usually rocket-propelled, air- or space-traversing missile, distinguished from an ordinary missile by its being capable of having its course corrected during its flight. It can be ground-launched, air-launched, surface-ship-launched, or submarine-launched. Among water-traversing missiles containing guidance systems, guided torpedoes are generally not called guided missiles, but sea-launched tactical antiship missiles, such as the French Exocet and the American Harpoon, are. Inventing missile guidance systems required the prior development of radar, radio, and computers.

Guisarme. A type of pole arm whose head includes two blades curving away from each other, sharpened on the outer, or concave, edges. Invented in Europe in the eleventh century, it was used until the fifteenth for slashing, unhorsing, tripping, and thrusting.

Gun. In military parlance, always a cannon, never a personal firearm. As a piece of ordnance, it is usually a big, powerful, long-range cannon firing with a flat trajectory and thus is distinguished from howitzers and mortars.

Guncotton. An explosive compound, also called nitrocotton, a variety of nitrocellulose invented by German chemist Christian Friedrich Schönbein (1799-1868) in 1845 and produced by soaking plain cotton in nitric acid and sulfuric acid. Guncotton burns too fast to be a safe and efficient smokeless propellant for firearms, but it was later used in the invention and manufacture of practical smokeless powders.

Gunpowder. Although Roger Bacon (c. 1220-c. 1292) was the first Westerner to give exact directions for making gunpowder (in 1242), gunpowder had been developed by the Chinese many centuries earlier. A simple mixture of potassium nitrate, sulfur, and charcoal, gunpowder revolutionized warfare by enabling projectiles to be fired long distances from hollow tubes closed or partially closed at one end. Later improvements, such as powder B, ballistite, and cordite, include less volatile and less smoky varieties.

Halberd. A versatile type of pole arm whose head includes an ax on one side, a spike, pick, or hook on the other side, and a spear point at the tip. Developed in Switzerland in the thirteenth century, gradually improved through the sixteenth, and still carried by the Swiss Guards of the Vatican, it was an important multipurpose weapon of European foot soldiers during the Renaissance, employed to unhorse, thrust, parry, or slash. Horsemen would frequently become intimidated by companies of well-seasoned infantry armed with halberds.

Hand cannon. A primitive European muzzle-loading personal firearm, developed about 1400, featuring a long stock, short barrel, smooth bore, and large caliber. Intended to be fired from a bench-rest position, it featured, under the stock near the muzzle, a protruding spike to hook over the rest to prevent recoil. It was superseded by the harquebus about 1450.

Hand grenade. Invented in the sixteenth century and in constant military use ever since, a small explosive device designed to be thrown by hand and detonated by either impact or a time fuse. Among its most prominent users were the British Grenadiers of the eighteenth century. Twentieth century examples include the German Steilhandgranate (potato masher), the Japanese 97, and the American Mk2 "pineapple."

Harquebus. A European muzzle-loading firearm developed about 1450. Fired by either a matchlock or a wheel-lock mechanism, it was in general use until about 1550, when the snaphance was invented and the flintlock musket became possible. Also called an arquebus, hackbut, or hagbut, it evolved from the hand cannon, was heavy, bulky, short-range, and inaccurate, and was typically fired from a monopod or tripod.

Hazara. A relatively small unit within the Mongol army, sometimes called a minghan, consisting of 1,000 soldiers, similar in size to a Roman legion or modern battalion. Subsequently the Mongol army was reorganized into ming bashi, which also consisted of 1,000 soldiers.

Heavy artillery. Large cannons that differ from light artillery not only by weight but also by caliber, mobility, and purpose. Such guns are suitable for fortress defense, shore batteries, and siege work, but not for battlefield situations where quick adaptability could be the key to victory. The peak use of heavy artillery was in World War I (1914-1918), when guns of 40 centimeters and larger were moved by railroad or mounted on battleships.

Horse artillery. A type of field artillery in which the gunners ride horses. Until the end of the eighteenth century, guns, carriages, and caissons were pulled by horses while the gun crews and drivers walked. One of Napoleon's most important tactical innovations was to develop the horse artillery, dramatically increasing the versatility, mobility, and effectiveness of his cannon. In the American Civil War (1861-1865), the term referred to the Confederate practice of disassembling small howitzers, loading the components on packhorses, running them with the cavalry through terrain where normal gun carriages could not pass, then quickly reassembling them at the next battle.

Host. The term used in ancient Egypt to designate 250 chariots, which were subdivided into corps of 25 chariots each.

Howitzer. A type of cannon, originating in the seventeenth century, with a barrel longer than that of a mortar but shorter than that of a gun, designed to fire medium-velocity projectiles at medium to high trajectories.

Hundertschaft. A term that arose in early medieval times to describe a unit of about 100 fighting men. Subsequently it continued to be used to denote a unit of around 100 men, notably by the German State Police and the German Federal Police.

Huo. The smallest subunit of a Chinese medieval army. During the Tang Dynasty (618-907), it consisted of 10 soldiers.

Hydrogen bomb (H-bomb). A thermonuclear device that uses the power of an atomic fission reaction to fuse heavy hydrogen atoms, deuterium and tritium, into helium. Fused in this way, hydrogen releases about four times as much destructive energy as the same mass of uranium or plutonium in an atomic bomb. The United States tested its first hydrogen bomb in 1952, the Soviet Union in 1953.

Ikhanda. A corps within the Zulu army from the 1820's to the 1870's. During the Zulu (or Anglo-Zulu) War of 1879, the number of soldiers in a Zulu ikhanda varied considerably. The entire Zulu army was divided into three of these, and they consisted of between 2,400 and 15,000 warriors, each with a number of amabuthos, or regiments.

Impi. A nonspecific term referring to a number of Zulu warriors. The size of impi units varied considerably.

Incendiary bomb. Any chemical device intended to cause an outbreak of flames among the enemy, including fire bombs, napalm bombs, Molotov cocktails, and firepots. Some commonly used inflammatory agents are white phosphorus, gasoline, thermite, and magnesium.

Intercontinental ballistic missile (ICBM). A strategic weapon of mass destruction, the focus of the Cold War (1945-1991) arms race between the Soviet Union and the United States; a very long range, nuclear-armed guided missile, such as the Soviet SS-9, SS-16, SS-17, SS-18, and SS-19, and the American Minuteman III and Titan II, land-launched from underground silos. Similar, but shorter-range, missiles, such as the American Polaris and Trident, can be launched from submarines.

Ironclad. A motorized or, less commonly, sailing wooden warship armored with metal plates on its hull and topsides, developed early in the American Civil War (1861-1865). As demonstrated in the classic draw between the USS *Monitor* and the CSS *Virginia* (formerly the USS *Merrimack*) at Hampton Roads, Virginia, on March 9, 1862, it revolutionized naval warfare.

Jacketed bullet. A small arms projectile consisting of a soft metal core, usually lead, coated with a harder metal, often copper, which is still soft enough to grip the rifling inside a gun barrel. It was standard military issue throughout the world as of the late nineteenth century. The main advantage of such ammunition is that it can be fired at higher velocity, thereby gaining a flatter trajectory and hence a longer range.

Javelin. The generic term for any light, usually short, spear whose sole purpose is to be thrown, sometimes with a throwing device to extend the arm and increase the weapon's range. Invented during the Stone Age, it was common among most ancient troops, especially the Greek hoplite infantry. One famous type of javelin is the Roman light pilum.

Jeddart ax. A type of pole arm whose head consists of a grappling hook on one side and, on the other side, a long ax-blade with an undulating edge and a spear point. Developed from the halberd and voulge, contemporaneous with the Lochaber ax in the sixteenth century, it could be used for scaling walls and unhorsing riders, as well as for thrusting, chopping, and slashing.

Jeep. Named by altering the acronym "GP" for "general purpose," a small, light, fast, tough, dependable, all-terrain motor vehicle with four-wheel drive, an 80-inch wheelbase, and often a machine gun mounted in the back, developed by the Americans in the late 1930's and used extensively in World War II (1939-1945), Korea (1950-1953), and Vietnam (1961-1975). (Jeep became a trademark for a civilian vehicle based on the military original.)

Judo. *See* Jujitsu.

Jujitsu. An unarmed Japanese martial art whose origins are lost in antiquity but whose basic principles were codified by samurai in the seventeenth century. Named from two Japanese words mean-

ing "gentle skill," it is not the same as judo, "gentle art," a more recent derivative that emphasizes leverage and throwing. True jujitsu also involves complex maneuvers of kicking, punching, and holding.

Karate. Based on ancient Chinese boxing techniques, this hard-hitting, unarmed Japanese martial art features extraordinary leaps, chops, and kicks. It became systematized during the seventeenth century on the island of Okinawa and was named from two Japanese words meaning "empty hand." Tae kwon do, or "Korean karate," evolved from it in the 1950's.

Kidney dagger. Sometimes called ballock dagger, a symmetrical, double-edged, usually ornate European dagger of the thirteenth to seventeenth centuries, so called from the shape of its guard.

Knife. A hand weapon with a multipurpose short cutting blade, dating from prehistoric times and differing from a dagger in its versatility, from a sword in its length, and from a bayonet in its independence.

Knobkerrie. A Zulu striking or throwing club, carved from a single piece of hardwood, with a long, thin, straight handle and a smooth, small to medium-sized spherical or ovoid knob for the warhead.

Korps. *See* Corps.

Kris. A traditional Malay dagger, common throughout Southeast Asia, characterized by a long, asymmetric, double-edged, distinctively wavy or serpentine blade. A spur on one side of the base of the blade typically blends into a sort of hand guard. The handle is often ornate and the blade is sometimes ridged, laminated, and inlayed with elaborate designs or battle scenes.

Kukri. A traditional, single-edged, guardless, long knife or short sword of the Gurkhas of Nepal, characterized by the distinctive shape of its blade: straight out from the hilt to about a third of its length, then bent abruptly downward toward the edge at an angle of about 35 degrees. The back of the blade thus resembles a hockey stick, but the edge is sinuous and, from the vertex of the angle to the point, usually convex.

Lance. A light, long, narrow spear, often with a hand guard, carried by horsemen. An ancient weapon, it was used for tournament jousting in the Middle Ages, fell out of military favor in the Renaissance, but was revived by Napoleon. Throughout the nineteenth century until World War I (1914-1918), the lance was common among European and Asian cavalry regiments and Native American horsemen.

Land mine. An explosive obstacle or booby trap, typically buried just under the surface of the ground and easily detonated by pressure or a tripwire. A mainstay of twentieth century warfare, most land mines are antipersonnel devices, but some, set to detonate only from heavy pressures, are used as antitank or antivehicle weapons.

Langue-de-bœuf. A type of pole arm whose head consists mainly of a long, double-bladed spear point named for its shape, like that of the tongue of an ox (*langue de bœuf* in French). Developed by the Swiss and French in the fifteenth century, it was an early form of the partisan.

Laser. An acronym for "light amplification by stimulated emission of radiation." This emission of light in a continuous narrow beam of all the same wavelength (visible, ultraviolet, or infrared) was developed in the late 1950's. Its most successful military use is in rangefinding and guidance systems for precision-guided munitions (PGMs). The United States used laser-guided bombs with great effectiveness in the 1991 Persian Gulf War (1990-1991).

Legion. This division of the Roman army consisted of approximately 4,500-5,500 soldiers. In early Rome, at full strength, it was formed by 4,200 legionaries and 300 equites, but during the Roman Republic it had 5,200 legionnaires, as well as a range of auxiliaries.

Lewisite. A poison gas, $C_2H_2AsCl_3$, a colorless or brown, fast-acting blistering agent and eye irritant, smelling of ammonia and geraniums, synthesized in 1918 by Winford Lee Lewis (1878-1943), then a captain in the U.S. Army Chemical Warfare Service. It was used briefly by the Americans toward the end of World War I (1914-1918).

Light artillery. A cannon with a small to medium caliber and a light barrel, distinguished from heavy artillery mainly by its superior versatility. Usually wheeled and sometimes portable by as few as two or three soldiers, it can be quickly redeployed, realigned, and redirected amid volatile battlefield predicaments. The category includes field artillery, tank guns, automatic cannons, anti-aircraft guns, antitank mortars, and most howitzers.

Limpet mine. Named after the marine gastropod mollusk that clings to undersea surfaces, a twentieth century naval explosive device containing magnets for divers or amphibious saboteurs to attach it to an enemy ship's metal hull below the water line. American versions from World War II (1939-1945) weighed about 10 pounds and used a time-delay fuse to detonate a high-explosive charge, usually torpex.

Lochaber ax. A type of pole arm whose head includes, on one side, a hook for scaling walls or unhorsing riders and, on the other side, a long, wide, convex blade. About half the length of the blade extends beyond the end of the staff. Developed in Scotland late in the sixteenth century, it was popular with clansmen in their struggles against the English until Culloden in 1746.

Long-range bomber. During World War II (1939-1945), the Americans developed aircraft that improved offensive punch by flying faster and farther for bombing runs. Early in the war, they replaced their B-17 Flying Fortress with the B-29 Superfortress, which flew at 350 miles per hour and could bomb a target 2,000 miles from base and return safely. The *Enola Gay*, which dropped the atomic bomb on Hiroshima, was a B-29. From the 1950's until the 1990's, the B-52 Stratofortress was the world standard for long-range jet bombers.

Longbow. The mainstay of English military success from the thirteenth to the sixteenth centuries, the longbow made archery more accurate and deadly, as well as inexpensive and uncomplicated. It was a simple bow about 6 feet long, drew about 80 or 90 pounds, and shot a 3-foot arrow about 270 yards (250 meters). In its time, the only personal weapon that could outrange it was the crossbow, but the crossbow was slow, and a practiced archer could shoot ten or twelve arrows per minute. The longbow proved devastating against the French at Crécy in 1346.

Longship. A long, low, slender, shallow-draft vessel of the eighth to eleventh centuries, usually propelled by a single square sail amidships but also equipped with oars. Developed in Scandinavia by expert seafarers, it was the swiftest ship of its time and struck terror throughout coastal Europe as the preferred raiding ship of the Vikings. From the name of its flat rudder, "steer-board," always lashed to the right side of the ship, derives the word "starboard."

Lucerne hammer. A type of pole arm that evolved from the voulge in the fifteenth century and whose head consists of a heavy, four-pronged warhead: a stout, thick spear point for thrusting; a pick perpendicular to the staff; and two claws opposite the pick and also perpendicular to the staff. Its sole purpose was to smash or penetrate armor.

Mace. A type of club, developed early in the Bronze Age and refined during the Middle Ages, consisting of a short, thick staff and a massive metal warhead with four to six blunt blades or flanges parallel to the shaft and equally spaced around the head. Alternately, a mace warhead could be a solid metal sphere studded with spikes. It was used extensively by mounted knights to smash or dent armor. After knights in armor disappeared from warfare, the mace continued to be used as a ceremonial symbol of authority.

Machete. A long knife or short sword that originated in the tropical Spanish colonies in the sixteenth century, with a short, thick, single-edged, heavy blade for cutting sugarcane, hacking through jungle, or slashing enemies.

Machine gun. Developed in the second half of the nineteenth century, a complex automatic rifle capable of rapid fire with ordinary small arms ammunition. Prototypes were developed by James Puckle (1667-1724), Richard Jordan Gatling, and Thorsten Nordenfelt (1842-1920), but the first successful true machine gun was invented around 1884 by Hiram Stevens Maxim (1840-1916) and adopted by Britain, Germany, and the United States in the 1890's. Loosely, the term can refer to any automatic weapon.

Man-of-war ship. Developed in Britain early in the seventeenth century, any large sailing warship, especially either a frigate or a ship of the line, square-rigged and with at least two gun decks. Bigger, faster, more fully rigged, and more heavily armed than the ship it replaced, the galleon, it survived until the end of the age of sail and made the British navy supreme.

Mangonel. A medieval torsion-powered catapult closely related to the onager but smaller and, because its throwing arm traveled through an arc of only 90 degrees, less efficient. When cocked, the arm was horizontal; when released, it hit the padded leather buffer at the vertical, thus dissipating all its follow-through energy. Like all torsion engines, it was adversely susceptible to changes in humidity affecting the twisted skein.

Maniple. A subunit in the Roman Republican army that consisted of 120 legionnaires. There were thirty maniples in each legion.

Matchlock. Introduced in Europe in the early fifteenth century and used until the early eighteenth century in the West and until the mid-nineteenth century in Asia, muzzle-loading firearm ignition mechanism consisting of a lighted wick or match that the trigger action brought into contact with the pan of powder after the pan cover was lifted by hand.

Meros (*pl.* meroi). A unit within the Byzantine army consisting of about 3,000 soldiers. It was further divided into ten tagmata. Three meroi formed an army.

Metal-case cartridge. The earliest cartridge cases were either paper or cloth. They were satisfactory for muzzle-loaders but impractical for breech-loaders, especially when the shooter wanted to reload quickly and cleanly. The metal case replaced the paper case in the 1870's and had several important advantages, chief among which was that it expanded to seal the breech as soon as the weapon was fired. It not only made breech-loading efficient but also made automatic weapons possible.

Militia. Traditionally, any nonregular military unit made up of volunteers drawn from areas about to be attacked. In Britain, militias originated with the Anglo-Saxons during the Viking raids.

Mine. A naval or land booby trap, an explosive weapon usually set to detonate by pressure. Floating mines, moored just below the surface, were typically equipped in both world wars with Herz horns, a German invention that, when hit, triggers an electrochemical reaction that detonates the high explosive charge. Land mines can be laid by sappers or sown by mortars or from cluster bombs. Antimine apparatus includes probes, metal detectors, bangalore torpedoes, tanks equipped with flails, ploughs, or rollers, and minesweeping ships.

Minenwerfer. Literally, a mine thrower; a rifled, muzzle-loading, short-barreled, 25-centimeter German mortar of World War I (1914-1918), often loaded with gas shells.

Ming bashi. Sometimes known as a minghan, a division in the Mongol army, which previously had been divided into hazara. The ming bashi was further divided into ten yuz bashi.

Minié ball. Not really a ball, but a conical lead bullet with a hollow, expanding base, invented in 1849 by French army officer Claude-Étienne Minié (1804-1879). Firing the weapon pushed the bullet tightly into the rifling of the barrel, thus dramatically increasing its range and accuracy. The Crimean War (1853-1856) and the American Civil War (1861-1865) proved the superiority of the Minié rifle over both the smoothbore musket and the rifled musket, which used spherical ammunition.

MIRV. *See* Multiple independently targetable reentry vehicle.

Missile. Any self-propelled ammunition or projectile; loosely, the term can mean any hurled object. Its three main types of self-propulsion are jet engines, propellers, and rockets. Because rocket propulsion is by far the most common, some missiles, especially small ones, are loosely called rockets. In the late twentieth century, the term became mostly synonymous with "guided missile."

Mitrailleuse. A hand-cranked machine gun developed in 1869 for France and characterized by thirty-seven barrels in a hexagonal pattern inside a single air-cooled barrel. A metal ammunition block inserted vertically into the breech, transverse to the barrels, held all thirty-seven rounds. The French used the mitrailleuse too far back from the front lines for it to be effective in the Franco-Prussian War (1870-1871). The term later became the ordinary French word for machine gun.

Molotov cocktail. A terrorist and insurrectionist incendiary weapon developed in Europe in the early twentieth century and named after Soviet statesman Vyacheslav Mikhailovich Molotov (1890-1986). Consisting of a glass bottle filled with gasoline and plugged with an oil-soaked rag, it is thrown like a hand grenade as soon as the rag is ignited.

Morning star. A medieval clublike weapon with a spiked end (hence its name). Used by both infantry and cavalry, it became popular in the fourteenth century and was soon replaced by the more effective flail.

Mortar. A short-barreled, large-caliber, usually muzzle-loading cannon designed to lob shells at low velocity and high trajectory with moderate accuracy for short distances, such as over the walls of a besieged fortress. It has been in constant military use since the fifteenth century, but in the late twentieth it became mostly an antiarmor, guided-missile-launching weapon.

Multiple independently targetable reentry vehicle (MIRV). A type of nuclear warhead on either an intercontinental ballistic missile (ICBM) or a sea-launched ballistic missile (SLBM), developed in the 1970's, consisting of a cluster of guided missiles to saturate the general area of the target and make antimissile defense more difficult for the enemy.

Musket. Any muzzle-loading, long-barreled, personal firearm, originally smoothbore, though it could be either smoothbore or rifled. Invented in the fifteenth century, it was a standard infantry weapon for four hundred years until superseded by the breech-loading rifle in the 1860's.

Mustard gas. A poison gas, $C_4H_8Cl_2S$, an acrid, noxious substance that penetrates and irritates skin, causes severe blisters, and can cause blindness. It was used extensively by both sides in World War I (1914-1918).

Muzzle-loader. Any firearm, either a personal weapon or an artillery piece, that loads its charge and projectile through the front end of the bore. Muzzle-loaders dominated for almost six hundred years, but, with the exception of mortars, most military firearms since the late nineteenth century have been breechloaders. The greatest drawback to muzzle-loaders is that they cannot repeat.

Naginata. A traditional Japanese pole arm whose head consists of a long, high-quality, curved, saberlike sword blade rigidly attached to the staff with an overly long shank or tang. An expert in naginatajutsu, the martial art of wielding this weapon, was a very deadly warrior.

Não. A sailing, deep-draft, broad-beam Portuguese merchantman and warship, called *nau* in Spain and carrack in England, developed in the late thirteenth or early fourteenth century, probably by Basque shipbuilders. Usually with three or four masts, armed with one or two decks of bronze cannons, and full-rigged, it was sturdy but slow. Famous nãos include the *Santa Maria*, Christopher Columbus's flagship; most of Ferdinand Magellan's fleet that circumnavigated the world from 1519 to 1522; and the *Henry Grâce à Dieu*, Henry VIII's naval flagship.

Napalm. An incendiary substance, ammunition for flamethrowers and firebombs, developed by the United States in 1942 and used extensively in the Pacific theater of World War II (1939-1945) and in Vietnam (1961-1975). Also called jellied gasoline (especially in its early years), it exists in several formulas, the most successful of which is napalm-B: 50 percent polystyrene, 25 percent benzene, and 25 percent gasoline. The name derives from two of its original ingredients, naphthenic acid, or aluminum naphthene, and palmitic acid, or aluminum palmate. Napalm adheres to its target, making it difficult to extinguish.

Nerve gas. Any gas composed of a nerve agent or agents that forms a chemical weapon capable of being used against opponents. It was first developed in Germany in 1936 but was most extensively used against the Kurds in the Iran-Iraq War of 1980-1988.

Neutron bomb. The so-called dirty bomb, developed in the 1970's, an enhanced radiation bomb intended as an antipersonnel tactical nuclear weapon, designed to do minimal damage to nonliving structures but to kill or incapacitate all animal life within a certain radius.

Niru. A subunit in the Chinese army during the Qing (Ch'ing) Dynasty (1644-1912) consisting of about 300 bannermen who were drawn from the Manchu minority.

Nuclear-powered warship. The technology of substituting nuclear fuel for diesel in oceangoing vessels, especially effective for submarines, enabling them to stay submerged much longer and refuel less frequently, thus increasing the threat of the sea-launched ballistic missile (SLBM). The first nuclear-powered submarine, the USS *Nautilus*, was launched in 1954.

Nunchaku. A Japanese weapon developed from the flail used in the threshing of rice. It consists of two sections of wood (or later metal), attached by a chain, and was similar in some ways to the European flail.

Oil pot. Defensive weapon for besieged medieval garrisons, a large metal cauldron containing hot oil to be poured on attackers trying to scale the walls.

Onager. A light, versatile, mobile catapult developed by the Romans, probably in the third century, so called because, after launching its load, when the throwing arm landed on the padded leather buffer at the front of the stout wooden frame, it kicked like its namesake, the Asian wild ass. Its power came from a skein twisted around one end of its arm, which traveled through an arc of about 135 degrees.

Ordnance. A term with two distinct meanings in military parlance, depending on context. On one hand, it means military equipment and hardware in general—not only weapons and ammunition, but also vehicles, tools, and durable supplies. On the other hand, and more properly, it means artillery, cannons, and their ammunition. Ordnance officers are responsible for procuring and maintaining this matériel and ensuring that the artillery is in good working order.

Pack. A grouping of submarines, specifically German U-boats in World War I (1914-1918) and World War II (1939-1945).

Parang. The Malay name for the jagged-edged, oddly angled sword traditionally used by the Dyak headhunters and pirates of Borneo. The tip is sometimes squared off, with three or more separate points in line. The hilt is usually guardless and often elaborately decorated with horn, hair, or feathers.

Partisan. A type of pole arm whose head consists mainly of a long, broad, double-bladed spearhead, characterized by two small, winglike extensions or flanges at the base of the spearhead curving up toward the point. It evolved from the langdebeve (French langue-de-bœuf) in the sixteenth century and was common throughout the seventeenth. In William Shakespeare's *Hamlet* (act I, scene i, line 144), Marcellus asks whether he should strike the ghost with his partisan.

Patriot missile. This U.S. missile was developed in 1981 as a surface-to-air missile, used mainly to shoot down incoming enemy missiles. There was much publicity about its deployment and use during the Gulf War of 1990-1991.

Patrol. A military unit involved in a specific task, on land, at sea, or in the air. It has no fixed size.

Patrol-torpedo (PT) boat. A very small, very fast, shallow-draft, motorized vessel, typically armed with torpedoes, machine guns, and depth charges, used extensively by the Americans in the Pacific theater during World War II (1939-1945). John F. Kennedy became a war hero while commanding PT-109.

Percussion cap. A small container of priming substance that is detonated when struck in a specific way, thus setting off the main charge and propelling the projectile down the barrel of the firearm.

Alexander John Forsyth (1769-1843), a Scottish minister, patented the first practical percussion firing mechanism in 1807. His invention proved to be among the most important in the history of firearms, because it eventually made possible metal-case cartridges, breech-loading, rapid fire, and quick reloading. Cartridges are designated according to the placement of their internal percussion caps: rimfire, centerfire, and the obsolete pinfire.

Petard. Explosive demolition device of the sixteenth century, consisting of a container of gunpowder which could be placed against a wall, gate, portcullis, or drawbridge, then detonated in an attempt to open a breach. Because of its extraordinarily loud report, it was named after the French word for "to break wind." Because so many of its users were killed by the explosion before they could get away, the phrase, "hoist with (or by) one's own petard" arose, meaning literally to be "blown up by one's own bomb," or defeated by one's own designs.

Petronel. A large-caliber matchlock carbine developed in France in the late sixteenth century, featuring a banana-shaped butt, curved sharply downward for bracing the weapon against the chest.

Phosgene. Poison gas, $COCl_2$, a colorless lung irritant that smells like freshly cut grass. It causes choking death by pulmonary edema (that is, by drowning in one's own mucus) and was used extensively by both sides in World War I (1914-1918).

Pike. A very long type of pole arm whose head consists mainly of a heavy but narrow spear point rigidly attached to the staff with a long metal shank. The pike dates from ancient times, but its most celebrated tactics involved infantrymen creating defensive formations such as the mobile cheval de frise against enemy cavalry in the sixteenth to eighteenth centuries to allow musketeers safety while reloading. Such pikes could be 16 feet (5 meters) long.

Pilum. A Roman spear, standard equipment for foot soldiers in the legions. It existed in two forms: one long, heavy, often with a hand guard midway down the shaft, and used mainly for thrusting; the other short, light, without a hand guard, basically a javelin with a small head designed to break off upon impact.

Pistol. A short-barreled handgun, invented in the late fifteenth or early sixteenth century, frequently in military use as an officer's sidearm. Its one-handed operation made it suitable for cavalrymen. In automatic or semiautomatic pistols, the magazine can be conveniently contained in the handle.

Plastic explosive. A stable, moldable, high-explosive mixture created by combining a plasticizing agent such as oil or wax with a high-explosive compound such as RDX (cyclo-1,3,5-trimethylene-2,4,6-trinitramine) or TNT (trinitrotoluene). First developed in the 1890's, research into plastic explosives expanded dramatically during and after World War II (1939-1945), resulting in such products as composition C.

Platoon. A subunit of an army company; in the case of the British army, there are three platoons in a company. At full strength, it consists of between 30 to 40 soldiers, and it is commanded by a subaltern. It is further divided into sections.

Polaris missile. This missile, first developed in 1960 in the United States, was an early submarine-launched missile used by the U.S. Navy and the (British) Royal Navy.

Pole arm. Any long, multipurpose spear. Pole arms have been developed at every time and in every culture, but especially in Europe throughout the Middle Ages. The typical pole arm was used extensively by foot soldiers and palace guards until the nineteenth century and consisted of a large, finely crafted metal head rigidly affixed to a wooden staff. Varieties include the bill, guisarme, glaive, halberd, jeddart ax, langue-de-bœuf, Lochaber ax, Lucerne hammer, partisan, pike, poleax, spetum, and voulge.

Poleax. A type of pole arm whose head includes a broad-bladed ax on one side. There may be a spear point at the tip of the head and either a spike, pick, or hook on the other side, so that the weapon would resemble a halberd. It was developed in Europe in the late Middle Ages and used throughout the Renaissance and early modern era.

Pom-pom. So named from the sound of its report, a small-caliber automatic cannon whose reloading mechanism is powered by the firing of each previous round. Developed in the 1880's and 1890's by Hiram Stevens Maxim and originally intended as a mounted naval gun, its first use was as a field piece by both the British and the Boers in the Second Boer War (1899-1902). In subsequent naval and antiaircraft use, it was typically mounted in pairs. The British used a 37-millimeter version as a field piece in World War I (1914-1918).

Poniard. A Renaissance French dagger with a long, slender, triangular or square blade, somewhat resembling a stiletto. In combat it was often wielded in conjunction with the rapier as a parrying weapon. The name derives from *poing*, the French word for fist.

Powder B. The first successful smokeless powder, invented in 1885 by Paul Vieille (1854-1934) and soon adopted by the French army. It consists of nitrocelluose gelatinized with ether and alcohol, evaporated, rolled, and flaked.

Pursuit plane. From 1920 to 1948, American fighter aircraft were officially designated "Pursuit" and were numbered with the prefix "P." Among the outstanding planes in this series were the Curtiss P-1 Hawk, the Boeing P-26 Peashooter, the Lockheed P-38 Lightning or Fork-Tailed Devil, and the Curtiss P-40 Flying Tiger.

Quarterstaff. A particularly stout medieval English stave of oak or ash, about 8 feet long and 1.5 inches thick, occasionally banded with iron at both ends and commonly wielded with one hand in the middle and the other near one end. A surprisingly versatile weapon in the quick hands of an expert, it can stun, stab, crush, unhorse, fracture, or even kill. The legendary meeting of Robin Hood and Little John involved their famous quarterstaff duel on a narrow bridge.

Rapier. A long thrusting sword developed in Europe in the sixteenth century and popular until the eighteenth. With a rigid, slender, straight blade of fine steel and usually an elaborate hilt and hand guard, it served the privileged classes, both civilian and military, as a dueling weapon, an instrument of stealth and assassination, and a symbol of rank and authority.

RDX (cyclo-1,3,5-trimethylene-2,4,6-trinitramine). Also called cyclonite or hexogen, one of the most common military explosives of the twentieth century, especially in World War II (1939-1945). Invented in 1899 by the Germans and named by the British, its name is an acronym for "Research Department Explosive." More powerful than TNT (trinitrotoluene) and comparatively stable, RDX is often mixed with TNT (trinitrotoluene), as in torpex, the standard torpedo load, or in aerial bombs and artillery shell fillings.

Recoilless rifle. Invented by the Americans during World War II (1939-1945), a hollow tube, open at both ends, allowing a single soldier to fire an artillery shell from the shoulder. The American M20 superseded the M9A1 after World War II (1939-1945). The Swedish Miniman and the German Armbrust are late twentieth century disposable recoilless antitank guns firing just one load of shaped charge, that is, a shell that explodes on the outer surface of the armor and bores a hole through it.

Regiment. In the British army, a permanently established unit within the infantry, and also the Royal Armoured Corps, Royal Artillery, Royal Engineers, Royal Signals, or Army Air Corps, being commanded by a lieutenant colonel. It could consist of a number of battalions, and most regiments had county or regional names showing where they were raised or had connections. Within the German army in World War I (1914-1918), regiments were assigned names of a king, prince, or other military identity.

Repeating rifle. A breech-loading personal firearm, using manual action to feed the next round from a magazine into the firing chamber. Developed independently and gradually by many inventors in the mid-nineteenth century, its eventual perfection early in the twentieth century was made possible by two innovations: the metal-case cartridge and smokeless powder. The repeating action can be a lever, as in the Winchester 1873; slide, as in the Colt Lightning; or bolt, as in most World War I (1914-1918) repeaters.

Revolver. A type of breech-loading pistol, invented in the mid-nineteenth century, classified in four basic kinds according to how the multichambered cylinder is exposed for reloading: side-gate, where a flap opens on one side of the weapon; break-open, where the barrel swings down on a hinge; swing-out, where the cylinder swings to one side on its hinge; and removable cylinder. A revolver is either single-action, if it needs to be cocked manually, or double-action, if the trigger cocks the hammer. Famous manufacturers include Tranter, Webley, Colt, and Smith and Wesson.

Rifle. Any long-barreled personal firearm, either muzzle-loading or breech-loading, that has spiral grooves machined inside the barrel to spin the bullet, thus increasing its accuracy, range, and power. Invented in the fifteenth century and first popularized by the American colonists in the mid-eighteenth century, it superseded smoothbore weapons in the 1860's. Outstanding examples are the Winchester, M-1, Springfield, and Enfield.

Robot bomb. An early type of guided missile developed by both sides in the European theater late in World War II (1939-1945), a small drone, or pilotless airplane, loaded with high explosives and sent on a descending course toward its target. The best known is the jet-powered Nazi V-1 (Vergeltungswaffe Eins), used against England in 1944.

Rocket. A self-propelled airborne missile, powered by the rearward thrust of gases from burning either solid or liquid fuel, invented by the Chinese about 1000, developed in Europe in the sixteenth century, and made practical for warfare by Sir William Congreve (1772-1828). It was developed into a major element of modern warfare by Konstantin Eduardovich Tsiolkovsky (1857-1935), Robert Hutchings Goddard (1882-1945), and Wernher von Braun (1912-1977). The first important military rocket was the German V-2 of World War II (1939-1945).

Rocket launcher. Developed by all sides during World War I (1914-1918), any device designed to make small rockets more portable, versatile, and mobile as artillery ammunition. In the form of a mortar or recoilless rifle, a rocket launcher and its ammunition can be mounted on a tank, jeep, or gun carriage, or carried by one or two infantrymen, who fire it either handheld or from a bipod or tripod mount.

Rubber bullet. Also called a baton round, a large-caliber antimob projectile, typically 37-millimeter, developed by the British in the 1960's and designed to stun and intimidate rather than kill, although it can kill if fired at close range. The same specialized weapons that fire it can also fire canisters of tear gas, smoke screen, and other antiriot ammunition.

Sa. A subunit of the ancient Egyptian army that consisted of between 200 and 250 soldiers. Each fought under a different standard in New Kingdom Egypt (sixteenth-fourteenth dynasties, 1570-1070 B.C.E.).

Saber. A long slashing sword invented in Europe in the eighth century. Used in most wars since then, it achieved its greatest prominence as a cavalry weapon in the nineteenth century. Usually curved with a blade-length single edge on the convex side, it could also be edged a few inches down from the point on the concave side for back-slashing.

Sai. A Japanese three-pronged weapon, a long dagger. Often it was attached to a long pole, which in some ways made it similar to the European trident. It was effective against cavalry.

Samurai sword. A traditional weapon of the feudal Japanese warrior class who followed the military religion of bushidō. This high-quality, gently curved, single-edged, two-handed, long sword features a small guard, long handle, and elaborate workmanship. Known in Japan as a daisho, no-dachi, tachi, or katana, depending on length and style, its standard design was established in the early ninth century by the great swordsmith Yasutsuna.

Sax. Also called a scramasax, a long dagger or short, straight, iron sword of the Northern European tribes in the Dark Ages.

Scimitar. A traditional saber of Islamic nations, developed prior to the Crusades, characterized by a long, thin, single-edged, crescent-shaped blade. It was made from Damascus steel, which was prepared at a very low temperature. Varieties include the Persian shamshir, the Turkish kilij, and the Arab saif.

Scud missile. A Soviet tactical nuclear or high-explosive missile, liquid-fueled, relatively short-ranged, and equipped with an inertial guidance system. Scuds with nonnuclear warheads were used ineffectively against Israel by Iraq in the 1991 Persian Gulf War.

Section. A subunit of a platoon in the British army. At full strength, it consists of between 7 and 10 men, serving under the command of a noncommissioned officer. There are generally three sections in a platoon.

Semiautomatic firearm. Any firearm that loads automatically but fires only one shot for each squeeze of the trigger. Mechanically, it is midway between a repeating rifle and a fully automatic weapon. The earliest was the 1893 Borchardt pistol.

Shell. Any cannon-fired projectile filled with explosive, typically designed to explode at a given point in its flight or upon impact. The earliest artillery shells, in the fifteenth century, were hollow iron spheres filled with gunpowder and fitted with fuses. Besides varieties of gunpowder or black powder, common explosive shell fillings include picric acid, ammonium picrate, TNT (trinitrotoluene), amatol, RDX (cyclo-1,3,5-trimethylene-2,4,6-trinitramine), and PETN (pentaerythitol tetranitrate).

Ship of the line. A large three-masted, square-rigged, sailing warship with at least two and usually three fully armed gun decks, carrying between 64 and 140 guns, so called either because it was powerful enough to hold the line of battle or because, with sister ships fore and aft, they formed an impregnable line. Developed by the British in the seventeenth century, it was the mainstay of naval power in general and the British navy in particular for the next two hundred years, superseded only by ironclad and motorized vessels.

Shrapnel. An antipersonnel explosive shell invented in the 1790's by British artillery officer Henry Shrapnel (1761-1842), consisting of a case of small shot with a fuse designed to detonate over the heads of enemy soldiers. The term also loosely refers to any small airborne metal fragments or debris from an explosion.

Siege artillery. Class of large weapons, originally only mechanical instruments such as catapults and trebuchets, but later also explosion-powered weapons such as mortars and other large firearms, employed during sieges to breach walls, destroy defensive works, and keep besieged garrisons confined.

Siege tower. A tall, shielded platform that could be wheeled up to a besieged wall for archers inside the platform to shoot down on defenders. Because they were so vulnerable to fire, siege towers were covered with water-soaked hides or metal plates. In a famous incident during the Siege of Acre (1191) by King Richard I of England (1157-1199) in the Third Crusade, the Muslim defenders first saturated a huge copper-plated Christian siege tower with a flammable liquid, then set it afire with a burning log hurled from within the fortress by a trebuchet.

Sling. Invented in the Stone Age and existing in myriad forms ever since, a simple flexible or elastic device for extending the range and velocity of hurled objects. The basic weapon is just a small pouch in the middle of a thong. The warrior places a stone in the pouch, grabs both ends of the thong, whirls the sling, and releases one end at the optimal moment, as David did in his famous encounter with Goliath in 1 Samuel 17. Slings are sometimes attached to certain kinds of catapults, such as the trebuchet.

Sloop of war. A single-masted, sailing, wooden warship, rigged fore and aft with a lone jib, carrying between ten and twenty-eight guns on a single deck. Sometimes called a corvette, a ship of this class could also have a small foremast, and if so, it could be square-rigged. Developed by the British in the late seventeenth and early eighteenth centuries, it was a staple of naval warfare until the middle of the nineteenth century.

Smokeless powder. Several attempts were made in the mid-nineteenth century to find an explosive that would burn more completely, produce less smoke, and thus be a more effective propellant for firearms than gunpowder. Prussian major Johann Schultze offered a prototype in 1864, but it burned too quickly, violently, and uncontrollably. The first successful smokeless powder was powder B, developed in France in 1884. The French produced the first smokeless powder cartridge in 1886. Other successful smokeless powders include ballistite and cordite. Such powders are either single-base, consisting of mostly nitrocellulose or guncotton, or double-base, consisting of nitrocellulose or guncotton and nitroglycerin. Conventional munitions typically use double-base powder.

Snaphance. Invented in Europe, perhaps by the Dutch, sometime between 1550 and 1570, a major technological advance in muzzle-loading firearm ignition mechanisms. When the trigger is pulled, the powder-pan cover swings up and the hammer swings down so that, when the two collide, sparks are produced which, as the hammer continues down into the pan, ignite the priming powder and fire the weapon. The snaphance achieved great popularity in the seventeenth century and made the flintlock possible.

Snickersnee. From two Dutch words meaning "thrust" and "cut," a large knife or short, saberlike sword used in Europe in the eighteenth century for both thrusting and cutting. The term has also become generic for any swordplay.

Spatha. An ancient Roman sword with a broad blade for slashing. Longer than the gladius, it was used by both infantry and cavalry in the last centuries of the Roman Empire.

Spear. Any long, pointed shaft for either thrusting or throwing. In prehistoric times it was first just a sharp stick, but later in the Stone Age hunters and warriors added sharp heads of stone, bone, teeth, or ivory. As knowledge of metallurgy grew, so did the sophistication and keenness of spearheads. By the Renaissance, European spears were highly specialized, some involving the functions of the ax or sword as well as the spear. By the twentieth century, most spears were only ceremonial.

Spetum. Type of pole arm evolved from the trident. In the middle of the warhead was a langdebeve (French langue-de-bœuf) spear point and at the sides were a symmetrical pair of shorter pointed blades, each with one or more bill hooks on the outer edge. A very versatile weapon for both thrusting and slashing, it combined the best features of the partisan, the guisarme, and the bill.

Squadron. A unit from the (British) Royal Armoured Corps, the Royal Engineers, the Royal Corps of Signals, or the Army Air Corps. At full strength, it consisted of between 50 and 100 men, often further divided into troops, sections, or flights. After 1882, in the United States, cavalry were divided into squadrons; before then there were cavalry battalions.

Star shell. A nineteenth century artillery projectile that explodes in midair, optimally at the high point of its arc, releasing a bright display of sparks, either to illuminate a target or to signal friendly forces. Used during the British night attack on Fort McHenry on September 13, 1814, these shells were immortalized by Francis Scott Key (1779-1843) in "The Star-Spangled Banner" as "the bombs bursting in air."

Stave. A peasant weapon of the Middle Ages, especially in England, where it evolved from the walking stick into a long club and became the standard defense for pedestrian travelers as well as a popular infantry weapon. The toughest kind of stave is the quarterstaff.

Stealth bomber. The American B-2 Spirit bomber, developed in the 1980's as part of President Ronald Reagan's Strategic Defense Initiative (SDI), characterized by its unique bat-wing appearance and its ability to avoid detection by enemy radar. Even though it first flew in 1988, it was not flown in the 1991 Persian Gulf War because it was not capable until 1996 of delivering nonnuclear bombs. It flew against Serbia during the Kosovo crisis of 1999.

Sten gun. A British 9-millimeter light, simple, inexpensive submachine gun invented in 1940 by Major Reginald Vernon Sheppard and Harold John Turpin. The name comes from the "S" in Sheppard, the "T" in Turpin, and the "En" in either Enfield Small Arms Company or England. Versatile, effective, and often having a collapsible stock, nearly four million Sten guns were manufactured during World War II (1939-1945). American soldiers in the European theater, equipped with more sophisticated weapons, called it the Stench gun.

Stiletto. A thin, symmetrical, Renaissance Italian dagger with a round, square, or triangular blade and no edge, used only for stabbing. Also called a stylet, some round-hilted varieties were used by infantrymen as plug bayonets. A highly specialized stiletto, the fusetto, had a slender, graduated, cone-shaped or isosceles-shaped blade for early artillerymen to gauge the bore, clean the vent, and puncture the powder bags of muzzle-loading cannons.

Stones. Always available, and with deadly power obvious even to the most prehistoric of our hominid ancestors, small, jagged rocks picked off the ground and hurled are the most ancient of all weapons. Still in prehistoric times, early humans learned to chip stones into sharper hand weapons, rudimentary knives, and later arrowheads, spearheads, and ax-heads. Naturally smooth or artificially smoothed stones became ammunition for slings.

Submachine gun. A fully automatic personal firearm, small and light enough to be fired by a single individual without support, developed between the world wars, in particular by John Taliaferro Thompson (1860-1940), inventor of the most famous submachine gun, the "tommy gun." The "sub-" prefix refers only to size and weight, not to either the mechanism or the degree of automatic operation.

Submarine. An undersea naval craft. David Bushnell (1742-1824) used a one-man submarine, the *Turtle*, in the American Revolution (1775-1783). A Confederate nine-man, hand-cranked submarine, the CSS *Hunley*, sank the USS *Housatonic*, and itself, in 1864. The first practical motorized submarines were developed in the United States by John Philip Holland (1840-1914). During World War I (1914-1918), the deadliness of the German U-Boat wolf packs proved submarines an indispensable aspect of effective naval warfare. The first nuclear submarine, the USS *Nautilus*, was launched in 1954. Torpedoes are the standard armament of submarines, but since the Cold War (1945-1991) many have also carried missiles.

Surface-to-air missile (SAM). A small, defensive, guided missile launched from a usually mobile ground station toward an airborne target. As either an antimissile missile or an antiaircraft weapon, it can be equipped with a small nuclear warhead. The smallest have a range of about 6 miles (10 kilometers) and can be fired by one soldier from a shoulder-held recoilless launcher. The largest have a range of about 40 miles (65 kilometers) and are launched from a semipermanent launch vehicle.

Sword. Any edged weapon with a long blade and usually a sharp point. Invented in the Near East about 6000 B.C.E., it may have been one of the earliest things that humans learned to make out of metal, though its technology did not become practical until the Iron Age, about 1000 B.C.E. Some varieties of sword, such as the rapier, are mainly for thrusting; others, such as the saber, mainly for slashing; and a few, such as the cutlass, are dual-purpose. A basic weapon in nearly every war until the end of the nineteenth century, the sword since then has been used for mainly ceremonial purposes.

Tae kwon do. *See* Karate.

Tagma (*pl.* tagamata). A tactical unit in the Byzantine army consisting of about 300 soldiers. Ten tagmata formed a meros.

Tank. A motorized, fully armored attack vehicle running on self-contained tracks, usually with guns mounted in a revolving turret, invented by the British in 1915 and first used in battle at Flers-Courcelette on September 15, 1916. The Allies used nearly five hundred tanks at Cambrai in November, 1916. The Germans were slower to recognize the value of this new technology, and the first tank-versus-tank battle occurred at Villers-Bretonneux on April 24, 1918. Early in World War II (1939-1945), German Panzers dominated, and it was the Allies' turn to play catch-up, which the Americans did very well with the Sherman tank. Tanks were a mainstay of ground warfare throughout the twentieth century.

Tear gas. Any solid, liquid, or gaseous substance that irritates the mucous membranes when dispersed. Although used primarily in riot control rather than in military operations, it is also useful as a nonlethal system of disabling enemy combatants. As a result it is often used in hostage situations.

Thermonuclear device. Any bomb that relies upon the principle of the fusion of atoms of low atomic weight. At the dawn of the twenty-first century, they were the most powerful bombs yet produced. To fuse the nucleus of one atom with another requires tremendous heat as a trigger and produces tremendous heat when accomplished. Since the early 1950's, these bombs have been extensively tested, manufactured, deployed, and stockpiled, although never used in warfare.

Time bomb. Any explosive device with a time-delay fuse set to detonate at an exact, predetermined time and usually hidden in or near its target. Invented in the nineteenth century, it comes in three types, classified according to their means of detonation: burning-fuse, the most primitive, first made practical in 1831 by the British; clockwork-fuse, developed in the twentieth century and used extensively in World War II (1939-1945); and chemical-reaction-fuse, the most sophisticated, invented by an Anglo-American team in World War II and common among demolition engineers, terrorists, and saboteurs ever since.

TNT (trinitrotoluene). A high explosive first synthesized in the 1860's but not used as a military explosive until the German armed forces adopted it in 1902 and not extensively used in warfare until World War I (1914-1918). Ideal military explosives are powerful, are nonreactive, are safe to handle, have a long storage life in any climate, and can detonate only under specific conditions. TNT meets all these criteria. The power of nuclear bombs is measured by kiloton, a unit equal to 1,000 tons of TNT, or by megaton, equal to 1 million tons of TNT.

Toledo. A finely tempered, very sharp, elegant steel sword produced in Toledo, Spain. Swords manufactured in this Spanish city have had the reputation for high quality since perhaps as early as the first century B.C.E. They have been commonly called Toledos since the sixteenth century.

Tomahawk. A small, light ax or hatchet invented in pre-Columbian times, probably by the Algonquins, but carried by most Eastern North American native tribes. Its head was originally stone, but metal after the seventeenth century. It could be either wielded as a hand weapon or thrown. Its name was adopted for one of the best-known cruise missiles.

Torpedo. A naval waterborne antiship missile, either guided or not, launched from a ship, submarine, patrol-torpedo boat, or aircraft, and driven by a propeller. The first practical torpedo, developed by British engineer Robert Whitehead (1823-1905), was invented in Britain in 1866. Earlier, for example in the American Civil War (1861-1865), the word referred to antiship mines. The first extensive use of true torpedoes in war was by the German submarines, U-boats, in World War I (1914-1918). Among the explosives commonly used in torpedo warheads is torpex, a mixture of 42 percent RDX (cyclo-1,3,5-trimethylene-2,4,6-trinitramine), 40 percent TNT (trinitrotoluene), 18 percent aluminum powder, and a tiny bit of wax, developed by the British during World War II (1939-1945).

Tracer bullet. Used in the nineteenth century but developed comprehensively in the twentieth, any projectile, usually from a machine gun and often for antiaircraft fire, either containing or coated with chemicals to produce a visible trail of luminous smoke, especially useful at night to verify the gunner's aim. A variant is the spotter bullet, which contains chemicals to provide a visible flash upon impact. Tracers or spotters can also be armor-piercing or incendiary.

Trebuchet. The largest, most efficient, and most effective of medieval catapults, developed in the thirteenth century and used exclusively as a siege engine. Essentially a first-class lever whose effort was about 20,000 pounds (9,000 kilograms) of rocks in a bucket on the short arm, whose load was a boulder of about 300 pounds (140 kilograms) at the end of the long arm, and whose fulcrum was a massive wooden frame, it had a range of several hundred yards at a medium to high trajectory. Often the throwing arm incorporated a sling to increase the range and velocity of the projectile. As the short arm was very short and the long arm could be up to 50 feet (15 meters), the machine had to be cocked with a complex system of pulleys.

Trident. The ancestor of most pole arms except the pike, evolving from the agricultural pitchfork and at first indistinguishable from it. Intended only for thrusting, its three points created a broad warhead that increased the likelihood of wounding the enemy. It was used in most ancient and medieval wars but is best known as a weapon of Roman gladiators. A later, more sophisticated version is the spetum.

Trireme. A galley with three banks of oars. Developed from the bireme for speed and power around 650 B.C.E. and reaching its height of development during the fifth century B.C.E., it had an overall length between 115 and 130 feet (35-40 meters), a crew of about 170, a draft of only 3 feet (1 meter), and a top oared speed between 9 and 11 knots per hour. Each higher bank of oars was mounted on outrigger fulcrums farther abeam than the next lower bank. Because rowing required precise timing by all crew members, only carefully trained freemen, not slaves, were used, to ensure high morale. By 500 B.C.E., the trireme dominated the Mediterranean.

Troop. A subunit of a cavalry squadron or an artillery battery in the British army roughly comparable to a platoon in the infantry. More recently, when used in the plural form, the term has been popularly used, coupled with a number, to refer to individual soldiers (for example, "25,000 troops" means the same number of soldiers).

Tulwar. A traditional saber of India, characterized by a large, disk-shaped pommel, a knobbed crosspiece at the guard, and a broad, deeply curved blade sharpened along the length of the convex edge. Some varieties had knuckle guards, and many had elaborately engraved or inlaid blades.

Tumen (*tuman* in Arabic). Originally a geographical division of the Mongol Empire that was organized in such a manner as to provide the Mongol ruler with 10,000 soldiers. Later, the subunit of a Mongol army that had 10,000 soldiers in it. This unit was further divided into the hazara or minghan. The term is still used in the Turkish army to denote a unit of between 6,000 and 10,000 soldiers.

Vanguard. The soldiers who are in a military tactical formation that serves in the front of any army. There is no prescribed number of soldiers that may serve in any vanguard action.

Voulge. A type of pole arm whose head consists of a very large, broad single-edged ax blade with small, sharp spikes or hooks at the top and back. One of the earliest pole arms, it evolved from the ancient pruning hook, a farm tool. The Lochaber ax, the jeddart ax, and the Lucerne hammer all evolved from it.

War hammer. A medieval, especially late medieval, sophisticated, metal-headed, European club, sometimes called a battle-hammer, either a short-handled hand weapon or a pole arm, designed with both a pick head to break armor and a blunt head to cause concussions, trauma, or fractures inside the armor without breaking it.

Wheel lock. A complex muzzle-loading firearm ignition mechanism, invented around 1500. When the trigger was pressed, a wheel turned, opening the pan, creating sparks from friction with iron pyrites, and igniting the powder. It was superseded by the snaphance in the mid-sixteenth century.

Whizbang. A British trench soldiers' onomatopoeic name for a German high-velocity, low-trajectory artillery shell in World War I (1914-1918), usually 88-millimeter. The soldiers believed that if they could hear the "whiz," then the "bang" would not get them.

Xiquipilli. A unit within the Aztec army that consisted of around 8,000 soldiers.

Yataghan. A Turkish short saber without a cross-piece or hand guard. The blade is nearly straight, but in the shape of an S-curve with the edge concave near the hilt and convex near the point.

Yeomanry. During the eighteenth century, volunteer cavalry units in the British army, generally made up of yeomen, freeholders of land, or tenant farmers. Subsequently it became a term for some cavalry units in the British army, and later still for units in the Royal Armoured Corps.

Yuz bashi. A division in the Mongol army, often also called a yaghun, consisting of about 100 soldiers. Ten yuz bashi constituted a ming bashi.

Zeppelin. A rigid airship or dirigible, a steerable lighter-than-air aircraft, as opposed to the blimp, which is nonrigid, and the balloon, which is rudderless. Invented in 1900 by German Count Ferdinand Graf von Zeppelin (1838-1917), it was originally intended for civilian passenger service and performed that function until the *Hindenburg* disaster in Lakehurst, New Jersey, on May 6, 1937. The Germans bombed England by zeppelin during World War I (1914-1918) but abandoned that practice because airships are difficult to defend.

Eric v.d. Luft, updated by Justin Corfield

MILITARY THEORISTS

Although weaponry has changed substantially, some of the fundamental military tactics remain the same. Essentially generals have learned to choose their own battlefield, if possible, and to disengage if they face inevitable defeat. Over history, various generals have tried to adapt these and other tactics, and theoreticians have refought battles to identify the causes of victory and defeat, as well as plan future strategies. The ancient Daoist general Sunzi wrote the oldest surviving manual on military tactics, and the books by Julius Caesar are the oldest surviving accounts of battles by a commander. The works of Caesar and later Carl von Clausewitz were heavily studied in Europe, and many of the recommendations by all three are still followed, albeit with changes to incorporate new technologies, such as cannons, guns, machine guns, tanks, and aircraft.

Abd el-Krim (Moroccan, 1880-1963): Abd el-Krim led the Rif Revolt against the French and the Spanish, managing to wage an effective guerrilla war against two major European powers with very little outside help.

Afonso de Albuquerque (Portuguese, 1453-1515): Albuquerque employed a system of strategically placed forts to expand Portuguese control of the trade route from the Red Sea along the coasts of India and Indonesia to Macao on the Chinese coast. Eventually Portuguese control was undermined by rival European powers and the Ottoman Empire.

Alexander the Great (Macedonian, 356-323 B.C.E.): Perhaps history's most famous conqueror, Alexander used a well-disciplined army inherited from his father, Philip II (382-336 B.C.E.), to dismantle the vast Persian Empire. Eventually his overreaching exhausted both his troops and himself; he died in Babylon returning from India. Alexander proved that smaller, better-trained armies with motivated troops could consistently defeat larger, more unwieldy forces. When asked to whom he would bequeath his empire, he replied simply to the strongest.

Alfred the Great (Anglo-Saxon, 849-899): The Anglo-Saxon king of Wessex defeated the Vikings on several occasions and established the English navy, which became the Royal Navy, later dominating much of the world from the eigh-

teenth to the early twentieth centuries. He is quoted as saying, "A King's raw materials and instruments of rule are a well-peopled land, and he must have men of prayer, men of war, and men of work."

Ardant du Picq, Charles Jean Jacques Joseph (French, 1821-1870): Killed during the Franco-Prussian War (1870-1871), Ardant du Picq is known for his posthumous work *Études sur le combat: Combat antique et combat moderne* (1880; *Battle Studies: Ancient and Modern Battle*, 1914), which stressed the importance of morale in war. He believed that officers must instill confidence in their troops, especially given the impersonal nature of the modern battlefield. In his book, he stated, "Man does not enter battle to fight, but for victory. He does everything he can to avoid the first and obtain the second."

Ashurnasirpal II (Assyrian, c. 915-859 B.C.E.): As creator of the Neo-Assyrian Empire, Ashurnasirpal established the traditions of military excellence and unrelenting cruelty that made Assyria a dominant and feared power from the Euphrates Valley to the Mediterranean. On one of his inscriptions, he exhorted his armies, "If it pleases, kill! If it pleases you, spare! If it pleases you, do what you will!"

Attila (Hunnic, 406?-453): By uniting all the Hunnic tribes from the northern Caucasus to the upper Danube, Attila led his armies on a swath of conquest that took them to the gates of Rome itself. Attila's tactics relied on the speed, skill, and savagery of his troops, as well as the terror they inspired.

Augustus (Roman, 63 B.C.E.-14 C.E.): After defeating Marc Antony at the great Battle of Actium, as first emperor of Rome, following the loss of three legions to German forces in the Teutoburg Forest in 9 C.E., Augustus fixed the boundaries of the Roman Empire along strong defensive lines. Gaius Suetonius Tranquillus, in *De vita Caesarum* (c. 120 C.E.; *History of the Twelve Caesars*, 1606), notes that, obviously fearing mutiny, "he never kept more than three companies on duty at Rome, and even these had no permanent camp, but were billeted in various City lodging houses."

Bayinnaung (Burmese, r. 1551-1581): As king of Burma (now known as Myanmar), Bayinnaung unified the country and made it the most powerful in Southeast Asia, dominating its neighbors and imposing Buddhism throughout the region.

Belisarius (Byzantine, c. 500-565): The greatest of Byzantine generals, Belisarius served on all imperial frontiers as well as crushing the Nika Uprising (532) that nearly toppled the emperor Justinian I (483-565). Belisarius wrested North Africa from the Vandals, conquered Sicily, and expelled the Ostrogoths from southern Italy—victories achieved with probably never more than about 18,000 troops at any one time. In one speech, he is quoted as saying, "Ours is a real enemy in the field; we march to a battle, and not to a review."

Ben Boulaid, Mustapha (Algerian, 1917-1956): Benboulaid served in the French army and then used French tactics against the French during the Algerian War of Independence, coordinating many attacks on that colonial power until his death. The French would withdraw from Algeria four years later.

Bolívar, Simón (Colombian, 1783-1830): Bolívar led the South American independence movement against the Spanish, which saw the formation of Gran Colombia and later the independent nations of Venezuela, Colombia, Ecuador, Peru, Bolivia, and Panama. He is reported to have said, "The army is a sack with no bottom."

Braun, Wernher von (German American, 1912-1977): A pioneer in German rocketry and a visionary of space flight, von Braun helped develop the German rocket program during World War II, which included the V-2, the first large military rocket. After the war he was a key member of the American space program.

Briggs, Sir Harold (British, 1894-1952): In 1950, Briggs devised the plan that bears his name, the Briggs Plan, which allowed the British to win the Malayan Emergency by the establishment of so-called new villages. The success led to the Strategic Hamlets program in South Vietnam, which was a dismal failure.

Bywater, Hector (British, 1884-1940): As a spy in World War I and then as a British diplomat, Bywater recognized the importance of the emerging power of Japan, warning that the Japanese navy could dominate the Pacific during a European war. Most British experts ignored his book *The Great Pacific War* (1925), which, however, was avidly read by the Japanese. In 1920, Maurice Prendergast (who illustrated R. H. Gibson's 1931 *The German Submarine War, 1914-1918*) summed up Bywater's ideas: "Naval policies still appeared to revolve, but in a dull and unnatural manner, round that vacuum where once the German Fleet had existed. The magnetic pole of maritime affairs had not vanished with German sea power; it had only altered its position and required re-discovery."

Cabral, Amilcar (Cape Verdean, 1921-1973): He helped plan the defeat of the Portuguese by training people in Guinea-Bissau against the colonial power, using a trade-and-barter system in parts of the country his forces had taken, and using political ideology as well as nationalism to hold together his supporters.

Caesar, Julius (Roman, 100-44 B.C.E.): A nephew of the Roman general Marius, Julius Caesar rose rapidly in public life and in 60 B.C.E. was elected consul. The following year he was named governor of Cisalpine and Transalpine Gaul and seized the opportunity to conquer the whole of Gaul. Caesar next marched into Italy, precipitating a civil war with his rival, Pompey the Great (106-48 B.C.E.).

In a whirlwind campaign, Caesar pushed Pompey out of Italy, captured Spain, and defeated Pompey at Pharsalus (48 B.C.E.). Master of the Roman world, Caesar was preparing for a campaign against the Parthian Empire when he was assassinated. He was bold to the point of rashness, but his brilliant mind and swift reactions made him master of any battlefield. He recorded his Gallic and civil war campaigns in his *Commentarii de Bello Gallico* (52-51 B.C.E.) and *Commentarii de Bello Civili* (45 B.C.E.), collectively translated as *Commentaries* (1609). Plutarch quotes Caesar as telling his men during the civil war, when sailing from Italy to modern-day Albania, "Go ahead my friends. Be bold and fear nothing. You have Caesar and Caesar's fortune with you in your boat."

Castro, Fidel (Cuban, born 1926): As leader of the Cuban revolutionaries, he not only led his insurgents to victory in Cuba against the Batista government but also proved to be an inspiration to many other Latin American revolutionaries. After his rise to power in Cuba, he supported revolution elsewhere in the world, notably in Angola. A keen reader, he wrote, "When I read the work of a famous author, the history of a people, the doctrine of a thinker, the theories of an economist or the theses of a social reformer, I am filled with the desire to know everything that all authors have written, the doctrines of all philosophers, the treatises of all economists, and the theses of all apostles."

Charlemagne (Frankish, 742-814): King of the Franks and, after 800, Holy Roman Emperor, Charlemagne returned a strategic vision to European warfare. Thanks to an effective system of communications with his subordinate commanders, Charlemagne directed independent campaigns that established a large, relatively stable state in Western Europe.

Chin Peng (Malayan, born 1924): As the leader of the Malayan Communist Party, Chin Peng succeeded in hit-and-run tactics based on heavy use of sympathizers, which nearly caused him to win the Malayan Emergency despite being outnumbered fifty to one. In his memoirs, *My Side of History* (2003), he summed up his strategy: "Our hit-and-run tactics, though more often than not devoid of centralized control, had been successful to the point that public morale on the enemy side had clearly deteriorated. In order to maintain this trend we resolved to hit the British even harder with the specific aim of racking up a higher killing rate among government security forces."

Churchill, John, first duke of Marlborough (English, 1650-1722): During the War of the Spanish Succession (1701-1714), Marlborough made effective use of the allied forces through a blend of battlefield brilliance, logistical thoroughness, and diplomatic skills.

Churchill, Winston S. (British, 1874-1965): A British soldier and politician who planned the ill-fated Gallipoli operation in 1915, Churchill displayed skill and tenacity during World War II, as well as doggedness, which contributed to Britain's triumph in 1945. Although some of his speeches are well known, his determination was best summed up by this famous quotation: "[W]e shall fight on the beaches, we shall fight on the landing grounds, we shall fight in the fields and in the streets, we shall fight in the hills; we shall never surrender...."

Clausewitz, Carl von (German, 1780-1831): Although he served as general in the Prussian army and fought against Napoleon in the Russian campaign of 1812, Clausewitz made his most important contribution when he wrote the posthumously published book *Vom Kriege* (1832-1834; *On War*, 1873). His representation of war as an instrument of the state to coerce an enemy into desired action is often paraphrased as "the continuation of politics by other means." Warfare, therefore, should be guided by political leaders who understand it. Political leaders and generals alike must also recognize what is known as the "Clausewitzian trinity" of violence, chance, and reason, represented in war respectively by the people, the military, and the government. Finally, war brings uncertainty—the "fog of war" and "friction"—in the context of which military decisions must be made and executed. Clausewitz thought commanders should reduce uncertainty, noting that courage and self-confidence are absolutely essential, especially for the general who seeks the most effective way to victory, that of destroying the enemy army in a single, decisive battle. Initially Clausewitz was regarded as a lesser military thinker, subordinate to his near-contemporary Antoine-Henri Jomini, and some have faulted him for not presenting specific rules or principles for waging war. Although historical and technological changes have made parts of his work less relevant today, Clausewitz remains one of the few essential military theorists in the history of warfare.

Colt, Samuel (American, 1814-1862): Colt invented the revolver that continues to bear his name, a pistol with a rotating cylinder holding six bullets that could all be fired before reloading. It proved a success in the Mexican War (1846-1848), and by 1855 Colt had built the world's largest private gun-making facility in Hartford, Connecticut, where he improved mass manufacturing through the use of assembly lines and interchangeable parts.

Crazy Horse (Native American, 1842?-1877): Chief of the Oglala Sioux, Crazy Horse joined with Sitting Bull (1831-1890) to use mobile warfare to destroy the forces under General George A. Custer (1839-1870) at the Battle of the Little Bighorn (1876). At that battle he rallied his warriors before battle, telling them, "Come on, it is a good day to die!"

Cromwell, Oliver (English, 1599-1658): The eventual commander of the Parliamentarian forces during the English Civil War, Cromwell recognized the importance of training and of professional soldiers through the creation of the New Model Army. He was also to establish an English Republic. After he dissolved the Parliament in 1649, a Presbyterian cleric said to him, "'Tis against the will of the nation: there will be nine in ten against you," to which Cromwell replied, "But what if I should disarm the nine, and put a sword in the tenth man's hand?"

Cyrus the Great (Persian, c. 601 to 590-530 B.C.E.): Founder of the Persian Empire, Cyrus was the world's first great cavalry commander and an expert at siege warfare. His conquests stretched from modern Turkey to the Persian Gulf, and the Greek writer Xenophon quoted him as telling his soldiers, "Remember my last saying: show kind-

ness to your friends, and then shall you have it in your power to chastise your enemies."

Darius the Great (Persian, 550-486 B.C.E.): Darius established a strong central government in Persia with excellent roads and a powerful army. He extended the empire into northern India and conquered Thrace and Macedonia in Europe and Libya in Africa. Around 500 B.C.E., Ionian Greeks revolted, beginning the Greco-Persian Wars (499-448 B.C.E.). Darius died before he could mount his invasion of the Greek mainland.

Dayan, Moshe (Israeli, 1915-1981): As Israel's minister of defense, Dayan's rapid strike at his country's opponents led to victory in the Six-Day War in 1967. In an interview with the British newspaper *The Observer* in 1972, he said, "War is the most exciting and dramatic thing in life. In fighting to the death you feel terribly relaxed when you manage to come through."

Douhet, Giulio (Italian, 1869-1930): Originally an artillery officer, Douhet commanded Italy's Aeronautical Battalion from 1912 to 1915 and became convinced of the superiority of airpower. Like the American William "Billy" Mitchell, Douhet argued with such vehemence that he was court-martialed and forced into retirement. However, Italy's poor performance in World War I brought about his recall. Douhet's *Il dominio dell'aria* (1921; *The Command of the Air*, 1921) argued for an independent air force capable of strategic bombing. In his book, he wrote, "Victory smiles upon those who anticipate the changes in the character of war, not those who wait to adapt themselves after they occur."

Drake, Francis (English, c. 1540-1596): Drake combined the roles of pirate, privateer, and admiral in England's struggle against Spain. He contributed to the tactics of fast, hard-hitting raids on Spanish ports and shipping. His concentration of the English fleet in the western entrance to the English Channel was a key factor in the defeat of the Armada in 1588. Although the most famous statement ascribed to him was made when he was playing bowls and said of the Spanish Armada, "There is time enough to finish the game and beat the Spaniards too," his 1587 letter to Lord Walshingham is more prescient: "There must be a beginning of any great matter, but the continuing unto the end until it be thoroughly finished yields the true glory."

Eisenhower, Dwight D. (American, 1890-1969): Eisenhower oversaw the D day Operation in June, 1944, one of the best-planned and -executed military operations and one of the most difficult yet successful seaborne invasions during World War II. In an address in London in June, 1945, he said, "Humility must always be the portion of any man who receives acclaim earned in the blood of his followers and the sacrifices of his friends."

Epaminondas (Greek, c. 410-362 B.C.E.): Commander of the Theban army at the Battle of Leuctra (371 B.C.E.), Epaminondas defeated a much larger Spartan force by concentrating his forces on his left wing and overwhelming the enemy's right. This use of the "oblique order" was an important development in phalanx warfare. He described the battlefield as "the dance floor of Aries," referring to the god of war.

Eugène of Savoy (French, 1663-1736): Although French-born, Eugène was rejected by King Louis XIV (1638-1715) and became instead an Austrian general and statesman. He was a master of coalition warfare and cooperated successfully with the duke of Marlborough in victories over the French at Blenheim (1704), Oudenarde (1708), and Malplaquet (1709). He wrote, "I never saw better horses, better clothes, finer belts and accoutrements; but money, which you do not want in England, will buy fine clothes and horses, but it cannot buy the lively air I see in every one of these troopers."

Fabius (Roman, c. 275-203 B.C.E.): Called to defend Rome during Hannibal's invasion of Italy, Fabius was nicknamed "the Delayer" for his refusal to meet his Carthaginian opponent in open battle. Instead, he wore down his foes by harassing them in their movements and denying them supplies, a logistical approach to warfare that had great implications for future commanders.

Fisher, John "Jackie" (English, 1841-1920): Fisher revolutionized naval warfare with the introduction of the HMS *Dreadnought* in 1906, the first all-big-gun battleship, which began a new arms race. Fisher instituted other sweeping changes in British naval policy, including concentrating the Royal Navy in home waters for quicker mobilization against a European enemy.

Foch, Ferdinand (French, 1851-1929): A supporter of the offensive and the power of morale, Foch believed a defeat to be final only when an army lost the will to fight. In the last year of World War I, the Allies named Foch as supreme commander, and his positive attitude, along with the arrival of American troops, brought an end to the war. In *Des principes de la guerre* (1903; *The Principles of War*, 1918), he wrote, "A battle won is a battle in which one will not confess himself beaten."

Franco, Francisco (Spanish, 1892-1975): As commander of the Nationalists during the Spanish Civil War, Franco devised a system of war by attrition in which he saw his role as to destroy all opposition in areas captured before advancing any farther. He was to become the longest-serving European dictator during the twentieth century.

Frederick the Great (Prussian, 1712-1786): With the hope of promoting Prussia to great-power status, Frederick relied upon both his superb army and his ability to draw the maximum from his troops. At battles such as Leuthen (1757), he used the famous "oblique order," massing troops on one flank to achieve a decisive local superiority. Even more important was his genius at combining his arms, as at Rossbach (1757). The result was to establish the Prussian army as the most powerful in Europe, a position that remained unchallenged more than a decade after Frederick's death. In one letter, he noted, "The lifetime of one man is not sufficiently long to enable him to acquire perfect knowledge and experience; theory helps to supplement it; it provides youth with early experience and makes him skilful through the mistakes of others." In his *Die Instruktion Friedrichs des Grossen für seine Generale* (1747; *Military Instructions, Written by the King of Prussia, for the Generals of His Army*, 1762; also known as *Instructions for His Generals*, 1944), he noted that "battle is lost less through the loss of men than by discouragement."

Fuller, J. F. C. (British, 1878-1966): During World War I, Fuller planned the Battle of Cambrai (1916-1917), the first to employ tanks. As both an author and an instructor at the British Staff College, he strenuously advocated the extensive use of armor and airpower. In his book *The Reformation of War* (1923), he noted, "I have not written this book for military monks, but for civilians who pay for their alchemy and mysteries. In war there is nothing mysterious, for it is the most common-sense of all sciences."

Genghis Khan (né Temüjin; Mongol, between 1155 and 1162-1227): Genghis Khan united the Mongol tribes and organized the Mongolian army into a powerful force. After his conquests of northern China and central Asia, he established a vast empire that was peaceful, well administered, and strategically positioned. He encouraged trade and opening routes between Europe and China. Genghis Khan's military skill in battle was matched by his attention to organization and administration. His armies were highly disciplined and well supplied. Campaigns were carefully prepared using intelligence gathered by spies and scouts. His reputation and that of his army were his most powerful weapons. He is quoted as saying, "The greatest happiness is to vanquish your enemies, to chase them before you, to rob them of their wealth, to see those dear to them bathed in tears, to clasp to your bosom their wives and daughters."

Geronimo (Native American, 1829-1909): With only a handful of supporters, Geronimo managed to evade capture by the U.S. forces for decades, preventing them from taking control of the Apache lands for much of that period.

Goddard, Robert H. (American, 1882-1945): The "father of modern rocketry," Goddard developed rockets using liquid hydrogen and liquid oxygen as fuels and invented steering systems, multistage rockets, and other technologies that allowed rockets to be used in modern warfare. From 1930 until the mid-1940's, Goddard conducted much of his research in Roswell, New Mexico.

Gribeauval, Jean-Baptiste Vacquette de (French, 1715-1789): As inspector general of French artillery, Gribeauval significantly modernized that military arm. By making cannons bored instead of cast, he improved range, power, and accuracy. His cannons were smaller, lighter, and exceptionally mobile when harnessed to a new design of gun carriage.

Grotius, Hugo (Huigh de Groot; Dutch, 1583-1645): The "father of international law," Grotius developed the first systematic set of laws to govern warfare. His masterpiece, *De iure belli ac pacis libri res* (1625; *On the Law of War and Peace*, 1654), became the foundation for international law regarding the conduct of warfare.

Guderian, Heinz (German, 1888-1954): A combat officer in World War I, Guderian recognized early the value of motorized armor. His book *Achtung-Panzer! Die Entwicklung der Panzerwaffe, ihre Kampfstatik, und ihre operative Möglickeiten* (1937; *Achtung-Panzer! The Development of Armoured Forces, Their Tactics, and Operational Potential*, 1937) outlined the tactics he and other German commanders would use in World War II. He condemned aspects of the Nuremberg war crimes trials in his book *Erinnerungen eines Soldaten* (1950; *Panzer Leader*, 1952), arguing, "All the reproaches that have been leveled against the leaders of the armed forces by their countrymen and by the international courts have failed to take into consideration one very simple fact: that policy is not laid down by soldiers, but by politicians. This has always been the case and is so today."

Guevara, Che (Argentine/Cuban, 1928-1967): Guevara gained legendary status in Cuba after the victory of Fidel Castro in his Cuban Revolution. Guevara planned to extend the revolution to all of Latin America. Although this plan failed and Guevara himself was killed, he proved an inspiration to revolutionaries not only in Latin America but also throughout the world. In his book *La guerra de guerrillas* (1960; *Guerrilla Warfare*, 1961), he noted, "Guerrilla warfare incites no nuclear retaliation. It avoids the troops-cross-border criterion needed to activate our defensive treaties. For the aggressor, guerrilla warfare has none of the heavy costs of all-out warfare. It exploits the Communists' long experience in revolutionary activities.

It can be conducted in countries not contiguous to the Communist land mass. The aggressor merely finds a suitably vulnerable nation, then supplies a few catalysts."

Gustavus II Adolphus (Swedish, 1594-1632): Called the "father of modern warfare," Swedish king Gustavus II Adolphus improved infantry by mixing pikemen and musketeers in battalions. His lighter cannons introduced mobile field artillery that could support infantry on the battlefield. He also reintroduced cavalry, especially heavy cavalry, as a major element in warfare, giving it a critical role to play. Ironically, he was killed leading a cavalry charge in his victory at the Battle of Lützen (1632). His religious beliefs led him to explain in 1632, "My lord God is my armour."

Hadrian (Roman, 76-138): As Roman emperor, Hadrian helped strengthen the borders of the Roman Empire. He is most remembered for the construction of one of the most massive military structures of his time, Hadrian's Wall (c. 122-136 C.E.), in northern England.

Hannibal (Carthaginian, 247-182 B.C.E.): Hannibal was a brilliant battlefield commander, and his victory at Cannae (216 B.C.E.) remains the standard by which all battles are judged. Hannibal's contribution to military theory comes mainly from his invasion of Italy during the Second Punic War. Hannibal cast himself as a "liberator" of the Italian cities and sought to detach them from Rome. When this proved unsuccessful, his unbroken string of tactical victories proved strategically useless. In *Ab urbe condita libri* (c. 26 B.C.E.-15 C.E.; *The History of Rome*, 1600; also known as *Annals of the Roman People*), Livy quoted Hannibal as telling Scipio Africanus just before the Battle of Zama in 202 B.C.E., "It is difficult for a man to whom fortune has never proved false to reflect upon its uncertainties."

Henry V (English, 1387-1422): In his victory at Agincourt in 1415, Henry skillfully employed the long-range firepower of English archers and mobile field fortifications, consisting of sharpened stakes driven into the ground, to defeat a larger army of mounted French knights, thus undermining the basis of traditional feudal military theory.

In a play named for him, William Shakespeare has Henry heroically ordering his soldiers at Harfleur, "Once more into the breach dear friends,/ or close up the walls with our English dead."

Heraclius (Byzantine, c. 575-probably 641): Threatened along his borders, Byzantine emperor Heraclius reformed the Byzantine military and administrative system by establishing the "theme system," in which military commanders were placed in complete control of provinces, or "themes."

Hideyoshi, Toyotomi (Japanese, 1537-1598): A peasant who rose to command armies and ultimately Japan itself, Hideyoshi combined military ability, diplomacy, and political skills to unite the island. His career is an excellent example of the interrelated nature of warfare and politics.

Hitler, Adolf (German, 1889-1945): Influenced by his experience in World War I and his own racist views, Hitler believed that Germany must conquer both Western Europe, to gain security, and Eastern Europe, especially the Soviet Union, to secure *Lebensraum*, or "living room," for Germany's population. He was successful in wedding traditional military strategy to this malign political theory and in maintaining the support of the German people and military throughout most of World War II. Hitler was a supporter of new weaponry, such as the Luftwaffe's tactical bombers and fighters, the V-1 and V-2 rockets, and advanced submarines. He also encouraged innovative military techniques such as the Blitzkrieg. In a 1942 speech to the Reichstag, the German parliament, he said of World War II, "This war is one of those elemental conflicts which usher in a new millennium and which shake the world."

Jomini, Antoine-Henri de (French, 1779-1869): A French general, Jomini entered Russian service after being denied a promotion. Jomini's *Précis de l'art de la guerre* (1838; *Summary of the Art of War*, 1868) was a systematic distillation of his thoughts on military science. He emphasized the immutable principles of war and the importance of maneuvering the mass, or main portion, of an army to make it most effective. He thought the mass should be concentrated at the decisive theater of war, threatening the enemy's communications if possible; that a commander should place the mass of his entire army against a part of his opponent's forces; that the mass of the army should concentrate on the decisive point on the battlefield; and that attacks should be coordinated for maximum impact. Jomini's ideas were highly influential, especially among commanders in the American Civil War (1861-1865). In his book he wrote, "A general thoroughly instructed in the theory of war but not possessed of military coup d'oeil, coolness and skill, may make an excellent strategic plan and be entirely unable to apply the rules of tactics in the presence of an enemy. His projects will not be successfully carried out, [and] his defeat will be probable. If he is a man of character he will be able to diminish the evil results of his failure, but if he loses his wits, he will lose his army."

Juárez, Benito (Mexican, 1806-1872): As leader of the Indians and poor in Mexico, Juárez managed to wage a successful guerrilla war against the Mexican government and then against the Royalists under Emperor Maximilian.

Kangxi (K'ang-Hsi; Chinese, 1654-1722): The fourth emperor of the Qing (Ching) Dynasty (1644-1912), who ruled China from 1669 to 1722, Kangxi consolidated Manchu power and legitimized Manchu rule in China. He defended his realm against incursions from the Russians to the north, seized the island of Taiwan, and overcame a serious internal revolt. In these efforts he made great use of Western technology, particularly cartography and cannons.

Khair ed-Dīn (Ottoman, 1483-1546): Creator of the Ottoman navy, Khair ed-Dīn was also known as Barbarossa because of his red beard. In 1533 Turkish sultan Süleyman I the Magnificent (1494/1495-1566) ordered him to reorganize the imperial navy, a task he accomplished with speed and ability. The new galleys were used in raids on Christendom and in the conquest of Tunis and Nice in France. Khair ed-Dīn used galleys to evacuate the Spanish Moors from Spain in 1533, a task of great logistic complexity. He noted, "He who rules on the sea will very shortly rule on the land also."

Krupp family (German, 1587-1968): The Krupp family was for four centuries the premier weapons manufacturer in Germany and perhaps the world. Alfred Krupp (1812-1887) perfected techniques to manufacture modern weapons and was known as "the cannon king." Krupp guns contributed to Prussia's victory in the Franco-Prussian War (1870-1871) and were important to Germany's efforts in World War I. The Krupp family supported Adolf Hitler, and a second Alfred Krupp helped devise the 88-millimeter gun, one of the most deadly artillery weapons of World War II. In 1968, following financial reverses, the Krupp family left the armaments business.

Lawrence, T. E. (British, 1888-1935): Part military adviser, part visionary, Lawrence directed operations of Arab irregular forces during World War I desert campaigns in 1917 and 1918 and helped the Arabs liberate themselves from the Ottoman Empire.

Lee, Robert E. (American, 1807-1870): Offered command of the Union armies at the start of the American Civil War, Lee sided with his native state of Virginia and rose to command the Army of Northern Virginia. He was noted for his aggressiveness, ever willing to defy military convention and divide his smaller forces in the face of the enemy to achieve a devastating flank attack. At the Battle of Gettysburg (1863), he said, "To be a good soldier, you must love the army. To be a good commander, you must be able to order the death of the thing you love." Later he said to Lieutenant General James Longstreet, "We are never quite prepared for so many to die. Oh, we do expect the occasional empty chair; a salute to fallen comrades. But this war goes on and on and the men die and the price gets ever higher. We are prepared to lose some of us, but we are never prepared to lose all of us. And there is the great trap General. When you attack, you must hold nothing back. You must commit yourself totally. We are adrift here in a sea of blood and I want it to end. I want this to be the final battle."

Lettow-Vorbeck, Paul von (German, 1870-1964): As commander of the German forces in Tanganyika (now Tanzania), Lettow-Vorbeck developed a system of guerrilla warfare that allowed him to avoid defeat by the British throughout World War I. In his memoirs, *Meine Erinnerungen aus Ostafrika* (1920; *My Reminiscences of East Africa*, 1920; also known as *East African Campaigns*, 1957), he wrote, "There is almost always a way out, even of an apparently hopeless position, if the leader makes up his mind to face the risks."

Liddell Hart, Basil Henry (British, 1895-1970): Liddell Hart's contributions to military theory include his concept of the "expanding torrent" of armed forces through the enemy's line, which was a precursor of the later German Blitzkrieg. He also advocated attacking key aspects of the enemy's civilian sector. In 1929, he wrote in the *Encyclopedia Britannica*, "In war, the chief incalculable is the human will." In his *Thoughts on War* (1944), he noted, "Those who are naturally loyal say little about it, and are ready to assume it in others. In contrast, the type of soldier who is always dwelling on the importance of loyalty usually means loyalty to his own interests."

Louvois, marquis de (French, 1639-1691): As war minister under Louis XIV, Louvois strengthened the French army, making it possible for Louis to wage his numerous wars. Louvois also supported Sébastien Le Prestre de Vauban and others who helped modernize the French military.

Lumumba, Patrice (Congolese, 1925-1961): Trained in Moscow, Lumumba led the Congolese to independence from Belgium and became a hero to many African revolutionaries.

MacArthur, Douglas (American, 1880-1964): From a family of career soldiers, MacArthur was defeated in the Philippines by the Japanese in early 1942 but became the author of the island-hopping strategy that would lead to the defeat of Japan in August of 1945. He later commanded U.S. forces (and others serving as part of the United Nations) in the Korean War. At the Republican National Convention in 1952, he said, "It is fatal to enter any war without the will to win it."

Machiavelli, Niccolò (Italian, 1469-1527): Best known for *Il principe* (1532; *The Prince*, 1640), Machiavelli also wrote *Dell'arte della guerra* (1521; *The Art of War*, 1560). Machiavelli looked to Republican Rome to argue that a truly stable and secure nation required a disciplined, well-trained citizen army instead of mercenaries. Machiavelli directly linked politics and war, anticipating the simplification of Carl von Clausewitz that "war is the continuation of politics by other means." *The Art of War* was held in high regard by readers such as Frederick the Great, Napoleon, and Clausewitz. Machiavelli wrote from experience: He drafted the Florentine *Ordinanza* of 1505, a military law to end use of mercenary troops. In *The Art of War*, he wrote, "It is better to subdue an enemy by famine than by sword, for in battle, *fortuna* has often a much greater share than *virtu*."

Maginot, André (French, 1877-1932): Maginot, French minister of defense, advocated the building of forts on France's eastern border to protect France from invasion by Germany. Built during the 1930's, these became known as the Maginot line during World War II.

Mahan, Alfred Thayer (American, 1840-1914): An American naval officer, Mahan published *The Influence of Sea Power upon History, 1660-1783* in 1890, arguing that sea power was the decisive factor in national strength. *The Influence of Sea Power upon the French Revolution and Empire, 1793-1812* (1892) extended and solidified his influence. Both books were widely read and studied in Great Britain and Germany prior to World War I and contributed to the naval arms race, which helped spark that conflict. In his book *Naval Strategy Compared and Contrasted with the Principles and Practices of Military Operations on Land* (1911), he wrote, "Where evil is mighty and defiant, the obligation to use force that is war arises."

Mahan, Dennis Hart (American, 1802-1871): Instructor at West Point and writer, Mahan published editions of his *An Elementary Treatise on Advanced-Guard, Out-Post, and Detachment Service of Troops and the Manner of Posting and Handling Them in Presence of an Enemy* in 1847, 1853, and 1863. *Out-Posts*, as it came to be known, was a comprehensive review of strategy and tactics. Mahan helped teach Civil War generals to believe in an active offensive campaign of maneuver as a means of victory. He wrote, "How different is almost every military problem except in the bare mechanism of tactics. In almost every case the data on which a solution depends is lacking."

Mao Zedong (Mao Tse-tung; Chinese, 1893-1976): As a military and revolutionary theorist, Mao believed that the countryside, not the city, was the seedbed of a people's revolution. He stated that "political power comes out of the barrel of a gun" and that "all reactionaries are paper tigers." He advocated a small but dedicated revolutionary force that would move among the general population until it could seize total control of the nation. His most famous comments on fighting were published in *Six Essays on Military Affairs* (1971).

Marius, Gaius (Roman, 157-86 B.C.E.): Gaius Marius was the prime mover behind the second century B.C.E. evolution of Roman armies from groups of citizens serving for limited periods to standing armies raised and paid by their commander, to whom they were therefore loyal. He also instituted the cohort as the principal unit of the Roman army and improved training and discipline. In one battle, his opposing commander is said to have claimed, "If you are a great general, come down and fight me," to which Marius replied, "If you are a great general, come and make me fight you."

Maurice of Nassau (Dutch, 1567-1625): Commander of the Dutch forces in their revolt against Spain, Maurice introduced drill, discipline, organization, standardized equipment, and clear command structure. He drew upon classical examples to make his troops more flexible and responsive, and he effectively utilized artillery and engineers.

Maxim, Hiram Stevens (British, 1840-1916): Born in the United States, Maxim became a British subject in 1900. He invented the automatic machine gun, the basis for one of the most important of modern weapons.

Mehmed II (Ottoman, 1432-1481): The sultan Mehmed II completed the defeat of the Byzantine Empire with the Siege of Constantinople (1453), in which he used the largest cannons yet known, specifically cast for the purpose. After capturing Constantinople, he famously is reported to have said, "The city and the buildings are mine, but I resign to your valor the captives and the spoil, the treasures of gold and beauty; be rich and be happy."

Minié, Claude-Étienne (French, 1804-1879): In 1849, Minié, a French officer, invented a bullet with a conical point and an iron cup at the bottom. When the "Minié ball" was fired from a muzzle-loading rifle, the cup caused the bullet to expand and fit snugly against the rifling grooves of the barrel, increasing the accuracy. The Minié ball was quickly adopted by Western armies.

Mitchell, William "Billy" (American, 1879-1936): An advocate of airpower in armed forces and of the creation of a separate air force, Mitchell commanded the U.S. Army Air Service in Europe during World War I. He was a friend of British air corps commander Hugh Trenchard, an equally strong proponent of airpower. Mitchell's forceful arguments that airpower would be the decisive factor in warfare and his attacks on his superiors led to his court-martial and resignation. In his book *Winged Defense: The Development and Possibilities of Modern Air Power—Economic and Military* (1925), he noted, "It is probable that future war will be conducted by a special class, the air force, as it was by the armored knights of the Middle Ages."

Monash, John (Australian, 1865-1931): As a commander in World War I, Monash oversaw the broad attack at Villers-Bretonneux in 1918 that forced the German to retreat, the first major defeat for the Germans after four years of trench warfare. In spite of his success in the war, he did say, "I do not regard and have never regarded permanent soldiering as an attractive proposition for any man who has some other profession at his command. I would recommend to him to stick to private practice every time."

Napoleon I (Napoleon Bonaparte; Corsican French, 1769-1821): Napoleon's rise from a position of relative obscurity to that of French emperor in 1804 and his final defeat at Waterloo (1815) and ensuing exile to the barren island of St. Helena are romantic aspects of his life. His reputation rests solidly on his reforms of the French legal and administrative system and, especially, his military genius. Napoleon inherited an army that had made major improvements in artillery, infantry tactics, and organization, and he incorporated these into a coherent system that improved the army's logistics, speed, and fighting power. He evolved a command system that allowed him to control operations in an extensive battlefield so he could menace one portion of an enemy's line and at the decisive moment strike at the most vulnerable point. With this flexibility, he won complex battles at Castiglione (1796) and Austerlitz (1805), both of which relied upon careful timing. Above all, Napoleon brought a vision to warfare that moved beyond the immediate battle to a strategic plan to win the war. He commented, "In war, everything depends on morale; and morale and public opinion comprise the better part of reality."

Nasution, Abdul Haris (Indonesian, 1918-2000): This Indonesian general developed the concept of territorial warfare and also the tactics of guerrilla warfare against the Dutch during the Dutch-Indonesian War. In his book *Pokok-Pokok Gerilya* (1953; *Fundamentals of Guerilla Warfare*, 1953), he argued, "The guerrilla should be a revolutionary vanguard; this was our ideal in the past and should be our ideal in the future."

Nelson, Horatio (British, 1758-1805): During the Napoleonic Wars (1793-1815), Nelson's victories at the Battle of the Nile (1798), Copenhagen (1801), and Trafalgar (1805) ensured English naval domination. Nelson's tactics, never formalized and always open to innovation, consisted of breaking the line of enemy ships and then concentrating on the scattered elements. At the Battle of Trafalgar, he noted, "England expects every man to do his duty."

Nimitz, Chester W. (American, 1885-1966): Commander in chief of the United States Pacific fleet during World War II, Nimitz used an "island-hopping" strategy that seized key points and left Japanese forces isolated. He combined airpower and military intelligence to win the decisive Battle of Midway in 1942. In March, 1945, he noted of his soldiers, "Among the men who fought on Iwo Jima, uncommon valor was a common virtue."

Oppenheimer, J. Robert (American, 1904-1967): As director of the Los Alamos Laboratories during World War II, Oppenheimer was in charge of the team of scientists who developed the nation's first nuclear weapons, a program called the Manhattan Project. An excellent administrator as well as a scientist, he also was a member of the scientific panel that supported the use of the atomic bomb against Japan.

Philip II (Macedonian, 382-336 B.C.E.): As king of a marginal state on the edge of the Greek world, Philip transformed the Macedonian army into his era's most potent force, largely through effective use of the military formation known as the phalanx. He was preparing an invasion of the Persian Empire when he was assassinated by a Macedonian youth. He was then succeeded in rule, ambition, and achievement by his son, Alexander the Great, who would go on to conquer much of the known world.

Qi Jiguang (Ch'i Chi-Kuang; Chinese, 1528-1587): Qi Jiguang incorporated the precepts in Sunzi's (Sun Tzu's) *Bingfa* (c. 510 B.C.E.; *The Art of War*, 1910) in reforms that allowed large Chinese armies to cross the steppes and fight against mounted, more mobile opponents. He thereby made China a more unified and stable nation.

Saladin (Seljuk Turk, c. 1137-1193): As leader of the Seljuk Turks, he led his troops to victory at the Battle of Hattin, and he managed to destroy the Kingdom of Jerusalem, and blunt the Third Crusade, holding together an Empire which included modern-day Egypt, Syria, Iraq, Saudi Arabia, and Yemen.

San Martín, José (Argentine, 1778-1850): San Martín managed to rally Latin Americans who supported independence from Spain, lead them across the Andes, and attack Spanish-dominated Peru, thereby ensuring independence for Argentina, Chile, and Peru.

Schlieffen, Alfred von (German, 1833-1913): The German chief of staff from 1891 to 1905, Schlieffen devised an intricate plan for Germany to strike first against France and then move against the slower Russian armies. The plan was the supreme example of war by timetable and went through more than fifty revisions. When war finally came, however, it failed.

Schwarzkopf, H. Norman (American, born 1934): Schwarzkopf oversaw the victory of the U.S.-dominated coalition forces in the Gulf War of 1991 with relatively few casualties. His role was not only to lead a sometimes uneasy coalition but also to use the media to make the Iraqis believe that he was about to launch a seaborne invasion instead of attacking on land. In an interview in 1991, he said, "It is very important that if we commit again to any kind of battle we are sure to understand the ramifications of what happens if we do accomplish our objectives," an observation that appeared prescient following the U.S.-led invasion of Iraq mounted in 2003.

Scipio Africanus (Roman, 235-183 B.C.E.): During the Punic Wars, Scipio Africanus managed to defeat Hannibal by embarking on a risky invasion of North Africa and forcing the Carthaginians to leave Italy in order to save their capital. His dislike of politicians was shown when he was later tried for bribery. Warning the Roman people against politicians, Scipio exclaimed, "Ungrateful country, you will not possess even my bones."

Scott, Winfield (American, 1786-1866): A veteran of the War of 1812, a victor in the Mexican War (1846-1848), and a long-serving army commander, Scott instilled professionalism in the new American nation's army. His amphibious expedition against Mexico in 1847 used maneuvering more than frontal assault to achieve victory. In 1861, in his mid-seventies, he proposed the Anaconda Plan, which eventually defeated the Southern Confederacy by blockade, driving down the Mississippi River into the heart of the South.

Servius Tullius (Roman, 578-534 B.C.E.): Servius was a possibly fictitious Etruscan king credited with revising the Roman state, including its military. His army was organized around "centuries" of one hundred men capable of providing their own arms and armor. Servius is said to have built the first walls around Rome, the first bridge across the Tiber, and Rome's seaport at Ostia. During his reign (or during this time), Rome emerged as the leading power in central Italy.

Severus, Lucius Septimius (Roman, 146-211): Severus restored military strength to the Roman Empire after a period of civil war. He increased the number of Roman legions, created a mobile reserve, used native troops, and tied the army to the throne by increased pay. His dying words to his sons were, in effect, "Be generous to the soldiers and don't care about anyone else."

Shaka (Zulu, c. 1787-1828): Founder of the Zulu Empire in southern Africa, Shaka introduced the *assagai*, or the short stabbing spear, and organized disciplined units that could be effectively commanded on the battlefield. The empire he founded resisted European control until 1897.

Sherman, William Tecumseh (American, 1820-1891): The commander of Union armies in the western theater during the American Civil War, Sherman declared that "war is hell and you cannot refine it," believing that the morale of an enemy civilian population was as much a target as its armies in the field. He employed this doctrine during his devastating March to the Sea (1864) and his subsequent advance across the Carolinas. Looking back on the war, in 1880 he said, "There is many a boy here to-day who looks on war as all glory, but, boys, it is all hell."

Shihuangdi (Shih Huang-ti; Chinese, 259-210 B.C.E.): The first emperor (also known as Qin Shihuangdi) to rule a unified China, Shihuangdi came to power in 246 B.C.E. as ruler of Qin (Ch'in), a feudal state that unified China in 221 B.C.E. He centralized government and military administration. He divided the country into thirty-six military districts and standardized weights, measurements, and even the axle lengths of carts to make roads more uniform. He built much of the Great Wall.

Shrapnel, Henry (British, 1761-1842): An English artillery officer, Shrapnel developed an artillery projectile with many small metal pieces. When exploded, these were effective against enemy troops. The name for his device, first used in 1804 and known as "shrapnel," has come to be used for similar fragments from artillery shells or bombs.

Skanderbeg (Albanian, 1405-1468): As prince of Albania, Skanderbeg was able to lead a spirited resistance against the Ottoman Turks for two decades, developing a system of hit-and-run raids yet managing to maintain some strategic strongholds.

Slim, Viscount (Sir William Slim; British, 1891-1970): A commander of guerrilla groups harassing the Japanese in Burma (now called Myanmar) in World War II, Viscount Slim noted in 1957, in *Courage and Other Broadcasts,* "The more modern war becomes, the more essential appear the basic qualities that from the beginning of history have distinguished armies from mobs."

Sunzi (Sun Tzu; Chinese, fl. c. fifth century B.C.E.): Little is known about the author of *Bingfa* (c. 510 B.C.E.; *The Art of War*, 1910) except that he was active in military affairs during the Zhou (Chou) Dynasty (1066-256 B.C.E.) and had a profound influence on Asian military thought. He was largely unknown in the West until the eighteenth century, and he received widespread appreciation only in the twentieth. Sunzi stressed moral more than physical force, seeing defeat as a psychological condition that a successful commander imposes upon an opponent. A proponent of Daoist thought, Sunzi preached that a commander must use the natural flow of conditions—terrain, weather, enemy strength, and morale—to shape the battle plan. To dominate an enemy morally, one must understand the enemy completely, necessitating the use of intelligence gathering, deception, and trickery. In Sunzi's concept of warfare, the ultimate goal is to make the enemy's plans fit one's own strategy so that his strengths become weaknesses and lead to his ultimate defeat. A quote he ascribed to Wu Ch'i was "The troops must have confidence in the orders of their seniors. The orders of their superiors [form] the source whence discipline is born."

Templer, Gerald (British, 1898-1979): As commander of the British in Malaya, Templer managed to use intelligence and strong-arm tactics to win the Malayan Emergency, in one of the most successful counterinsurgency campaigns in the twentieth century. When asked how he won the conflict, he said, "It all depended on intelligence."

Themistocles (Greek, c. 524-c. 460 B.C.E.): After the Greek victory over the Persians at Marathon (490 B.C.E.), Themistocles established a strong Athenian navy. In 480 B.C.E., the combined Greek fleet defeated the Persians at Salamis. Although Themistocles was exiled from Athens, he laid the foundation for the Athenian Empire.

Thompson, Robert (British, 1916-1992): A leading British counterinsurgency expert, Thompson advised the British military in Malaya and later the Americans in Vietnam. He started his book *No Exit from Vietnam* (1969) by noting that war as a continuation of politics is comprehensible only in relation to the achievement of its political aim.

Tiglath-pileser III (Assyrian, r. 745-727 B.C.E.): Assyrian ruler Tiglath-pileser III established a strong, centralized government and army that allowed the Assyrian Empire to conquer Syria, Phoenicia, Israel, and much of the Middle East.

Tito (Josip Broz; Yugoslav, 1892-1980): As leader of the Partisans, Tito managed to defeat the Germans in Yugoslavia and outmaneuver the Yugoslav Royalists. In 1942 he wrote that success would come from "swift, surprise assaults, night forays, surrounding the enemy and regularly attacking him from the rear."

Torstenson, Lennart (Swedish, 1603-1651): A Swedish general and artillery commander, Torstenson served under Gustavus II Adolphus and was expert in the use of the new mobile field artillery. After rising to the command of the Swedish army in 1641, he won a series of victories that relied on his skillful use of field artillery.

Trenchard, Hugh (British, 1873-1956): After serving in the British Army, Trenchard became the Royal Flying Corps' field commander in 1913. In 1918 he established the Independent Air Force as a separate branch. He supported strategic bombing and instituted its first use against Germany in the closing days of the war.

Trotsky, Leon (Russian, 1879-1940): Known as a political leader of the Bolshevik Revolution (1917-1921), Trotsky was the creator of the Red Army during the Russian Civil War (1918-1921). As the first modern military force motivated and guided by ideology, the Red Army preserved the

Soviet revolutionary government against its internal and external enemies. In 1921, Trotsky wrote, "If we happen to be too weak for attack, then we strive to detach ourselves from the embraces of the enemy in order later to gather ourselves into a gist and to strike at the enemy's most vulnerable spot." This and other comments were published as *Military Writings* (1969). As his long-term strategy, he noted, "First of all you must build the morale of your own troops. Then you must look to the morale of your civilian population. Then, and only then, when these are in good repair, should you concern yourself with the enemy morale. And the best way to destroy the enemy morale is to kill him in large numbers. There is nothing more demoralizing than that."

Tsuji, Masanobu (Japan, 1902-1961): Tsuji was a Japanese army officer who helped plan the invasion of Malaya, oversaw the war in Malaya, and later served in Burma and Guadalcanal. His book *Shingapōru: Unmei no tenki* (1952; *Singapore: The Japanese Version*, 1960) is one of the few accounts in English by a senior Japanese officer. He noted famously, "Patience is a virtue in staff discussions."

Vauban, Sébastien Le Prestre de (French, 1633-1707): Vauban is chiefly remembered as Europe's best and most prolific military engineer at a time when siegeworks and fortifications were crucial to the art of military affairs. He developed a system of geometric, angular, defensive works that were mutually reinforced by firepower and difficult to attack. Vauban was equally adept using counterwalls or circumvallations; indirect approaches, such as zigzagging trenches; and explosives, such as mines, in capturing enemy fortresses.

Vegetius Renatus, Flavius (Roman, fifth century C.E.): Vegetius's *De Re Militari* (383-450 C.E.; *The Fovre Bookes of Flauius Vegetius Renatus: Briefelye Contayninge a Plaine Forme and Perfect Knowledge of Martiall Policye, Feates of Chiualrie, and Vvhatsoeuver Pertayneth to Warre*, 1572; also translated as *Military Institutions of Vegetius*, 1767) provided an excellent description of Roman infantry doctrine, especially its empha-

sis on drill and maneuver. This work was consulted as a practical manual on military matters well into the nineteenth century.

Vo Nguyen Giap (Vietnamese, born 1911): Viet Minh general Giap believed revolutionary warfare should follow a three-step progression: guerrilla fighting, equality with the opponent, and final victory. During the long struggle in Vietnam, he employed this strategy against the French, South Vietnamese, and Americans, leading to military victories, such as that at Dien Bien Phu in 1954, as well as politically beneficial military defeats, such as the 1968 Tet Offensive. Commenting on his military tactics, in 1982 he said famously, "There is only one rule in you: you must win."

Wallenstein, Albrecht Wenzel von (Bohemian, 1583-1634): As a general in the forces of the Holy Roman Empire during the Thirty Years' War (1618-1648), Wallenstein raised his own armies and provided for them from the lands of his opponents. His maxim was that "war must feed war."

Washington, George (American, 1732-1799): As commander of the American forces during the American Revolution, Washington transformed the militia into the Continental Army after training them at Valley Forge. In 1796 he stated, "It is our true policy to steer clear of permanent alliance with any portion of the foreign world."

Weinberger, Caspar (American, 1917-2006): As U.S. secretary of defense (1981-1987), Weinberger oversaw the massive expansion of the U.S. military, including nuclear submarines, that prompted the Soviet Union to compete, bankrupting itself in the process. In 1990 he published an account of his time in the Pentagon, *Fighting for Peace: Seven Critical Years in the Pentagon*.

Wellington, duke of (Arthur Wellesley; British, 1759-1852): As commander of the British forces in the Peninsular War and then at Waterloo, Wellington invoked planning, shrewdness, and conservatism to achieve many victories against Napoleon. In 1810 he said of the French, "They won't draw me from my cautious system. I'll fight them only where I am pretty sure of victory."

Wet, Christiaan de (South African, 1854-1922): As commander of the Boer guerrillas, de Wet was able to wage a long war against a massively superior British army during the Second Boer War. In his book *De strijd tusschen Boer en Brit* (1902; *Three Years' War*, 1902), he said, "[W]e had always felt that no one is worthy of the name of man who is not ready to vindicate the right, be the odds what they may."

Whitney, Eli (American, 1765-1825): American inventor Whitney perfected the manufacture of interchangeable parts in 1798, standardizing the machine-made parts of a musket to predetermined specifications and bringing mass production to warfare.

Yamamoto, Isoroku (Japanese, 1884-1943): Japan's most successful admiral during World War II, Yamamoto devised the surprise attack on Pearl Harbor. He forced the "decisive battle" with the American fleet at Midway; the American victory there was the turning point in the Pacific war. In 1937 he urged that "Japan should never be so foolish as to make enemies of Great Britain and the United States."

Yi Sun-sin (Korean, 1545-1598): Yi developed probably the first ironclad battleship, the *kobukson* or "turtle ship," whose upper deck was covered with iron plates and with cannons mounted along the sides and stern. When the Japanese invaded Korea in 1592, Yi's fleet cut them off from supplies and reinforcements. His naval victories are ranked with those of the Battle of Lepanto (1571) and the defeat of the Spanish Armada (1588).

Zhukov, Georgy (Soviet, 1896-1974): A Red Army commander during World War II, Zhukov earned a reputation for tenacity and planning, which led to the destruction of the Axis forces at Stalingrad and later their defeat in Europe.

Žižka, Jan (Bohemian, c. 1360-1424): Military leader of the Hussites, Žižka used linked, stoutly built wagons filled with troops and small cannons as mobile field fortifications known as Wagenburgs. Žižka was never defeated in battle, despite the fact that he was, for much of his life, blind.

BOOKS AND ARTICLES

Alexander, Bevin. *How Wars Are Won: The Thirteen Rules of War from Ancient Greece to the War on Terror*. New York: Crown, 2002.

Haas, Jonathan, ed. *The Anthropology of War*. New York: Cambridge University Press, 1990.

Lider, Julian. *Military Theory: Concept, Structure, Problems*. Aldershot, Hampshire, England: Gower, 1983.

Montgomery of Alamein, Viscount. *A History of Warfare*. London: Collins, 1968.

Murray, Williamson, and Richard Hart Sinnreich, eds. *The Past Is Prologue: The Importance of History to the Military Profession*. New York: Cambridge University Press, 2006.

Tsouras, Peter G. *Changing Orders: The Evolution of World Armies, 1945 to the Present*. New York: Facts On File, 1994.

Tsouras, Peter G., ed. *The Greenhill Dictionary of Military Quotations*. London: Greenhill Books, 2000.

Michael Witkoski, updated by Justin Corfield

TIME LINE

c. 13,000 B.C.E.	Spears and spear-throwers appear as weapons.
c. 10,000 B.C.E.	Bows and arrows appear as weapons in Neolithic cave paintings.
c. 9th millen. B.C.E.	The sling makes its first known appearance.
c. 7000 B.C.E.	The inhabitants of Jericho construct massive fortifications around their city.
c. 7th millen. B.C.E.	The stone-headed mace makes its first known appearance.
c. 5000 B.C.E.	The city of Jericho becomes arguably the first town to be fortified with a stone wall.
c. 5000 B.C.E.	Sailing ships make their first appearance in Mesopotamia.
c. 4000 B.C.E.	Horses are first domesticated and ridden by people of the Sredni Stog culture.
c. 4000 B.C.E.	Copper is used to make the first metal knives, in the Middle East and Asia.
c. 3500 B.C.E.	The Sumerians employ wheeled vehicles.
c. 3200 B.C.E.	The Bronze Age is inaugurated in Mesopotamia as new metal technology allows more lethal weapons and more effective armor.
c. 2500 B.C.E.	The Sumerian phalanx is first employed.
c. 2500 B.C.E.	Metal armor is developed in Mesopotamia, making the stone-headed mace obsolete.
2333 B.C.E.	The emergence of King Tangun, who establishes what becomes Korea.
c. 2300 B.C.E.	After the composite bow is introduced by Sargon the Great, the use of the Sumerian phalanx declines.
c. 2250 B.C.E.	The composite bow is depicted in Akkadian Stela of Naram-Sin.
c. 2100 B.C.E.	The Sumerians reassert their supremacy over southern Mesopotamia, precipitating a renaissance of Sumerian culture and control that lasts for approximately two hundred years.
c. 2000 B.C.E.	The first metal swords, made from bronze, appear.
c. 1950-1500 B.C.E.	Assyrians first rise to power during the Old Empire period.
c. 1900 B.C.E.	Primitive battering rams are depicted in Egyptian wall paintings.
c. 1810 B.C.E.	Neo-Babylonian leader Hammurabi unifies the Mesopotamian region under his rule and establishes a capital at the city-state of Babylon.
c. 1800-1000 B.C.E.	Aryan invaders conquer India, mixing with earlier cultures to produce a new Hindu civilization in the area of the Ganges River Valley.

c. 1700 B.C.E.	Assyrians employ integrated siege tactics with rams, towers, ramps, and sapping.
c. 1674 B.C.E.	The Hyksos people introduce the horse-drawn chariot during invasions of Egypt.
c. 1600 B.C.E.	Chariot archers are increasingly used in warfare.
1600-1066 B.C.E.	The Shang Dynasty rules in China.
c. 1500-900 B.C.E.	During their Middle Empire period, the Assyrians drive the Mitanni from Assyria, laying foundations for further expansion.
1469 B.C.E.	At the Battle of Megiddo, the first recorded battle in history, the ancient Egyptians win a resounding victory against their opponents.
1400-1200 B.C.E.	Mycenaean civilization flourishes, with a wealth of political, economic, and religious centers.
c. 1384-1122 B.C.E.	The crossbow is originated during China's Shang Dynasty.
c. 1300 B.C.E.	Chariot design undergoes major innovations, with an increase in the number of spokes and the relocation of axles.
c. 1300-700 B.C.E.	Semitic desert dwellers infiltrate southern Mesopotamia to establish Chaldean culture during a period of Assyrian domination in the Near East.
c. 13th cent. B.C.E.	The Hebrews conquer Transjordan and Canaan under the leadership of Joshua.
1274 B.C.E.	At the Battle of Kadesh, the Egyptian Pharaoh uses massed chariots against the Hittites, wining a great victory in spite of his opponents' possession of iron weapons against the Egyptian soldiers, who are armed with bronze ones.
c. 1200 B.C.E.	The use of the chariot in warfare declines and foot soldiers increasingly come into use, as "barbarian" tribes, fighting on foot and armed with javelins and long swords, overrun many ancient Middle Eastern kingdoms.
c. 1200 B.C.E.	The chariot is introduced to China from the northwest and is later adapted for use in siege warfare.
1200-1100 B.C.E.	The Mycenaean order collapses during a period of upheaval.
c. 1200-1100 B.C.E.	The fortified city of Troy is besieged by the Greeks for ten years, with many leaders on both sides involved in single combat. The city falls only after succumbing to the Greek deception tactic of the Trojan horse placed outside the city's gates.
c. 1122 B.C.E.	Shang Dynasty armies introduce the chariot to northern China in warfare against the Zhou (Chou) Dynasty.
1100-750 B.C.E.	In the period known as the Greek Dark Age, petty chieftains replace the Mycenaean kings.
1066-256 B.C.E.	The Zhou Dynasty rules in China.
c. 1000 B.C.E.	Metal-headed maces become common in Europe.
c. 1000 B.C.E.	Cimmerians first produce bronze battle-axes.

c. 1000 B.C.E.	Iron begins to replace bronze in the making of weapons in Assyria.
1000-990 B.C.E.	David consolidates the reign of Judah and Israel and defeats neighboring kingdoms of Moab, Edom, Ammon, and Aramaea, among others.
c. 1000-600 B.C.E.	The Aryan Hindu civilization comes to dominate most of northern and central India while smaller states wage war for control in the southern region of the subcontinent.
c. 900 B.C.E.	Cavalry begins to compete with chariotry as a method of warfare in the Neo-Assyrian Empire.
c. 900 B.C.E.	Scyths and succeeding steppe warriors master the use of bows while on horseback.
c. 900 B.C.E.	Iron weapons become increasingly popular. Smiths master the use of iron to make stronger, more lethal swords.
900-600 B.C.E.	Assyria undergoes its Late Empire period, its greatest era of military expansion.
850 B.C.E.	The principles of fortress building are evidenced in an Assyrian relief sculpture.
753 B.C.E.	The city of Rome is said to be founded on the banks of the Tiber River by Romulus, one of the twin sons of Mars, the Roman god of war.
c. 750-650 B.C.E.	Hoplite armor and tactics are developed.
745-727 B.C.E.	After years of domestic turmoil, Tiglath-pileser III reestablishes control over Assyrian homeland and institutes military reforms.
721 B.C.E.	Sargon II conquers Israel.
705-701 B.C.E.	Judean king Hezekiah leads a rebellion against Assyrian domination.
c. 700 B.C.E.	Tight-formation hoplite tactics, well suited to the small plains of the ancient Greek city-states, are first introduced in Greece.
c. late 7th cent. B.C.E.	The Greeks develop the trireme, a large ship powered by three rows of oarsmen.
626 B.C.E.	Nabopolassar Nebuchadnezzar leads a revolt against Assyrian rule and establishes the Chaldean (Neo-Babylonian) kingdom.
612 B.C.E.	The Assyrian city of Nineveh is conquered by Medes and Babylonians, marking the final destruction of the Assyrian Empire.
c. 6th cent. B.C.E.	The lance is first used by the Alans and Sarmatians, and the chariot is first used by various tribes in battle.
587 B.C.E.	Jerusalem falls to the Neo-Babylonians.
587-586 B.C.E.	Nebuchadnezzar II uses siege warfare to conquer Jerusalem.
c. 546 B.C.E.	Persian king Cyrus the Great uses chariots to great advantage at the Battle of Thymbra.
539 B.C.E.	The Chaldean Empire is conquered by Persian king Cyrus the Great.
c. 510 B.C.E.	Sunzi writes his classic work *Bingfa* (*The Art of War*).

c. 5th cent. B.C.E.	The crossbow is developed in China; it provides more power, speed, and accuracy than the composite bow.
c. 5th cent. B.C.E.	Athens establishes itself as a major naval power in the Mediterranean.
c. 5th cent. B.C.E.	The Republican Revolt in Rome leads Horatius and two others to hold back a large Etruscan army as the bridge over the River Tiber is destroyed.
499-448 B.C.E.	The Persian Wars are fought between Persia and the Greek city-states.
480 B.C.E.	The Persians advance into Greece, but their massive force is held back at Thermopylae and their navy is later defeated at Salamis.
431-404 B.C.E.	Thc Peloponnesian Wars are fought between Athens and Sparta.
c. 429-427 B.C.E.	A wall of circumvallation is used in the Siege of Plataea by Sparta and Thebes at the beginning of the Peloponnesian War.
c. 401 B.C.E.	Slings are used to great effect against the Persians at the Battle of Cunaxa, outranging Persian bows and arrows, and charioteers are overwhelmed by more flexible cavalry, ending the dominance of chariots in warfare.
c. 400 B.C.E.	The development of the *gastraphetes*, or belly bow, allows the shooting of more powerful arrows.
c. 4th cent. B.C.E.	The earliest known stirrups, made from leather or wood, are used by the Scyths.
c. 4th cent. B.C.E.	Onboard catapults are added to ships, effectively rendering them as floating siege engines.
c. 4th cent. B.C.E.	The *Arthaśāstra* (*Treatise on the Political Good*), an influential treatise on Indian politics, administration, and military science, is reputedly written by the prime minister Kauṭilya.
c. 4th-3d cent. B.C.E.	Mediterranean city-states undertake the building of massive walls during a period of warfare.
c. 4th-3d cent. B.C.E.	Protective bone breastplates are used regularly.
c. 399 B.C.E.	The catapult is invented at Syracuse under Dionysius I, significantly advancing the art of siege warfare.
c. 390 B.C.E.	Gallic warriors overwhelm the Republic's forces, capturing and plundering the city of Rome.
371 B.C.E.	Thebes defeats Sparta at Leuctra, ending Spartan supremacy in hoplite warfare.
c. 350 B.C.E.	Philip II of Macedon develops the Macedonian phalanx and adopts the use of the sarissa, a pike nearly 15 feet long and wielded with two hands.
338 B.C.E.	Philip II of Macedon defeats a united Greek army at Chaeronea.
334 B.C.E.	Alexander the Great uses stone-throwing torsion catapults at the Siege of Halicarnassus.

333 B.C.E.	Alexander uses combined infantry and cavalry forces to rout the Persian cavalry under Darius III at the Battle of Issus.
332 B.C.E.	Alexander begins the Siege of Tyre.
331 B.C.E.	Alexander defeats main army of Darius III at Gaugamela, which sees Alexander charge the center of a much larger army, forcing Darius to flee prematurely.
326 B.C.E.	The Indian king Porus employs war elephants against Alexander's forces at the Battle of the Hydaspes, seriously disrupting the Macedonian phalanx.
323 B.C.E.	The death (or murder) of Alexander the Great leads to the start of the Diadochi Wars, which will see fighting throughout the Near East and Middle East over much of the next century.
c. 321 B.C.E.	Chandragupta Maurya expels Alexander's forces from India and establishes the Mauryan Dynasty.
307 B.C.E.	King Wu Ling of Zhao (Chao), inspired by steppe nomad tribes to the north, introduces the use of cavalry in China.
305-304 B.C.E.	Macedonians employ a huge siege tower known as a *helepolis* during the Siege of Rhodes.
c. 3d cent. B.C.E.	The Parthians, a steppe nomad people, perfect the Parthian shot, fired backward from the saddle while in retreat.
c. 3d cent. B.C.E.	Romans utilize the corvus, a nautical grappling hook that allows sailors to board and capture opposing vessels.
280 B.C.E.	Pyrrhus from Macedonia defeats the Romans at the Battle of Heraclea, but his losses are so great that similar battles become known as a Pyrrhic victories.
275 B.C.E.	The guards in Rome associated with the Scipio family become known as the Praetorian Guards, later the guards for the Roman emperors.
c. 274 B.C.E.	Aśoka the Great, grandson of Chandragupta Maurya and a military genius in his own right, solidifies the strength of the Mauryan Empire.
264 B.C.E.	Outbreak of the First Punic War, the first major war in the central Mediterranean.
247 B.C.E.	Hamilcar Barca is appointed Carthaginian military commander, marking the emergence of Carthage as a major military threat.
241 B.C.E.	In the final naval victory of the First Punic War, Rome expels the Carthaginians from Sicily.
237 B.C.E.	Hamilcar begins a Spanish military campaign in preparation for ultimate war with Rome.
221 B.C.E.	Hamilcar's son Hannibal takes command of the Carthaginian military.
221-206 B.C.E.	The Qin (Ch'in) Dynasty rules in China, vastly expanding the area under imperial control.

218 B.C.E.	Hannibal leads a force of war elephants, cavalry, and foot soldiers across the Alps to trap and defeat the Romans at Trebia. The Second Punic War begins.
216 B.C.E.	Hannibal issues Rome its greatest defeat in battle at Cannae.
214 B.C.E.	Chinese emperor Qin Shihuangdi (Ch'in Shih huang-ti) orders that the many portions of the Great Wall be joined to form a unified boundary.
c. 206 B.C.E.-220 C.E.	Crossbows come into regular usage in China.
206 B.C.E.-220 C.E.	The Han Dynasty rules in China.
202 B.C.E.	The Romans succeed in driving back Carthaginian war elephants, gaining a surprisc victory and leading to the end of the Second Punic War.
197 B.C.E.	The Romans defeat the main army of Macedonian king Philip V at Cynoscephalae.
168 B.C.E.	The Romans defeat Philip V's son, Perseus, at Pydna, eventually organizing Macedonia as a Roman province.
167-161 B.C.E.	Judas Maccabeus leads campaigns against Greek rule in Judea.
146 B.C.E.	Rome defeats Carthage in the Third Punic War, destroying its greatest enemy and assuring its long-term dominion.
c. 1st cent. C.E.	Aksumite Ethiopians emerge as dominant players in the control of Red Sea trade.
87 B.C.E.	The rise of Sulla as dictator of Rome leads to a power struggle that lasts for the next sixty years.
73 B.C.E.	Hsiung-nu (Huns) invade and attack Turkestan, heading westward from China.
73-71 B.C.E.	The Third Servile War sees slaves revolt and fight under the command of Spartacus. Crassus, a wealthy Roman politician, pays for the furnishing of soldiers.
62 B.C.E.	Defeat of Roman populist leader Catiline, who stages a revolt to bring down the Roman Republic. His supporters essentially form the basis for those who will support Julius Caesar in the Roman Civil War.
58-45 B.C.E.	Julius Caesar employs independently operating cohorts in the Gallic Wars and the Roman Civil Wars against Pompey.
55 B.C.E.	Caesar's soldiers build a bridge over the River Rhine to help with the invasion of Germany.
53 B.C.E.	Parthian mounted archers defeat heavily armed Roman infantry at the Battle of Carrhae, destroying the army of Marcus Licinus Crassus.
c. 50 B.C.E.-50 C.E.	The earliest horseshoes are made in Gaul.
39-37 B.C.E.	Herod is named king of Judea by the Roman senate and leads campaigns to establish his kingdom.
c. 31 B.C.E.	Specialist corps of slingers largely disappear from ancient armies.

20 B.C.E.	Augustus manages to reach a treaty with Parthians.
66-70 C.E.	The Jews wage war against the Romans.
70 C.E.	The Romans besiege Jerusalem, taking the city's population captive and leveling its buildings.
70-73 C.E.	The Romans employ ramps and siege towers in their successful three-year Siege of Masada.
c. 2d cent. C.E.	The use of armor spreads from the Ukraine to Manchuria.
c. 100	With the increasing use of cavalry in Roman warfare, the spatha, a long slashing sword, becomes popular.
c. 122-136	Hadrian's Wall is constructed in northern England, marking the northernmost border of the Roman Empire.
c. 3d-4th cent.	Despite the increasing role of cavalry due to barbarian influence, infantry remains the dominant component of the Roman legions.
220-280	The Wei (220-265), Shu-Han (221-263), and Wu (222-280) Dynasties rule in China during Three Kingdoms period.
226	Establishment of the Sāsānian Empire in Persia.
c. 250	The decline of the Kushān Empire leads to instability in Central Asia.
265-316	The Western Jin (Chin) Dynasty rules in China.
267	Zenobia, the female ruler of Palmyra, defeats the Romans.
270	The Romans start fighting the Goths again.
284	Roman emperor Diocletian reduces the power of the Praetorian Guard.
c. 4th cent.	The use of stirrups is introduced in China, allowing cavalry armor to become heavier and more formidable.
300-1763	During the miasma-contagion phase of biological warfare, environments are deliberately polluted with diseased carcasses and corpses.
312	At the Battle of the Milvian Bridge, the Roman commander Constantine sees a cross in the sky and promises to become a Christian if he wins the battle. The cross inspires his soldiers, who defeat Maxentius, leader of the Gauls. After the battle Constantine disbands the Praetorian Guard.
317-420	The Eastern Jin (Chin) Dynasty rules in China.
320	Chandragupta II establishes the Gupta Dynasty, recalling the glory days of the Mauryan Empire and employing a feudal system of decentralized authority.
324	Roman emperor Constantine builds a new eastern capital at Constantinople, which will become the capital of the Eastern Roman Empire.
370	Rome rebuilds its walls as protection against barbarian invasions.

378	The Second Battle of Adrianople sees Goths advancing into Thrace and threatening Constantinople.
386-588	The Southern and Northern Dynasties rule concurrently in China.
c. 400	The bow and arrow is introduced in eastern North America.
c. 400	Cavalry replaces infantry as the most important element in Roman armies.
c. 400	Horseshoes come into general use throughout Europe.
c. 400	The Chinese first make steel by forging cast and wrought iron together.
c. 400	Japanese clans start fighting for control of Kyushu.
410	Romans withdraw their soldiers from Britain.
451	Attila the Hun invades Roman Gaul.
476	The Sack of Rome by barbarians brings about an "age of cavalry," during which foot soldiers play a diminished role in warfare.
500	Central Asian invaders appear in India, bringing superior fighting techniques and concentrated use of cavalry.
507	Clovis defeats the Visigoths at Vouille and unifies Gaul.
527-565	Roman emperor Justinian reigns, definitively codifying Roman law, waging war against the Germans and Persians, and changing the empire from a constitutional to an absolute monarchy.
536	Goths capture and sack Rome.
553	The T'u-chüeh Empire is founded in Mongolia.
568	Lombards start invading Italy.
c. 580	Maurice from Byzantium (Flavius Tiberius Mauricius) writes *Strategikon*, outlining military tactics.
581	The rise of the Sui Dynasty reestablishes a central government in China.
c. 7th cent.	The Aksumite kingdom in eastern Africa is weakened by the spread of Islam throughout Arabia and North Africa.
610-641	Heraclius reigns over the Byzantine Empire, Hellenizing the culture and introducing the theme system of Byzantine provinces ruled by military governors.
622	In a journey known as the Hegira, the Islamic prophet Muḥammad (c. 570-632) flees from Mecca to Medina to avoid persecution.
632-661	Muḥammad is succeeded after his death in 632 by the four legitimate successors of the rashidun (from Arabic *rāshidūn*, "rightly guided") caliphate.
674-678	Greek fire, an inflammable liquid, is used by the Byzantines against Arab ships during the Siege of Constantinople.
680	Arabs invade Anatolia.

680	The forces of Muḥammad's grandson Ḥusayn are ambushed and massacred at the Battle of Karbalā, marking the beginning of Shia as a branch of Islam.
687	Pépin of Herstal wins the Battle of Tertry, solidifying rule over all Franks, and unifies the office of Mayor of the Palace.
c. mid-8th cent.	Islam becomes the dominant religio-political power structure of the Middle East, from the Atlantic to the Indian frontier, including the Mediterranean coast and Spain.
c. 700-1000	Ghana emerges as the dominant kingdom and military power of the western Sudan in Africa.
714	Pépin's illegitimate son, Charles Martel, seizes control over Frankish kingdom in a palace coup.
732	Rise of the Carolingians in France.
740	The Berber Revolt in northern Africa expands into Spain.
740-840	Uighurs destroy the T'u-chüeh Empire and dominate Mongolia.
c. 750	Carbon-steel swords first appear in Japan.
c. 757-796	Offa's Dyke is built in the kingdom of Mercia to protect the kingdom's Welsh border.
793	Vikings sack Lindisfarne Abbey in northern England.
800	Charlemagne is crowned Holy Roman Emperor by Pope Leo III, establishing a new military system that is compared to that of the Romans but that lacks the coherence of the Roman or Byzantine system.
839	Byzantine emperor Theophilus starts hiring foreign mercenaries, who later become the Varangian Guard.
840-920	The Kirghiz invade Mongolia and drive out the Uighurs, thereafter dominating the region.
843	Vikings sack Dorestadt and Utrecht.
845	Charles the Bald, king of the Franks, pays Vikings money to retreat.
880's	King Alfred the Great begins constructing a series of *burhs*, or garrisons, to defend Wessex from Vikings. He later founds the (British) Royal Navy to prevent raids on England.
886	The Vikings mount their last siege of Paris.
891	Vikings suffer a rare defeat at Louvain.
900	Leo IV the Wise writes *Tactica*, outlining Byzantine military strategy.
980	The Byzantine warrior emperor Nicephorus Phocas inspires a third Byzantine military manual.

c. 10th cent.	Ghaznavid Turks invade India from Afghanistan, introducing an Islamic influence that will continue almost uninterrupted until the early sixteenth century.
911	The Viking Rollo receives the county of Normandy from the French king.
920	The Khitans drive out the Kirghiz and establish an empire in Mongolia and China.
c. 930	Vikings settle in Iceland.
954	The English expel the last Viking king from York.
990's	The first stone keeps appear in northwestern Europe.
c. 10th-11th cent.	The crossbow makes its first European appearance, in Italy.
1013	Danish king Sweyn I Forkbeard defeats English king Æthelred I and forces him into exile.
1017-1035	Sweyn's son Canute I (the Great) rules both England and Denmark.
1044	The first precise recipe for gunpowder is given, in a Chinese work.
Aug. 15, 1057	The death of Macbeth, usurper of the Scottish throne.
1066	The defeat and death of Harold Hardrada at the Battle of Stamford Bridge ends Viking invasions of Britain. William of Normandy defeats the English at the Battle of Hastings, using cavalry armed with lances against a shield wall, and a rapid proliferation of motte-and-bailey castles follows.
1082	At the battle of Durazzo (or Dyrrachium), Norman cavalry tactics from the Battle of Hastings are used against Byzantines to great effect.
1089-1094	El Cid (Rodrigo Díaz de Vivar) captures Valencia, leading a mixed Christian-Moorish army.
1095-1099	During the First Crusade, initiated by Pope Urban II, European Crusaders, fighting to protect the Holy Land for Christianity, capture Jerusalem.
1100	European knights adopt the use of the couched lance, which provides more force than previous hand-thrust weapons.
1125	Jürcheds conquer northern China, driving out Khitans, and Mongolia descends into tribal warfare.
1139	The use of the crossbow in Christian Europe is prohibited by Pope Innocent II at the Lateran Council.
1145-1149	The Second Crusade, unsuccessfully led by the kings of France and Germany, is prompted by Muslim conquest of the principality of Edessa in 1144.
1187-1192	The Third Crusade succeeds, especially through the efforts of English king Richard I, in restoring some Christian possessions.
1192	The samurai Minamoto Yoritomo establishes the first shogunate at Kamakura, bringing order to Japan after four centuries of feudal chaos and political vacuum.

1196-1198	King Richard I of England builds Château Gaillard with three baileys, which had to be captured before the castle could be taken and hence served as multiple lines of defense.
1198-1204	The Fourth Crusade, initiated by Pope Innocent III, captures Constantinople and seriously damages the Byzantine Empire.
c. 1200	In North America, the southwestern Anasazi culture is destroyed, possibly by raiding Ute, Apache, Navajo, and Comanche tribes.
c. 1200	As forged steel processes are refined, several European cities, including Sheffield, Brussels, and Toledo, emerge as sword-making centers.
1206	Genghis Khan is named ruler of the Mongols.
1213	The Mongols invade China.
1215	The Magna Carta is signed by King John of England, granting rights to the people of England, especially the barons; King John outlaws the use of the crossbow and the deployment of mercenaries in England.
1217-1221	The Fifth Crusade, organized to attack the Islamic power base in Egypt, succeeds in capturing the Egyptian port city of Damietta but ends in defeat when the crusading army attempts to capture Cairo.
1228-1229	In what is sometimes referred to as the Sixth Crusade, the excommunicated Holy Roman Emperor Frederick II sails to the Holy Land and negotiates a reoccupation of Jerusalem.
c. mid-13th cent.	The cog, with high sides that offer protection against other vessels, is developed in northern Europe.
1230	The kingdom of Mali is founded by a Mandinka prince after the defeat of the Susu kingdom.
1236-1242	The Mongols achieve conquests in Russia, Eastern Europe, Iran, and Transcaucasia.
1248-1254	The Seventh (or Sixth) Crusade is led by Louis IX of France and follows a course similar to that of the Fifth Crusade.
1258	Mongols capture Baghdad and end the ʿAbbāsid Caliphate.
1260	Mongols invade Syria and capture Damascus but are defeated at the Battle of Ain Jalut by Mamlūk slave cavalry, trained by the Egyptians to steppe nomad levels.
1261	A war between the Il-Khanate of Persia and the Golden Horde of Russia begins.
1269-1270	The Eighth (or Seventh) Crusade is organized by the now elderly Louis IX, whose death upon landing in Tunisia leads to the breakup of his army.
1270-1272	Edward I, the son of Henry III of England, decides to press on alone to Palestine after the French abandon the Eighth Crusade and achieves some modest success with a truce before the ultimate fall of Acre, the last bastion of the Crusader states, in 1291.

1274, 1281	The Mongol fleet is destroyed in an attempt to invade Japan.
1277-1297	King Edward I of England builds a series of ten Welsh castles, with an implicitly offensive function as continuances of the king's campaigns.
1279	Kublai Khan establishes the Yuan Dynasty.
1298	The English army, employing large numbers of Welsh archers, uses the longbow to great effect against the Scots at Falkirk.
c. 14th cent.	An "infantry revolution," spurred by the greater use of the pike and bow, takes place in Europe.
c. 1300	An increase in separate tribal identities among North American indigenous peoples develops in response to the increasing importance of agriculture and a clearer definition of gender roles.
c. 1300	The Chinese first use black powder to propel projectiles through bamboo tubes, revolutionizing warfare.
1300	Japanese craftsmen perfect the art of sword making, creating the katana, a curved sword used by samurai warriors.
1302	Flemish pikemen defeat French knights with an advantageous choice of terrain at Courtrai.
1314	Emperor Amda Tseyon comes to power in Ethiopia, expanding and solidifying the Solomonid Dynasty.
1315	Swiss pikemen begin a string of victories against mounted knights by defeating the Austrians at Morgarten, leading to their dominance of infantry warfare in the fourteenth and fifteenth centuries.
1331	The first recorded European use of gunpowder weaponry occurs at the Siege of Friuli in Italy.
1335	The Il-Khanate of Persia ends.
1340	Definitive use of gunpowder weapons is made at the Siege of Tournai.
1346	English longbowmen defeat French knights at the Battle of Crécy, which also marks the first definitive use of gunpowder artillery on a battlefield.
1346-1347	Cannons are deployed by the English at the Siege of Calais.
c. mid-14th cent.	The carrack, an efficient sailing ship with multiple masts, becomes popular in Atlantic and Mediterranean waters.
1360	Sir John Hawkwood forms his White Company, English mercenaries operating in Italy.
1368	The Chinese Yuan Dynasty ends, and the Mongols are driven back to Mongolia, where a period of civil war ensues.
1369	Tamerlane (Timur) becomes ruler of Central Asia.

1377	Cannons are first used successfully to breach a wall at the Siege of Odruik in the Netherlands.
1398	Mongol invasions by Tamerlane devastate North India.
1415	English archers and infantry inflict a major defeat upon mounted French knights at the Battle of Agincourt, initiating the decline of the heavily armored cavalry knight.
1420	Hussite leader Jan Žitka stymies German knights during the Hussite Wars with his Wagenburg, a defensive line of wagons and cannons.
c. 1425	The corning, or granulating, process is developed to grind gunpowder into smaller grains, leading to corned powder and matches.
June 18, 1429	French cavalry succeed in defeating English longbowmen for the first time in the Hundred Years' War.
1432	The sacking of Angkor ends the domination by the Khmer kingdom of mainland Southeast Asia.
1450	In West Africa, Songhai incorporates the former kingdom of Mali and comes to control one of the largest empires of the time.
c. 14th-15th cent.	The increasing predominance of firearms in Europe results in the diminishing use of archers in warfare.
1450-1700	Sword blades become lighter, narrower, and longer, gradually evolving into the familiar rapier design.
1453	With use of large cannons, the Muslim Turks besiege and capture Constantinople from the Byzantines and establish the Ottoman Empire, a watershed event often used to mark the transition from the medieval to the early modern world.
1468	Songhai armies invade Timbuktu, execute Arab merchants and traitors, and sack and burn the city, thereby heralding a period of anti-Islamic sentiment in West Africa.
1471	The Battle of Barnet, north of the English capital, London, involves cannons for the first time on an English battlefield, but bad weather prevents their use.
1477-1601	Perpetual civil war is waged throughout the Sengoku (Warring States) period.
c. 1480	Fortifications begin to undergo design changes, such as lower, wider walls to accommodate the use of cannons.
Aug. 22, 1485	The Battle of Bosworth Field, which results in the death of King Richard III and victory for King Henry VII, effectively ends the Wars of the Roses in England.
1492	Spanish troops capture Granada, ending the Reconquista; later the same year, Christopher Columbus sails to the New World.
1494	Charles VIII introduces the modern siege train in his invasion of Italy, confirming the obsolescence of high medieval defenses.

1494	The Treaty of Tordesillas leads to a "division" of the world by Pope Alexander VI between the Spanish and the Portuguese.
c. 1500	The Iroquois Confederacy, an alliance of separate tribes formed to fight hostile western and southern neighbors, is established in the American Northeast.
c. 1500	The development of gunpowder muskets, pistols, and cannons forces tactical and strategic changes in the use of spears, bows and arrows, swords, cavalry, and armor.
c. 1500	As European plate armor becomes more prevalent, the sharper, narrower rapier is developed to combat it.
c. 1500	Leonardo da Vinci draws what could arguably be the first design for a helicopter.
c. 1500	A Chinese scientist is killed by the explosion of gunpowder rockets he had tied to a chair in an effort to develop a flying machine.
1501	The development of gunports allows a ship's heaviest guns to be mounted on its lowest decks, stabilizing its center of gravity.
1503	The first effective use of the combination of firearms and pikes, a formation called the Spanish Square, is made at the Battle of Cerignola.
Jan. 21, 1506	The Swiss Guards are formed to protect the pope.
1520-1521	Hernán Cortés and a small force of Spanish conquistadors destroy the Aztec Empire.
1522	Spanish harquebusiers slaughter Swiss pikemen in the service of the French at the Battle of Bicocca.
1525	The Spanish Square formation of pikemen and harquebusiers is used to defeat French cavalry at the Battle of Pavia.
Apr. 20, 1526	Bābur makes effective use of artillery to defeat Sultan Ibrāhīm Lodī at the famous Battle of Pānīpat, establishing the Mughal Empire.
1527	The Mughals defeat the Rajputs at the Battle of Kanwa.
1529	Muslim leader Aḥmad Grāñ defeats forces of Lebna Dengel at the Battle of Shimbra-Kure, opening southern Ethiopia to Islamic rule.
1529	The Mughals defeat the Afghans at the Battle of Ghāghara.
c. 1530	King Henry VIII of England builds a series of forts on England's southern coastline to guard against European invasion.
1531-1532	The Spanish under Francisco Pizarro start the sacking of the Inca Empire.
c. mid-1500's	European cavalries begin to appear armed with short muskets that can be fired from both mounted and dismounted positions.
1541	Portuguese musketeers arrive to help defend Ethiopia, ending the Islamic threat two years later, under the emperor Galawdewos.

1541	The English start making iron cannons in Ashdown Forest.
1543	Firearms are first used in Japan.
1544	At Cerisolles, French knights fighting in the traditional style play a major role in gaining victory over the Swiss, the last battle in which they are to do so.
1545-1550	Formation of the Streltsy in Moscow by Ivan the Terrible, as guards of the Russian czars.
1556	Bābur's grandson Akbar is victorious at the second Battle of Pānīpat, against the Sur descendants of Shīr Shāh, and eventually conquers most of northern and eastern India, Afghanistan, and Baluchistan.
1562	The caracole maneuver is first executed by Huguenot pistolers against Catholic forces at the Battle of Dreux.
1565	The Siege of Malta ends the Turkish advance across the Mediterranean.
1571	The Battle of Lepanto II, fought between the Ottoman Turks and the Christian forces of Don Juan de Austria, is the last major naval battle to be waged with galleys.
1575	Three thousand musketeers help General Oda Nobunaga win control of central Japan.
Aug. 4, 1578	In the Battle of the Three Kings in Morocco, a Portuguese army is destroyed by Moroccans, precipitating a crisis in the Portuguese royal family leading to King Philip II of Spain becoming king of Portugal.
1588	The English employ galleons to attack the larger ships of the formidable Spanish Armada individually, thereby defeating the Spanish and revolutionizing naval tactics.
1591	Songhai is conquered by a Moroccan army consisting primarily of European mercenaries armed with muskets, the first to be used in West African warfare.
c. late 16th cent.	Japanese sword-making techniques reach a peak of sophistication, with a variation of the hammer-welding process.
c. 17th cent.	The howitzer is developed by the English and Dutch for use against distant targets.
c. 1600	The military reforms of Maurice of Nassau reduce the size and depth of pike formations to facilitate maneuverability and increase the number of muskets in units.
1600	The Battle of Nieuwpoort in the Netherlands is the first battlefield test of Maurice of Nassau's linear infantry tactics.
1603	Tokugawa Ieyasu establishes the Tokugawa shogunate, with its capital at Edo, marking the beginning of early modern Japanese history.
1605	Miguel de Cervantes writes *El ingenioso hidalgo don Quixote de la Mancha* (*Don Quixote de La Mancha*), ridiculing the role of the armored knight in Spain.

1609	The Netherlands forces Spain to grant a truce tacitly recognizing Dutch independence after more than thirty years of revolution of Dutch Protestant provinces against Spanish occupation.
1609	The Kalmyk people on the Caspian Sea become a part of the Russian Empire, and their horsemen start serving in the Russian cavalry.
1618-1648	The Thirty Years' War leads to mass destruction of Central Europe, with major atrocities and killing of civilians. It is estimated that some eight million people in Germany alone die in the war.
1631	Gustavus II Adolphus's military reforms prove their value at the Battle of Breitenfeld, as Gustavus's disciplined cavalrymen combine firepower and shock tactics.
1632-1653	The fifth Mughal emperor, Shāh Jahān, builds the Taj Mahal as a monument to his love for his wife.
1642-1651	During the English Civil Wars, the Royalist Army is the first to use horse artillery in the form of a small brass cannon mounted onto a horse-drawn cart.
1645	Oliver Cromwell establishes the New Model Army.
1653	The line of battle is developed as a naval tactic, allowing for more effective use of broadside firepower.
1657	ʿĀlamgīr becomes the sixth Mughal emperor and ultimately expands the Mughal Empire to its greatest extent.
c. 1660	Sébastien Le Prestre de Vauban emerges as a genius of military engineering, designing bastioned fortifications.
Jan. 1, 1660	The Coldstream Guards (from a unit raised by Colonel George Monck from 1650) become the first part of a standing army in Britain.
1673	The first transportable mortar, invented by Baron Menno van Coehoorn, is used at the Siege of Grave.
1673	The use of saps and parallels is introduced by Sébastien Le Prestre de Vauban at the Siege of Maastricht.
1673	Dutch scientist Christiaan Huygens develops a motor driven by the explosion of gunpowder.
Sept. 11-12, 1683	Polish King John III Sobieski leads 3,000 Polish landers and hussars and 17,000 other cavalry against the Ottoman army, in the largest cavalry charge in history at the Battle of Vienna.
1688	Sébastien Le Prestre de Vauban introduces the socket bayonet, which fits over a musket's muzzle and allows the musket to be loaded and fired with the bayonet attached. As the socket bayonet replaces the pike, specialized pike troops disappear from use. At the Siege of Philippsburg that year, he introduces ricochet fire.

1689	Russian czar Peter II "the Great" disbands the Streltsy Corps, which has protected the czars since the 1550's (but became involved in many court intrigues).
1690	The Brown Bess flintlock musket is developed, and its variations remain in use by all European nations until the mid-nineteenth century.
c. 1700	The introduction of rifling and patched-ball loading increases the accuracy of firearms.
c. mid-1700's	Advances in cannon technology allow smaller guns to shoot farther with less powder.
1712-1786	King Frederick the Great of Prussia is the first to use Jaegers, or "huntsmen," expert mounted marksmen.
1754-1763	Large muskets are first used successfully by Americans in the French and Indian War.
1757	Frederick the Great wins renown and respect with his masterful use of the oblique attack at Leuthen.
1759	Frederick the Great introduces the first true horse artillery units, which, because of their unprecedented mobility and firepower, are quickly adopted by other European nations to become a staple of most eighteenth and nineteenth century armies.
Sept. 13, 1759	British troops under General James Wolfe land secretly and attack Montreal, suprising the French commander, Louis-Joseph de Montcalm. Both Wolfe and Montcalm are killed in the battle.
1763-1925	During the fomites phase of biological warfare, specific disease agents and contaminated utensils are introduced as weapons, with smallpox, cholera, and the bubonic plague as popular agents.
1769	French military engineer Joseph Cugnot develops a steam-driven carriage, arguably the first true automobile. It is essentially designed for the transportation of field artillery for sieges.
1775	David Bushnell invents a one-man submarine, the *Turtle*, which is used in the American Revolutionary War.
Dec. 19, 1777	George Washington starts training his soldiers at Valley Forge, continuing until June 19, 1778.
1778-1779	Frederick the Great begins deploying semi-independent detachments during the War of Bavarian Succession, foreshadowing use of independent army divisions.
1781	The Siege of Yorktown effectively ends the American War of Independence.
1790's	British artillerist Henry Shrapnel invents the "shrapnel shell," packed with gunpowder and several musket balls and designed to explode in flight.
1792	Modern French military techniques and arms are introduced into Turkey.
1792	War rockets are used by the sultan of Mysore to terrorize British soldiers.

1795	The Springfield Armory is founded in Massachusetts.
1798	British admiral Horatio Nelson abandons traditional line tactics, achieving victory over the French at Abū Qīr Bay.
1799	The Royal Military College is established at Woolwich to train British army officers.
1802	The Royal Military College at Sandhurst is founded to train British army officers.
1802	The Tay Son Rebellion ends, leading to the emergence of the Nguyen Dynasty in Vietnam.
Mar. 16, 1802	The United States Military Academy at West Point is founded.
1803	The École Speciale Militaire de Saint-Cyr, the French military academy, is established.
1804-1815	French emperor Napoleon I (Bonaparte) develops his cavalry to the height of its quantity and quality, making it as significant as infantry in the outcomes of battles and campaigns.
1805	British artillerist William Congreve develops the first warfare rockets and launching tubes.
1807	American inventor Robert Fulton invents the first steamship, which by the time of the Crimean War (1853-1856) has largely replaced the sail-powered ships in British, French, and American navies.
Feb. 8, 1807	Joachim Murat leads 11,000 French cavalry in an attack on the Russians at the Battle of Eylau, allowing Napoleon Bonaparte to win the battle.
July-Dec., 1809	The Walcheren Expedition sees British forces in the Netherlands destroyed by disease, probably malaria caused when Napoleon opened the dikes and much low-lying land was flooded.
1812	In the opening part of the War of 1812, the British capture Washington, D.C.
Dec. 12, 1812	Napoleon's Grande Armée, consisting of French and allied soldiers, retreats from Moscow and is destroyed by Cossacks and by disease, especially typhus, in their retreat.
1814	The Russian cavalry enter Paris as Napoleon flees and later abdicates. He is sent into exile on the island of Elba.
1814-1815	The Conference of Vienna is followed by the inauguration of the Congress System to help promote collective security in Europe.
June 18, 1815	The defeat of Napoleon at Waterloo signals the end of the Napoleonic Wars and the end of French military dominance in Europe. Napoleon is sent into exile at St. Helena.
1816-1819	The rise of Shaka and the establishment of the Zulu Kingdom in southern Africa.
1817	Gurkhas start serving in the Pindaree War, alongside the British, under a contract between them and the East India Company.

July 26, 1822	José de San Martín and Simón Bolívar meet at Guayaquil, Ecuador, drawing up plans for an independent South America.
1826	The janissary corps are destroyed and the Turkish army is modernized.
1831	The duke of Wellington establishes the Royal United Services Institute in London.
Mar. 9, 1831	The French Foreign Legion is founded.
1832	The last of the classical sieges occurs at Antwerp.
1834	Turkey creates its first military academy.
1836	The Colt revolver is first manufactured in the United States by Colt's Patent Firearms Manufacturing Company, later renamed Colt's Manufacturing Company. It was patented by its inventor, Samuel Colt, and quickly emerged as a popular handgun in the United States.
Feb., 1836	Mexicans capture the Alamo but are defeated soon afterward at the Battle of San Jacinto.
Dec. 16, 1838	Voortrekkers in South Africa win the Battle of Blood River against the Zulus by forming a laager with their wagons.
1838-1842	The First Anglo-Afghan War leads to defeat for the British.
1840's	The telegraph becomes widely used and links governments with field commanders.
1840's-1850's	The Paraguayan government embarks on modernization, including the establishment of its own arms industry.
1845-1920	Asphyxiating gas weapons are developed for chemical warfare, using chlorine and phosgene.
Oct. 10, 1845	The United States Naval Academy at Annapolis is established.
1846-1848	Although military swords have entered a period of decline, cavalry sabers prove decisive during the Mexican War.
1847	Anesthesia is first used during a battlefield operation.
1848	The Sharps carbine, a single-shot, dropping-block breechloader firing paper and metallic cartridges, is developed.
1848	Revolutions throughout much of the Habsburg Empire lead to a political restructuring of Europe.
Aug. 22, 1849	The Austrian army uses balloons loaded with explosives to attack the Italian city of Venice.
1853-1856	The Crimean War sees major improvements in military medical hygiene, spearheaded by Florence Nightingale, as well as the "first" full-time war correspondent, William Howard Russell of the London newspaper *The Times*.
Oct. 25, 1854	The Charge of the Light Brigade, during the Crimean War.

1856	The Bessemer process of economical steel production is invented.
1856	The Victoria Cross, the highest British medal for bravery in battle, is awarded for the first time.
1857	A mutiny of Indian soldiers serving in British India leads to a widespread revolt against the British and the massacre of many Britons at Cawnpore (Kanpur).
1860	England launches HMS *Warrior*, its first ironclad warship.
1861	The first machine gun, the Gatling gun, is designed by Richard Gatling.
Apr. 12, 1861	Confederate forces attack Fort Sumter, South Carolina, starting the American Civil War.
Mar. 9, 1862	The Battle of Hampton Roads, between the ironclads USS *Monitor* and CSS *Virginia*, revolutionizes naval warfare.
May 5, 1862	Confederate General Gabriel J. Rains uses the first land mines to cover his retreat from Williamsburg, Virginia.
May 31-June 1, 1862	At the Battle of Seven Pines (Fair Oaks), Virginia, a machine gun is used for the first time in war.
Sept. 17, 1862	At the Battle of Antietam, Union General Ambrose Burnside blunders his way into a defeat, becoming one of the least successful commanders in the war.
1863	Establishment of the Red Cross by Henri Dunant, inspired by the treatment of casualties at the Battle of Solferino in the previous year.
July 1-3, 1863	The Confederate general Robert E. Lee is defeated at the Battle of Gettysburg, during a Confederate attempt to "take" the war into the North.
1864	Paraguayan president Francisco Solano López intervenes in the Uruguayan Civil War and soon ends up at war with Argentina, Brazil, and Uruguay.
Feb. 17, 1864	The Confederate submarine CSS *H. L. Hunley* becomes the first underwater vessel to sink an enemy ship, the USS *Housatonic*, near Charleston, South Carolina.
May, 1864	General William T. Sherman starts his Atlanta Campaign, which will see the destruction of a large part of Georgia.
1866	British engineer Robert Whitehead develops the first practical torpedo.
1867	The last Tokugawa shogun surrenders power to imperial forces, paving the way for the Meiji Restoration and Japan's reentry into world politics and culture.
June 19, 1867	The execution of Emperor Maximilian I of Mexico ends the establishment of a pro-French Mexican Empire.
Feb., 1868	The Brazilian navy destroys Paraguayan fortifications at Humaita, allowing Brazil to attack the Paraguayan capital, Asunción.
1870	The Russians order Smith and Wesson pistols, the first military order for these.

1870-1871	The Franco-Prussian War sees the French quickly defeated and the Prussians take Paris.
1873	German arms manufacturer Alfred Krupp invents one of the first practical recoil systems for field artillery pieces.
1873	The Bofors iron and arms company is established in Sweden; it is later owned by Alfred Nobel.
1873	The Nordenfelt gun, designed by Swedish engineer Helge Palmcrantz, is patented and named after the steel producer Thorsten Nordenfelt.
Sept., 1878- Nov., 1880	The Second Anglo-Afghan War.
Jan. 22, 1879	The Battle of Isandhlwana sees the defeat of a British expeditionary force by the Zulus at the start of the Anglo-Zulu War; on the following day, at Rorke's Drift, the British are victorious.
1880's	The French develop high-explosive artillery, rendering all existing forts obsolete.
Aug., 1880	The Enfield rifle is tested and approved for use by the British Army.
1884	Hiram Stevens Maxim invents the first practical machine gun.
Jan. 26, 1885	The Siege of Khartoum, Sudan, ends in the capture of Khartoum and the death of Charles Gordon.
1889	John M. Browning begins developing his guns in the United States.
1892	The Model 1892 "Lebel" revolver is developed by the French.
Mar. 1, 1896	The Italian army is defeated at the Battle of Adowa, the first major defeat of a European army in Africa.
1897	The French develop the first antiaircraft gun for use against balloons.
1898	The Mauser Model 1898 is produced; it is the culmination of military bolt action design.
1898	The Germans invent the Luger revolver.
Sept. 2, 1898	Some 400 British lancers charge and rout 2,500 Sudanese at the Battle of Omdurman.
1900	The Siege of the Foreign Legations in Beijing, China, results in the dispatch of a large, multinational European force to China to rescue diplomats and others in the Legations.
1900	The zeppelin, also known as a rigid airship or dirigible, a steerable lighter-than-air aircraft, is invented in 1900 by German count Ferdinand Graf von Zeppelin.
May 17, 1900	The Relief of Mafeking in South Africa (modern-day Botswana) follows a siege that captured the imagination of the press around the world.

1903	The Wright brothers, William and Orville, launch the first successful airplane at Kitty Hawk, North Carolina.
1904	Japan attacks the Russian-controlled port of Lüshun, traditionally known as Port Arthur, beginning the Russo-Japanese War, a conflict between Russia and Japan for control over Korea and Manchuria.
1904-1905	Trinitrotoluene (TNT) is first used as a military explosive during the Russo-Japanese War.
1904-1905	The effective use of indirect fire during the Russo-Japanese War spurs American and European leaders to adopt it for their own armies in order to defend their guns against counterbattery and infantry weapon fire.
1905	The Japanese navy wins a stunning victory at Battle of Tsushima, devastating the Russian fleets and forcing Russia to surrender Korea and other territory to Japan.
1905	The paramilitary Legion of Frontiersmen is formed.
1905	The French build the first airplane factory, near Paris.
1906	HMS *Dreadnought*, the first all-big-gun battleship, is launched at Portsmouth, England, transforming the nature of ship architecture.
1908	The Luger P.08 is adopted as the official German service pistol.
1910	A plane takes off for the first time from the deck of a ship, presaging the modern aircraft carrier.
Oct. 11, 1911	After an Italian pilot flies the first combat mission, using his plane for reconnaissance, during the Italo-Turkish War, Italy begins using airplanes and dirigibles for bombing attacks.
1912	"Bangalore torpedoes" are produced for the first time by Captain McClintock.
1912	Manufactured by Krupp for the Germans, Big Bertha was a howitzer capable of firing artillery long distances, used extensively in World War I.
1912	World War I armies form large cavalry components, which are converted into infantry as the war evolves into stagnant trench warfare, and high casualty rates occur.
1914	Rolls-Royce manufactures an armored car for the British Royal Naval Air Service, designed to protect the Belgian airfields from attack by the Germans. These were used in Palestine in 1917-1918.
Aug., 1914	German planes bomb Paris.
Aug. 28, 1914	The Battle of the Heligoland Bight is the first naval battle of World War I.
Sept., 1914	German U-9 submarines torpedo Allied ships.
Nov. 1, 1914	In the Battle of Coronel, the German East Asiatic Fleet destroys a smaller British force and then is itself destroyed at the Battle of the Falklands.
1915	The Beretta pistol is developed in Italy; the Beretta machine gun follows in 1918.

Jan. 24, 1915	During the Battle of the Dogger Bank, the British fleet is warned by radio intercepts.
Feb. 4, 1915	A major German submarine campaign against British shipping begins.
Apr., 1915	The first aerial "dogfight" takes place after German aircraft are fitted with machine guns that are coordinated to fire between the blades of a moving propeller.
Apr., 1915	The ultimately unsuccessful Allied attack on Turkey at Gallipoli begins.
Apr. 22, 1915	The Second Battle of Ypres sees the first use of poison gas in battle on the western front.
May, 1915	German zeppelins bomb London.
May 7, 1915	The sinking of the *Lusitania* leads to a major public outcry in the United States.
1915-1917	"Young Turk" Ottomans massacre between 1 and 1.5 million Armenians in Anatolia and historic western Armenia.
1916	Unmanned aerial vehicles (drone aircraft) are developed for attacking zeppelins; they are later used for reconnaissance and for bombing of enemy targets.
Apr. 20, 1916	Defeat of British forces after the Siege of Kut, which started on December 7, 1915.
Apr. 24-30, 1916	Easter Uprising in Ireland.
May 30-31, 1916	In the Battle of Jutland, the German fleet destroys the British fleet.
June 10, 1916	The Turks surrender their garrison in Mecca.
July 1, 1916	On the first day of the Battle of the Somme, 19,000 British soldiers are killed, the highest loss by the British army on any single day.
Feb., 1917	Czar Nicholas II abdicates during the First Russian Revolution.
May, 1917	The World War I Allies establish the Atlantic convoy system.
May 21, 1917	The Imperial War Graves Commission (later the Commonwealth War Graves Commission) is formed by Fabian Ware to look after the war dead from Britain and its empire.
July, 1917	T. E. Lawrence leads the Arabs in their capture of Aqaba from the Turks.
Oct. 31, 1917	In the Battle of Beersheba, the Australian Light Horse charge at Turkish positions in Beersheba, capturing the city.
Nov. 7, 1917	The second Russian Revolution sees communists seize power in Petrograd (St. Petersburg), leading to the start of the Russian Civil War. (The date was October 25 in Russia, then still using the Gregorian calendar.)
Nov. 20, 1917	The British make a successful tank attack at the Battle of Cambrai.
Apr. 21, 1918	The "Red Baron," Manfred Richthofen, the most famous air ace of World War I, is shot down.

Nov. 11, 1918	A cease-fire ends World War I.
1919	The restrictions imposed on the German military by the Treaty of Versailles at the end of World War I meet almost universal disapproval across the political spectrum in Germany.
1919	The Government Communications Headquarters (GCHQ) are established in Britain to listen in to radio transmissions in Europe, initially operating as a government code and cipher school.
1920	American John Taliaferro Thompson invents the most famous submachine gun, known as the "tommy gun," fully automatic and small and light enough to be fired by a single individual without support.
1920-1960	Nerve gases, such as tabun and sarin, are developed for chemical warfare to inhibit nerve function, leading to respiratory paralysis, or asphyxia.
Jan. 16, 1920	The League of Nations holds its first meeting to mediate in disputes between nations.
Aug. 31, 1920	At the Battle of Komarow, the Poles are involved in the last great cavalry charge in history.
Sept., 1920	Mohandas K. Gandhi, the "Mahatma," starts a campaign of nonviolent resistance against British rule in India.
Oct., 1920	The Spanish Foreign Legion is founded.
Oct., 1920	The Arab Legion is founded.
1921	British spy and later naval analyst Hector Bywater publishes *Sea-Power in the Pacific*, describing how the Japanese could win a Pacific war. The book prompts great interest in Japan.
1922	Turks capture Smyrna, signaling the defeat of the Greeks in the Greco-Turkish War.
1923	The Treaty of Lausanne creates the Republic of Turkey, bringing the Ottoman Empire to its official end.
1923	HMS *Hermes*, the first purpose-built aircraft carrier, is commissioned by the British government.
1923	The building of the Singapore Naval Base to protect British interests in East Asia and Southeast Asia is announced.
1925-1940	During the cell-culture phase of biological warfare, biological weapons are mass-produced and stockpiled; Japan's research program includes direct experimentation on humans.
1925	The Schutzstaffel (SS) is formed to protect members of the Nazi Party, later becoming a government "agency" in Germany. Its members perpetrate major crimes during World war II.
1926	Robert Goddard achieves the first free flight of a liquid-fueled rocket.

1928	Chiang Kai-shek captures Beijing and, as leader of the Nationalist Party, heads China's first modern government.
Nov., 1928	*Am westen nichts neues* (*All Quiet on the Western Front*), an antiwar novel by German World War I veteran and writer Erich Maria Remarque, is published in Germany.
Dec. 19-22, 1929	Britons and other Europeans are airlifted from Kabul, Afghanistan, in the first major airlift in war.
Sept. 18, 1929	German President Paul von Hindenburg repudiates German responsibility for World War I.
1930	As the building of extensive fortified lines begins, the French start work on the Maginot line along the eastern border of France, naming the fortifications for André Maginot, French minister of defense.
1930's	German scientist Wernher von Braun develops the first liquid-fueled rockets.
1931	The Japanese bomb Mukden in the first major aerial bombing of any city in history.
1932	The nationalist Chinese government of Chiang Kai-shek starts "extermination campaigns" against the Chinese communists.
1933	Adolf Hitler, leader of the National Socialist German Workers' (Nazi) Party, is appointed chancellor of Germany and calls for the abolition of the Treaty of Versailles and the rearmament of Germany.
1934-1935	Mao Zedong leads his Chinese communist forces on a 6,000-mile strategic retreat known as the Long March.
1935	The Italian invasion of Abyssinia leads to the collapse of collective security arrangements formulated by the League of Nations.
1935	British scientists develop the first radar.
1935	The Germans first develop the Stuka dive-bombers; the Stuka is used in combat for the first time in 1936 during the Spanish Civil War.
Mar. 28, 1935	The Catalina flying boat is first used for reconnaissance by the (British) Royal Navy.
Mar., 1936	The German government remilitarizes the Rhineland, leading to increased tensions in Europe.
July, 1936	The Spanish Civil War begins; during this conflict, much of Spain's infrastructure will be destroyed and new weapons will be tested.
July, 1936	German air force volunteers fighting on the Nationalist side in the Spanish Civil War form the Condor Legion.
1936	The M-1 Garand rifle is the first standard-issue semiautomatic military rifle.
1936	The first practical helicopter is developed by German engineer Heinrich Focke.

1936	The International Brigades are established in Spain.
Oct., 1936	The first tank-versus-cavalry and tank-versus-tank engagements of the Spanish Civil War take place near Esquivias, south of Madrid.
Apr., 1937	German air forces supporting the Nationalist cause in the Spanish Civil War bomb the Spanish town of Guernica, killing approximately 2,100 of the town's 8,000 inhabitants in arguably the first premeditated use of terror bombing.
May 6, 1937	The crashing of the *Hindenburg* airship results in the decline of interest in airships.
July, 1937	Japan invades China, initiating the Second Sino-Japanese War (1937-1945).
1938	The British use the Bren gun after its original design in Czechoslovakia.
Mar., 1938	In what has come to be known as the Anschluss, Germany annexes Austria, forming a country which dominates Central Europe.
Sept., 1938	With the agreement of other European powers, Germany annexes the Sudetenland from Czechoslovakia, and then the rest of Czechoslovakia in March, 1939.
Apr., 1939	Italy launches a joint naval and air attack on Albania, quickly capturing the country and annexing it.
Sept., 1939	German chancellor Adolf Hitler uses combined arms forces to invade Poland, which is then partitioned between Germany and the Soviet Union.
Sept. 1, 1939	Polish cavalry at Krojanty charge Germans, leading to the myth surrounding cavalry attacking tanks.
May 10, 1940	The German Luftwaffe conducts the first combat parachute and glider troop landings to open Germany's western-front attack on the Netherlands.
June, 1940	The Stern Gang, or Lehi, an extremist Zionist organization, is formed to fight against the British in the British-mandated territory of Palestine.
June 22, 1940	The French sign an armistice after their defeat by Germany in less than six weeks. British prime minister Winston Churchill announces that the battle of France is over; the battle of Britain is about to begin.
Aug., 1940	Germans begin the Battle of Britain, a series of air raids over Britain aimed at destroying British infrastructure and morale.
Nov. 10, 1940	The British Royal Navy produces a decisive aerial victory at Taranto Harbor, Italy, crippling the anchored Italian fleet with nighttime bomb and torpedo attacks.
1940-1969	During the vaccine development and stockpiling phase of biological warfare, there are open-air tests of biological dispersal in urban environments in the United States.
May 20, 1941	German parachutists land in Crete in the first mainly airborne invasion in history.
June, 1941	The Germans begin Operation Barbarossa, their invasion of Russia, advancing as far as Moscow and Leningrad.

1941	U.S. pilots form the Flying Tigers to assist the Chinese in fighting the Japanese.
July 25, 1941	Spanish volunteers form the Blue Division to fight on the eastern front in World War II.
Nov. 20, 1941	The Australian Army develops the Owen gun.
Dec. 7, 1941	The Japanese navy launches a morning surprise air raid against the U.S. fleet at Pearl Harbor, Hawaii, sinking or damaging several U.S. battleships and bringing the United States into World War II.
Jan. 20, 1942	During the Wannsee Conference, the Germans inaugurate plans for the Holocaust.
Feb. 15, 1942	Singapore falls to the Japanese.
Apr., 1942	Soviet leader Joseph Stalin discovers information about the U.S. nuclear program.
May, 1942	The Battle of the Coral Sea is the first naval battle fought entirely by carrier-based aircraft.
May, 1942	Navajo Indians are first used to transmit messages that cannot be decoded by the Japanese.
June 13, 1942	The United States forms the Office of Strategic Services (OSS), forerunner of the Central Intelligence Agency (CIA).
Aug., 1942- Jan., 1943	With the use of aerial resupply, the Russians withstand the German Siege of Stalingrad, marking the ultimate German failure on the Russian front.
Aug. 23, 1942	The Italian cavalry charge the Soviet artillery near the River Don in the last successful cavalry charge.
May 16-17, 1943	During the Dam Buster raids, the British Royal Air Force drops bouncing bombs on dams in Germany.
Apr. 19- May 16, 1943	Jews in the Warsaw Ghetto revolt against the Germans.
July, 1943	The Russians defeat the Germans at the Battle of Kursk, one of the largest tank battles in history.
1944	Germany launches the first long-range ballistic missiles, the V-1 and V-2, against England during World War II.
1944	The Japanese begin kamikaze attacks on Allied ships in the Pacific.
1944-1946	The AK-47, the Kalashnikov rifle, is developed in the Soviet Union.
June 6, 1944	On what is known as D day, the Allies begin an invasion of Normandy, France, the largest amphibious operation in history and the beginning of Allied victory in Europe.
June 13, 1944	The Germans fire the Fieseler Fi 103 (V-1) for the first time at London. It is later followed by the V-2 rocket bombs, used to strike terror in southern Britain.

Feb. 24-25, 1945	The U.S. Air Force firebombs Tokyo, and General Curtis LeMay promotes U.S. airpower.
Apr., 1945	In the last major amphibious offensive of World War II, U.S. forces invade Okinawa and, after meeting fierce resistance, seize the island from Japan.
Apr.-May, 1945	The Russians wage air, artillery, and tank attacks in the Battle for Berlin, which ultimately leads to German surrender.
June 26, 1945	Replacing the ineffective League of Nations, the United Nations is formed to mediate disputes between countries, providing a platform for dialogue.
July 16, 1945	The first atomic bomb is successfully tested at Alamogordo, New Mexico.
Aug. 6, 1945	The first atomic bomb to be used in war is dropped by the United States on the Japanese city of Hiroshima, killing more than 70,000 civilians and hastening the end of the war. Four days later, the second bomb was dropped on Nagasaki, killing 40,000.
Aug. 15, 1945	Emperor Hirohito announces the surrender of Japan.
1945	As World War II concludes, Indochinese Communist Party leader Ho Chi Minh proclaims a Democratic Republic of Vietnam, and France begins reasserting its colonial rule in Indochina.
1945	The International Court of Justice is established in The Hague by United Nations Charter.
1945-1946	An international tribunal to try Germans accused of war crimes is conducted at Nuremberg, establishing the concept of war crimes in international law.
1946	Air America is founded as a U.S. civilian airline. It is later revealed to be covertly owned and operated by the Central Intelligence Agency (CIA).
1946-1949	Civil war rages in China between Nationalist and Communist Party forces, resulting in the triumph of Communism and in Nationalist leader Chiang Kai-shek's flight to Taiwan.
Feb. 22, 1946	George F. Kennan's "Long Telegram" articulates the rationale behind Soviet aggression and advocates a firm U.S. response, with force if necessary, beginning the Cold War era.
July 22, 1946	King David's Hotel in Jerusalem is bombed, the first modern major bombing in the Middle East.
1947	The Kalashnikov AK-47 becomes the first widely deployed modern assault rifle.
Mar. 12, 1947	U.S. president Harry S. Truman introduces the Truman Doctrine, committing the United States to responsibility for defending global democracy—a clear signal that the United States intends to check Soviet expansion and influence.
Sept. 18, 1947	The Central Intelligence Agency is established.
Jan. 4, 1948	The assassination of Burmese independence leader Aung San is followed by an independent Burma.

Aug., 1949	The Soviet Union tests its first atomic bomb.
June 25, 1950	The Korean War begins, becoming the first conflict to involve the United Nations.
Sept. 15-19, 1950	U.N. soldiers under General Douglas MacArthur land at Inchon, the first major seaborne operation since D day.
1952	The world's first hydrogen bomb is exploded at Enewetak Atoll in the Pacific Ocean.
1953	The Soviet Union tests its first hydrogen bomb.
1954	The Geneva Conference, after discussions on the Korean War, calls for a partition of Indochina into four countries—North Vietnam, South Vietnam, Laos, and Cambodia—and for an election within two years to unify the two Vietnams.
1954	The USS *Nautilus*, the first nuclear-powered submarine, is commissioned.
1955	The United States starts actively supporting South Vietnam, taking over from the French.
1955	The first practical hovercraft is developed by Christopher Cockerell.
1956	The Chinook Boeing Vertol is designed as a U.S. Army medium-lift helicopter.
1956	The United States and the U.S.-backed South Vietnamese president, Ngo Dinh Diem, reject the Geneva-mandated reunification elections, knowing that the popular Ho Chi Minh would win.
July 26, 1956	The Suez Crisis leads to Egypt's capturing and nationalizing the Suez Canal Company.
Oct. 23- Nov. 10, 1956	The Hungarian Uprising resists the influence of the Soviet Union in Hungary.
1957	The Soviet Union successfully tests an intercontinental ballistic missile.
Oct. 4, 1957	The Soviet Union launches the world's first artificial Earth satellite, inaugurating the space race, sparking a reassessment of U.S. military and technological capabilities, and providing impetus for the development of both a space program and more sophisticated weapons-delivery systems.
1959-1970	Psychoactive chemical weapons are developed to produce hallucinations in exposed individuals.
Jan., 1959	Formation of the Viet Cong launches an armed struggle, backed by North Vietnam, against U.S. soldiers and South Vietnamese loyal to the Diem government.
Jan., 1960	U.S. president Dwight D. Eisenhower warns about the rise in the military-industrial complex.
July 11, 1960	Katanga tries to break away from the Congo.
1961	Agent Orange is used as a defoliant in the Vietnam War.

Oct. 14-26, 1962	A U.S. pilot takes pictures indicating that Soviets are placing missiles on Cuba. The ensuing Cuban Missile Crisis takes the world to the brink of nuclear war.
1963	The United States deploys Polaris submarine-launched missiles. The British introduce them in 1968.
May, 1963	The British manufacture the Chieftain Tank.
Oct. 7, 1963	The United States and the Soviet Union sign the Partial Test Ban Treaty.
Nov. 1, 1963	The South Vietnamese government of Ngo Dinh Diem precipitates instability in the country, leading to increased U.S. military involvement in the region. The assassination of John F. Kennedy three weeks later sees Lyndon B. Johnson becoming U.S. president.
1964	The People's Republic of China conducts its first successful nuclear weapons test.
1964	War in Congo involves the use of mercenaries, including "Mad" Mike Hoare.
1964	The Palestine Liberation Organization is founded.
1965	The United States pursues a policy of escalated military involvement in Vietnam.
Mar. 2, 1965	The U.S. Air Force begins Operation Rolling Thunder, which involves sustained bombing of North Vietnam.
1966	Mao Zedong initiates the decadelong Chinese Cultural Revolution to purge his opponents from the Communist Party and renew the people's revolutionary spirit.
Jan. 27, 1967	More than sixty (and later many more) countries sign the Outer Space Treaty, banning the use of outer space for warfare.
Apr., 1967	The Rapier surface-to-air missile is developed and manages to shoot down a Meteor drone.
May, 1967	Biafra's attempt to break away from Nigeria starts the Nigerian Civil War.
June 5, 1967	The Israeli Air Force (IAF) launches devastating surprise counter-air raids against threatening Arab nations, beginning the Six-Day War.
Oct. 21, 1967	Egypt sinks the Israeli destroyer *Eilat* with a Soviet Styx cruise missile.
1968	The Soviet Union invades Czechoslovakia, establishing the Brezhnev Doctrine of Soviet military domination over Warsaw Pact states.
Jan., 1968	The North Vietnamese and Viet Cong launch the Tet Offensive, which, although unsuccessful, contradicts U.S. reports that a decisive end to the war is near at hand.
Jan. 23, 1968	The North Korean navy captures the USS *Pueblo*, according to U.S. Navy intelligence.
Mar. 18, 1969	The United States starts secret bombings of Cambodia during Operation Menu, in an attempt to destroy the Ho Chi Minh Trail.

1969-present	During the genetic engineering phase of biological warfare, recombinant DNA biotechnology opens new frontiers in the design and production of biological weapons.
1970-1979	During an era of détente, stable relations, relative to the earlier Cold War, prevail between the Soviet Union and the United States and their respective allies.
1970-present	Binary chemical weapons, stored and shipped in their component parts, are developed to allow chemical weapons to be safely transported to deployment sites.
Mar. 31, 1971	The British deploy Poseidon submarine-launched missiles.
1973	The last American fighting forces withdraw from Vietnam in late March, following a January 27 peace agreement.
Oct. 6, 1973	Egypt launches an air strike against Israel, beginning Arab-Israeli October War, also known as the Yom Kippur War.
May 18, 1974	India tests its first atomic bomb, known as the "Smiling Buddha."
Jan., 1975	The Cambodian Communists (Khmer Rouge) massacre the entire population of the town of Ang Snuol, after capturing it.
Apr. 17, 1975	The fall of Phnom Penh, the Cambodian capital, is accompanied by the rising rule of the Khmer Rouge.
Apr. 30, 1975	Saigon finally falls to the North Vietnamese forces, and Vietnam is united under communist rule following a referendum held the following year.
1976	The emergence of Khun Sa and his private army in northern Burma is financed by drug sales.
May, 1976	The Liberation Tigers of Tamil Elam (known as the Tamil Tigers) emerge in Sri Lanka.
July 4, 1976	Israeli commandos storm the old terminal building at Entebbe International Airport, Uganda, freeing Israeli hostages in one of the most daring antiterrorist raids of the modern era.
1978	The United States develops the Abrams tank, named after General Creighton Abrams, U.S. Army chief of staff and commander of the U.S. military forces in South Vietnam from 1968 until 1972. The U.S. military begins using it in 1980.
1978	The United States begins production of the first precision-guided artillery munitions.
May 13, 1978	Ex-Congo mercenary Bob Denard takes the Comoros Islands.
Dec., 1978	Vietnam invades Cambodia, capturing the vast majority of the country in two weeks, and establishes the People's Republic of Kampuchea.
1979	Soviet forces enter Afghanistan ostensibly to overthrow the government of Prime Minister Hafizullah Amin and install a puppet government loyal to Moscow.

1979	The Iranian Revolution ends Iran's close military ties with the United States and replaces the shah's regime with an Islamic theocracy.
Feb. 17- Mar. 16, 1979	Chinese soldiers invade northern Vietnam. The war quickly ends in a stalemate, and subsequently the Chinese government overhauls its army structure.
Oct., 1979	The British replace Poseidon submarine-launched missiles with Trident missiles.
Jan. 23, 1980	After an Iranian mob takes over the U.S. embassy, taking hostages, and the Soviet Union invades Afghanistan, U.S. president Jimmy Carter declares that the United States will consider any threat against the Persian Gulf a threat against its vital interests and will react, if necessary, with military force. The so-called Iranian hostage crisis ensues.
1981	Demonstrations against U.S. cruise missiles start at Greenham Common in England.
Mar., 1981	The Soviets launch their first well-planned offensive in Afghanistan, inaugurating the decadelong Soviet-Afghan War.
1982	Hezbollah, the "Party of God," forms in Lebanon.
May 4, 1982	The firing of an Exocet missile, manufactured by the French, by the Argentine air force against the British HMS *Sheffield* leads to major changes in British naval tactics during the Falklands War.
June 13-14, 1982	British soldiers on the Falkland Islands charge Argentines at the Battle of Mount Tumbledown, the last successful bayonet charge until 2004.
Mar. 11, 1985	Mikhail Gorbachev is chosen as the new general secretary of the Soviet Communist Party, and his reforms initiate a thaw in relations between the Soviet Union and the United States.
July 28, 1986	Soviet leader Mikhail Gorbachev announces a limited withdrawal of Soviet troops from Afghanistan.
Dec. 8, 1987	The first intifada between Palestinians and Israelis begins.
Dec. 8, 1987	U.S. president Ronald Reagan and Soviet general secretary Gorbachev sign the Intermediate Nuclear Forces (INF) Treaty, which calls for the destruction of U.S. and Soviet missiles and nuclear weapons.
Mar. 16, 1988	In Iraq, Saddam Hussein uses nerve gas against the Kurds in Halabja.
Dec. 21, 1988	After Pan American Flight 103 explodes over Lockerbie, Scotland, killing hundreds, state terrorism mounted by Libya is blamed.
1989	The Afghan Interim Government (AIG) is established, and the Soviet Union completes its withdrawal from Afghanistan.
1989	Gorbachev is elected Soviet president in the first pluralist elections since 1917, and by the end of the year all Warsaw Pact nations have overthrown their communist leadership.

1989	The dismantling of Germany's Berlin Wall signifies the end of the Cold War, as U.S president George H. W. Bush promises economic aid to the Soviet Union.
1989	Vietnam announces the withdrawal of all its soldiers from Cambodia.
July 17, 1989	The first flight of the Stealth bomber, made by Northrop Corporation and Northrop Grumman, herald's the aircraft's role in combat after April, 1997.
Jan. 17, 1991	A U.S.-led U.N. coalition leads a well-orchestrated air attack against Iraqi dictator Saddam Hussein in an effort to oust his forces from Kuwait, which he invaded in the summer of 1990.
Jan. 18, 1991	U.S. Patriot missiles are used in combat against Scud missiles fired by Iraq at Saudi Arabia during the First Gulf War.
Feb., 1991	U.N. forces undertake a decisive ground assault on Iraqi positions in Kuwait.
Apr., 1991	No-fly zones are established and enforced in Iraq to prevent repression of Kurds in northern Iraq.
1991	After the Baltic states of Estonia, Latvia, and Lithuania are granted independence and other former soviets join the Commonwealth of Independent States, Gorbachev resigns as president and the Soviet Union is officially dissolved.
Feb. 26, 1993	A bomb attack on New York's World Trade Center kills 6 people and injures more than 1,000.
May 25, 1993	The International Criminal Tribunal for the former Yugoslavia is established at The Hague, following passage of Resolution 827 by the United Nations Security Council.
1994	The Australian company Metal Storm forms to develop machine guns and electronically initiated superimposed-load weapons technology.
1995	The April bombing of a federal office building in Oklahoma City, Oklahoma, by one or more individuals allegedly affiliated with militia groups kills 168. Within the same week, the Japanese religious cult Aum Shinrikyo mounts a sarin gas attack in a Tokyo subway, hospitalizing 400.
1996	Millionaire Islamic extremist Osama Bin Laden issues a declaration of war against the United States.
Jan., 1996	An international force composed largely of troops under the auspices of the North Atlantic Treaty Organization (NATO) is deployed in Bosnia to ensure the implementation of the Dayton Accords.
1998	Pakistan successfully tests its first fission device.
Aug. 7, 1998	The simultaneous bombings of U.S. embassies in Kenya and Tanzania in August kill 224, and Osama Bin Laden's supporters are suspected. Shortly thereafter, the United States conducts a counterattack against Bin Laden's training base in Afghanistan.

2000	The October 12 suicide bombing of the USS *Cole* in the Persian Gulf kills 17 sailors.
Aug. 12, 2000	During a Russian naval exercise, the *Kursk* submarine sinks.
Apr., 2001	A U.S. spy plane is brought down over China in the Hainan Island incident.
Sept. 11, 2001	Two hijacked planes are deliberately crashed into the World Trade Center in New York, another is crashed into the Pentagon, and a fourth crashes in a field in Pennsylvania, in a coordinated series of attacks organized by Osama Bin Laden's terrorist group al-Qaeda.
Oct. 7, 2001	U.S. president George W. Bush announces the start of the War on Terrorism in response to the September 11, 2001, attacks on U.S. soil. A U.S.-led invasion of Afghanistan starts to bring down the Taliban government of the country that has been harboring Osama bin Laden.
Mar. 20-May 1, 2003	A U.S.-led invasion of Iraq topples Saddam Hussein. Justification for the Bush administration's preemptive strike, previously presented before the United Nations, includes controversial and, some maintain, poorly substantiated evidence that the Iraqi dictator is refusing to be transparent about programs to develop weapons of mass destruction and suspected use of Iraqi soil to provide terrorist groups with safe harbor.
2003-2009	Fighting in the Darfur region leads to atrocities and severe humanitarian problems for the people of southern Sudan.
Oct. 15, 2003	Yang Liwei becomes the first Chinese taikonaut in space.
2004	An attempt to overthrow the government of Equatorial Guinea is executed by mercenaries hired in South Africa.
Oct. 9, 2006	The North Korean government issues an announcement that it has successfully conducted its first nuclear test.
Aug., 2008	A brief war erupts between the Russian Federation and Georgia over South Ossetia.
Jan. 22, 2009	On his second day in office, U.S. president Barack Obama issues an executive order to close the terrorist detention camp at Guantánamo Bay, Cuba.
Mar. 4, 2009	The International Criminal Court (ICC) issues a warrant for the arrest of Sudanese president Omar Hassan al-Bashir for war crimes, in its first action against a head of state since the ICC's founding in 2002.
May 18, 2009	The Sri Lankan Civil War ends folllowing more than a quarter century of conflict.
May 27, 2009	After conducting nuclear tests, North Korea issues an announcement stating that it is no longer bound by the 1953 armistice it signed at the end of the Korean War. The United Nations issues sanctions in mid-June, in response to which North Korea promises to step up its weaponization of plutonium.

BIBLIOGRAPHY

Recently published secondary print resources are categorized by subject, such as General Studies, Military Theory and Strategy, and type of weapon or technology. Abbreviations are used at the end of each entry, summarizing features of the work as follows: "ill" for illustrations, "M" for maps, "tab" for tables, "chr" for chronology, "app" for appendixes, "glo" for glossary, "B" for bibliography, and "i" for index. These abbreviations are enclosed in brackets, for example: [ill, M, glo, B, i]

Several prominent publishers universally identified with series of works of compilation and collection in military, naval, air, and space matters, often published annually, are not included in the bibliographical listing but may be consulted for their ongoing and more professionally targeted publications. Important examples are *Jane's Fighting Ships*, *Jane's Weapons Systems*, *Jane's Infantry Weapons*, *Jane's All the World's Fighting Aircraft*, *Brassey's Naval Annual*, *Naval Institute Guide to Combat Fleets*, *Naval Institute Guide to World Military Aviation*, *Conway's All the World's Fighting Ships*, *Royal United Services Institute and Brassey's Defence Yearbook*, *Putnam Aviation Series*, *Guinness Book of Air Warfare*, *Guinness Book of Decisive Battles*, and *SIPRI Yearbook: Armaments, Disarmament, and International Security*.

GENERAL STUDIES

Addington, Larry H. *The Patterns of War Since the Eighteenth Century*. 1984. Rev. ed. Bloomington: Indiana University Press, 1994. A synthesis of the massive changes in warfare since the eighteenth century, describing sociopolitical, technological, and organizational patterns and covering the dynastic wars up to the post–World War II period. [ill, M, B, i]

————. *Patterns of War Through the Eighteenth Century*. Bloomington: Indiana University Press, 1990. A companion to the previous entry, incorporating ancient, medieval, and early modern land and naval warfare, including the age of sailing ship warfare and the expansion of European overseas empires. [ill, M, B, i]

Bell, Martin. *Through Gates of Fire: a Journey into World Disorder*. London: Weidenfeld & Nicolson, 2003. A veteran war reporter analyzes the evolution of warfare over the 1980's, 1990's, and 2000's, by looking at the integration of the roles of war, journalism, and politics in how modern warfare is presented and justified to the general public. [i]

Black, Jeremy. *The Age of Total War, 1860-1945*. Westport, Conn.: Praeger Security International, 2006. Defines "total war" in terms of the geographic and chronological scope of warfare, the intensity of the conflict, and the involvement of civilians in the conflict. The author sets aside the period roughly from the American Civil War to the end of World War II as being different from both the eras before and after, in that the wars fought during these periods had immense consequences for large parts of the world and were fought by entire societies, not just their armies. [B, i]

Boog, Horst, ed. *The Conduct of the Air War in the Second World War: An International Comparison*. New York: St. Martin's Press, 1992. The proceedings from a conference in Germany in 1988, containing thirty-four essays about various aspects of the air war, including surveys and comparisons of the performance of seven nations, including the United States, Great Britain, Germany, Russia, Japan, and Italy. [B, i]

Brodie, Bernard, and Fawn Brodie. *From Crossbow to H-Bomb*. New York: Dell, 1962, 1973. A useful introduction to weapons development. [ill, B]

Clodfelter, Michael D. *Warfare and Armed Conflicts: A Statistical Reference to Casualty and Other Figures, 1618-1991.* 2 vols. London: McFarland, 1992. A statistical record of all military casualties of modern warfare, discussing the impact of weapons since the introduction of gunpowder. [tab, B, i]

Contamine, Philippe. *War in the Middle Ages.* Translated by Michael Jones. Oxford, England: Blackwell, 1980. A good survey of medieval European warfare, neglecting naval aspects, by a prominent French authority. [ill, B, i]

Cordesman, Anthony H., and Abraham R. Wagner. *The Lessons of Modern War.* 3 vols. Boulder, Colo.: Westview Press, 1990-1996. A study of the changes that faced military planners at the end of the Cold War. [ill, M, B, i]

Craig, Gordon A. *The Politics of the Prussian Army, 1640-1945.* New York: Oxford University Press, 1955. A classic study of the enormous influence of the Prussian Army Officer Corps, and of armies that were based on the Prussian military system. [B, i]

De Moor, J. A., and H. L. Wesseling, eds. *Imperialism and War: Essays on Colonial Wars in Asia and Africa.* Leiden, Netherlands: E. J. Brill, 1989. A collection of academic essays on the nature of the European colonial powers involving themselves in warfare around the world before the start of World War I. [M, B, i]

DeVries, Kelly. *Medieval Military Technology.* Peterborough, Ont.: Broadview Press, 1992. An encyclopedic production divided into four sections: arms and armor, artillery, fortifications, and warships. [ill, B, i]

Diagram Group. *Weapons: An International Encyclopedia from 5000 B.C. to 2000 A.D.* New York: St. Martin's Press, 1980. A profusely illustrated, folio-sized reference work featuring all types of weapons developed in all cultures over seven thousand years. [ill, glo, B, i]

Echevarris, Antulio J., II. *Imagining Future War: The West Technological Revolution and Visions of Wars to Come, 1880-1914.* Westport, Conn.: Praeger Security International, 2007. A short history and analysis of the changes in warfare in the three decades before World War I. [ill, B, i]

Elgood, Robert. *The Arms and Armour of Arabia in the Eighteenth, Nineteenth, and Twentieth Centuries.* New York: Scholar, 1994. A folio-sized, profusely illustrated survey of Islamic arms. [ill, app, glo, B, i]

Fuller, J. F. C. *The Decisive Battles of the Western World.* London: Eyre & Spottiswoode, 1954. A detailed account of thirty-four battles from Salamis to D day, by a leading British military authority. [M, B, i]

Glete, Jan. *Navies and Nations: Warships, Navies, and State Building in Europe and America, 1500-1860.* 2 vols. Stockholm, Sweden: Almqvist, 1993. A comprehensive and definitive reassessment by a remarkable Swedish scholar of the role of naval warfare in the development of hegemonic expansive powers of Europe and America; a multinational review and comparison in statistical and quantitative detail of twelve major and more than forty minor navies during the period. [ill, tab, B, i]

_____. *Warfare at Sea, 1500-1650: Maritime Conflicts and the Transformation of Europe.* London: Routledge, 2000. A brilliant synthesis incorporating themes of naval technology, tactics, strategy, personnel, administration, logistics, and national states as related to maritime wars during the early modern period. [M, B, i]

Hall, Bert S. *Weapons and Warfare in Renaissance Europe: Gunpowder, Technology, and Tactics.* Baltimore: Johns Hopkins University Press, 1997. A discussion of gunpowder as a catalyst for historical change and related technological developments in gun casting and gun carriages. [ill, M, B, i]

Hanson, Victor D., ed. *Hoplites: The Classical Greek Battle Experience.* London: Routledge, 1991. Papers by experts on ancient warfare, covering men and weapons, battlefield environment, and rules of war. [ill, B, i]

Harkavy, Robert E., and Stephanie G. Neuman. *Warfare and the Third World.* New York: Palgrave, 2001. A survey of the nature of warfare in the Third World from the end of the Cold War. [B, i]

Haythornthwaite, Philip J. *The Colonial Wars Source Book.* London: Arms & Armour, 1995. A detailed reference work that includes vast amounts of information on colonial wars, colonial armies, and weapons in use at the time, as well as biographies of the major figures involved. [ill, M, tab, chr, glo, B, i]

_____. *The Napoleonic Souce Book*. London: Arms & Armour, 1990. An important reference work on the Napoleonic Wars, starting with a general survey and then covering (alphabetically) all involved countries, the types of weapons used by them, and biographies of the major commanders, with copious illustrations and quotations from original sources. [ill, M, tab, chr, glo, B, i]

_____. *The World War I Source Book*. London: Arms & Armour, 1992. Like others in this series, this book provides much detail on the armies involved in the conflict, as well as the political background to their involvement and then the nature of the fighting and the weaponry and biographies of the important commanders, as well as a detailed list of contemporary and secondary source material. [ill, M, tab, chr, glo, B, i]

Haywood, John. *Dark Age Naval Power: A Reassessment of the Frankish and Anglo-Saxon Seafaring Activity*. London: Routledge, 1991. A look at a neglected subject: the impressive maritime achievements of Germanic seafarers before the Vikings, with coverage of warfare, piracy, migration, and trade. [ill, M, glo, B, i]

Headrick, Daniel R. *Tools of Empire: Technology and European Imperialism in the Nineteenth Century*. New York: Oxford University Press, 1981. A discussion of nineteenth century imperialism as facilitated by innovations in technology such as steamships, submarine cables, guns, and gunboats. [B]

Hedges, Chris. *What Every Person Should Know About War*. New York: Free Press, 2003. A short overview of warfare in the post-Cold War period. [B, i]

Hogg, O. F. G. *The Royal Arsenal: Its Background, Origin, and Subsequent History*. 2 vols. New York: Oxford University Press, 1963. A comprehensive and heavily documented history of the British ordnance industry since the eleventh century. [ill, app, B]

Holsinger, M. Paul, ed. *War and American Popular Culture: A Historical Encyclopedia*. Westport, Conn.: Greenwood Press, 1999. A large and detailed encyclopedia including not only conflicts within the United States but also those overseas involving the U.S. armed forces, such as Korea, Vietnam, and other conflicts after 1975. [ill, B, i]

Howard, Howard E., ed. *The Theory and Practice of War*. New York: Praeger, 1965. A series of fifteen essays dedicated to Basil Liddell Hart, written by noted scholars such as Peter Paret, Gordon Craig, Jay Luvaas, Brian Bond, Norman Gibbs, and Henry Kissinger. [B]

Ion, A. Hamish, and Keith Neilson, eds. *Elite Military Formations in War and Peace*. Westport, Conn.: Praeger, 1996. A series of seven scholarly presentations of the history of special units from ancient times to the present. [B, i]

Isby, David C., and Charles Kamps, Jr. *Armies of NATO's Central Front*. London: Jane's Publishing Company Limited, 1985. A detailed survey of the military forces of the member countries of the North Atlantic Treaty Organization in the last part of the Cold War. [ill, i]

Jensen, Geoffrey, and Andrew Wiest, eds. *War in the Age of Technology: Myriad Faces of Modern Armed Conflict*. New York: New York University Press, 2001. An analysis of how warfare has changed from the end of the Cold War and the increasing importance of technology. [B, i]

Jones, Archer. *The Art of War in the Western World*. London: Harrap, 1987. An overview of twenty-five hundred years of land-based warfare in the West from the social-history perspective, with a focus on institutions, comparative analysis, and interactions. [ill, tab, M, B, i]

Jordan, Gerald, ed. *Naval Warfare in the Twentieth Century, 1900-1945*. New York: Russak, 1977. Thirteen essays in honor of Arthur Marder, by noted scholars such as Paul Kennedy, on John Fisher and Alfred von Tirpitz; Robin Higham, on peripheral weapons; Peter Gretton, on U-boats; Sadao Asada, on Japanese admirals; and W. A. B. Douglas, on the Canadian navy. [B]

Keegan, John, ed. *The Book of War: Twenty-five Centuries of Great War Writing*. London: Viking,

1999. A collection of eighty-two contemporary accounts from Thucydides to Desert Storm. [B, i]

Keen, Maurice, ed. *Medieval Warfare: A History*. New York: Oxford University Press, 1999. Twelve expert historians on methods of warfare from 700 to 1500, including H. B. Clarke on the Vikings, Clifford Rogers on the Hundred Years' War, and Felipe Fernandez-Armesto on naval warfare. [ill, M, B, i]

Kierman, Frank A., and J. K. Fairbank, eds. *The Chinese Ways in Warfare*. Cambridge, Mass.: Harvard University Press, 1974. A historical survey focusing on distinctive elements in Chinese warfare. [ill, B]

Kightly, Charles. *Strongholds of the Realm: Defenses in Britain from Prehistory to the Twentieth Century*. New York: Thames, 1979. A history of fortresses from early times to the present. [ill, B, i]

Laffin, John. *Brassey's Battles: Thirty-five Hundred Years of Conflicts, Campaigns, and Wars from A-Z*. New York: Barnes & Noble Books, 1995. A substantial alphabetical survey of seven thousand battles, campaigns, and wars. [ill, M, i]

Lynn, John A., ed. *Feeding Mars: Logistics in Western Warfare from the Middle Ages to the Present*. Boulder, Colo.: Westview Press, 1993. A dozen articles by expert scholars, such as Lynn, on Martin van Creveld's *Supplying War*; Bernard Bachrach, on logistics for the Crusades; Jon Sumida, on British industrial logistics and naval war production during World War I; and Timothy Runyan, on naval logistics during the Hundred Years' War. [B, i]

_____, ed. *Tools of War: Instruments of Warfare, 1445-1871*. Urbana: University of Illinois Press, 1990. A series of papers from a conference on how weapons shaped military thought and organization of armed forces, including Simon Adams on the late sixteenth century Habsburg hegemony, William Maltby on sailing ship tactics, Dennis Showalter on the Prussian army, and Hew Strachan on the British army. [B, i]

McElwee, William L. *The Art of War: Waterloo to Mons*. Bloomington: Indiana University Press, 1974. A general survey. [M, B, i]

McInnes, Colin J., and G. D. Sheffield, eds. *Warfare in the Twentieth Century: Theory and Practice*. Boston: Allen & Unwin, 1988. Nine essays by expert scholars, including McInnes, on nuclear strategy; Keith Jeffery, on colonial warfare; and Geoffrey Till, on naval power. [B, i]

Macksey, Kenneth. *For Want of a Nail: The Impact on War of Logistics and Communications*. Washington, D.C.: Brassey's, 1989. A study of technological developments in the fields of logistics and communications and their impact on warfare. [ill, M, B, i]

_____. *Technology and War: The Impact of Science on Weapon Development and Modern Battle*. London: Arms & Armour, 1986. Accounts of how science and scientific developments have influenced weaponry. [ill, i]

McNeill, William H. *The Age of Gunpowder Empires, 1450-1800*. Washington, D.C.: American Historical Association, 1989. An informative guide by an outstanding scholar on the role of gunpowder in imperial expansion. [B]

_____. *The Pursuit of Power: Technology, Armed Force, and Society Since 1000*. Chicago: University of Chicago Press, 1982. One volume in a trilogy by the premier scholar on world history, extending the concept of the military-industrial complex back several centuries to 1000 and presenting its practical and far-reaching impact on world society. [B, i]

Mallet, M. E., and J. R. Hale. *The Military Organization of a Renaissance State: Venice, 1400-1617*. New York: Cambridge University Press, 1984. A history of one of the earliest, and most innovative and formative, military states, including coverage of its standing army, the institutionalization of its armed forces, its galley navy, and its famous arsenal. [ill, M, app, B, i]

Messenger, Charles. *The Century of Warfare: Worldwide Conflict from 1900 to the Present Day*. London: HarperCollins, 1995. A detailed overview of changes in warfare during the twentieth century based on the television documentary series of the same name. [ill, M, B, i]

Millett, Allan R., and Williamson Murray, eds. *Military Effectiveness*. 3 vols. Boston: Allen & Unwin, 1988. Twenty-four eminent scholars systematically assess twenty-one comparative case studies of military performance in similar categories—political, operational, strategic, and tactical—for three designated periods: World War I, the inter-war years, and World War II. [ill, M, B, i]

Moulton, James L. *A Study of Warfare in Three Dimensions: The Norwegian Campaign of 1940.* Athens: Ohio University Press, 1966. A participant's contention that the Norwegian Campaign of 1940 was the first major campaign with operations on the surface, subsurface, and in the air. [ill, M, B, i]

Murray, Williamson, and Allan R. Millett. *A War to Be Won: Fighting the Second World War.* Cambridge, Mass.: Harvard University Press, 2000. A substantial survey of World War II, focusing on traditional military operations on the battlefield and assessing commanders such as Douglas MacArthur, Omar N. Bradley, Chester W. Nimitz, and First Viscount Slim, categorized from bad to best. [ill, M, B, i]

Nicolle, David. *Medieval Warfare Source Book: Christian Europe and Its Neighbours.* London: Brockhampton Press, 1996. One of two volumes in an important reference book covering medieval warfare over various time periods, with copious illustrations, and original source material covering Europe and also the Crusades, and Central Asia. [ill, M, tab, chr, glo, B, i]

_____. *Medieval Warfare Source Book: Warfare in Western Christendom.* London: Brockhampton Press, 1999. The second volume of Nicolle's reference work covering warfare within Europe, arranged chronologically. [ill, M, tab, chr, glo, B, i]

Norman, Vesey B., and Don Pottinger. *A History of War and Weapons, 449-1660: English Warfare from the Anglo-Saxons to Cromwell.* New York: Prentice-Hall, 1966. A survey of medieval warfare, exclusive of naval warfare, aimed at the introductory student. [ill, i]

Oakeshott, R. Ewart. *European Weapons and Armour: From the Renaissance to the Industrial Revolution.* Rochester, N.Y.: Boydell Press, 2000. A general survey. [ill, B, i]

O'Connell, Robert L. *Of Arms and Men: A History of War, Weapons, and Aggression.* New York: Oxford University Press, 1989. A general review of the development of weapons, with the observation that military leaders disliked revolutionary breakthroughs in weaponry. [ill, B, i]

Partington, J. R. *A History of Greek Fire and Gunpowder.* Baltimore: Johns Hopkins University Press, 1960, 1998. A study of how these pyrotechnics and firearms went from China to the Mediterranean through the Muslim world. [ill, tab, glo, B, i]

Payne, Samuel B. *The Conduct of War: An Introduction to Modern Warfare.* Oxford, England: Blackwell, 1989. A survey of contemporary warfare, including nuclear war; conventional land war, sea, and air actions; and guerrilla warfare. [ill, B, i]

Perrett, Bryan. *The Battle Book: Crucial Conflicts in History from 1469 B.C. to the Present.* New York: Sterling, 1996. An easy-to-use, encyclopedic guide covering 566 battles during more than three thousand years of warfare. [B]

Pollington, Stephen. *The Warrior's Way: England in the Viking Age.* New York: Sterling, 1990. A nicely illustrated, folio-sized volume covering the period from Alfred the Great to William the Conqueror. [ill, app, M, B, i]

Porter, Bruce D. *War and the Rise of the State: The Military Foundations of Modern Politics.* New York: Free Press, 1994. An important synthesis of the increasingly popular topic of war and state formation, exclusive of the United States, delineating dynastic, national, collectivist, and totalitarian state patterns. [B, i]

Porter, Patrick. *Military Orientalism: Eastern War Through Western Eyes.* New York: Columbia University Press, 2009. An account illustrating different techniques of fighting and how this has transformed thinking with different forms of asymmetrical warfare. [B, i]

Quick, John. *Dictionary of Weapons and Military Terms.* New York: McGraw-Hill, 1973. A profusely illustrated, folio-sized dictionary defining thousands of terms. [ill, B]

Ralston, David B. *Importing the European Army: The Introduction of European Military Techniques and Institutions into the Extra-European World, 1600-1914.* Chicago: University of Chicago Press, 1990. This book covers the transfer of European technology within Africa, the Middle East, and elsewhere, and the changes which have resulted. [B, i]

Reardon, Carol. *Soldiers and Scholars: The U.S. Army and the Uses of Military History, 1865-1920.* Lawrence: University of Kansas Press, 1990. A description of the process of professionalization within the U.S. Army, from an author with an outstanding record of historical writing. [B, i]

Roth, Jonathan P. *War and World History.* Chantilly, Va.: The Teaching Company, 2009. Presented by the well-known military historian and director of the University of Calilfornia's Burdick Military History Project, these forty-eight lectures, captured on individual DVDs, cover such topics as "The Stone Age War," "The Chariot Revolution," "Monotheisms and Militaries," "The Weaponization of Information," and "The Struggle for Peace and Justice."

Southworth, Samuel A., ed. *Great Raids in History: From Drake to Desert One.* New York: Sarpedon, 1997. Accounts of nineteen small-unit, irregular warfare actions, both failed and successful, during the last four hundred years, including raids by or identified with Sir Francis Drake, George A. Custer, Jimmy Carter, and Benjamin Netanyahu. [B, i]

Stewart, Richard W. *The English Ordnance Office, 1585-1625: A Case Study in Bureaucracy.* Rochester, N.Y.: Boydell Press, 1996. An outstanding example of the importance of logistics in warfare, a case study of England's supply of all ordnance facilities to all services during a formative period. [tab, B, i]

Stradling, R. A. *The Armada of Flanders: Spanish Maritime Policy and European War, 1568-1668.* New York: Cambridge University Press, 1992. A thesis that proposes that Spanish arms at sea in the long war against the Dutch produced a change in the nature of warfare at sea; key factors were the use of Dunkirk as base, the frigate warship, the process of prize taking, and even the wages of seamen. [tab, glo, app, M, B, i]

Thompson, Julian. *The Lifeblood of War: Logistics in Armed Conflict.* Washington, D.C.: Brassey's,

1991. Presents eight case studies to form a comprehensive analysis of this vital aspect of war, including North Africa, Italy, and Burma in World War II; Korea; Vietnam; the Arab-Israeli October War; and the Falkland Islands, the latter reported from firsthand participation. [ill, M, B, i]

Thompson, Sir Robert, ed. *War in Peace: An Analysis of Warfare from 1945 to the Present Day.* London: Orbis, 1985. A detailed study by the British counterinsurgency expert who advised successfully on the Malayan Emergency, and later advised the United States on Vietnam. [ill, M. B, i]

Townshend, Charles, ed. *The Oxford Illustrated History of Modern War.* New York: Oxford University Press, 1997. A beautifully illustrated collection of stimulating essays by prominent authorities, such as Richard Overy, Richard Holmes, and Martin van Creveld. [ill, M, B, i]

Toy, Sidney. *Castles: Their Construction and History.* 1939. Reprint. Mineola, N.Y.: Dover, 1985. A survey of the general characteristics and history of castles, with examples. [ill, B, i]

————. *A History of Fortification from 3000 B.C. to A.D. 1700.* New York: Macmillan, 1955. A popular history presenting a general overview covering five thousand years. [ill]

Unger, Richard W. *The Ship in the Medieval Economy, 600-1600.* London: Croom Helm, 1980. A comprehensive and highly technical survey based primarily upon extensive discoveries in underwater archaeology, a relatively new discipline that has contributed vastly to knowledge in this field. Stresses the economic, social, and cultural aspects of ship design and how developments stimulated commercial, military, and imperial expansion. [ill, B, i]

Unsworth, Michael E., ed. *Military Periodicals: United States and Selected International Journals and Newspapers.* Westport, Conn.: Greenwood Press, 1990. A comprehensive reference guide to military journals and periodicals such as *Armed Forces and Society, Proceedings of the Naval Institute, Royal United Services Institute Journal, Air Power History, Aviation Week,* and *Space Technology.* [chr, app, i]

Van Creveld, Martin L. *Supplying War: Logistics*

from Wallenstein to Patton. New York: Cambridge University Press, 1977. A provocative early analysis from an innovative and controversial author, an Israeli professor who contends that logistics is nine-tenths of the business of war. [M, B, i]

———. *Technology and War: From 2000 B.C. to the Present.* New York: Free Press, 1989. A survey of dramatic changes in warfare over four thousand years due to advances in technology, concentrating on the systematization of war and its increasing remoteness from reality; divided into chronological sections such as the age of tools, the age of machines, the age of systems, and the age of automation. [ill, B, i]

———. *The Transformation of War.* New York: Maxwell Macmillan International, 1991. An account of the changes in warfare at the end of the Cold War. [B, i]

Verbruggen, J. F. *The Art of Warfare in Western Europe During the Middle Ages from the Eighth Century to 1340.* Translated by Sumner Willard and Mrs. R. W. Southern. 2d rev. ed. Rochester, N.Y.: Boydell Press, 1998. A classic by a noted Belgian scholar of land warfare, featuring warfare of knights and foot soldiers and their tactics and strategies. [ill]

Warner, Philip. *Firepower: From Slings to Star Wars.* London: Grafton Books, 1988. A good general history about the invention and use of new weaponry. [ill, B, i]

Wright, Quincy. *A Study of War: An Analysis of the Causes, Nature, and Control of War.* Chicago: University of Chicago Press, 1942. An encyclopedic and monumental study, with brilliant observations and analyses, originally formulated in the 1920's but updated during World War II. [ill, tab, app, B, i]

MILITARY THEORY AND STRATEGY

Albion, Robert G. *Makers of Naval Policy, 1798-1947.* Edited by Rowena Reed. Annapolis, Md.: Naval Institute Press, 1980. An official study of the making of naval administration and policy for the United States up until the time of amalgamation of the armed services. [B, i]

Armitage, M. J., and R. A. M. Mason, eds. *Air Power in the Nuclear Age: Theory and Practice.* London: Macmillan, 1983. Nine essays assessing the role of airpower during the Cold War. [B, i]

Asprey, Robert B. *War in the Shadows: The Guerrilla in History.* 2 vols. Garden City, N.Y.: Doubleday, 1975. Rev. ed. Boston: Little, Brown, 1994. The classic history describing dozens of instances of the employment of irregular forces in conjunction with a larger political-military strategy. [M, B, i]

Bacon, Benjamin W. *Sinews of War: How Technology, Industry, and Transportation Won the Civil War.* Novato, Calif.: Presidio Press, 1997. An account of how the Union created and sustained a logistical advantage during the American Civil War. [ill, i]

Ball, Desmond, and Jeffrey Richel, eds. *Strategic Nuclear Targeting.* Ithaca, N.Y.: Cornell University Press, 1986. A description of an essential aspect of nuclear weapons development, covering, for example, the Single Integrated Plan formulated by the United States. [ill, M, B, i]

Barker, A. J. *Suicide Weapon: Japanese Kamikaze Forces in World War II.* New York: Ballantine, 1971. A study of the variety of kamikaze forces, including aircraft, submarines, and entire fleets, used during and especially toward the end of World War II. [ill, B]

Bartlett, Merrill L., ed. *Assault from the Sea: Essays on the History of Amphibious Warfare.* Annapolis, Md.: Naval Institute Press, 1983. Fifty articles describing amphibious campaigns, such as the Norman Conquest, the Mongols against Japan, Gallipoli, Dieppe, and the Falkland Islands. [ill, B]

Bartusis, Mark C. *The Late Byzantine Army: Arms and Society, 1204-1453.* Philadelphia: University of Pennsylvania Press, 1992. A synthesis describing military institutions of Byzantium from the Fourth Crusade until the empire's fall to the Ottoman Turks. [ill, M, tab, glo, B, i]

Bateman, Robert L., ed. *Digital War: A View from the Front Lines.* Novato, Calif.: Presidio Press, 1999. Eight essays by experts on the strategy and tactics for the "digital battlefield." [tab, B]

Beaumont, Roger A. *Military Elites: Special Fighting Units in the Modern World*. Indianapolis, Ind.: Bobbs-Merrill, 1974. A study of several modern elite units, including the French Foreign Legion, the Green Berets, and Combined Operation Headquarters. [ill, B, i]

Bellamy, Chris. *The Evolution of Modern Land Warfare: Theory and Practice*. London: Routledge, 1990. An analysis of land warfare at the very end of the Cold War. [ill, B, i]

Bidwell, Shelford, and Dominick Graham. *Fire-Power: British Army Weapons and Theories of War, 1904-1945*. Boston: Allen & Unwin, 1982. A description of the process aimed to link together artillery, infantry, tactical air, and communication, all to create a doctrine leading to effective command and control. [ill, M, B, i]

Brodie, Bernard. *A Layman's Guide to Naval Strategy*. Princeton, N.J.: Princeton University Press, 1943. A classic text on sea power, tools, command of the sea, bases, and the air arm. [ill, M, B, i]

_____. *Strategy in a Missile Age*. 1959. Reprint. Princeton, N.J.: Princeton University Press, 1965. An early analysis of the significance of the nuclear age, pointing out the danger of precipitating total war. [B]

Chaliand, Gerard, ed. *Guerrilla Strategies: An Historical Anthology from the Long March to Afghanistan*. Berkeley: University of California Press, 1982. A collection of case studies—for example, Burma, China, Cuba, South Africa, and Yugoslavia. [B]

Colomb, Philip H. *Naval Warfare: Its Ruling Principles and Practice Historically Treated*. 3d ed. London: W. H. Allen, 1891. Reprint. Annapolis, Md.: Naval Institute Press, 1990. An early treatise on the strategic implications of the study of naval history to demonstrate certain laws governing naval warfare. [ill, tab, M]

Corbett, Julian S. *Some Principles of Maritime Strategy*. New York: Longmans, Green, 1911. Reprint. Annapolis, Md.: Naval Institute Press, 1988. A treatise seen by some experts as the most appropriate and important of all relating to naval, and even national, strategy. [ill, B, i]

Corum, James S. *The Luftwaffe: Creating the Operational Air War, 1918-1940*. Lawrence: University of Kansas Press, 1997. A German perspective on air warfare.

Cox, Sebastian, ed. *The Strategic Air War Against Germany, 1939-1945: The Official Report of the British Bombing Survey Unit*. London: Cass, 1998. An extensive British investigation, originally withheld, now published, into controversial strategic bombing. [ill, B, i]

Douhet, Giulio. *The Command of the Air*. Translated by Dino Ferrari. New York: Coward, 1921. A treatise by the Italian officer, the original theorist and advocate of airpower. [B]

Ellis, John. *Brute Force: Allied Strategy and Tactics in the Second World War*. New York: Viking, 1990. A revisionist assessment positing that the Allies won the war because of industrial capacity only and that Allied commanders were incapable of effective warfare. [tab, app, M, B, i]

Gat, Azar. *The Development of Military Thought: The Nineteenth Century*. Oxford, England: Clarendon, 1992. A continuation of the author's *The Origins of Military Thought*, about strategy and military theory during the nineteenth century, in which the French Revolution introduced a new mode of warfare, Prussia and the mass army developed, and total war began to be anticipated. [B, i]

_____. *The Origins of Military Thought: From the Enlightenment to Clausewitz*. Oxford, England: Clarendon, 1989. An examination of how conceptions of military theory emerged from the Enlightenment and Counter-Enlightenment. [B, i]

Gray, Colin S. *Strategy for Chaos: Revolutions in Military Affairs and the Evidence of History*. Portland, Oreg.: Frank Cass, 2002. Conceptually analyzes the idea of "revolutions in military affairs," the adoption of wholesale changes in military strategies by numerous or important nations, comparing the changes that took place during the Napoleonic Era, World War I, and the nuclear era as context for the revolution taking place in the 1990's and 2000's due to the application of information technology to warfare. [B, i]

Guilmartin, John F. *Gunpowder and Galleys: Chang-*

ing *Technology and Mediterranean Warfare at Sea in the Sixteenth Century*. New York: Cambridge University Press, 1974. A look at how the sixteenth century domination of the galley over the Mediterranean culminated in the Battle of Lepanto (1571) and how the development of gunpowder and heavy cannons contributed to the decline of southern, and the rise of northern, Europe. [ill, B, i]

Hague, Arnold. *The Allied Convoy System, 1939-1945: Its Organization, Defence, and Operation*. Annapolis, Md.: Naval Institute Press, 2000. An intensive study based on convoy records. [ill, B, i]

Handel, Michael I. *Masters of War: Classical Strategic Thought*. 1992. 3d ed. London: Cass, 2000. A detailed textual analysis of the great military strategists, such as Sunzi (Sun Tzu); Niccolò Machiavelli; Carl von Clausewitz; Antoine Henri, baron de Jomini; and Mao Zedong (Mao Tse-tung). [tab, M, B, i]

Hanzhang, Tao. *Sun Tzu's "Art of War": The Modern Chinese Interpretation*. Translated by Yuan Sibling. New York: Sterling, 2000. The classical work on military affairs, dealing with war, politics, economics, diplomacy, geography, and astronomy. [ill, M, i]

Hawkes, Sonia Chadwick, ed. *Weapons and Warfare in Anglo-Saxon England*. New York: Oxford University Press, 1989. A collection of papers by experts from several disciplines, including history, archaeology, anthropology, and metallurgy. [ill, B, i]

Honan, William H. *Bywater: The Man Who Invented the Pacific War*. London: Macdonald, 1990. A detailed account of the Bywater plan, outlined in a number of books, on the strategy Japan would eventually use to fight the Pacific war. [ill, M, B, i]

Hughes, B. P. *Open Fire: Artillery Tactics from Marlborough to Wellington*. London: Bird, 1983. A focused study of artillery in the formative eighteenth century, including the dominance of smoothbore field artillery weapons and the tactics, organization, and operations that were developed along with them. [ill, M, B, i]

Hughes, Wayne P. *Fleet Tactics: Theory and Practice*. Annapolis, Md.: Naval Institute Press, 1986.

A major contribution to naval literature; a comprehensive survey of naval tactics over five distinct periods, such as those of sailing ships, big gunships, and carriers. [ill, tab, app, B, i]

Inoguchi, Rikihei, and Nakajima Tadashi. *The Divine Wind: Japan's Kamikaze Force in World War II*. Annapolis, Md.: Naval Institute Press, 1958. The Japanese perspective and rationale for the unique kamikaze force used on an increasing scale during the war. [ill, i]

Jacobsen, Carl G., ed. *The Uncertain Course: New Weapons, Strategies and Mind-sets*. New York: Oxford University Press, 1987. An account of the changing nature in war in the last years of the Cold War. [B, i]

Joes, Anthony James. *Guerrilla Warfare: A Historical, Biographical, and Bibliographical Sourcebook*. Westport, Conn.: Greenwood Press, 1996. A series of case studies and 151 profiles of guerrilla leaders, including those of the American Revolution, Haiti, the Boer War, the Chinese Civil War, and the Vietnam War. [M, B, i]

Johnson, David E. *Fast Tanks and Heavy Bombers: Innovation in the U.S. Army, 1917-1945*. Ithaca, N.Y.: Cornell University Press, 1998. A critical analysis with extensive documentation of how and why the United States was unprepared for World War II. [B, i]

Jones, Archer. *Civil War Command and Strategy: The Process of Victory and Defeat*. New York: Free Press, 1995. A sophisticated analysis of strategy during the American Civil War, focusing on key decisions. [ill, M, B, i]

_____. *Elements of Military Strategy: An Historical Approach*. Westport, Conn.: Praeger, 1996. A conceptualization supported by extensive statistics, using history as a source of ideas; a series of case studies considering strategy, logistics, tactics, and operations. [ill, M, B, i]

Kane, Thomas M. *Ancient China on Postmodern War: Enduring Ideas from the Chinese Strategic Tradition*. New York: Routledge, 2007. Outlines the social context in which Chinese military philosophers, such as the vaunted Sunzi (Sun Tzu), wrote, noting that it, like the early 2000's, was a time of social, economic, and military change.

Using both Chinese military strategists and later European military thought, the book looks at how such classical military thought can benefit modern debates over military strategy. [B, i]

Kemp, Paul. *Convoy Protection: The Defence of Seaborne Trade*. London: Arms & Armour, 1993. A study of the development and strategy of convoy protection, as used, for example, by France during the early modern period, against German U-boats during World War I, and against American submarines in the Pacific during World War II. [ill, tab, B, i]

Kennedy, Paul M., ed. *Grand Strategies in War and Peace*. New Haven, Conn.: Yale University Press, 1991. Ten essays on national strategies by noted scholars such as Kennedy, on Britain; John Hattendorf, on the War of the Spanish Succession; Michael Howard, on World War I; Dennis Showalter, on Germany; and Douglas Porch, on France. [B, i]

Laqueur, Walter. *Guerrilla: A Historical and Critical Study*. Boston: Little, Brown, 1976. A general and historical survey of guerrilla warfare, covering partisans against Adolf Hitler, National Liberation movements, and fictional accounts by Honoré de Balzac, Leo Tolstoy, and Ernest Hemingway. [chr, B, i]

_____. *The New Terrorism: Fanaticism and the Arms of Mass Destruction*. New York: Oxford University Press, 1999. An important review and discussion on the history and psychology of terrorists, including animal rights activists, UFO (unidentified flying object) cultists, and religious extremists, linking them to literature and popular culture. [B, i]

_____, ed. *The Guerrilla Reader: A Historical Anthology*. New York: New American, 1977. Accounts from forty authors taken from the eighteenth century to the present. [B]

_____, ed. *The Terrorism Reader: A Historical Anthology*. Philadelphia: Temple University Press, 1978. A series of writings selected by the author. An examination, based on terrorism as it existed in the 1970's, of the origins of terrorism as a tactic and the military, social, and religious philosophies from which it flows. [B]

Leighton, Richard, and Robert W. Coakley. *Global Logistics and Strategy*. 2 vols. Washington, D.C.: Government Printing Office, 1955-1968. A study of the intricate and complicated logistical process worldwide and its impact on strategy. [ill, M, B, i]

Liddell Hart, Basil H. *The Strategy of Indirect Approach*. London: Faber and Faber, 1941. A survey, by one of the most influential strategic thinkers of the twentieth century, of the history and making of strategy; later editions include a chapter on unconventional warfare. [M]

Luttwak, Edward N. *The Political Uses of Sea Power*. Baltimore: Johns Hopkins University Press, 1974. A study of alternative operations related to diplomacy and international affairs, such as naval "presence," interposition, and blockade. [B]

_____. *Strategy and History*. New Brunswick, N.J.: Transaction Books, 1985. A volume containing essays by Luttwak covering the strategy of military deterrence, and the use of seapower, as well as other topics. [i]

McNeilly, Mark. *Sun Tzu and the Art of Modern Warfare*. New York: Oxford University Press, 2003. A treatise on the continued relevance of Sunzi (Sun Tzu), including references to terrorism. [B, i]

Mahan, Alfred Thayer. *The Influence of Sea Power upon the French Revolution and Empire, 1793-1812*. Boston: Little, Brown, 1892. The second and continuing treatise about the impact of sea power based on Mahan's understanding of the classic case study, the British success against France. [ill, M, B, i]

_____. *The Influence of Sea Power upon History, 1660-1783*. Boston: Little, 1890. An enormously influential treatise on the decisive influence of naval battle fleets on national development and expansion, based on Mahan's perceptions of British history during the early modern period; said to be read and heeded by political and naval officials of all the major powers during the 1890's and later, and considered the "bible of the Blue Water School" of naval expansionists. [ill, M, B, i]

_____. *Naval Strategy: Compared and Contrasted with the Principles and Practices of Military Operations on Land*. London: Sampson, 1911. A later treatise of Mahan, demonstrating the differences between military and naval strategies. [ill, M, i]

Mao Zedong. *Six Essays on Military Affairs*. Beijing: Foreign Languages Press, 1971. Six essays, written between 1936 and 1948, that were influential in the thinking of the Chinese Communist army.

Mao Zedong and Che Guevara. *Guerilla Warfare*. London: Cassell & Company, 1962. An account of the nature of guerrilla warfare by two of its leading protagonists, involving comments not just on conflicts in which they were involved but on the philosophical underpinnings of their strategies as well. [i]

Martin, Laurence W. *The Sea in Modern Strategy*. New York: Praeger, 1967. A review and critique of notable naval strategists, such as Alfred Thayer Mahan, Julian S. Corbett, and Bernard Brodie, exclusive of important factors such as aircraft, submarines, and missiles. [ill, B]

Miller, Edward S. *War Plan Orange: The U.S. Strategy to Defeat Japan, 1897-1945*. Annapolis, Md.: Naval Institute Press, 1991. An extensively researched and award-winning study of the famous American war plan, first formulated about 1900, in case of war with Japan and further developed as opposing schools of thought, "thrusting" versus "cautionary," pressured for decisive influence. [ill, M, B, i]

Mitchell, William L. *Winged Defense: The Development and Possibilities of Modern Air Power, Economic and Military*. New York: G. P. Putnam's Sons, 1925. Reprint. Mineola, N.Y.: Dover, 1988. The classic advocacy of airpower by Billy Mitchell. [ill]

Murray, Williamson, MacGregor Knox, and Alvin Bernstein, eds. *The Making of Strategy: Rulers, States, and War*. New York: Cambridge University Press, 1994. A study similar to Paret's *Makers of Modern Strategy*, with more emphasis on the process and coverage of earlier times, including seventeen case studies on topics such as the Peloponnesian War, Rome versus Carthage, Ming Dynasty China, Philip II of Spain, Winston Churchill, and Israel. [ill, B, i]

Murray, Williamson, and Richard Hart Sinnreich, eds. *The Past as Prologue: The Importance of History to the Military Profession*. New York: Cambridge University Press, 2006. Although the study of history is clearly important to military strategists, the book analyzes the challenges of applying historical events and ideas to modern warfare. Military conflict has long provided fertile ground for historians, and there are problems that have recurred throughout military history for which having a good contextual knowledge is vital. [B, i]

Nasution, Abdul Haris. *Fundamentals of Guerilla Warfare, and the Indonesian Defence System, Past and Future*. Djakarta: Indonesian Army Information Service, 1953. A detailed history of the nature of successful guerrilla warfare during the Dutch-Indonesian War, and also how this can be used in other conflicts. [ill, M]

O'Neill, Richard. *Suicide Squads: Axis and Allied Special Attack Weapons of World War II, Their Development, and Their Missions*. New York: Salamander, 1981. A review of the use, mostly by the Japanese, of torpedoes, midget submarines, and aircraft. [ill, M, B, i]

Paret, Peter, ed. *Makers of Modern Strategy: From Machiavelli to the Nuclear Age*. Princeton, N.J.: Princeton University Press, 1986. Based on the 1943 classic edited by Edward Mead Earle, a superb guide to modern strategy; twenty-eight essays by eminent scholars, twenty-two of them new, including Felix Gilbert on Niccolò Machiavelli, R. R. Palmer on Frederick the Great, Paret on Carl von Clausewitz, Hajo Holborn on the Prussian-German school, and David McIsaac on airpower theory. [B, i]

Parker, Geoffrey. *The Grand Strategy of Philip II*. New Haven, Conn.: Yale University Press, 1998. An argument by a noted expert on the early modern European military that Philip II of Spain formulated a grand strategy based on imperialism and expansion, a view contrary to some prominent scholars, such as Fernand Braudel, Paul Kennedy, and Henry Kamen. [ill, B, i]

Perla, Peter P. *The Art of Wargaming*. Annapolis, Md.: Naval Institute Press, 1990. An analysis of the techniques of war-gaming as essential to grand strategy. [ill, app, B, i]

Reynolds, Clark G. *Command of the Sea: The History and Strategy of Maritime Empires*. 2 vols. New York: William Morrow, 1974. A substantial historical synthesis by a prominent authority, characterized by depth and balance and an especially impressive bibliography. [M, B, i]

Robison, Samuel S., and Mary L. Robison. *A History of Naval Tactics from 1530 to 1930: The Evolution of Tactical Maxims*. Annapolis, Md.: Naval Institute Press, 1942. An old classic, a substantial survey focusing on technical aspects of naval warfare, from King Richard I's Third Crusade to the Armada and Jutland campaigns. [ill, M]

Roskill, Stephen W. *The Strategy of Sea Power: Its Development and Application*. London: Collins, 1962. Reprint. Westport, Conn.: Greenwood Press, 1981. A collection of the Lees-Knowles lectures given at Cambridge University, with extensive use of historical analysis as an apology for Julian S. Corbett, who had been ignored during World War I. [B]

Ross, Steven T. *American War Plans, 1919-1941*. 5 vols. New York: Garland, 1992. Almost two thousand pages describing in detail the making of a series of American war plans during the interwar period, the responsibility of the Joint Army-Navy Board; individual volumes cover peacetime war plans, plans for war against the British and Japanese, plans to meet the Axis threats, coalition plans, and plans for global war. [ill, M]

_____. *American War Plans, 1939-1945*. London: Cass, 1996. The story after the making of the various plans as described in the previous entry; a more complicated and challenging process, dealing with problems within the coalition, interservice rivalries, disagreements between field commanders and headquarters, and logistical restraints. [ill, M]

Ryan, Alan. *Thinking Across Time: Concurrent Historical Analysis on Military Operations*. Duntroon, Australia: Land Warfare Studies Centre, 2001. A short working paper on Australian military thinking.

Strachan, Hew, and Andreas Herberg-Rothe, eds. *Clausewitz in the Twenty-first Century*. New York:

Oxford University Press, 2007. A series of articles showing the continued relevance of Clausewitz in the post-Cold War period. [B, i]

Van Creveld, Martin. *Command in War*. Cambridge, Mass.: Harvard University Press, 1985. A series of loosely connected essays about land warfare, presenting the historical evolution of the function of command, control, and communication in warfare, with an emphasis on the uncertainties. [ill, B, i]

Wegener, Wolfgang. *The Naval Strategy of the World War*. Translated by Holger Herwig. 1929. Reprint. Annapolis, Md.: Naval Institute Press, 1989. A classic treatise written in approximately 1915 by a German vice admiral highly critical of Alfred von Tirpitz's strategy and "risk fleet theory" and celebrated for his perceptiveness, his appreciation of the importance of geopolitics in naval strategy, and his "Atlantic vision," which Germany should possibly have followed in World War I. [B, i]

Weigley, Russell F. *The Age of Battles: The Quest for Decisive Warfare from Breitenfeld to Waterloo*. Bloomington: Indiana University Press, 1991. By a preeminent authority, a look at war from the initiation of conflict to the "the grand-scale battle," a feature of military and naval professionalism. [M, B, i]

_____. *The American Way of War: A History of U.S. Military Strategy and Policy*. New York: Macmillan, 1973. A study of American military institutions and a survey of American strategy, including coverage of George Washington and attrition, Robert E. Lee and Napoleonic strategy, Ulysses S. Grant and annihilation, Alfred Thayer Mahan and Stephen B. Luce and sea power and empire, Billy Mitchell and airpower, and Douglas MacArthur and the frustrations of limited war in Korea. [M, B, i]

Wilt, Alan F. *War from the Top: German and British Military Decision Making During World War II*. Bloomington: Indiana University Press, 1990. A masterful analysis of the only two powers that fought throughout World War II, using a comparative approach to conclude that the overall direction of the war was better handled by the British and that, after 1940, all of Adolf Hitler's decisions were flawed. [M, B, i]

Wintringham, Thomas, and J. N. Blashford-Snell. *Weapons and Tactics*. London: Faber and Faber, 1943. Reprint. Baltimore: Penguin, 1973. A thought-provoking but dated analysis. [B, i]

WEAPONS AND TECHNOLOGIES

AIR WEAPONS

Batchelor, John, and Bryan Cooper. *Fighter: A History of Fighter Aircraft*. New York: Charles Scribner's Sons, 1974. A general survey. [ill, B]

Beaver, Paul. *Attack Helicopters*. London: Arms & Armour, 1987. A survey of attack helicopters, first used for armed battlefield reconnaissance during the Korean War and later used as "gunships." [ill]

Boyce, Joseph C., ed. *New Weapons for Air Warfare: Fire-Control Equipment, Proximity Fuzes, and Guided Missiles*. Boston: Little, Brown, 1947. A post-World War II assessment by the Office of Scientific Research and Development of past technological accomplishments and anticipated future successes. [ill]

Boyne, Walter J., ed. *Air Warfare: An International Encyclopedia*. Santa Barbara, Calif.: ABC-CLIO, 2002. A detailed encyclopedia by the former director of the National Air and Space Museum, covering entries alphabetically for aircraft, conflicts, biographies, themes such as air war in the arts, and also the role of women. Covers wars through the initial war in Afghanistan. [ill, M, B]

Buckley, John D. *Air Power in the Age of Total War*. London: University College, London, Press, 1999. An analysis of the changes in airpower after the end of the Cold War. [ill, B, i]

Burrows, William E. *By Any Means Necessary: America's Secret Air War in the Cold War*. New York: Farrar, Strauss and Giroux, 2001. A detailed account of the use of military and civilian airplanes during the Cold War. [B, i]

Constant, Edward W. *The Origins of the Turbojet Revolution*. Baltimore: Johns Hopkins University Press, 1980. A discussion of the impact of an important technological advance. [ill, B, i]

Cross, Wilbur. *Zeppelins of World War I: The Dramatic Story of Germany's Lethal Airships*. New York: Paragon, 1991. A collection of accounts of little-publicized aerial warfare, German zeppelins bombing British cities. [ill, B, i]

Everett-Heath, John. *Helicopters in Combat: The First Fifty Years*. London: Arms & Armour, 1992. A survey. Presents a detailed history of military helicopters from their first implementation as evacuation vehicles to the 2000's, through their evolution during the Korean War, the Vietnam War (when aerial gunships first saw action), to the modern era, where they are one of the most ubiquitous and deadly weapons available on the battlefield. [ill, app, B, i]

Godden, John, ed. *Harrier: Ski Jump to Victory*. Washington, D.C.: Brassey's, 1983. A case study of the success of the Harrier jump-jet during the Falkland Islands campaign. [ill, i]

Gooch, John, ed. *Airpower: Theory and Practice*. London: Cass, 1995. A series of essays about the development of airpower, including the contributions of Giulio Douhet, Billy Mitchell, and Hugh Trenchard and the debate between advocates of precision and area bombing. [ill, M, B, i]

Harris, Arthur T. *Bomber Offensive*. London: Collins, 1947. Reprint. London: Greenhill, 1990. Apologetics by the controversial commander of British strategic bombing. [M]

Hastings, Max. *Bomber Command: The Myths and Realities of the Strategic Bombing Offensive, 1939-1945*. New York: Dial, 1979. An examination of the controversial question about the effectiveness of the Strategic Bombing Offensive. [ill, B, i]

Hearn, Chester G. *Carriers in Combat: The Air War at Sea*. Westport, Conn.: Praeger Security International, 2005. Covers naval air power, aircraft carriers at war, air admirals, strategies, and tactics in several twentieth century conflicts. [ill, M, B, i]

Higham, Robin. *Air Power: A Concise History*. Rev. 3d ed. Manhattan, Kans.: Sunflower University Press, 1988. A historical survey. [ill, B, i]

Homze, Edward L. *Arming the Luftwaffe: The Reich*

Air Ministry and the German Aircraft Industry, 1919-1939. Lincoln: University of Nebraska Press, 1976. A case study of industry, logistics, politics, and air force officials involved in the making of a major airpower. [ill, B, i]

Hone, Thomas C., Norman Friedman, and Mark D. Mandeles. *American and British Aircraft Carrier Development, 1919-1941*. Annapolis, Md.: Naval Institute Press, 1999. A study of the extraordinary, fateful, and decisive innovations in the creation of British and American aircraft carriers. [ill, B, i]

Kennett, Lee B. *A History of Strategic Bombing*. New York: Charles Scribner's Sons, 1982. A survey of airpower, from the initial fear of bomber aircraft to industrial preparation for massive production and eventual "total war." [ill, B, i]

Kozak, Warren. *Lemay: The Life and Wars of General Curtis Lemay*. Washington, D.C.: Regnert, 2009. A detailed history of General Curtis LeMay and his belief in the superiority of airpower. [ill, B, i]

Marriott, Leo. *Royal Navy Aircraft Carriers, 1945-1990*. London: Ian Allan, 1985. A detailed history of the developments in aircraft carriers by the Royal Navy from the end of World War II. [ill, B, i]

Mason, R. A. *Air Power: An Overview of Roles*. London: Brassey's, 1987. A short account of the nature of airpower in the last years of the Cold War. [ill, B, i]

Meilinger, Phillip S. *Airwar: Theory and Practice*. Portland, Oreg.: Frank Cass, 2003. An analysis of the changes in aerial warfare from the end of the Cold War. [B, i]

———, ed. *The Paths of Heaven: The Evolution of Airpower Theory*. Maxwell Air Force Base, Ala.: Air University Press, 1997. Essays by teachers and students reviewing the origins and evolution, covering theorists such as Giulio Douhet, Billy Mitchell, and Hugh Trenchard. [B, i]

Mikesh, Robert C. *Zero Fighter*. New York: Crown, 1980. An exquisite, double-folio publication production with foldout pages, covering the Mitsubishi Type 0 Japanese fighter, the Zero, a completely original aircraft design that achieved notable early success during World War II. [ill]

Murphy, James T. *Skip Bombing*. Westport, Conn.: Praeger, 1993. The story of the development of an effective low-altitude bombing tactic, used against Japanese supply and troop ships in the Pacific war, that increased "hits" from 1 to 72 percent. [ill, i]

Nordeen, Lon O. *Air Warfare in the Missile Age*. Washington, D.C.: Smithsonian Institution Press, 1985. A detailed academic account of the changes in air warfare during the last period of the Cold War. [B, i]

Rimal, Raymond L. *Zeppelin! A Battle for Air Supremacy in World War I*. London: Conway, 1984. A profusely illustrated, folio-sized volume telling the story of British and German developments in the use of the zeppelin during World War I and including photographs of bomb damage. [ill, M, B, i]

Robinson, Douglas H. *Giants of the Sky: A History of the Rigid Airship*. Seattle: University of Washington Press, 1973. A scholarly survey and overview covering about forty years of development of 161 rigid airships in four nations. [B, i]

Sherry, Michael S. *The Rise of American Air Power: The Creation of Armageddon*. New Haven, Conn.: Yale University Press, 1987. A winner of the Bancroft Prize, the story of the creation and development of the American strategic bombing campaign and a cultural study of attitudes toward bombing. [ill, B, i]

Smith, Peter C. *Dive-Bomber: An Illustrated History*. Annapolis, Md.: Naval Institute Press, 1982. A history of the development of the dive-bomber and its impact. [ill, B, i]

Winton, John. *Air Power at Sea: 1945 to Today*. London: Sidgwick & Jackson, 1987. An account of the nature of airpower during the Cold War. [ill, M, B, i]

AMPHIBIOUS WARFARE

Alexander, Joseph H. *Storm Landings: Epic Amphibious Battles in the Central Pacific*. Annapolis, Md.: Naval Institute Press, 1997. Covers amphibious operations during World War II. [ill, M, glo, B, i]

Bartlett, Merrill L., ed. *Assault from the Sea: Essays*

on the History of Amphibious Warfare. Annapolis, Md.: Naval Institute Press, 1983. Fifty articles describing amphibious campaigns, such as the Norman Conquest, the Mongols against Japan, Gallipoli, Dieppe, and the Falkland Islands. [ill, B, i]

Croizat, Victor J. *Across the Reef: The Amphibious Tracked Vehicle at War*. New York: Sterling, 1989. An account of an early amphibious vehicle. [ill, M, B, i]

Keyes, Lord. *Amphibious Warfare and Combined Operations*. New York: Cambridge University Press, 1943. The chapters of the book, covering military conflicts from the eighteenth century through the mid-twentieth century, consist of lectures delivered by Britain's first wartime director of combined operations during World War II, at the annual Lees Knowles Lectures at Trinity College, Cambridge University.

McGee, William L. *Amphibious Operations in the South Pacific in World War II*. 2 vols. Santa Barbara, Calif.: BMC, 2000-2002. A detailed history of the U.S. Marine Corps, especially the operations on the Solomons and Bougainville. [ill, M, B, i]

Polmar, Norman, and Peter B. Mersky. *Amphibious Warfare: The Illustrated History*. London: Blandford, 1988. A profusely illustrated, folio-sized volume beginning with early combined operations, moving toward the massive invasions of World War II, and culminating in more recent amphibious operations, such as Suez, Vietnam, and the Falkland Islands. [ill, M, B, i]

ARMY WEAPONS

Croll, Mike. *The History of Landmines*. London: Cooper, 1998. A short, disjointed survey about the use of land mines, consciousness-raising about their implications, and international efforts to limit their use. [ill, B, i]

Dastrup, Boyd L. *The Field Artillery: History and Sourcebook*. Westport, Conn.: Greenwood Press, 1994. The history, use, and users of field artillery from 1350 to the present. [glos, app, B, i]

Duffy, Christopher. *Siege Warfare: The Fortress in the Early Modern World, 1494-1660*. New York: Routledge, 1979. A comprehensive study of siege warfare by country, including Italy, France, England, the Baltic states, China, and Japan. [ill, M, B, i]

Griffith, Paddy. *British Fighting Methods in the Great War*. London: Cass, 1996. An effort to evaluate and rehabilitate opinion of British military tactical leaders and their methods, which, the author insists, deserve more credit than they have been given. [tab, B, i]

Gudmundsson, Bruce I. *On Artillery*. Westport, Conn.: Praeger, 1993. A short academic account of the use of artillery. [B, i]

Hazlett, James C., et al. *Field Artillery Weapons of the Civil War*. Newark, N.J.: University of Delaware Press, 1983. An excellent reference work, with a detailed analysis of developments in artillery. [ill, tab, app, B, i]

Hogg, O. F. G. *Artillery: Its Origin, Heyday, and Decline*. Hamden, Conn.: Archon, 1970. A history of artillery. [ill, B]

Hughes, B. P. *Firepower: Weapons Effectiveness on the Battlefield, 1630-1850*. New York: Charles Scribner's Sons, 1974. A profusely illustrated, folio-sized assessment of the performance of combined infantry, cavalry, and artillery during the formative seventeenth through nineteenth centuries. [ill, B, i]

Macksey, Kenneth. *Tank Warfare: A History of Tanks in Battle*. New York: Stein, 1971. A history of development with an emphasis on tactics by a veteran armor officer. [ill, chr, B, i]

McLean, Donald B., ed. *Japanese Tanks, Tactics, and Antitank Weapons*. Wickenburg, Ariz.: Normount Technical, 1973. The story of tank developments and the use of the tank in the Japanese army. [ill]

Marsden, Eric W. *Greek and Roman Artillery: Technical Treatises*. Oxford: Clarendon Press, 1971. A detailed history of artillery used by and against the Greeks and Romans. [ill, B, i]

Messenger, Charles. *The Art of Blitzkrieg*. New York: Simon & Schuster, 1976. The story of developments in tank warfare, especially during the interwar period. [ill, B, i]

Needham, Joseph. *Military Technology: The Gun-*

powder Epic. New York: Cambridge University Press, 1987. The story of the increasing dominance of gunpowder in warfare during the early modern period. [ill, B, i]

Perrett, Bryan. *A History of Blitzkrieg*. New York: Stein, 1983. A popular history describing Germany's use of the Blitzkrieg from Poland to Kursk, as well as the Blitzkrieg's use by Americans, Japanese, and Israelis. [ill, B, i]

Roland, Paul M. *Imperial Japanese Tanks, 1918-1945*. New York: Bellona, 1975. A survey of tank developments by the Japanese before and during World War II. [ill]

Showalter, Dennis E. *Railroads and Rifles: Soldiers, Technology, and the Unification of Germany*. Hamden, Conn.: Archon, 1975. A critical and scholarly analysis by an eminent authority of the military impact of advanced technological developments on politics and international events. [M, B, i]

Strachan, Hew. *European Armies and the Conduct of War*. London: Routledge & Kegan Paul, 1983. An outstanding example of the relation of strategic theory to actual practice. [ill, M, B, i]

Van Creveld, Martin. *Fighting Power: German and U.S. Army Performance, 1939-1945*. Westport, Conn.: Greenwood Press, 1982. A comparative analysis of German and American fighting power. [tab, app, B, i]

Vuksic, V., and Z. Grbasic. *Cavalry: The History of a Fighting Elite, 650 B.C.-A.D. 1914*. New York: Sterling, 1993. A profusely illustrated, folio-sized volume including one hundred color plates and a short narrative essay. [ill, i]

Watson, Bruce A. *Sieges: A Comparative Study*. Westport, Conn.: Praeger, 1993. An analysis of five case studies, including Jerusalem in 1099 and Singapore in 1942. [ill, M, B, i]

Wright, Patrick. *Tank: The Progress of a Monstrous War Machine*. London: Faber, 2000. An anecdotal history of the tank, from its beginnings in 1914, when the crisis in trench warfare prompted British analysts to look toward engines and tracked vehicles to break the deadlock, to its evolution for use in Blitzkrieg warfare. [ill]

CHEMICAL AND BIOLOGICAL WARFARE

Adams, Valerie. *Chemical Warfare, Chemical Disarmament: Beyond Gethsemane*. New York: Macmillan, 1989. An analysis of the nature of chemical warfare at the end of the Cold War. [B, i]

Barnaby, Wendy. *The Plague Makers: The Secret World of Biological Warfare*. New York: Continuum, 2002. A detailed account of the possibility of biological warfare, including its potential use by terrorists. [B, i]

Gander, Terry. *Nuclear, Biological, and Chemical Warfare*. London: Ian Allan, 1987. A survey of different forms of warfare during the Cold War. [ill, B, i]

Hammond, James W. *Poison Gas: The Myths and Reality*. Westport, Conn.: Greenwood Press, 1999. Definitions, history, various scientific factors, and "myths" are reviewed. [B, i]

Hoenig, Steven L. *Handbook of Chemical Warfare and Terrorism*. Westport, Conn.: Greenwood Press, 2002. A reference book giving a detailed survey on the nature of chemical warfare and also its possible use by terrorists. [B, i]

Mauroni, Albert J. *America's Struggle with Chemical-Biological Warfare*. Westport, Conn.: Greenwood Press, 2000. A detailed review of the problems, challenges, and technicalities of chemical and biological warfare. [ill, tab, glo, B, i]

Solomon, Brian, ed. *Chemical and Biological Warfare*. New York: H. W. Wilson, 1999. A post-Cold War survey of chemical and biological weaponry and scenarios for their possible deployment. [B, i]

Spiers, Edward M. *Chemical and Biological Weapons: A Study of Proliferation*. New York: St. Martin's Press, 1994. A survey of the problems of proliferation, using the Middle East as a focus. [tab, app, B, i]

_____. *Chemical Warfare*. Urbana: University of Illinois Press, 1986. A brilliant analysis presenting the origins and nature of chemical warfare. [app, B, i]

_____. *Weapons of Mass Destruction*. New York: St. Martin's Press, 2000. An overview and analysis, incorporating revelations of 1990's terrorism proliferation and counterproliferation.

ELECTRONICS

Brown, Louis. *A Radar History of World War II: Technical and Military Imperatives*. Bristol: Institute of Physics, 1999. A detailed history of the radar. [ill, B, i]

Buderi, Robert. *The Invention That Changed the World: How a Small Group of Radar Pioneers Won the Second World War and Launched a Technological Revolution*. New York: Simon & Schuster, 1998. The story of the making of radar. [ill, glo, B, i]

De Archangelis, Mario. *Electronic Warfare: From the Battle of Tsushima to the Falklands and the Lebanon Conflicts*. New York: Sterling, 1985. A survey of the development and use of electronic warfare. [ill, M, B, i]

Fisher, David E. *A Race on the Edge of Time: Radar, the Decisive Weapon of World War II*. New York: Paragon, 1989. A slightly exaggerated, but timely and insightful, account of radar use in World War II. [ill, tab, app, i]

Hackmann, Willem D. *Seek and Strike: Sonar, Antisubmarine Warfare, and the Royal Navy, 1914-54*. London: H.M.S.O., 1984. The story of the development of sonar technology, the science of acoustics, and associated tactics. [ill, app, B, i]

Kiely, D. G. *Naval Electronic Warfare*. Washington, D.C.: Brassey's, 1987. A general survey, including coverage of radar and HF/DF, the radio direction-finding technology that was a key process in defeating German U-boats during World War II. [ill, i]

Latham, Colin, and Anne Stobbs. *Radar: A Wartime Miracle*. Dover, N.H.: Sutton, 1996. A historical survey of radar's use and performance during World War II. [ill, glo, app, B, i]

Macksey, Kenneth. *Technology in War: The Impact of Science on Weapon Development and Modern Battle*. New York: Prentice Hall Press, 1986. An important work on the nature of changing technology toward the end of the Cold War. [ill, B, i]

Mendelsohn, Everett, Merritt Roe Smith, and Peter Weingart, eds. *Science, Technology, and the Military*. 2 vols. Boston: Kluwer Academic, 1988. A very detailed academic account of the nature of science technology and its effects on military thinking at the end of the Cold War. [ill, B. i]

Page, Robert M. *The Origins of Radar*. 1962. Reprint. Westport, Conn.: Greenwood Press, 1979. The story of the development of radar (an acronym for radio detection and ranging), first used in 1934 by an electronic engineer. [ill, i]

Schleher, D. Curtis. *Introduction to Electronic Warfare*. Dedham, Mass.: Artech House, 1986. A historic account of the nature of electronic warfare during the latter period of the Cold War. [ill, B, i]

Williams, Kathleen B. *Secret Weapons: U.S. High-Frequency Direction-Finding in the Battle of the Atlantic*. Annapolis, Md.: Naval Institute Press, 1996. Details of the sophisticated and elaborate system of electronic warfare whereby the origin of the transmission of radio waves is pinpointed by antennas in various locations, a highly effective process that located German U-boats. [ill, M, B, i]

FIREARMS

Allsop, D. F., and M. A. Toomey. *Small Arms*. Washington, D.C.: Brassey's, 1999. A useful survey. [ill]

Ayalon, David. *Gunpowder and Firearms in the Mamlūk Kingdom: A Challenge to a Medieval Society*. London: Cass, 1978. A study of the early use of firearms in Egypt. [B, i]

Bailey, J. B. *Field Artillery and Firepower*. New York: Military Press, 1987. A survey of more than 650 years of development in the area of field artillery, looking both at the technical aspects of different weapons systems and at the ways in which they have changed the tactics and strategy of warfare. [ill, B, i]

Bradley, Iain. *Firearms*. Edinburgh: W. Green & Sweet and Maxwell, 1995. An overview of firearms laws and regulations. [il, i]

Chase, Kenneth Warren. *Firearms: A Global History to 1700*. New York: Cambridge University Press, 2003. A general history of firearms. [ill, B, i]

Ford, Roger. *The Grim Reaper: Machine Guns and Machine Gunners in Action*. New York: Sarpedon, 1997. A history of the invention, development, and use of the machine gun. [ill, B, i]

Hobart, F. W. A. *Pictorial History of the Machine Gun*. London: Ian Allan, 1971. A detailed illustrated history of the development of the machine gun. [ill, i]

Kelly, Jack. *Gunpowder: A History of the Explosive That Changed the World.* London: Atlantic Books, 2004. A history of the development of gunpowder. [ill, B, i]

Pope, Dudley. *Guns: From the Invention of Gunpowder to the Twentieth Century.* New York: Delacorte, 1965. A general survey of military and naval ordnance. [ill]

INTELLIGENCE TECHNOLOGY

Alvarez, David J. *Secret Messages: Codebreaking and American Diplomacy, 1930-1945.* Lawrence: University Press of Kansas, 2000. A detailed account of the use of code breaking by the United States in the run-up to the Pacific war and during World War II. [ill, B, i]

Andrew, Christopher M., ed. *Codebreaking and Signals Intelligence.* London: Cass, 1986. A series of essays by experts on signals intelligence (SIGINT), the most important method of intelligence collection in the twentieth century, including coverage of interception, code breaking, and cryptanalysis. [B]

Budiansky, Stephen. *Battle of Wits: The Complete Story of Codebreaking in World War II.* New York: Free Press, 2000. A detailed history of the nature of code breaking in World War II, making use of many sources that did not become available until after the end of the Cold War. [ill, M, B, i]

Copeland, B. Jack, et al., ed. *Colossus: The Secrets of Bletchley Park's Codebreaking Computers.* New York: Oxford University Press, 2006. A history of Bletchley Park making copious use of British government records that became available only at the end of the twentieth century. [ill, B, i]

Hartcup, Guy. *Camouflage: A History of Concealment and Deception in War.* New York: Charles Scribner's Sons, 1980. A study of camouflage as used in air, land, and naval contexts, with a series of national examples. [ill, B, i]

Hesketh, Roger. *Fortitude: The D-Day Deception Campaign.* London: St. Ermin, 1999. A previously classified report, revealing details about the successful deception campaign for the Normandy invasion in which the focus was on Calais. [ill, app, glo, M, B, i]

Hinsley, F. H. *British Intelligence in the Second World War.* London: H.M.S.O., 1983. An abridged edition of the original five volumes of official history published in the late 1970's, which revealed for the first time the unprecedented and massive intelligence operation based at Bletchley Park, seventy miles northwest of London, where ten thousand expert Allied operatives broke German, Italian, and Japanese codes and quickly informed pertinent commanders. [M, B, i]

Hinsley, F. H., and Alan Stripp, eds. *Code Breakers: The Inside Story of Bletchley Park.* New York: Oxford University Press, 1993. A personalized and informative presentation of accounts by participants in the massive intelligence operation conducted during World War II. [ill, i]

Kahn, David. *The Codebreakers: The Story of Secret Writing.* New York: Scribner, 1996. A detailed history of codes and code breaking from ancient times through to the Cold War, by one of the acknowledge experts in the field. [ill, B, i]

Neilson, Keith, and B. J. C. McKercher. *Go Spy the Land: Military Intelligence in History.* Westport, Conn.: Praeger, 1992. A survey of the history of military intelligence. [B, i]

Stripp, Alan. *Codebreaker in the Far East.* London: Frank Cass, 1989. An account of code breaking in East Asia and the Pacific war, including a detailed account of how the Japanese devised their own codes. [ill, B, i]

Welchman, Gordon. *The Hut Six Story: Breaking the Enigma Code.* New York: McGraw-Hill, 1982. The extraordinary story by a major participant of Bletchley Park and the breaking of the German codes, describing the Bletchley Park environment and the process of decryption in an understandable manner. [ill, app, B, i]

NAVAL WEAPONS

Baxter, James P. *The Introduction of the Ironclad Warship.* Cambridge, Mass.: Harvard University Press, 1933. Reprint. Annapolis, Md.: Naval Institute Press, 2001. The best account of the nineteenth century transition to ironclad warships, describing five innovations: steam power, shell guns, the screw propeller, rifled guns, and armor. [ill, B]

Boudriot, Jean. *The Seventy-four Gun Ship: A Practical Treatise on the Art of Naval Architecture.* Translated by David Roberts. 4 vols. Annapolis, Md.: Naval Institute Press, 1986-1988. An exquisitely comprehensive description of the standard ship of the line, with volumes on hull construction, fittings, rigging, and manning and ship handling. [ill]

Breyer, Siegfried. *Battleships and Battle Cruisers, 1905-1970.* Translated by Alfred Kurti. New York: Doubleday, 1970, 1973. A short history of the battleship, followed by descriptions and more than nine hundred illustrations of every battleship of every country during the period from 1905 to 1970. [ill, tab, B]

Brogger, A. W., and Haakon Shetelig. *The Viking Ships: Their Ancestry and Evolution.* Translated by Katherine John. Oslo: Dreyersforlag, 1951. An account not just of Viking longboats but also the orgin of their design and how they were later adapted in medieval Europe. [ill, M, i]

Busk, Hans. *The Navies of the World.* London: Routledge, Warnes and Routledge, 1859. Facsimile. Annapolis, Md.: Naval Institute Press, 1973. When originally published, this book provided a survey of the navies around the world just before the start of the American Civil War. Republished, this is an important contemporary source about naval power during the mid-nineteenth century. [ill, M]

Campbell, N. J. M. *Jutland: An Analysis of the Fighting.* Annapolis, Md.: Naval Institute Press, 1986. An extraordinarily detailed study and analysis of the performance of all guns of all calibers on both the British and German sides, with statistics on ammunition expended, the disposition of each round, the damage sustained, and the resulting damage-control measures. [ill, tab, B, i]

————. *Naval Weapons of World War II.* Annapolis, Md.: Naval Institute Press, 1985. An extensive, folio-sized, country-by-country survey of all naval weapons, with 750 illustrations. [ill, tab, i]

Cipolla, Carlo M. *Guns, Sails, and Empires: Technological Innovation and the Early Phases of European Expansion, 1400-1700.* London: Collins, 1965. Reprint. New York: Barnes & Noble Books, 1996. A substantial survey of the crucial, much-debated question of whether naval armaments and related technological advances made European expansion and hegemony inevitable during the early modern period. [ill, B]

Clancy, Tom. *Submarine: A Guided Tour Inside a Nuclear Warship.* New York: G. P. Putnam's Sons, 1993. An extraordinarily detailed report on an official tour of a nuclear submarine. [ill]

Friedman, Norman. *U.S. Naval Weapons: Every Gun, Missile, Mine, and Torpedo Used by the U.S. Navy from 1883 to the Present Day.* Annapolis, Md.: Naval Institute Press, 1982. A comprehensive review of naval weaponry. [ill, B, i]

Gardiner, Robert, ed. *Cogs, Caravels, and Galleons, 1000-1650.* Annapolis, Md.: Naval Institute Press, 1994. A large-folio-format survey of warships during the transition from medieval to modern times, from the Vikings to the Dutch. [ill, glo, B, i]

Garzke, William H., Jr., and Robert O. Dulin, Jr. *Battleships: Axis and Neutral Battleships in World War II.* Annapolis, Md.: Naval Institute Press, 1985. An account of battleships operated by the Axis Powers as well as neutral countries in the early 1940's. [ill, M, B, i]

Gray, Edwyn. *The Devil's Device: Robert Whitehead and the History of the Torpedo.* Rev. ed. Annapolis, Md.: Naval Institute Press, 1991. The story of how an English engineer working in Austria invented and developed the torpedo. [ill, B, i]

Griffiths, Maurice. *The Hidden Menace: Mine Warfare, Past, Present, and Future.* London: Conway, 1981. A review of the numerous types of naval mines in language understandable by the layperson. [ill, i]

Hobson, Rolf, and Tom Kristiansen. *Navies in Northern Waters 1721-2000.* Portland, Oreg.: Frank Cass, 2004. An account of navies in northern Europe, with heavy emphasis on the Baltic. [B, i]

Howarth, Stephen. *The Fighting Ships of the Rising Sun: The Drama of the Imperial Japanese Navy, 1895-1945.* New York: Atheneum, 1983. The story of the Imperial Japanese Navy, a massive and innovative naval force that achieved spectacular victories and equally devastating defeats, from its origin in 1894 until its demise in 1945. [ill, B, i]

Kaufmann, Robert Y., et al. *Submarine*. Annapolis, Md.: Naval Institute Press, 1993. A profusely illustrated, folio-sized volume supporting a televised documentary about submarines during and after World War II. [ill, B]

Lane, Frederic C. *Venetian Ships and Shipbuilders of the Renaissance*. 1934. Reprint. Baltimore: Johns Hopkins University Press, 1992. The history of one of the earliest and most important naval powers and its associated features, such as galleys, shipwrights, craft guilds, the construction process, timber supplies, and the famous Venice Arsenal. [ill, B, i]

Lavery, Brian, ed. *The Line of Battle: The Sailing Warship, 1650-1840*. London: Conway, 1992. Part of an important series, The History of the Ship, this volume includes essays on types of ships and fittings. [ill, B, i]

Lawliss, Chuck. *The Submarine Book: A Portrait of Nuclear Submarines and the Men Who Sailed Them*. New York: Thames, 1991. A short history of submarines and more details on modern nuclear-powered submarines. [ill]

Macintyre, Donald G. F. W. *Aircraft Carrier: The Majestic Weapon*. New York: Ballantine, 1968. A popular account of the development of the aircraft carrier, seen especially as the decisive factor in the Pacific campaign of World War II. [ill, B]

————. *Wings of Neptune: The Story of Naval Aviation*. New York: Norton, 1964. A historical survey. [ill, B, i]

Macintyre, Donald G. F. W., and Basil W. Bathe. *The Man-of-War: A History of the Combat Vessel*. London: Methuen, 1969. A profusely illustrated, folio-sized historical survey. [ill, B, i]

Manson, Janet M. *Diplomatic Ramifications of Unrestricted Submarine Warfare, 1939-1941*. Westport, Conn.: Greenwood Press, 1990. A survey of international law and its implications, including case studies of U-boats during World War I, World War II, and American submarines in the Pacific, which all resorted to the same rationale. [M, B, i]

Massie, Robert K. *Dreadnought: Britain, Germany,*

and the Coming of the Great War. New York: Random House, 1991. A history of the political impetus by the European navies to build the dreadnoughts in an arms race before the outbreak of World War I. [ill, M, B, i]

Neilson, Keith, and Elizabeth Jane Errington, eds. *Navies and Global Defense: Theories and Strategy*. Westport, Conn.: Praeger, 1995. Papers from a symposium held at the Royal Military College of Canada in 1994. [B, i]

O'Connell, Robert L. *Sacred Vessels: The Cult of the Battleship and the Rise of the U.S. Navy*. New York: Oxford University Press, 1991. A virtual indictment, critical of the U.S. Navy's excessive emphasis and reliance on the battleship, which, the author contends, was never an effective weapon. [ill, tab, B, i]

Padfield, Peter. *Guns at Sea*. New York: St. Martin's Press, 1973. A profusely illustrated, folio-sized historical survey from the time of projecting stones to the present, with an emphasis on the technical and tactical aspects of guns at sea. [ill, B]

Pivka, Otto von. *Navies of the Napoleonic Era*. New York: Hippocrene, 1980. A general overview that fills a void in a neglected area with accounts of spectacular Napoleonic battles, such as those of St. Vincent, Camperdown, Nile, Copenhagen, and Trafalgar. [ill, app, M, B]

Polmar, Norman, et al. *Aircraft Carriers: A Graphic History of Carrier Aviation and Its Influence on World Events*. New York: Doubleday, 1969. A full, detailed, scholarly, and engaging presentation. [ill, app, B, i]

Reynolds, Clark G. *The Fast Carriers: The Forging of an Air Navy*. New York: McGraw-Hill, 1968. Reprint. Annapolis, Md.: Naval Institute Press, 1992. A contribution to a controversial debate, arguing that fast carriers were the most significant naval development of World War II and especially decisive in the Pacific war. [ill, M, B, i]

Robertson, Frederic L. *The Evolution of Naval Armament*. London: Constable, 1921. Reprint. London: Storey, 1968. A classic, comprehensive survey featuring progressive developments in gunnery, gun carriages, propelling machinery, and armor. [ill, B, i]

Rodgers, William L. *Naval Warfare Under Oars: Fourth to Sixteenth Centuries: A Study of Strategy, Tactics, and Ship Design*. Annapolis, Md.: Naval Institute Press, 1939. Reprint. Norwalk, Conn.: Easton Press, 1991. A narrative history of events related to the use of galleys in the Mediterranean, by the Vikings, and during naval wars of England, France, and Italy. [ill, M, B]

Sondhaus, Lawrence. *Navies of Europe: 1815-2002*. Harlow: Longman, 2002. An overview of the changes in the nature of navies from the end of the Napoleonic Wars through to the end of the twentieth century. [ill, M, B, i]

Unger, Richard W., ed. *Cogs, Caravels, and Galleons: The Sailing Ship, 1000-1650*. London: Conway, 1994. A profusely illustrated, folio-sized volume focused on the technological advances of the sailing ship and its navigation. [ill, glo, B, i]

Whitley, M. J. *Battleships of World War II: An International Encyclopedia*. London: Arms & Armour Press, 1988. A detailed encyclopedia covering battleships by all countries during World War II. [ill, M, glo, B, i]

NONLETHAL WEAPONS

Alexander, John B. *Future War: Nonlethal Weapons in Modern Warfare*. New York: St. Martin's Press, 1999. An argument that innovative electromagnetic, acoustical, and psychological weapons are called for in the post-Cold War era of peacekeeping, humanitarian, and antiterrorist military missions. [ill, B, i]

Morehouse, David A. *Nonlethal Weapons: War Without Death*. Westport, Conn.: Praeger, 1996. The story of the development of nonlethal weapons in the twentieth century, associated with the search for alternative methods of combat. [ill, tab, B, i]

Rappert, Brian. *Non-lethal Weapons as Legitimizing Forces? Technology, Politics, and the Management of Conflict*. Portland, Oreg.: Frank Cass, 2003. Addresses state-of-the-art nonlethal weapons such as acoustic weapons, electromagnetic pulse beams, and calmative chemical agents. [ill, B, i]

NUCLEAR WEAPONS

Bernstein, Barton J., ed. *The Atom Bomb: The Critical Issues*. Boston: Little, Brown, 1976. A comprehensive assessment, featuring arguments both for and against the development and use of the atomic bomb. [B]

Caldicott, Helen. *The New Nuclear Danger: George W. Bush Military-Industrial Complex*. New York: New Press, 2004. An account of the increased importance of the military-industrial complex by one of the leading Australian antinuclear campaigners. [ill, B, i]

Cimbala, Stephen J. *Nuclear Weapons and Strategy: U.S. Nuclear Policy for the Twenty-first Century*. New York: Routledge, 2005. An important survey of the nature of nuclear weapons. [B, i]

Gerson, Joseph. *Empire and the Bomb: How the U.S. Uses Nuclear Weapons to Dominate the World*. Ann Arbor, Mich.: Pluto Press, 2007. A detailed account of the use and the threat of use of nuclear weapons, especially in Asia, including scenarios in China, during the Korean War, during the Vietnam War, and in the Middle East. [B, i]

Gray, Colin S. *The Second Nuclear Age*. Boulder, Colo.: Rienner, 1999. A discussion of the role of nuclear weapons in the post-Cold War era, concluding that nuclear arms control is not working and that China is a future potential antagonist. [B, i]

Groueff, Stephane. *Manhattan Project: The Untold Story of the Making of the Atomic Bomb*. Boston: Little, Brown, 1967. A report by a French journalist about the extraordinary and massive endeavor, with much interesting information from interviews of participants. [ill, B]

Groves, Leslie R. *Now It Can Be Told: The Story of the Manhattan Project*. New York: Harper, 1962. A firsthand account by the project's nonscientist director, an American general. [ill, i]

Harris, John B., and Eric Markusen, eds. *Nuclear Weapons and the Threat of Nuclear War*. New York: Harcourt, 1986. A presentation based on Cold War situations. [B]

Herf, Jeffrey. *War by Other Means: Soviet Power, West German Resistance, and the Battle of the Euromissiles*. New York: Free Press, 1991. A detailed account, from a political viewpoint, of the introduction of nuclear missiles into Western Europe during the 1980's. [B, i]

Hilsman, Roger. *From Nuclear Military Strategy to a World Without War: A History and a Proposal*. Westport, Conn.: Praeger, 1999. An account of U.S. nuclear strategy by an adviser to President John F. Kennedy. [B, i]

Irving, David J. C. *The German Atomic Bomb: The History of Nuclear Research in Nazi Germany*. New York: Simon & Schuster, 1967. By a controversial author, the definitive history of the attempt by Germany to develop the atomic bomb; based on extensive primary research. [ill, M, B]

Kahn, Herman. *On Thermonuclear War*. Princeton, N.J.: Princeton University Press, 1960. Three lectures on the nature and feasibility, plans and objectives, and analysis of thermonuclear war. [ill, tab, i]

Maddox, Robert James. *Weapons for Victory: The Hiroshima Decision Fifty Years Later*. Columbia: University of Missouri Press, 1995. An assessment of the controversial decision to drop the atomic bomb at the end of World War II. [B, i]

Paul, T. V., and James J. Wirtz, eds. *The Absolute Weapon Revisited: Nuclear Arms and Emerging International Order*. Ann Arbor: University of Michigan Press, 1998. An essential and timely study, reevaluating nuclear weapons policies in the post-Cold War environment and analyzing their problems and potential. [i]

Perkovich, George. *India's Nuclear Bomb: The Impact on Global Proliferation*. Berkeley: University of California Press, 1999. A report on a particularly crucial issue: India and the proliferation of nuclear weapons in one of the most dangerous hot spots in the world. [M, B, i]

Quester, George H. *Nuclear First Strike: Consequences of a Broken Taboo*. Baltimore: Johns Hopkins University Press, 2006. An account of the problems with nuclear escalation and likely scenarios in which the United States could resort to nuclear warfare. [B, i]

Rhodes, Richard. *Dark Sun: The Making of the Hydrogen Bomb*. New York: Simon & Schuster, 1995. A clear and understandable narrative about the hydrogen bomb, with expert analysis and informative detail. [ill, glos, B, i]

_____. *The Making of the Atomic Bomb*. New York: Simon & Schuster, 1986. Awarded the Pulitzer Prize and the National Book Award, a comprehensive account focusing on developments in nuclear physics and the scientific aspects and technical complexities of the atomic bomb. [ill, B, i]

Wainstock, Dennis. *The Decision to Drop the Atomic Bomb*. Westport, Conn.: Praeger, 1996. A history of the thinking that went behind the decision by President Harry S. Truman to bomb Hiroshima and Nagasaki, written on the fortieth anniversary of the bombing. [B, i]

Walker, J. Samuel. *Prompt and Utter Destruction: Truman and the Use of Atomic Bombs Against Japan*. Chapel Hill: University of North Carolina Press, 2004. Analyzes President Harry S. Truman's decision to use atomic weapons against Japan in 1945, looking not only at what was and was not known by Truman himself but also at Japanese attitudes toward surrender. Provides the context in which the decision was made to use atomic weapons and examines an array of factors that eventually convinced Japan to end the war. [B, i]

PRIMITIVE AND ANCIENT WEAPONS

Annis, P. G. W. *Naval Swords: British and American Naval Edged Weapons, 1600-1815*. Harrisburg, Pa.: Stackpole, 1970. A general survey. [B, i]

Bartlett, Clive. *English Longbowman, 1530-1515*. London: Osprey, 1997. Explains how the success of the English military during the Late Middle Ages was built on the effective use of the longbow. A characteristically English weapon, it was not overcome in its ability to pierce armor or in its rate of fire until the early twentieth century. [ill, B]

Bishop, M. C., and J. C. N. Coulston. *Roman Military Equipment: From the Punic Wars to the Fall of Rome*. London: Batsford, 1993. An important history showing the changes in Roman military hardware. [ill, M, B, i]

Bradbury, Jim. *The Medieval Archer*. New York: St. Martin's Press, 1985. An important and useful, if somewhat dated, survey. [ill, B, i]

De Souza, Philip. *The Ancient World at War*. London: Thames & Hudson, 2008. This study includes chapters on warfare in various regions around the world. [ill, M, B, i]

Drews, Robert. *The End of the Bronze Age: Changes in Warfare and the Catastrophe ca. 1200 B.C.* Princeton, N.J.: Princeton University Press, 1993. Gives a military explanation for the fall of the Levantine, Hittite, Mycenaean, and Trojan kingdoms and the "dark age" that followed the end of the Bronze Age in the early twelfth century B.C.E. [ill, M, B, i]

Featherstone, Donald. *Bowmen of England*. London: Jarrolds, 1967. An account of how English archers were to change the nature of warfare in western Europe in the fourteenth and fifteenth centuries, by one of the leading British authors on war gaming.

Hamblin, William J., ed. *Warfare in the Ancient Near East c.1600 B.C.* New York: Routledge, 2005. A detailed account of the nature of fighting in the Eastern Mediterranean and Mesopotamia. [ill, M, B, i]

Kern, Paul Bentley. *Ancient Siege Warfare*. Bloomington: Indiana University Press, 1999. This book covers various different parts of the ancient world and is based on the premise that siege warfare was responsible for unleashing violence throughout the ancient world. [ill, M, glo, B, i]

Malone, Patrick M. *The Skulking Way of War: Technology and Tactics Among the Indians of New England*. Lanham, Md.: Madison Books, 1991. A survey of the ways of war among North American indigenous peoples. [ill, M, B, i]

Osgood, Richard. *Warfare in the Late Bronze Age of North Europe*. Oxford: Archaeopress, 1998. An account of the nature of warfare among the Germanic tribes from Roman sources. Makes heavy use of archaeological evidence. [ill, M, B, i]

Osgood, Richard, and Sarah Monks, with Judith Toms. *Bronze Age Warfare*. Stroud, Gloucestershire, England: Sutton, 2000. Using contemporary written sources, mainly Roman, this history makes extensive use of the latest archaeological finds. [ill, M, B, i]

Sidebottom, Harry. *Ancient Warfare*. New York: Oxford University Press, 2004. An account of warfare in the ancient world, including descriptions on ancient military philosophy. [M, glo, B, i]

Snodgrass, Anthony. *Early Greek Armour and Weapons: From the End of the Bronze Age to 600 B.C.* Edinburgh, Scotland: Edinburgh University Press, 1964. With profuse illustrations and literary sources such as Homer, a collection of descriptions of helmets, shields, armor, swords, spears, bows and arrows, and chariots. [ill, B, i]

Underwood, Richard. *Anglo-Saxon Weapons and Warfare*. Stroud, Gloucestershire, England: Tempus, 1999. A study based on an extensive and informative survey from the artifacts, such as helmets, shields, mail coats, swords, spears, and knives, recovered from the famous Sutton Hoo ship burial in East Anglia. [ill, B, i]

Eugene L. Rasor, revised by Justin Corfield

WEB SITES

The AK Site
http://kalashnikov.guns.ru/
Affiliated with: Military Parade magazine
Contains detailed specifications and history of the development of the Kalashnikov rifle, in all of its variants the most widely adopted infantry weapon of the late twentieth century.

American Battle Monuments Commission
http://www.abmc.gov
Affiliated with: Same
Contains information on all American military personnel who died in World War I or World War II, and all foreign cemeteries where they are buried.

Arador Armour Library
http://www.arador.com/main.html
Affiliated with: Sword Forum magazine
In addition to discussion forums on arms and armor, this site features photographic galleries from many of the world's leading military museums, as well as detailed discussions on the manufacture and use of armor throughout history.

Arms and Armor Collection of the Metropolitan Museum of Art
http://www.metmuseum.org/collections/
department.asp?dep=4
Affiliated with: Metropolitan Museum of Art
The Metropolitan Museum of Art has one of the world's leading collections of military equipment, and this site presents an online version of a growing percentage of the museum's collection of arms and armor, focusing on Europe and Japan but with some representation from other regions.

Army Technology
http://www.army-technology.com/index.html
Affiliated with: Net Sources International
Provides current information about modern military equipment used by the armies of the world, in-cluding tanks, armored fighting vehicles, artillery, missiles, and helicopters.

Australian War Memorial
http://www.awm.gov.au
Affiliated with: Same
Contains photographs and reports, as well as vast array of genealogical information on Australians in World War I, World War II, and other conflicts.

The Aviation History On-line Museum
http://www.aviation-history.com/
Affiliated with: Aviation Internet Group
Details the history of civilian and military aircraft and includes text and photographic galleries primarily for U.S. engines, armaments, and aircraft, as well as discussions of avionics and the theory of flight.

British Association for Cemeteries in South Asia
http://www.bacsa.org.uk
Affiliated with: Same
Contains details on Britons and others from the British Empire who are buried in India and other parts of Asia, including much on soldiers and monuments in the region.

Center for Arms Control, Energy, and Environmental Studies
http://www.armscontrol.ru/
Affiliated with: Moscow Institute of Physics and Technology
Focuses on arms control connected with the various phases of the Strategic Arms Reduction Talks (START), beginning in 1986, between the United States and the Soviet Union, and details the ongoing nuclear capabilities of the two powers as well as the technical specifications for their arsenals.

Chemical and Biological Weapons Site
http://www.cdi.org/issues/cbw/
Affiliated with: Center for Defense Information

Presents an examination of the current chemical and biological capabilities of major nations and rogue states, as well as details about the effects of chemical and biological weapons on military and civilian populations.

Commonwealth War Graves Commission

http://www.cwgc.org
Affiliated with: Same

Contains details on the war graves maintained by the Commonwealth War Graves Commission, including details on all service personnel from the British Empire killed in World War I or World War II.

Documents in Military History

http://www.hillsdale.edu/academics/history/
    Documents/War/index.htm
Affiliated with: Hillsdale College

This primary source site contains more than three hundred documents on military history from ancient times to the modern era, including land, sea, and air campaigns. Although its focus is not primarily on military technology, many of the documents do discuss weapons, armor, and fortifications.

First Empire

http://www.firstempire.net
Affiliated with: First Empire magazine

Established by the leading magazine about the Napoleonic period, this site contains a number of sample articles from the magazine.

The French Army Museum

http://www.invalides.org/
Affiliated with: Government of France

Home of Le Musée de l'Armée, Hôtel National des Invalides, this site contains extensive selections from the holdings of the museum. Much of the focus is on the Napoleonic Era and World Wars I and II, although there are important images and texts from France's colonial history as well. Much of the collection is in French.

The Geometry of War

http://info.ox.ac.uk/departments/hooke/geometry/
    content.htm
Affiliated with: Oxford University

Applies and interprets geometry in its military application to Renaissance warfare. These applications include cartography, gunnery, and ballistics. Based on an exhibition at Oxford University.

The High Energy Weapons Archive: A Guide to Nuclear Weapons

http://www.fas.org/nuke/hew/
Affiliated with: Federation of American Scientists

Dedicated to nonproliferation and disarmament, this site provides extensive detail on the history, capabilities, and spread of nuclear weapons and technology over the past decades.

History and Archaeology of the Ship

http://www.history.bangor.ac.uk/Shipspecial/
    SHIP_int.htm
Affiliated with: Department of History and Welsh History, University of Wales, Bangor

An outlined history of military and commercial ships, from ancient vessels to early modern galleys, this site focuses on archaeological evidence to account for changes in technology and military applications.

The History Channel

http://www.historychannel.com/war/
Affiliated with: Same

Provides links to previous History Channel programs on military equipment and conflicts, as well as to book and video resources. The site also contains a detailed time line of history from 500 B.C.E. to the present, which includes many events of military significance.

The History Net

http://www.thehistorynet.com/
Affiliated with: Primedia History Group

Primedia is a publisher of a variety of military history journals, and this site features articles and source material from these periodicals, as well as additional materials on weapons and warfare from all periods of history.

Imperial War Museum

http://www.iwm.org.uk/

Affiliated with: Government of the United
    Kingdom

Contains representative text, photographic, and image collections from the holdings of the museum, taken primarily from British and Commonwealth military history.

Jane's Defense Information

http://www.janes.com/index.shtml

Affiliated with: Jane's Information Group

Provides extensive information about military equipment, contractors, arms purchases, weapons specifications, and intelligence about world events. Jane's is the world's leading private consulting group on military affairs and publishes standard works on military hardware.

**Land Forces of Britain, the Empire, and
    Commonwealth**

http://regiments.org/milhist/

Affiliated with: T. F. Mills, University of Denver

Provides detailed information about the historical structure, military equipment, weapons, personnel, and campaigns of the armed forces of the United Kingdom and its associated territories.

MagWeb

http://www.magweb.com

Affiliated with: Network Solutions

This subscription site contains thousands of articles from military and war-gaming magazines from around the world.

MILNET

http://www.milnet.com/milnet/index.html

Affiliated with: Same

This open-source intelligence site provides current information about the military forces of the world, including their equipment, interests, and rivals, with particular focus on those of the United States. Areas of military technology covered include ground forces, military aviation, space-based weapons, intelligence capabilities, and naval warships.

Museum of Antiquities

http://museums.ncl.ac.uk/archive/index.htm

Affiliated with: Society of Antiquaries of
    Newcastle upon Tyne and the University of
    Newcastle upon Tyne

This museum of archaeology in northeast England concentrates on the Roman era in Britain. In the collection are photographs of Roman weapons, fortifications, and armor, along with a virtual book on Roman military equipment.

Museum of Archaeology and Anthropology

http://www.museum.upenn.edu/Greek_World/
    Index.html

Affiliated with: University of Pennsylvania

Contains a text discussion of warfare in the lives of the ancient Greeks as well as photographs of Greek artifacts of war and representations of combat in artistic forms, taken from the museum's collection. Relevant sections of the online museum include warfare, hunting, chariots, horses, and daily life.

Napoleon

http://www.napoleon.org/index_flas.html

Affiliated with: Napoleon Foundation, Paris, France

Provides detail about the military campaigns of Napoleon I (Bonaparte) and Napoleon III through extensive image and text databases.

National Atomic Museum

http://www.atomicmuseum.com/

Affiliated with: U.S. Air Force

Provides image and text representations of the U.S. nuclear weapons program, including information about the Manhattan Project, the Cold War arms race, and the history of disarmament efforts.

Naval Historical Center

http://www.history.navy.mil/

Affiliated with: U.S. Navy

Provides image and photographic galleries, technical specifications, and the history of naval campaigns of the U.S. Navy since the American Revolutionary War.

Nihon Kaigun: Imperial Japanese Navy Page

http://www.combinedfleet.com/

Affiliated with: Jon Parshall, independent researcher

Based on years of research into the history of the Japanese navy, this site includes detailed representations of the armaments and equipment of Japan's air and sea forces of World War II. In addition, it provides operational histories of major Japanese vessels during the war and thorough discussions of ballistics, ship armor, and other technical areas, as well as details of both major and minor naval campaigns.

Official History of New Zealand

http://www.nzetc.org/projects/wh2/

Affiliated with: New Zealand Department of Internal Affairs and Victoria University of Wellington

Provides the official history of New Zealand in World War II.

Photos of the Great War

http://listproc.cc.ukans.edu/~kansite/ww_one/
   photos/greatwar.htm#TOP

Affiliated with: University of Kansas and Brigham Young University

This photographic database includes almost two thousand images of World War I, mostly from U.S. sources. Main areas of focus include weapons, equipment, military aviation, animals at war, and naval campaigns. Features include liberal rules for using images, as well as an accompanying link to a World War I text site.

Redstone Arsenal Historical Information

http://www.redstone.army.mil/history/

Affiliated with: U.S. Army

Provides historical, photographic, and technical information about U.S. military capabilities in space and about missile technology since World War II.

Regia Anglorum

http://www.regia.org/index.html

Affiliated with: Same

This living-history site includes photographs, descriptions, and illustrations of Anglo-Saxon, Viking, Norman, and British weapons, armor, and daily life from the period from 950 to 1066.

Royal Museum of the Army and Military History

http://www.klm-mra.be/

Affiliated with: Government of Belgium

The Royal Museum of the Army and Military History contains more than ten centuries of texts and artifacts from Belgian and world military history, and its Web site includes online exhibitions of main galleries and holdings, as well as a text and image database.

Springfield Armory National Historic Site

http://www.nps.gov/spar/home.html

Affiliated with: U.S. Park Service

The Springfield Armory, a National Historic Site, was for almost two hundred years a critical manufacturer of weapons for the U.S. military. Its online site demonstrates most of the equipment produced during the history of the armory, and its archive contains more than twenty-five thousand documents.

A Storm of Shot and Shell: Weapons of the Civil War

http://www.chipublib.org/003cpl/
   civilwar_catalog.html

Affiliated with: Chicago Public Library

This exhibit presents photographs, engravings, and illustrations of weapons of the American Civil War, taken from the collection of the library and including artillery, ammunition, and small arms.

Strategic Air Command Museum

http://www.sacmuseum.org

Affiliated with: U.S. Air Force

Contains an online exhibit of the bomber aircraft and other equipment used by the Air Force, as well as a virtual reality tour of the museum. The museum also features special exhibitions online, on a rotating basis.

The Tank Museum

http://www.tankmuseum.org/home.html

Affiliated with: Same

This online museum for the Tank Museum of Bovington in the United Kingdom presents some of the collection from the actual museum, which contains more than three hundred tanks and armored fighting vehicles from more than twenty-five countries. In addition to photographs and illustrations, the site has detailed technical information for an increasing portion of its collection.

Trenches on the Web: An Internet History of the Great War

http://www.worldwar1.com/index.html
Affiliated with: History Channel Affiliate Program

Provides images, documents, maps, and other material about World War I. Also contains a book-search engine, discussion forums, poster sales, and extensive links to other sites.

U.S. Air Force Museum

http://www.wpafb.af.mil/museum/index.htm
Affiliated with: U.S. Air Force

This online presence of the U.S. Air Force Museum has special image collections, taken from the holdings of the Air Force, and is especially strong in the areas of aircraft weaponry, fighter and bomber engines, and ground equipment.

U.S. Army Ordnance Museum

http://www.ordmusfound.org/
Affiliated with: U.S. Army

The museum contains more than eight thousand artifacts, with the online collection focused on photographs and technical specifications primarily for U.S. tanks, armored fighting vehicles, and artillery.

U.S. Civil War Navies

http://www.tfoenander.com
Affiliated with: Terry Foenander, military historian

This site has a vast array of material on the Union and Confederate navies in the American Civil War.

War, Peace, and Security

http://www.cfcsc.dnd.ca/links/milhist/index.html
Affiliated with: Information Resource Centre,
    Canadian Forces College

A detailed site, organized by period, subject, and conflict, with links to archives, photograph galleries,

texts, and other resources from the ancient era to the late twentieth century.

The War Times Journal

http://www.wtj.com/
Affiliated with: Same

Provides extensive archival information, photographs, and other materials about warfare from the Napoleonic era to World War II. Also contains an extensive collection of articles about conflicts in the nineteenth and twentieth centuries, as well as war-gaming information and hundreds of links to other military history sites.

Warfare in the Ancient World

http://www.fiu.edu/~eltonh/army.html
Affiliated with: Department of History, Florida
    International University

The focus of this site is on Greek, Roman, and Byzantine warfare, with sections devoted to bibliographies of specific as well as comparative weaponry, fortifications, and other areas of military technology.

Web Sources for Military History

http://home.nycap.rr.com/history/military.html
Affiliated with: Richard Jensen, University of
    Illinois, with support from the Gilder-Lehrman
    Foundation, the National Endowment for the
    Humanities, the Japan Foundation, and the Luce
    Foundation

Provides a bibliography and extensive Web links to hundreds of military history and technology sites, especially those dealing with the modern era.

World War II Armed Forces Orders of Battle and Organizations

http://freeport-tech.com/wwii/index.htm
Affiliated with: Dr. Leo Niehorster, independent
    military historian and publisher

Thoroughly details the equipment, weapons, personnel, and campaigns of nearly all military forces involved in World War II down to the company level.

Wayne H. Bowen

INDEX

INDEX

Cuba Libre (Leonard), 1070
Cuban Missile Crisis (1962), 458, 744, 750, 1012, 1058
Cuban Revolution (1956-1959), 744, 931; fiction about, 1087
Cudgels, 273
Cuirasses, 347, 492
Cuirassiers, 490, 542
Cultural Revolution (China, 1966-1976), 732
Culture and warfare. *See* Categorized Index of Essays
Culverins, 38, 419, 1044, 1099
Cummings, E. E., 1073
Cunaxa, Battle of (401 B.C.E.), 6, 34
Cuneiform tablets; Hittites, 93
Cuneus (wedge tactic), 187, 238
Cunnae, Battle of (216 B.C.E.), 1033
Curtis, George William, 917
Curtius Rufus, Quintus, 147
Curzon, George, 630
Custer, George Armstrong, 496, 863
Cutlasses, 1099
Cutters, 953
Cutting weapons. *See* Categorized Index of Essays
Cuzco, Battle of (1438), 359
Cyaxares (Median king), 100, 102
Cyclonite, 1113
Cynoscephalae, Battle of (197 B.C.E.), 158
Cyprus, 72; colony of Britain, 652; independence movement, 774
Cyril, Saint, 272
Cyrus the Great (king of Persia), 33, 42, 102, 118, 202, 1123
Cyrus the Younger (king of Persia), 34, 124, 132
Czar cannon, 521
Czechoslovakia, 753; Soviet invasion, 756, 793

D day (June 6, 1944), 514, 696, 1054-1055; in film, 866
Dadullah, Mullah, 808
Dagestan, 931
Daggers, 21, 23, 25, 108, 265, 1099; Egyptian, 112; Hittite, 90; India, 212; kidney, 1106; Lombard, 245; modern, 393, 395, 397
Dahomey, 611, 613, 615-616, 619
Daidoji Yuzan, 324
Daimyos (Japanese warlords), 322, 632, 637-638
Daito (Japanese sword), 397
Daladier, Édouard, 693
Damascus, Syria, 23
Damascus steel, 1025
Dana, Charles A., 917
Dandanqan, Battle of (1040), 288-289
Danelaw, 253
Daniel, Aubrey, 996
Danish Vikings, 253, 255, 257, 259
Danube frontiers (Rome), 169
Daoism, 319
Daoud, Mohammed Khan, 791
Dar al-Funun (military academy), 630
Dar-al-Islam, 281-282, 838
Dardanelles (1915), 676
Darius I the Great (king of Persia), 42, 140, 202, 1123
Dark Ages, 916; economy, 934; mercenaries during, 977. *See also* Middle Ages
Darwin, Charles, 581
Das Boot (film), 1053
Dau tranh, 1029
Daulambapur, Battle of (1612), 609
Dauntless dive-bomber, 444
Davach, 1099
David (king of Israel), 106
David, Jacques-Louis, 854

Davis, Jefferson, 559
Davout, Louis-Nicolas, 541
Dawn Patrol, The (film), 864
Day After, The (film), 1057
Dayan, Moshe, 1123
Dayton Agreement, 822-823
De re militari (Vegetius), 907
Deal (English fort), 474
Deane, Richard, 503
Death of Che Guevara, The (Cantor), 1087
"Death of the Ball Turret Gunner, The" (Jarrell), 1078
Deborah (biblical figure), 939
Deccan (India), 599
Deception, 199; Napoleonic era, 545; Trojan horse, 59
Decimation (Roman punitive practice), 160
Deeds of the Hungarians, The (Simon de Kéza), 252
Deer Hunter, The (film), 1059
Défense du système de guerre moderne (Guibert), 1030
Defense economics, 1013, 1015, 1017
Defensive weapons. *See* Categorized Index of Essays under Siegecraft and defensive weapons
Defiance (film), 1053
Defoliants, 774, 1099
Deighton, Len, 1077
Deir el-Bahri, 115
Delhi, Muslim Sultanate of, 338
Delhi, Sack of (1739), 609
Delian League, 1064
Deluge, The (Sienkiewicz), 1068
Demaratus, 1002
Demetrius I Poliorcetes (king of Macedonia), 57, 72
Demobilization, 1052
Democracy; vs. fascism, 654; and imperialism, 657
Deng Xiaoping, 732
Dengizich (Hun chieftan), 204

Rabanus Maurus, 907
Race-built galleons, 502
Radar, 435, 437; antisubmarine,
513; counterbattery artillery
fire, 424; detection, 456; radar
missiles, 439
Radio, 422, 678
Raids, 4, 1013
Railroads, 543, 679; American
Civil War, 571; Crimean War,
548; French use, 667
Rainbow Plans (World War II),
700
Rains, Gabriel J., 566
Raison d'état, 1009
Rajput Indians, 601
Rāmāyaṣa, 209, 212
Ramesseum, 93
Ramillies-Offus, Battle of
(1706), 533
Ramps, 171
Ramrods, 486
Ramses II (Egyptian Pharaoh),
14, 91-92, 115, 976; funerary
temple, 93
Ramses III (Egyptian Pharaoh),
106, 116
Ran (film), 1045
Range finders on ships, 510
Rank; American Civil War, 568;
weapons as badges of, 400
Rank system, 1029
Rapid Deployment Joint Task
Force, 747
Rapid dominance, 759
Rapiers, 394, 1112
Rashīd ad-Dīn, 334
Rashidun caliphs, 281
Ratzel, Friedrich, 870
Ravelins, 473
Ravenna, Battle of (1512), 418
Rawlinson, Henry Creswicke,
629
Razées, 505
RDX (explosive), 406, 1113
Reagan, Ronald, 746, 799, 1013

Reagan Doctrine, 747
Realpolitik, 1010
Rebellions, 929, 931-932;
colonial, 585, 652-653, 655,
657, 659
Rebels' Hour, The (Joris), 1090
Recapitulatio (Rabanus), 907
Recoil, 376, 421
Recoilless rifle, 1113
Reconnaissance planes, 437
Reconquista, 912
Recruiting; feudal, 260; Roman,
157
*Recueil des historiens des
Croisades* (William of Tyre),
291
Red Army (Soviet Union), 756
Red Badge of Courage, The
(Crane), 874, 1070
Red Badge of Courage, The
(film), 863
Red-hot shot, 506
Red Sorghum (Yan Mo), 1076
Red Turban movement, 315
Red Wheel, The (Solzhenitsyn),
1085
Reed, John, 682
Reeves, Joseph Mason, 443
Reformation, 519, 521, 523-524,
885; pacifism, 982;
propaganda during, 923
Refuges, 47, 49
Regeneration Trilogy (Barker),
1074
Regiment (army unit), 568, 678,
1031, 1113
Regulus (Roman consult), 149
Reîtres (pistolers), 383
Rejewski, Marian, 1006
Religion, European Wars of
(c. 1517-1618), 519, 521,
523-524; England vs. Spain,
579
Religion and warfare, 838, 883,
885, 887-888; Buddhism, 347;
Byzantine Empire, 228;

Catholicism, 525; China, 645;
and colonialism, 579; Egypt,
116; Hinduism, 346; India,
215; Judaism, 107; Mughal
Empire, 600
Remarque, Erich Maria, 875,
1071
Remington, Frederic, 925
Remotely piloted vehicles, 423
Renaissance war art, 853
RENAMO. *See* Resistência
Nacional Moçambicana
Renaudot, Théophraste, 916
Repeating crossbow, 17
Repeating rifles, 564, 1113
Reporters. *See* Journalism
Republican Guard (Iraq), 802
Republican Popular Army
(Spanish Civil War), 685
Resettlement plans, 778
Resistance (World War II), 1055
Resistência Nacional
Moçambicana, 913
Retreat, Hell! (film), 1059
Retrograde defense strategy, 649
Revere, Paul, 924
Revolts, 929, 931-932
Revolutionary Armed Forces
(Colombia), 818
Revolutionary People's
Liberation Party (Turkey),
818
Revolutionary United Front
(Sierra Leone), 818
Revolvers, 1113
Reynold, John, 495
Reza Shah Pahlavi, 623
Rhine frontier (Rome), 169
Rhodes, Siege of (305-304
B.C.E.), 57, 72
Ribauld (small cannon), 36, 375
Ricasso (blade), 395
Richard I "Lion-Heart" (king of
England), 18, 52, 266
Richard II (king of England),
995

REF
132

LIBRARY

3 1220 00676 7766

WITHDRAWN